Why Do You Need This Ne

If you're wondering why you should buy this of *Social Problems in a Diverse Society*, here are 11 good reasons!

1. Chapter 1 includes more extensive coverage of how various theoretical and political perspectives might be used to reduce or solve social problems such as gun violence.
2. In Chapter 2, a revised Social Problems and Social Policy box, titled "More Than a Decade after Reforms: Welfare Rolls Down—Poverty Up," looks at the effects of welfare reform since the 1996 welfare reform laws were passed.
3. Food prices around the world have been soaring, and more people already in poverty are going hungry. A revised and updated Chapter 2 discusses the problems of world hunger and poverty in a new Social Problems in Global Perspective box, entitled "A New Way of Looking at World Hunger."
4. Chapter 3 offers more extensive coverage of how various theoretical and political perspectives might be used to reduce or solve social problems such as racism and discrimination.
5. Chapter 5 updates its coverage of inequality based on age, and opens with a powerful new vignette about an older individual victimized by telemarketing fraud.
6. Chapter 6 includes a new Social Problems in the Media box titled "Getting Better All the Time? Representations of Gay Life on TV."
7. Chapter 10 provides more extensive coverage of how various theoretical and political perspectives might be used to reduce or solve social problems related to illness and health care.
8. Chapter 13 opens with a new narrative quoting the 2008 U.S. presidential candidates regarding their divergent stands on the U.S. economy.
9. Chapter 17 includes a revised Social Problems in the Media box titled "Weapons of Mass Destruction: Political Spin and Media Framing of a War" in which former White House Press Secretary Scott McClellan is quoted on his opinion of the Iraq war.
10. Chapter 18 offers expanded discussion of solutions to social problems and why it is so difficult to bring about social change in contemporary nations.
11. 2010 Census Update: The inclusion of data from the 2010 Census throughout brings this edition thoroughly up-to-date.

PEARSON

Fifth Edition

Social Problems in a Diverse Society

Census Update

DIANA KENDALL

Baylor University

Allyn & Bacon

Boston Columbus Indianapolis New York San Francisco Upper Saddle River
Amsterdam Cape Town Dubai London Madrid Milan Munich Paris Montreal Toronto
Delhi Mexico City Sao Paulo Sydney Hong Kong Seoul Singapore Taipei Tokyo

Publisher, Social Sciences: Karen Hanson
Editorial Assistant: Christine Dore
Development Editor: Maggie Barbieri
Executive Marketing Manager: Kelly May
Production Project Manager: Maggie Brobeck
Editorial Production Service: PreMediaGlobal
Manufacturing Buyer: Megan Cochran
Electronic Composition: PreMediaGlobal
Interior Design: Elm Street Publishing Services
Photo Researcher: Jessica Riu
Cover Designer: Joel Gendron

CIP information not available at time of publication.

10 9 8 7 6 5 4 3 2 1 RRD-W 15 14 13 12 11

Allyn & Bacon
is an imprint of

www.pearsonhighered.com

ISBN-10: 0-205-02487-4
ISBN-13: 978-0-205-02487-2

Contents

CHAPTER 3

Racial and Ethnic Inequality 45

CHAPTER 4

Gender Inequality 68

CHAPTER 5

Inequality Based on Age 90

CHAPTER 6

Inequality Based on Sexual Orientation 109

CHAPTER 7

Prostitution, Pornography, and the Sex Industry 128

CHAPTER 8

Alcohol and Other Drugs 148

CHAPTER 9

Crime and Criminal Justice 174

CHAPTER 10

Health Care: Problems of Physical and Mental Illness 202

CHAPTER 11

The Changing Family 224

CHAPTER 12

Problems in Education 248

CHAPTER 15

Population, Global Inequality, and the Environmental Crisis 309

CHAPTER 16

Urban Problems 333

CHAPTER 17

CHAPTER 18

Preface

A glimpse at the headline of any daily newspaper or at the TV screen shows us that we are living in difficult times: Our social problems are many in number, diverse in their causes and consequences, and often global in their reach. Clearly, 24/7 (twenty-four hours a day, 7 days a week) access to news and current events can either keep us informed or create a sense of "media overload" in regard to these problems. Sometimes, it is easy to get discouraged or to believe that some problems simply can't be reduced or solved. However, studying social problems can provide us with new insights on the complexities of everyday life and the problems in our nation and world. Although we live in difficult and challenging times, the social problems course provides us with an excellent way in which to develop our critical thinking skills and to learn how to use sociological concepts and perspectives to analyze specific social concerns ranging from terrorism and war to social inequalities rooted in factors such as one's race, class, gender, age, or sexual orientation.

My first and foremost goal in writing this book is to make the study of social problems *interesting* and *relevant* to you, the student. To stimulate your interest in reading the chapters and participating in class discussions, I have used lived experiences (personal narratives of *real* people) and statements from a wide variety of analysts to show how social problems affect people at the individual, group, and societal levels. Moreover, I have applied the sociological imagination and relevant sociological concepts and perspectives to all the topics in a systematic manner.

This Fifth Edition of *Social Problems in a Diverse Society* continues, like the very popular previous editions, to focus on the significance of race, class, and gender as key factors in our understanding of social problems in the United States and around the globe. Throughout the text, all people—but particularly people of color and white women—are shown not merely as "victims" of social problems but as individuals who resist discrimination and inequality and seek to bring about change in families, schools, workplaces, and the larger society. To place specific social problems within a larger social inequality framework, Chapters 2 through 6 conduct a systematic evaluation of wealth and poverty, racial and ethnic inequality, gender inequality, and inequalities based on age and sexual orientation. Thereafter, concepts and perspectives related to race, class, and gender are intertwined in the discussion of specific social problems in institutions such as education and health care.

Like prior editions, the fifth edition is balanced in its approach to examining social problems. *Social Problems in a Diverse Society* includes a comprehensive view of current feminist and other contemporary perspectives on a vast array of subjects—such as the effect of new technologies on social life and how the media depict social issues. As a sociologist who specializes in social theory, I was disheartened by the minimal use of sociological theory in most social problems texts. Those texts that discuss theory typically do so in early chapters, but then fail to use these theories as a systematic framework for examining specific social issues in subsequent chapters. Similarly, many texts give the impression that social problems can be solved if people reach a consensus on what should be done, but *Social Problems in a Diverse Society,* Fifth Edition, emphasizes that the way people view a social problem is related to how they believe the problem should be reduced or solved. Consider poverty, for example: People who focus on individual causes of poverty typically believe that individual solutions (such as teaching people the work ethic and reforming welfare) are necessary to reduce the problem, whereas those who focus on structural causes of poverty (such as chronic unemployment and inadequate educational opportunities) typically believe that solutions must come from the larger society. Moreover, what some people perceive as a *problem* is viewed by others as a *solution* for a problem (e.g., the sex industry as a source of income, or abortion to terminate a problematic pregnancy). In the final chapter (Chapter 18), I ask students to more fully explore the question, "Can Social Problems Be Solved?"

Finally, I wrote *Social Problems in a Diverse Society,* Fifth Edition, to provide students and instructors with a text that covers all the major social concerns of our day but does not leave them believing that the text—and perhaps the course—was a "depressing litany of social problems that nobody can do anything about anyway," as one of my students stated about a different text. I believe the sociological perspective has much to add to our national and global dialogues on a host of issues such as environmental degradation; terrorism and war; discrimination based on race, class, gender, age, sexual orientation, or other attributes; and problems in education. Welcome to an innovative examination of social problems—one of the most stimulating and engrossing fields of study in sociology!

SPECIAL FEATURES AND PEDAGOGY IN THE FIFTH EDITION

Critical Thinking and You

A boxed feature, "Critical Thinking and You," encourages students to use the sociological imagination in thinking and answering questions about issues such as:

- "Determining What Constitutes a Social Problem" (Chapter 1, "Studying Social Problems in the Twenty-First Century")
- "Calling on a Higher Power or Using Self-Reliance? Alcohol and Drug Abuse Programs" (Chapter 8, "Alcohol and Other Drugs")
- "Are You a Conservative or a Liberal? The Language of the Political Economy" (Chapter 13, "Problems in Politics and the Global Economy")
- "Do We Have a Problem or Not? Learning from Environmental Sociology" (Chapter 15, "Population, Global Inequality, and the Environmental Crisis")
- "Applying Sociology to the Ordinary and the Extraordinary in Everyday Life" (Chapter 18, "Can Social Problems Be Solved?")

New and updated material has been added throughout the text, on topics including the following:

- using sociological insights to study social problems
- media framing of social problems
- violence on college campuses
- victimization of older people
- campaigning in the presidential election of 2008
- how environmental problems harm everyone

Exciting Features

A number of special features have been designed to incorporate race, class, and gender into our analysis of social problems and to provide you with new insights on the social problems that we hear about on the evening news.

Lived Experiences Throughout Each Chapter

These authentic, first-person accounts are used as vignettes—"real words from real people"—to create interest and show how the problems being discussed affect people as they go about their daily lives. Lived experiences provide opportunities for instructors to systematically incorporate into lectures and class discussions examples of relevant, contemporary issues that have recently been on the evening news and in newspaper headlines, and for you to examine social life beyond your own experiences ("to live vicariously," as one student noted). Some examples of lived experiences include:

- Rosabelle Walker describes her problems with lack of food and hunger in her retirement years even though she was employed for many years (Chapter 2, "Wealth and Poverty: U.S. and Global Economic Inequalities").

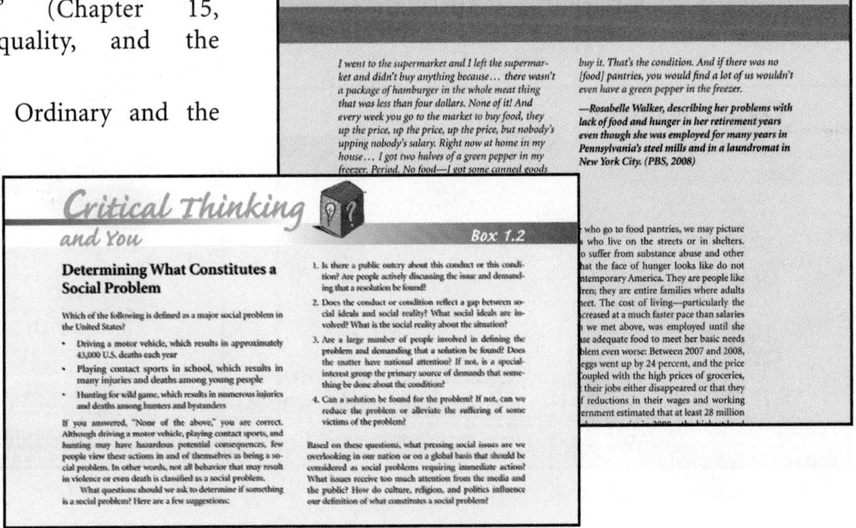

I went to the supermarket and I left the supermarket and didn't buy anything because… there wasn't a package of hamburger in the whole meat thing that was less than four dollars. None of it! And every week you go to the market to buy food, they up the price, up the price, up the price, but nobody's upping nobody's salary. Right now at home in my house… I got two halves of a green pepper in my freezer. Period. No food—I got some canned goods … buy it. That's the condition. And if there was no [food] pantries, you would find a lot of us wouldn't even have a green pepper in the freezer.

—Rosabelle Walker, describing her problems with lack of food and hunger in her retirement years even though she was employed for many years in Pennsylvania's steel mills and in a laundromat in New York City. (PBS, 2008)

Critical Thinking and You — Box 1.2

Determining What Constitutes a Social Problem

Which of the following is defined as a major social problem in the United States?

- Driving a motor vehicle, which results in approximately 43,000 U.S. deaths each year
- Playing contact sports in school, which results in many injuries and deaths among young people
- Hunting for wild game, which results in numerous injuries and deaths among hunters and bystanders

If you answered, "None of the above," you are correct. Although driving a motor vehicle, playing contact sports, and hunting may have hazardous potential consequences, few people view these actions in and of themselves as being a social problem. In other words, not all behavior that may result in violence or even death is classified as a social problem.

What questions should we ask to determine if something is a social problem? Here are a few suggestions:

1. Is there a public outcry about this conduct or this condition? Are people actively discussing the issue and demanding that a resolution be found?
2. Does the conduct or condition reflect a gap between social ideals and social reality? What social ideals are involved? What is the social reality about the situation?
3. Are a large number of people involved in defining the problem and demanding that a solution be found? Does the matter have national attention? If not, is a special-interest group the primary source of demands that something be done about the condition?
4. Can a solution be found for the problem? If not, can we reduce the problem or alleviate the suffering of some victims of the problem?

Based on these questions, what pressing social issues are we overlooking in our nation or on a global basis that should be considered as social problems requiring immediate action? What issues receive too much attention from the media and the public? How do culture, religion, and politics influence our definition of what constitutes a social problem?

- Author Abigail Garner explains how she and other children of gay parents feel when they are treated differently and stigmatized (Chapter 6, "Inequality Based on Sexual Orientation").
- "Liz," an Internet blogger, discusses the death of Jesse Drews, a college student, when he attempted to quickly consume 21 alcoholic drinks in celebration of his 21st birthday (Chapter 8, "Alcohol and Other Drugs.")
- Zainub Razvi in Pakistan and Amanda Hirsch in the United States describe their similar problems with Internet addiction because they spend large amounts on time online to the exclusion of people and other activities (Chapter 14, "Problems in the Media.")

Interesting and Highly Relevant Boxed Features

In addition to the Critical Thinking and You boxes, four other types of boxes—Social Problems in the Media, Social Problems and Social Policy, Social Problems in Global Perspective, and Social Problems and Statistics—highlight important current topics regarding pressing social problems:

- *Social Problems in the Media:* Boxes include "Video Games, Racial Stereotypes, and Glamorized Violence" (Chapter 3, "Racial and Ethnic Inequality"), "Middle-aged Women: Over the Hill and in Need of Repair?" (Chapter 5, "Inequality Based on Age"), "TV Shows and the Framing of Alcohol Use" (Chapter 8, "Alcohol and Other Drugs"), and "Run! Hide! Media Framing of the Illegal Border-Crossing Experience" (Chapter 15, "Population, Global Inequality, and the Environmental Crisis").

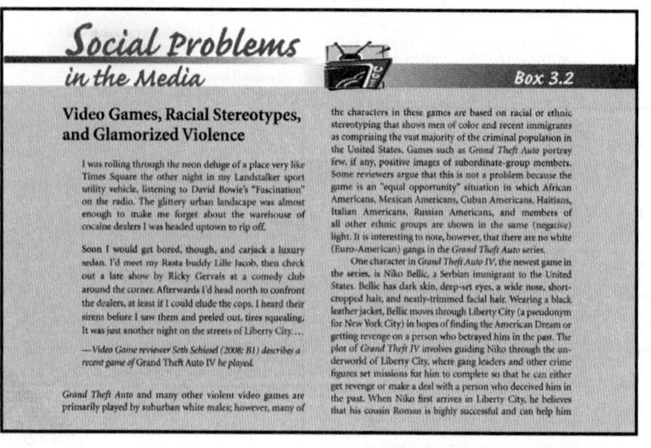

Social Problems in the Media — Box 3.2

Video Games, Racial Stereotypes, and Glamorized Violence

> I was rolling through the neon deluge of a place very like Times Square the other night in my Landstalker sport utility vehicle, listening to David Bowie's "Fascination" on the radio. The glittery urban landscape was almost enough to make me forget about the warehouse of cocaine dealers I was headed uptown to rip off.
>
> Soon I would get bored, though, and carjack a luxury sedan. I'd meet my Rasta buddy Lille Jacob, then check out a late show by Ricky Gervais at a comedy club around the corner. Afterwards I'd head north to confront the dealers, at least if I could elude the cops. I heard their sirens before I saw them and peeled out, tires squealing. It was just another night on the streets of Liberty City....
>
> —*Video Game reviewer Seth Schiesel (2008: B1) describes a recent game of* Grand Theft Auto IV *he played.*

Grand Theft Auto and many other violent video games are primarily played by suburban white males; however, many of the characters in these games are based on racial or ethnic stereotyping that shows men of color and recent immigrants as comprising the vast majority of the criminal population in the United States. Games such as *Grand Theft Auto* portray few, if any, positive images of subordinate-group members. Some reviewers argue that this is not a problem because the game is an "equal opportunity" situation in which African Americans, Mexican Americans, Cuban Americans, Haitians, Italian Americans, Russian Americans, and members of all other ethnic groups are shown in the same (negative) light. It is interesting to note, however, that there are no white (Euro-American) gangs in the *Grand Theft Auto* series.

One character in *Grand Theft Auto IV*, the newest game in the series, is Niko Bellic, a Serbian immigrant to the United States. Bellic has dark skin, deep-set eyes, a wide nose, short-cropped hair, and neatly-trimmed facial hair. Wearing a black leather jacket, Bellic moves through Liberty City (a pseudonym for New York City) in hopes of finding the American Dream or getting revenge on a person who betrayed him in the past. The plot of *Grand Theft IV* involves guiding Niko through the underworld of Liberty City, where gang leaders and other crime figures set missions for him to complete so that he can either get revenge or make a deal with a person who deceived him in the past. When Niko first arrives in Liberty City, he believes that his cousin Roman is highly successful and can help him

- *Social Problems and Social Policy:* Boxes include "'Packing Heat:' Should College Students Be Allowed to Carry Guns on Campus?" (Chapter 1, "Studying Social Problems in the Twenty-First Century"), "Who Pays for Health Care? A Brief Look at Canada, the United Kingdom, and Sweden" (Chapter 10, "Health Care: Problems of Physical and Mental Illness"), and "Persons Living with HIV/AIDS and Homelessness: What Should the Government Do?" (Chapter 16, "Urban Problems").

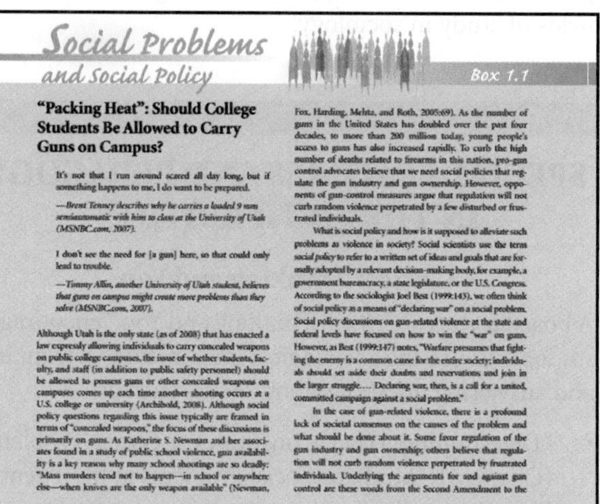

Social Problems and Social Policy — Box 1.1

"Packing Heat": Should College Students Be Allowed to Carry Guns on Campus?

> It's not that I run around scared all day long, but if something happens to me, I do want to be prepared.
>
> —*Brent Tenney describes why he carries a loaded 9 mm semiautomatic with him to class at the University of Utah (MSNBC.com, 2007).*
>
> I don't see the need for [a gun] here, so that could only lead to trouble.
>
> —*Timmy Allin, another University of Utah student, believes that guns on campus might create more problems than they solve (MSNBC.com, 2007).*

Although Utah is the only state (as of 2008) that has enacted a law expressly allowing individuals to carry concealed weapons on public college campuses, the issue of whether students, faculty, and staff (in addition to public safety personnel) should be allowed to possess guns or other concealed weapons on campuses comes up each time another shooting occurs at a U.S. college or university (Archibold, 2008). Although social policy questions regarding this issue typically are framed in terms of "concealed weapons," the focus of these discussions is primarily on guns. As Katherine S. Newman and her associates found in a study of public school violence, gun availability is a key reason why many school shootings are so deadly: "Mass murders tend not to happen—in school or anywhere else—when knives are the only weapon available" (Newman, Fox, Harding, Mehta, and Roth, 2005:69). As the number of guns in the United States has doubled over the past four decades, to more than 200 million today, young people's access to guns has also increased rapidly. To curb the high number of deaths related to firearms in this nation, pro-gun control advocates believe that we need social policies that regulate the gun industry and gun ownership. However, opponents of gun-control measures argue that regulation will not curb random violence perpetrated by a few disturbed or frustrated individuals.

What is social policy and how is it supposed to alleviate such problems as violence in society? Social scientists use the term *social policy* to refer to a written set of ideas and goals that are formally adopted by a relevant decision-making body, for example, a government bureaucracy, a state legislature, or the U.S. Congress. According to the sociologist Joel Best (1999:143), we often think of social policy as a means of "declaring war" on a social problem. Social policy discussions on gun-related violence at the state and federal levels have focused on how to win the "war" on guns. However, as Best (1999:147) notes, "Warfare presumes that fighting the enemy is a common cause for the entire society; individuals should set aside their doubts and reservations and join in the larger struggle.... Declaring war, then, is a call for a united, committed campaign against a social problem."

In the case of gun-related violence, there is a profound lack of societal consensus on the causes of the problem and what should be done about it. Some favor regulation of the gun industry and gun ownership; others believe that regulation will not curb random violence perpetrated by frustrated individuals. Underlying the arguments for and against gun control are these words from the Second Amendment to the

- *Social Problems in Global Perspective:* Boxes include "The Polish Plumber in France: Negative Stereotypes about 'Cheap Labor'" (Chapter 3, "Racial and Ethnic Inequality"), "Who Am I? Identity Theft in the Global Village" (Chapter 9, "Crime and Criminal

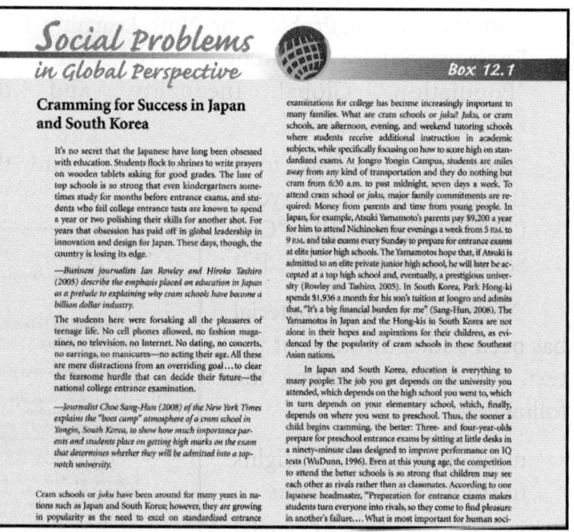

Social Problems in Global Perspective — Box 12.1

Cramming for Success in Japan and South Korea

> It's no secret that the Japanese have long been obsessed with education. Students flock to shrines to write prayers on wooden tablets asking for good grades. The lure of top schools is so strong that even kindergartners sometimes study for months before entrance exams, and students who fail college entrance tests are known to spend a year or two polishing their skills for another shot. For years that obsession has paid off in global leadership in innovation and design for Japan. These days, though, the country is losing its edge.
>
> —*Business journalists Ian Rowley and Hiroko Tashiro (2005) describe the emphasis placed on education in Japan as a prelude to explaining why cram schools have become a billion dollar industry.*
>
> The students here were forsaking all the pleasures of teenage life. No cell phones allowed, no fashion magazines, no television, no Internet. No dating, no concerts, no earrings, no manicures—no acting their age. All these are mere distractions from an overriding goal...to clear the fearsome hurdle that can decide their future—the national college entrance examination.
>
> —*Journalist Choe Sang-Hun (2008) of the New York Times explains the "boot camp" atmosphere of a cram school in Yongin, South Korea, to show how much importance parents and students place on getting high marks on the exam that determines whether they will be admitted into a top-notch university.*

Cram schools or *juku* have been around for many years in nations such as Japan and South Korea; however, they are growing in popularity as the need to excel on standardized entrance examinations for college has become increasingly important to many families. What are cram schools or *juku*? *Juku*, or cram schools, are afternoon, evening, and weekend tutoring schools where students receive additional instruction in academic subjects, while specifically focusing on how to score high on standardized exams. At Jongro Yongin Campus, students are miles away from any kind of transportation and they do nothing but cram from 6:30 a.m. to past midnight, seven days a week. To attend cram school or *juku*, major family commitments are required: Money from parents and time from young people. In Japan, for example, Atsuki Yamamoto's parents pay $9,200 a year for him to attend Nichinoken four evenings a week from 5 P.M. to 9 P.M. and take exams every Sunday to prepare for entrance exams at elite junior high schools. The Yamamotos hope that, if Atsuki is admitted to an elite private junior high school, he will later be accepted at a top high school and, eventually, a prestigious university (Rowley and Tashiro, 2005). In South Korea, Park Hong-ki spends $1,936 a month for his son's tuition at Jongro and admits that, "It's a big financial burden for me" (Sang-Hun, 2008). The Yamamotos in Japan and the Hong-kis in South Korea are not alone in their hopes and aspirations for their children, as evidenced by the popularity of cram schools in these Southeast Asian nations.

In Japan and South Korea, education is everything to many people: The job you get depends on the university you attended, which depends on the high school you went to, which in turn depends on your elementary school, which, finally, depends on where you went to preschool. Thus, the sooner a child begins cramming, the better: Three- and four-year-olds prepare for preschool entrance exams by sitting at little desks in a ninety-minute class designed to improve performance on IQ tests (WuDunn, 1996). Even at this young age, the competition to attend the better schools is so strong that children may see each other as rivals rather than as classmates. According to one Japanese headmaster, "Preparation for entrance exams makes students turn everyone into rivals, so they come to find pleasure in another's failure.... What is most important for human soci-

Justice"), "Cramming for Success in Japan and South Korea" (Chapter 12, "Problems in Education"), and "International Migration: Problem or Solution?" (Chapter 15, "Population, Global Inequality, and the Environmental Crisis").

- *Social Problems and Statistics:* Boxes include "Poverty in the United States" (Chapter 2, "Wealth and Poverty"), "Accurate and Inaccurate Comparisons" (Chapter 3, "Racial and Ethnic Inequality"), and "The Odds of Getting Divorced" (Chapter 11, "The Changing Family").

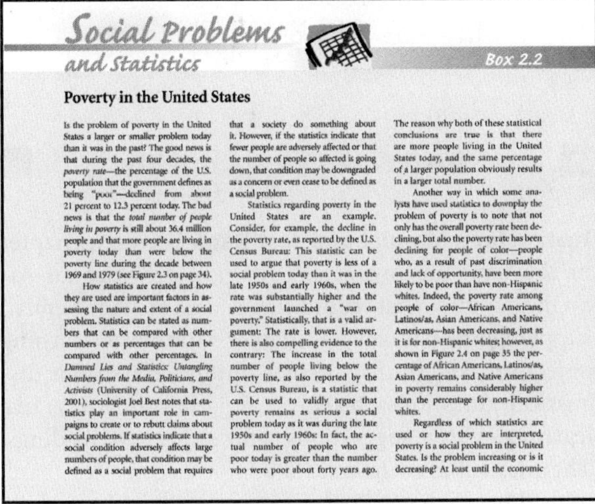

Social Problems and Statistics

Box 2.2

Poverty in the United States

Is the problem of poverty in the United States a larger or smaller problem today than it was in the past? The good news is that during the past four decades, the *poverty rate*—the percentage of the U.S. population that the government defines as being "poor"—declined from about 21 percent to 12.3 percent today. The bad news is that the *total number of people living in poverty* is still about 36.4 million people and that more people are living in poverty today than were below the poverty line during the decade between 1969 and 1979 (see Figure 2.3 on page 34).

How statistics are created and how they are used are important factors in assessing the nature and extent of a social problem. Statistics can be stated as numbers that can be compared with other numbers or as percentages that can be compared with other percentages. In *Damned Lies and Statistics: Untangling Numbers from the Media, Politicians, and Activists* (University of California Press, 2001), sociologist Joel Best notes that statistics play an important role in campaigns to create or to rebutt claims about social problems. If statistics indicate that a social condition adversely affects large numbers of people, that condition may be defined as a social problem that requires that a society do something about it. However, if the statistics indicate that fewer people are adversely affected or that the number of people so affected is going down, that condition may be downgraded as a concern or even cease to be defined as a social problem.

Statistics regarding poverty in the United States are an example. Consider, for example, the decline in the poverty rate, as reported by the U.S. Census Bureau: This statistic can be used to argue that poverty is less of a social problem today than it was in the late 1950s and early 1960s, when the rate was substantially higher and the government launched a "war on poverty." Statistically, that is a valid argument: The rate is lower. However, there is also compelling evidence to the contrary: The increase in the total number of people living below the poverty line, as also reported by the U.S. Census Bureau, is a statistic that can be used to validly argue that poverty remains as serious a social problem today as it was during the late 1950s and early 1960s: In fact, the actual number of people who are poor today is greater than the number who were poor about forty years ago. The reason why both of these statistical conclusions are true is that there are more people living in the United States today, and the same percentage of a larger population obviously results in a larger total number.

Another way in which some analysts have used statistics to downplay the problem of poverty is to note that not only has the overall poverty rate been declining, but also the poverty rate has been declining for people of color—people who, as a result of past discrimination and lack of opportunity, have been more likely to be poor than have non-Hispanic whites. Indeed, the poverty rate among people of color—African Americans, Latinos/as, Asian Americans, and Native Americans—has been decreasing, just as it is for non-Hispanic whites; however, as shown in Figure 2.4 on page 35 the percentage of African Americans, Latinos/as, Asian Americans, and Native Americans in poverty remains considerably higher than the percentage for non-Hispanic whites.

Regardless of which statistics are used or how they are interpreted, poverty is a social problem in the United States. Is the problem increasing or is it decreasing? At least until the economic

Built-in Study Features

These pedagogical aids promote students' mastery of sociological concepts and perspectives:

- *Thinking Sociologically.* A bulleted list of critical thinking questions at the beginning of each chapter gives students an overview of major topics.
- *Summary in Question-and-Answer Format.* Each chapter concludes with a concise summary in a convenient question-and-answer format to help students master the key concepts and main ideas in each chapter.
- *Key Terms.* Major concepts and key terms are defined and highlighted in bold print within the text. Definitions are provided the first time a concept is introduced; they are also available in the Glossary at the back of the text.

ORGANIZATION OF THIS TEXT

Social Problems in a Diverse Society, Fifth Edition, has been organized with the specific plan of introducing disparities in wealth and poverty, race and ethnicity, gender, age, and sexual orientation early on, so that the concepts and perspectives developed in these chapters may be applied throughout the text. Chapter 1 explains the *sociological perspective* and highlights the issue of violence to draw students into an examination of such debates as whether "guns kill people" or "people kill people."

Chapter 2 looks at *wealth and poverty* in the United States and around the world. The chapter provides new insights on wealth compared with income inequality and on problems such as homelessness, low-income and poverty-level neighborhoods, and the relationship between "cheap labor" and the global economy. Chapter 3 integrates the previous discussion of class-based inequalities with an examination of *racial and ethnic inequality.* Chapter 4, disusses *gender inequality* and highlights factors such as mainstream gender socialization and social barriers that contribute to the unequal treatment of women in the workplace and family and at school and other social institutions. Ageism and *inequality based on age* are discussed in Chapter 5. *Inequality based on sexual orientation* is examined in Chapter 6, where concerns such as how gay men and lesbians are portrayed on television shows are discussed and problems regarding an accurate count of the number of gays and lesbians are described.

Chapter 7 links previous discussions of race, class, and gender to an analysis of *prostitution, pornography, and the sex industry.* In Chapter 8, *alcohol and other drugs* are discussed in depth, and students are provided with information about the so-called date rape drug and the abuse of prescription drugs, over-the-counter drugs, and caffeine. Chapter 9 discusses *crime and criminal justice* and takes an incisive look at sociological explanations of crime.

Beginning with Chapter 10, a look at *health care and its problems,* we examine some of the major social institutions in our society and note aspects of each that constitute a social problem for large numbers of people. Chapter 10 discusses global enemies of health in low-income nations, and examines the Canadian

Chapter 6

Inequality Based on Sexual Orientation

THINKING SOCIOLOGICALLY

- Why is sexual orientation an emotionally-charged legal and social issue in the United States?
- What types of discrimination are based on sexual orientation?
- How do biological and psychological explanations differ from sociological perspectives on sexual orientation?

109

health care model. Chapter 11 explores *the changing family,* emphasizing diversity in intimate relationships and families, and child-related family issues such as problems with day care. Chapter 12 presents contemporary *problems in education,* tracing the problems to such issues as what schools are supposed to accomplish, how they are financed, and why higher education is not widely accessible. Chapter 13 focuses on *problems in politics and the global economy* and provides a variety of perspectives on political power and the role of the military-industrial complex in U.S. politics and the economy. Chapter 14, a discussion of *problems in the media,* looks at how the recent concentration in the media industries affects the news and entertainment that people receive. Chapter 15 provides a survey of problems associated with *population and the environmental crisis,* particularly focusing on the causes and consequences of overpopulation and high rates of global migration. Chapter 16, a look at *urban problems,* details the powerful impact of urbanization on both high-income and low-income nations of the world. Chapter 17 discusses *global social problems related to war and terrorism.* After discussing such topics as militarism, military technology, and war in historical context, the text examines current issues of war and terrorism. Chapter 18 asks "*Can social problems be solved?*" and includes a review of the sociological theories used to explain social problems, plus an analysis of attempts at problem solving at the microlevel, midrange, and macrolevel of society.

SUPPLEMENTS

Instructor Supplements

Instructor's Manual and Test Bank For each chapter in the text, the *Instructor's Manual* provides an At-a-Glance grid that coordinates use of the Kendall supplements package, a chapter summary, learning objectives, key terms, chapter outline, classroom discussion questions, teaching suggestions for active learning, video suggestions, and suggested readings. The manual also includes a comprehensive test bank with hundreds of test items: true/false, multiple choice, and essay questions.

Computerized Test Bank The printed *Test Bank* is also available through Allyn & Bacon's online test generating system, MyTest. The user-friendly interface allows you to view, edit, and add questions; transfer questions to tests; and print tests. Search and sort features allow you to locate questions quickly and arrange them in whatever order you prefer.

PowerPoint Presentation These PowerPoint presentations available online, created for the Fifth Edition, feature lecture outlines for every chapter.

Student Supplement

Study Guide This student guide contains practice tests and exercises to help students prepare for quizzes and exams. Each chapter contains Before You Read, As You Read, and After You Read sections—with chapter outlines, chapter summaries, learning objectives, and practice tests. The *Study Guide* for the Fifth Edition is available for sale separately or packaged with the text at a special price.

Online Supplement

MySocKit MySocKit (*www.mysockit.com*) is a new online resource that contains web links, learning objectives, chapter summary, and practice tests (with multiple-choice, true/false, and essay questions), *New York Times* articles, audio and video activities, writing and research tutorials, and access to scholarly literature through Research Navigator. MySocKit is available with *Social Problems in a Diverse Society*, Fifth Edition, when a MySocKit access code card is value-packed with the text.

Census Update

2010 Census Update Edition Features fully updated data throughout the text—including all charts and graphs—to reflect the results of the 2010 Census.

A Short Introduction to the U.S. Census A brief seven-chapter overview of the Census, including important information about the Constitutional mandate, research methods, who is affected by the Census, and how data is used. Additionally, the primer explores key contemporary topics such as race and ethnicity, the family, and poverty. The primer can be packaged at no additional cost, and is also available online in MySeachLab, as a part of MySocLab.

A Short Introduction to the U.S. Census Instructor's Manual with Test Bank Includes explanations of what has been updated, in-class activities, homework activities, discussion questions for the primer, and test questions related to the primer.

MySocKit 2010 Census Update gives students the opportunity to explore 2010 Census methods and data and apply Census results in a dynamic interactive online environment. It includes a series of activities using 2010 Census results , video clips explaining and exploring the Census , primary source readings relevant to the Census, and an online version of the 2010 Census Update Primer.

ACKNOWLEDGMENTS

I wish to thank personally the many people who have made this fifth edition a reality. First, I offer my profound thanks to the following reviewers who provided valuable comments and suggestions on how to make this text outstanding. Whenever possible, I have incorporated their suggestions into the text. The reviewers are:

Fifth Edition

Michele Bogue, Texas Christian University
Leslie Cintron, Washington & Lee University
Brian Hawkins, University of Colorado–Boulder
Jason Mazaik, Massbay Community College

Fourth Edition

Todd F. Bernhardt, Broward Community College
Ann Marie Hickey, University of Kansas
Amy Holzgang, Cerritos College
Dr. Fred Jones, Simpson College
Dr. Gordon W. Knight, Green Mountain College

Third Edition

Joanne Ardovini-Brooker, Sam Houston State University
Bernadette Barton, Morehead State University
Tody Buchanan, Dallas Baptist University
Janice DeWitt-Heffner, Marymount University
Marcie Goodman, University of Utah
Judith Greenberg, Georgia State University
Patricia A. Joffer, Mesa State College
Thomas G. Sparhawk, Central Virginia Community College

Second Edition

Susan Cody, Brookdale Community College
William A. Cross, Illinois College
Jennifer A. John, Germanna Community College
James J. Norris, Indiana University, South Bend
Anne R. Peterson, Columbus State Community College

First Edition

Allan Bramson, Wayne County Community College
Scott Burcham, University of Memphis
Keith Crew, University of Northern Iowa
Mike Hoover, Western Missouri State College
Mary Riege Laner, Arizona State University
Patricia Larson, Cleveland State University
Kathleen Lowney, Valdosta State College
Edward Morse, Tulane University
Charles Norman, Indiana State University
James Payne, St. Edward's University
Anne R. Peterson, Columbus State Community College
Margaret Preble, Thomas Nelson Community College
Dale Spady, Northern Michigan University
John Stratton, University of Iowa

This fifth edition of *Social Problems in a Diverse Society* has involved the cooperative efforts of many people who have gone above and beyond the call of duty to make the book possible. I wish to thank Karen Hanson, Publisher, for her efforts throughout the publishing process. Likewise, I wish to thank Emily Winders of Elm Street Publishing Services, who made everything run smoothly. I am extremely grateful to Liz Napolitano, Production Editor, and Courtney Shea, Editorial Assistant.

To each of you reading this preface, I wish you the best in teaching or studying social problems and hope that you will share with me any comments or suggestions you have about *Social Problems in a Diverse Society,* Fifth Edition. The text was written with you in mind. Let's hope that our enthusiasm for "taking a new look at social problems" will spread to others so that together we may seek to reduce or solve some of the pressing social problems we encounter during our lifetime.

Diana Kendall

Chapter 1

Studying Social Problems in the Twenty-First Century

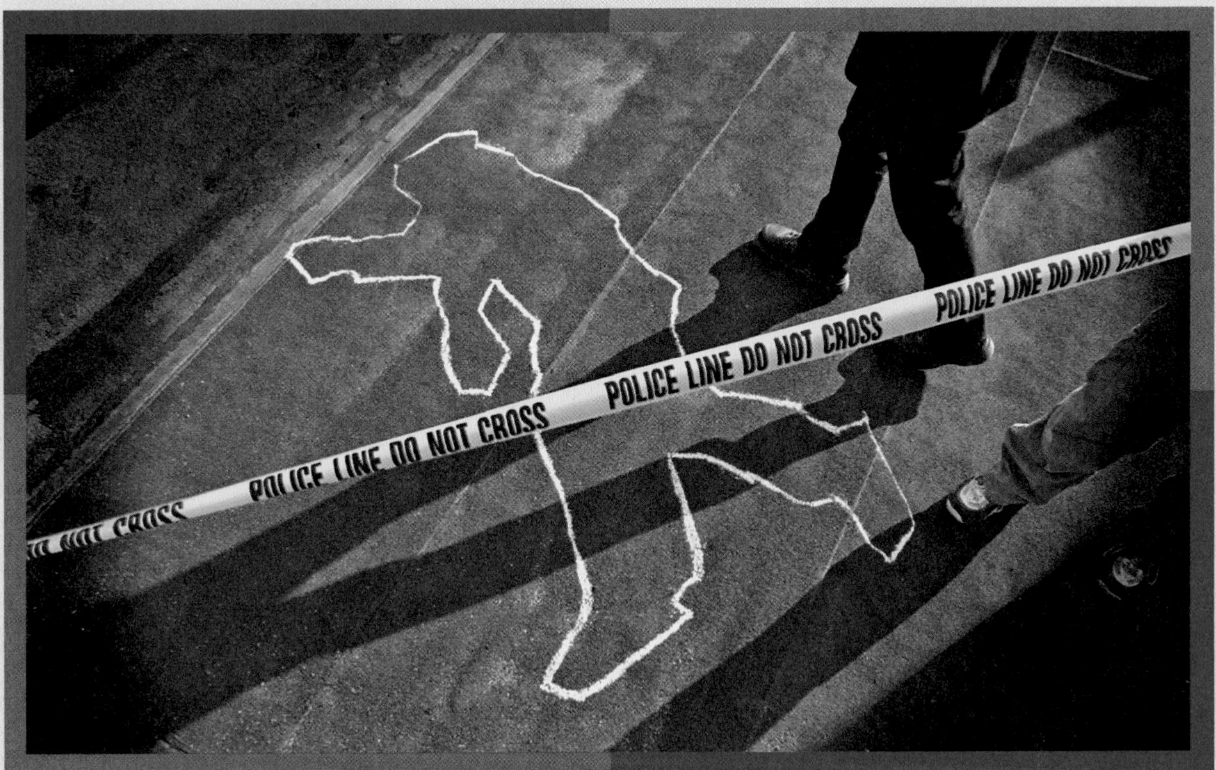

THINKING SOCIOLOGICALLY

- Why are social problems everybody's problem?
- How does sociology differ from "common sense" in explaining social problems?
- Do you agree with this statement: "Guns don't kill people; people kill people"? Is this sound sociological thinking?

None of us thought it was gunshots. [The shooter] didn't say a single word the whole time. He didn't say get down. He didn't say anything. He just came in and started shooting.... I'm not sure how long it lasted. It felt like a really long time but was probably only a minute or so. He looked like, I guess you could say, serious. He didn't look frightened at all. He didn't look angry. Just a straight face....

—Trey Perkins, a Virginia Tech University student, describes a scene of violence in the lecture hall where his German class met. Before the lone gunman ended his shooting spree, 33 people were dead and more than two dozen others were wounded. (MSNBC.com, 2007)

I was in my office in Northern Illinois's Department of Teaching and Learning when the shooting started. The gravity of the situation did not hit me until later, when I picked up my boy from preschool and showed my wife where the shooting was in relation to my office—literally around the corner. The full extent of it did not dawn on me until the next morning, when all of the news outlets were still talking about it. Then I looked at myself in the mirror and realized: Students were shot and killed at my university.

—Joseph Flynn, a Northern Illinois University professor, explains his reaction to the violence that occurred on his campus when a person opened fire inside a lecture hall, killed five students and wounded 20 others, and then took his own life. (Flynn, Kemp, and Madrid, 2008:C1)

For those of us who spend our days in a college setting, few things scare us more than the thought that violence might shatter our "protected" social environment in a lecture hall or other campus facility. Sadly, however, such shootings are becoming an all-too-common occurrence in educational settings, from elementary and secondary schools to colleges and universities, across the United States. And schools are only one of the many settings in which seemingly random acts of violence, typically involving guns and multiple injuries or deaths, take place. Violence has also become all too common in locations such as shopping malls, workplaces, hospitals, and other public spaces. Regardless of where the violence occurs, it leaves behind shock and anguish. ***Violence* is the use of physical force to cause pain, injury, or death to another or damage to property.** On an almost daily basis, the Internet and global television news channels quickly spread word of the latest bombing, the latest massacre, or the latest murder. In the United States today, gunfire is one of the leading causes of death—only vehicular accidents take a higher toll on the lives of young people in this country. Indeed, this country has the highest homicide rate of any high-income nation. In this chapter, we explore what we can learn from sociology about social problems such as this.

USING SOCIOLOGICAL INSIGHTS TO STUDY SOCIAL PROBLEMS

Sociologists who specialize in the study of social problems often focus on violence as a pressing social issue because it inflicts harm not only on victims and their families but also on entire communities and the nation. The study of social problems is one area of inquiry within ***sociology*—the academic discipline that engages in the systematic study of human society and social interactions.** A sociological examination of social problems focuses primarily on issues that affect an entire ***society*—a large number of individuals who share the same geographical territory and are subject to the same political authority and dominant cultural expectations**—and the groups and organizations that make up that society. ***Culture* refers to the knowledge, language, values, customs, and material objects that are passed from person to person and from one generation to the next in a human group or society.** Culture helps us to define what we think is right or wrong and to identify the kinds of behavior we believe should be identified as a social problem.

What Is a Social Problem?

A social problem is a social condition (such as poverty) or a pattern of behavior (such as substance abuse) that harms some individuals or all people in a society and that a sufficient number of people believe warrants public concern and collective action to bring about change. Social conditions or certain patterns of behavior are defined as social problems when they systematically disadvantage or harm a significant number of people or when they are seen as harmful by many of the people who wield power, wealth, and influence in a group or society. Problems that disadvantage or harm a significant number of people include violence, fear of crime, environmental pollution, and inadequate access to health care. Problems that may be viewed as harmful to people who have power, wealth, and influence are conditions that adversely affect their economic livelihood and social well-being, such as a weakening economy, inadequate schools that do not produce the quality of workers that employers need, and high rates of crime that threaten their safety and security. To put it another way, social problems are social in their causes, consequences, and sources of possible resolution. Because social problems are social in their causes, public perceptions of what constitutes a social problem change over time (see Table 1.1 on page 4). It is no surprise, for example, that concerns about war and terrorism are important to people in the United States today, whereas in times of peace concerns focus on issues such as drug abuse, poverty, and homelessness.

Sociologists apply theoretical perspectives and use a variety of research methods to examine social problems. Some social problems—such as violence and crime—are commonly viewed as conditions that affect all members of a population. Other social problems—such as racial discrimination—may be viewed (correctly or incorrectly) as a condition that affects some members of a population more than others. However, all social problems may be harmful to all members in a society whether they realize it or not. Sociological research, for example, has documented the extent to which racial discrimination by whites against African Americans and other people of color wastes the energies and resources of those individuals who engage in such racist actions as well as harming the targets of their actions (see Feagin and Sikes, 1994; Feagin and Vera, 1995).

Social problems often involve significant discrepancies between the ideals of a society and their actual achievement. For example, the United States was founded on basic democratic principles that include the right to "Life, Liberty, and the pursuit of Happiness," as set forth in the Declaration of Independence. The rights of individuals are guaranteed by the U.S. Constitution, which also provides the legal basis for remedying injustices. Significant discrepancies exist, however, between the democratic ideal and its achievement. One such discrepancy is ***discrimination*—actions or practices of dominant group members (or their representatives) that have a harmful impact on members of subordinate groups.** Discrimination may be directed along class, racial, gender, and age lines. It also may be directed against subordinate group members whose sexual orientation, religion, nationality, or other attributes are devalued by those who discriminate against them. Sometimes, discrimination is acted out in the form of violence. This type of violent act is referred to as a ***hate crime*—a physical attack against a person because of assumptions regarding his or her racial group, ethnicity, religion, disability, sexual orientation, national origin, or ancestry.** Hate crime laws have been adopted on the federal and state level that increase the penalties for crimes committed when the perpetrator is motivated by the race, color, national origin, religion, sexual orientation, gender, or disability of the victim. However, these laws vary widely, and seven states have no hate crime laws. Among those states that

TABLE 1.1 Changing Perceptions of What Constitutes a Social Problem, 1950–2008

Nationwide polls taken over the last half century reflect dramatic changes in how people view social problems. Notice how responses to the question "What do you think is the most important problem facing the country today?" have changed over the years.

1950		1965		1975	
War	40%	Civil rights	52%	High cost of living	60%
The economy	15%	Vietnam War	22%	Unemployment	20%
Unemployment	10%	Other international problems	14%	Dissatisfaction with government	7%
Communism	8%	Racial strife	13%	Energy crisis	7%
1990		**2005**		**2008**	
Budget deficit	21%	War in Iraq	19%	The economy	35%
Drug abuse	18%	The economy/jobs	18%	Situation in Iraq/War	21%
Poverty, homelessness	7%	Terrorism (general)	6%	Health care	8%
The economy	7%	Health care	5%	Fuel/oil prices	8%
		Social Security	4%	Immigration/Illegal aliens	6%
		Moral/family values	4%	Unemployment/jobs	5%

Sources: New York Times, 1996b; The Polling Report, 2005; Gallup, 2008.

have passed hate crime laws, some of the laws do not protect sexual orientation, which has been the most hotly debated issue regarding hate crime legislation. For many people, hate crimes are a personal problem because they believe that they have been the victim of violent attacks based on their race, sexual orientation, or both. Some analysts believe that people of color in the gay, lesbian, bisexual, and transgendered (GLBT) community are at greater risk of violence. As a Human Rights Campaign activist explained, "When a GLBT person of color is targeted for hate violence, it is difficult—if not impossible—to separate out race, sexual orientation, or gender identity discrimination in the treatment of the victim and the victim's family and loved ones" (Human Rights Campaign, 2003).

When hate crimes have been reported prominently by the news media, some political leaders have taken a stronger stand against such violence, thus moving the problem from the personal to the social level. For example, when an African-American man in New York City was attacked with a baseball bat, leaving him with a fractured skull, the city's mayor made public appearances around the city to show that the city would actively confront racial violence and would not tolerate it. As Mayor Michael R. Bloomberg stated, "I cannot stress it enough: We are going to live together, and nobody, nobody, should ever feel that they will be attacked because of their ethnicity, their orientation, their religion, where they live, their documented status, or anything else. Period. End of story" (quoted in Rutenberg and Kilgannon, 2005:A15). Public statements such as this and corresponding changes in social policy and law are the point at which personal problems and social issues begin to connect. Sociologists use a perspective known as the sociological imagination to explain this phenomenon.

The Sociological Imagination: Bringing Together the Personal and the Social

How do our personal problems relate to the larger social problems in our society and around the world? Although each of us has numerous personal problems, ranging from how to pay our college tuition and where to find a job to more general concerns about safety, health, and war, we are not alone in these problems, and there are larger societal and global patterns that we can identify that are related to these issues. In one of the most popular phrases in the social sciences, the sociologist C. Wright Mills uniquely captured the essence of how our personal troubles are related to the larger social issues in society. According to Mills, the ***sociological imagination* is the ability to see the relationship between individual experiences and the larger society.** The sociological imagination enables us to connect the private problems of individuals to public issues. Public issues (or social problems) are matters beyond a person's control that originate at the regional or national level and can be resolved only by collective action. Mills (1959b) used unemployment as an example of how people may erroneously separate personal troubles from public issues in their thinking. The unemployed individual may view his or her unemployment as a personal trouble concerning only the individual, other family members, and friends. However, widespread unemployment resulting from economic changes, corporate decisions (downsizing or relocating a plant abroad), or technological innovations (computers and advanced telecommunications systems displacing workers) is a public issue. The sociological imagination helps us to shift our focus to the larger social context and see how personal troubles may be related to public issues. For example, it is easy for the victims of violent crimes and their families to see themselves as individual victims rather than placing such attacks within the larger, collective context of a society that often tolerates violence.

Although some people think that being unemployed is a personal problem, widespread unemployment is a public issue. These laid-off employees are only a few of the thousands of U.S. workers who have lost their jobs in recent years. What can we gain by applying a sociological perspective to social problems such as unemployment?

Sociologists make connections between personal and public issues in society through microlevel and macrolevel analysis. ***Microlevel analysis* focuses on small-group relations and social interaction among individuals.** Using microlevel analysis, a sociologist might investigate how fear of unemployment affects workers and their immediate families. In contrast, ***macrolevel analysis* focuses on social processes occurring at the societal level, especially in large-scale organizations and major social institutions such as politics, government, and the economy.** Using macrolevel analysis, a sociologist might examine how the loss of millions of jobs in recent decades has affected the U.S. economy. As Mills suggested, a systematic study of a social problem such as unemployment gives us a clearer picture of the relationship between macrolevel structures such as the U.S. economy and microlevel social interactions among people in their homes, workplaces, and communities.

What can we gain by using a sociological perspective to study social problems? A sociological examination of social problems enables us to move beyond myths and common-sense notions, to gain new insights into ourselves, and to develop an awareness of the connection between our own world and the worlds of other people. According to sociologist Peter Berger (1963:23), a sociological examination allows us to realize that "things are not what they seem." Indeed, most social problems are multifaceted. When we recognize this, we can approach pressing national and global concerns in new ways and make better decisions about those concerns. By taking a global perspective on social problems, we soon realize that the lives of all people are closely intertwined and that any one nation's problems are part of a larger global problem. Examining violence as a social problem, for example, makes it possible for us to look at the causes and consequences of this type of behavior on a global basis. It also makes it possible for us to look more closely at our own society to see how we respond to such problems through social policy.

An example is the renewed call by many members of society for gun control in the aftermath of each new episode of gun-related violence and the contradictory assertion from organizations such as the National Rifle Association that gun-control laws are neither needed nor effective (see Box 1.1). As this example shows, what constitutes a social problem and what should be done about that problem is often a controversial topic.

DO WE HAVE A PROBLEM? SUBJECTIVE AWARENESS AND OBJECTIVE REALITY

A subjective awareness that a social problem exists usually emerges before the objective reality of the problem is acknowledged. Subjective awareness tends to be

Social Problems and Social Policy

Box 1.1

expressed as a feeling of uneasiness or skepticism about something, but the feeling is not founded on any concrete evidence that a problem actually exists. A subjective awareness that there is potential for violent acts in public settings such as schools, day-care centers, businesses, and churches exists even when there has been no recent violence in one of these settings. However, when new killings take place, our subjective awareness shifts to being an objective reality.

Consider, for example, the differences in subjective awareness and objective reality when it comes to violence in the media. Many people feel uncomfortable with the increasingly graphic nature of portrayals of violence on television and in films and video games. Initially, parents have a subjective awareness that these depictions might be harmful for their children and perhaps for the larger society. However, it is only when we have facts to support our beliefs that there is a link between media violence and actual behavior that we move beyond a subjective awareness of the issue. Indeed, recent studies show that media violence may influence how people think and act. According to one study, boys and girls who watch a lot of violence on television have a heightened risk of aggressive adult behavior including spousal abuse and criminal offenses (Huesmann, Moise-Titus, Podolski, and Eron, 2003).

Box 1.1 *(continued)*

U.S. Constitution: "A well regulated Militia, being necessary to the security of a free State, the right of the people to keep and bear Arms, shall not be infringed." Those in favor of legislation to regulate the gun industry and gun ownership argue that the Second Amendment does not guarantee an individual's right to own guns: The right "to keep and bear Arms" applies only to those citizens who do so as part of an official state militia (Lazare, 1999:57). However, in 2008, the U.S. Supreme Court ruled that the Second Amendment protects an individual's right to own a gun for personal use. In other words, people have a constitutionally protected right to keep a loaded handgun at home for self-defense. This is in keeping with an argument long made by spokespersons for the National Rifle Association (NRA), a powerful group with about 4 million members nationwide and a $20 to $30 million lobbying budget, which has stated that gun control regulations violate the individual's constitutional right to own a gun (Schwartz, 2008) and would not be an effective means of curbing random acts of violence on school campuses and elsewhere.

What solutions exist for the quandary over gun regulations? Best notes that declaring war on a social problem such as gun-related violence is difficult for several reasons. First, social problems are not simple issues: Most problems have multiple causes and a variety of possible solutions. Second, it is difficult to determine what constitutes victory in such a war. Third, it takes a long time to see the outcome of changes in social policies, and efforts to produce change may receive reduced funding or be eliminated before significant changes actually occur. Finally, it is impossible to rally everyone behind a single policy, and much time is therefore spent arguing over how to proceed, how much money to spend, and who or what is the real enemy (Best, 1999). In the final analysis, the problem of gun violence is a chronic problem in the United States that has yet to be successfully addressed by social policy and its implementation.

In the meantime, we return to the question we initially raised about students possessing guns at college. Those persons who believe that students should be allowed to carry guns on campus for self-defense assert that no acts of violence have occurred at universities where students are legally allowed to carry concealed handguns. They also note that many states set the legal age limit at 21 for obtaining a concealed handgun license, which means that the students who obtain such a license typically are juniors or seniors, not beginning college students. By contrast, those individuals and organizations that strongly object to non–law enforcement personnel "packing heat" on college campuses argue that when guns are readily available, there is a greater likelihood of lethal outcomes because people have violent force right at their fingertips when they fear for their safety or become involved in an emotionally volatile situation.

What will be the future of guns on college campuses? If the past is any indication, people will let the issue drop during the time period when no violence occurs, but when the next episode of violence transpires, there will be new demands from state lawmakers, gun-control advocates, and gun rights lobbyists to turn their specific point of view into legislation, perhaps including a law granting students the right to carry firearms at their college or university. How do you feel about this very polarizing social policy issue? Would you feel more—or less—safe if you knew that more people were carrying concealed weapons on your campus?

Moreover, the American Psychological Association has concluded that viewing violence on television and in other media does promote aggressive behavior in children as well as in adults (Ritter, 2003). Children's identification with television characters and the perceived realism of television violence may be linked to aggression in adulthood, regardless of a child's intellectual ability or his or her family income level. The more that children watch media violence, the more likely they are to participate in rough play and eventually to engage in violence as adults (Zimring and Hawkins, 1997; Huesmann, Moise-Titus, Podolski, and Eron, 2003). As researchers gather additional data to support their arguments, the link between extensive media watching and the potential for violence grows stronger, moving into the realm of objective reality rather than being merely a subjective awareness of isolated individuals.

However, even the gathering of objective facts does not always result in consensus on social issues. Individuals and groups may question the validity of the facts, or they may dispute the facts by using other data that they hope demonstrate a different perspective. Examples of objective conditions that may or may not be considered by everyone to be social problems include environmental pollution and resource depletion, war, health care, and changes in moral values. Religious and political views influence how people define social problems and what they think the possible solutions might be. Often, one person's solution to a problem is viewed as a problem by another person. For example, some people see abortion as a solution to an unwanted pregnancy, whereas others believe that abortion is a serious social problem. Abortion and end-of-life decisions (such as assisted suicide and "right to die" cases) are only two of the many issues that are strongly influenced by religion and politics in the United States. To analyze the conditions that must be met before an objective reality becomes identified as a social problem, see Box 1.2.

Just like other people, sociologists usually have strong opinions about what is "good" and "bad" in society and what might be done to improve conditions. However, sociologists know their opinions are often subjective. Thus, they use theory and systematic research techniques and report their findings to other social scientists for consideration. In other words, sociologists strive to view social problems *objectively.* Of course, complete objectivity may not be an attainable—or desirable—goal in studying human behavior. Max Weber, an early German sociologist, acknowledged that complete objectivity might be impossible but pointed out that *verstehen* ("understanding" or "insight") was critical to any analysis of social problems. According to Weber, *verstehen* enables individuals to see the world as others see it and to empathize with them. *Verstehen,* in turn, enables us to use the sociological imagination and employ social theory rather than our own opinions to analyze social problems.

USING SOCIAL THEORY TO ANALYZE SOCIAL PROBLEMS

To determine how social life is organized, sociologists develop theories and conduct research. A ***theory*** **is a set of logically related statements that attempt to describe, explain, or predict social events.** Theories are useful for explaining relationships between social concepts or phenomena, such as age and unemployment. They also help us to interpret social reality in a distinct way by giving us a framework for organizing our observations. Sociologists refer to this theoretical framework as a ***perspective*****—an overall approach or viewpoint toward some subject.** Three major theoretical perspectives have emerged in sociology: the functionalist perspective, which views society as a basically stable and orderly entity; the conflict perspective, which views society as an arena of competition and conflict; and the interactionist perspective, which focuses on the everyday, routine interactions among individuals. The functionalist and conflict perspectives are based on macrolevel analysis because they focus on social processes occurring at the societal level. The interactionist perspective is based on microlevel analysis because it focuses on small-group relations and social interaction.

The Functionalist Perspective

The functionalist perspective grew out of the works of early social thinkers such as Auguste Comte (1798–1857), the founder of sociology. Comte compared society to a living organism. Just as muscles, tissues, and organs of the human body perform specific functions that maintain the body as a whole, the various parts of society contribute to its maintenance and preservation. According to the ***functionalist perspective,*** **society is a stable, orderly system composed of a number of interrelated parts, each of which performs a function that contributes to the overall stability of society** (Parsons, 1951). These interrelated parts are social institutions (such as families, the economy, education, and the government) that a society develops to organize its main concerns and activities so that social needs are

Critical Thinking and You

Box 1.2

Determining What Constitutes a Social Problem

Which of the following is defined as a major social problem in the United States?

- Driving a motor vehicle, which results in approximately 43,000 U.S. deaths each year
- Playing contact sports in school, which results in many injuries and deaths among young people
- Hunting for wild game, which results in numerous injuries and deaths among hunters and bystanders

If you answered, "None of the above," you are correct. Although driving a motor vehicle, playing contact sports, and hunting may have hazardous potential consequences, few people view these actions in and of themselves as being a social problem. In other words, not all behavior that may result in violence or even death is classified as a social problem.

What questions should we ask to determine if something is a social problem? Here are a few suggestions:

1. Is there a public outcry about this conduct or this condition? Are people actively discussing the issue and demanding that a resolution be found?
2. Does the conduct or condition reflect a gap between social ideals and social reality? What social ideals are involved? What is the social reality about the situation?
3. Are a large number of people involved in defining the problem and demanding that a solution be found? Does the matter have national attention? If not, is a special-interest group the primary source of demands that something be done about the condition?
4. Can a solution be found for the problem? If not, can we reduce the problem or alleviate the suffering of some victims of the problem?

Based on these questions, what pressing social issues are we overlooking in our nation or on a global basis that should be considered as social problems requiring immediate action? What issues receive too much attention from the media and the public? How do culture, religion, and politics influence our definition of what constitutes a social problem?

met. Each institution performs a unique function, contributing to the overall stability of society and the well-being of individuals (Merton, 1968). For example, the functions of the economy are producing and distributing goods (such as food, clothing, and shelter) and services (such as health care and dry cleaning), whereas the government is responsible for coordinating activities of other institutions, maintaining law and order, dealing with unmet social needs, and handling international relations and warfare.

Manifest and Latent Functions

Though the functions of the economy and the government seem fairly clear-cut, functionalists suggest that not all the functions of social institutions are intended and overtly recognized. In fact, according to the functionalist perspective, social institutions perform two different types of societal functions: manifest and latent. *Manifest functions* are intended and recognized consequences of an activity or social process. A manifest function of education, for example, is to provide students with knowledge, skills, and cultural values. In contrast, *latent functions* are the unintended consequences of an activity or social process that are hidden and remain unacknowledged by participants (Merton, 1968). The latent functions of education include the babysitter function of keeping young people off the street and out of the full-time job market and the matchmaking function whereby schools provide opportunities for students to meet and socialize with potential marriage partners. These functions are latent because schools were not created for babysitting or matchmaking, and most organizational participants do not acknowledge that these activities take place.

Dysfunctions and Social Disorganization

From the functionalist perspective, social problems arise when social institutions do not fulfill their functions or when dysfunctions occur. *Dysfunctions* are the undesirable consequences of an activity or social process that inhibit a society's ability to adapt or adjust (Merton, 1968). For example, a function of education is to prepare students for jobs, but if schools fail to do so, then students have problems finding jobs, employers have to spend millions of dollars on employee training programs, and consumers have to pay higher prices for goods and services to offset worker training costs. In other words, dysfunctions in education threaten other social institutions, especially families and the economy.

Dysfunctions can occur in society as a whole or in a part of society (a social institution). According to functionalists, dysfunctions in social institutions create social disorganization in the entire society. ***Social disorganization*** **refers to the conditions in society that undermine the ability of traditional social institutions to govern human behavior.** Early in the twentieth century, sociologists Robert E. Park (1864–1944) and Ernest W. Burgess (1886–1966) developed a social disorganization theory to explain why some areas of Chicago had higher rates of *social deviance,* which they defined as a pattern of rule violation, than other areas had. Social disorganization causes a breakdown in the traditional values and norms that serve as social control mechanisms, which, under normal circumstances, keep people from engaging in nonconforming behavior. ***Values*** **are collective ideas about what is right or wrong, good or bad, and desirable or undesirable in a specific society** (Williams, 1970). Although values provide ideas about behavior, they do not state explicitly how we should behave. Norms, on the other hand, have specific behavioral expectations. ***Norms*** **are established rules of behavior or standards of conduct.** French sociologist Emile Durkheim (1858–1917) suggested that social problems arise when people no longer agree on societal values and norms. According to Durkheim, periods of rapid social change produce *anomie*—a loss of shared values and sense of purpose in society. During these periods, social bonds grow weaker, social control is diminished, and people are more likely to engage in nonconforming patterns of behavior such as crime.

Early sociologists, examining the relationship between social problems and rapid industrialization and urbanization in Britain, western Europe, and the United States in the late nineteenth and early twentieth centuries, noted that rapid social change intensifies social disorganization. ***Industrialization*** **is the process by which societies are transformed from a dependence on agriculture and handmade products to an emphasis on manufacturing and related industries.** At the beginning of the Industrial Revolution, thousands of people migrated from rural communities to large urban centers to find employment in factories and offices. New social problems emerged as a result of industrialization and ***urbanization,*** **the process by which an increasing proportion of a population lives in cities rather than in rural areas.** During this period of rapid technological and social change, a sharp increase occurred in urban social problems such as poverty, crime, child labor, inadequate housing, unsanitary conditions, overcrowding, and environmental pollution.

Applying the Functionalist Perspective to Problems of Violence

Some functionalists believe that violence arises from a condition of anomie, in which many individuals have a feeling of helplessness, normlessness, or alienation. Others believe that violence increases when social institutions such as the family, schools, and religious organizations weaken and the main mechanisms of social control in people's everyday lives are external (i.e., law enforcement agencies and the criminal justice system).

One functionalist explanation of violence, known as the ***subculture of violence hypothesis,*** **states that violence is part of the normative expectations governing everyday behavior among young males in the lower classes** (Wolfgang and Ferracuti, 1967). Violence is considered a by-product of their culture, which idealizes toughness and even brutality in the name of masculinity. According to criminologists Marvin E. Wolfgang and Franco Ferracuti (1967), violent subcultures (for example, violent juvenile gangs, neo-Nazi skinhead groups, and some organized crime groups) are most likely to develop when young people, particularly males, have few legitimate opportunities available in their segment of society and when subcultural values accept and encourage violent behavior. In this context, young people come to consider aggression or violence a natural response to certain situations. However, this explanation has been criticized for exclusively focusing on violence among young males in the lower classes but providing no explanation regarding violence perpetrated by people in the middle or upper classes.

Still other functionalist explanations of violence focus on how changes in social institutions put some people at greater risk of being victims of violent crime than others. According to the ***lifestyle-routine activity approach,*** **the patterns and timing of people's daily movements and activities as they go about obtaining the necessities of life—such as food, shelter, companionship, and entertainment—are the keys to understanding violent personal crimes and other types of crime in our society** (Cohen and Felson, 1979). Among the changes over the past fifty years that have increased violent crime in the United States are more families in which both parents (or the sole parent) work outside the home, more people living by themselves, shopping hours extended into the night, and more people eating outside the home (Parker, 1995). Social structure may also put constraints on behavior, thus making certain people more vulnerable to violent attack (e.g., people who are required to work at night). The lifestyle-routine activity approach suggests that people who willingly put themselves in situations that expose them to the potential for violent crime should modify their behavior or that society should provide greater protection for people whose lifestyle routine leaves them vulnerable to attackers. The lifestyle-routine activity approach is good as far as it goes, but it does not address the issue of violence in the home and other supposedly safe havens in society.

How would a functionalist approach the problem of violence? Most functionalists emphasize shared moral values and social bonds. They believe that when rapid social change or other disruptions occur, moral values may erode and problems such as school violence or hate crimes are likely to occur. Functionalists believe that to reduce violence, families, schools, religious organizations, and other social institutions should be strengthened so that they can regenerate shared values and morality. Most functionalists also believe that those who engage in violent criminal behavior should be prosecuted to the full extent of the law.

The functional approach to social problems has been criticized for its acceptance of the status quo and for its lack of appreciation of how problems in society are associated with vast economic and social inequality, racism, sexism, ageism, and other forms of discrimination that keep our society from being an equal playing field for everyone.

The Conflict Perspective

The ***conflict perspective* is based on the assumption that groups in society are engaged in a continuous power struggle for control of scarce resources.** Unlike functionalist theorists, who emphasize the degree to which society is held together by a consensus on values, conflict theorists emphasize the degree to which society is characterized by conflict and discrimination. According to some conflict theorists, certain groups of people are privileged while others are disadvantaged through the unjust use of political, economic, or social power. Not all conflict theorists hold the same views about what constitutes the most important form of conflict. We will examine two principal perspectives: the value conflict perspective and the critical-conflict perspective.

The Value Conflict Perspective

According to value conflict theorists, social problems are conditions that are incompatible with group values. From this perspective, value clashes are ordinary occurrences in families, communities, and the larger society, in which individuals commonly hold many divergent values. Although individuals may share certain core values, they do not share all values or a common culture. As previously stated, culture refers to the knowledge, language, values, customs, and material objects that are passed from person to person and from one generation to the next in a human group or society.

Discrepancies between ideal and real culture are a source of social problems in all societies. *Ideal culture* refers to the values and beliefs that people claim they hold; *real culture* refers to the values and beliefs that they actually follow. In the United States, for example, members of the National Association for the Advancement of Colored People (NAACP), La Raza, the Ku Klux Klan, and the White Aryan Resistance all claim to adhere to ideal cultural values of equality, freedom, and liberty; however, these ideal cultural values come into direct conflict with real cultural values when issues of racial-ethnic relations arise. Urban marches and protest rallies held by members of the NAACP and the Ku Klux Klan on Martin Luther King Day, which celebrates the birthday of the African-American minister and civil rights activist who was murdered in 1968, are a concrete example of the clash between ideal and real cultural values. The value conflict perspective has been criticized by critical-conflict theorists, who argue that it overlooks the deeper social problems of inequality and oppression based on class, race, and gender.

Critical-Conflict Perspective

Unlike the value conflict approach, critical-conflict theorists suggest that social problems arise out of the major contradictions inherent in the way societies are organized. Some critical-conflict perspectives focus on class inequalities in the capitalist economic system; others focus on inequalities based on race, ethnicity, or gender.

Most class perspectives on inequality have been strongly influenced by Karl Marx (1818–1883), a German economist and activist, who recognized that the emergence of capitalism had produced dramatic and irreversible changes in social life. ***Capitalism* is an economic system characterized by private ownership of the means of production, from which personal profits can be derived through market competition**

■ *Business scandals such as the one involving Enron Corporation show the wide gap between those corporate executives who made millions of dollars from questionable business practices that eventually brought down their companies and the employees who lost their jobs and benefits when those companies folded.*

and without government intervention. In contemporary capitalist economies, businesses are privately owned and operated for the profit of owners and corporate shareholders. According to Marx, members of the *capitalist class* (*the bourgeoisie*), who own and control the means of production (e.g., the land, tools, factories, and money for investment), are at the top of a system of social stratification that affords them different lifestyles and life chances from those of the members of the *working class* (the *proletariat*), who must sell their labor power (their potential ability to work) to capitalists. In selling their labor power, members of the working class forfeit control over their work, and the capitalists derive excessive profit from the workers' labor.

Marx believed that capitalism led workers to experience increased levels of impoverishment and alienation—a feeling of powerlessness and estrangement from other people and from oneself (Marx and Engels, 1847/1971:96). He predicted that the working class would eventually overthrow the capitalist economic system. Although Marx's prediction has not come about, Erik Olin Wright (1997) and other social scientists have modified and adapted his perspective to apply to contemporary capitalist nations. In today's capitalist nations, according to Wright, ownership of the means of production is only one way in which people gain the ability to exploit others.

Two other ways in which individuals gain control are through control of property and control over other people's labor. In this view, upper-level managers and others in positions of authority gain control over societal resources and other individuals' time, knowledge, and skills in such a manner that members of the upper classes are able to maintain their dominance (Wright, 1997).

Some critical-conflict perspectives focus on racial and gender subordination instead of class-based inequalities. Critical-conflict theorists who emphasize discrimination and inequality based on race or ethnicity note that many social problems are rooted in the continuing exploitation and subordination of people of color by white people. For example, some scholars suggest that Native Americans have the highest rates of poverty in the United States because of extended periods of racial subordination and exploitation throughout this country's history (see Feagin and Feagin, 2008).

Critical-conflict theorists who use a feminist approach focus on *patriarchy,* a system of male dominance in which males are privileged and women are oppressed. According to a feminist approach, male domination in society contributes not only to domestic violence, child abuse, and rape but also to poverty and crimes such as prostitution. Feminist scholars state that gender inequality will not be eliminated in the home, school, and workplace until patriarchy is abolished and women and men are treated equally.

Finally, there are some critical-conflict theorists who note that race, class, and gender are interlocking systems of privilege and oppression that result in social problems. For example, black feminist scholar Patricia Hill Collins (1990) has pointed out that race, class, and gender are simultaneous forces of oppression for women of color, especially African-American women. Critical-conflict analysts focusing on these intersections believe that equality can come about only when women across lines of race and class receive equal treatment (Andersen and Collins, 2001; Collins, 1995). Throughout this text, we will use critical-conflict theory (rather than the value conflict approach) to highlight the power relations that result in social problems.

Applying the Conflict Perspective to Problems of Violence

Conflict theorists who focus on class-based inequalities believe that the potential for violence is inherent in capitalist societies. In fact, say these theorists, the wealthy engage in one form of violence, and the poor engage in another. They note that the wealthy often use third parties to protect themselves and their families from bodily harm as well as to secure their property and investments in this country and elsewhere in the world. For example, the wealthy who live in the United States or other high-income nations and own factories (or own stock in factories) in middle- and low-income nations use the governments and police of those nations—third parties—to control workers who threaten to strike. The wealthy also influence U.S. government policy. For instance, they are likely to support U.S. military intervention—and thus violence—in nations where they have large investments at stake. However, sometimes the wealthy want the U.S. government to look the other way and not intervene in these nations in order to protect investments in countries in which dictators have made their investments profitable.

■ *Low-income African American women are disproportionately affected by flooding, property damage, and housing displacement that occur as a result of hurricanes and other natural disasters. Feminist critical-conflict theorists believe that African American women face a system of interlocking oppression of race, class, and gender that intensifies this problem.*

In contrast, these theorists say, when the poor engage in violence, the violence is typically committed by the individual and is a reaction to the unjust social and economic conditions he or she experiences daily on the bottom rung of a capitalist society. The economic exploitation of the poor, these theorists note, dramatically affects all aspects of the individual's life, including how the person reacts to daily injustices, stress, and other threatening situations. In violent street crimes, the vast majority of offenders—as well as victims—are poor, unemployed, or working in low-level, low-paying jobs. In fact, most violent street crime is an intraclass phenomenon: Poor and working-class people typically victimize others who are like themselves.

The conflict perspective argues that the criminal justice system is biased in favor of the middle and upper classes. Because it is, its definition of violence depends on where a person's race, class, and gender locate him or her in the system of stratification. In this way, violent crimes are but one part of a larger system of inequality and oppression. Sexism and racism are reinforced by the overarching class structure that benefits the powerful at the expense of the powerless. Exploitation of people of color and the poor creates a sense of hopelessness, frustration, and hostility in them that may boil over into violent acts such as rape or murder. At the same time, it is important to note that violent acts, including murder, occur across all class and racial-ethnic categories in the United States.

The conflict perspective that focuses on feminist issues specifically examines violence against women, for example, rape and most spousal abuse. One feminist perspective suggests that violence against women is a means of reinforcing patriarchy. According to the feminist perspective, in a patriarchal system, the sexual marketplace is characterized by unequal bargaining power, making transactions between men and women potentially coercive in nature. Gender stratification is reinforced by powerful physical, psychological, and social mechanisms of control, including force or the threat of force. Fear of violence forces women to change their ways of living, acting, and dressing and thus deprives them of many basic freedoms (see Gardner, 1995).

The conflict perspective that focuses on racial-ethnic inequalities points out that racism is an important factor in explaining such violent acts as hate crimes. Some analysts trace contemporary brutality against African Americans, particularly men, to earlier periods when hanging or dragging was used to punish slave insurrections and to keep African Americans subservient during the Reconstruction and the subsequent years of legal racial segregation in the South (see Feagin and Feagin, 2008).

No matter what approach conflict theorists take, they all agree on one thing: Violence is unlikely to diminish significantly unless inequalities based on class, gender, and race are reduced at the macrolevel in society. However, social problems must also be examined at the microlevel, where individuals actually live their daily lives.

The Symbolic Interactionist Perspective

Unlike the conflict perspective, which focuses on macrolevel inequalities in society, the symbolic interactionist perspective focuses on a microlevel analysis of how people act toward one another and how they make sense of their daily lives. The ***symbolic interactionist perspective*** **views society as the sum of the interactions of individuals and groups.** Most symbolic interactionists study social problems by analyzing how certain behavior comes to be defined as a social problem and how individuals and groups come to engage in activities that a significant number of people and/or a number of significant people view as a major social concern.

What is the relationship between individuals and the society in which they live? One early sociologist attempted to answer this question. German sociologist Georg Simmel (1858–1918), a founder of the interactionist approach, investigated the impact of industrialization and urbanization on people's values and behavior within small social units. Simmel (1902/1950) noted that rapid changes in technology and dramatic urban growth produced new social problems by breaking up the "geometry of social life," which he described as the web of patterned social interactions among the people who constitute a society. According to Simmel, alienation is brought about by a decline in personal and emotional contacts. How people interpret the subjective messages that they receive from others and the situations that they encounter in their daily life greatly influences their behavior and their perceptions of what constitutes a social problem.

Labeling Theory and the Social Construction of Reality

While Simmel focused on how people interpret their own situations, other symbolic interactionists have examined how people impose their shared meanings on others. According to sociologist Howard Becker (1963), *moral entrepreneurs* are people who use their own views of right and wrong to establish rules and label others as deviant (nonconforming). Labeling theory, as this perspective is called, suggests that behavior that deviates from established norms is deviant because it has been labeled as such by others. According to this theory, deviants (nonconformists) are people who have been successfully labeled as such by others. Labeling theory raises questions about why certain individuals and certain types of behavior are labeled as deviant but others are not.

According to some symbolic interaction theorists, many social problems can be linked to the *social construction of reality*—the process by which people's perception of reality is shaped largely by the subjective meaning that they give to an experience (Berger and Luckmann, 1967). From this perspective, little shared reality exists beyond that which people socially create. It is, however, this social construction of reality that influences people's beliefs and actions.

Other symbolic interactionists suggest that how we initially define a situation affects our future actions. According to sociologist W. I. Thomas (1863–1947), when people define situations as real, the situations become real in their consequences. Elaborating on Thomas's idea, sociologist Robert Merton (1968) has suggested that when people perceive a situation in a certain way and act according to their perceptions, the end result may be a ***self-fulfilling prophecy*****—the process by which an unsubstantiated belief or prediction results in behavior that makes the original false conception come true.** For example, a teenager who is labeled a "juvenile delinquent" may accept the label and adopt the full-blown image of a juvenile delinquent as portrayed in television programs and films: wearing gang colors, dropping out of school, and participating in gang violence or other behavior that is labeled as deviant. If the teenager subsequently is arrested, the initial label becomes a self-fulfilling prophecy.

Applying Symbolic Interactionist Perspectives to Problems of Violence

Symbolic interactionist explanations of violence begin by noting that human behavior is learned through social interaction. Violence, they state, is a learned response, not an inherent characteristic, in the individual. Some of the most interesting support for this point of view comes from studies done by social psychologist Albert Bandura, who studied aggression in children (1973). Showing children a film of a person beating, kicking, and hacking an inflatable doll produced a violent response in the children, who, when they were placed in a room with a similar doll, duplicated the person's behavior and engaged in additional aggressive behavior. Others have noted that people tend to repeat their behavior if they feel rewarded for it. Thus, when people learn that they can get their way by inflicting violence or the threat of violence on others, their aggressive behavior is reinforced.

Symbolic interactionists also look at the types of social interactions that commonly lead to violence. According to the ***situational approach*****, violence results from a specific interaction process, termed a "situational transaction."** Criminologist David Luckenbill (1977) has identified six stages in the situational transaction between victim and offender. In the first stage, the future victim does something behavioral or verbal that is considered an affront by the other (e.g., a glare or an insult). In the second, the offended individual verifies that the action was directed at him or her personally. In the third, the offended individual decides how to respond to the affront and might issue a verbal or behavioral challenge (e.g., a threat or a raised fist). If the problem escalates at this point, injury or death might occur in this stage; if not, the participants enter into the fourth stage. In this stage, the future victim further escalates the transaction, often prodded on by onlookers siding with one party or the other. In the fifth stage, actual violence occurs when neither party is able to back down without losing face. At this point, one or both parties produce weapons, which may range from guns and knives to bottles, pool cues, or other bludgeoning devices, if they have not already appeared, and the offender kills the victim. The sixth and final stage involves the offender's actions after the crime; some flee the scene, others are detained by onlookers, and still others call the police themselves.

The situational approach is based, first, on the assumption that many victims are active participants in the violence perpetrated against them and, second, on the idea that confrontation does not inevitably lead to violence or death. As Robert Nash Parker (1995) has noted, in the first four stages of the transaction, either the victim or the offender can decide to pursue another course of action.

According to symbolic interactionists, reducing violence requires changing those societal values that encourage excessive competition and violence. At the macrolevel, how the media report on violence may influence our thinking about the appropriateness of certain kinds of aggressive behavior (see Box 1.3 on page 16). However, change must occur at the microlevel, which means that agents of socialization must transmit different attitudes and values toward violence. The next generation must learn that it is an individual's right—regardless of gender, race, class, religion, or other attributes or characteristics—to live free from violence and the devastating impact it has on individuals, groups, and the social fabric of society.

USING SOCIAL RESEARCH METHODS TO STUDY SOCIAL PROBLEMS

Sociologists use a variety of research methods to study social problems such as violence. Research methods are strategies or techniques for systematically collecting data. Some methods produce *quantitative data* that can be measured numerically and lend themselves to statistical analysis. For example, the *Uniform Crime Report* (UCR), published annually by the Federal Bureau of Investigation, provides crime statistics that sociologists and others can use to learn more about the nature and extent of violent crime in the United States. Other research methods produce *qualitative data* that are reported in the form of interpretive descriptions (words) rather than numbers. For example, *qualitative data* on violence in the United States might provide new insights on how the victims or their families and friends cope in the aftermath of a violent attack such as school shootings or terrorist bombings.

Sociologists use three major types of research methods: field research, survey research, and secondary analysis of existing data. Although our discussion focuses on each separately, many researchers use a combination of methods to enhance their understanding of social issues.

Field Research

Field research **is the study of social life in its natural setting: observing and interviewing people where they live, work, and play.** When sociologists want firsthand information about a social problem, they

Social Problems

Box 1.3 (continued)

unemployment, violence in the media, lack of education, abuse as a child, witnessing violence in the home or neighborhood, isolation of the nuclear family, and belief in male dominance over females" (Stevens, 2001:8). Episodic framing highlights the importance of individual responsibility for acts of violence and reinforces the dominant ideology that individuals must be held accountable for their actions. This type of framing suggests to media audiences that public officials, business leaders, and other influential people are not accountable for any part that they may have played in creating a situation that produced the violence. For example, lobbyists who pressure legislators to pass lenient gun-control legislation (or none at all) are seldom held accountable for gun-related deaths, nor are the legislators and politicians who control the political process.

Standing in sharp contrast to episodic framing is thematic framing, which provides a more impersonal view of what the nature of the social problem is. Journalists using thematic framing often tell the story through the use of statistics and discussions of trends ("Is the problem growing worse?" "Should we fear for our safety?"). Thematic framing emphasizes "facts" based on statistical data, such as the number of people killed in drive-by shootings or school violence in recent years. Thematic framing does not focus on the human tragedy of social problems such as violence or poverty, and when bombarded by continuous coverage of this sort, television viewers may conclude that little can be done about the problem. Rather than hearing from the victims of gun violence or poverty, for example, media reports typically emphasize "expert opinion" from "talking heads" who provide information that often supports the reporter's own point of view.

Would you like to more closely study how the media frame stories about social problems? Select one or more of these problems and identify recurring framing patterns you can find in media coverage:

War in Iraq	Social Security
Economy/Jobs	Terrorism
Health care	Education

Based on Kendall, 2005; Iyengar, 1990, 1991.

Using field research, sociologists have studied gang violence and found that gang members are not all alike. Some do not approve of violence; others engage in violence only to assert authority; still others may engage in violence only when they feel threatened or want to maintain their territory.

often use participant observation—field research in which researchers collect systematic observations while participating in the activities of the group they are studying. Field research on social problems can take place in many settings, ranging from schools and neighborhoods to universities, prisons, and large corporations.

Field research is valuable because some kinds of behavior and social problems can be studied best by being there; a more complete understanding can be developed through observations, face-to-face discussions, and participation in events than through other research methods. For example, field research on gang violence led sociologist Martin Sánchez Jankowski (1991) to conclude that most gang members do not like violence and fear that they might be injured or killed in violent encounters. As a result, gang members engage in collective violence only to accomplish specific objectives such as asserting authority or punishing violations by their own members who are incompetent or who break the gang's code. Violence against other gangs occurs primarily when gang members feel threatened or need to maintain or expand their operations in a certain area. According to Jankowski, gang members use collective violence to achieve the goals of gang membership (proving their masculinity and toughness, providing excitement, and maintaining their reputation) mainly when they are provoked by others or when they are fearful.

Sociologists who use field research must have good interpersonal skills. They must be able to gain and keep the trust of the people they want to observe or interview. They also must be skilled interviewers who can keep systematic notes on their observations and conversations. Above all, they must treat research subjects fairly and ethically. The Code of Ethics of the American Sociological Association provides professional standards for sociologists to follow when conducting social science research.

Survey Research

Survey research is probably the research method that is most frequently used by social scientists. ***Survey research*** **is a poll in which researchers ask respondents a series of questions about a specific topic and record their responses.** Survey research is based on the use of a sample of people who are thought to represent the attributes of the larger population from which they are selected. Survey data are collected by using self-administered questionnaires or by interviewers who ask questions of people in person or by mail, telephone, or the Internet.

The Bureau of Justice Statistics, for example, conducts survey research every year with its national crime victimization survey (NCVS), which fills in some of the gaps in the UCR data. The NCVS interviews 100,000 randomly selected households to identify crime victims, whether the crime has been reported or not. These surveys indicate that the number of crimes committed is substantially higher than the number reported in the UCR.

Survey research allows sociologists to study a large population without having to interview everyone in that population. It also yields numerical data that may be compared between groups and over periods of time. However, this type of research does have certain limitations. The use of standardized questions limits the types of information researchers can obtain from respondents. Also, because data can be reported numerically, survey research may be misused to overestimate or underestimate the extent of a specific problem such as violence.

Secondary Analysis of Existing Data

Whereas the NCVS is primary data—data that researchers collected specifically for that study—sociologists often rely on ***secondary analysis of existing data*****—a research method in which investigators analyze data that originally were collected by others for some other purpose.** This method is also known as *unobtrusive research* because data can be gathered without the researcher's having to interview or observe research subjects. Data used for secondary analysis include public records such as birth and death records, official reports of organizations or governmental agencies such as the U.S. Census Bureau, and information from large databases such as the general social surveys, which are administered by the National Opinion Research Center.

Secondary analysis often involves *content analysis,* a systematic examination of cultural artifacts or written documents to extract thematic data and draw conclusions about some aspect of social life. For example, for the National Television Violence Study, researchers at several universities conducted content analyses of violence in television programming. During a nine-month period each year from October 1994 to June 1997, researchers selected a variety of programs, including drama, comedy, movies, music videos, reality programs, and children's shows on twenty-three television channels, thus creating a composite of the content in a week of television viewing. The viewing hours were from 6:00 A.M. until 11:00 P.M., for a total of seventeen hours a day across the seven days of the week (National Television Violence Study, 1998). Although the study's findings are too numerous to list all of them, here are a few (NTVS, 1998: 26–31):

- Much of television violence is glamorized, sanitized, and trivialized. Characters seldom show remorse for their actions, and there is no criticism or penalty for the violence at the time that it occurs.
- Across the three years of the study, violence was found in 60 percent of the television programs taped—only a few of which carried anti-violence themes—and the networks and basic cable stations increased the proportion of programs containing violence during prime time (the three-hour period each night that draws the most viewers).
- "High-risk" depictions (those that may encourage aggressive attitudes and behaviors) often involve: (1) "a

perpetrator who is an attractive role model"; (2) "violence that seems justified"; (3) "violence that goes unpunished"; (4) "minimal consequences to the victim"; and (5) "violence that seems realistic to the viewer."

- The typical preschool child who watches cartoons regularly will come into contact with more than 500 high-risk portrayals of violence each year. For preschoolers who watch television for two to three hours a day, there will be, on average, about one high-risk portrayal of violence per hour in cartoons.

Clearly, researchers can learn much from content analysis that they could not learn through other research methods because it allows them to look in more depth at a specific topic of concern and to systematically analyze what they find.

A strength of secondary analysis is its unobtrusive nature and the fact that it can be used when subjects refuse to be interviewed or the researcher does not have the opportunity to observe research subjects firsthand. However, secondary analysis also has inherent problems. Because the data originally were gathered for some other purpose, they might not fit the exact needs of the researcher, and they might be incomplete or inaccurate.

IS THERE A SOLUTION TO A PROBLEM SUCH AS GUN VIOLENCE?

Sociologists view social problems from a variety of perspectives. As shown in Table 1.2 on page 20, each sociological perspective is rooted in different assumptions, identifies differing causes of a problem, and suggests a variety of possible solutions for reducing or eliminating a social problem such as gun violence.

Functionalists, who emphasize social cohesion and order in society, commonly view social problems as the result of institutional and societal dysfunctions, social disorganization, or cultural lag, among other things. Conflict theorists, who focus on value conflict or on structural inequalities based on class, race, gender, or other socially constructed attributes, suggest that social problems arise either from disputes over divergent values or from exploitative relations in society, such as those between capitalists and workers or between women and men. In contrast, symbolic interactionists focus on individuals' interactions and on the social construction of reality. For symbolic interactionists, social problems occur when social interaction is disrupted and people are dehumanized, when people are labeled deviant, or when the individual's definition of a situation causes him or her to act in a way that produces a detrimental outcome.

No matter what perspectives sociologists employ, they use research to support their ideas. All research methods have certain strengths and weaknesses, but taken together, they provide us with valuable insights that go beyond commonsense knowledge about social problems and stereotypes of people. Using multiple methods and approaches, sociologists can broaden their knowledge of social problems such as violence in the United States and other nations.

In this chapter, we have looked at violence from these sociological perspectives. Like many other social problems, people do not always agree on the extent to which gun violence really is a major social problem in the United States or if the media tend to overblow each isolated incident because it can easily be sensationalized by tying it to other, previous occurrences. For example, how was the shooting at Virginia Tech similar to, or different from, the one that occurred at Northern Illinois University? Just as people do not share a consensus on what constitutes a social problem, they often do not agree on how to reduce or solve problems such as gun violence.

Functionalist/Conservative Solutions

Those who adhere to a functionalist approach argue that violence can be reduced by strengthening major social institutions (such as the family, education, and religion) so that agents (such as parents, teachers, and spiritual leaders) can be effective in instructing children and young adults and thereby repressing negative attitudes and antisocial behaviors that might otherwise result in violent behavior, such as school and mall shootings.

Some people who embrace a functionalist theoretical perspective on violence also view themselves as being aligned with conservative political sectors that are comprised of individuals who believe that people should be free of government intervention and control when it comes to their "fundamental" rights, including the right to bear arms. From this side of the political arena, social policy solutions to reducing violence, such as passing and enforcing more stringent gun-control measures, are unacceptable means of trying to reduce the number of acts of violence that take place each year. Some political conservatives argue that gun control constitutes an aggressive disarmament strategy that violates the individual's constitutional rights while

TABLE 1.2 Sociological Perspectives on Social Problems

Perspective	Analysis Level	Nature of Society and Origins of Social Problems	Causes and Solutions to Violence
Functionalism	Macrolevel	Society is composed of interrelated parts that work together to maintain stability within society. Social problems result from dysfunctional acts and institutions.	The weakening of social institutions such as schools, families, and religion has produced an increase in violent behavior. Social institutions must be strengthened, and individuals should be taught to conform to society's rules, which must be reinforced by the criminal justice system.
Conflict Theory	Macrolevel	Society is characterized by conflict and inequality. Value conflict theory attributes social problems to lack of agreement on values. Critical-conflict theory focuses on oppression due to class, race, gender, and other social divisions.	Factors such as sharp divisions on values, increasing social inequality, and unresolved discrimination contribute to violence in capitalist societies. To significantly reduce violence, fundamental changes are needed in political and economic institutions to bring about greater equality.
Symbolic Interactionism	Microlevel	Society is the sum of the interactions of people and groups. Social problems are based on the behavior people learn from others; how people define a social problem is based on subjective factors.	Violence is learned behavior, and children must be taught attitudes and values that discourage such behavior. At the societal level, we must change those societal values that encourage excessive competition and violence.

undermining the nation's overall well-being as a democratic and "free" society.

To reduce violence in the United States, the functionalist approach would suggest that it is important to maintain and preserve traditional moral and social values. Functionalists and political conservatives also believe that we should reinforce the importance of conformity to society's rules and laws through effective use of the criminal justice system, including the passage of tougher laws, more aggressive policing, and the imposition of more severe penalties in the courtroom. Conservative political viewpoints tend to reaffirm this approach by suggesting that positive social behavior, as well as violent behavior, is passed down from generation to generation through families. As a result, positive behavior must be reinforced through positive family life. Child abuse, domestic violence, and other antisocial behavioral problems within the family must not be tolerated because these contribute to larger societal problems of violence and crime.

Conflict/Liberal Solutions

Unlike functionalist sociological perspectives and conservative political approaches to solving the problem of violence, conflict theorists and liberal political analysts generally view increasing social inequality and unresolved discrimination as major factors that contribute to violence in societies. Some conflict theorists highlight the ways in which social problems are linked to the lack of agreement on values in our society. Critical-conflict theorists emphasize that oppression, based on class, race, gender, and other social divisions, is a major factor that contributes to social problems such as gun violence. In the political arena, liberal analysts similarly emphasize how a lack of economic opportunities encourages violence in a society. Based on these viewpoints, if we are to significantly reduce violence in our society, we must push for major changes in our nation's political and economic institutions. From this approach, one factor contributing to gun violence is poverty and growing inequality. Research has shown, for example, that the risk of sustaining a firearm injury is greatest for young males who have already been involved in the criminal justice system and who have few opportunities for legitimate jobs. Although functionalist theorists might view this situation as being one in which behavioral interventions should occur that target these high-risk people and those individuals who supply them with guns and other contraband items, conflict analysts argue that the problem can only be solved if underlying problems such as poverty, racism, and chronic unemployment are systematically addressed rather than focusing on the people who commit gun-related violence or on suppressing the availability of firearms throughout the nation. From this approach, ways to eventually reduce gun-related violence might include passing legislation that requires that workers be paid a wage high enough that they can adequately support their families, improving public schools so that young people will receive a better education and be able to find decent jobs, and having community, state, and national economic development programs that create good jobs and benefit all people, not just a small percentage of the world's wealthiest people. This approach is most useful in explaining violence in low-income urban areas and other communities where few legitimate opportunities exist for individuals and most economic opportunities are of an illegal nature. It does not explain, however, why recent gun violence has been perpetrated by middle- and upper-middle-class high school students living in the suburbs and by college students with good academic records who appear to have a bright future in front of them.

Symbolic Interactionist Solutions

Finally, symbolic interactionist perspectives focus on how violence is learned behavior that comes from people's interactions in their daily lives. As a result, if we are to prevent violence, we must teach children the attitudes and values that discourage such behavior. If children are exposed to aggressive behavior or violence in their own homes, they may come to view such behavior as the norm rather than the exception to the norm. Some analysts believe that those children who spend large amounts of unsupervised time watching violence in films and on television or playing violent video games will demonstrate more violent behavior themselves. However, other analysts disagree with this assessment, claiming that violence in the media and gaming worlds provides people with an opportunity to vicariously vent their frustrations and feelings without ever actually engaging in violence themselves. Since peer groups are an important source of social learning for children and young people, some symbolic interactionists might suggest that parents, teachers, and other adult caregivers must become aware of the friends and acquaintances of the children for whom they are responsible.

Based on symbolic interactionist perspectives, one way to reduce violence is to teach people of all ages to engage in nonviolent conflict resolution where they learn how to deal with frustrating situations, such as when tensions are running high among individuals or social relationships are breaking down. The focus on competition in nations such as ours encourages people to think of everyone else as their competitors and that, in all situations, what one individual gains is another person's loss. Beliefs such as this tend to foster conflict rather than cooperation, and individuals who think that they have been marginalized (and thus taken out of the competition for friends, material possessions, or other valued goods, services, or relationships) may act out toward their perceived enemies in an aggressive or violent manner. If people learn socially acceptable ways of responding to conflict and intense competition, they may be less likely to engage in violent behavior. However, according to symbolic interactionists and other theorists who use a microlevel approach, we must first recognize as a community or nation that violence is a problem that must be solved, and then we must work collectively to reduce the problem. Although the symbolic interactionist approach is a microlevel perspective, some advocates suggest that changes must also be made at the societal level if we hope to change those societal values that encourage excessive competition and may contribute to negative behavior including gun violence.

Critique of Our Efforts to Find Solutions

How successful are our attempts to solve the problem of gun violence? The answer to this question is mixed. The United States has been somewhat successful in reducing certain types of violence, at least for several years running; however, most of our efforts have focused on particular types of violence or particular populations or categories of people, rather than on bringing about systemic change throughout the nation. Unless our nation and its political leaders face up to the fact that violence in this country is a major social problem that may lie dormant for a period of time but then rise up to leave us frightened and astonished, we are unlikely as a nation to seriously deal with the underlying causes and consequences of such violent actions, which is a necessary prerequisite for reaching the point where we might successfully reduce the problem. The following words in an editorial in the *Journal of the American Medical Association,* published ten years ago, perhaps said it best:

> We know that violence is widespread, long lasting, and harmful to human health—in short, a major public health problem. Violence prevention is a maturing discipline, and there are still opportunities to characterize poorly understood violent outcomes. However, the current state of knowledge is more than sufficient to emphasize the urgent nature of finding solutions. The problems and questions are complex, yet clear. It's time for some real answers. (Cole and Flanagin, 1999:482)

And so it remains a decade later: When we think about the problem of gun violence or other pressing social issues that we will examine in this book, we must acknowledge that we have a long way to go in identifying real solutions to many of these problems, and that is why it is important that you are enrolled in this course and pursuing new ideas for the future. Please join me now as we explore a number of crucial problems we face in the twenty-first century.

SUMMARY

■ *How do sociologists define a social problem?*

According to sociologists, a social problem is a social condition (such as poverty) or a pattern of behavior (such as substance abuse) that people believe warrants public concern and collective action to bring about change.

■ *How do sociologists view violence?*

Sociologists view violence as a social problem that involves both a subjective awareness and objective reality. We have a subjective awareness that violence can occur in such public settings as schools, day-care centers, businesses, and churches. Our subjective awareness becomes an objective reality when we can measure and experience the effects of violent criminal behavior.

■ *How do sociologists examine social life?*

Sociologists use both microlevel and macrolevel analyses to examine social life. Microlevel analysis focuses on small-group relations and social interaction among individuals; macrolevel analysis focuses on social processes occurring at the societal level, especially in large-scale organizations and major social institutions.

■ *How does the functionalist perspective view society and social problems?*

In the functionalist perspective, society is a stable, orderly system composed of interrelated parts, each of which performs a function that contributes to the overall stability of society. According to functionalists, social problems such as violence arise when social institutions do not fulfill the functions that they are supposed to perform or when dysfunctions occur.

■ *How does the conflict perspective view society and social problems?*

The conflict perspective asserts that groups in society are engaged in a continuous power struggle for control of scarce resources. This perspective views violence as a response to inequalities based on race, class, gender, and other power differentials in society.

■ *How does the value conflict perspective differ from the critical-conflict perspective?*

According to value conflict theorists, social problems are conditions that are incompatible with group values. From this perspective, value clashes are ordinary occurrences in families, communities, and the larger society, in which people commonly hold many divergent values. In contrast, critical-conflict theorists suggest that social problems arise out of major contradictions inherent in the way societies are organized.

■ *Why are there so many different approaches in the conflict perspective?*

Different conflict theorists focus on different aspects of power relations and inequality in society. Perspectives based on the works of Karl Marx emphasize class-based inequalities arising from the capitalist system. Feminist perspectives focus on patriarchy—a system of male dominance in which males are privileged and women are oppressed. Other perspectives emphasize that race, class, and gender are interlocking systems of privilege and oppression that result in social problems. However, all of these perspectives are based on the assumption that inequality and exploitation, rather than social harmony and stability, characterize contemporary societies.

■ *How does the symbolic interactionist perspective view society and social problems?*

Unlike the functionalist and conflict perspectives, which focus on society at the macrolevel, the symbolic interactionist perspective views society as the sum of the interactions of individuals and groups. For symbolic interactionists, social problems occur when social interaction is disrupted and people are dehumanized, when people are labeled deviant, or when the individual's definition of a situation causes him or her to act in a way that produces a detrimental outcome.

■ *How do sociological research methods differ?*

In field research, sociologists observe and interview people where they live, work, and play. In survey research, sociologists use written questionnaires or structured interviews to ask respondents a series of questions about a specific topic. In secondary analysis of existing data, sociologists analyze data that originally were collected for some other purpose.

KEY TERMS

capitalism, p. 11
conflict perspective, p. 11
culture, p. 3
discrimination, p. 3
field research, p. 15
functionalist perspective, p. 8
hate crime, p. 3
industrialization, p. 10
lifestyle-routine activity approach, p. 10
macrolevel analysis, p. 5
microlevel analysis, p. 5
norms, p. 10
perspective, p. 8
secondary analysis of existing data, p. 18
self-fulfilling prophecy, p. 14
situational approach, p. 15
social disorganization, p. 10
social problem, p. 3
society, p. 3
sociological imagination, p. 5
sociology, p. 3
subculture of violence hypothesis, p. 10
survey research, p. 18
symbolic interactionist perspective, p. 14
theory, p. 8
urbanization, p. 10
values, p. 10
violence, p. 2

QUESTIONS FOR CRITICAL THINKING

1. The functionalist perspective focuses on the stability of society. How do acts of violence undermine stability? Can a society survive when high levels of violence exist within its borders? Do you believe that violence can be controlled in the United States?
2. Value conflict theorists suggest that social problems are conditions that are incompatible with group values. How would value conflict theorists view debates over gun-control laws?
3. Some critical-conflict theorists believe that social problems arise from the major contradictions inherent in capitalist economies. What part do guns play in a capitalist economy?
4. Using feminist and symbolic interactionist perspectives, what kind of argument can you make to explain why males are more frequently involved in acts of physical violence than females? What do your own observations tell you about the relationship between social norms and aggressive or violent behavior?

Chapter 2

Wealth and Poverty: U.S. and Global Economic Inequities

THINKING SOCIOLOGICALLY

- How important is a person's social class in achieving the "American Dream"?
- Why do great disparities exist between the rich and the poor in the United States?
- How do sociologists explain poverty?

I went to the supermarket and I left the supermarket and didn't buy anything because... there wasn't a package of hamburger in the whole meat thing that was less than four dollars. None of it! And every week you go to the market to buy food, they up the price, up the price, up the price, but nobody's upping nobody's salary. Right now at home in my house... I got two halves of a green pepper in my freezer. Period. No food—I got some canned goods on the shelf—no food in the house. No money to go buy it. That's the condition. And if there was no [food] pantries, you would find a lot of us wouldn't even have a green pepper in the freezer.

—Rosabelle Walker, describing her problems with lack of food and hunger in her retirement years even though she was employed for many years in Pennsylvania's steel mills and in a laundromat in New York City. (PBS, 2008)

When many of us think about the people who go to food pantries, we may picture these individuals as homeless persons who live on the streets or in shelters. Sometimes we may see them as single men who suffer from substance abuse and other problems. However, these perceptions about what the face of hunger looks like do not accurately reflect who the hungry really are in contemporary America. They are people like you and me; they are young mothers with children; they are entire families where adults hold down several jobs trying to make ends meet. The cost of living—particularly the spiraling price of housing, fuel, and food—has increased at a much faster pace than salaries or retirement benefits. Rosabelle Walker, whom we met above, was employed until she reached her 80s, but she cannot afford to purchase adequate food to meet her basic needs in her "golden" years. Inflation has made the problem even worse: Between 2007 and 2008, for example, milk prices went up by 26 percent, eggs went up by 24 percent, and the price of bread increased by 13 percent (PBS, 2008). Coupled with the high prices of groceries, gas, and electricity, many people have found that their jobs either disappeared or that they are now receiving smaller paychecks because of reductions in their wages and working hours (Goodman, 2008b). Recently, the U.S. Government estimated that at least 28 million Americans will be using food stamps to help purchase groceries in 2008—the highest level since the food stamp program was started in the 1960s (PBS, 2008).

For centuries, the United States has been described as the "land of opportunity"—home of the "American Dream." Simply stated, the American Dream is the belief that each generation can have a higher standard of living than that of its parents. Implicit in the American Dream is the belief that all people—regardless of race, creed, color, national origin, sex, sexual orientation, or religion—should have an equal opportunity for success. But do all the people in this nation have an equal opportunity for success?

In this chapter, we look at inequality and poverty in the U.S. class system and worldwide. **A *class system* is a system of social inequality based on the ownership and control of resources and on the type of work people do**. A primary characteristic of any class system is social mobility. *Social mobility* refers to the upward or downward movement in the class structure that occurs during a person's lifetime and from one generation to another. The research of many social analysts and journalists suggests that upward social mobility is an elusive goal for many people.

WEALTH AND POVERTY IN GLOBAL PERSPECTIVE

Although there is a disparity in the distribution of economic resources in the United States, the disparity is even wider both across nations and within many other nations. In any one nation, there are both very wealthy and very poor individuals and families. When sociologists conduct research on these disparities, they frequently analyze secondary data that originally were collected by the World Bank and the United Nations. These data focus on quality-of-life indicators such as wealth; income; life expectancy; health; sanitation; the treatment of women; and education for high-income, middle-income, and low-income nations. ***High-income nations* are countries with highly industrialized economies; technologically advanced industrial, administrative, and service occupations; and relatively high levels of national and per capita (per person) income.** Examples include Australia, New Zealand, Japan, the European nations, Canada, and the United States. ***Middle-income nations* are countries undergoing transformation from agrarian to industrial economies.** Colombia, Guatemala, Panama, Poland, and Romania are examples of middle-income nations. These nations still have many people who work the land, and national and per capita incomes remain relatively low. ***Low-income nations* are primarily agrarian countries that have little industrialization and low levels of national and personal income.** For example, the countries in sub-Saharan Africa have experienced little or no benefit from recent changes in global economic markets (United Nations Development Programme, 1999). Today, low-income nations include countries such as Rwanda, Mozambique, Ethiopia, Nigeria, Cambodia, Vietnam, Afghanistan, Bangladesh, and Nicaragua.

Comparisons of high-income and low-income nations reveal a growing gap between the rich and the poor, both within and among nations. Indeed, throughout the world today, the wealthiest and poorest people are living in increasingly separate worlds. The wealthiest 10 percent of the world's population, almost all of whom live in high-income nations, account for 54 percent of the world's gross domestic product (United Nations Development Programme, 2005). The gross domestic product (GDP) is all of the goods and services produced within a country's economy during a given year (revenue from sources outside the country is not included in the GDP). The world's GDP, then, is the total of the GDP for each nation. By contrast, the bottom 40 percent of the world's population—approximately 2.5 billion people, most of whom live in low-income nations—exist on less than $2 a day and account for only 5 percent of the world's GDP. More than 1 billion people live on less than $1 per day (United Nations Development Programme, 2005).

Disparity in the GDPs of high-income and low-income nations reflects disparity in the life chances of the populations of these nations. ***Life chances* are the extent to which individuals have access to important societal resources such as food, clothing, shelter, education, and health care.** Poverty, food shortages, hunger, and rapidly growing populations are pressing problems in many middle- and low-income nations (see Box 2.1). Today, more than 1.3 billion people live in ***absolute poverty*, a condition that exists when people do not have the means to secure the most basic necessities of life.** Absolute poverty is often life-threatening. People living in absolute poverty may suffer from chronic malnutrition or die from hunger-related diseases. Current estimates suggest that more than 600 million people suffer from chronic malnutrition and more than 40 million people die each year from hunger-related diseases. To put this figure in perspective, the number of people worldwide dying from hunger-related diseases each year is the equivalent of more than 300 jumbo jet crashes a day with no survivors and half the passengers being children.

Despite the disparity in life chances and the prevalence of absolute poverty, experts project that the populations of middle- and low-income nations will increase by almost 60 percent by the year 2025 while the populations of high-income nations will increase by about 11 percent. Because half of the world's population of more than 6 billion people already lives in low-income nations (see Map 2.1 on page 29), this rapid increase in population can only compound existing problems and increase inequality on a global basis.

How do social scientists explain the disparity between wealth and poverty in high-income and low-income nations? According to the "new international division of labor" perspective, the answer lies in the global organization of manufacturing production. Today, workers in a number of low-income nations primarily produce goods such as clothing, electrical machinery, and consumer electronics for export to the United States and other high-income nations. Using this global assembly line, transnational corporations find that they have an abundant supply of low-cost (primarily female) labor, no corporate taxes, and no labor unions or strikes to

Social Problems in Global Perspective

Box 2.1

A New Way of Looking at World Hunger

Port-Au-Prince, Haiti:

> They look at me and say, "Papa, I'm hungry," and I have to look away. It's humiliating and it makes you angry.
>
> —*Saint Louis Meriska describes his anguish on the days when he has nothing to feed his children or when he can provide them with only two spoonfuls of rice each (Lacey, 2008: A1).*

> It's salty and it has butter and you don't know you're eating dirt. It makes your stomach quiet down.
>
> —*Olwich Louis Jeune explains how Haiti's most destitute residents offset their hunger pangs by eating patties made of mud, oil, and sugar (Lacey, 2008: A11).*

Cairo, Egypt:

> We never thought it would reach this level. The prices of some foods have doubled since the end of [2007]. One Egyptian pound used to feed the whole household; now five Egyptian pounds barely covers it. We used to go to the market and buy whatever we laid eyes upon, but now we have to think first. I buy more fruit and vegetables and we eat meat just once a week instead of every day.
>
> —*Aza Hedar tells how her family survives in Imbaba, a poor section of Cairo, where her family now spends 80 percent of its total income on food because of spiraling international food prices (BBC, 2008a).*

Hunger and other problems associated with poverty, such as the ones described here, can be found around the globe as food prices continue to soar, wages remain extremely low, and millions of people are unemployed. More than 100 million people in low-income and middle-income nations are being pushed deeper into poverty by spiraling prices and lack of money (BBC, 2008b). In nations such as Haiti and Egypt, the problem of hunger has grown so great that food riots have become a common occurrence. The problem is even worse in areas of sub-Saharan Africa, such as Burkina Faso, where dire poverty, absolute deprivation, and potential starvation loom heavily over residents (Lacey, 2008). Today, sub-Saharan Africa has the highest prevalence of chronic hunger in the world, affecting about one-third of its entire population (United Nations Food and Agricultural Organization, 2006). Arif Husain, the World Food Program's senior food security analyst, explains the cause of food riots: "The human instinct is to survive, and people are going to do no matter what to survive. And if you're hungry you get angry quicker" (Lacey, 2008: A11). However, some of the world's poorest people do not riot at all and merely suffer in silence because they are physically too weak to engage in activism or they must channel what little energy they have into helping their children survive.

The sociological issues associated with hunger and poverty are complex. The most popular answer to the question of why so much hunger exists worldwide typically relates to the issue of *scarcity*, and the solution is seen as more effectively producing and distributing food so that fewer people will be hungry (Lappé, 2008). However, many analysts believe that this explanation is seriously flawed. According to social scientist Frances Moore Lappé, plenty of food exists throughout the world to feed everyone, but hunger remains a major problem for reasons that cannot be explained by scarcity. According to Lappé (2008), hunger is not *caused* by scarcity: Hunger is a *symptom* of deeper causes, including widely-held

(continued)

■ *Many thousands of people in India's cities are forced to live in the streets and scrounge a living by either begging or working in the recycle industry. Here, a poverty stricken father uses basic cooking tools to prepare a meal on the ground for his children near the Amritsar railway station.*

Box 2.1 (continued)

beliefs regarding human relationships that generate *artificial* scarcity. In other words, wealthy and powerful individuals and corporations often make decisions that serve their best interests while casting aside millions of the world's people who are deprived of life's most basic and important necessities, such as food, as a result of those decisions. For example, India and Africa have millions of hungry people even though these areas export millions of tons of food to higher-income nations around the globe (Lappé, 2008).

If we are to curb world hunger, we must focus on human needs and values, not on profits that are enjoyed by only a tiny percentage of the world's population. According to Lappé, the real roots of world hunger lie in the answers to questions such as these: (1) Who owns and controls the land where food can be grown? (2) Why do small farmers and producers continue to see their share of profits shrink while global transnational corporations have extremely high profit margins? (3) Why do trade rules favor those who are already wealthy? and (4) Why does the debt burden—the debt repayments that poor nations make to wealthy nations each year—fall disproportionately on poor people? Although these questions may cause us to think that we cannot do much to alleviate world hunger, we must have hope that the situation can change (Lappé, 2008). For example, we may encourage people to view hunger as more than a lack of basic resources and instead to see how the problem is rooted in large-scale economic inequalities and social injustices in the twenty-first century. The first step in applying our sociological imagination to the problem is to view hunger as everyone's problem, not as something that affects only people living in the poorest, most distressed nations of the world and on the margins of life in the United States. Consider these challenging words of Frances Moore Lappé (2008):

> It is tempting to view hunger as a moral crisis, when it is more usefully understood as a crisis of imagination.... Humanity is trapped in a failed frame, a way of seeing that underestimates both nature's potential and the potential of human nature....Mounting sociological evidence reveals that most humans have, inherently, what it takes to end hunger: deep needs for fairness, efficacy and meaning. The challenge is therefore to reframe hunger as a crisis of human relationships that is within our proven power to address, to search out and broadcast lessons of success, and most importantly, to fearlessly engage oneself....

What steps might you take in your own community to reduce the problem of hunger? What social policies do you think the United States might implement to help alleviate world hunger?

interfere with their profits. Owners and shareholders of transnational corporations, along with subcontractors and managers in middle- and low-income nations, thus benefit while workers remain in poverty despite long hours in sweatshop conditions.

ANALYZING U.S. CLASS INEQUALITY

Despite the American Dream, one of this country's most persistent social problems is that the United States is a highly stratified society. ***Social stratification* is the hierarchical arrangement of large social groups on the basis of their control over basic resources.** Today, the gap between the rich and the poor in this nation is wider than it has been in half a century.

This widening gap, which is linked with global systems of stratification, has a dramatic impact on everyone's life chances and opportunities. Affluent people typically have better life chances than the less affluent because the affluent have greater access to quality education, safe neighborhoods, high-quality nutrition and health care, police and private security protection, and an extensive array of other goods and services. In contrast, people who have low and poverty-level incomes tend to have limited access to these resources.

How are social classes determined in the United States? Most contemporary research on class has been influenced by either Karl Marx's means of production model or Max Weber's multidimensional model. In Marx's model, class position is determined by people's relationship to the means of production. Chapter 1 described Marx's division of capitalist societies into two classes: the bourgeoisie, or capitalist class, which owns the means of production, and the proletariat, or working class, which sells its labor power to the capitalists to survive. According to Marx, inequality and poverty are inevitable by-products of the exploitation of workers by capitalists (Vanneman and Cannon, 1987).

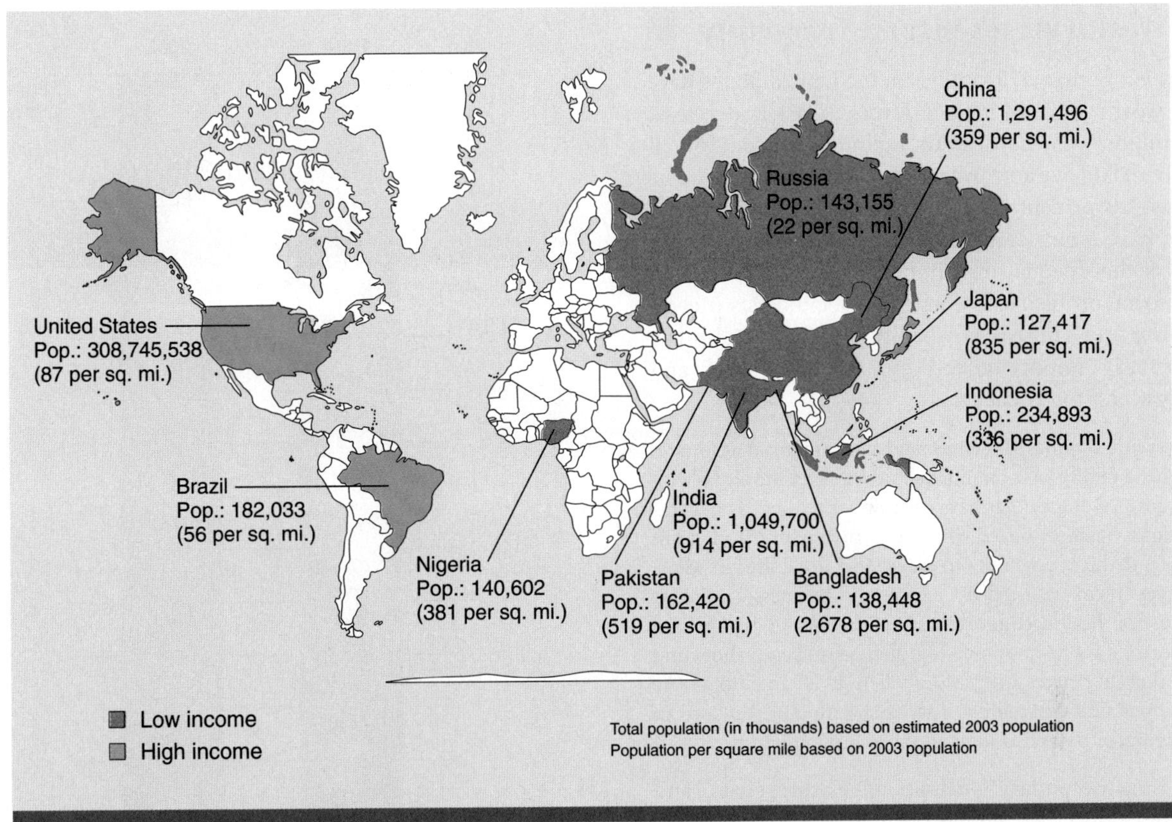

■ *Map 2.1* ***The most rapid population growth is occurring primarily in low-income nations that can least afford to take care of greater numbers of people.***

Source: U.S. Census Bureau, 2010.

Like Karl Marx, early German sociologist Max Weber (1864–1920) believed that economic factors were important in determining class location and studying social inequality, but he also believed that other factors were relevant. Consequently, Weber developed a multidimensional class model that focused on the interplay of wealth, power, and prestige as determinants of people's class position. ***Wealth* is the value of all economic assets, including income, personal property, and income-producing property.** While some people have great wealth and are able to live off their investments, others must work for wages. ***Power* is the ability of people to achieve their goals despite opposition from others.** People who hold positions of power can achieve their goals because they can control other people; on the other hand, people who hold positions that lack power must carry out the wishes of others. ***Prestige* is the respect, esteem, or regard accorded to an individual or group by others.** Individuals who have high levels of prestige tend to receive deferential and respectful treatment from those with lower levels of prestige.

Recent theorists have modified Marx's and Weber's theories of economic inequality. According to the sociologist Erik O. Wright (1997), neither Weber's multidimensional model of wealth, power, and prestige nor Marx's two-class system fully define classes in modern capitalist societies or explain economic inequality. Wright sets forth four criteria for placement in the class structure: (1) ownership of the means of production, (2) purchase of the labor of others (employing others), (3) control of the labor of others (supervising others on the job), and (4) sale of one's own labor (being employed by someone else). On the basis of these criteria, Wright (1979, 1985) has identified four classes in the U.S. economy: the capitalist class, the managerial class, the small-business class, and the working class.

Wealth versus Income Inequality

Today, more than 470 families in the United States have a net worth above $1 billion (*Forbes,* 2008), and at least 7.5 million U.S. households (about 7 percent of all households) have a net worth of at least $1 million. The poorest 20 percent of U.S. households, on the other hand, have a net worth close to zero (D'Souza, 1999). How is the unequal distribution of wealth associated with social problems? According to sociologists Melvin L. Oliver and Thomas M. Shapiro (1995:2), wealth is a particularly important indicator of individual and family access to life chances:

> Wealth signifies the command over financial resources that a family has accumulated over its lifetime along with those resources that have been inherited across generations. Such resources, when combined with income, can create the opportunity to secure the "good life" in whatever form is needed—education, business, training, justice, health, comfort, and so on. Wealth is a special form of money not used to purchase milk and shoes and other life necessities. More often it is used to create opportunities, secure a desired stature and standard of living, or pass class status along to one's children.

Using secondary analysis of existing data and in-depth interviews with African-American and white American families, Oliver and Shapiro found that African Americans have accumulated much less wealth than white Americans because whites, especially well-off whites, have had the opportunity to amass assets and pass them on from generation to generation, whereas African Americans have not. According to Oliver and Shapiro, African Americans have experienced the cumulative effects of racial discrimination as evidenced by poor schooling, high unemployment rates, and low wages. As a result, it has been difficult, if not impossible, for multiple generations of African Americans to acquire wealth, which has kept them cemented to the bottom of the U.S. economic hierarchy. This is not to say, however, that no African Americans have achieved middle-class and upper-class levels of wealth. Recent research has described the presence of a wealthy black elite in the United States (see Graham, 2000; Kendall, 2002).

Like wealth, income is extremely unevenly divided in the United States. ***Income* is the economic gain derived from wages, salaries, income transfers (governmental aid such as Temporary Aid to Needy Families, known as TANF), or ownership of property** (Beeghley, 1989). The income gap between the richest and poorest U.S. households has been wide for many years. The top 20 percent of households earned about half of the nation's aggregate income in 2005 and the top 5 percent alone earned more than 20 percent of aggregate income (see Figure 2.1). As

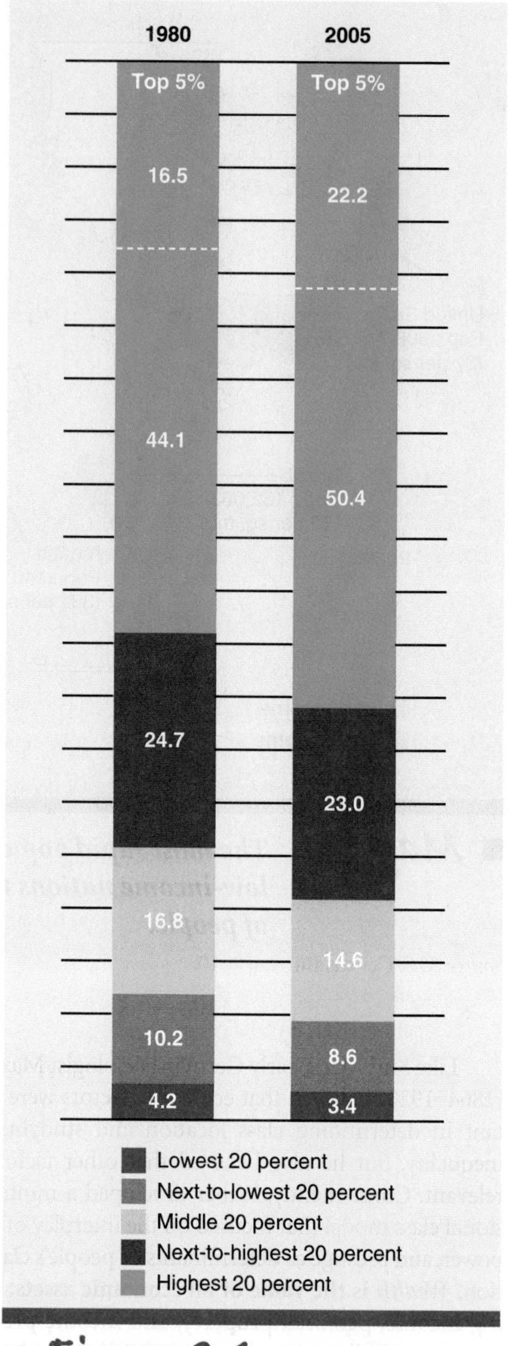

Figure 2.1 ***Share of aggregate income, 1980 and 2005***

Source: U.S. Census Bureau, 2008.

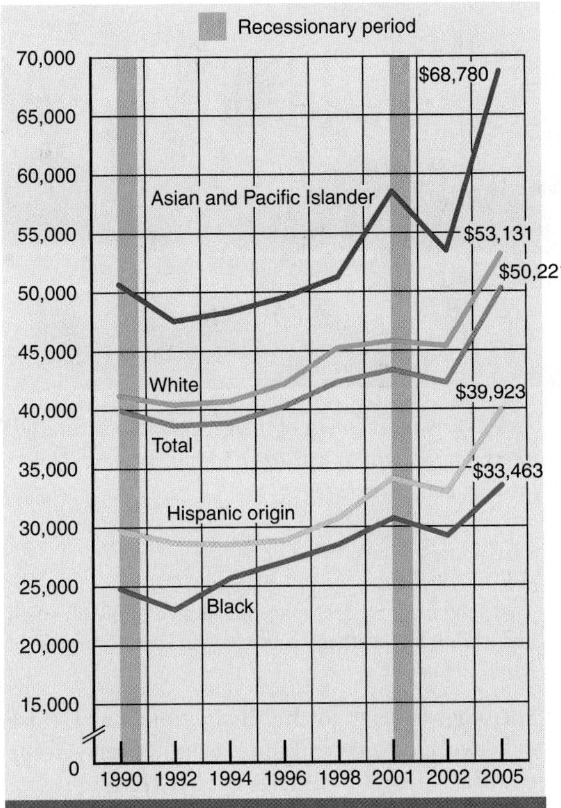

■ *Figure 2.2* **Median U.S. household income by race and Hispanic origin, 1990–2005 (median income in 2005 dollars)**

Note: People of Hispanic origin may be of any race. Data points represent the midpoints of the respective years.

Source: U.S. Census Bureau, 2009. (1-Year Estimates)

shown in Figure 2.2, median income for households across racial and ethnic lines has remained relatively constant over the last decade. Although African Americans and Latinas/os have made some gains in income in recent years, median income for both African American and Latina/o households remains far behind median income for white households.

Divisions in the U.S. Class Structure

The United States has a number of class divisions that are characterized by widely diverse lifestyles and life chances. The *upper*, or capitalist, *class*—the wealthiest and most powerful class—is made up of investors, heirs, and executives. Some members of the capitalist class derive their income from investments in income-producing property such as media conglomerates, high-rise hotels, apartment buildings, and office parks; others earn their wealth as entrepreneurs, presidents of major corporations, sports or entertainment celebrities, or top-level professionals. For example, the top ten corporate executives in a recent survey of executive compensation had 2004 salaries, bonuses, and stock options ranging from about $38.8 million to more than $109 million. The *upper-middle class* is composed of professionals (for example, physicians and attorneys), business analysts, owners of small businesses, stockbrokers, and corporate managers. These individuals generally do not own the means of production but have substantial control over production and other workers (Wright, 1979, 1985). The *middle class* includes white-collar office workers, middle-management personnel, and people in support positions (for example, medical technologists, nurses, and legal and medical secretaries), semiprofessionals, and nonretail salesworkers.

The *working class* is composed of people who work as semiskilled machine operators in industrial settings and in nonmanual, semiskilled positions (for example, day-care workers, checkout clerks, cashiers, and counter help in fast-food restaurants). The *working poor* are those who work full-time in unskilled positions such as seasonal or migrant agricultural workers or the lowest-paid service sector workers but still remain at the edge of poverty. In an interview with sociologist Mark Robert Rank, Jack Collins, a married father with six children, described the transitory nature of work for the working poor:

> You name it, I've done it. I started out cooking. I've been a janitor. I've been an auto mechanic. I drove a school bus for five years. I drove a semi [truck] coast to coast. I've worked in a foundry. I've worked in a shoe factory. I've worked in other factories, warehouses. I'll do just about anything.... The main problem was findin' [a job] with starting pay that's enough to really get by on. (Rank, 1994:43)

Jack Collins and his family might be only one paycheck away from the chronically poor, the bottom division in the U.S. class system.

The *chronically poor* constitute about 20 percent of the U.S. population but receive only 3.6 percent of the overall U.S. income. People in this category have an average net worth of −$7,075 (i.e., they owe more than they

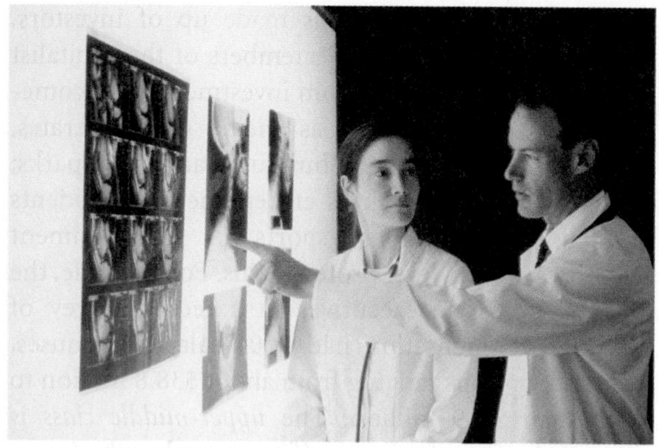

Upper-middle-class professionals, such as the doctors shown on the left, are one segment of the U.S. class structure, whereas people in the working class, including these fast-food workers on the right, constitute another segment. How do functionalist and conflict views differ in their descriptions of the U.S. class structure?

own). In 2006, almost 36.5 million people (12.3 percent of the U.S. population) fell below the poverty threshold, which ranged from $9,669 for a single-person household to $20,614 for a family of four. Individuals who are chronically poor include people of working age who are unemployed or outside the labor force and children who live in poor families caught in long-term deprivation. Overrepresented among low-income and poverty-level individuals are those who are unable to work because of age or disability and single mothers who are heads of households. The term "underclass" is sometimes used to refer to people who are chronically poor, but this term not only negatively labels poor people, it also puts them outside the mainstream of society.

POVERTY IN THE UNITED STATES

When sociologist Mark Robert Rank asked Denise Turner, an African-American mother of four living in poverty, to describe her daily life, Denise Turner replied,

> … it can be summarized in one word, and that's survival. That's what we're tryin' to do. We're tryin' to survive. And … I talk to a lot of people, and they say, "Well, hey, if you went to Ethiopia, you know, survival would be one thing. And that … eating." But, damn it, I'm not in Ethiopia! You know. So I want a little bit more than just … having some food. Having a coupla meals. So, if I can just summarize it, in one word, it would be we're tryin' to survive. We're tryin' to stay together. That's my major concern, keepin' all my family together, my children together. And to survive. (quoted in Rank, 1994:88)

Sociologists refer to the distinction that Denise makes between poverty in Ethiopia and poverty in the United States as the difference between absolute poverty and relative poverty. As defined earlier, absolute poverty exists when people do not have the means to secure the most basic necessities of life (food, clothing, and shelter). ***Relative poverty*** **exists when people may be able to afford basic necessities such as food, clothing, and shelter but cannot maintain an average standard of living in comparison to that of other members of their society or group** (Ropers, 1991). By this definition, Denise Turner does not suffer from absolute poverty, but she does experience relative poverty on the basis of what is available to other people in the United States.

The United States has the highest poverty rate of any advanced industrial nation. The ***poverty rate*** **is the proportion of the population whose income falls below the government's official poverty line—the level of income below which a family of a given size is considered to be poor.** As is discussed in Box 2.2 on page 33, the U.S. poverty rate has declined over the past four decades, although both the rate and the number of people living in poverty rose slightly in 2006. The official poverty line is based on money income and cash government assistance programs such as Social Security payments; however, it does not reflect the value of in-kind benefits such as public housing subsidies, Medicare, or Medicaid.

The Poverty Line

How is the U.S. poverty line determined? Established in 1965 by the Social Security Administration, the poverty line is based on an assumption that the average family must spend about one-third of its total income on food. Therefore the official poverty line is determined by a minimum family *market basket*—a low-cost food budget that contains a minimum level of nutrition for a family—multiplied by 3 to allow for nonfood costs such as rent and utilities. Although the poverty line is adjusted for the number of people in the household and is corrected at least annually for changes in the cost of living, essentially the same poverty test has been used since the 1960s.

Today, many social analysts argue that the official poverty line is too low. According to economist Patricia Ruggles (1990, 1992), the poverty line is based on outdated (pre-1960) standards that were established at a time when fewer households were composed of two working parents

Social Problems and Statistics

Box 2.2

Poverty in the United States

Is the problem of poverty in the United States a larger or smaller problem today than it was in the past? The good news is that during the past four decades, the *poverty rate*—the percentage of the U.S. population that the government defines as being "poor"—declined from about 21 percent to 12.3 percent today. The bad news is that the *total number of people living in poverty* is still about 36.4 million people and that more people are living in poverty today than were below the poverty line during the decade between 1969 and 1979 (see Figure 2.3 on page 34).

How statistics are created and how they are used are important factors in assessing the nature and extent of a social problem. Statistics can be stated as numbers that can be compared with other numbers or as percentages that can be compared with other percentages. In *Damned Lies and Statistics: Untangling Numbers from the Media, Politicians, and Activists* (University of California Press, 2001), sociologist Joel Best notes that statistics play an important role in campaigns to create or to rebutt claims about social problems. If statistics indicate that a social condition adversely affects large numbers of people, that condition may be defined as a social problem that requires that a society do something about it. However, if the statistics indicate that fewer people are adversely affected or that the number of people so affected is going down, that condition may be downgraded as a concern or even cease to be defined as a social problem.

Statistics regarding poverty in the United States are an example. Consider, for example, the decline in the poverty rate, as reported by the U.S. Census Bureau: This statistic can be used to argue that poverty is less of a social problem today than it was in the late 1950s and early 1960s, when the rate was substantially higher and the government launched a "war on poverty." Statistically, that is a valid argument: The rate is lower. However, there is also compelling evidence to the contrary: The increase in the total number of people living below the poverty line, as also reported by the U.S. Census Bureau, is a statistic that can be used to validly argue that poverty remains as serious a social problem today as it was during the late 1950s and early 1960s: In fact, the actual number of people who are poor today is greater than the number who were poor about forty years ago. The reason why both of these statistical conclusions are true is that there are more people living in the United States today, and the same percentage of a larger population obviously results in a larger total number.

Another way in which some analysts have used statistics to downplay the problem of poverty is to note that not only has the overall poverty rate been declining, but also the poverty rate has been declining for people of color—people who, as a result of past discrimination and lack of opportunity, have been more likely to be poor than have non-Hispanic whites. Indeed, the poverty rate among people of color—African Americans, Latinos/as, Asian Americans, and Native Americans—has been decreasing, just as it is for non-Hispanic whites; however, as shown in Figure 2.4 on page 35 the percentage of African Americans, Latinos/as, Asian Americans, and Native Americans in poverty remains considerably higher than the percentage for non-Hispanic whites.

Regardless of which statistics are used or how they are interpreted,

(continued)

or of single parents who faced employment-related expenses such as work clothes, transportation, child care, and quick and convenient foods. Ruggles believes that poverty thresholds should be increased by at least 50 percent.

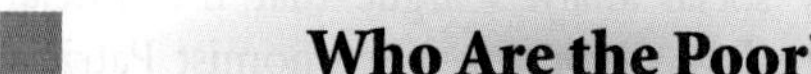

Who Are the Poor?

If poverty were equally distributed among all social groups in the United States, all people regardless of their age, race or ethnicity, sex, household composition, or other attributes would have an equal statistical chance of being among the poor in any given year. However, poverty is not distributed equally: People in some categories are at greater risk for poverty than are people in other categories.

Age, Gender, Household Composition, and Poverty

The vast majority of poor people in the United States are women and children. Children under age eighteen—25 percent of the U.S. population—account for more than 40 percent of the poor. About one in six children age eighteen and under lives in poverty (see Table 2.1 on page 35). The percentage of children under six years of age who live in poverty-level households is even higher: In 2006 about one in four was considered poor. When children under age six live in households headed by women with no adult male present, almost 53 percent are poor. Children of working-poor parents are the fastest growing segment of children living in poverty. More than half of all poor children live in

Box 2.2 (continued)

TABLE 2.1 Children (under 18 Years Old) below the U.S. Poverty Level, 1990 and 2006

		Percentage below Poverty Level			
Year	All Races	Non-Hispanic White	Asian or Pacific Islander	African American	Hispanic Origin
1990	20.6	12.3	17.6	44.8	38.4
2006	17.4	10.0	11.4	33.4	26.9

Source: Dalaker, 2001; DeNavas-Walt, Proctor, and Smith, 2007.

families in which one or both parents work outside the home (DeNavas-Walt, Proctor, and Smith, 2007).

About two-thirds of all adults living in poverty are women; households headed by women are the fastest growing segment of the overall poverty population. Researchers have discovered a number of reasons why single-parent families headed by women are at such a great risk of poverty. Single-parent families typically have fewer employed adults in them and therefore a lower annual income than most two-parent households in the first place, and women generally earn less money than men, even for comparable work. Thus, a single-parent family headed by a woman usually faces a greater risk of poverty than a single-parent family headed by a man. Women also bear the major economic burden for their children. Contributions from absent fathers in the form of child support and alimony payments account for less than 10 percent of family income. About 43 percent of unmarried mothers with incomes above poverty level receive child support from the fathers; however, only 25 percent of unmarried mothers at or below the poverty line receive such support (U.S. House of Representatives, 1994). Sociologist Diana Pearce (1978) refers to the association between gender and poverty as the ***feminization of poverty*—the trend whereby women are disproportionately represented among individuals living in poverty.** On the basis of research on the feminization of poverty, some sociologists suggest that high rates of female poverty are related to women's unique vulnerability to event-driven poverty—poverty resulting from the loss of a job, disability, desertion by a spouse, separation, divorce, or widowhood (Weitzman, 1985; Bane, 1986; Kurz, 1995).

Race, Ethnicity, and Poverty

Despite fluctuations in poverty rates from one year to the next, African Americans, Latinos/as, and Native Americans remain overrepresented among people living in poverty (see Figure 2.4). Across racial-ethnic categories, about three times as many African-American families and Latina/o families lived in poverty in 2006 as non-Latina/o white families (DeNavas-Walt, Proctor, and Smith, 2007). Within

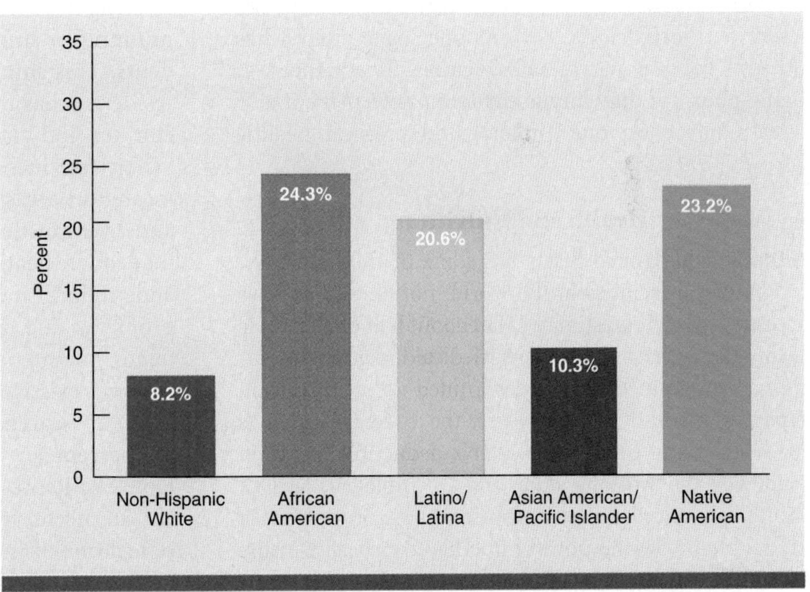

Figure 2.4 *People below the U.S. poverty level, 2006, by race*

Note: Data on Native Americans are based on 2001–2003 average.

Source: DeNavas-Walt, Proctor, and Smith, 2007.

racial-ethnic categories, fewer than one in eight (non-Latino/a) whites fell below the official poverty level in 2006 in contrast to 23.2 percent of all Native Americans, 24.3 percent of all African Americans, 20.6 percent of all Latinos/as, and 10.3 percent of Asian and Pacific Island Americans.

The contrast in poverty rates within racial-ethnic categories becomes especially evident when household composition is considered. In households headed by women with no husband present, about one-third of all Latina/o families (34.2 percent) and African-American families (34.6 percent) had incomes below the official poverty level in 2001, in contrast to 16.9 percent of white (non-Latino/a) families. According to sociologist Demie Kurz (1995), the feminization of poverty is intensified by the racialization of poverty—the process by which the effects of low income are made even worse by racial discrimination, which is experienced by all people of color but particularly by women who are single heads of household.

Consequences of Poverty

Poverty statistics are more than just a snapshot of who is poor and how the poor live: These statistics are predictors. As such, they tend to predict a grim future for individuals who live below the poverty line and for the entire nation (Gleick, 1996). As one social analyst has noted, "Poverty narrows and closes life chances.... Being poor not only means economic insecurity, it also wreaks havoc on one's mental and physical health" (Ropers, 1991:25).

Health and Nutrition

Although the United States has some of the best high-tech medical facilities in the world, not all people have access to them. It is estimated that about half of all people below the poverty line receive Medicaid, a government-funded program that provides limited access to certain types of medical care; however, the coverage often is inadequate and begins only after a deductible has been paid. For the working poor and unemployed, lack of health insurance is a major problem. About 30 percent of all people below the poverty line have no health insurance. The highest rates of uninsured persons are among African Americans and Latinas/os, and many of these uninsured persons are infants and children who do not receive the care they need for illnesses and disease.

Like health care, good nutrition is essential to an individual's well-being. Good nutrition depends on the food purchased, and when people are poor, they are more likely to go without food or to purchase cheap but filling foods such as beans, rice, and potatoes that typically do not meet all daily nutritional requirements. Poor children particularly are at risk for inadequate nutrition and hunger. It is estimated that about 4 million U.S. children under age twelve are hungry during some part of any twelve-month period. Prolonged malnutrition can contribute to or result in such medical problems as rickets, scurvy, parasitic worms, and mental retardation. About 40 percent of all children living in poverty consume significantly less than the federally recommended guidelines for caloric and nutritional intake (Brown, 2002). Problems associated with food and shelter are intricately linked. When parents have to decide between paying the rent and putting food on the table, many choose to pay the rent in hopes of keeping a roof over the heads of family members. Sometimes, however, they cannot afford to do either.

Housing

Many regions of the United States lack affordable housing for low-income families. Frequently, housing costs have risen dramatically even for marginal places of residence. The problem has been heightened by the loss of many lower-cost housing units. In cities with rapid urban and suburban growth patterns, low-cost housing units have been replaced by expensive condominiums or single-family residences for affluent residents. This shift to condominiums and single-family residences has made finding housing even more difficult for individuals and families living in poverty. When low-income housing is available, it may be located in areas that are plagued by high crime rates and overcrowded conditions. The housing often has inadequate heating and plumbing facilities, cockroach and rodent infestation, and dangerous structural problems due to faulty construction or lack of adequate maintenance. Although much substandard housing exists in central cities where there is a high level of segregation, rural areas have more than 50 percent of all inadequate housing units (U.S. House of Representatives, 1994).

In recent years, increasing rates of homelessness reflect one of the most devastating effects of poverty. Today, homeless people include single men, single women, increasing numbers of teenage runaways, older people, and entire families (see studies by Rossi, 1989; Liebow, 1993; Lundy, 1995). Families with children accounted for about 40 percent of all homeless people in 2004, up from about

Housing is one reflection of larger economic inequalities that exist in the United States. What economic realities are shown by this multistory house in a wealthy suburban neighborhood (left) as compared with these apartment units in a low-income urban area (right)?

27 percent a decade earlier (U.S. Conference of Mayors, 2004). Regardless of age or marital status, homeless people are among the poorest of the poor, and people of color are overrepresented in the homeless population.

Education

A crucial relationship exists between educational opportunities and life chances. Children from low-income families tend to have inadequate educational opportunities, which keeps them at the bottom of the class system (Bowles and Gintis, 1976). They get fewer years of schooling and are less likely to graduate from high school or college than are children from more affluent families. The schools that poor children attend are more likely to be in areas with lower property values and more limited funding bases for education than are the schools attended by more affluent students, who often live in property-rich suburbs. Schools located in high-poverty rural areas or central cities often are dilapidated, have underpaid and overworked teachers, and must rely on outdated equipment and teaching materials. Lack of educational opportunity results in lower levels of educational attainment among people from lower-income and poverty-level families and tends to perpetuate poverty by making it significantly more difficult for these individuals to acquire well-paying jobs or a more secure economic future.

SOCIAL WELFARE IN THE UNITED STATES

The initial wave of U.S. welfare programs was established by Roosevelt's New Deal during the Great Depression of the 1930s. These programs marked the beginning of the ***welfare state*****—a program under which the government takes responsibility for specific categories of people by offering them certain services and benefits, such as employment, housing, health, education, or guaranteed income.** From their inception, government assistance programs have been viewed as "good" if recipients are thought to be deserving of assistance and "bad" if recipients are considered undeserving (see Box 2.3 on page 38).

The second wave of welfare programs began with the passage of the Economic Opportunity Act of 1964 and the implementation of the War on Poverty programs, which focused on education and vocational training for low-income children and adults to help them escape poverty. These programs included preschool education (Head Start), compensatory education, and vocational training programs such as Job Corps, Neighborhood Youth Corps, and Manpower Development (Kelso, 1994). With these programs in place, the percentage of people living in poverty dropped from 22 percent in 1960 to 12 percent in 1976

The faces of people seeking welfare tell the story of how intertwined the problems of poverty and welfare are in our nation. How do individual, cultural, and structural explanations for poverty differ?

(see Coleman, 1966; Jencks et al., 1972). However, in the 1980s and early 1990s, funding for many of these programs was greatly reduced or eliminated, and in 1996, President Clinton signed into law a welfare reform plan that dramatically changed the U.S. welfare system by requiring recipients to work in exchange for time-limited assistance (see Box 2.3).

Are welfare programs a problem or a solution for poverty? The answer to this question depends on how poverty itself is explained.

Explanations for Poverty

Poverty can be explained in individualistic, cultural, or structural terms. The framework that is applied influences people's beliefs about how poverty might be reduced. Individual explanations for poverty view poverty as the result of either attitudinal and

Box 2.3

motivational problems that cause individuals to be poor or the amount of human capital that a person possesses (Rank, 1994). Attitudinal and motivational explanations focus on the United States as the "land of opportunity" and suggest that people who do not succeed have no one to blame but themselves for their lack of motivation, laziness, or other flaws (Feagin, 1975). In contrast, human capital explanations of poverty highlight the individual's lack of human capital—the assets that a person brings to the labor market such as education, job training, experience, and specialized knowledge or skills (Becker, 1964). Those favoring human capital explanations of poverty have noted, for example, that the introduction of new workplace technologies has resulted in many people having limited human capital to bring to the job market. As discussed in Box 2.3, the 1996 workfare program for welfare recipients appears to be based on individual explanations for poverty and welfare dependency. To many sociologists, however, individual explanations of poverty amount to ***blaming the victim*—a practice used by people who view a social problem as emanating from within the individual who exhibits the problem** (Ryan, 1976).

Cultural explanations of poverty focus on how cultural background affects people's values and behavior. Among the earliest of these explanations is the culture of poverty thesis by anthropologist Oscar Lewis (1966). According to Lewis, some—but not all—poor people develop a separate and self-perpetuating system of attitudes and behaviors that keeps them trapped in poverty. Among these attitudes and behaviors are an inability to defer gratification or plan for the future; feelings of apathy, hostility, and suspicion toward others; and deficient speech and communication patterns. The culture of poverty thesis has provided political leaders and social analysts with a rationale for labeling the poor as lazy and perpetually dependent on "government handouts."

Box 2.3 *(continued)*

health problems or disability or because of the need to care for relatives with such problems, have remained on the welfare rolls and have been granted an exemption from the law's work requirements. Others who periodically sign up for TANF are referred to as *cyclers*—individuals who return to the welfare rolls for a period of time as a result of pregnancy, the birth of a child, or other major life crises or events (Moffitt et al., 2002). Mysheda Autry is typical of women who have remained on TANF for more than the five-year limit under the law. With a tenth-grade education, few job skills, and three children, Ms. Autry was granted a temporary reprieve from being "booted off" the rolls when she became pregnant with her fourth child provided that she agreed to return to her full-time job-skill classes and to reestablish her job search within eight and one-half months after the child was born (Eckholm, 2006). Although some people might blame Ms. Autry for "causing her own problems," some sociologists suggest that leaving welfare is tough for anyone in a society that is characterized by inadequate wages for lower level positions, lack of affordable child care and public transportation, and rapid increases in the cost of living. Many of the jobs that are most readily available to welfare recipients do not pay a living wage—the salary that is necessary for an individual or family to have some minimum standard of living. As a result, many past and current welfare recipients need cash, health care, child care, and job training if they are going to have any chance of making the transition from welfare to work (Goodman, 2008a). Today, about 1 million poor mothers are neither employed nor receive welfare benefits (Goodman, 2008a). Some of these women rely on their family members or social service agencies for housing and other assistance; others live in shelters or on the street, where they attempt to acquire food from community pantries or by panhandling.

Have we been successful in ending welfare as we knew it? Not really. In the twenty-first century, regulations pertaining to welfare programs such as TANF are continually being changed, but welfare—and the need for a social safety net of this type—has not gone away. Furthermore, it appears that some problems of the most needy in our nation may only grow worse in the future. With job losses, low wages, large numbers of housing foreclosures, and spiraling costs of food, fuel, and transportation, the U.S. economy appears to be turning down more sharply than it has at any other time since these welfare changes were imposed in the 1990s (Goodman, 2008b). What this means for the future is problematic: In tough economic times, political leaders are often hesitant to adopt broad new social policies that might assist the most needy persons in society and, as a result, the poorest people may fall farther behind—rather than experiencing any kind of upward mobility—even in one of the world's wealthiest nations.

What social policies do you believe might be helpful in reducing poverty? How should welfare programs in the United States be funded? What do you think?

More recent cultural explanations of poverty have focused on the lack of ***cultural capital*—social assets such as the values, beliefs, attitudes, and competencies in language and culture that are learned at home and required for success and social advancement** (Bourdieu and Passeron, 1990). From this perspective, low-income people do not have adequate cultural capital to function in a competitive global economy. According to some sociologists, cultural explanations deflect attention from the true sources of poverty and shift blame from the affluent and powerful to the poor and powerless (Sidel, 1996).

Unlike individual and cultural explanations of poverty, which operate at the microlevel, structural explanations of poverty focus on the macrolevel, the level of social organization that is beyond an individual's ability to change. One structural explanation of poverty points to changes in the economy that have dramatically altered employment opportunities for people, particularly those who have the least wealth, power, and prestige (see Wilson, 1996). According to the functionalists who espouse this explanation, social inequality serves an important function in society because it motivates people to work hard to acquire scarce resources.

Another structural explanation for poverty is based on a conflict perspective that suggests that poverty is a side effect of the capitalist system. Using this explanation, analysts note that workers are increasingly impoverished by the wage squeeze and high rates of unemployment and underemployment. The wage squeeze is the steady downward pressure on the real take-home pay of workers that has occurred over the past three decades. During these same decades, shareholders in major corporations have had substantial increases in dividends and chief executive officers have received extremely lucrative salaries and compensation packages (Gordon, 1996). Corporate downsizing and new technologies that take the place of workers further enhanced capitalists' profits and contributed to the impoverishment of middle- and low-income workers by creating a reserve army of unemployed people whom the capitalists use for labor and as a means to keep other workers' wages low. In sum, corporations' intense quest for profit results in low wages for workers, a wide disparity in the life chances of affluent people and poor people, and the unemployment and impoverishment of many people. Although some analysts suggest that high rates of poverty will always exist in advanced capitalist societies, others believe that inequality and poverty can be reduced if not eliminated.

IS THERE A SOLUTION TO POVERTY?

As we saw in Chapter 1, how people view a social problem has a direct effect on how they believe the problem should be reduced or solved. Poverty, hunger, and social inequality are no exception. Functionalist analysts and those who follow a conservative political outlook typically view these issues quite differently—and offer different solutions—from conflict or symbolic interactionist theorists and liberal political analysts, who possess divergent assumptions about the causes for, effects of, and possible solutions to these pressing social problems.

Functionalist/Conservative Solutions to the Problem of Poverty

How big a problem is poverty in the United States? Some functionalist theorists and conservative political analysts begin any discussion of poverty by noting that, although poverty *is* a problem, it is not *as big a problem* as some people might believe. To some of

Reprinted by permission

these analysts, for example, "official" poverty statistics issued by agencies of the federal government and some other organizations exaggerate the nature and extent of poverty in this country. Some functionalists and conservatives believe that, if we take into account all of the available anti-poverty benefits (including health care for the poor, subsidized housing, and food stamps), the number of people living in poverty is much lower than many estimates suggest. In other words, if we include all of the benefits available to so-called poor people when we calculate rates of poverty, we will find that the "real poverty rate has been cut in half" (Ways and Means Republicans, 2007).

From a functionalist viewpoint, there will always be poverty in any society: Some people will earn more than other people, there will always be people on the "bottom rungs" of society, and those on the bottom rungs will live in poverty when contrasted with those who earn more. The issue, from this point of view, is not whether society can eliminate poverty but rather what can be done to strengthen those social institutions that help individuals lift themselves out of poverty. Based on functionalist and conservative perspectives, putting more resources into welfare benefits for the poor would be the equivalent of simply throwing away money in an effort the solve the problem. According to these analysts, you do not eliminate poverty-related problems by paying people to stay poor and/or unemployed, and throwing money at the problem of poverty therefore neither reduces the nation's poverty rate nor helps make poor individuals self-sufficient. Instead, it increases public spending and red tape while giving "faceless bureaucrats" in the government more of an opportunity to meddle in the lives of people who are turned into passive individuals who depend on "handouts" from others to survive (Cato Institute, 2006). Functionalist theorizing and conservative political perspectives further suggest that contemporary U.S. welfare programs have seriously weakened many people's work ethic, contributed to rising rates of crime, and created a "pathology" of dependency that is passed on "from parent to child, from generation to generation" (Cato Institute, 2006).

Based on this functionalist/conservative assessment of the causes of poverty, what are the possible ways to reduce or eliminate poverty? Those who adhere to a functionalist approach often argue that poverty-related problems can be reduced by strengthening our major social institutions. We must improve our schools and strengthen our families, churches, and communities, so that these groups can more effectively meet the needs of people. Not only should school systems be greatly improved, for example, but parents and teachers should motivate students to remain in school so that they can find a decent job when they graduate (Cato Institute, 2006). By motivating low-income and poverty-level people to change their attitudes, beliefs, and work habits, they will have a better chance of escaping poverty. According to some analysts, we must educate children and young people in low-income or poverty-level families to see that the "surest way for them to stay out of poverty is to finish school, not get pregnant outside marriage, and get a job— any job—and stick with it" (Cato Institute, 2006). Equally important to these analysts, if we are to reduce poverty, we must eliminate high taxes and regulatory excesses that make it prohibitive for individual employers and large corporations to create new jobs.

Conflict/Liberal Solutions to the Problem of Poverty

Some of the strongest critiques of functionalist/conservative perspectives on poverty come from conflict theorists and liberal political analysts who argue that this approach amounts to "blaming the victim." When we blame people living in poverty for their own plight, we place the focus on their "faulty" beliefs, values, or actions; we do not give proper attention to larger societal issues such as the role that out-of-control capitalists or greedy and corrupt political elites play in maintaining and perpetuating vast inequalities and social injustices in society. This perspective is in keeping with the ideas of Karl Marx, who believed that poverty was a side effect of capitalism, an economic system that made a few people very wealthy but pushed the vast majority further and further into poverty.

Different schools of thought within the larger umbrella of conflict theory offer different views of poverty and what its solutions might be. According to feminist conflict theorists, for example, poverty is partly based on gender. Patriarchy in society and discrimination against women in the home and workplace produce a harmful effect on women and children. The feminization of poverty makes women particularly vulnerable to event-driven poverty such as the loss of a job or a downturn in the economy that makes it more difficult for those on the lower rungs of the economic ladder to find a job at all, much less to find decent-paying work. From this perspective, solving the problem of poverty requires solving problems within the labor market itself, especially the problems that women face within that market.

Conflict theorists who focus on the issue of racial and ethnic inequality believe that poverty is rooted in past and present prejudice and discrimination that keeps people of color out of the economic mainstream. The high poverty rate among African Americans, Latinos/as, and other people of color is caused by structural factors such as substandard schools, inadequate housing, and crime-ridden neighborhoods. The lack of social policies that address ongoing problems of economic inequality, such as the large number of subordinate-group members who do not have health insurance or access to legal counsel, also contributes to the continued subordination of these populations. Based on this perspective, the problem of poverty can be solved only if we are able to reduce racial and ethnic inequality, as well as economic inequality, in our nation.

Overall, conflict theorists and liberal political analysts view increased social inequality and unresolved race, class, and gender discrimination as major factors that contribute to the problem of poverty: These structural problems are beyond the control of individuals who live in poverty. Liberal political analysts argue that, to reduce the problem of poverty, federal and state governments must play a larger role by enacting and implementing social policies that stimulate the economy, create new jobs, and provide workers with a living wage: People must be better rewarded for working by raising the federal minimum wage, as well as tax credits for low-income families. We must also overhaul housing policies and strengthen job training programs. In other words, to significantly reduce poverty, we must not blame people for being poor. Our nation's political and business leaders must devise new ways to fund needed social service programs and must cut excessive "corporate welfare" programs that primarily benefit the wealthiest people.

Symbolic Interactionist Solutions to the Problem of Poverty

As discussed in Chapter 1, analysts using a symbolic interactionist perspective typically focus on how human behavior is learned through social interaction and how people impose their shared meanings on others. One of the ways in which meanings—both positive and negative—are shared is through the labeling of other individuals and groups. *Labeling theory* is based on the assumption that how people are viewed by others has a strong influence on how they perceive themselves, particularly if they accept the label placed upon them as being valid. When people are labeled as "deviant," for example, they have fewer resources and opportunities than those who are not so labeled. Persons labeled as "deviant" are more likely to engage in nonstandard patterns of behavior, and they have a much greater chance of being stigmatized by others. *Stigma* is a negative social label that singles out people as "deviants" because of some characteristic they possess that is devalued by other individuals.

In the United States, being financially self-sufficient is the minimum norm for social acceptance by many people. Individuals who are poor are considered to be a burden upon society and may be labeled as "lazy," "ignorant," or "useless" in a society that values high achievement and self-sufficiency. In sociologist Erving Goffman's (1963) discussion of social stigma, he stated that individuals are stigmatized when their appearance, behavior, or assumed beliefs and attitudes go against cultural norms. Those who are stigmatized experience social disapproval from others and are blamed for being the cause of their own problems. Although some of the poor, homeless, and hungry in our nation may escape stigmatization because they are largely invisible to middle- and upper-class people, poverty-level individuals who are visible on the streets and busy corners in major cities are often the object of labeling ("Bum!") and derision ("Get a job!"). They also experience informal and official stigmatization (such as city ordinances that prohibit homeless people from being on the streets if they have no visible means of support). Based on Goffman's assessment of stigma, we may assume that labeling and stigmatization strongly affect people and have a profound effect on human interactions across class lines.

Symbolic interactionists suggest that, in order to reduce or eliminate poverty, we should fine more constructive ways to think about poor people individually and better ways to envision what might reduce poverty at a societal level. Although improving how affluent people perceive of the poor will not immediately resolve the larger structural issue of how to reduce vast economic inequalities, the process of changing people's perceptions about the poor might result in significant social policy changes. When poor people are viewed as *being the problem*, our political, business, and social leaders see little reason to take action to reduce poverty. By contrast, if the poor are viewed as *needing assistance to overcome poverty* because of factors largely beyond their control, political leaders may be more likely to seek ways to provide that assistance.

People who are poor are hurt psychologically and socially by being stigmatized and have little chance of escaping poverty. According to Goffman, going through the process of stigmatization spoils a person's identity and makes the individual feel inadequate and even inferior. If poor individuals who are labeled as having some sort of personal flaw that keeps them in poverty come to accept this label, they may lose any motivation to try to rise out of poverty: Why try to escape poverty when it is an inevitable consequence of their own personal flaws?

Although the symbolic interactionist perspective does not provide a list of ways to deal with social problems such as poverty, it does provide us with insights on the social-psychological issues that are associated with being poor, such as how labeling and stigmatization may affect individuals living in poverty. This approach makes us aware that social change must occur at both the microlevel and macrolevel to reduce poverty. Many individuals living in poverty are not passive victims of their situation: They want to bring about positive changes in their own lives and that of their families if they are only given the opportunity to do so. Amazingly, many people living in poverty have not given up on the American Dream of upward mobility for themselves and their children. In one study of poverty, Sara, a woman struggling to find such opportunities for advancement, said,

> I got my vision, I got my dreams.... I have goals—I want to be something different from what I have right now.... I guess to be somebody in poverty, to see that generation that's coming behind us—it's sad, it's real sad, what do they have to strive for? ... I just got to believe I only can make the difference.... even though obviously the system doesn't really want you to succeed.... I can become what statistics has designed me to be, a nothing, or I can make statistics a lie.... Today, I am making statistics a lie. (Polakow, 1993:73)

SUMMARY

■ *Why is social stratification a social problem?*

Social stratification refers to the hierarchical arrangement of large social groups based on their control over basic resources. In highly stratified societies, low-income and poor people have limited access to food, clothing, shelter, education, health care, and other necessities of life.

■ *What are the major problems of the low-income nations?*

Studies of global inequality distinguish between high-income nations—countries with highly industrialized economies and relatively high levels of national and per capita (per person) income, middle-income nations—countries that are undergoing transformation from agrarian to industrial economies, and low-income nations—countries that are primarily agrarian with little industrialization and low levels of national and personal income. Poverty, food shortages, hunger, and rapidly growing populations are pressing problems in many low-income nations.

■ *How does the "new international division of labor" perspective explain global inequality?*

According to this perspective, transnational corporations have established global assembly lines of production in which workers in middle- and low-income nations, earning extremely low wages, produce goods for export to high-income nations such as the United States and Japan.

■ *How is the U.S. class structure divided?*

The U.S. population is divided into a number of classes. The upper, or capitalist, class is the wealthiest and most powerful class and is made up of investors, heirs, and executives. The upper-middle class is composed of professionals, business analysts, owners of small businesses, stockbrokers, and corporate managers. The middle class includes white-collar office workers, middle-management personnel, people in technical-support positions, semiprofessionals, and nonretail salesworkers. Members of the working class hold occupations such as semiskilled machine operators and counter help in fast-food restaurants. The chronically poor include individuals of working age who are outside the labor force and children who live in poor families.

■ *Who are the poor in the United States?*

The major categories of poor people in the United States are women, children under age eighteen, and people of color, especially African Americans, Latinas/os, and Native Americans.

■ *What are individual and cultural explanations of poverty?*

Individual explanations of poverty focus on the attitudinal and motivational problems of individuals or the amount of human capital a person possesses. Cultural explanations of poverty focus on how cultural background affects people's values and behavior. These explanations focus on the microlevel, and many sociologists view them as attempts to blame the victim for the problem.

■ *What are structural explanations of poverty?*

Structural explanations of poverty focus on the macrolevel, the level of social organization that is beyond an individual's ability to change. These explanations consider how changes in the economy have altered employment opportunities or how inequality and exploitation are inherent in the structure of class relations in a capitalist economy.

■ *What solutions have been suggested for poverty?*

Most individual and cultural solutions focus on the importance of work. Individual perspectives suggest that people should work harder. Cultural perspectives suggest enhancing people's cultural capital to make them better prepared for employment. Structural perspectives are based on the assumption that society can reduce poverty by creating job and training programs and investing in people through provision of child care, health care, and affordable housing.

KEY TERMS

absolute poverty, p. 26
blaming the victim, p. 39
class system, p. 25
cultural capital, p. 40
feminization of poverty, p. 35
high-income nations, p. 26
income, p. 30
life chances, p. 26
low-income nations, p. 26
middle-income nations, p. 26
poverty rate, p. 32
power, p. 29
prestige, p. 29
relative poverty, p. 32
social stratification, p. 28
wealth, p. 29
welfare state, p. 37

QUESTIONS FOR CRITICAL THINKING

1. You have decided to study wealth and poverty in your community. Which of the research methods described in Chapter 1 would provide the best data for analysis? What secondary sources might provide useful data? What kinds of information would be easiest to acquire? What kinds of information would be most difficult to acquire?
2. What would happen if all the wealth in the United States were redistributed so that all adults had the same amount? Some analysts suggest that within five years, most of the wealth would be back in the possession of the people who hold it today. What arguments can you give to support this idea? What arguments can you give to disprove this idea?
3. How do the lives of assembly line workers in middle- and low-income nations compare with the lives of people who live in poverty in central cities and rural areas of the United States? Should U.S. foreign policy include provisions for reducing the problems of people in middle- and low-income nations? Should it be U.S. government policy to help disadvantaged people in our own country? Why or why not?
4. Pretend that cost is no object and develop a plan for solving the problem of poverty in the United States. What are your priorities and goals? How long will your plan take to implement? Who will be the primary beneficiaries of your plan? Will the plan have any effect on you?

Chapter 3

Racial and Ethnic Inequality

THINKING SOCIOLOGICALLY

- How does a sociological definition of race differ from a biological one?
- Why are some forms of discrimination more difficult to identify and remedy than others?
- What similarities can we identify in the experiences of various subordinate racial and ethnic groups in the United States? What are some of the differences?

Commercial #1:

"It's so easy to use GEICO.com, a caveman could do it," recites a blow-dried actor smiling into the camera. "What?" we hear off-screen. The camera pans and reveals that the boom operator on this film shoot is, in fact, a caveman (wearing a backward baseball cap). Huffily dropping his boom mic to the floor, the caveman shouts, "Not cool!" and storms off the set. The GEICO spokesperson awkwardly yells back, "I didn't know you were there!" (Stevenson, 2007)

Commercial #2:

A caveman—with a plane ticket in one hand and a canvas bag containing a wooden tennis racket slung over one shoulder—is riding a moving sidewalk at an airport when he spots a billboard ad for GEICO. The ad shows a caveman wearing a loincloth made out of animal hide. He is holding a large club in one hand and making the "Okay" sign with two fingers of the other hand as he stands near a computer: The purpose is to show that he found GEICO's website easy to use. The "real" caveman walks back on the moving sideway to take another look at the ad, and then shakes his head in disgust. Playing in the background is the Röyksopp song, "Remind Me," which states, "Everywhere I go, there's something to remind me..." and this is what the ad does for the "traveling" caveman. The next ad in the GEICO series shows the same caveman talking on his cell phone and complaining intently about the ad. (GEICO.com, 2008)

ABC Promotion for *Cavemen:*

They have been around since the dawn of time, survived the Ice Age, and witnessed the evolution of the Homo sapiens, making them one of the world's oldest minorities. Keeping mostly to themselves over the millennia and living in remote communities, a small number of cavemen—and cavewomen—have been slowly migrating from these sub-societies and attempting to acclimate themselves to the Homo sapiens' world. Needless to say, this has proven difficult.

Meet three cavemen who have successfully made the move to San Diego and are just trying to fit in.... Joel, Nick, and Andy have to overcome prejudice from most of the Homo sapiens' world and the misconceptions that modern society has of its earliest ancestors. In order for these cavemen to survive in the twenty-first century, they must work together to render those misconceptions extinct. (ABC TV, 2007)

What do commercials and television shows about make-believe cavemen have to do with a discussion about racial and ethnic inequality? Although the stereotypic portrayal of cavemen as subordinate-group members who need everything to be "easy" for them to accomplish because they lack intelligence may seem like a small concern in our society, many scholars believe that media portrayals such as these are a reflection of lingering racial prejudice and contribute to discrimination. In the short-lived *Cavemen* series, for example, negative stereotypes once used against African Americans, such as being "good dancers, great athletes, and grand sexual partners," were revived in caveman-form for a cheap laugh (Garvin, 2007). According to one blogger, "We finally get to laugh at all the stereotypes in the world directed at cavemen, without feeling guilty" (Garvin, 2007).

By contrast, the sociologist Matthew W. Hughey (2008:39) argues that such portrayals have many negative effects on individuals and on the larger society:

> ...the troubling import of [the *Cavemen*] is that it minimizes, commercializes, and makes comedic fodder out of *modern* discrimination and inequality, as well as the tactic of "identity politics" that is *still* used to combat it.... *Cavemen* activates racialized comedic discourse and allows the viewer enjoyment without the danger of being called insensitive, politically incorrect, or a racist. After all, you can't be called a racist if you're laughing at cavemen because it's not *really* about race. Even better, one can always dismiss such claims of racism as: "It's just a joke, don't take it seriously."

From this perspective, caveman portrayals (and other stereotypes found in ads and cartoons) trivialize our nation's larger problems regarding racial and ethnic discrimination. When the media attempt to satirize racial differences and poke fun at people based on their appearance or perceived attributes—such as how intelligent or unintelligent they are—they actually open wider the doors of prejudice and discrimination with these "humorous" spots. In this chapter, we examine both overt and covert forms of discrimination, ranging from "joking" media portrayals to larger scale discrimination in education, employment, law enforcement, and other areas of social life. As was described in Chapter 1, *discrimination* is the actions or practices of dominant group members that have a harmful impact on members of subordinate groups (Feagin and Feagin, 2008). Like many other social problems, racial and ethnic discrimination signals a discrepancy between the ideals and realities of U.S. society today. Although equality and freedom for all—regardless of race, color, creed, or national origin—are stated ideals of this country, many subordinate-group members experience oppression regardless of their class, gender, or age.

RACIAL AND ETHNIC INEQUALITY AS A SOCIAL PROBLEM

Race is among the most divisive social problems facing the United States today. However, sociologists such as William J. Wilson (1996) suggest that we all, regardless of racial or ethnic background, share certain interests and concerns that cross racial and class boundaries. Some of the problems are unemployment and job insecurity, declining real wages, escalating medical and housing costs, a scarcity of good-quality child-care programs, a sharp decline in the quality of public education, and the toll of crime and drug trafficking in all neighborhoods. From this perspective, racial and ethnic inequality is a problem for everyone, not just for people of color.

What Are Race and Ethnicity?

Many sociologists view race as a social construct—a classification of people based on social and political values—rather than a biological given (see Omi and Winant, 1994). How does a sociological definition of race differ from a biological one? A biological definition of a race is a population that differs from other populations in the incidence of some genes. In the past, some anthropologists classified diverse categories of peoples into races on the basis of skin color (pigmentation) and features and build (morphology). However, contemporary anthropologists classify races in terms of genetically determined immunological and biochemical differences. In the process, they have concluded that no "pure" races exist because of multiple generations of interbreeding.

In contrast with the biological definition of race, sociologists define a ***racial group*** **as a category of people who have been singled out, by others or themselves, as inferior or superior, on the basis of subjectively selected physical characteristics such as skin color, hair texture, and eye shape.** African American, Native American, and Asian American are examples of categories of people that have been designated racial groups.

Sociologists note that racial groups usually are defined on the basis of real or alleged physical characteristics; ethnic groups are defined on the basis of cultural or nationality characteristics. An ***ethnic group*** **is a category of people who are distinguished, by others or by themselves, as inferior or superior primarily on the basis of cultural or nationality characteristics** (Feagin and Feagin, 2008). Briefly stated, members of an ethnic group share five main characteristics: (1) unique cultural traits, (2) a sense of community, (3) a feeling that one's own group is the best, (4) membership from birth, and (5) a tendency, at least initially, to occupy a distinct geographic area (such as Chinatown, Little Italy, or Little Havana). "White ethnics," such as Irish Americans, Italian Americans, and Jewish Americans, are also examples of ethnic groups.

"Official" Racial and Ethnic Classifications

Racial and ethnic classifications have been used for political, economic, and social purposes for many years. During the sixteenth century, northern Europeans used the concept of race to rationalize the enslavement of Africans, who were deemed an "inferior race" (Feagin and Feagin, 2008).

Before the Civil War, race was used to justify the subordination of African Americans—whether they were classified as "slaves" in the South or "freemen" in the North. In some southern states, people were classified on the basis of the "one-drop rule"—a person with any trace of African blood was considered "black" and treated as inferior (Davis, 1991). Other states traced "black blood" by fractions, such as one-sixteenth African ancestry, or used an "eyeball test" based on physical features such as hair texture, eye color, and shape of nose, ears, lips, and skull (Funderburg, 1994). Being classified as "Negro," "black," or "colored" had a profound effect on people's life chances and opportunities during slavery and the subsequent era of legally sanctioned segregation of the races. Gregory Howard Williams describes how he felt when he learned from his father in the 1950s that he was "colored" rather than white, as he previously had been led to believe:

> [My father said,] "Life is going to be different from now on. In Virginia you were white boys. In Indiana, you're going to be colored boys. I want you to remember that you're the same today that you were yesterday. But people in Indiana will treat you differently. . . ."
>
> No, I answered, still refusing to believe. I'm not colored, I'm white! I look white! I've always been white! I go to "whites only" schools, "whites only" movie theaters, and "whites only" swimming pools! I never had heard anything crazier in my life! How could Dad tell us such a mean lie? I glanced across the aisle [of the bus] to where he sat grim-faced and erect, staring straight ahead. I saw my father as I never had seen him before. . . . My father was a Negro! We were colored! After ten years in Virginia on the white side of the color line, I knew what that meant. (Williams, 1996:33–34)

When Williams and his younger brother went to live with their African-American grandmother in Muncie, Indiana, they quickly saw the sharp contrast between the "white" and "black" worlds: The first was one of privilege, opportunity, and comfort, and the second was one of deprivation, repression, and struggle. Since that time, Williams has become a lawyer and a law school dean; however, his memories of the prejudice and discrimination he experienced in Muncie because of the change in his racial classification remain with him (Williams, 1996).

Government racial classifications are based primarily on skin color. One category exists for "whites" (who vary considerably in actual skin color and physical appearance); all the remaining categories are considered "nonwhite." Until the 2000 census, the U.S. Census Bureau required respondents to choose from the categories of White, Black, Asian and Pacific American, American Indian, Eskimo or Aleut, or "Other" in designating their racial classification. In an effort to overcome inadequacies in the previous system, the 2000 census allowed people to place themselves in more than one racial category. Although racial classifications might seem unimportant, they affect people's access to employment, housing, social services, federal aid, and many other publicly and privately valued goods and services (Omi and Winant, 1994).

Dominant and Subordinate Groups

The terms *majority group* and *minority group* are widely used, but their meanings are less clear as the composition of the U.S. population continues to change. Accordingly, many sociologists prefer the terms *dominant* and *subordinate* to identify power relationships that are based on perceived racial, ethnic, or other attributes and identities. A ***dominant or (majority group)*** **is one that is advantaged and has superior resources and rights in a society** (Feagin and Feagin, 2008). Dominant groups (sometimes referred to as majority groups regardless of their proportion in the overall U.S. population) often are determined on the basis of race or ethnicity, but they can also be determined on the basis of gender, sexual orientation (homosexuality, heterosexuality, or bisexuality), or physical ability. A ***subordinate (or minority) group*** **is one whose members, because of physical or cultural characteristics, are disadvantaged and subjected to unequal treatment by the majority group and regard themselves as objects of collective discrimination** (Wirth, 1945). In the United States, people of color, all women, people with disabilities, and gay men and lesbians tend to be considered subordinate-group members.

In the United States, the racial and ethnic dominant group typically is associated with the white-skin privilege, which is afforded to the people who trace their ancestry to northern Europe and think of themselves as European Americans or WASPs (white Anglo-Saxon Protestants). Women's studies scholar Peggy McIntosh describes white-skin privilege as

> an invisible package of unearned assets that I can count on cashing in each day, but about which I was "meant" to

> remain oblivious. White privilege is like an invisible weightless knapsack of special provisions, assurances, maps, guides, codebooks, passports, visas, clothes, compass, emergency gear, and blank checks. (McIntosh, 1995:76–77)

Most white Americans are unaware of the benefits that they derive from white-skin privilege (see Frankenberg, 1993; Wellman, 1993; Hacker, 1995; McIntosh, 1995). Nevertheless, the advantage/disadvantage and power/exploitation relationships of dominant and subordinate groups in this country are deeply rooted in patterns of prejudice and discrimination.

Although the United States has come a long way in race relations, we are occasionally reminded of the lingering problem of racism. As recently as 2007, an African American professor at Columbia University found this four-foot-long twine noose (left) hanging from her office doorknob. Members of the university community (right) quickly made it known that this act constituted unacceptable behavior at their institution.

RACISM, PREJUDICE, AND DISCRIMINATION

***Racism* is a set of attitudes, beliefs, and practices used to justify the superior treatment of one racial or ethnic group and the inferior treatment of another racial or ethnic group.** In the United States, racism is sometimes referred to as white racism. *White racism* refers to socially organized attitudes, ideas, and practices that deny people of color the dignity, opportunities, freedoms, and rewards that are typically available to white Americans (Feagin and Vera, 1995:7). From this perspective, people of color pay a *direct, heavy, and immediately painful price* for racism, while white discriminators pay an *indirect and seldom-recognized price.*

***Prejudice* is a negative attitude based on faulty generalizations about members of selected racial and ethnic groups.** These generalizations may involve such characteristics as race, age, religion, or sexual orientation. If we think of prejudice as a set of negative attitudes toward members of another group simply because they belong to that group, we quickly realize that all people have prejudices, whether or not they acknowledge them. Prejudice is rooted in ***ethnocentrism*—the assumption that one's own group and way of life are superior to all others.** For example, most schoolchildren are taught that their own school and country are the best. The school song, the pledge to the flag, and the national anthem are forms of *positive ethnocentrism*. However, *negative ethnocentrism* can result if individuals come to believe, because of constant emphasis on the superiority of one's own group or nation, that other groups or nations are inferior and should be treated accordingly (Feagin and Feagin, 2008). Negative ethnocentrism is manifested in stereotypes that adversely affect many people.

***Stereotypes* are overgeneralizations about the appearance, behavior, or other characteristics of all members of a group.** For example, second-generation Filipino-American Steven De Castro and his friends were the objects of stereotyping throughout their school years:

> "What's up, monkey?" "Hey Ching Chong! Hey eggroll!" "Here comes the gook!" If you are Filipino in America, that is what you grow up hearing in the schoolyard. All you want to do is belong, but white and black classmates never let you forget that you will never belong in their America. (De Castro, 1994:303–304)

Box 3.1 on page 50 discusses stereotyping and discrimination that occur in most nations that have diverse populations. Discrimination may be carried out by individuals acting on their own or by individuals operating within the context of large-scale organizations or institutions such as schools, corporations, and government agencies. ***Individual discrimination* consists of one-on-one acts by members of the dominant group that harm members of the subordinate group or their property** (Carmichael and

Hamilton, 1967). Individual discrimination results from the prejudices and discriminatory actions of bigoted people who target one or more subordinate-group members. The taxi driver who refuses to pick up African-American passengers is practicing individual discrimination.

In contrast, ***institutional discrimination*** **consists of the day-to-day practices of organizations and institutions that have a harmful impact on members of subordinate groups.** For example, many mortgage companies are more likely to make loans to whites than to people of color (see Squires, 1994). Institutional

Social Problems in Global Perspective

Box 3.1

The Polish Plumber in France: Negative Stereotypes about "Cheap Labor"

> Live in France? Got leaky pipes? The Polish plumber—muscled, square jawed, and downright handsome—won't be there to help. But with his wrench at the ready, the man who came to symbolize cheap labor in France traveled to Paris [recently] to prove he is harmless—and to welcome the French to Poland.... "I will stay in Poland" [he said]. "Come [visit in large] numbers."
>
> —*Journalist Elaine Ganley describes an advertising campaign, featuring a model dressed as a Polish plumber who seeks to lure tourists to Poland by spoofing fears of cheap foreign labor that supposedly would diminish the quality of life in France. (Ganley, 2005)*

In a bitter 2005 referendum (which failed) in France on whether to ratify the proposed European Union constitution, many voters feared that affluent western Europe would be overrun by low-wage, immigrant workers from less affluent nations (such as Poland) that had recently joined the union. To fuel this fear and encourage a vote against ratifying the constitution, opponents bombarded voters with negative stereotypes of low-wage workers—such as the "Polish plumber"—who would flood into France, take jobs away from French citizens, and lower living standards if national borders became more open as called for in the constitution. The "Polish plumber" became a negative icon symbolizing the threat of cheap labor (Fuller, 2005).

The use of stereotypes that are derogatory regarding a person's race, ethnicity, nationality, or religion is not new in global politics. Over the centuries, recent immigrants to countries such as England, France, Sweden, and the United States have often been stereotyped as "cheap labor" that threatens the quality of life for longer-term residents. Whether the stereotypes are of the low-wage Latvian construction worker in Sweden or of the Mexican worker in the United States, these negative images fuel a fear of outsiders (referred to by sociologists as "the Other") and heighten citizens' anxieties about jobs and economic security. Stereotypes of "cheap labor" typically are contradictory: Immigrant workers are portrayed as wanting jobs so badly that they will work for less money and take more hazardous jobs than longer-term residents, but they are also depicted as being ignorant, lazy, and deviant individuals who will place an unnecessary burden on the nation's schools, hospitals, and welfare system.

Is it possible to turn a negative stereotype into a positive image? In the case of the mythical Polish plumber in France, the Polish National Tourism Office decided to shift the image of the Polish plumber from its xenophobic (that is, abnormal fear or hatred of strangers or foreigners) overtones to a focus on the welcoming nature of the Polish people toward the French. The Polish ad campaign featured the new face of the Polish plumber, portrayed by Piotr Adamski, a smiling model who wore blue overalls and gripped a wrench in his hand, and who came to Paris to invite the people of France to come to Poland for a visit (Ganley, 2005). Did it work? The result is not yet known, but according to Pierre Lequiller, head of the French parliament's delegation to the European Union, "It's extraordinary, this welcome for a plumber...humor will triumph over stupidities" (Ganley, 2005). Can humor also triumph over stupidities in regard to negative stereotypes in the United States?

Questions for Consideration

1. Do political leaders influence how we think about people of other racial and ethnic groups and nationalities by the manner in which they frame social issues and public policy?
2. What examples can you give of racial or ethnic minorities that have been stereotyped as "cheap labor" in the United States?
3. Is it possible to convert a negative stereotype into a positive image? If so, how might this be accomplished?

discrimination is carried out by the individuals who implement policies and procedures that result in negative and differential treatment of subordinate-group members. Jewish immigrants in the late 1800s experienced institutional discrimination in accommodations and employment. Signs in hotel windows often read "No Jews Allowed," and many "help wanted" advertisements stated "Christians Only" (Levine, 1992:55). Such practices are referred to as ***anti-Semitism*—prejudice and discriminatory behavior directed at Jews.**

PERSPECTIVES ON RACIAL AND ETHNIC INEQUALITY

Over the course of the past 100 years, sociologists have developed different perspectives to explain why racial and ethnic inequality occurs and why it persists. Some perspectives are social-psychological; others focus on sociological factors such as migration, assimilation, conflict, and exploitation.

Social-Psychological Perspectives

Are some people more prejudiced than others? Social-psychological perspectives on prejudice emphasize psychological characteristics or personality traits. We will look at the frustration-aggression hypothesis and the authoritarian personality.

Aggression is behavior intended to hurt someone, either physically or verbally, that results from frustration (Weiten and Lloyd, 1994). According to the *frustration-aggression hypothesis*, individuals who are frustrated in their efforts to achieve a highly desired goal tend to develop a pattern of aggression toward others (Dollard et al., 1939). If they have a very high level of frustration and are unable to strike out at the source of their frustration, they may take out their hostility and aggression on a ***scapegoat*—a person or group that is blamed for some problem causing frustration and is therefore subjected to hostility or aggression by others** (Marger, 1994). For example, illegal aliens (people who have entered the United States without permission) have been blamed for a wide variety of societal woes, such as unemployment ("they take our jobs"), economic recession ("things were good until they came"), or high taxes ("we pay more taxes to give them health care").

Another major social-psychological perspective suggests that people who have an authoritarian personality are most likely to be highly prejudiced. According to psychologist Theodore W. Adorno and his colleagues (1950), the *authoritarian personality* is characterized by excessive conformity, submissiveness to authority, intolerance, insecurity, a high level of superstition, and rigid, stereotypic thinking. Individuals with this type of personality typically view the world as a threatening place and are highly intolerant of members of subordinate racial, ethnic, or religious groups.

Symbolic Interactionist Perspectives

Somewhat related to social-psychological explanations of prejudice and discrimination are theories based on the symbolic interactionist perspective. One symbolic interactionist approach emphasizes how racial socialization contributes to feelings of solidarity with one's own racial-ethnic group and hostility toward all others. *Racial socialization* is a process of social interaction that contains specific messages and practices concerning the nature of one's racial-ethnic status as it relates to (1) personal and group identity, (2) intergroup and interindividual relationships, and (3) one's position in the social stratification system. Although racial socialization may occur through direct statements about race made by parents, peers, teachers, and others, it may also include indirect modeling behaviors, which occur when children imitate the words and actions of parents and other caregivers (Thornton et al., 1990). Racial socialization also occurs indirectly through media representations of people in various racial and ethnic categories. Video games are an example: Some video games use racial stereotyping to create a digital cast of characters that players encounter as they play the game (see Box 3.2 on page 52).

Racial socialization affects how people view themselves, other people, and the world. Here, for example, racial relations scholar and historian Manning Marable (1995:1) describes how racial socialization makes race a prism through which African Americans and other people of color view their daily lives:

> Black and white. As long as I can remember, the fundamentally defining feature of my life, and the lives of my family, was the stark reality of race.... It was the social gravity which set into motion our expectations and emotions, our language and dreams.... Race seemed granite-like, fixed and permanent, as the center of the social universe. The reality of racial discrimination constantly fed the pessimism and

Social Problems in the Media

Box 3.2

Video Games, Racial Stereotypes, and Glamorized Violence

> I was rolling through the neon deluge of a place very like Times Square the other night in my Landstalker sport utility vehicle, listening to David Bowie's "Fascination" on the radio. The glittery urban landscape was almost enough to make me forget about the warehouse of cocaine dealers I was headed uptown to rip off.
>
> Soon I would get bored, though, and carjack a luxury sedan. I'd meet my Rasta buddy Lille Jacob, then check out a late show by Ricky Gervais at a comedy club around the corner. Afterwards I'd head north to confront the dealers, at least if I could elude the cops. I heard their sirens before I saw them and peeled out, tires squealing. It was just another night on the streets of Liberty City. . . .
>
> —*Video Game reviewer Seth Schiesel (2008: B1) describes a recent game of* Grand Theft Auto IV *he played.*

Grand Theft Auto and many other violent video games are primarily played by suburban white males; however, many of the characters in these games are based on racial or ethnic stereotyping that shows men of color and recent immigrants as comprising the vast majority of the criminal population in the United States. Games such as *Grand Theft Auto* portray few, if any, positive images of subordinate-group members. Some reviewers argue that this is not a problem because the game is an "equal opportunity" situation in which African Americans, Mexican Americans, Cuban Americans, Haitians, Italian Americans, Russian Americans, and members of all other ethnic groups are shown in the same (negative) light. It is interesting to note, however, that there are no white (Euro-American) gangs in the *Grand Theft Auto* series.

One character in *Grand Theft Auto IV*, the newest game in the series, is Niko Bellic, a Serbian immigrant to the United States. Bellic has dark skin, deep-set eyes, a wide nose, short-cropped hair, and neatly-trimmed facial hair. Wearing a black leather jacket, Bellic moves through Liberty City (a pseudonym for New York City) in hopes of finding the American Dream or getting revenge on a person who betrayed him in the past. The plot of *Grand Theft IV* involves guiding Niko through the underworld of Liberty City, where gang leaders and other crime figures set missions for him to complete so that he can either get revenge or make a deal with a person who deceived him in the past. When Niko first arrives in Liberty City, he believes that his cousin Roman is highly successful and can help him

> doubts that we as black people felt about the apparent natural order of the world, the inherent unfairness of it all, as well as limiting our hopes for a better life somewhere in the distant future.

Though all groups practice racial socialization, white racial socialization emphasizes white racial bonding. According to Christine E. Sleeter (1996), white racial bonding occurs when white people act in ways that reaffirm the common stance on race-related issues and draw we–they boundaries, thus perpetuating racism and discrimination. Such people choose to live near other whites, to socialize with other whites, and to vote for other whites, thus maintaining racial solidarity. Although many whites do not support racist beliefs, actions, or policies, they fear breaking bonds with other whites and may simply remain silent in the face of prejudice and discrimination (Sleeter, 1996).

Functionalist Perspectives

To functionalists, social order and stability are extremely important for the smooth functioning of society. Consequently, racial and ethnic discord, urban unrest, and riots are dysfunctional and must be eliminated or contained. One functionalist perspective focuses on ***assimilation*—the process by which members of subordinate racial and ethnic groups become absorbed into the dominant culture.** Functionalists view assimilation as a stabilizing force that minimizes differences that otherwise might result in hostility and violence (Gordon, 1964). In its most complete form, assimilation becomes ***amalgamation*, also referred to as the *melting-pot model*, a process in which the cultural attributes of diverse racial-ethnic groups are blended together to form a new society**

Box 3.2 *(continued)*

get ahead because the cousin sent numerous e-mails claiming he was living a fabulous life, with a mansion, women, hot tubs, and sports cars. After his arrival, however, Niko learns that Roman owns a small taxi business and owes gang bosses large sums of money. As a result, Roman enlists Niko to help kill the bosses, and Niko becomes involved in crime rather than in making his legitimate fortune.

Although excessive violence is commonplace in video games such as *Grand Theft Auto*, the negative portrayal of racial and ethnic minorities is also a central concern of social scientists who study representations of people of color. The digital cast of *Grand Theft Auto IV*, for example, includes numerous African-American and Latino characters who exhibit negative racial stereotypes and are involved in criminal conduct. Among the stereotypes shown are young African-American men continually engaging in violent street crime and Latinos operating as hard-core gang members. According to some social analysts, depictions of African Americans and Latinos such as these influence not only how some white, dominant-group individuals may perceive people of color but also how some people of color may come to view themselves. When dark-skinned men are always engaged in violent behavior in video games, a negative image is cast on men of color and on immigrant populations. Niko Bellic, who initially came to this country to pursue the American Dream, became involved in drugs and violence. This image is not a positive reflection on millions of hardworking, law-abiding immigrants from Eastern Europe and other regions of the world.

What effect does racial stereotyping in video games have on young people? Manufacturers of video games such as *Grand Theft Auto* emphasize that their games are geared for an audience over the age of seventeen and that younger people should not be playing them at all. However, many younger individuals play the games for hours at a time. Video-game makers say that the games are just a way for people to relax and have fun; however, critics warn that some games may have harmful consequences as they reinforce negative images of subordinate-group members and perpetuate violence.

Questions for Consideration

1. In violent video games, does the over-representation of characters patterned on subordinate racial or ethnic groups influence our thinking regarding who commits crime in this country? Why or why not?
2. Should any controls be placed on the content of video games and other forms of entertainment? If so, should the government, parents, or the purchasers of video games be the primary agents of social control?

incorporating the unique contributions of each group. Amalgamation occurs when members of dominant and subordinate racial-ethnic groups intermarry and procreate "mixed-race" children.

Early assimilation in the United States focused primarily on the Anglo-conformity model, rather than the melting-pot model. The ***Anglo-conformity model* refers to a pattern of assimilation whereby members of subordinate racial-ethnic groups are expected to conform to the culture of the dominant (white) Anglo-Saxon population.** Assimilation does not always lead to full social acceptance. For example, many successful African Americans and Jewish Americans have been excluded from membership in elite private clubs and parties in the homes of coworkers.

Recently, political conservatives have focused on assimilation and, particularly, adopting English as the country's official language. In her influential book *Out of the Barrio* (1991), social analyst Linda Chavez says that Latinas/os in the United States must learn English and adopt the dominant culture if they want economic success and social acceptance. According to Chavez, Latinos/as should forget about entitlement programs such as affirmative action and focus on assimilating into the U.S. economic mainstream.

Another functionalist perspective emphasizes ***ethnic pluralism*—the coexistence of diverse racial-ethnic groups with separate identities and cultures within a society.** In a pluralistic society, political and economic systems link diverse groups, but members of some racial-ethnic groups maintain enough separation from the dominant group to guarantee that their group and ethnic cultural traditions continue (Gordon, 1964). Ethnic pluralism in the United States typically has been based on *segregation* because subordinate racial-ethnic groups have less power and privilege than do members of the dominant group (Marger, 1994). ***Segregation* is the spatial and social separation of people by race/ethnicity, class, gender, religion, or other social characteristics.** Sociological studies have found that when high levels of racial segregation are followed by interracial contact, racial competition may ensue, tending to increase ethnic and racial unrest and the potential for urban riots (Olzak et al., 1996).

Conflict Perspectives

Conflict theorists explain racial and ethnic inequality in terms of economic stratification and access to power. As was discussed in Chapter 1, there are a number of conflict perspectives. However, in this chapter, we focus on the critical-conflict approach, which explains racial and ethnic inequality in terms of economic stratification and unequal access to power. We will briefly examine class perspectives, split-labor market theory, gendered racism, internal colonialism, and the theory of racial formation.

Class perspectives on racial and ethnic inequality highlight the role of the capitalist class in racial exploitation. For example, according to sociologist Oliver C. Cox (1948), the primary cause of slavery was the capitalist desire for profit, not racial prejudice. African Americans were enslaved because they were the cheapest and best workers that owners of plantations and mines could find to do the heavy labor. One contemporary class perspective suggests that members of the capitalist class benefit from a split-labor market that fosters racial divisions among workers and suppresses wages. According to the *split-labor market theory*, the U.S. economy is divided into two employment sectors: a primary sector composed of higher-paid workers in more secure jobs and a secondary sector composed of lower-paid workers in jobs that often involve hazardous working conditions and little job security (Bonacich, 1972, 1976). Dominant group members are usually employed in primary sector positions; subordinate-group members usually are employed in the secondary sector. Workers in the two job sectors tend to have divergent interests and goals; therefore worker solidarity is unlikely (Bonacich, 1972, 1976). Members of the capitalist class benefit from these divisions because workers are less likely to bind together and demand pay increases or other changes in the workplace. White workers in the primary sector attempt to exclude subordinate-group members from higher-paying jobs by barring them from labor unions, supporting discriminatory laws, and opposing immigration.

A second critical-conflict perspective links racial inequality and gender oppression. ***Gendered racism* may be defined as the interactive effect of racism and sexism in exploiting women of color.** According to social psychologist Philomena Essed (1991), not all workers are exploited equally by capitalists. For many years, the majority of jobs in the primary sector of the labor market were held by white men, while most people of color and many white women were employed in secondary-sector jobs. Below the secondary sector, in the underground sector of the economy, many women of color worked in sweatshops or the sex trade to survive. Work in this underground sector is unregulated, and people who earn their income in it are vulnerable to exploitation by many people, including unscrupulous employers, greedy pimps, and corrupt police officers (Amott and Matthaei, 1991).

A third critical-conflict perspective examines ***internal colonialism*—a process that occurs when members of a racial-ethnic group are conquered or colonized and forcibly placed under the economic and political control of the dominant group.** According to sociologist Robert Blauner (1972), people in groups that have been subjected to internal colonialism remain in subordinate positions in society much longer than do people in groups that voluntarily migrated to this country. For example, Native Americans and Mexican Americans were forced into subordination when they were colonized by European Americans. These indigenous groups lost property, political rights, components of their culture, and often their lives. Meanwhile, the capitalist class acquired cheap labor and land, frequently through government-sanctioned racial exploitation (Blauner, 1972). Vestiges of internal colonialism remain visible today in the number of Native Americans who live in poverty on government reservations, as well as Mexican Americans in *colonias*—poor subdivisions that usually lack essential services such as water, electricity, and sewage disposal—located along the U.S.-Mexico border (see Valdez, 1993).

The last critical-conflict perspective we will look at is the ***theory of racial formation*, which states that the government substantially defines racial and ethnic relations.** From this perspective, racial bias and discrimination tend to be rooted in government actions ranging from passage of race-related legislation to imprisonment of members of groups that are believed to be a threat to society. According to sociologists Michael Omi and Howard Winant (1994), the U.S. government has shaped the politics of racial inequality in this country through actions and policies that have resulted in the unequal treatment of people of color. Immigration legislation, for example, reveals specific racial biases. The Naturalization Law of 1790 permitted only white immigrants to qualify for naturalization, and the Immigration Act of 1924 favored northern Europeans and excluded Asians and southern and eastern Europeans.

INEQUALITIES AMONG RACIAL AND ETHNIC GROUPS

Although all subordinate racial and ethnic groups have been the objects of prejudice and discrimination and share many problems, each has its own unique identity and concerns. In our examination of Native Americans, African Americans, Latinos/as, and Asian and Pacific Americans, we will note commonalities and differences in the discriminatory practices each group has experienced when in contact with members of the dominant group.

Native Americans (American Indians)

Perhaps because they are often somewhat invisible in daily life, Native Americans tend to be viewed more as artifacts of "Indian culture" than as real people. As such, they are associated with turquoise jewelry and deerskin clothing, "Indian" Barbie dolls, vehicles such as the Jeep "Cherokee," and the stereotypical images utilized by sports teams with names like "Braves," "Redskins," "Chiefs," and "Seminoles." Although such movies as *Dances with Wolves, The Last of the Mohicans, Pocahontas,* and *The Indian in the Cupboard* have increased public awareness of Native Americans to some extent, some also have perpetuated myths and stereotypes.

Colonized Migration and Genocide

When Christopher Columbus arrived in 1492, approximately 15 million indigenous people lived on this continent. They had many distinct cultures, languages, social organizations, technologies, and economies (Thornton, 1987; Sale, 1990; Mohawk, 1992). The arrival of the white Europeans changed the native inhabitants' ways of life forever as *colonization migration*—a process whereby a new immigrant group conquers and dominates an existing group in a given geographical area—occurred (Lauber, 1913; Feagin and Feagin, 2008). During this period of conquest, white European immigrants engaged in ***genocide*, the deliberate, systematic killing of an entire people or nation.** Hundreds of thousands of Native Americans died during this period. This widespread murder was rationalized by stereotypes depicting Native Americans as subhuman "savages" and "heathens" (Takaki, 1993).

Forced Migration and "Americanization"

After the Revolutionary War, the newly founded federal government negotiated treaties with various Native-American nations to acquire additional land for the rapidly growing white population. Even with these treaties in place, federal officials ignored boundary rights and gradually displaced Native Americans from their lands. When the demand for land escalated, Congress passed the Indian Removal Act of 1830, forcing entire nations to move to accommodate white settlers. During the "Trail of Tears," perhaps the most disastrous of the forced migrations, over half of the Cherokee nation died while being relocated from the southeastern United States to what was called the Indian Territory in Oklahoma during the bitter cold winter of 1832 (Thornton, 1984). After the forced relocation, Native Americans were made wards of the government—a legal status akin to that of a minor or a mental incompetent—and by 1920, about 98 percent of all native lands were controlled by the U.S. government (McDonnell, 1991).

Because Native Americans were regarded as less "civilized" than whites, Native-American children were subjected to an extensive Americanization process. Boarding schools and mission schools, cosponsored by the government and churches, were located some distance from the reservations to facilitate assimilation. In these schools, white teachers cut Native-American boys' braids, eliminated the children's traditional clothing, handed out new names, and substituted new religious customs for old ones (Oxendine, 1995).

Contemporary Native Americans

Today, Native Americans number slightly more than 4.5 million, about 1.5 percent of the U.S. population. Most Native Americans live in Oklahoma, California, Arizona, and New Mexico (U.S. Census Bureau, 2008). Although the majority of Native Americans live in cities, about one-third live on reservations or other officially designated areas. They are the most disadvantaged racial or ethnic group in the United States. They have the highest unemployment and school dropout rates in the country. The median family income of Native Americans is $35,381, compared with a national median of $50,221 for all races (U.S. Census Bureau, 2009 (1-Year Estimates)). The average life expectancy on reservations is less than forty-five years for men and

Some Native American groups on government controlled reservations have found a new source of revenue through ownership and operation of casinos. However, these casinos have not been without controversy.

less than forty-eight years for women. Infant mortality rates and adult death rates from substance abuse and suicide are much higher than the national averages (National Center for Health Statistics, 2004).

Many Native Americans have organized to resist discrimination and oppression. They actively oppose mining, logging, hunting, and real estate development on native lands without permission or compensation (Serrill, 1992). Groups such as the American Indian Movement and Women of All Red Nations have struggled to regain control of native lands, to end centuries of colonization, and to stop cultural exploitation.

African Americans

The term *African American* does not reflect the diversity of the more than 38 million African Americans who currently make up about 13 percent of the U.S. population. Although some are descendants of families that have been in this country for many generations, others are recent immigrants from the West Indies, South America, Africa, and the Caribbean. Many have Native-American, white, or Latino/a ancestors (Feagin and Feagin, 2008; Kivel, 1996).

Although media coverage has improved somewhat over the past decade, stereotypic depictions of African Americans continue to "demonize blackness" (Gray, 1995). Television and films frequently depict African-American women as "welfare mothers"; drug addicts; sex objects; prostitutes; and elderly, overweight, aggressive family matriarchs who are made the object of derision by their families and others (see Gray, 1995). African-American men are depicted as "menacing black male criminals" who murder, rape, pimp, and sell drugs (Feagin and Feagin, 2008; Kivel, 1996).

Slavery and the Racial Division of Labor

From its beginnings in 1619, when the first Africans were brought to North America for forced labor, slavery created a rigid, castelike division of labor between white slave owners and overseers and African slave labor. Southern plantation owners derived large profits from selling raw materials harvested by the slaves. Northern capitalists became rich by converting those raw materials into finished products that could be sold at market (e.g., the cotton fiber used in textile manufacturing). Even white immigrants benefited from slavery because it provided the abundant raw materials needed for their factory jobs.

Segregation and Lynching

After slavery was abolished in 1863, this division of labor was maintained through *de jure segregation*, the passage of laws that systematically enforced the physical and social separation of African Americans from whites in all areas of public life, including schools, churches, hospitals, cemeteries, buses, restaurants, water fountains, and restrooms. (These laws were referred to as *Jim Crow laws* after a derogatory song about a black man.) African Americans who did not stay "in their place" were subjected to violence by secret organizations such as the Ku Klux Klan and by lynch mobs (Franklin, 1980).

While African Americans in the South experienced de jure segregation, those who migrated to the North experienced *de facto segregation*—racial separation and inequality enforced by custom. African Americans seeking northern factory jobs encountered *job ceilings*—specific limits on the upward job mobility of targeted groups—set up by white workers and their unions (see Baron, 1969; Allen, 1974). Because African-American men were barred from many industrial jobs, African-American women frequently became their families' primary breadwinners. Most African-American women were employed as domestic workers in private households or as personal service workers such as hotel chambermaids (Higginbotham, 1994).

Reprinted by permission.

of the job ceiling and racial division of labor is evident today in many corporations, including Fortune 1000 companies (the 1000 highest revenue-producing companies), only a few of which have African-American chief executive officers. Approximately one-fourth of the African-American workforce is employed in the public sector, that is, in federal, state, city, and county governments (Higginbotham, 1994).

The unemployment rate for African Americans (9.0 percent in 2007) has remained twice as high as that for white Americans (4.4 percent in 2007) for more than three decades (U.S. Bureau of Labor Saistics, 2008). As new

Protests and Civil Disobedience

During World War II, new job opportunities opened up for African Americans in northern defense plants, especially after the issuance of a presidential order prohibiting racial discrimination in federal jobs. After the war, increasing numbers of African Americans demanded an end to racial segregation. Between the mid-1950s and 1964, boycotts, nonviolent protests, and civil disobedience—nonviolent action seeking to change a policy or law by refusing to comply with it—called attention to racial inequality. The civil rights movement culminated in passage of the Civil Rights Acts of 1964 and 1965, which signified the end of *de jure* segregation; however, *de facto* segregation was far from over.

Contemporary African Americans

Since the 1960s, African Americans have made significant political gains. Between 1964 and 1999, the number of African-American elected officials increased from about 100 to almost 9,000 (Joint Center for Political and Economic Studies, 2000). African Americans won mayoral elections in many major cities that had large African-American populations, including Houston, Philadelphia, New Orleans, Atlanta, and Washington, D.C. Even with these gains, however, fewer than 3 percent of all elected officials in this country are African Americans.

The proportion of African Americans in professional, managerial, sales, clerical, crafts, and factory jobs grew steadily between 1955 and 1972, but this growth slowed dramatically in the late 1970s and 1980s. The continuation

Dr. Martin Luther King, Jr., was perhaps the most influential person in obtaining passage of the Civil Rights Act in the 1960s, which has profoundly affected the lives of many African Americans.

technology has been introduced in the workplace and more jobs have moved to suburban areas and to other countries, employment opportunities for African Americans in central cities have declined (see Neckerman and Kirschenman, 1991; Tienda and Stier, 1996; Wilson, 1996).

As is shown in Figure 3.1, a wide disparity exists between the median income of white Americans and that of African Americans. Whereas African-American households had median earnings of $33,463 in 2009, the median earnings of white non-Latino families were about 60 percent higher ($53,131).

Contemporary scholars suggest that the legacies of slavery, segregation, and individual and institutionalized discrimination are evident in both the persistent—though informal—racial discrimination practiced by banks, real estate agencies, mortgage lenders, and other businesses that has resulted in the high percentage of racially segregated schools and residential areas and the daily bias that many African Americans face in the workplace and other public spaces (see Feagin and Sikes, 1994; Feagin and Feagin, 2008). Residential discrimination has proved to be one of the more persistent inequalities experienced by African Americans (Ross and Turner, 2005). Today, a typical African American lives in a neighborhood that is only 33 percent white, whereas the typical white person lives in a neighborhood that is only 7 percent black (Mumford Center for Comparative Urban and Regional Research, 2001). Residential segregation produces a ripple effect on all other areas of social life, including the schools that children attend, the quality of education they receive, the types of jobs people have access to, and the availability and quality of such public facilities as hospitals and transportation systems (Massey and Denton, 1992).

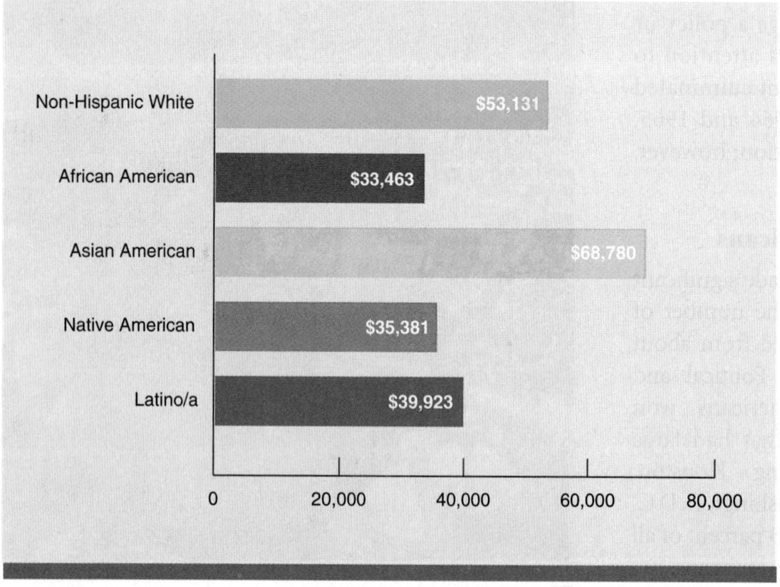

Latinos/as (Hispanic Americans)

Today, almost two-thirds of the more than 44 million Latinos/as who make up over 14 percent of the U.S. population are of Mexican origin. After Mexican Americans, the largest groups of Latinos/as are Puerto Ricans, Cuban Americans, Dominican Americans, and Salvadoran Americans (Logan, 2001). The remainder trace their ancestry to elsewhere in Central and South America.

Latinos/as have been the objects of stereotyping based on skin color and perceived cultural differences, including food preferences and language. In the media, Latinos/as are often depicted as either rich drug lords or illegal aliens (McWilliams, 1968; Morales, 1996).

Internal Colonialism and Loss of Land

Beginning in the late 1400s and continuing into the early 1500s, Spanish soldiers took over the island of Puerto Rico, Central America, and that area of the United States now known as the Southwest. Although Mexico gained its independence from Spain in 1810, it lost Texas and most of the Southwest to the United States in 1848. Under the treaty ending the Mexican-American War, Texans of Mexican descent (Tejanos/as) were granted U.S. citizenship; however, their rights as citizens were violated when Anglo Americans took possession of their lands, transforming them into a landless and economically dependent laboring class.

When Spain lost the Spanish-American War, it gave Puerto Rico and the Philippine Islands to the United States. Gradually, U.S.-owned

Figure 3.1 ***Median U.S. family income by race and Hispanic origin of householder, 2006***

Source: U.S. Census Bureau, 2009. (1-Year Estimates)

corporations took over existing Puerto Rican sugarcane plantations, leaving peasant farmers and their families with no means of earning a living other than as seasonal sugarcane laborers. In time, nearly one-third of the Puerto Rican population migrated to the U.S. mainland. The majority of this population settled in the Northeast and found work in garment factories or other light manufacturing.

Migration

In the late 1950s and early 1960s, waves of Latinos/as escaping from Fidel Castro's Communist takeover of Cuba were admitted to the United States. Unlike Puerto Ricans, who have been allowed unrestricted migration between the mainland and the island since Puerto Rico became a U.S. possession in 1917 (Melendez, 1993), these immigrants were admitted as political refugees (Rogg, 1974). Mexicans have been allowed to migrate to the United States whenever there has been a need here for agricultural workers. However, during times of economic depression or recession in this country, Mexican workers have been excluded, detained, or deported (see Moore, 1976; Acuna, 1984).

Many Latinos/as have experienced discrimination as a result of the Immigration Reform and Control Act (IRCA) of 1986. Although IRCA was passed to restrict illegal immigration into the United States, it has adversely affected many Latinos/as. To avoid being penalized for hiring undocumented workers, some employers discriminate against Latinas/os who "look foreign" on the basis of facial features, skin color, or clothing (see Chavez and Martinez, 1996).

Contemporary Latinos/as

Today, Latinos/as comprise a growing percentage of the U.S. population (see Box 3.3 on page 60). Although the full effect of this young and growing populace has not yet been fully evidenced in U.S. politics and business, many analysts predict that Latinos/as will be increasingly visible in all areas of public life by 2020. However, progress has been slow for some Latinos/as up to now: Currently, only about 1 percent of the top executives in Fortune 1000 corporations are Latinos/as (Hispanic Association on Corporate Responsibility, 2004), and they usually work for companies that actively pursue Latina/o consumers, for example beverage, entertainment, and soap and cosmetic companies (Zate, 1996). In secondary-sector employment, the other end of the employment spectrum, low wages, hazardous workplaces, and unemployment are pressing problems for Latinos/as. The unemployment rate for Latinos/as is 6.3 percent as compared with 4.4 percent for non-Latino/a whites. Almost one-fifth (19.7 percent) of Latinas/os lived below the poverty level in 2006, and Latino/a children are three times more likely to be poor than their non-Latino/a white peers.

Many Latinas/os continue to experience high levels of segregation in housing and education (Ross and Turner, 2005). According to a study by anthropologist Martha Menchaca (1995), landlords, realtors, and bankers in many communities have colluded to keep Mexican Americans in barrios and out of predominantly Anglo neighborhoods. Segregated schools are a major problem for many Latino/a children and their parents. The average Latina/o student attends a school that is 57 percent Latino/a; in some schools in California, New Mexico, and Texas, more than 80 percent of the students are Latina/o (Mumford Center, 2002).

Cesar Chavez has been hailed as one of the leaders most responsible for gaining better wages and working conditions for Latino/a farm workers. Since his death, leaders of Mexican-American social movements have continued to take inspiration from Chavez's civil rights activities.

Asian and Pacific Americans

Asian and Pacific Americans are one of the fastest growing racial-ethnic groups in the United States; their numbers have risen from 1 million in 1960 to 13.5 million today. In the 1990s, about half of all legal immigrants to this country had Asian or Pacific Island ancestry. Constituting about 4.4 percent of the U.S. population, most Asian and Pacific Americans reside in California, New York, and Hawaii (U.S. Census Bureau, 2008).

Asian and Pacific Americans have been stereotyped as "Orientals." Advertisements often depict Asian and Pacific American women as exotic beauties with silky black hair, heavy eye makeup, and seductive clothing (Shah, 1994). Because many are college-educated and have middle- or upper-income occupations, Asian and Pacific Americans also have been stereotyped as the model minority. However, the model minority stereotype ignores the reality that many Asian and Pacific Americans, especially recent immigrants, are employed in low-paying service jobs or sweatshops.

Immigration and Oppression

Among the first Asian and Pacific people to arrive in this country were Chinese immigrants, who came between 1850 and 1880. Some were fleeing political

Social Problems and Statistics

Box 3.3

Accurate and Inaccurate Comparisons

According to data from the U.S. Census Bureau for 2006 (the most recent year for which data are available), 14.6 percent of the U.S. population is of Hispanic (or Latino/a) origin, representing a significant increase from previous years. Approximately 80 percent of the population is white, 12.8 percent is black or African American, 4.4 percent is Asian American, 1.0 percent is Native American, 0.2 percent is Native Hawaiian or other Pacific Islanders, and 1.6 percent is of two or more races (see Figure 3.2). These are valid statistics, and they come from a very good source of data: the U.S. Census Bureau.

On the basis of these statistics, we can conclude that Latinos/as comprise the largest subordinate racial-ethnic group in the United States and that African Americans (who until recently were the largest such group) comprise the second-largest subordinate racial-ethnic group. However, it would be incorrect to conclude that Latinos/as (14.6 percent) and African Americans (12.8 percent) represent 27.4 percent of the U.S. population. Why is this true?

Whereas African Americans are considered to be members of a racial group, Latinos/as are considered to be

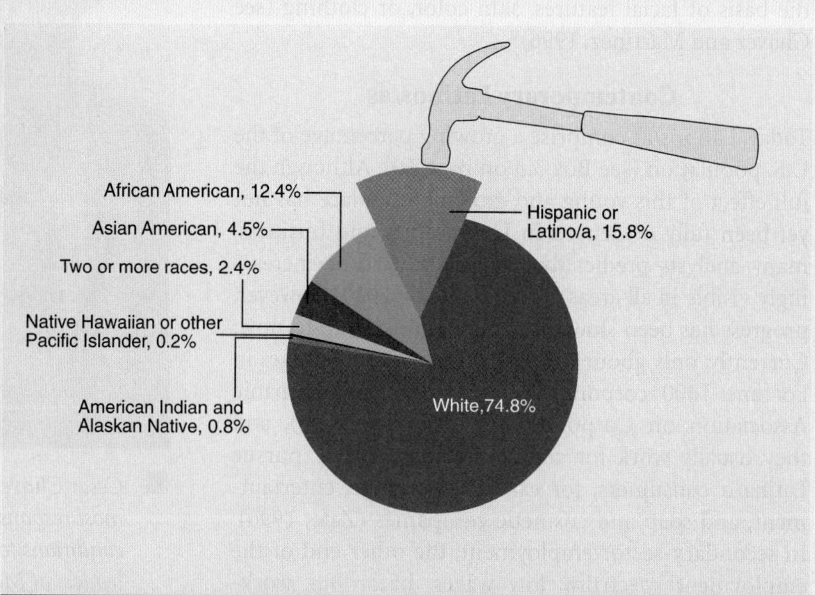

■ Figure 3.2 Race and Hispanic origin

oppression and harsh economic conditions in China; others were recruited to build the transcontinental railroad. Almost immediately, these immigrants were labeled "the yellow peril," a reflection of nineteenth-century prejudice that Asians constituted a threat to Western civilization. In response to demands from white workers who were concerned about cheap labor (employers paid Chinese laborers far less than white workers [Takaki, 1993]), Congress passed the Chinese Exclusion Act of 1882, bringing all Chinese immigration to an abrupt halt. This law wasn't repealed until World War II, when Chinese-American workers contributed to the U.S. war effort by working in defense plants (see Chan, 1991).

Facing high levels of overt discrimination, many Chinese Americans opened laundries, stores, and restaurants, doing business primarily with each other (Takaki, 1993). More recently, however, young second- and third-generation Chinese Americans have left these ethnic niches to live and interact with people from diverse racial-ethnic groups (see Chen, 1992).

Internment

Although Japanese Americans experienced high levels of prejudice and discrimination almost as soon as they arrived in this country, their internment in U.S. concentration camps during World War II remains the central event of the Japanese-American experience (Kitano and Daniels, 1995). After Japan bombed Pearl Harbor in 1941, anti-Japanese sentiment soared in the United States. Japanese Americans were forcibly removed to concentration camps on remote military bases surrounded by barbed wire fences and guard towers. During their internment, which lasted for

Box 3.3 (continued)

members of an ethnic group. A Latino/a may be of any one or more racial categories: Some Latinos/as are also whites; other Latinos/as are also African American, Asian American, and/or Native American. Therefore the Census Bureau asks separate questions regarding a person's race and regarding whether or not he or she is of Hispanic origin, and each person answers both questions.

The thing to be noted here is that in using statistics, it is important that we not make inaccurate comparisons of statistics. As sociologist Joel Best (2001:97–98) states,

> Good comparisons involve comparable items: they pair apples with apples, and oranges with oranges. Comparable statistics count things in the same ways. Comparisons among statistics that are not comparable confuse and distort. Before accepting any statistical comparison, it is important to ask whether the numbers are comparable.

As was noted above, it would be inappropriate to add the percentage of the U.S. population that is African American to the percentage that is Latino/a and conclude that these two categories represent 27.4 percent of the overall U.S. population: Because one is based on race and the other on ethnicity, there is some overlap between the two. For the same reason, combining the percentage of the U.S. population that is white with the percentage that is Latino/a would not produce a useful statistic: Most Latinos/as self-identify as white.

However, the census data in Figure 3.2 do provide valid bases for other comparisons. For example, the proportion of the U.S. population that is Latino/a (about 14.6 percent) can be compared with the proportion that is non-Hispanic (about 85.2 percent) to validly conclude that the vast majority of the population is non-Latino/a, although Latinos/as are a significant and growing minority of the U.S. population. Likewise, the proportion that is Latino/a (14.8 percent) can be compared with the proportion that is African American (12.8 percent) to validly conclude that these two categories are of somewhat similar size although there are slightly more persons who self-identify as Latino/a than as African American. Similarly, the proportion that is African American can be compared with the proportion that is Asian American, and so on. In each instance, these are good comparisons involving comparable items.

In each instance in this text where comparisons are made, every effort is made to ensure that they involve comparable statistics. Even so, that can be a difficult task: As Figure 3.2 reflects, 1.6 percent of the U.S. population self-identifies as being of two or more races, meaning that we must keep in mind that the statistics shown represent only those people who self-identify as being of only one race and that such statistics therefore ignore the growing number of people in this country who see themselves as being of mixed racial backgrounds.

Source: U.S. Census Bureau, 2009. (1-Year Estimates)

more than two years, most Japanese Americans lost their residences, businesses, and anything else they had owned. Four decades later, the U.S. government issued an apology for its actions and agreed to pay $20,000 to each Japanese American who had been detained in a camp (Kitano and Daniels, 1995). For Japanese Americans and other Asian and Pacific Americans, the struggle for rights has often been played out in the U.S. Supreme Court and other judicial bodies (see Box 3.4).

Colonization

A bloody guerrilla war between Filipino Islanders and U.S. soldiers followed Spain's surrender of the Philippine Islands, as well as Puerto Rico, to the United States in the aftermath of the Spanish-American War. When the battle ended in 1902, the United States established colonial rule over the islands, and Filipinos were "Americanized" by schools that the U.S. government established (Espiritu, 1995).

Social Problems and Social Policy

Box 3.4

Most early Filipino migrants were recruited as cheap labor for sugar plantations in Hawaii, agriculture in California, and fish canneries in Seattle and Alaska. Like members of other racial-ethnic groups, Filipino Americans were accused of stealing jobs and suppressing wages during the Great Depression, and Congress restricted Filipino immigration to fifty people per year until after World War II.

Newer Waves of Asian Immigration

Today, many of the Asian and Pacific immigrants arriving from India and Pakistan are highly educated professionals. Although some immigrants from Korea are also professionals, many have few years of formal schooling. They have developed an ethnic niche in "Koreatowns," which are similar to the communities of earlier generations of Chinese Americans (Kim and Yu, 1996).

Since the 1970s, many Indochinese American refugees have arrived in the United States from Vietnam, Cambodia, Thailand, and Laos. About half of these immigrants live in Western states, especially California. Although many early Vietnamese refugees were physicians, pharmacists, and engineers who were able to reenter their professions in the United States, more recent immigrants have had less formal education, fewer job skills, and therefore much higher rates of unemployment. Recent immigrants are more likely to live in poverty and rely on assistance from others (Du Phuoc Long, 1996).

Pacific Islanders

More than 1.6 million people live on the Hawaiian Islands. About 13 percent are native or part-native Hawaiians who can trace their ancestry to the original Polynesian inhabitants of the islands. Originally governed as a monarchy and then as a republic, the Hawaiian Islands were annexed by the United States in 1898. In 1959, Congress passed legislation that made Hawaii the fiftieth state. Because of widespread immigration and high rates of intermarriage, contemporary Hawaiians include people of Chinese, Japanese, Filipino, Korean, Puerto Rican, and Portuguese ancestry.

Contemporary Asian and Pacific Americans

Asian and Pacific Americans have high educational levels compared to the overall U.S. population. Nearly nine out of ten Asian and Pacific Americans age twenty-five and over are high school graduates. Asian and Pacific Americans are almost twice as likely to have a bachelor's degree than are non-Latina/o whites: Almost 50 percent of Asian and Pacific Americans age twenty-five and over hold at least a bachelor's degree, and 19 percent hold an advanced degree (master's or doctor's degree, for example).

Many Asian Americans have created economic niches such as ownership of nail salons, restaurants, or other small businesses to provide them with a livelihood. Creation of economic niches has contributed to the financial survival of many immigrant groups throughout U.S. history.

The median income of households in this population category exceeded that of non-Latino/a whites: $68,780 to $53,131 in 2009. In fact, the median family income of Japanese Americans is more than 30 percent above the national average. Whereas about 10 percent of all Asian and Pacific American families live below the official poverty line, fewer than 4 percent of Japanese American families do.

IS THERE A SOLUTION TO RACIAL AND ETHNIC INEQUALITY?

Although most sociologists acknowledge that there will always be some inequality in the distribution of wealth, power, and prestige in the United States, some analysts are concerned about the vast social inequalities that exist along racial and ethnic lines. These inequalities affect people's opportunities, quality of life, and access to important goods and services such as education, housing, and health care. Discrimination based on race and ethnicity is a significant factor in determining people's life chances and their opportunities. Racial and ethnic inequality is intertwined with class-based inequality to produce strong distinctions in the life chances and opportunities for people who are in dominant, privileged groups and those who are in subordinate, oppressed groups where they may be subjected to unequal treatment and collective discrimination. Sociologists who apply functionalist, conflict, and symbolic interactionist perspectives to the study of racial and ethnic inequalities typically offer different analyses of the problem and suggest different ways to reduce or eliminate race- or ethnicity-based injustice and inequality. Similarly, social analysts applying various political approaches to the problem provide divergent outlooks on what causes racial inequality and what the possible solutions might be to this problem.

Functionalist/Conservative Solutions to the Problem of Racial and Ethnic Inequality

How do functionalists suggest reducing racial-ethnic inequality? High rates of immigration in the United States have raised new questions in recent decades about how to maintain social order and stability when people from throughout the world are arriving in this country, bringing with them a wide variety of languages, cultures, and traditions that are different from those of established residents. Older functionalist models of assimilation—based on the belief that members of subordinate racial and ethnic groups should absorb the dominant culture as soon as possible and become somewhat indistinguishable from it—are no longer effective in producing a homogeneous population where everyone speaks the same language, shares the same holidays, and participates in the same cultural traditions. Instead, these racial and ethnic differences have become a source of identity and pride for many people. But these differences are often used to "explain" why inequalities exist in educational attainment, job opportunities, income, health, and other valued goods and services along lines of race, ethnicity, and national origin. Based on this approach, individuals and groups are at least partly responsible for their own subordination because of decisions they make along the way.

For some functionalist analysts and political conservatives, lack of assimilation by recent immigrant groups is a major problem that can be reduced only by heightening legal requirements for entry into the country, controlling the borders more effectively, and demanding that people become part of the mainstream culture by making English the "official language." Functionalists and political conservatives often view families, schools, and churches as being key institutions that should foster achievement in minority youths by helping them to accept dominant U.S. cultural patterns. As previously discussed, some political analysts strongly advocate that people living in the United States should learn English and speak this language in public places. They also believe that individuals should adopt the dominant culture if they want to achieve academic and economic success, as well as social acceptance in the larger society. According to some conservative analysts, if subordinate group members continue to be the objects of prejudice and discrimination in the United States, they have no one to blame but themselves because they have been unwilling to embrace the dominant culture. Conservatives typically view programs such as affirmative action or others that are designed to specifically benefit minority group members as being divisive and harmful. By contrast, functionalist analysts and conservative political observers believe that individual achievement should be encouraged and highly rewarded because individuals such as Tiger Woods (the golfer) can serve as role models for other minority youths on how to get ahead in the United States and other nations.

Conflict/Liberal Solutions to the Problem of Racial and Ethnic Inequality

From a conflict perspective, racial and ethnic inequality can be reduced only through struggle and political action. Conflict theorists believe that if inequality is based on the exploitation of subordinate groups by the dominant group, political intervention is necessary to bring about economic and social change. They agree that people should mobilize to put pressure on public officials. According to social activist Paul Kivel (1996), racial inequality will not be reduced until there is, in this country, significant national public support and leadership for addressing social problems directly and forcefully.

Among the problems that conflict theorists and liberal political analysts believe need to be systematically addressed in the United States are persistent patterns of prejudice and discrimination, both at the individual and institutional levels. Conflict theorists who use a class perspectives approach often point out that discrimination in the workplace must be reduced before racial and ethnic inequality can be eliminated. Discrimination based on race and class play a key part in determining the amount of education people have, the kinds of jobs that they hold, how much they earn, what kind of benefits (if any) they have, and what opportunities they may have for future advancement. If the deck is stacked against people of color and recent immigrants in the labor market, these individuals will have few opportunities to get ahead in American society.

Conflict theorists and liberal political analysts who believe that the government substantially defines racial and ethnic relations emphasize that solutions to the problem of inequality will be found only through government programs that specifically attack racial inequality and actively reduce patterns of discrimination. For this reason, many conflict/liberal solutions to the problem are based on the assumption that we have reduced or eliminated affirmative action programs before they have been fully effective in bringing about social change. Clearly, affirmative action programs in the past opened up opportunities for many college students, workers, and minority businesses that otherwise would have remained out of the economic and social mainstream. Now, if conflict/liberal theorists' assertions are correct, programs such as this are still needed if all people are to have equal opportunities in this nation. For this to occur, political activism will be required because such changes typically occur only because of organized political pressure. Ironically, when the U.S. economy is in a recession and people are concerned about having a job and earning a living wage, it sometimes becomes more difficult to mobilize them to demand economic justice, even when they are low-income individuals and/or subordinate group members who are the most likely to be harmed by the vast divide between the rich and the poor.

Symbolic Interactionist Solutions to the Problem of Racial and Ethnic Inequality

According to symbolic interactionists, prejudice and discrimination are learned, and what is learned can be unlearned. As sociologist Gale E. Thomas (1995:339) notes, "In the areas of race, ethnic, and human relations, we must learn compassion and also to accept and truly embrace, rather than merely tolerate, differences... through honest and open dialogue and through the formation of genuine friendships and personal experiential... exchanges and interactions with different individuals and groups across cultures." In other words, only individuals and groups at the grass-roots level, not government and political leaders or academic elites, can bring about greater racial equality.

Racial socialization and personal identity are central to symbolic interactionist perspectives on inequality because how people are socialized has a profound effect on how people view themselves and other people. For this reason, children and young adults should be taught about cultural diversity and American history, including how members of some subordinate groups were treated by some members of dominant groups. They should also be encouraged to think of positive ways in which individuals of all races can acquire a positive self concept and interact positively with each other. By developing a better understanding of the past, it is reasoned, children and young adults of all races will be able to understand how race is a prism through which African Americans and other people of color view their lives. To reduce racial and ethnic inequality will require a better understanding of people across racial and ethnic categories. This must begin with a new social construction of reality which requires that people abandon those traditional prejudices which make it impossible for them to view others as people who are deserving of social justice and equality.

Whether or not the people of the United States work for greater equality for all racial-ethnic groups, one thing is certain: The U.S. population is becoming increasingly diverse at a rapid rate. African Americans, Latinos/as, Asian and Pacific Americans, Native Americans, and people who trace their ancestry to other regions of the world make up more than 35 percent of the U.S. population. In the year 2009 non-Hispanic white Americans made up less than 65 percent of the U.S. population (see Figure 3.3 on page 66); and by the year 2050, a lot of U.S. residents will trace their roots to Africa, Asia, the Hispanic countries, the Pacific Islands, and the Middle East, not white Europe (Henry, 1990). If we fail to recognize the challenges posed by increasing racial-ethnic and cultural diversity and we do not develop a more visionary and inclusive

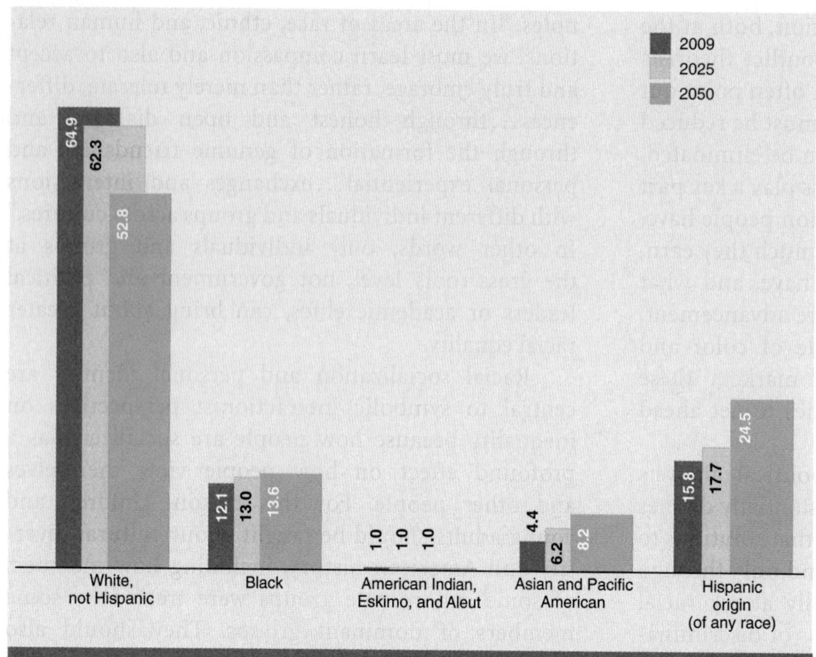

■ **Figure 3.3** ***Percentage of U.S. population by race and Hispanic origin: 2009, 2025, and 2050 (middle-series projections)***

Source: U.S. Census Bureau, 2009. (1-Year Estimates)

perspective, fires like those that occurred in Los Angeles in the 1960s and the 1990s may spread across the nation, as African-American activist James Baldwin (1963) suggested when he spoke of "the fire next time" (Thomas, 1995).

On a more optimistic note, perhaps the future of racial-ethnic relations in the United States is forecast by this newspaper reporter's description of a Chicago kindergarten class:

> They stand with arms outstretched, touching fingertip to fingertip on a yellow circle inscribed on the floor of a kindergarten classroom.
>
> A girl with braids who describes herself as a light-skinned black stands next to a boy who has a white mother and a black father. Just a few feet away is a boy whose mother is black and whose father is white. He is flanked by a classmate born in Sweden of Chinese parents.
>
> He stretches his fingertips to touch the hand of a close friend, a blond girl whose parents are from Idaho. She stands next to two girls with dark ponytails who whisper their secrets in Spanish. They smile at their neighbor, a shy and tiny girl most comfortable speaking Polish.
>
> They are the pupils in Mary Sigman's kindergarten at Ogden Elementary School in Chicago. To much of America, having all these diverse backgrounds in a kindergarten class remains atypical. But that may be changing: These children already are experiencing a multiracial, multiethnic world that increasingly will come to characterize this country...the year they graduate from high school. (Schreuder, 1996:F1)

SUMMARY

■ *How do racial and ethnic groups differ?*

According to sociologists, racial groups are defined on the basis of real or alleged physical characteristics, and ethnic groups are defined on the basis of cultural or nationality characteristics.

■ *What are dominant and subordinate groups?*

Although the terms *majority group* and *minority group* are widely used, many sociologists prefer the terms *dominant* and *subordinate* to identify power relationships that are based on perceived racial, ethnic, or other attributes and identities. A dominant (or majority) group is one that is advantaged and has superior resources and rights in a society. A subordinate (or minority) group is one whose members, because of physical or cultural characteristics, are disadvantaged and subjected to unequal treatment by the dominant group, and regard themselves as objects of collective discrimination.

■ *How are prejudice and discrimination related?*

Prejudice is a negative attitude that might or might not lead to discrimination, which is an action or practice of dominant group members that has a harmful impact on subordinate group members.

■ *How do individual discrimination and institutional discrimination differ?*

Although individual discrimination and institutional discrimination are carried out by individuals, individual discrimination consists of one-on-one acts by members of the dominant group; institutional discrimination refers to actions and practices that are built into the day-to-day operations of large-scale organizations and social institutions.

■ *How do the interactionist and functionalist perspectives view racial and ethnic relations?*

Interactionists focus on microlevel issues such as how people develop a racial-ethnic identity and how individuals from diverse racial-ethnic groups interact with each other. Functionalists focus on macrolevel issues such as how entire groups of people assimilate into the mainstream of the society.

■ *What are the major conflict explanations for racial-ethnic inequality?*

Conflict perspectives include class perspectives, split-labor market theory, gendered racism, internal colonialism, and racial formation theory.

■ *What types of discrimination have been experienced by Native Americans, African Americans, Latinos/as, and Asian and Pacific Americans in the United States?*

Native Americans have experienced internal colonization, genocide, forced migration, and Americanization. African Americans have experienced slavery, de jure segregation (Jim Crow laws), and de facto segregation—racial separation and inequality enforced by custom. Latinos/as have experienced internal colonialism, exclusionary immigration policies, and segregation in housing and education. Asian and Pacific Americans also have experienced exclusionary immigration policies; Japanese Americans uniquely experienced internment during World War II.

■ *What commonalities can be seen in the experiences of all subordinate racial-ethnic groups?*

Members of most subordinate racial-ethnic groups have these commonalities in their experiences in the United States: (1) Each has been the object of negative stereotypes and discrimination, (2) each has resisted oppression and continued to strive for a better life for its members and their children, and (3) each has been the object of some government policy that has shaped its place (or lack thereof) in U.S. race and ethnic relations over the past two centuries.

KEY TERMS

amalgamation, p. 52
Anglo-conformity model, p. 53
anti-Semitism, p. 51
assimilation, p. 52
dominant group (majority), p. 48
ethnic group, p. 47
ethnic pluralism, p. 53
ethnocentrism, p. 49
gendered racism, p. 54
genocide, p. 55
individual discrimination, p. 49
institutional discrimination, p. 50
internal colonialism, p. 54
melting pot model, p. 52
prejudice, p. 49
racial group, p. 47
racism, p. 49
scapegoat, p. 51
segregation, p. 54
stereotypes, p. 49
subordinate (minority) group, p. 48
theory of racial formation, p. 54

QUESTIONS FOR CRITICAL THINKING

1. Do you consider yourself part of the dominant racial-ethnic group or part of a subordinate racial-ethnic group in the United States? In what specific ways might your life be different if you were in the opposite group?
2. Sociologists suggest that we acquire beliefs about ourselves and others through socialization. What specific messages have you received about your racial-ethnic identity? What specific messages have you received about dealing with people from other racial-ethnic groups?
3. Have all white Americans, regardless of class, gender, or other characteristics, benefited from racial prejudice and discrimination in the United States? Why or why not?
4. Compare recent depictions of Native Americans, African Americans, Latinos/as, and Asian and Pacific Americans in films, television shows, and advertisements. To what extent have we moved beyond the traditional stereotypes discussed in this chapter? To what extent have the stereotypes remained strong?

Chapter 4

Gender Inequality

THINKING SOCIOLOGICALLY

- Why should we be concerned about sexual harassment? How is sexual harassment related to gender inequality?
- What types of gender socialization influence our ideas about what it means to be a woman or a man?
- How does gender-segregated work contribute to the larger picture of gender inequality in a society?

Our district manager ... learned he was in trouble because several [Wal-Mart] stores in his district had high [shrinkage or employee theft]. We (the district manager, the store managers, and the loss prevention staff) were told to drive to [Wal-Mart headquarters] to meet with senior management about the problems. We went in two cars, one driven by [the district manager] and the other by [the loss prevention manager]. I was the only woman in my car and there was another female store manager in the other. During the approximately sixteen-hour drive, the male managers talked ceaselessly about sex despite my repeated requests that they stop. We stopped for gas and several of the male managers wanted to go for a drink at the club adjacent to the station. When we entered, I realized that it was a strip club. Although I had never been in a place like this and had no interest in being there, I had no choice but to stay because I did not have my own car. I did not believe that it would have been safe for me to sit in the parking lot in the dark outside the club. I tried to ignore the show, but at one point, I was approached by one of the strippers and [the district manager] proposed that he pay one of the strippers $50 for a "threesome out back" with me. I refused....

On the return trip to Indiana, we stopped at two more strip clubs, including the "Pink Cadillac" somewhere in Missouri. The other female manager... and I sat in the back of the club as far away from the stage as possible, while several of the men sat up close and paid for lap dances. We repeatedly asked the male drivers whether we could leave. When we returned to the motel where we were to spend the night, [the district manager] and at least one other store manager dropped us off and announced that they were going to a massage parlor, which I understood to mean that they were planning to hire prostitutes.

—Sworn statement of Melissa Howard in a lawsuit brought by Betty Dukes and others against Wal-Mart Stores, Inc. (WalMartclass.com, 2005)

In what may be the largest employment discrimination case in U.S. history, a number of current and former female employees of Wal-Mart or Sam's Club have claimed that they have been the victims of sexual harassment by their supervisors and that Wal-Mart discriminated against women in the way it recruited and promoted managers. The suit also accuses the corporation of paying male employees more than females for performing comparable jobs. Melissa Howard's story, told in her own words above, is one of the many allegations brought by women against Wal-Mart Stores, Inc., the nation's largest private employer. One issue in the case is the extent to which Wal-Mart is responsible for the behavior of male employees when they are away from the workplace as was the case in the "stripper club incidents" that Howard describes. Whether this behavior fits the legal definition of sexual harassment in the workplace or not, it does constitute a form of sexism.

What is sexism? ***Sexism*** **is the subordination of one sex, usually female, based on the assumed superiority of the other sex**. Lewd comments, derogatory jokes, indecent gestures, and other conduct that makes women feel uncomfortable constitutes sexist behavior. Sexist behavior may create in-group solidarity among men, particularly in male-dominated groups and occupations, but it marginalizes women and makes them "sex objects," thus perpetuating gender inequality (Benokraitis and Feagin, 1995). From this perspective, pervasive sexism (along with racism and class-based inequalities) is deeply rooted in society, where it has a negative effect on women and men alike.

GENDER INEQUALITY AS A SOCIAL PROBLEM

Just as subordinate racial-ethnic group members experience discrimination based on innate character-istics, women experience discrimination based on their sex. Because 51 percent of the people in the United States are female, women constitute the numerical majority. However, they sometimes are referred to as the country's largest minority group because, typically, they do not possess as much wealth, power, or prestige as men.

Defining Sex and Gender

What is the difference between sex and gender? Although many people use these terms interchangeably, sociologists believe that there are significant differences in their meanings. ***Sex* is the biological differences between females and males.** A person's sex is the first label he or she receives in life. Before birth or at the time of birth, we are identified as male or female on the basis of our sex organs and genes. In comparison, ***gender* is the culturally and socially constructed differences between females and males that are based on meanings, beliefs, and practices that a group or society associates with "femininity" or "masculinity."** For many people, being masculine means being aggressive, independent, and not showing emotions; being feminine means the opposite—being unaggressive, dependent, and very emotional. Understanding the difference between sex and gender is important, according to sociologists, because what many people think of as sex differences—for example, being aggressive or independent—are actually socially constructed gender differences based on widely held assumptions about men's and women's attributes (Gailey, 1987). In other words, males are supposed to be aggressive and independent not because they have male sex organs but because that's how people in this society believe males should act.

Biological and Social Bases for Gender Roles

To study gender inequality, sociologists begin with an examination of the biological and social bases for gender roles, which are the rights, responsibilities, expectations, and relationships of women and men in a society (Benokraitis and Feagin, 1995). Gender roles have both a biological and a social basis. The biological basis for gender roles is rooted in the chromosomal and hormonal differences between men and women. When a child is conceived, the mother contributes an X chromosome, and the father contributes either an X chromosome (which produces a female embryo) or a Y chromosome (which produces a male embryo). As the embryo's male or female sex glands develop, they secrete the appropriate hormones (androgens for males, estrogens for females) that circulate through the bloodstream, producing sexual differentiation in the external genitalia, the internal reproductive tract, and possibly some areas of the brain. At birth, medical personnel and family members distinguish male from female infants by their *primary sex characteristics:* the genitalia that are used in the reproductive process. At puberty, hormonal differences in females and males produce *secondary sex characteristics,* the physical traits that, along with the reproductive organs, identify a person's sex. Females develop secondary sex characteristics such as menstruation, more prominent breasts, wider hips and narrower shoulders, and a layer of fatty tissue throughout the body. Male secondary sex characteristics include the development of larger genitals, a more muscular build, a deeper voice, more body and facial hair, and greater height. Although both males and females have androgens and estrogens, it is the relative proportion of each hormone that triggers masculine or feminine physical traits.

Is there something in the biological and genetic makeup of boys or girls that makes them physically aggressive or unaggressive? As sociologist Judith Lorber (1994:39) notes, "When little boys run around noisily, we say 'Boys will be boys,' meaning that physical assertiveness has to be in the Y chromosome because it is manifest so early and so commonly in boys." Similarly, when we say, "She throws like a girl" we mean, according to Lorber, that "she throws like a female child, a carrier of XX chromosomes." However, Lorber questions these widely held assumptions: "But are boys universally, the world over, in every social group, a vociferous, active presence? Or just where they are encouraged to use their bodies freely, to cover space, take risks, and play outdoors at all kinds of games and sports?"

According to Lorber, boys and girls who are given tennis rackets at the age of three and encouraged to become champions tend to use their bodies similarly. Even though boys gradually gain more shoulder and arm strength and are able to sustain more concentrated bursts of energy, after puberty girls acquire more stamina, flexibility, and lower-body strength. Coupled with training and physical exercise, these traits enhance, compensate for, or override different physical capabilities (Lorber, 1994). Thus the girl who throws like a girl is probably a product of her culture and time: She has had more limited experience than many boys at throwing the ball and engaging in competitive games at an early age.

The social basis for gender roles is known as the *gender belief system*—the ideas of masculinity and femininity that are held to be valid in a society (Lorber, 1994). The gender belief system is reflected in what sociologists refer to as the ***gendered division of labor*—the process whereby productive tasks are separated on the basis of gender.** How do people determine what constitutes "women's work" or "men's work"? Evidence from cross-cultural studies shows that social factors, more than biological factors, influence the gendered division of labor in societies. In poor agricultural societies, for example, women work in the fields and tend to their families' daily needs; men typically produce and market cash crops but spend no time in household work. In high-income nations, an increasing proportion of women are in paid employment but still have heavy household and family responsibilities. Across cultures, women's domain is the private and domestic, and men's domain is the public, economic, and political. This difference in how labor is divided and how workers are rewarded affects access to scarce resources such as wealth, power, and prestige. Given their domain, men have greater access to wealth, power, and prestige, a situation that leads to gender inequality in other areas.

To explain gender inequality, some sociologists use a *gender-role approach*, focusing on how the socialization process contributes to male domination and female subordination. Other sociologists use a structural approach, focusing on how large-scale, interacting, and enduring social structures determine the boundaries of individual behavior. Let's look first at how socialization can perpetuate gender stereotyping and inequality.

GENDER INEQUALITY AND SOCIALIZATION

Numerous sociological studies have found that gender-role stereotyping is one of the enduring consequences of childhood gender socialization. Socialization into appropriate "feminine" behavior makes women less likely than men to pursue male-dominated activities, and socialization into appropriate "masculine" behavior makes men more likely than women to pursue leadership roles in education, religion, business, politics, and other spheres of public life (Peterson and Runyan, 1993). We learn our earliest and often most lasting beliefs about gender roles from a variety of socializing agents—people, groups, or institutions that teach us what we need to know to participate in society. Among the most significant socializing agents are parents, peers, teachers and schools, sports, and the media.

Gender Socialization by Parents

From birth, parents create and maintain gender distinctions between girls and boys through differential treatment (Witt, 1997). Because boys are thought to be less fragile than girls, parents are more likely to bounce an infant son, to hold him up in the air, and to play with him more vigorously than they are an infant daughter (MacDonald and Parke, 1986). Parents tend to cuddle infant girls, treat them gently, and provide them with verbal stimulation through cooing, talking, and singing to them (Basow, 1992).

Parents reinforce gender distinctions through their selection of infants' and children's clothing. Most parents dress boys in boldly colored "rough and tough" clothing and girls in softly colored "feminine" clothing. They purchase sweatshirts that are decorated with hearts and flowers or female characters such as Cinderella, Ariel (the Little Mermaid), or Tinkerbell for girls and sweatshirts that feature male superheroes, athletic motifs, or characters such as Mickey Mouse, Spider-Man, or Superman for boys.

Parents further reinforce gender stereotyping and gender distinctions through the toys they buy. For example, parents buy blocks and building sets, vehicles, sporting equipment, and action toys such as guns, tanks, and soldiers for boys and dolls, doll clothing, dollhouses, play cosmetics, and homemaking items such as dishes and miniature ovens for girls (Leaper, 1994). However, toys and games do more than provide fun and entertainment; they develop different types of skills and can encourage children to participate in gender-typed activities.

Chores also reinforce gender distinctions. Most research confirms that parents use toys and chores to encourage their sons more than their daughters toward greater independence (Basow, 1992). Thus, boys frequently are assigned such maintenance chores as carrying out the garbage, cleaning up the yard, or helping dad or an older brother. Girls, on the other hand, are given domestic chores such as shopping, cooking, clearing the table, and doing laundry (Weisner et al., 1994). When parents purchase gender-specific toys and give children gender-specific household assignments, they send a powerful message about the gendered division of labor. However, gender socialization by parents does not stop at the end of childhood. Parents play a pivotal role in what many children do—and how they perceive of themselves in regard to gender, as well as class—well into adolescence and adulthood (see Box 4.1 on page 73).

Peers and Gender Socialization

Peer groups are powerful socializing agents that can reinforce existing gender stereotypes and pressure individuals to engage in gender-appropriate behavior. Peer groups are social groups whose members are linked by common interests and, usually, by similar age. Children are more widely accepted by their peer group when they conform to the group's notion of gender-appropriate behavior (Maccoby and Jacklin, 1987; Martin, 1989). Male peer groups place more pressure on boys to do "masculine" things than female peer groups place on girls to do "feminine" things. For example, most girls today wear jeans, and many play soccer and softball, but boys who wear dresses or play hopscotch with girls are banished from most male peer groups.

During preadolescence, male peer groups also reinforce gender-appropriate emotions in boys. In a study of a Little League baseball team, for example, sociologist Gary Fine (1987) found that the boys were encouraged by their peers to engage in proper "masculine" behavior—acting tough even when they were hurt or intimidated, controlling their emotions, being competitive and wanting to win, and showing group unity and loyalty. Boys who failed to display these characteristics received instantaneous feedback from their teammates.

Peers are important in both women's and men's development of gender identity and their aspirations for the future (Maccoby and Jacklin, 1987). Among college students, for example, peers play an important part in career choices and the establishment of long-term, intimate relationships (Huston, 1985; Martin, 1989). Even in kindergarten and the early grades, peers influence how we do in school and our perceptions of ourselves and others.

Education and Gender Socialization

Like parents and peers, teachers reinforce gender distinctions by communicating to students that males and male-dominated activities are more important than females

Across cultures, parents tend to socialize daughters and sons differently, including the clothes that the children are encouraged to wear. What gender-related messages do clothes convey? What messages about gender did you receive from your parents? Do you wish to convey the same messages to your children?

and female-dominated activities. Research on education continues to show the existence in schools of ***gender bias*****—a situation in which favoritism is shown toward one gender.** For example, education scholars Myra Sadker and David Sadker (1994) found that teachers subtly convey the message to their students that boys are more important than girls by devoting more time, effort, and attention to boys than to girls. In day-to-day interactions, teachers are more likely to allow boys to interrupt them and give boys more praise, criticism, and suggestions for remediation than girls. Boys are more likely to be called on in class, whether they volunteer or not. When boys make comments, teachers often follow up with additional questions or suggestions; but when girls make comments, teachers often respond with a superficial

Critical Thinking and You

Box 4.1

Does Class Position Influence How We Think about Gender?

> My mother is of a culture that believes girls aren't worth educating. . . . [My father thought] why reach for the sky when you can be happy on earth. My dad was trying to save me from disappointment. The daughter of peasant stock shouldn't strive to be in the ruling class, he thought. . . . If I had had parents who backed me, I could've owned my own company by now. I was always struggling against my parents.
>
> —*"Donna" (not her real name), a journalist for a national magazine, describes how her working-class parents thought that if the "working-class life was good enough for us, it's good enough for you, too." (quoted in Lubrano, 2004:33–34)*

> Being a debutante helped to define who I am as a woman and where I belong. I'm glad my mother insisted that I "come out" even though, at the time, I didn't want to because I thought it was "old fashioned" and "elitist." I think being a deb showed me I can be a woman with good manners and represent my family's position well.
>
> —*"Mary" (not her real name), a twenty-five-year-old white upper-class woman, explains how she felt about being presented as a society debutante at the encouragement of her mother. (Author's files, 2002)*

Although Donna and Mary are both women living in America, they have had different experiences as women based on their class location and what their families thought their "place" was in the social order. Donna represents those individuals who are raised in a blue-collar family but now live a white-collar, middle-class lifestyle. By contrast, Mary represents individuals who are raised in an upper-class family and continue to live a privileged lifestyle. Both women's stories reflect an interesting intersection of gender and class. To participate in the debutante ritual, Mary had to come from the "right families" with the proper social credentials and sufficient resources to pay for the many expenses associated with this ritual, while Donna's early life was a struggle, not only in regard to getting an education but also in facing parents who believed that she should not aspire to be upwardly mobile.

The lived experiences of these two women, as described by a sociologist (Kendall, 2002) and by a reporter for the *Philadelphia Inquirer* (Lubrano, 2004), are typical of thousands of women and men living in the United States where to be "male" or "female" does not fully explain a person's life chances and opportunities: Class is also a critical factor in understanding each individual's life. Consider, for example, how the intersections of gender and class have influenced the lives of people you know.

Putting Critical Thinking to Use

1. Think of a community you know well (perhaps your hometown or a city in which you lived for a lengthy period of time) and identify several families you consider to be in each of these categories: upper class, middle class, and working class. What are the key work and leisure activities of the men in each class? What are the key work and leisure activities of the women in each class?
2. Do these activities reflect the socialization of women and men based on their gender? Based on their class location?
3. What commonalities exist among women across class lines in the activities they typically perform? What activities are specific to women in the upper class? The middle class? The working class?
4. When is gender more important than class in helping us understand human behavior? When is class more important?
5. What type of sociological research might help you further explore the intersections of gender and class in your community?

"OK" and move on to the next student. Teachers praise girls for their appearance or for having a neat paper, but boys are praised for their accomplishments.

Teachers encourage gender-segregated activities when they organize classroom and playground activities by sex ("Boys line up on the left; girls on the right") and when they set up unnecessary competition between the sexes. One teacher divided her class into the "Beastly Boys" and the "Gossipy Girls" for a math game and allowed students to do the "give me five" handslapping ritual when one group outscored the other (Thorne, 1995).

The effects of gender bias become evident when teachers take a "boys will be boys" attitude about

Take a close look at this picture. What do you notice about the two lines? Social scientists have pointed out that gender socialization occurs in many ways, including how teachers organize school activities by sex.

derogatory remarks and aggressive behavior against girls. ***Sexual harassment*****—unwanted sexual advances, requests for sexual favors, or other verbal or physical conduct of a sexual nature—is frequently overlooked by teachers and school administrators.** Unfortunately, media stories like the one about the first-grade boy who was suspended from school for kissing a female classmate on the cheek trivialize gender bias and sexual harassment, both of which create a hostile environment that makes it more difficult for many girls and young women to learn and accomplish as much as their male counterparts (see Orenstein, 1996; Sadker and Sadker, 1994). Researchers have found that in some schools, male students regularly refer to girls as "sluts," "bitches," and "hos" without fear of reprimand from teachers, and the girls' fear of reprisal keeps them from speaking out against their harassers (Orenstein, 1996). One high school student described her experience in a shop class in this way:

> The boys literally pushed me around, right into tables and chairs. They pulled my hair, made sexual comments, touched me, told sexist jokes. And the thing was that I was better in the shop class than almost any guy. This only caused the boys to get more aggressive and troublesome. (Sadker and Sadker, 1994:127)

However, girls are not the only ones to experience sexual harassment at school. A recent report based on a national survey of more than 2,000 public school children in the eighth through eleventh grades states that 83 percent of girls and 79 percent of boys reported having experienced harassment at least once and that one in four of the students had experienced sexual harassment often (AAUW Educational Foundation, 2001). Nonphysical harassment (such as other students making comments or spreading rumors about them) and physical harassment (such as someone pulling off or down their clothing in a sexual way or forcing them to do something sexual other than kissing) were concerns of many of the students in the study. However, girls were more likely than boys to report negative consequences of these actions: Many stated that such harassment made them feel "self conscious," "embarrassed," or "less confident"(AAUW Educational Foundation, 2001).

Boys often are limited by stereotypical notions of masculinity and gender-appropriate behavior. According to Sadker and Sadker (1994:220), boys confront "frozen boundaries" of the male role at every turn in their school life. They are taught to "Be cool, don't show emotion, repress feelings, be aggressive, compete, and win"—the same messages that sociologist Gary Fine (1987) found Little Leaguers using to reinforce each other. Such teachings not only limit the range of emotions boys are allowed to feel but also encourage boys to see themselves—and other males—as better than girls and to distance themselves from any activity that is considered "feminine," even if it is an activity they enjoy.

Male gender norms, which require boys to be active, aggressive, and independent, often conflict with school norms, which require students to be quiet, passive, and conforming. Many boys walk a tightrope between compliance and rebellion. They tend to receive lower grades than girls do and are more likely to drop out of school (Sadker and Sadker, 1994). Although female gender norms conflict less with school norms than male gender norms, sociologist Michelle Fine (1991) has found in one study that for many girls, the price of academic success is being compliant and muting their own voice.

Sports and Gender Socialization

Although girls' participation in athletics has increased dramatically since the 1972 passage of Title IX, which mandates equal opportunities in academic and athletic programs, boys' participation is about one and one-half times that of girls. Emphasis on greater gender equity in sports has contributed to a more positive outlook for girls and women with regard to participation in a wider variety of athletic endeavors than was true a decade or two ago. For example, when students in a

1990 study were asked about sports participation, most students listed all sports as male domains with the exception of figure skating, gymnastics, and jumping rope, which were identified as female activities (Michigan Department of Education, 1990). Although this perception has changed somewhat in recent years as a much wider range of opportunities in sports has become available to women, some critics argue that women's gains have been at the expense of men in college sports (see Box 4.2).

Overall, for both women and men, sports participation is an important part of gender socialization. Across lines of race, ethnicity, and gender, sports and other extracurricular activities provide students with important opportunities for leadership and teamwork and for personal contact with adult role models. Consequently, athletic participation must be viewed as more than just "play"; it constitutes an important part of the learning experience and can promote greater equality in society.

The Media and Gender Socialization

The media—including newspapers, magazines, television, and movies—are powerful sources of gender stereotyping. Although some critics argue that the media simply reflect existing gender roles in society, others point out that the media have a unique ability to shape ideas. From children's cartoons to adult shows, television programs offer more male than female characters. Furthermore, the male

Social Problems and Social Policy

Box 4.2

Title IX and Gender Quotas in College Sports

> If we are forced to have gender quotas in college sports, men's programs will lose out to women's programs.
>
> —*An often-repeated statement made by critics of Title IX of the Education Amendments of 1972*

Has this pronouncement proved to be true over the past thirty-plus years since Title IX was enacted? Have men's teams felt great pain while women's teams obtained an advantage in college athletics? To gain insights on this controversial social policy, let's first look at what Title IX is all about.

Title IX prohibits discrimination on the basis of sex in any educational program or activity receiving financial assistance from the U.S. government and has been applied to athletic programs as well as to other academic endeavors. A three-part test was established to help colleges determine if they provide sufficient opportunities for female athletes to participate in athletic programs:

- Does the college have the same proportion of students and athletes who are female?
- Does the college have a "history and continuing practice" of expanding opportunities for women?
- Can the college show that it is fully and effectively accommodating the interests and abilities of women on campus? (Suggs, 2005:A25)

If the answer is "yes" to all three parts of the test, a college is considered to be in compliance with Title IX. However, there are serious limitations to the three-part test, according to *The Chronicle of Higher Education:* "The guidelines do not define how close the proportions of students and athletes must be to meet the first test; they do not state how often colleges must add women's teams to meet the second; and they do not indicate what the Education Department will accept as proof that women are satisfied with the sports opportunities they are receiving" (Suggs, 2005:A25). If these criticisms are valid, then it is very difficult to determine if a college is in compliance with Title IX. With all of the confusion and numerous pending court cases, is there anything we can tell at this time about the effect of Title IX as a social policy on gender equity in college sports?

Overall, statistics show that Title IX has had a very favorable effect on women's participation in college athletic programs. Statistics—in this instance, data about athletic participation—show that some women's teams have made progress in regard to equity, but that this typically has not been at the expense of men's athletic programs. As a result of Title IX, many more women are playing collegiate sports today than before this law was enacted, but the percentage *increase* in athletic participation during that period of time has not been as high for females as it has been for

Box 4.2 (continued)

males: More men are playing varsity sports today than in the past, even as their numbers on college campuses have become a smaller percentage of the undergraduate student population. Based on the latest data from the U.S. Department of Education, the number of male college athletes increased by about 2,700 between 2002 and 2004, and the total number of men's teams either increased or remained the same across all divisions (Suggs, 2005).

Although there has been a significant increase in the number of female athletes competing in college sports, the representation of female athletes remains far from proportional to the number of female students at most colleges. Consider, for example, that in 2003–2004, 41 percent of the 494,000 athletes who competed in college sports were women, but during that same period of time, women made up about 55 percent of all full-time undergraduate students at U.S. colleges (Suggs, 2005). At the same time that more women have become involved in college athletic programs, women have come to dominate undergraduate enrollments, making it more difficult to demonstrate the effect of Title IX in regard to athletic participation.

At the bottom line—the dollar figures—we can particularly see that men's athletic programs have not been losing out to women's programs. Men's collegiate sports still receive the lion's share of the money when it comes to budgets, coaches' salaries, facilities, and other resources. Some of the complaints of coaches and male athletes—particularly in programs such as swimming, wrestling, and other less visible sports—that they are losing out to women's programs might better be directed toward other men's programs, specifically football and basketball, that remain the powerhouses for both bringing in the money and spending it (Suggs, 2005).

Would you like to know more about Title IX or gain other information on National Collegiate Athletic Association (NCAA) sports? Go to the NCAA website at http://www.ncaa.org.

characters act in a strikingly different manner from female ones. Male characters in both children's programs and adult programs are typically aggressive, constructive, and direct, while some female characters defer to others or manipulate them by acting helpless, seductive, or deceitful (Basow, 1992). Daytime soap operas are an example of such gender stereotyping. As media scholar Deborah D. Rogers (1995) has noted, even though contemporary soaps feature career women, the cumulative effect of these programs is to reconcile women to traditional feminine roles and relationships. Whether the scene takes place at home or in the workplace, female characters typically gossip about romances or personal problems or compete for a man. Meanwhile, male characters are shown as superior beings who give orders and advice to others and do almost anything. In a hospital soap, for example, while female nurses gossip about hospital romances and their personal lives, the same male doctor who delivers babies also handles AIDS patients and treats trauma victims (Rogers, 1995). Prime-time television has provided better portrayals of women in medicine and in leadership positions in hospitals, but this change to more accurate depictions of women is not reflected throughout television programming.

Television and films influence our thinking about the appropriate behavior of women and men in the roles they play in everyday life. Because it is often necessary for an actor to overplay a comic role to gain laughs from the viewing audience or to exaggerate a dramatic role to make a quick impression on the audience, the portrayal of girls and women may (either intentionally or inadvertently) reinforce old stereotypes or create new ones. Consider, for example, the growing number of women who are depicted as having careers or professions (such as law or medicine) in which they may earn more income and have more power than female characters had in the past. Some of these women may be portrayed as well-adjusted individuals; however, many women characters are still shown as overly emotional and unable to resolve their personal problems even as they are able to carry out their professional duties. Women characters who are supervisors or bosses are sometimes portrayed as loud, bossy, and domineering individuals. Mothers in situation comedies frequently boss their children around and may have a Homer Simpson–type husband who is lazy and incompetent or who engages in aggressive verbal combat with the woman throughout most of the program.

Advertising further reinforces ideas about women and physical attractiveness. Women are bombarded with media images of ideal beauty and physical appearance (Cortese, 1999), and eating problems such as anorexia and bulimia are a major concern associated with many media depictions of the ideal body image for women. With anorexia, a person has lost at least 25 percent of body weight owing to a compulsive fear of becoming fat. With bulimia, a person consumes large quantities of food and then purges the food by induced vomiting, excessive exercise, laxatives, or fasting. In both forms of eating disorders, distorted body image plays an important part, and this distorted image may be perpetuated by media depictions and advertisements. According to the media scholar Jean Kilbourne (1994:395),

> The current emphasis on excessive thinness for women is one of the clearest examples of advertising's power to influence cultural standards and consequent individual behavior. Body types, like clothing styles, go in and out of fashion, and are promoted by advertising.... The images in the mass media constantly reinforce the latest ideal—what is acceptable and what is out of date.... Advertising and the media indoctrinate us in these ideals, to the detriment of most women.

Clearly, the dramatic increase in eating problems in recent years cannot be attributed solely to advertising and the mass media. However, their potential impact on the gender socialization of young girls and women in establishing role models with whom to identify is extremely important (Kilbourne, 1994:398).

Why is awareness of gender socialization important for understanding sex discrimination and gender inequality? Social analysts who use a gender-role approach say that because parents, peers, teachers, and the media influence our perceptions of who we are and what our occupational preferences should be, gender role socialization contributes to a gendered division of labor, creates a wage gap between women and men workers, and limits the occupational choices of women and men. However, some social analysts say that no direct evidence links gender role socialization to social inequality and that it is therefore important to use social structural analysis to examine gender inequality (see Reskin and Hartmann, 1986). In other words, these analysts believe that the decisions that people make (such as the schools they choose to attend and the occupations they choose to pursue) are linked not only to how they were socialized, but also to how society is structured. We now examine structural features that contribute to gender inequality.

CONTEMPORARY GENDER INEQUALITY

How do tasks in a society come to be defined as "men's work" or "women's work" and to be differentially rewarded? Many sociologists believe that social institutions and structures assign different roles and responsibilities to women and men and, in the process, restrict women's opportunities. According to feminist scholars, gender inequality is maintained and reinforced through individual and institutionalized sexism. The term *individual sexism* refers to individuals' beliefs and actions that are rooted in antifemale prejudice and stereotypic beliefs. The term *institutionalized sexism* refers to the power that men have to engage in sex discrimination at the organizational and institutional levels of society. This pattern of male domination and female subordination is known as ***patriarchy*—a hierarchical system of social organization in which cultural, political, and economic structures are controlled by men.** According to some analysts, the location of women in the workplace and on the economic pyramid is evidence of patriarchy in the United States (Epstein, 1988). In this section, we focus on five structural forms that contribute to contemporary gender inequality: the gendered division of labor, the wage gap, sexual harassment, the glass ceiling and the glass escalator, and the double shift.

The Gendered Division of Paid Work

Whether by choice or economic necessity, women have entered the paid labor force in unprecedented numbers in recent years. In 1940, about 30 percent of working-age women in the United States were employed. Today, women represent more than 45 percent of the

Television reality shows such as The Bachelor *often rely on stereotypical portrayals of women's behavior, such as these young women who are supposedly "out to get" a man at virtually any cost. How might such representations of women and men affect viewers' perceptions of what constitutes gender-appropriate behavior?*

workforce. Among women age twenty-five to fifty-four, the increase is even more dramatic: 75 percent currently are either employed or looking for a job. In fact, a higher proportion of women of all races, ages, and marital status groups are employed or seeking work than ever before. At the same time, the proportion of male employees has gradually declined because of layoffs in the industrial sector and the long-term trend toward early retirement.

Although many people who know these statistics are optimistic about the gains women in the United States have made in employment, it should be noted that women's position as a social category in the labor force is lower than men's in terms of status, opportunities, and salaries. Today, most women and men remain concentrated in occupations that are segregated by gender (see Table 4.1). The term *gender-segregated work* refers to the extent to which men and women are concentrated in different occupations and places of work (Reskin and Padavic, 1994). For example, women are predominant in word-processing pools and child-care centers, while men are predominant in the construction trades. Other individuals are employed in settings where both men and women are present. In these settings, however, women are employed predominantly in clerical or other support positions, while men hold supervisory, managerial, or other professional positions. For example, despite the increasing number of women entering the legal profession, almost 85 percent of all law firm partners (owners) are men (see Krufka, 2001). Gender-segregated work is most visible in occupations that remain more than 90 percent female (for example, secretary, registered nurse, and bookkeeper/auditing clerk) or more than 90 percent male (for example, carpenter, construction worker, mechanic, truck driver, and electrical engineer) (U.S. Department of Labor, 2007). In fact, to eliminate gender-segregated jobs in the United States, more than half of all employed men or women would have to change occupations (Reskin and Hartmann, 1986).

Observers who are optimistic about women's gains point out that government statistics show women employed in a wide variety of organizations and holding nearly every kind of job. It is important to note, however, that the types of work women and men do still vary significantly and that 60 percent of all employed women in the United States today are concentrated in ***pink-collar occupations*****—relatively low-paying, nonmanual, semi-skilled positions that are held primarily by women—** such as clerical work, counter help in fast-food restaurants, medical assistance, and child-care work.

Women are overrepresented in the contingent workforce as well. ***Contingent work*** **is part-time work,**

TABLE 4.1 Employment Percentages by Occupation and Sex, 2006

Occupation	Men	Women
Total percentage[1]	100	100
Managerial and professional specialty	31.3	41.3
Executive, administrative, managerial	14.3	14.9
Professional specialty	17.0	26.4
Sales and office occupations	16.3	34.4
Sales and related occupations	9.7	9.8
Office and administrative support	6.7	24.5
Service occupations	12.2	16.1
Healthcare support (nurses, dental assistants, home health aides)	0.4	4.3
Protective service	3.5	1.2
Food preparation and service	3.5	4.6
Other service occupations	4.8	6.1
Production, transportation, and material moving occupations	20.1	7.1
Production	10.0	5.2
Transportation and material moving	10.2	1.9
Natural resources, construction, and maintenance occupations	20.0	1.1

[1]Percentages might not add to 100 because of rounding.

Source: Calculated by author based on U.S. Bureau of Labor Statistics, 2007.

temporary work, and subcontracted work that offers advantages to employers but can be detrimental to workers' welfare. Many employers stress that having more contingent workers and fewer permanent, full-time employees keeps corporations competitive in the global marketplace. However, this type of employment actually makes it possible for employers to avoid providing benefits such as health insurance and pension plans to all employees. Although many women are found in contingent work because it often provides greater flexibility for those with family responsibilities, nearly 2 million women who accepted part-time or temporary work in 1995 did so because they were unable to find permanent jobs (Costello et al., 1996). All contingent workers experience problems related to this type of work, but women especially are affected by the fact that contingent workers are unlikely to qualify for unemployment compensation if they lose their jobs (see Bassi and Chasanov, 1996), and most do not qualify for pension coverage (see Hounsell, 1996; Patterson, 1996).

Although the degree of gender segregation in the workplace and in professions, such as accounting, law, and medicine, has declined in the last three decades, occupational segregation by race and ethnicity persists. Today, a larger percentage of white women (30 percent) than African American women (21 percent) or Latinas (17 percent) hold managerial and professional specialty jobs. When African-American women become professionals, they often find their employment opportunities more limited than those of white women and men. Sociologist Elizabeth Higginbotham (1994) has found that most African-American professional women are concentrated in public sector employment (as public school teachers, welfare workers, librarians, public defenders, or faculty members at public colleges) rather than in private sector employment (e.g., in large corporations, major law firms, and elite private universities).

Both Latinas and African-American women are more likely than white women to work in service occupations such as private household workers. Although private household work has become less common among African-American women in the last two decades, Latinas remain heavily represented among the 800,000 women who are employed as private household workers. Across racial and ethnic lines, women continue to be concentrated in jobs in which they receive lower wages and fewer benefits on average than men.

The Wage Gap

The ***wage gap*—the disparity between women's and men's earnings**—is the best-documented consequence of gender-segregated work (Reskin and Padavic, 1994). No matter what their race or ethnic group, men earn more than women of the same racial or ethnic group. The median earnings for women who worked full time in 2006 were $600 per week compared to $743 for men. This means that a woman who works full time makes about 81 cents for every dollar that a man makes.

The wage gap varies by age: The older the worker, the larger the gap. This may be true in part because younger workers tend to have about the same amount of work experience and to be concentrated in entry-level jobs. Thus between the ages of twenty and twenty-four, women earn an average of 94.9 cents for every dollar that men earn. However, women between the ages of twenty-five and thirty-four earn only 88.2 cents for every dollar that men earn. Women between the ages of thirty-five and forty-four earn only 77.1 cents per dollar; and by ages fifty-five to sixty-four, the amount has dropped to only 72.9 cents for each dollar men earn (U.S. Bureau of Labor Statistics, 2007).

Social analysts suggest that the higher wage gap for older workers probably reflects a number of factors, including the fact that women in those age groups tend to have, on average, less overall work experience and less time with their present employer than have men of the same age (Herz and Wootton, 1996). As Figure 4.1

www.CartoonStock.com

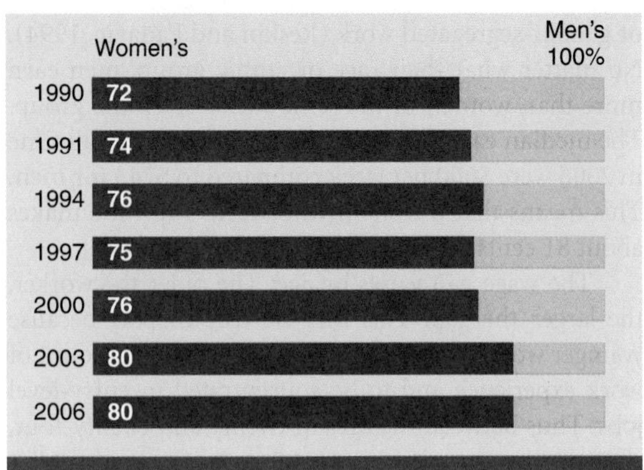

■ Figure 4.1 *The U.S. wage gap: Women's earnings compared with men's earnings, selected years 1990–2006*

Source: U.S. Bureau of Labor Statistics, 2007.

shows, the wage gap has narrowed somewhat between women and men over the last few years, but much of the decrease in wage disparity can be attributed to a decline in men's average earnings (adjusted for inflation) rather than to a significant increase in women's earnings.

For pay equity to occur between men and women, there has to be a broad-based commitment to ***comparable worth*—the belief that wages ought to reflect the worth of a job, not the gender or race of the worker** (Kemp, 1994). To determine the comparable worth of different kinds of jobs, researchers break a specific job into components to determine (1) how much education, training, and skills are required; (2) how much responsibility a person in that position has for others' work; and (3) what the working conditions are. Researchers then allocate points for each component to determine whether or not men and women are being paid equitably for their work (Lorber, 1994). For pay equity to exist, men and women in occupations that receive the same number of points must be paid the same. However, pay equity exists for very few jobs. (See Figure 4.2 for a comparison of men's and women's earnings in selected occupations.)

Comparable worth is an important issue for men as well as women. Male workers in female-dominated jobs such as nursing, secretarial work, and elementary teaching pay an economic penalty for their choice of work. If women were compensated fairly, an employer could not undercut men's wages by hiring women at a cheaper rate (Kessler-Harris, 1990).

Sexual Harassment

Sexual harassment is a form of intentional gender discrimination that includes all unwelcome sexual attention that affects an employee's job conditions or creates a hostile work environment. According to the U.S. Equal Employment Opportunity Commission (EEOC), sexual harassment in the workplace is a form of sex discrimination that violates Title VII of the Civil Rights Act of 1964:

> Unwelcome sexual advances, requests for sexual favors, and other verbal or physical conduct of a sexual nature constitutes sexual harassment when submission to or rejection of this conduct explicitly or implicitly affects an individual's employment, unreasonably interferes with an individual's work performance or creates an intimidating, hostile or offensive work environment. (EEOC, 2002)

As this definition suggests, sexual harassment can occur in various forms, including supervisor-subordinate harassment, subordinate-supervisor harassment, and peer-peer harassment. It also occurs in other types of institutions. Although most reported cases of sexual harassment involve the harassment of women by men, the victim as well as the harasser may be a woman or a man (EEOC, 2002).

People who are accused of sexual harassment frequently claim that their actions were merely harmless expressions of (supposedly) mutual sexual attraction. However, sexual harassment is not about attraction; it is about *abuse of power*. Sexual harassment constitutes a

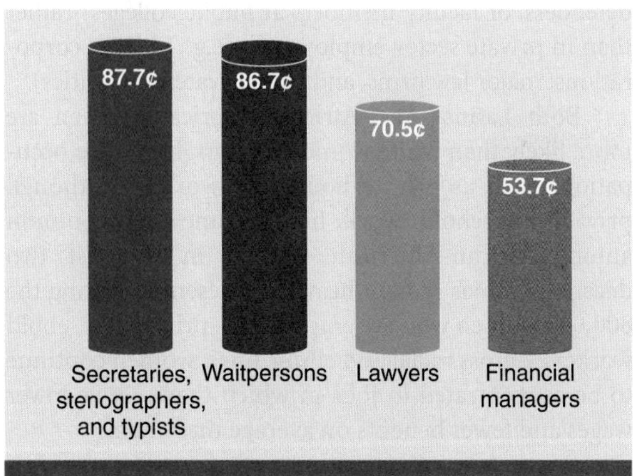

■ Figure 4.2 *U.S. wage gap in selected occupations*

Source: U.S. Bureau of Labor Statistics, 2007.

form of intimidation and aggression: The recipient has no choice in the encounter or has reason to fear repercussions if she or he declines. Some men are able to harass because they hold economic power over women (e.g., bosses, supervisors, and colleagues who have some say over promotions and raises); others are able to harass because they hold gender-based power (e.g., power rooted in cultural patterns of male dominance and backed up by the threat of violence and the ability to rape) (Langelan, 1993). In either case, sexual harassment serves as a means of boundary heightening between men and women in the workplace. For example, male lawyers might exaggerate the differences between women lawyers and themselves by directing unwanted sexual invitations, attention, and behavior at women in their firm. In her study of law firms, sociologist Jennifer L. Pierce interviewed many female lawyers who reported incidents similar to the one described by Gabriella, a twenty-six-year-old associate who had slapped a male partner who was harassing her at a firm cocktail party:

> "Everyone else knew about George, but I was new, I didn't know to avoid him. So, when he tried to grab my breasts, I didn't even think, I just came out swinging ....It was so humiliating. Then, afterwards...the snide remarks, the knowing glances, the comments, 'How's your left hook?' It was the second public humiliation." (Pierce, 1995:108–109)

According to Pierce, the comments made about Gabriella's reaction (slapping George) by the male attorneys show that they considered her behavior (not George's actions) to be inappropriate and worthy of derision.

Sexual harassment is a costly problem for women who may lose employment opportunities and for their employers who lose more than $7 million a year in low productivity, absenteeism, and employee turnover related to harassment (Basow, 1992). Sexual harassment and other forms of blatant and subtle discrimination in the workplace also contribute to the institutional barriers that limit women's opportunities to rise to the top positions in corporations and other occupational settings (see MacCorquodale and Jensen, 1993; Rosenberg et al., 1993).

The Glass Ceiling and the Glass Escalator

More recently, feminist researchers have used the advancement (or lack of advancement) of women into top-tier management jobs as a litmus test for how well women are faring in the labor force as a whole. They have found that women hold only a handful of top positions. Although they are inching their way up the corporate ladder, women almost always encounter barriers when they try to enter the lucrative and prestigious top positions of their occupations. This is because of what is known as the ***glass ceiling*—the invisible institutional barrier constructed by male management that prevents women from reaching top positions in major corporations and other large-scale organizations.** Among the reasons that have been cited for this barrier are male executives who believe that male workers will not work under women supervisors and that women workers are supposed to be in support roles (Benokraitis and Feagin, 1995).

The glass ceiling is particularly evident in the nation's 500 largest companies. In 2005, only 15.7 percent of the corporate officers among those companies were women; only eight of those companies had a woman as chief executive officer of the corporation (see Table 4.2). Women of color occupy fewer than 1 percent of top management positions.

Overall, women are most likely to reach top positions in the service sector (for example, banking and diversified finance, publishing, retailing, food services, and entertainment), a sector in which they have traditionally been employed in great numbers. Women fare the worst in male-dominated businesses such as mining, crude oil, brokerages, and manufacturing. In its research, Catalyst, a nonprofit research organization seeking to expand opportunities for women in business, found that women who continue to bump into glass ceilings tend to leave large corporations and start their own businesses.

Unlike women who enter male-dominated occupations, men who enter female-dominated occupations are

TABLE 4.2 Fortune 500 Companies with a Woman as CEO

Company	Rank
Sara Lee	114
Rite Aid	128
Xerox	132
Avon Products	278
Reynolds American	321
Mirant	424
Golden West Financial	435
Pathmark Stores	467

Source: Fortune, 2005.

apt to find little difficulty in rising to the top of their occupation. In research on men working as registered nurses, elementary teachers, librarians, and social workers, sociologist Christine L. Williams (1995) found that men tended to rise in disproportionate numbers to administrative positions at the top of these occupations. Williams (1995:12) calls the upward movement of men in "women's professions" the glass escalator effect because, as she notes, "like being on an invisible 'up' escalator, men must struggle to remain in the lower (i.e., 'feminine') levels of their professions." Men also move into more "masculine" specialties within traditionally female-dominated occupations. Male librarians, for example, often move into high-technology computer information specialties and administration. In contrast, women in male-dominated occupations typically find they are bumping their heads on the glass ceiling and working a double shift.

As more women have entered the paid workforce, they have encountered a double shift at home. According to researchers, employed women still do most of the daily household chores such as taking care of the children. Is this photo a hopeful sign for the future?

The Double Shift

Although there have been dramatic changes in the participation of women in the labor force, the division of labor by sex has remained essentially unchanged in many families. Although more married women now share responsibility for earning part—or all—of the family income, many married men do not participate in routine domestic chores (Reskin and Padavic, 1994). Consequently, many employed women must deal with a double work load. In the words of sociologist Arlie Hochschild (1989), women with dual responsibilities as wage earners and unpaid household workers work "the second shift."

Not only does the relative number of hours spent on housework differ widely between women and men, but the kinds of chores men and women do also vary significantly. Women do most of the daily chores such as taking care of children, making beds, and cooking and cleaning up after meals. Men are more likely to do chores that do not have to be done every day. For example, men typically mow the lawn, repair cars or other equipment, and do home improvements (Shelton, 1992). Although some kinds of housework can be put off, young children's needs cannot be ignored or delayed, so daily domestic duties in families with young children consume a great deal of time and energy. A sick child or a school event that cannot be scheduled around work causes additional stress for parents, especially mothers. Furthermore, more and more women are becoming members of "the sandwich generation." In other words, they are caught, sandwiched, between the needs of their young children and those of older relatives for whom they are often the primary caregivers. In an effort to keep up with family obligations while working full-time or part-time, many women spend a large portion of their earnings on day-care and elder-care centers, prepared foods and meals from fast-food restaurants, and laundry and dry cleaning (Bergmann, 1986).

When sociologists conduct research on participation in household work, both men and women state that working couples should share household responsibilities. However, when it gets down to who actually does what, most studies find that women, even those who hold full-time jobs, do most of the work. According to Arlie Hochschild (1989), many women try to solve their time crunch by forgoing leisure activities and sleep.

PERSPECTIVES ON GENDER INEQUALITY

Unlike functionalist and conflict perspectives, which focus on macrolevel sources of gender inequality, interactionist perspectives typically focus on social constructs such as language. It is language, interactionists say, that structures our thinking and discourse about domination and subordination.

The Symbolic Interactionist Perspective

For symbolic interactionists, who view society as the sum of all people's interactions, language is extremely significant in defining social realities because it provides people with shared meanings and social realities. Historically, what men have thought, written, and concluded have been the givens of our discourse (Peterson and Runyan, 1993). Today, however, English and other languages are being criticized for *linguistic sexism,* that is, for words and patterns of communication that ignore, devalue, or make sex objects of one sex or the other, most often women.

Linguistic sexism, some analysts believe, perpetuates traditional gender role stereotypes and reinforces male dominance. These analysts note that the idea that women are secondary to men in importance is embedded in the English language: The masculine form (he) is used to refer to human beings generally, and words such as *chairman* and *mankind* are considered to include both men and women (Miller and Swift, 1991). When a woman enters a profession such as medicine or law, she is frequently referred to as a "female doctor" or "woman lawyer"; such terms linguistically protect these male-dominated professions from invasion by females (Lindsey, 1994).

Language can also be used to devalue women by referring to them in terms that reinforce the notion that they are sex objects. Terms such as *fox, bitch, babe,* or *doll* further devalue women by ascribing petlike, childlike, or toylike attributes to them (Adams and Ware, 1995). According to one analyst, at least 220 terms exist for sexually promiscuous women, but only 22 terms exist for promiscuous men (Stanley, 1972).

Research by scholars in a variety of disciplines has demonstrated not only the importance of language in patterning our thoughts, but also how gender—and the hierarchy it constructs—is built into the English language (Peterson and Runyan, 1993). According to sociologists Claire M. Renzetti and Daniel J. Curran (1995:151), "Given that women are denigrated, unequally defined, and often ignored by the English language, it serves not only to reflect their secondary status relative to men in our society, but also to reinforce it."

According to symbolic interactionists, male dominance is also perpetuated through nonverbal communication such as bodily movement, posture, eye contact, use of personal space, and touching. Men typically control more space than women do, whether they are sitting or standing. Men tend to invade women's personal space by standing close to them, touching them, or staring at them. Such actions are not necessarily sexual in connotation, but to symbolic interactionists, they reinforce male dominance. However, when a man nudges and fondles a flight attendant or a coworker in the office, these actions do have sexual overtones that cannot be dismissed. Sexual harassment cases show that women do not appreciate such acts and feel threatened by them, especially if the toucher is the employer (Lindsey, 1994:79).

Although the symbolic interactionist perspective has been criticized for ignoring the larger, structural factors that perpetuate gender inequality, it is important to note that language and communication patterns are embedded in the structure of society and pass from generation to generation through the socialization process.

The Functionalist Perspective

In focusing on macrolevel issues affecting gender inequality, functionalists frequently examine employment opportunities and the wage gap between men and women.

According to such early functionalists as Talcott Parsons (1955), gender inequality is inevitable because of the biological division of labor: Men generally are physically stronger than women and have certain abilities and interests, whereas women, as the only sex able to bear and nurse children, have their own abilities and interests. Given the biological attributes, Parsons said, men find themselves more suited to *instrumental* (goal-oriented) *tasks* and women to *expressive* (emotionally oriented) *tasks*. In the home, therefore, husbands perform such instrumental tasks as providing economic support and making the most important decisions for the family, while wives perform such expressive tasks as nurturing children and providing emotional support for all family members. The division of labor by gender ensures that important societal tasks—such as procreation and the socialization of children—are fulfilled and that the family is socially and economically stable.

According to Parsons, this division of labor continues in the workplace, where women again do expressive work and men again do instrumental work. Thus, women cluster in occupations that require expressive work, such as elementary school teaching, nursing, and secretarial work because of their interests and abilities. Women also are concentrated in specific specialties within professions such as law and medicine because of their aptitude for expressive work and their desire to spend more time with their families than men, who are in more lucrative specialties, are able to spend. For example, many women in law specialize in family law, and many women in medicine specialize in pediatrics (infants and children), obstetrics and gynecology (women), or family practice. In corporations, women are thought to be more adept at public relations and human resources; men are viewed as more adept at financial management. In recent years, however, critics have rejected the dichotomy between men's instrumental work and women's expressive work set forth by functionalists (see Scott, 1996). These critics have noted that the functionalist explanation of gender inequality does not take into account sex discrimination and other structural barriers that make some educational and occupational opportunities more available to men than to women. It also fails to examine the underlying power relations between women and men and does not consider the fact that society places unequal value on tasks assigned to men and women (Kemp, 1994).

Other functionalist explanations of gender inequality focus on the human capital that men and women bring to the workplace. According to human capital explanations, what individuals earn is based on choices they have made, including choices about the kinds of training and experience they accumulate. For example, human capital analysts argue that women diminish their human capital when they leave the labor force to engage in childbearing and child-care activities. While women are out of the labor force, their human capital deteriorates from nonuse. When they return to work, they earn lower wages than men do because the women have fewer years of work experience and "atrophied human capital," that is, because their education and training may have become obsolete (Kemp, 1994:70).

Critics of the human capital model note that it is based on the false assumption that all people, regardless of gender, race, or other attributes, are evaluated and paid fairly on the basis of their education, training, and other job-enhancing characteristics. It fails to acknowledge that white women and people of color tend to be paid less even when they are employed in male-dominated occupations and take no time off for family duties (Lorber, 1994).

Conflict and Feminist Perspectives

Conflict perspectives on gender inequality are based on the assumption that social life is a continuous struggle in which members of powerful groups (males, in this case) seek to maintain control of scarce resources such as social, economic, and political superiority. By dominating individual women and commanding social institutions, men maintain positions of privilege and power. However, conflict theorists note, not all men are equally privileged: Men in the upper classes have greater economic power because they control elite positions in corporations, universities, the mass media, and government (Richardson, 1993).

Conflict theorists using a Marxist approach believe that gender inequality results primarily from capitalism and private ownership of the means of production. Basing their work on this Marxist approach, socialist feminists state that under capitalism, men gain control over property and over women. Thus, capitalism exploits women in the workplace, and patriarchy exploits women at home (Kemp, 1994). According to this perspective, capitalists benefit from the gendered division of labor in the workplace because they can pay women lower wages and derive higher profits. At the same time, individual men benefit from the unpaid work women do at home. The capitalist economic system is maintained because women reproduce the next generation of workers while providing current employees (often including themselves) with food, clean clothes, and other goods and services that are necessary for those who must show up at the workplace each day (Hartmann, 1976).

Unlike socialist feminists, *radical feminists* focus exclusively on patriarchy as the primary source of gender inequality. From this perspective, men's oppression of

According to conflict and feminist perspectives, many women continue to face sexism even after they attain top positions in the workplace. Zoe Cruz, shown here, was fired from Morgan Stanley, a Wall Street financial services firm, where she had risen to upper management because her boss "lost confidence" in her ability.

women is deliberate, with ideological justification provided by other institutions such as the media and religion. *Liberal feminists* believe that gender inequality is rooted in gender-role socialization, which perpetuates women's lack of equal civil rights and educational opportunities. *Black feminists* believe that women of color face inequalities based on the multiplicative effect of race, class, and gender as simultaneous forces of oppression (Andersen and Collins, 2001).

Conflict and feminist perspectives have been criticized for their emphasis on male dominance without a corresponding analysis of how men might be oppressed by capitalism and/or patriarchy.

GLOBAL GENDER INEQUALITY

Many social analysts argue that patriarchy and capitalism have maintained and perpetuated gender inequality worldwide. Today, millions of girls and women are the victims of physical and sexual abuse, and authorities believe that the number of cases is so seriously underreported that we do not know the full nature and extent of this problem. According to the World Bank, gender-based violence is a greater cause of ill health and death among women between the ages of fifteen and forty-four than cancer, and it is a greater cause of ill health than traffic accidents and malaria combined (Venis, 2002). Likewise, female infanticide reduces the number of girls born in some nations (see Box 4.3 on page 86), and patterns of female genital mutilation and violence against girls and women perpetuate women's powerless condition. Although infant mortality rates typically are higher for boys than for girls, there are regions of the world where gender-based discrimination has served to outweigh any biological advantage that girls otherwise might have. In regard to female genital mutilation, United Nations studies estimate that in some African countries, more than half of all girls and women have been subjected to female genital mutilation (referred to by some as "female circumcision").

Systematic patterns of gender discrimination are the result of centuries of maltreatment of girls and women, and these patterns are maintained and perpetuated based on tradition, customs, religious beliefs, family socialization, and prevalent economic and political conditions. Breaking the virtual chains that currently bind many women is extremely difficult. Despite calls from some international organizations for greater gender equality, women remain significantly underrepresented worldwide in governments, political parties, and at the United Nations.

Is paid employment the solution for producing greater gender equality? This is a difficult question to answer. It appears that employment alone does not greatly reduce the problem: Worldwide, more women are employed outside the household today than in previous decades. In all regions except northern Africa and western Asia, women constitute at least one-third of the workforce. In middle- and low-income nations, self-employment, part-time work, and home-based jobs have offered some opportunities for women, but these forms of employment typically provide little security, few benefits, and low income and sometime bring hazardous materials into the women's homes. Outside employment frequently is not much better: These jobs are often concentrated in a few occupations within employment sectors that are characterized by low wages, little or no authority and benefits for employees, and virtually no job security. From high-income nations (such as the United States and Japan) to low-income nations, women typically earn less than men in the paid workforce, and women's opportunities to attain the better-paid positions are restricted.

Problems of economic opportunity for women are further complicated by high rates of global illiteracy and low levels of educational attainment. It is estimated that women account for two-thirds of the more than 875 million illiterate people worldwide, and there is little hope that these numbers will be reduced in the early decades of the twenty-first century (United Nations, 2000). Levels of educational attainment in some countries among those women who are literate is also problematic. As the recent case of Afghanistan has shown, girls and women actively seek educational opportunities when they are able to do so; however, oppressive political regimes and local customs have conspired to keep women undereducated. This is a problem not only for the women but also for their children and other family members. It means that the women will be less equipped to educate their children for changing times in their nation and that the women will not have the necessary skills for becoming economically self-sufficient. Although the gender gap is closing somewhat in the United States, women worldwide still lag far behind men in educational attainment. This disparity is particularly pronounced in some countries in Africa and southern Asia.

Around the globe, women's problems—including violence, illiteracy, and lack of educational and employment opportunity—are further exacerbated by poor medical facilities and health crises such as HIV/AIDS. Although life expectancy has generally been increasing worldwide, AIDS has taken a devastating toll on the population in regions such as southern Africa, particularly among girls and women. Women now account for almost half of all HIV/AIDS cases worldwide, and in regions with high HIV prevalence such as southern Africa, young

Social Problems in Global Perspective

Box 4.3

Missing Girls: Facing Up to the Problem in China

> When a son is born, Let him sleep on the bed,
>
> Clothe him with fine clothes, And give him jade to play...
>
> When a daughter is born, Let her sleep on the ground,
>
> Wrap her in common wrappings, And give broken tiles to play...
>
> —*Traditional Chinese thinking on the divergent value of male and female babies as recorded in the 1000-700 B.C. "Book of Songs"(quoted in Baculinao, 2004)*

This age-old bias against girls, combined with a one-child-only policy implemented in China in 1980, has brought about a major social problem for that nation: Where have all the girls gone?

Recently, government officials in China announced that their country was going to intensify its efforts to protect girls and to address the gender imbalance of newborn babies (BBC News, 2004). What is the gender imbalance? In 2004, the ratio of births in China was close to 120 boys for every 100 girls, as contrasted with the international average of about 106 boys to every 100 girls (Baculinao, 2004).

How did this imbalance occur? With China's strict family planning policies, which in rural areas may bring stiff fines for having more than one or two children, some parents want to prevent female births so that they can count on their sons to help them out with the work and to take care of them when they are older. Since the 1990s, there has been a significant increase in the rate of sex-selective abortions, perhaps because of the greater availability of ultrasound scanners that provide couples with a way to learn the sex of a fetus. Sex-selective abortion refers to a situation in which an individual or couple decide to terminate a pregnancy solely on the basis of the sex of the fetus. This type of abortion does not include situations where an abortion is chosen for health-related concerns or any reason other than that the fetus is a member of the unwanted sex (Weiss, 1995). As Wu Zheng, a villager in China, stated, "If you're rich and you want a big family, you can just keep having babies until you get a boy. But if you can't pay the fines, or you don't want all the burdens of a large family, then you go get the [ultrasound] test" (quoted in Eckholm, 2002:A3). In some cases, the parents kill their infant daughters (infanticide). Other parents sell their infant girls to families who want a daughter, who want the girls to eventually work for them, or who want future brides for young sons (CBS News.com, 2003).

Today, sex ratios at birth and in the first years of life show that millions of female fetuses and infant girls are "missing" in China and a number of other nations (Watts and Zimmerman, 2002). Practices such as sex-selective abortion, infanticide, and the selling of baby girls constitute a global social problem that is harmful not only to girls and women in China but that also produces adverse effects on these nations—and their citizens—for decades to come. One problem is the rapidly growing number of human trafficking cases where young men have tried to "purchase" a wife because so few women are available for marriage. Another issue is China's increasing crime rate because of 80 million low-status, unmarried males who constitute a "floating" or transient population with little chance of forming their own families and who attempt to improve their lot in life through violent and criminal behavior (Baculinao, 2004).

One effort to reduce the imbalance between male and female infants, Girl Care Project, attempts to encourage the birth of girls and to encourage people to show more respect for females. The program speaks out against female infanticide, pre-birth sex selection, and other types of behavior that are detrimental to baby girls. Some analysts argue, however, that much of the Girl Care Project is framed in male-oriented terms that suggest the scarcity of females must be rectified for the benefit of men, so that they will be able to find sex partners and wives, rather than focusing on the many contributions that women can make in society (Baculinao, 2004). Will China's efforts be successful? Some hope to see the sex ratio reach a normal level by 2010 in that nation, but it remains to be seen if long-held beliefs and values will shift rapidly enough to bring about this change.

Questions to Consider

1. Do people in the United States equally value male children and female children? What examples can you give to support your answer?
2. How do social policy and law influence what we think of as the "ideal family"?
3. Should the government of any nation play a central role in determining how many children a couple should have? In determining the gender of the children?

women are at greater risk than young men. Another major problem is the high rate of maternal mortality (dying from pregnancy-related causes). Inadequate health care facilities and lack of access to the medical care that does exist contribute to high rates of maternal mortality and shorter life expectancies for many women. The disparities in maternal mortality vary widely across regions. According to a United Nations report, an African woman's lifetime risk of dying from pregnancy-related causes is 1 in 16; in Asia, 1 in 65; and in Europe, 1 in 1,400.

As concern increases among people in the United States and other high-income nations about threats of global terrorism, war, and economic instability, political and economic leaders often turn their attention to issues other than the rights of women, but as some women's advocacy groups have pointed out, the problems of girls and women worldwide are the problems of all people.

IS THERE A SOLUTION TO GENDER-RELATED INEQUALITY?

Although the rights and working conditions of women in the United States have improved during the past forty years, much remains to be done before gender equality truly can exist. In many families and in many workplaces, women's roles have changed significantly, and men's roles have undergone important changes as well. Men have greater opportunities to express their emotions, be active fathers in the lives of their children, and sometimes feel less pressure to be the sole or primary financial provider in the family. However, changes for both men and women have extracted their price as changing roles, responsibilities, and social norms have brought about new stresses and conflict within families, occupations, and the larger society. With regard to how we might specifically go about reducing or solving gender inequality, a point that was made in previous chapters bears repeating: How we view social problems affects how we think the problem should be solved.

Functionalist/Conservative Solutions to the Problem of Gender Inequality

Some functionalist analysts believe that although women and men have different gender roles, this does not necessarily mean that gender inequality exists. From this approach, the division of labor by gender ensures that important societal tasks, such as childbearing and the socialization of children, are fulfilled and that families remain stable, dependable social institutions. If we accept the assumption that *gender differences* do not necessarily equal *gender inequality,* then a social problem does not truly exist.

Most functionalists and conservative analysts acknowledge that, in day-to-day life, gender differences can *contribute* to the problems that at least some women face. By way of example, sexual harassment is more likely to be encountered by women than by men; some women may find job and pay opportunities limited by their lack of human capital in the workplace; and child-care responsibilities in some families are unequally and unfairly divided between the father and the mother. However, these are issues relating to specific aspects of social life, rather than a "catch all" category of sexism and gender inequality. In other words, there is not an all encompassing gender "problem," and there is no overall solution that would eliminate or reduce gender-related problems.

From this perspective, the primary "solution" to problems arising from gender differences is to be found in better education and in the strengthening of existing social institutions. Education contributes to women's human capital and thus to their ability to earn wages and hold positions that are comparable to those of men. Strengthening other social institutions such as the family promotes having a two-parent household in which both parents share household responsibilities and are active participants in rearing their children.

Conflict/Liberal Solutions to the Problem of Gender Inequality

Some conflict theorists view elimination of all gender-based discrimination as the primary solution for gender inequality, and they strongly disagree with functionalist/conservative ideas that efforts to promote gender equality are a threat to family life and family values. Instead, theorists using a Marxist approach state that gender equality will come about only when capitalism and patriarchy are abolished: Capitalism exploits women in the workplace, and patriarchy exploits women in the home. However, it would be extremely difficult, if not impossible, to end capitalism as we know it and to abolish all forms of male domination over women, so many theorists and political analysts look for less sweeping solutions to this problem. For example, some social activists and women's organizations establish funds to help women file lawsuits when they believe they have been the objects of sexual harassment or discrimination in the workplace. Although such activities do not solve the problem of gender inequality at the societal level, they call attention to the fact that such problems still exist, and they may help individuals and small groups of workers gain opportunities and social justice.

Liberal feminists and liberal political analysts typically believe that gender inequality can be reduced through legislation that seeks to reduce discrimination and by programs that provide more opportunities for women. These analysts emphasize the importance of equality in all areas of social life, including families, education, politics, and work. From this perspective, the best way to produce change is through government policies that are designed to bring about greater gender equality in activities ranging from college sports teams and politics to hiring and promotion in the workplace. Similarly, sexual harassment and violence against women must be actively discouraged, and perpetrators of such offenses must be vigorously prosecuted. Some liberal analysts also highlight the ways in which race, class, gender, and age intersect to produce multiple dimensions of inequality that are particularly harmful for women of color: Social change to reduce gender inequality must simultaneously deal with issues of race, class, and age if equality for all women is the goal.

Symbolic Interactionist Solutions to the Problem of Gender Inequality

Symbolic interactionists think that gender inequality can be reduced only when people redefine social realities and eliminate problems such as linguistic sexism. In their view, language is one way in which male superiority over women is expressed and reinforced in the culture. As a result, language should be modified so that it no longer conveys notions of male superiority and female inferiority, which are then transmitted intergenerationally through the socialization process.

Since symbolic interactionists focus on microlevel processes, one way to reduce or eliminate gender inequality is to change the process of socialization. Emphasis in popular culture on sexualized images of women contributes to the devaluation of all women, particularly those who are not young, thin, and comparable to media portrayals of what women should be like and how they should act. Similarly, the representation of men as either strong, wealthy, and powerful, or as "dudes," slackers, and evil men in media portrayals creates distorted images of men that others may seek to imitate. According to some symbolic interactionists, media representations such as these must be modified before people will truly accept the wider range of roles and responsibilities that should be available to women as well as men.

Finally, to some symbolic interactionists, gender and issues of gender inequality are—like beauty—"in the eye of the beholder," and individuals typically have their own perceptions about the social interactions that occur in their own life. Although symbolic interactionist views on the solution to gender inequality focus primarily on microlevel issues, these observations highlight the ways in which social interaction and popular culture influence not only our individual thinking but also beliefs and values that are embedded in the larger structure of society.

What do you think might reduce gender inequality in the United States? Could your solutions be applied to similar problems in other nations? Why or why not?

SUMMARY

■ *How does sex differ from gender?*

Sex is the biological aspects of being male or female; gender is the socially constructed differences between females and males. In short, sex is what we (generally) are born with; gender is what we acquire through socialization.

■ *What are the primary socializing agents?*

The key socializing agents are parents, peers, teachers and schools, sports, and the media, all of which may reinforce gender stereotypes and gender-based inequalities as they attempt to teach gender-appropriate behavior.

■ *How are sexism and patriarchy related?*

Individual and institutional sexism are maintained and reinforced by patriarchy, a hierarchical system in which cultural, political, and economic structures are dominated by males.

■ *What are some of the primary causes of gender inequality?*

Gender inequality results from economic, political, and educational discrimination against women as evidenced in gender-segregated work, which in turn results in a disparity—or wage gap—between women's and men's earnings. Even when women are employed in the same job as men, on average they do not receive the same (or comparable) pay.

■ *What is the second shift, and why is it a problem for women?*

The second shift is the unpaid household work performed by employed women. Many women have a second shift because of their dual responsibilities in the workplace and at home. The typical woman in the United States who combines paid work in the labor force and family work as a homemaker does not have enough hours in the average day to fulfill all her responsibilities, and many men have been unwilling or unable to pick up some of the slack at home.

■ *How do functionalist and conflict analysts explain the gendered division of labor?*

According to functionalist analysts, women's caregiver roles in contemporary industrialized societies are crucial in ensuring that key societal tasks are fulfilled. While the husband performs the instrumental tasks of economic support and decision making, the wife assumes the expressive tasks of providing affection and emotional support for the family. According to conflict analysts, the gendered division of labor within families and the workplace results from male control and dominance over women and resources.

■ *What are the major feminist perspectives and how do they explain gender inequality?*

In liberal feminism, gender equality is connected to equality of opportunity. In radical feminism, male dominance is seen as the cause of oppression. According to socialist feminists, women's oppression results from capitalism and patriarchy and women's dual roles as paid and unpaid workers. Black feminism focuses on race and class in analyzing gender inequality.

KEY TERMS

comparable worth, p. 80
contingent work, p. 78
gender, p. 70
gender bias, p. 72
gendered division of labor, p. 71
glass ceiling, p. 81
patriarchy, p. 77
pink-collar occupations, p. 78
sex, p. 70
sexism, p. 69
sexual harassment, p. 74
wage gap, p. 79

QUESTIONS FOR CRITICAL THINKING

1. Examine the various administrative and academic departments at your college. What is the gender breakdown of administrators and faculty in selected departments? Can you identify a gender-related pattern associated with women's and men's majors at your school? What conclusions can you draw about the relationship between gender and education on the basis of your observations?
2. Will the increasing numbers of women in higher education, the workplace, and the military tip the balance of power between men and women and result in greater gender equality in the future? Explain your answer.
3. What kind of study might you develop to examine the effects of children's clothing and toys on the socialization of children? How could you isolate the clothing or toy variable from other variables that influence children's socialization?
4. What steps do you think should be taken to reduce sexism and bring about greater gender equality in the United States? What resources would you need to implement your plan?

Chapter 5

Inequality Based on Age

THINKING SOCIOLOGICALLY

- How is our age related to what people expect of us? Is age always a good indicator of our abilities?
- What are some of the major problems experienced by older people?
- How do key sociological perspectives explain the aging process and how ageism contributes to social inequality?

I loved getting those calls. Since my wife passed away, I don't have any people to talk with. I didn't even know they were stealing from me until everything was gone.... One gal in particular loved to hear stories about when I was younger.... I was afraid if I didn't give her my bank information, I wouldn't have money for my heart medicine.... It's lonelier now. I really enjoy when those salespeople call. But when I tell them I can't buy anything now, they hang up. I miss the good chats we used to have.

—Richard Guthrie, a 92-year-old Army veteran, explains how he was tricked into giving banking data to telephone scam artists who then stole money from his account. (Duhigg, 2008: A1, A18)

Recent Ads Offering to Sell Lists of Older People to Telemarketers:

- Elderly Opportunity Seekers: Incredibly gullible, these buyers [have] responded to a number of different offers costing anywhere from $40 to $80 dollars that promised them big riches from following some simple money-making plan.
- Oldies but Goodies: These people are gullible. They want to believe that their luck can change and it's just a matter of catching a bit of star dust.
- Suffering Seniors is the perfect list for mailers targeting the ailing elderly who will be most responsive [4.7 million older individuals with Alzheimer's disease or cancer] (Duhigg, 2008:A1).

Only one kind of customer wants to buy lists of seniors interested in lotteries and sweepstakes: criminals.... If someone advertises a list by saying it contains gullible or elderly people, it's like putting out a sign saying, "Thieves welcome here."

—Sgt. Yves Leblanc, Royal Canadian Mounted Police (Duhigg, 2008:A1)

In one recent scandal, unscrupulous individuals stole millions of dollars from older people by purchasing lists of names and phone numbers from a company that compiles consumer information and specifically earmarks some elderly Americans as "gullible" because of their purchasing habits, willingness to gamble, or health status. How is such a scam possible? Fraud against the elderly often begins with "list brokers" who sell their prospect lists to telemarketers, often indicating a way in which the persons on the list might be gullible. The telemarketers then call persons on the list and attempt to get them to reveal pertinent bank information. If successful, the fraudulent telemarketer has checks printed with the victim's name, address, bank, and routing number on them. They deposit the checks—not signed by anyone—at a bank other than the victim's own bank and request that payment be credited to the telemarketer's account. When the bank pays the amount of the check, the illegal transaction is complete, and the victim has been successfully bilked of his or her money (Duhigg, 2008).

Previously, Mr. Guthrie's name was listed on several databases because he entered a number of sweepstakes contests. These databases were sold to thieves in Toronto, Canada, and in India over the Internet. The con artists then posed as government, banking, or insurance employees who were supposed to update the information in people's files, but they actually were gaining crucial financial information from people like Mr. Guthrie so that they could steal money from their banking and savings accounts. Preying on Mr. Guthrie's loneliness after the death of his wife, various telemarketers called him constantly and eventually tricked him into revealing information about his accounts. By the time the scam was over, the thieves had depleted all of the money in his bank and savings accounts, which amounted to more than $100,000, leaving Mr. Guthrie with no funds to purchase food, buy medicine, or pay his bills. Being ashamed of the fact that he had been conned, Mr. Guthrie did not inform law enforcement officials or his family about the problem: When past due bills began to come in and relatives noticed that he was not buying food to eat, the scam was finally revealed (Duhigg, 2008).

Con artists such as the ones who stole from Mr. Guthrie are a social problem, and his situation is not an isolated occurrence involving one "gullible" person. Many elderly persons are bilked of their life savings by unscrupulous individuals who prey on negative stereotypes of older people as weak and vulnerable. With the introduction of new information technologies during the past three decades, more older Americans are being targeted by unscrupulous Internet salespersons, telemarketers, and direct mail salespeople who routinely take advantage of them. Although a person of any age may be victimized by criminals, older individuals typically are viewed as being easier to manipulate because scam artists can prey on the victim's feelings of isolation and loneliness. In the twenty-first century, many elderly Americans already have much to deal with because of other age-related problems in society and various forms of age-based discrimination that they experience. Being crime victims further intensifies their worries that old age does not constitute the "Golden Years" that they had looked forward to when they were younger.

In this chapter, we discuss how age-based inequality has a variety of sources, and how these inequalities are exacerbated by negative stereotypes of older individuals as "gullible," "slow," or "easily tricked." These stereotypes are harmful to the individual's self image, and—if they are widely believed by the general population—they limit older people's opportunities. Age-based inequality is linked to age discrimination, which by definition involves negative and differential treatment of people over forty years of age.

AGEISM AS A SOCIAL PROBLEM

***Ageism*—prejudice and discrimination against people on the basis of age—is a social problem that particularly stigmatizes and marginalizes older people.** Gerontologist Robert Butler (1969) introduced the term *ageism* to describe how myths and misconceptions about older people produce age-based discrimination. According to Butler, just as racism and sexism perpetuate stereotyping and discrimination against people of color and all women, ageism perpetuates stereotyping of older people and age-based discrimination. Most research has therefore focused on the negative impact ageism has on older people.

Age-Based Stereotypes

There are more stereotypes about the physical and mental abilities of older people than there are about the abilities of people in any other age category. This does not mean that children and adolescents are exempt from

"My mom and dad are still very sharp."

age-based stereotypes. Comedians often refer to very young children as "crumb crunchers," "curtain climbers," and "little hellions." Animated television characters such as Bart and Lisa Simpson (*The Simpsons*) and young characters in many situation comedies and movies are simply stereotypic depictions of children and young adolescents.

Older people, however, are stereotyped in numerous ways. Some stereotypes depict them as slow in their thinking and movement; as living in the past and unable to change; and as cranky, sickly, and lacking in social value (Atchley, 2004). Other stereotypes suggest that older people are "greedy geezers," living an affluent lifestyle and ignoring the needs of future generations (Toner, 1995). When many people accept age-based stereotypes, they can affect how people vote and what types of social policies legislators enact. Negative stereotypes of older people reinforce ageism and influence how younger people interact with older people.

Although most of us do not believe that we engage in stereotypical thinking about older people, researcher William C. Levin (1988) found that college students in his study evaluated people differently on the basis of their assumed age. When Levin showed three photographs of the same man, who had been made up to appear twenty-five in the first photo, fifty-two in the second, and seventy-three in the third, to the students and asked them to evaluate these (apparently different) men for employment purposes, many students described the "seventy-three-year-old" as less competent, less intelligent, and less reliable than the "twenty-five-year-old" and the "fifty-two-year-old." Clearly, our place in the social structure changes during our life course, and if we live long enough, any of us may become the target of stereotyping and discrimination directed at older people (Hooyman and Kiyak, 2008).

Social Inequality and the Life Course

To study age and social inequality, many sociologists and social gerontologists focus on the life course—the age-based categories through which people pass as they grow older. In the United States, the life course tends to be divided into infancy and childhood, adolescence and young adulthood, middle age, later maturity, and old age. The field of gerontology examines the biological, physical, and social aspects of the aging process. We will focus primarily on ***social gerontology*—the study of the social (nonphysical) aspects of aging**—as we examine age classifications in the United States.

Childhood

Infants (birth to age two) and children (ages three to twelve) are among the most powerless individuals in society. In the past, children were seen as the property of their parents, who could do with their children as they chose (Tower, 1996). Although we have a more liberal attitude today, children remain vulnerable to problems such as family instability, poverty, maltreatment by relatives and other caregivers, and sexual exploitation.

The Children's Defense Fund (2004) points out the perils of childhood in the United States:

- one out of every six children lives in poverty
- one out of every eight children has no health insurance
- three out of every five children under age six are cared for by someone other than their parents
- three million children are reported as suspected victims of child abuse and neglect
- eight children and teens die from gunfire every day

Relatively high rates of single parenthood, a significant increase in the divorce rate in recent decades, and the fact that many parents work several jobs in an attempt to make ends meet have caused many children to face a complex array of problems and social relationships in their families. A large number of children believe that they do not receive enough attention from their parents. Raoul, an eleven-year-old Cuban American, is an example:

> I live with my mom. My dad moved to Miami when they broke up and I was about two. So I have a stepdad and a stepbrother.... My stepbrother and my mom get along, but not too good. He misses his mom. My stepdad took him because his mom was bad. And then my mom and his dad got married and we became a family. I think he would like to get his mom and dad back together 'cause he gets in trouble a lot....
>
> I've had a nice life so far, for eleven years, but I wish everybody would pay more attention to kids. That's something we really need. Sometimes grown-ups pay attention, but not a lot. They're kind of all wrapped up in their jobs and they don't really pay attention to little children. I think it wouldn't be so violent [in society] if people paid attention. (quoted in *Children's Express*, 1993:43–45)

Adolescence

Before the twentieth century, the concept of adolescence did not exist. When children grew big enough to do adult work, they were expected to fulfill adult responsibilities such as making money to support their families. Today, the line between childhood and adolescence is blurred. While some researchers define adolescence as the teenage years (ages thirteen to nineteen), others place the lower and upper ages at fifteen and twenty-four, respectively (Corr et al., 1994).

Adolescents tread a narrow path between childhood and adulthood. They are not treated as children, but they are not afforded the full status of adulthood. Early teens are considered too young to drive, to drink alcohol, to stay out late, and to do other things that are considered to be adult behavior by the media, particularly television and movies, and by members of some peer groups. Adolescents face an identity crisis in which they must figure out who they are and what they want to become. They also face difficult decisions pertaining to their sexuality and their relationships with people of the same sex and the opposite sex. Teen pregnancy and parenthood are major concerns for many adolescents.

Many adolescents must deal with conflicting demands for money and school attendance. Most states have compulsory school attendance laws that require young people to attend school from about ages six through sixteen or eighteen. However, some adolescents balk at this requirement; they cannot see what school is doing for them and would prefer to find employment. In fact, many teenagers who live in families that are trapped in poverty hold jobs to supplement the family income or support themselves. These adolescents might view being required to remain in school as a form of discrimination.

Although child labor laws allegedly control the amount of work and working conditions of young employees, recent studies show that many employed adolescents face hazardous working conditions and work more than the allowable number of hours per day. There are, for example, few restrictions on farm labor, and teenagers who harvest crops such as strawberries for thirteen hours a day, earning $2.80 per hour or less, may be exposed to harmful pesticides (Lantos, 1992). Teenagers employed in fast-food restaurants have been injured by electric knives that cut off fingers. In one case, a fifteen-year-old boy employed by a bakery died when he was pulled into a dough-mixing machine.

Unemployment rates among adolescents, particularly African-American males, are extremely high, and the available jobs are in the service sector, such as fast-food restaurants, which usually pay minimum wage or slightly above. Perceiving a lack of opportunity for themselves in the adult world, many teens, especially males, join gangs. Some social analysts suggest that we should not be surprised that individuals between the ages of fifteen and twenty-four account for almost half of all property crime arrests in the United States.

Young Adulthood

Typically beginning in the early to mid-twenties and lasting to about age thirty-nine, young adulthood is a period during which people acquire new roles and experience a sense of new freedom. However, many also experience problems finding their niche, particularly when it appears doubtful that they will have as high a standard of living as their parents had. Subsequent chapters examine a variety of issues affecting young adults, including alcohol and drug abuse, divorce, and employment instability. Many of these issues also concern people older than age forty.

Middle Age

Because life expectancy was lower in the past, the concept of middle age (age forty to sixty or sixty-five) did not exist until fairly recently. *Life expectancy*—the average length of time a group of individuals will live—increased dramatically during the twentieth century. Today, life expectancy at birth in the United States is approximately seventy-seven years, compared to only forty-seven years in 1900. Moreover, it is predicted that life expectancy will increase to about seventy-eight years by 2010 and about eighty-two years by 2050.

As people progress through middle age, they experience *senescence (primary aging)*, which results from molecular and cellular changes in the body. Some signs of senescence are visible (e.g., wrinkles and gray hair); others are not (e.g., arthritis or stiffness in connective tissue joints; a gradual dulling of senses such as taste, touch, and vision; and slower reflexes). Vital systems also undergo gradual change; lung capacity diminishes, and the digestive, circulatory, and reproductive systems gradually decline in efficiency (Atchley, 2004). In addition to primary aging, people experience *secondary aging*, which has to do with environmental factors and lifestyle choices. A MacArthur Foundation study on aging identified several factors that contribute to "successful aging," including regular physical activity, continued social connections, resiliency—the ability to bounce back readily after suffering a loss—and self-efficacy, a feeling of control over one's life. According to one gerontologist, "Only about 30 percent of the characteristics of aging are genetically based; the rest—70 percent—is not" (Brody, 1996:B9).

Some people fight the aging process by spending billions of dollars on products such as Oil of Olay, Clairol or Grecian Formula, and Buster's Magic

Tummy Tightener. Others have cosmetic surgery. In one study, an interviewee explained that she had decided to undergo liposuction (a surgical procedure in which fat is removed) because she had started to get a lot of "crepeyness" in her neck and her jowls were "coming down" owing to aging (Dull and West, 1991:57). As her remarks suggest, the United States is a youth-oriented society that tends to equate beauty, stamina, and good health with youth. Because of this, many of the changes associated with growing older are viewed as something to be avoided at all costs. Popular culture contributes to this perception by suggesting that middle-aged women become old and unattractive if they do not endeavor (and buy products) to prevent the aging process and to remain sexy (see Box 5.1 on page 96).

Whereas women in middle age may believe that they have become less sexually attractive than they were, middle-aged men tend to realize that their physical strength and social power over others are limited. As if to reinforce their awareness of the passage of time, many women and men also may have to face the fact that their children have grown and left home. However, for some people, middle age is a time of great contentment; their income and prestige are at their peak, the problems of raising their children are behind them, they are content with their spouse of many years, and they may have grandchildren who give them a tie to the future. Even so, all middle-aged people know that their status will change significantly as they grow older.

Later Maturity and Old Age

Later maturity is usually considered to begin in the sixties. The major changes associated with this stage are social. Although many people in their sixties retain sufficient physical strength to be able to carry on an active social life, their peer groups shrink noticeably as friends and relatives die. Many people in later maturity find themselves caring for people of their own age and older people.

Sociologists use an age pyramid to show the distribution of a given population by age and sex groupings at various points in time. As Figure 5.1 on page 96 shows, the United States is undergoing what some social analysts refer to as the graying of America, the aging of the population due to an increase in life expectancy combined with a decrease in the birth rate (Atchley, 2004). This is a long-term trend, and as Box 5.2 on page 99 shows, it is important to differentiate between short-term changes and long-term trends when we are comparing statistics.

Old age is usually considered to begin in one's late sixties or seventies. Although some people continue to work past age seventy, most have left paid employment by their seventieth birthday. Problems are not just social but also increasingly biological. Some physical changes, such as arteriosclerosis (the loss of elasticity in the walls of the arteries), are potentially life-threatening (Belsky, 1999). As bones become more porous, they become more brittle; a simple fall can result in broken bones that take longer to heal than those of a younger person. Strength, mobility, and height may decline; and the abilities to see, hear, taste, touch, and smell may diminish. Because taste and smell work together to allow us to enjoy food, eating may become less pleasurable and so contribute to poor nutrition in some older adults (Belsky, 1999). Although it is not true of all elderly people, the average person over age sixty-five does not react as rapidly (physically or mentally) as the average person who is younger than sixty-five (Lefrançois, 1999).

The chances of heart attacks, strokes, and cancer increase along with the likelihood of some diseases that primarily affect the elderly. Alzheimer's disease, a degenerative disease that attacks the brain and severely impairs memory, thinking, and behavior, may be the best-known example. People who have this disease have an impaired ability to function in everyday social roles; in time, they cease to be able to recognize people they have always known, and they lose all sense of their own identity. Finally, they may revert to a speechless childishness, at which point others must feed them, dress them, sit them on the toilet, and lead them around by the hand. Alzheimer's disease strikes one in ten people over age sixty-five and nearly half of those over eighty-five. It can last eight to twenty years, ending only with death (Lefrançois, 1999).

As older people have begun to live longer, gerontologists have come to realize that there are significant differences among the "young-old" (ages sixty-five to seventy-four), the "old-old" (ages seventy-five to eighty-four), and the "oldest-old" (ages eighty-five and older). Although more than half of all people age sixty-five and older are in the young-old category, the oldest-old category has grown more rapidly over the past three decades than has any other age group in the United States (Angier, 1995). As with other age categories, it is difficult to make generalizations about older people, as gerontologists Nancy R. Hooyman and H. Asuman Kiyak (1996:5) have noted:

> Older people vary greatly in their health status, their social and work activities, and their family situations. Some are still employed full- or part-time; most are

Social Problems in the Media

Box 5.1

Box 5.1 *(continued)*

Questions to Consider

1. What values in our society might contribute to women's fear of looking "old"? Do these same values apply to men? Why or why not?
2. What ads can you find that reaffirm the worth of women and men across age categories, racial and ethnic groupings, and class locations? Do these ads primarily emphasize the physical appearance of people? What other attributes do the ads highlight?
3. How do television programs promote ideas about what it means to be young, middle-aged, or old in America? Are middle-aged men portrayed differently from middle-aged women? If so, how?

> retired. Most are healthy; some are frail, confused, or home-bound. Most still live in a house or apartment; a small percentage are in nursing homes. Some receive large incomes from pensions and investments; many depend primarily on Social Security and have little discretionary income. Most men over age 65 are married, whereas women are more likely to become widowed and live alone as they age.... It is ... impossible to define aging only in chronological terms, since chronological age only partially reflects the biological, psychological, and sociological processes that define life stages.

As a spokesperson for the AARP (formerly the American Association of Retired Persons) has said, "Age is simply not a measure of competence in any way, shape or form and people need to be judged on their own individual characteristics" (quoted in Berke, 1996:E1). Or, in the words of Virginia McCalmont, age eighty-five, "I feel like I'm about 30 or 40—until I look in a mirror. So I try not to look in the mirror" (quoted in Kolata, 1996b:B10).

Death and Dying

In previous generations, death was a common occurrence in all stages in the life course, but today most deaths occur among older people. Because of medical advances and the increase in life expectancy, death is now viewed as that stage of the life course that usually occurs in old age. According to social gerontologists, the increased association of *death* with the process of *aging* has caused many people to deny the aging process and engage in ageism as a means of denying the reality of death, particularly their own (Atchley, 2004). Euphemisms, such as "pass away" or "sleep," are often used to refer to death by those who are trying to avoid its reality. Researchers have found, however, that many people do not actually fear death itself as much as they fear the possibility of pain and suffering, loss of control, and the consequences of their death for survivors (Marshall and Levy, 1990). Given a chance to choose, most people would choose a painless death over prolonged physical and mental deterioration and the prospect of being a burden on their families. Some researchers have also found that older people have less fear of death than younger people do; others have found that education and religious beliefs are important factors in how people view death and dying (Kalish, 1985). However, little research has focused on attitudes toward death among African Americans, Latinas/os, and other people of color, so it is important to be wary of overgeneralizations about the fear of death (see Kalish and Reynolds, 1981).

There are three widely known frameworks for explaining how people cope with the process of dying: the *stage-based approach*, the *dying trajectory*, and the *task-based approach*. The stage-based approach was popularized by Elisabeth Kübler-Ross (1969), who proposed five stages in the dying process: (1) denial ("Not me"), (2) anger ("Why me?"), (3) bargaining and asking for divine intervention to postpone death ("Yes me, but..."), (4) depression and sense of loss, and (5) acceptance. According to some social scientists, Kübler-Ross's study is limited because she focused primarily on the attitudes of younger people who had terminal illnesses. These scientists argue that the same stages might not apply to older people who believe that they have already lived a full life (Marshall, 1980; Kalish, 1985).

In contrast to Kübler-Ross's five stages, the concept of the *dying trajectory* focuses on the perceived course of dying and the expected time of death. From this perspective, not all people move toward death at the same speed and in the same way. A dying trajectory may be sudden

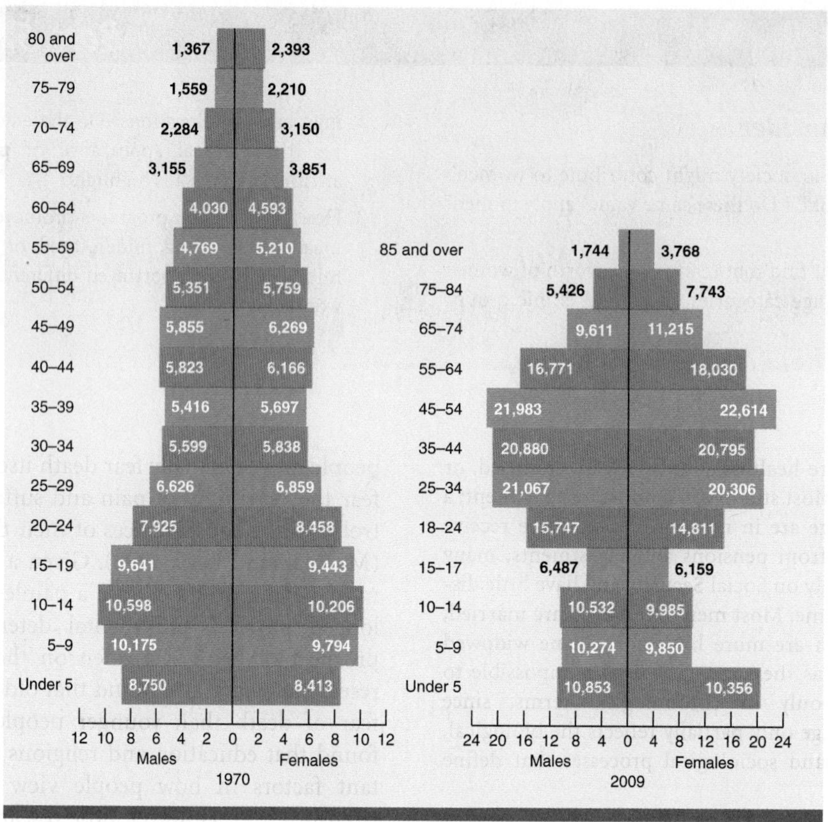

■ ***Figure 5.1*** ***U.S. age pyramid by age and sex, 1970 and 2009***

Source: U.S. Census Bureau, 2009. (1-Year Estimates)

(e.g., a heart attack) or slow (e.g., lung cancer) and is usually shaped by the condition causing death. A dying trajectory involves three phases: the acute phase, in which maximum anxiety or fear is expressed; the chronic phase, in which anxiety declines as the person confronts reality; and the terminal phase, in which the dying person withdraws from others (Glaser and Strauss, 1968).

The *task-based approach* suggests that daily activities can still be enjoyed during the dying process and that fulfilling certain tasks makes the process of death easier on everyone involved, not just the dying person. *Physical tasks* are performed to satisfy bodily needs and to minimize physical distress. *Psychological* tasks help to maximize psychological security, autonomy, and richness of experience. *Social tasks* sustain and enhance interpersonal attachments and address the social implications of dying. *Spiritual tasks* are performed to identify, develop, or reaffirm sources of spiritual energy and to foster hope (Corr et al., 1994). Most important in any approach are the rights of the dying person and how care is provided to him or her.

Technological advances in medicine have helped to focus attention on the physical process of dying and, in recent years, the needs of dying patients and their families. Many people are choosing to sign a *living will*—a document stating their wishes about the medical circumstances under which their life should be allowed to end. Some people reject the idea of being kept alive by elaborate life-support systems and other forms of high-tech medicine, choosing to die at home rather than in a hospital or nursing home. The hospice movement has provided additional options for caring for the terminally ill. ***Hospices*** **are organizations that provide a homelike facility or home-based care (or both) for people who are terminally ill.** Some hospices have facilities where care is provided, but hospice is primarily a philosophy that affirms life, not death, and offers holistic and continuing care to the patient and family through a team of visiting nurses, on-call physicians, and counselors. Home care enables many people to remain in familiar surroundings and maintain dignity and control over the dying process (Corr et al., 1994). Sophia Mumford summarizes the feelings of many older people about death:

> I'm afraid of one thing. I want my death to be dignified. My fear is that something will cause me to live past the point where my life has value. I don't want to live on.... From now on, if life says it's leaving, I'm not doing anything about it. If I get a bad pain and it's diagnosed as cancer, then I won't wait, I'll go. I'm ready, because I feel I've had a good life. (Terkel, 1996:429)

Given Mumford's feelings, which mirror the feelings of many others, and a variety of other factors, it is not altogether surprising that older people around the world have a relatively high rate of suicide.

Social Problems and Statistics

Box 5.2

Drawing the Wrong Conclusion

In its 2000 survey, the U.S. Census Bureau found that for the first time, the population age sixty-five years and above did not increase at a faster rate than the rate of the total U.S. population (see Figure 5.2 for comparison). On the basis of this statistic, it might be easy for us to draw the conclusion that the "graying of America" (aging of the population) has already occurred and will decrease in the future. However, the slower growth rate in the number of people age sixty-five and above actually resulted from low rates of birth in the 1920s and early 1930s and is not an accurate reflection of the future. The Census Bureau predicts that the increase in the older population will be at least double that of the total population during the current decade (2000–2009) and will increase to more than three times the growth in the total population beginning in the year 2011. By 2050, people age sixty-five and over will account for one in five individuals in the United States, so the "graying" trend is far from over.

Whenever we compare statistics at different points in time or over different periods of time, we need to keep in mind what this example shows: that a short-term change is not necessarily proof of a long-term trend.

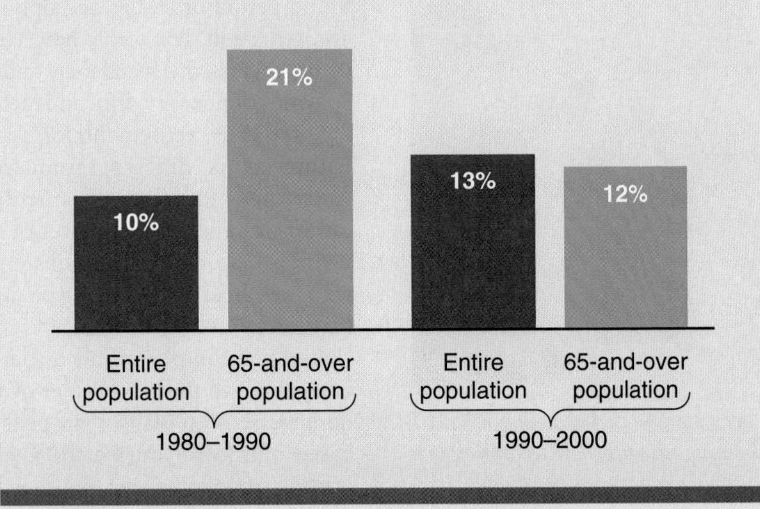

■ Figure 5.2 U.S. population growth

PROBLEMS ASSOCIATED WITH AGING

Age stratification—the inequalities, differences, segregation, or conflict between age groups—occurs throughout the life course (Atchley, 2004). It is a determinant of how education, jobs, and other scarce resources and opportunities are allocated in society. But age stratification also limits roles and opportunities. Many people automatically assume that at age fourteen, a person should be in school; that at age thirty, a person should be married; and that at age sixty-five, a person should retire from full-time employment. Such perceptions about age may create problems for people in all age categories, but the problems typically are most pronounced among older people.

Workplace Discrimination

Despite the Age Discrimination in Employment Act that was passed in 1967 to protect workers age forty and above from unfair employment practices based on age, many subtle forms of age discrimination in the workplace remain. Some employers prefer younger workers to older workers, whom they believe have health problems, poor motivation, and low ability. Employers might hire younger workers because they believe that they can pay them less than older workers and make more demands on their time and energy. Older employees might find that their employers have downgraded their job descriptions, have failed to promote them or grant them raises, and sometimes are trying to push them out of their jobs so that cheaper workers can be hired. Despite the negative stereotypes, some employers have found it profitable to hire older employees. Travelers Insurance Company of Hartford, Connecticut, and Days Inn of America, a major hotel chain, both hire a number of older workers, whom they have found to have lower rates of absenteeism than younger workers (valic.com, 2003). Days Inn has also found that older people quickly learned to use computers, stayed on the job three times as long, and booked more reservations than their younger counterparts did (Foreman, 1993). Still, at some point, retirement becomes an expected part of the life course for many individuals.

Older people have been stereotyped as being behind the times and not keeping up with new technology. However, this stereotype is inaccurate for people, like the couple shown here, who use computers regularly for sending e-mail, gathering information, and paying bills.

Retirement and Changing Roles

Retirement is the institutionalized separation of an individual from her or his occupational position, with continuation of income from a retirement pension based on prior years of service (Atchley, 2004). In the past, people in many occupations and professions (including tenured faculty members at universities, police officers, and firefighters) faced mandatory retirement at age sixty-five regardless of their health or desire to continue working. It was simply assumed that everyone experienced a decline in physical and mental ability at a specific age. Changes in compulsory retirement laws have led many people to view retirement less as a sign of decline than as a newfound period of leisure and opportunity for adaptation and reflection. For some, however, adapting to less income, increased dependency, and the loss of roles and activities can be very difficult (Atchley, 2004).

Typically, retirement for African Americans and Latinos/as is different from retirement for white Americans. Racial discrimination in the workplace diminishes the earning power of many minority group members, so older Latinos/as and African Americans who have held lower-paying positions throughout their lifetime often have no employer-sponsored or self-purchased pension plans, only Social Security. When these individuals in the bottom tier of the dual labor market do have pension plans, their pension checks, which are based on income during the working years, are small, leading some to believe that they have no choice but to work into their seventies (Uchitelle, 1995).

Women who are over sixty-five today are less likely to have access to pension and Social Security income in

Retirement is a time of leisure and reflection if it comes by choice and the individual is healthy and financially prepared. These individuals are participating in a water exercise class for their health and recreation. However, for some people, adapting to less income, increased dependency, and the loss of roles can be difficult.

their own name than younger women who are currently employed will. However, many employed women—as well as many men—are losing out on traditional pension coverage because of changes in the economy and the workplace. Many unionized industrial jobs that used to provide pension coverage have virtually disappeared, and more women than men are employed as part-time workers, who are less likely to have pension coverage than full-time workers. In fact, companies rarely offer pension plans or health insurance to part-time, contingent, and temporary workers.

Health, Illness, and Health Care

At age ninety-three, Malcolm Clarke plays doubles tennis four times a week and sails his boat; he also shops and cooks for himself (Brody, 1996). Although Clarke attributes his longevity and good health to "luck," studies show that many older people are not developing the disabling diseases that were common in the past, and the vast majority function quite well. Improvement in the health status of older people has been attributed, at least in part, to better education (knowing what to do and not do to stay healthy), nutrition, and health insurance through Medicare and sometimes Medicaid (see Box 5.3 on page 102). Because most people over age sixty-five are covered by Medicare, health care coverage is a greater problem for the young and middle-aged. Lack of health insurance affects substantial portions of all age groups below age sixty-five.

Malnutrition and disease are life-threatening problems for some older people. Although malnutrition is sometimes related to poverty, nutritionists suggest that the condition is pervasive even among older people who are not poor, perhaps in part because diminishing senses make food less appealing. Malnutrition is a problem for 25 percent of people over age sixty-five, and studies have found that 15 percent of all older people consume fewer than 1,000 calories per day.

About seven of every ten deaths among older people are due to heart disease, cancer, or stroke. By far, the leading killer of persons over age sixty-five is heart disease. Among white women, cancer has overtaken heart disease as the leading cause of death; breast cancer and lung cancer are responsible for nearly half of all cancer deaths in women. African-American women are more likely than white women to die from strokes or diabetes. Men, particularly African Americans, are highly vulnerable to cancer of the prostate, a reproductive gland. Many people over age eighty-five die of multiple organ failure or pneumonia, which has been referred to as the "old folk's friend" (Angier, 1995). Recently, the number of AIDS cases has risen at a faster rate among older people than among other age groups, and AIDS educators are seeking to make older people aware of the risk of becoming infected with HIV, the virus that causes AIDS (Anderson, 2005).

People age sixty-five and older account for about one-third of all dollars spent on health care, and this figure is expected to rise dramatically with the aging of the U.S. population. Many believe the cost problems associated with health care will be further intensified by the feminization of aging—the increasing proportion of older women—because these women, on average, have a greater likelihood of being poor and having no spouse to care for them (Weitz, 2004). Chapter 10 discusses health care issues in greater detail.

Victimization

Although older people are in fact less likely than younger people to be victims of violent crime, they fear this type of crime more than people in other age categories do. However, as discussed at the beginning of this chapter, older people are often the targets of other types of crime. Con artists frequently contact them by mail or telephone to perpetrate scams that often promise prizes or involve a "stockbroker" selling a "hot" stock or other commodity (Hays, 1995). In one scam, an older person would receive a message to call a number beginning with the area code 809 for important information about a family member who had become ill or died or about a prize he or she had won. Callers were charged $25 per minute for the call and often were kept on the line for an extended period of time. Some people received phone bills for more than $100.00 per call, not knowing that the 809 area code covers the Dominican Republic and is a pay-per-call number that is not covered by U.S. regulations regarding 900 numbers (City of Austin, 1996).

Another form of victimization is elder abuse. According to the U.S. Administration on Aging, the abuse may be physical, emotional, sexual, financial, and/or the result of neglect. According to the best available estimates, between 1 and 2 million people over age sixty-five in the United States have been injured, exploited, or otherwise mistreated by someone on whom they depended for care (see National Center on Elder Abuse, 2005). Many analysts believe that elder abuse is underreported because people who know of the abuse are unwilling to report it and older people who are the victims are either too ashamed or afraid to notify authorities. As a government official noted, "Seniors are . . . embarrassed to admit that a relative, a loved one, a child is abusing them, either physically or financially, or neglecting or exploiting them" (*Austin American-Statesman*, 1995:A6). Although some analysts initially believed that younger people were likely to exploit older people who were psychologically and economically dependent on them, just the opposite has often proven true: Younger people are more likely to exploit elders on whom they themselves are dependent (Atchley, 2004).

Family Problems and Social Isolation

Older people can easily become socially isolated from their families. Younger members who once asked for advice stop asking, perhaps because they think that their older relatives are out of touch or perhaps because of some miscommunication. Sometimes, younger family members feel unduly burdened by the concerns of

Social Problems and Social Policy

Box 5.3

their elders, which don't seem truly important to them. For one reason or another, older people come to believe (rightly or wrongly) that they are isolated from the rest of the family.

In 2000, 49 percent of women and 21 percent of men age seventy-five and above lived alone, the difference reflecting the fact that fewer males attain that age (Fields and Casper, 2001). Many older people live alone voluntarily, but others live by themselves because they are divorced, widowed, or single. Living alone is not the equivalent of social isolation. Many older people have networks of friends with whom they engage in activities. To a large degree, the extent to which they associate with others has to do with social class: People with more money are able to pursue a wider array of activities and take more trips than are those with more limited resources.

Perhaps one of the saddest developments in contemporary society is the growing number of older people who are homeless. Some older homeless people have lived on the streets for many years; others have become homeless because they have been displaced from low-income housing such as single-room occupancy (SRO) hotels. In recent years, many SROs in cities such as New York and San Francisco have been replaced by high-rise office buildings, retail space, and luxury condominiums. Older people who are homeless typically lack nutritious food, appropriate clothing, adequate medical care, and a social support network. They tend to die prematurely of disease, crime victimization, accidents, and weather-related crises such as a winter blizzard, when an individual without shelter can freeze to death on a park bench. Fortunately, the picture is not this bleak for many older people who remain in residences they have occupied for many years.

Housing Patterns and Long-Term Care Facilities

Many people mistakenly assume that most older people live in long-term care facilities such as nursing homes. In fact, however, only about 5 percent of older people live in any kind of institution. More than people of any other age category, older people are likely to reside in the housing in which they have lived for a number of years and own free and clear of debt. White Americans are significantly more likely than African Americans and Latinas/os to own their homes, and married couples are more likely to own their homes than are single people. Because of the high cost of utilities, insurance, taxes, and repairs and maintenance, older women, who are more likely to live alone than are older men, are at a distinct disadvantage if they attempt to maintain their own homes (Hooyman and Kiyak, 2008).

Box 5.3 *(continued)*

health services, long-term care such as nursing homes, or custodial or nonmedical service such as adult day care or homemaker services (Atchley, 2004). Because of these serious gaps in coverage, older people who can afford it often purchase *medigap policies*, supplementary private insurance.

Some low-income older people are eligible for Medicaid, a joint federal-state *means-tested welfare program* that provides health care insurance for poor people of any age who meet specific eligibility requirements. People over age sixty-five constitute about 13 percent of Medicaid recipients but account for more than 40 percent of the program's total expenditures (Hooyman and Kiyak, 2008). However, Medicaid recipients have been stigmatized because Medicaid is a "welfare program." Furthermore, because the administrative paperwork is burdensome and reimbursements are so low—typically less than one-half of what private insurance companies pay for the same services—many physicians refuse to take Medicaid patients.

In sum, Medicare and Medicaid provide broad coverage for older people, but both programs have major flaws: (1) they are extremely expensive, (2) they are highly vulnerable to costly fraud by health care providers and some recipients, and (3) they typically provide higher-quality health care to older people who are white and more affluent than to African Americans, Latinos/as, people with disabilities, and individuals living in rural areas (Pear, 1994). Chapter 10 discusses U.S. health care in greater detail.

What impact do you think the aging of the U.S. population will have on government-funded programs such as Medicare and Medicaid? What solutions can you suggest for providing more adequate health care for older people at less cost?

Assisted living facilities are a popular housing option for many middle- and higher-income older people because they provide needed services but offer more home-like settings and greater freedom than other long-term care facilities such as nursing homes.

Some low-income older people live in planned housing projects that are funded by federal and local government agencies or private organizations such as religious groups. Older people with middle and upper incomes are more likely to live in retirement communities (for example, Sun City) or in *congregate housing*, which provides amenities such as housekeeping, dining facilities, and transportation services (Hooyman and Kiyak, 2008). In recent years, religious organizations and for-profit corporations have developed *multilevel* facilities, which provide services ranging from independent living to skilled nursing care all at the same site. Such facilities often are quite expensive. Residents may have to purchase their housing units, pay a substantial initial entry fee, and/or sign life care contracts, which provide for nursing home care if it becomes necessary.

Today, only 1.1 percent of people age sixty-five to seventy-four live in nursing homes; however, the percentage increases to 18.2 percent among people age eighty-five and over. Because of their greater life expectancy, higher rates of chronic illness, and higher rates of being unmarried, women are disproportionately represented among the 1.5 million people who reside in nursing homes (Hetzel and Smith, 2001). According to social gerontologists, the primary factors related to living in a nursing home are age (eighty-five and over), being female, having been in the hospital recently, living in retirement housing, having no spouse at home, and having some cognitive or physical impairment that interferes with the activities of daily living (Greene and Ondrich, 1990).

White Americans constitute more than 90 percent of all nursing home residents; 7 percent are African American; 2.5 percent are Latino/a; and fewer than 0.5 percent are Native American or Asian or Pacific American. Ethnic minorities may be underrepresented because their families are less willing to institutionalize them or because more caregivers exist to help meet the needs of older relatives. Racial discrimination and a lack of consideration of residents' ethnic backgrounds also might contribute to the perception among many subordinate-group members that nursing homes are no place for their older family members. Sociologists have found that many nursing home assistants, who often are recent immigrants to the United States, do not speak the same language as the residents (Diamond, 1992). Although some nursing home facilities may be excellent, others have undergone extensive media scrutiny and public criticism for violations of regulations and harmful practices such as elder abuse. As a result, many people select home care, adult day care, or assisted living for older relatives rather than institutional settings, which tend to depersonalize individuals and "reify the image of age as inevitable decline and deterioration" (Friedan, 1993:516).

PERSPECTIVES ON AGING AND SOCIAL INEQUALITY

Although each of the major sociological perspectives focuses on different aspects of aging and social inequality, they all provide insights into how people view the aging process and how ageism contributes to social inequality in society.

The Functionalist Perspective

According to functionalists, dramatic changes in such social institutions as the family and religion have influenced how people look at the process of growing old. Given this, both the stability of society and the normal and healthy adjustment of older people require that they detach themselves from their social roles and prepare for their eventual death (Cumming and Henry, 1961). Referred to as *disengagement theory*, this theory suggests that older people want to be released from societal expectations of productivity and competitiveness. At the same time, disengagement facilitates a gradual and orderly transfer of statuses and roles from one generation to the next instead of an abrupt change, which might result in chaos. Retirement policies, then, are a means of ensuring that younger people with more up-to-date training (for example, computer skills) move into occupational roles while ensuring that older workers are recognized for years of service (Williamson et al., 1992).

Critics of this perspective object to the assumption that disengagement is functional for society and that all older people want to disengage even though they are still productive and gain satisfaction from their work. In fact, according to some social analysts, disengagement as evidenced by early retirement policies has been dysfunctional for society. Social Security and other pension systems have been strained by the proportionately fewer workers who are paying into the plan to support an increasing number of retired workers. Contrary to disengagement theory, these analysts say, older people may disengage not by choice but because of a lack of opportunity for continued activity.

The Symbolic Interactionist Perspective

Symbolic interactionist perspectives on aging and inequality focus on the relationship between life satisfaction and levels of activity. The interactionist *activity theory* is based on the assumption that older people who are active are happier and better adjusted than are less active older persons. According to this theory, older people shift gears in late middle age and find meaningful substitutes for previous statuses, roles, and activities (Havighurst et al., 1968). Those who remain active have a higher level of life satisfaction than do those who are inactive or in ill health (Havighurst et al., 1968). In contrast to disengagement theory, activity theory suggests that older people must deny the existence of old age by maintaining middle-aged lifestyles for as long as possible. However, an eight-year study found that death rates among older Mexican Americans and whites were not significantly reduced by engaging in such activities as hunting or fishing or by attending movies and sporting events (Lee and Markides, 1990).

Other symbolic interactionist perspectives focus on role and exchange theories. Role theory poses the question "What roles are available for older people?" Some theorists note that industrialized, urbanized societies typically do not have roles for older people (Cowgill, 1986). Other theorists note that many older people find active roles within their own ethnic group. Although their experiences might not be valued in the larger society, they are esteemed within their ethnic subculture because they are a rich source of ethnic lore and history. According to sociologist Donald E. Gelfand (1994), older people can exchange their knowledge for deference and respect from younger people.

The Conflict Perspective

Conflict theorists focus on the political economy of aging in analyzing the problems of older people in contemporary capitalistic societies. From this perspective, class constitutes a structural barrier to older people's access to valued resources, and dominant groups attempt to maintain their own interests by perpetuating class inequalities. According to conflict theorists, aging itself is not the social problem. The problem is rooted in societal conditions that older people often face without adequate resources such as income and housing. People who were poor and disadvantaged in their younger years become even more so in old age. Women age seventy-five and over are among the most disadvantaged because, having often outlived their spouses and sometimes their children, many in this age group must rely solely on Social Security (Harrington Meyer, 1990).

In a capitalist economy, older people are viewed as a growing consumer market for services and products that promise to reduce the effects of aging.

In the capitalist system, middle- and upper-income older people might be viewed as consumers to whom a range of products and services can be sold specifically based on the consumers' age. As the "baby boomers," those born between 1946 and 1964, grow older, advertisers focus on them as a target audience for pharmaceutical products, such as pills to reduce the effects of arthritis, high blood pressure, and sexual impotency, and for foods and automobiles that are thought to be appropriate for older individuals (*The Economist*, 2002). In this way, people over age sixty might be more positively portrayed as having active and healthy lifestyles, but these lifestyles appear to be available only to those people who purchase the particular products or services that are being advertised. According to some conflict analysts, this is yet another way in which people are exploited by capitalist societies, in which the primary emphasis is on profits rather than on the real needs of individuals.

IS THERE A SOLUTION TO AGE-BASED INEQUALITY?

As we have seen, technological innovations and advances in medicine have contributed to the steady increase in life expectancy in the United States. Advances in the diagnosis, prevention, and treatment of diseases associated with old age, such as Alzheimer's disease, may revolutionize people's feelings about growing older (Atchley, 2004). Technology may bring about greater equality and freedom for older people. Home-based computer services such as banking and shopping make it possible for older people to conduct their daily lives without having to leave home to obtain services. Computerized controls on appliances, lighting, and air conditioning make it possible for people with limited mobility to control their environment. Technology also brings recreation and education into the home. For example, Senior Net is a nationwide computer network that encourages discussion of diverse topics and provides hands-on classes in computer use. Robotics and computer systems may eventually be used by frail older people who otherwise would have to rely on family or paid caregivers to meet their needs or move to a nursing home. However, class is again a factor: More than 75 percent of home accessibility features currently are paid for by users or their families (Hooyman and Kiyak, 2008).

Economic concerns loom large in the future as baby boomers begin to retire in about 2010, bringing about a dramatic shift in the ***dependency ratio*—the number of workers necessary to support people under age fifteen and over age sixty-three.** Instead of *five* workers supporting one retiree by paying Social Security taxes, *three* workers will be providing support for each retiree. Some social analysts suggest that increased age-based inequality may bring about a "war" between the generations (Toner, 1995). However, advocates of *productive aging* suggest that instead of pitting young and old against each other, we should change our national policies and attitudes. We should encourage older people to continue or create their own roles in society, not to disengage from it. Real value should be placed on unpaid volunteer and caregiving activism, and settings should be provided in which older people can use their talents more productively (Hooyman and Kiyak, 2008).

To distribute time for family responsibilities and leisure more evenly throughout the life course, changes must occur in the workplace. Today, younger workers struggle to care for their families, without the support of employers in many cases, and leisure is associated with old age and "being put out to pasture." But people who have had no opportunity to engage in leisure activities earlier in their life are unlikely to suddenly become leisure-oriented. Employment, family responsibilities, and leisure must become less compartmentalized, and changes in technology and employment may make this possible. At present, however, it is difficult for most people to have *free time* and *money* at the same time.

Functionalists suggest that changes must occur in families and other social institutions if we are to resolve problems brought about by high rates of divorce, single-parent households, and cohabitation by unmarried couples, which tend to reduce the individual's commitment to meet the needs of other family members. These analysts argue that individuals must be socialized to care for an increasing number of living generations in their family and must be given economic incentives such as tax breaks for fulfilling their responsibility to children and older relatives. Because adult children might have to provide economic and emotional support for aging parents and grandparents at the same time as they are caring for their own children, more community services are needed, particularly for adult children who are "suitcase caregivers" for frail, elderly relatives living many miles away (Foreman, 1996). Communities should create or expand existing facilities such as day-care centers for children and seniors; provide affordable housing; and build low-cost, community-based health facilities.

Other social analysts suggest that people need to rely more on themselves for their retirement and old age. Younger workers should be encouraged to save money for retirement and not to assume that Social Security, Medicare, and other entitlement programs will be available when they reach old age. As conflict theorists have pointed out, however, many young people do not have jobs or adequate income to meet their current economic needs, much less their future needs. A 1995 Gallup poll found that people with children under age eighteen indicated that they were saving primarily for their children's education and did not have adequate resources to put aside money for retirement (Golay and Rollyson, 1996).

From the conflict perspective, age-based inequality is rooted in power differentials, and short of dramatic changes in the structure of political and economic power in society, the only way for older people to hold onto previous gains is through continued activism. However, this approach does not take into account the fact that some older people have benefited more than others from social programs such as Medicare, Social Security, and the Older Americans Act (the federal law that authorizes and funds direct services such as senior centers, nutrition programs, and referral services). Groups such as the Gray Panthers and the AARP work for passage of specific legislation that has benefited many older people. Nevertheless, older people as a category are devalued in a society that prizes youth over old age and in a social structure that defines productivity primarily in terms of paid employment.

According to interactionists, however, individuals who maintain strong relationships with others and remain actively involved throughout their lifetime have reason to be optimistic about life when they reach old age. An example is Victor Reuther, age eighty-one, a founder—with his brother Walter—of the United Auto Workers:

> I still have hope. When you lose hope, you bury yourself. I'm not ready for that. I have too much work to do yet. I never did find it comfortable to sit in a rocking chair complaining about my aches and pains. I think society has a lot of aches and pains. We shouldn't become obsessed with them. We've got to be pragmatic and say: There's a challenge. Let's change. Let's turn things over. (Terkel, 1996:96)

SUMMARY

■ *What is ageism and why is it considered a social problem?*

Ageism is prejudice and discrimination against people on the basis of age. Ageism is a social problem because it perpetuates negative stereotypes and age-based discrimination, particularly against older people.

■ *What is the life course and why are different stages problematic for some people?*

The life course is generally divided into infancy and childhood, adolescence and young adulthood, middle age, later maturity, and old age. During infancy and childhood, we are dependent on other people and so are relatively powerless in society. Adolescence is a stage in which we are not treated as children but also are not afforded the full status of adulthood. In young adulthood, we acquire new roles and have a feeling of new freedom but also may have problems ranging from alcohol and drug abuse to employment instability that may make life complicated. During middle age, we begin to show such visible signs of aging as wrinkles and gray hair, and roles begin to change in the workplace and family as children leave home. In later maturity, we increasingly find ourselves involved in caring for people of our own age and older people. Problems of older adults vary widely because of the diverse needs of the young-old (ages sixty-five to seventy-four), the old-old (ages seventy-five to eighty-four), and the oldest-old (ages eighty-five and older).

■ *What types of problems do older people face today?*

Despite laws to the contrary, older workers may experience overt or covert discrimination in the workplace. Retirement brings about changing roles and a loss of status for those older people whose identity has been based primarily on their occupation. For some older people, malnutrition, disease, and lack of health care are life-threatening problems. Older people may become the victims of scams by con artists and elder abuse by family members or nursing home personnel. For most older people, moving into a nursing home represents a loss of autonomy.

■ *How do people cope with the process of dying?*

Three explanations have been given for how people cope with dying. Kübler-Ross identified five stages that people go through: (1) denial, (2) anger, (3) bargaining, (4) depression, and (5) acceptance. However, the dying trajectory suggests that individuals do not move toward death at the same speed and in the same way. The task-based approach suggests that daily activities can still be enjoyed during the dying process and that fulfilling certain tasks makes the process of death easier on everyone involved (not just the dying person).

■ *How do functionalist and symbolic interactionist explanations of age-based inequality differ?*

According to functionalists, disengagement of older people from their jobs and other social positions may be functional for society because it allows the smooth transfer of roles from one generation to the next. However, symbolic interactionists suggest that activity is important for older people because it provides new sources of identity and satisfaction later in life.

■ *How do conflict theorists explain inequality based on age?*

According to conflict theorists, aging itself is not a social problem. The problem is rooted in societal conditions that older people often face when they have inadequate resources in a capitalist society. In the capitalist system, older people are set apart as a group that depends on special policies and programs.

KEY TERMS

ageism, p. 92
dependency ratio, p. 106
hospices, p. 98
social gerontology, p. 93

QUESTIONS FOR CRITICAL THINKING

1. If you were responsible for reducing ageism, what measures would you suggest to bring about greater equality? What resources would be required to fulfill your plan?
2. Should retirement be compulsory for neurosurgeons (brain surgeons), airline pilots, police officers, and firefighters? Explain your answer.
3. Does disengagement theory or activity theory more closely reflect how you plan to spend your later years? What other approaches to aging can you suggest?
4. Will future technological advances change how people view growing old? Explain your answer.

Chapter 6

Inequality Based on Sexual Orientation

THINKING SOCIOLOGICALLY

- Why is sexual orientation an emotionally-charged legal and social issue in the United States?
- What types of discrimination are based on sexual orientation?
- How do biological and psychological explanations differ from sociological perspectives on sexual orientation?

Many times throughout my life people have been shocked when they find out my father is gay. "I had no idea," they say. "You'd never know just by looking at you." They make me feel like a rare species as their eyes scan me for any abnormalities they missed that could have tipped them off. Ladies and Gentlemen, step right up! Look closely at the child of a gay dad. No horns! No tail! In fact, she could pass for anybody's child.

—Author Abigail Garner (2005:13) explains in her book,* Families Like Mine, *how she and other children of gay parents feel when they are treated differently and stigmatized by individuals who are sure they know what the child of a gay parent* should *look like.

It's hard to grow up under a microscope. As kids, we are expected to talk about very adult issues—sex, civil rights, legal and political issues. What other situations are there where people talk to kids and then legislate from there?

—Jesse Gilbert, age 30, describes how the children of gay or lesbian parents feel when they are constantly asked about their parents. (Garner, 2005:13)

The comments by these two individuals show the extent to which the children of lesbian and gay parents may be stereotyped by individuals who identify themselves as heterosexual. When Abigail Garner (above) was five years old, her parents divorced, her father came out as gay, and she found herself in the middle of many discussions regarding the children of people who are lesbian, gay, bisexual, or transgendered (LGBT). As a result, she wrote a book describing the unique issues and problems that such children face, including negative stereotyping and homophobia at school. Garner's research shows that LGBT parents and their children experience discrimination based on ***sexual orientation*—a preference for emotional-sexual relationships with individuals of the same sex (homosexuality), the opposite sex (heterosexuality), or both (bisexuality)** (Lips, 1993). People in LGBT families have been widely criticized because some people believe that gay and lesbian parents are not only different from heterosexual parents but that they are inferior to them because of their sexual orientation, lifestyle, and acceptance of non-traditional family values (O'Briant, 2008). The terms *homosexual* and *gay* are most often used in association with males who prefer same-sex relationships; the term *lesbian* is used in association with females who prefer same-sex relationships. Heterosexual individuals, who prefer opposite-sex relationships, are sometimes referred to as *straight* (e.g., "What's it like to be straight?"). It is important to note, however, that heterosexual people are much less likely to be labeled by their sexual orientation than are people who are gay, lesbian, or bisexual.

What criteria do social scientists use to classify individuals as gay, lesbian, or bisexual? In a definitive study of sexuality that was published in the mid-1990s, researchers at the University of Chicago established three criteria for identifying people as homosexual or bisexual: (1) sexual *attraction* to persons of one's own gender, (2) *sexual involvement* with one or more persons of one's own gender, and (3) *self-identification* as a gay man, lesbian, or bisexual (Michael et al., 1994). According to these criteria, then, engaging in a homosexual act does not necessarily classify a person as homosexual. In fact, many respondents in the Chicago study indicated that although they had had at least one homosexual encounter when they were younger, they no longer were involved in homosexual conduct and never identified themselves as lesbians, bisexuals, or gay.

NATURE AND EXTENT OF INEQUALITY BASED ON SEXUAL ORIENTATION

How many homosexuals and bisexuals are there in the United States? Although the U.S. Census Bureau keeps track of numbers in sex, age, and racial-ethnic categories, it does not specifically count people on the basis of their sexual orientation. Estimates of the homosexual population range from fewer than 2 percent to more than 10 percent of all U.S. men and from about 1 percent to at least 5 percent of all U.S. women; however, the exact percentages are not known (see Box 6.1). Based on the latest available data from the American Community Survey, approximately 8.8 million gay, lesbian, and bisexual persons reside in the United States with the states of California, Florida, New York, Texas, and Illinois having the largest LG... lations (Gates, 2006). Few studies have attempted t... transgendered persons—individuals who exhibit appearances or behaviors that are the opposite of their birth sex. In other words, their *gender identity* differs from their *physical sex*. Although many transgendered persons identify themselves as heterosexual, they still experience anti-gay prejudice and discrimination because outsiders assume that they are homosexual (DignityUSA.com 2008).

Although homosexuality has existed in most societies throughout human history, for most of the last two thousand years, there have been groups—sometimes entire societies—that considered homosexuality "a crime against nature," "an abomination," or "a sin" (Doyle, 1995:224). Most societies have norms pertaining to ***sexuality*—attitudes, beliefs, and practices related to sexual attraction and intimate relationships with others**. The norms are based on the assumption that some forms of

Social Problems and Statistics

Box 6.1

How Many Gays and Lesbians?

According to sociologist Joel Best (2001:87), "bad statistics often take on a life of their own." In other words, when statistics are frequently repeated, they are assumed to be valid and are taken for granted. Best uses the discrepancy between estimates of how many gays and lesbians live in the United States as one example. Gay and lesbian activists frequently argue that at least 10 percent of the population is homosexual and therefore constitutes a significant group that must be reckoned with in this country. Family values activists assert that the percentage is much less—as low as 1 or 2 percent.

The earliest estimates of the number of gays and lesbians residing in the United States arose from studies by biologist Alfred Kinsey and his colleagues in the 1930s and 1940s. On the basis of interviews with more than 11,000 people, the researchers developed the so-called Kinsey Report (Kinsey et al., 1948), which suggested that about 10 percent of the male population and a slightly lower percentage of the female population in the United States was more or less exclusively homosexual at some point between the ages of 16 and 55. Although Kinsey's research has been widely criticized because it included a much higher proportion of prisoners (who did not have options for heterosexual sexual encounters), middle-class whites, and college-educated people than resided in the general population, the 10 percent figure became widely accepted.

Other studies have produced estimates quite different from that of the Kinsey Report. On the basis of a 1992 survey of more than 3,000 noninstitutionalized U.S. residents, for example, Edward O. Laumann and colleagues (1994) concluded that about 2.8 percent of adult males and 1.4 percent of adult females in this country self-identify as gays or lesbians and that about 4.9 percent of males and 2.7 percent of females had engaged in homosexual conduct at some point since age 18.

The differences in these various estimates can be attributed to a number of factors. First, how representative is the population that is being surveyed in comparison with the overall population that the statistics allegedly represent? Second, how accurate are the responses with regard to the conclusions that are drawn from those responses? By way of example, in face-to-face interviews, will people sometimes give inaccurate responses with regard to questions about things such as sexual orientation or conduct? Either of those factors (and many others) can greatly skew the results of the survey. As a result, we should be careful in assuming that statistics about such subjects are accurate.

As gay rights advocates suggest, however, whether homosexuals make up 2 percent or 20 percent of the U.S. population, the central issue is not about numbers but rather about reducing discrimination. Social policy should seek to do this, regardless of the exact number of people the policy affects.

attraction and sexual relationships are *normal* and appropriate and others are *abnormal* and *inappropriate*. In many societies, homosexual conduct has been classified as a form of ***deviance*—a behavior, belief, or condition that violates social norms**. This classification can make people targets of prejudice, discrimination, and even death. Extreme prejudice toward gay men and lesbians is known as ***homophobia*—excessive fear or intolerance of homosexuality**. According to sociologists, homophobia is a *socially determined prejudice*, not a medically recognized *phobia* (Lehne, 1995). Homophobia is intensified by the ideology of *compulsory heterosexism*, a belief system that denies, denigrates, and stigmatizes any gay, lesbian, or bisexual behavior, identity, relationship, or community. Somewhat like institutional racism and sexism, compulsory heterosexism is embedded in a society's social structure and maintained by ideologies that are rooted in religion and law (Herek, 1995).

IDEOLOGICAL BASES OF INEQUALITY BASED ON SEXUAL ORIENTATION

Social analysts such as Bruce Bawer (1994:81), an author and cultural critic, believe that homophobia differs significantly from other forms of bigotry:

> In a world of prejudice, there is no other prejudice quite like [homophobia]. Mainstream writers, politicians, and cultural leaders who hate Jews or blacks or Asians but who have long since accepted the unwritten rules that forbid public expression of those prejudices still denounce gays with impunity. For such people, gays are the Other in a way that Jews or blacks or Asians are not. After all, they can look at Jewish or black or Asian family life and see something that, in its chief components—husband, wife, children, workplace, school, house of worship—is essentially a variation of their own lives; yet when they look at gays—or, rather, at the image of gays that has been fostered both by the mainstream culture and by the gay subculture—they see creatures whose lives seem to be different from theirs in every possible way.

According to Bawer, heterosexuals cannot identify with the daily lives of lesbians and gay men, who—unlike them—exist as identifiable categories primarily because there is such strong antigay prejudice in the United States. In fact, the stereotypic beliefs that dominant (heterosexual) group members hold about gay men and lesbians are a major impediment to achieving gay rights and reducing inequalities based on sexual orientation (Nava and Dawidoff, 1994).

Stereotypic beliefs about lesbians and gay men often equate people's sexual *orientation* with sexual *practice*. For example, all gay men and lesbians, regardless of the nature and extent of their sexual activity, are stereotyped as "sex obsessed, sexually compulsive, and sexually predatory" (Nava and Dawidoff, 1994:32). Media depictions often reinforce stereotypes of gay men as sexual exploiters or "limp-wristed sissies," while lesbians are "stomping macho soldiers" (Nava and Dawidoff, 1994:32). Recently, some television shows have sought to bring gay lifestyles into prime-time programming. Although a few of these shows have perpetuated negative stereotypes about lesbians and gay men, others have attempted to change public perceptions about issues related to sexual orientation (see Box 6.2).

Religion and Sexual Orientation

Most of the major religions of the world—Judaism, Christianity, Islam, and Hinduism, as well as Confucianism—historically have regarded homosexuality as a sin. Indeed, the only major world religion that does not condemn homosexuality is Buddhism (Dynes, 1990). Religious fundamentalists in particular denounce homosexual conduct as a sign of great moral decay and societal chaos. In the Judeo-Christian tradition, religious condemnation of homosexuality derives from both the Hebrew Scriptures (e.g., Genesis 19 and Leviticus 18:33) and the New Testament (e.g., Romans 1:26–27 and I Corinthians 6:9) (Kosmin and Lachman, 1993).

Since the early 1990s, same-sex marriages and the ordination of "practicing" lesbians and gay men have been vigorously debated by various religious organizations. For example, the Vatican has directed Roman Catholic bishops in the United States to oppose laws that protect homosexuals, promote public acceptance of homosexual conduct, or give gay relationships equal footing with traditional, heterosexual marriage. However, many Roman Catholics disagree with the directive, stating that it is based on the faulty assumption that lesbians and gay men seek to influence the sexual orientation of children or youths with whom they live or work, that gay people are erotically attracted to every person of their own gender, and that they cannot control their sexual impulses in same-sex environments (cited in Bawer, 1994). Roman Catholics are not the only religious group debating same-sex marriage and the ordination of lesbians and gay men: The Southern Baptist Convention voted to expel two congregations—one for blessing the union of two gay men and the other for licensing a gay divinity student to preach. Although Baptist congregations usually are allowed to be autonomous, religious leaders determined that this autonomy did not

Social Problems in the Media

Box 6.2

Getting Better All the Time? Representations of Gay Life on TV

> When we give up on what was, well that's when things we thought improbable or impossible, even, happen right before your eyes.
>
> —*"Kitty" (a character played by Calista Flockhart) on ABC's prime time network series,* Brothers & Sisters, *explains how she found herself—a former conservative television pundit who strongly objected to gay marriage—presiding at the wedding (civil commitment ceremony) of Kevin, her gay brother, in the show's season finale (Gilbert, 2008).*

Unlike past controversies that have surrounded some prime time network televisions programs showing gay characters coming out, kissing, getting married, or adopting children, recent episodes on series such as *Ugly Betty* and *Brothers & Sisters* have produced little public controversy. The wedding of Kevin and Scotty on *Brothers & Sisters* (shown in May 2008) was the first same-sex commitment ceremony of series regulars shown on American network television. Although cable television programs (such as *Six Feet Under* and *The L Word*) have dealt with such issues previously, the major networks had been slow to embrace change in this regard even though corporate executives knew that a significant number of their viewers were "gay-friendly" and that advertisers would like to reach this audience. In fact, record numbers of viewers tuned in to see Kevin and Scotty's ceremony and to admire the couple's four-tier wedding cake, which was decorated with flowers, blackberries, and a cake topper with two men wearing formal attire (rather than the traditional one featuring a bride and groom). In the show's storyline, only Scotty's parents overtly expressed displeasure over the union, and they choose not to attend the ceremony (Keck, 2008).

Are issues such as gay marriage or same-sex adoptions becoming less controversial to media audiences? There is a lack of consensus about the answer to this question. However, unlike controversies generated by earlier shows such as *Dawson's Creek* and *Roseanne*, which showed gay or lesbian kisses and drew network boycotts by viewers, hate campaigns, and withdrawal of support by major advertisers, the "Prior Commitments" episode showing the gay commitment ceremony on ABC barely created a buzz among media critics and viewers. According to one media critic, for example, "While gay marriage can still be a polarizing political issue, the realities of gay life—coming out, kissing, weddings—have become normalized in popular culture enough to pass by almost unnoticed on prime time" (Gilbert, 2008).

Do shows such as this constitute a significant change in how gay men and lesbians are depicted in prime time television programming? Although the writers of some television series now include one or more gay characters in the permanent cast of their show, the actual number of these characters overall on the networks continues to decline. According to a study conducted by the Gay & Lesbian Alliance Against Defamation (GLAAD), lesbian, gay, bisexual, and transgender scripted representations (as opposed to reality shows) on prime time broadcast television have improved in quality but not in quantity: The actual number of these characters on the networks continues to decline. Among the findings of the study were these:

- LGBT representations account for only 1.1 percent of all series regular characters on prime time broadcast networks even though they have reached an all-time high on scripted cable programming.

(continued)

Popular television series such as Brothers and Sisters *have featured more gay, lesbian, bisexual, and transgendered characters in recent years. Does this mean that problems associated with sexual orientation will soon be eliminated? Why or why not?*

Box 6.2 (continued)

- Only one LBGT person of color was a series regular during the 2007–2008 prime time television season.
- Most of the LGBT characters are found on a single network, ABC—home of *Brothers & Sisters* and *Ugly Betty*, which includes both the openly gay Marc and transgender Alexis in major roles (GLAAD, 2007a).

As this study suggests, some positive changes have occurred in regard to LGBT representations on network and cable television channels, including the introduction of Logo, a lesbian and gay cable network, by the popular MTV network. GLAAD has also noted that the positive representations of gay characters on shows such as *Ugly Betty, Brothers & Sisters*, and another ABC hit, *Desperate Housewives*, may be partly attributed to the fact that the creators and/or Showrunners of these series are all openly gay individuals (GLAAD, 2007b).

Despite these positive changes, a number of media analysts believe that much remains to be done in regard to the manner in which gay, lesbian, bisexual, and transgendered characters are portrayed in media and popular culture. For example, some television shows and films with a gay or lesbian character present a one-dimensional representation of the individual that focuses only on the person's sexual orientation or some quirk or mannerism supposedly associated with the "gay lifestyle," such as being heavily into fashion or standing in a certain way. According to one analyst, the best way to portray gay characters is so "their sexuality is not a punch line to laugh at or something used to make the other characters—or the audience—feel uncomfortable" (Jensen, 2007). In this regard, we have a long way to go both in media representations of gays and lesbians and in their treatment in everyday life: These individuals are often viewed as one-dimensional people rather than as whole persons who possess many different—and praiseworthy—attributes and talents.

How do you think that the portrayal of people, specifically in relation to their sexual orientation, might be improved on television, in films, and in other forms of popular entertainment? What positive and negative examples can you give of media portrayals of people based on their sexual orientation?

extend to "acts to affirm, approve or endorse homosexual behavior" because these acts are deemed to be "contrary to the Bible on human sexuality and the sanctity of the family" (cited in Kosmin and Lachman, 1993:230). Episcopalians have been debating for two decades whether or not "practicing homosexuals" should be ordained. In 2003, the confirmation of Gene Robinson—the first openly gay bishop in the Episcopal Church's history—as bishop of New Hampshire threatened to split the U.S. denomination apart and to distance it from the worldwide Anglican Communion, to which it belongs.

Still, increasing numbers of lesbians and gay men are carving out their own niches in religious organizations. Some gay men and lesbians have sought to bring about changes in established religious denominations; others have formed religious bodies, such as the Metropolitan Community Church, that focus on the spiritual needs of the gay community. Even so, many gay men and lesbians believe that they should not have to choose between full participation in their church and committed same-sex relationships (Dunlap, 1996).

Law and Sexual Orientation

Throughout U.S. history, moral and religious teachings have been intertwined with laws that criminalize homosexual conduct. It is important to note that the law deals with homosexual *conduct* differently from the way in which it deals with *homosexuality*. To be a homosexual is not a crime, but to engage in homosexual conduct is a crime in some states. Although only a few states today have *sodomy laws* that criminalize oral or anal intercourse between persons of the same sex, about twenty states have laws pertaining to "deviant sexual conduct," "crimes against nature," or "unnatural intercourse." Under these laws, people can be imprisoned for oral or anal intercourse. According to lesbian and gay rights advocates, these laws are unconstitutional or indefensible for two reasons: (1) If the acts are conducted between consenting adults in *private*, any reported violation invades the privacy of their relationship; and (2) in some states, this conduct becomes a crime only if it is between persons of the same sex. However, in 1986, in *Bowers v. Hardwick*, the U.S. Supreme Court upheld state laws banning sodomy whether or not the conduct is between persons of the same sex. Thus, in effect, the Court ruled that people do not have a constitutionally protected right to engage in private homosexual conduct. For homosexuals, the Court's ruling virtually eliminates protection for sexual activities and creates the impression that gay or lesbian couples have no privacy rights (Aday, 1990). In fact, Justice Harry A. Blackmun's dissenting opinion in this case stated that the Supreme Court had invited the state to "invade the houses, hearts and minds of citizens who choose to live their life differently" (cited in Nagourney, 1996:E4).

Since *Bowers v. Hardwick*, the Supreme Court has been asked to rule on civil rights issues pertaining to lesbians and gay men. In 1996, the Court struck down an initiative that Colorado voters had passed, which banned all measures protecting gay men and lesbians against discrimination (Nagourney, 1996). The initiative was a reaction to ordinances passed by such Colorado municipalities as Boulder, Denver, and Aspen that barred discrimination against lesbians and gay men (N. A. Lewis, 1995). Many gay rights issues, including those pertaining to same-sex marriages, are won or lost on a case-by-case or state-by-state basis, and some gay rights advocates believe that the fight for equality is far from over (Bawer, 1994).

DISCRIMINATION BASED ON SEXUAL ORIENTATION

As the campaigns for equal rights and an end to antigay discrimination have progressed, more people have come forward to declare that they are gay, lesbian, or bisexual and to indicate their support for gay organizations. Many lesbian or gay couples have sought the statutory right to marry, to obtain custody of their children if they are fit parents, to adopt, and to have their property pass to one another at death—in sum, to do all the things that people in heterosexual marriages are permitted to do. However, because ideas about marriage and the family are at the core of many people's moral or religious objections to homosexuality, gay marriage is still among the most controversial social issues today.

Lack of Marital Rights

In most states, gay and lesbian couples cannot legally-recognized marital relationships either b ause the states have passed constitutional amendments that limit marriage to a union between a man and a woman or because legislators have passed statutes that restrict marriage to two persons of the opposite sex. At the time of this writing, same-sex marriage in the United States is recognized in only two states, California and Massachusetts. Thus, many same-sex partners who have united but are unable to legally marry have chosen to cohabit. *Cohabitation* refers to the practice in which partners live together in a sexual relationship where they assume the same responsibilities as a "married couple" but are not considered by law to have all of the rights and privileges of those who are considered to be legally "married."

Some cities and states have given legal recognition to the concept of a ***domestic partnership*****—a household partnership between two individuals of the same gender who live together in a long-term relationship of indefinite duration and share a common domestic life but are not legally married or joined by a civil union.** Initially, some gay rights advocates saw the recognition of domestic partnerships as a major step forward because it was believed that same-sex partners would derive more of the rights and benefits, such as health insurance coverage through employers, that were provided to heterosexual married couples. However, gay and lesbians quickly found that certain rights came only with a marriage license and that there was strong opposition to efforts by unmarried lesbian or gay couples to attempt to exercise such rights as joint parenting through birth or adoption; the right to file joint income tax returns; legal immigration and residency for partners from other countries; benefits such as annuities, pensions, and Social Security for surviving spouses; wrongful death benefits for surviving partners; and immunity from having to testify in court against a spouse.

Because of the many limitations placed on domestic partnerships and the desire to be legally married, many same-sex couples in the United States have chosen to get married in countries such as Canada, Belgium, Spain, and the Netherlands, which provide legal recognition for same-sex unions. Other couples have chosen to marry in states such as Massachusetts

Although several states have legalized same-sex marriages, controversy continues over the rights of gay and lesbian couples in the United States. The men shown here were married, along with about 50 other gay or lesbian couples, in the state of Massachusetts shortly after that state legally sanctioned same-sex marriage.

or California, where same-sex marriages are currently recognized. It should be noted, however, that the U.S. federal government does not recognize same-sex marriages performed in other countries or in states such as California and Massachusetts because of the Defense of Marriage Act passed by Congress in 1996. This law denies federal recognition of same-sex marriages and allows states to ignore unions that are legalized elsewhere. Currently various advocacy groups across the United States continue their efforts to get same-sex marriage laws revoked in California and Massachusetts and to bring passage of an amendment to the U.S. Constitution that would define marriage as strictly a union between one man and one woman (see Box 6.3).

As battles over same-sex marriage have continued in states such as California, some analysts have compared the discrimination faced by lesbian and gay couples with that of earlier bans on interracial marriage in the United States. In deciding a recent case regarding same-sex marriage in the California Supreme Court, for example, the Chief Justice quoted from that court's 1948 decision in *Perez v. Sharp* that struck down a state ban on interracial marriage: "The essence of the right to marry is freedom to join in marriage with the person of one's choice" (quoted in Liptak, 2008:A10). However, opponents of same-sex marriage argue that this comparison is not valid because they believe marriage has nothing to do with *race* and everything to do with the union of *a man and a woman* (Liptak, 2008). It remains to be seen what the longer-term implications of the California Supreme Court's decision and similar ones will be for the future of marital rights for gay and lesbian couples. Yet another murky area of rights that contributes to inequality based on sexual orientation is the issue of parental rights in the United States.

Parental Rights

There are as many as 5 million lesbian mothers and 3 million gay fathers in the United States. An estimated 6 million to 14 million children have a gay or lesbian parent (Patterson, 1992). Sometimes, when a gay father or lesbian mother has previously had a child with an opposite-sex partner, the other biological parent seeks custody of the child on the grounds that the lesbian or gay parent is "unfit" because of sexual orientation. In several widely publicized cases, lesbian mothers lost custody of their children when their fitness was challenged in court by ex-spouses or the children's grandparents (Gover, 1996a). Gay fathers sometimes face double jeopardy in child custody struggles: Both their sexual orientation and the widespread belief that women make better parents can work against them (Gover, 1996a).

Parental rights are a pressing concern for gay or lesbian partners who are raising children together, particularly when only one partner is legally recognized as the parent or guardian. Many couples rely on legal documents such as special powers of attorney, wills, and guardianship agreements to protect both partners' rights, but these documents do not have the legal force of formal adoption (Bruni, 1996). As more lesbian couples choose donor insemination to become parents, issues arise about the rights of nonbiological gay parents, whose claims often are the least recognized (Gover, 1996c). In recent court custody cases, the nonbiological parent has had no standing because he or she has neither biological nor legal ties to the child. Some lesbian and gay couples draft their own parenting contracts, but for the most part, these agreements are not enforceable in court and can be revoked by the biological parent at any time (Gover, 1996c). As more states allow unmarried partners—whether gay or straight—to adopt children, more same-sex couples will probably seek joint legal custody of their children. However, the process is extremely time consuming and expensive and involves an invasion of personal privacy (Bruni, 1996).

Many gay men and lesbians experience discrimination when they seek to become foster parents or to adopt a child. Widespread myths about the "homosexual lifestyle" lead to the notion that children living with

Social Problems and Social Policy

Box 6.3

Should We Amend the U.S. Constitution to Define "Marriage"?

> Hello. My name is Michael, and I am 15 years old and a sophomore at West Springfield High School. I live... with my mother, who is a lesbian. I wanted to thank you for being here because a lot of people have been talking about "gay marriage" and the proposed amendment banning it.... The people who wrote this amendment are basically saying that families that have gay and lesbian parents—like mine—aren't real families. Not only are they not real families...but the supporters of the amendment want to take away the few rights and protections that our families might obtain through local governments.... I am here today because I believe in America and the freedoms with which the country was founded. The Constitution was written by the people, for the people, and some of those people are gay. Writing discrimination into the Constitution is simply wrong and goes against the spirit of the document. That's not what America is about. It's about freedom, and I, for one, think every family should have the freedom and the right to be a family.
>
> *—High school student Michael Cooper explaining to Congress why he opposes the proposed Federal Marriage Amendment to the U.S. Constitution (Cooper, 2004)*

Should two people of the same sex be allowed to marry each other? There have been several roadblocks placed in the way of same-sex marriages in the United States. First, when it appeared that some states were about to legalize gay marriage, Congress enacted the Defense of Marriage Act ("DOMA") in 1996 to ensure that no state would be required to recognize a same-sex marriage that was conducted under the laws of another state. Second, as some city and state officials began issuing permits and conducting same-sex marriages, antigay–marriage advocates strongly argued that the United States needed a constitutional amendment to ban same-sex marriages throughout the nation. Wording of the proposed Federal Marriage Amendment states that a marriage must consist only of the union between one man and one woman, and that no other union shall be construed as a marriage.

Proponents of the amendment argue that since the U.S. Constitution requires that each state give "full faith and credit" to actions lawfully taken under the laws of another state, the courts might hold that a statute such as DOMA could not override that constitutional requirement and that same-sex partners who became married in a state that permits such unions would have to be accorded the rights of a married couple in every other state. Proponents therefore argue that a federal definition of marriage needs to be stated in the Constitution.

(continued)

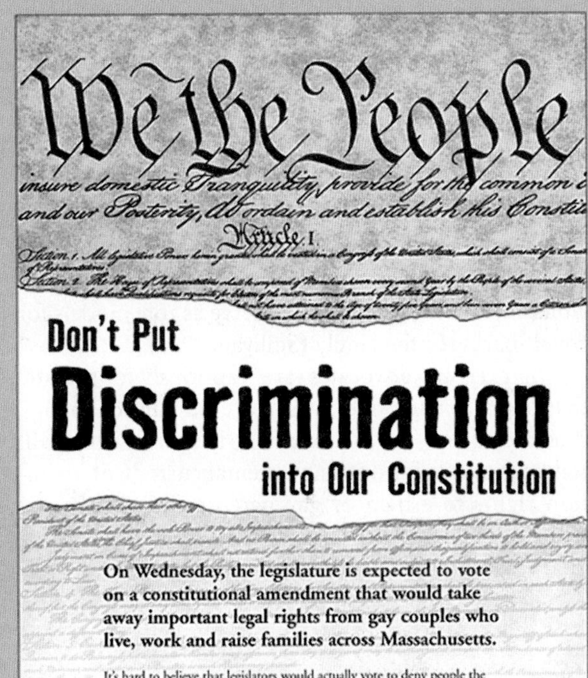

Box 6.3 *(continued)*

Some opponents of the amendment—such as Michael—argue that gays and lesbians should have the right to marry each other if they so desire. However, not all opponents of the amendment favor same-sex marriage: They are "states rights" advocates who believe that the definition of what constitutes a marriage is an issue best left to the people of each state, rather than to the federal government. According to this school of thought, the Constitution was established to promote individual freedoms rather than to impose moral judgments of what is right and wrong, and it should remain that way (Barr, 2004).

In order for the Federal Marriage Amendment to become law, two-thirds of the Congress and three-fourths of the states must approve this change to the Constitution. Over the past 200 years, only twenty-seven Constitutional amendments (out of more than 14,000 that were proposed) have been adopted (Rios, 2004). Should the Federal Marriage Amendment become number twenty-eight? What do you think?

Questions for Critical Thinking

1. Would the Federal Marriage Amendment primarily limit individuals' freedom of choice or would it be in the best interests of the country to have a national definition, stated in the Constitution, of what constitutes a legal marriage in the United States?
2. Do you agree with Michael's statement that the Federal Marriage Amendment amounts to "writing discrimination into the Constitution"? Why or why not?

lesbian or gay parents may witness immoral conduct or be recruited into homosexuality (Singer and Deschamps, 1994). In fact, research shows that children raised by lesbian or gay parents typically are well adjusted, and the parents often serve as role models for equal sharing in the family (Sullivan, 1996).

Gay rights advocates are cautiously optimistic that social norms and laws are gradually changing. They hope that, in time, sexual orientation alone will not be grounds for denying parental custody or visitation rights to esbian or gay parents and that courts will rule solely on the basis of which parent can provide a better home for the child.

Housing Discrimination

In recent years, opponents of gay rights have worked to pass state constitutional amendments that would remove any existing protection afforded to gay men, lesbians, and bisexuals against discrimination in housing, public accommodations, and other areas of life. Carrying signs that say, for example, "God Made Adam and Eve, NOT Adam and Steve," opponents of gay rights maintain that they are not "bashing gays" but rather upholding the family (Dunlap, 1995:10).

Some lesbian and gay people are denied housing because they are gay; others are evicted from apartments where they have lived for some period of time. Even those who successfully rent or purchase property tend to remain targets of discrimination from some heterosexual residents, building managers, and custodial personnel, as Bruce Bawer explains:

> When two gay people decide to move in together, they commit themselves to insult and discrimination and attack. At one apartment building in which [a male partner] and I lived, the superintendent spit on me one day without provocation; at our next address, members of the building staff, not knowing that I understood Spanish, joked with one another in my presence about the maricones (faggots). Living alone, most gay people can conceal their sexuality; living together, a gay couple advertises theirs every time they step out of the house together. (Bawer, 1994:254)

Discrimination in Medical Care

Like housing, medical care is not exempt from discrimination based on sexual orientation. Studies by the American Medical Association have found that some physicians do not ask about patients' sexual orientation, and many lesbians and gay men do not tell (*JAMA*, 1996). As a result of their failure to ask, when physicians make diagnoses, they may overlook diseases that gay men or lesbians are more prone to contract. For example, the risk of developing anal cancer is 25 to 84 times higher for gay men than it is for heterosexual men (*JAMA*, 1996). Gay men also have a greater likelihood than heterosexual men of acquiring gastrointestinal and rectal diseases.

Some physicians and nurses adopt a judgmental stance when dealing with gay and lesbian patients. One study of 100 nurses teaching in nursing programs found that 34 percent believed that lesbians are "disgusting" and 17 percent believed that lesbians molest children (Stevens, 1992). Other physicians and nurses might provide reduced care to gays and lesbians or deny them medical care altogether (*JAMA*, 1996). For example, lesbians might be at risk for terminal breast or ovarian cancer because some doctors do not provide adequate information about the importance of early cancer detection through routine gynecological examinations and mammography screening (Gessen, 1993).

Probably the most controversial topic in health care for gay men, lesbians, and bisexuals is HIV/AIDS. Although physicians, dentists, nurses, and other health professionals might learn about treating patients who are HIV-positive, many feel inadequate to deal with these patients' psychological and social needs. Today, HIV/AIDS is the third leading cause of death among African Americans between the ages of twenty-five and thirty-four and the sixth leading cause of death for Latinos/as and non-Latino/a whites in this age group. Women now account for about one out of every four new cases of HIV/AIDS in the United States (The Henry J. Kaiser Family Foundation, 2004). Despite the prevalence of HIV/AIDS among gay men and bisexuals in certain age groups, many medical professionals do not inform their patients about the risks associated with various types of sexual conduct and intravenous drug use or about measures that can be taken to prevent exposure to sexually transmitted diseases and HIV. Although HIV/AIDS has been referred to as "the gay disease," social analysts suggest that it should be viewed as *everyone's* problem.

Occupational Discrimination

Fearing that they might be stigmatized or discriminated against in the workplace, many gay and lesbian people do not reveal their sexual orientation (Woods, 1993). Their fears have some ground in reality. Despite laws in many states prohibiting discrimination in employment on the basis of sexual orientation, openly lesbian and gay people often experience bias in hiring, retention, and promotion in private and public sector employment. More than 100 major companies have stated that they do not discriminate on the basis of sexual orientation. Nevertheless, studies show that about two-thirds of gay employees in private sector employment (e.g., small businesses and large corporations) have witnessed some type of hostility, harassment, or discrimination at their place of employment (Singer and Deschamps, 1994). Many chief executive officers are reluctant to put a lesbian or gay man at the top of the corporate hierarchy, and some employees express concern about working around gay men and lesbians (Woods, 1993). Many who do not reveal their sexual orientation to coworkers are subjected to a general disparagement of gays, as Brian, a gay executive in a large New York corporation, explains:

> I was in an office with the boss and another person who is my same level, and we were talking about another professional that we should probably get involved in this transaction. The person who was at the same level as me said, "Oh, he's really good, but he's a flaming faggot." What was very shocking to me was that it was an attack on this person in a professional context. You are sort of used to the way straight men sort of banter around, calling each other queer, on a social level. But it's really strange when they talk about it in a professional setting. But this person thought it was okay. I assume that he thought there were three straight men there, so he could still say these things that in mixed company he would never say. (quoted in Mead, 1994:40)

Although the Equal Employment Opportunity Commission, a federal agency, acknowledges that same-sex sexual harassment occurs in the workplace, supervisors frequently do not take it seriously. To prove sexual harassment, victims must show that the harasser targeted a specific category of people such as gay men; therefore charges of harassment reflect the victim's sexual orientation. Victims of same-sex harassment may be blamed for causing the incident. Many fear that they will lose their job if they file a grievance, even though gay rights advocates believe that sexual orientation should be irrelevant in determining whether harassment has occurred (Gover, 1996b).

Same-sex sexual harassment and blatant discrimination in hiring and promotion are also problems in public sector positions at the federal and state government level, as well as in local law enforcement agencies. Consider, for example, the blatant discrimination of the executive order signed in 1953 by President Dwight D. Eisenhower mandating that "sexual perverts" be fired from federal jobs. For many years, most law enforcement agencies and police departments did not employ lesbian or gay people. Until 1993, the Dallas police department refused to hire gay men or lesbians because of Texas sodomy laws criminalizing same-sex conduct. Today, gay and lesbian people are employed in law enforcement agencies throughout the country because of antibias policies that preclude the agencies from asking job applicants about their sexual orientation. Despite such provisions, sociologist Stephen Leinen (a former lieutenant in the New York City police department) found in his study of "gay cops" that many remain "totally closeted" for fear of how other police officers and gay people will treat them. The total secrecy among lesbians and gay men in many large police departments is illustrated by one gay police officer's surprise on learning that his partner, with whom he had worked for some time, also was gay: "I was deeply shocked when he told me. We had worked together for over three years and neither of us knew about the other. He said, 'How the hell could we have worked together for so long and neither one of us knew it?'" (Leinen, 1993:3)

In recent years, some gay advocates have encouraged people to "come out" (identify their sexual orientation) at work and to make the biases against people based on their sexual orientation known to the media and the general public so that demands for change will be met. As long as people remain "in the closet," the advocates argue, workplace discrimination will not be eliminated (Nava and Dawidoff, 1994). However, extensive media coverage about openly lesbian and gay soldiers in the U.S. armed forces has not led to lifting the ban against gays and lesbians in the military.

Discrimination in the Military

According to the U.S. military, the nation's largest employer, lesbians and gay men are unfit to serve their country, especially if they make their sexual orientation known to others. Although many closeted gay men and lesbians have served in various branches of the military over the years, the official government policy has been one of exclusion, based on the assumption that homosexuals are a security risk because they might be blackmailed by someone who finds out about their sexual orientation. Accordingly, tens of thousands of gay and lesbian military service personnel have sought to appear as conventional as possible and behave exactly like heterosexual people. This course of action often has devastating personal consequences for closeted soldiers and sailors (see Shilts, 1993).

When the Clinton administration attempted to lift the ban on gays in the military, the outcry by many military and religious leaders forced the administration to promulgate a compromise policy known as "don't ask, don't tell." Under this policy, commanders may no longer ask about a serviceperson's sexual orientation, and gay men and lesbians can serve in the military as long as they do not reveal their sexual orientation. Although some social analysts believe that the policy provides gay men and lesbians with the same opportunity to serve their country as heterosexuals have, others believe that this compromise is a form of institutionalized discrimination: "While heterosexuals would continue to enjoy their right to lead private lives and to discuss those lives freely, gays would be allowed to remain in the armed forces only so long as they did not mention that they were gay or lesbian or have relationships on or off base" (Bawer, 1994:61).

Studies by the Servicemembers Legal Defense Network appear to support the belief that the "don't ask, don't tell" policy has led to differential treatment of some gay men and lesbians in the military. Some commanders continue to ask about sexual orientation. Internal U.S. Navy documents have shown, for example, that the Navy has sought evidence of homosexual conduct if sailors have acknowledged being gay or were reported to have told friends or others that they were gay. In some cases, heterosexual women have indicated that they were falsely accused of being lesbians after they filed sexual assault or sexual harassment charges against male military personnel (Shenon, 1996b).

Victimization and Hate Crimes

Before the early 1990s, few acts of violence against gays and lesbians were ever reported in the media. Indeed, hate crimes against gay men and lesbians were not acknowledged as such, even though civil rights groups had been tracking increasing violence motivated by group prejudice for over a decade.

The brutal murder of Matthew Shepard, a gay college student in Wyoming, produced an outcry from many people. Some were concerned that hate crimes against individuals because of race, class, gender, or sexual orientation might go unpunished; others used their own beliefs or moral values to harshly judge categories of people who often are the victims of hate crimes.

Hate crimes appear to be most prevalent where homophobic attitudes and behaviors are tolerated or at least overlooked. However, some behaviors are too reprehensible to be overlooked. One of the most brutal hate crimes perpetrated against a gay man occurred when Matthew Shepard, a college student, was brutally murdered because of his sexual orientation. In 1999, Shepard's killer, a twenty-two-year-old man, was given two life sentences for beating the gay University of Wyoming student to death. Shepard had been lured from a bar by two men posing as homosexuals. They drove him to the outskirts of Laramie, Wyoming, tied him to a fence, savagely pistol-whipped him, and left him to die in a snowstorm. Had it not been for an appeal for mercy in remarks to the jury by Matthew's father, Dennis Shepard, the killer might have received the death penalty. But Dennis Shepard ended his remarks with one final comment to the killer: "You robbed me of something very precious, and I will never forgive you for that" (Matthew's Place, 1999).

The Shepard incident was not an isolated hate crime. In other incidents around the country, pipe-wielding youths yelling "Kill the faggot" beat a gay man unconscious in Laguna Beach, California; a gay man was so seriously injured in an act of "gay bashing" in Boston that doctors initially believed that he might not survive; and another gay man was killed by an antigay cruiser who had "picked up" his victim on the Internet (Meers, 1996). Lesbians have been assaulted, raped, and sometimes killed when they have been seen in public with their partners (Dunlap, 1995).

Before enactment of the Hate Crimes Statistics Act of 1990, hate crimes were classified as such only on the basis of race, ethnicity, or religion. However, during debate over the passage of the act, gay rights advocates argued that not including sexual orientation in the law created a double standard in the United States: Crimes against gay men and lesbians would be classified as "less significant, less pervasive, and less reprehensible" than crimes motivated by racial, religious, or ethnic prejudice. In contrast, some senators argued that the law gave undue protection and respectability to gay men and lesbians (Fernandez, 1991). Information that has been gathered since passage of the act shows that more than 50 percent of all reported antigay harassment and violence is perpetrated by young males age twenty-one or under (Comstock, 1991). In some situations, police officers and judges do not take hate crimes against lesbians and gay men seriously. According to a former Dallas judge, "I put prostitutes and queers at the same level...and I'd be hard-put to give somebody life for killing a prostitute" (quoted in Singer and Deschamps, 1994:68).

PERSPECTIVES ON SEXUAL ORIENTATION AND SOCIAL INEQUALITY

Sexual orientation and social inequality can be understood from various perspectives. Biologists take one approach, and psychologists take another. Sociological explanations focus primarily on how sexual orientation and homophobia are associated with social learning and/or social structural factors in society. We'll look at each perspective separately.

Biological and Psychological Perspectives

If biologists could determine that sexual orientation was genetic in origin and that gay men and lesbians do not choose to be homosexuals, would homophobia decrease? There is no simple answer to this question, but some gay advocates applaud recent studies that suggest that sexual orientation might be determined by a person's genetic inheritance. According to this view, homosexuality—like heterosexuality—is an ascribed characteristic, present from birth, that cannot be changed through counseling or therapy; therefore gay men and lesbians cannot be blamed for their sexual orientation.

Over the past two decades, research has produced some evidence that sexual orientation is partially linked to genetic inheritance. For example, some researchers believe that they have isolated a specific marker on the sex chromosome that might increase the likelihood of homosexuality among members of the same family (LeVay and Hamer, 1994). Other researchers are searching for a "gay gene." So far, they have found some support for the presence of such a gene in their studies of identical twins (twins who have the same genetic material), and fraternal twins (twins who share some, but not all, genetic material), which have shown that identical twins are much more likely to both be gay (if one is gay) than are fraternal twins (see Bailey and Pillard, 1991; Bailey and Benishay, 1993). A recently released study by researchers in Europe found that the hypothalamus—the part of the brain that governs sexual arousal—of gay men is stimulated by a testosterone-related scent derived from male sweat that also sexually arouses most women but does not sexually arouse heterosexual men (Lemonick, 2005), lending credence to the belief that there may be a genetic predisposition in some individuals for homosexuality. Although these studies are promising, some critics suggest that biological explanations alone cannot account for sexual orientation (Doyle, 1995).

Unlike biologists, who typically focus on genetic determinants of sexual orientation, psychologists associate homosexuality with mental processes and childhood experiences. Early psychological approaches considered homosexuality a form of maladjustment. Sigmund Freud, founder of the psychoanalytic approach, believed that humans are constitutionally bisexual—meaning that masculine and feminine currents coexist in everyone—but that as children progress toward adulthood, they move toward heterosexuality. According to Freud, not everyone makes it down the difficult path to heterosexuality because it is fraught with dangers and problems. According to Freud, for example, sons whose mothers were domineering and overprotective found it difficult to achieve heterosexuality. Following in Freud's footsteps, later psychologists equated heterosexuality with good mental health and homosexuality with mental illness (see Bieber et al., 1962).

In 1942, the American Psychiatric Association formally classified homosexuality as a form of mental illness and suggested that treatments ranging from castration to electroshock therapy might remedy the problem (Marcus, 1992). However, the association's classification did not go undisputed. By administering standard personality tests to two groups of men—one heterosexual and the other homosexual—and asking a panel of psychiatrists and psychologists to tell her the sexual orientation of each subject on the basis of those tests, psychologist Evelyn Hooker (1957, 1958) showed that not all homosexuals are maladjusted or mentally ill. The judges were unable to differentiate between the heterosexuals and homosexuals. In 1973, the American Psychiatric Association removed homosexuality from its list of mental disorders.

Many psychologists believe that biological and psychosocial factors interact in the formation of sexual orientation. Psychologist Daryl J. Bem, for example, thinks that genetic factors and gender roles in childhood interact to produce sexual orientation. According to Bem, "In most societies, including our own, most boys and girls are raised so that they tend to feel more similar to children of their own sex and different from children of the opposite sex" (cited in Shea, 1996:All). These feelings of similarity and difference are often formed on the playground, where boys are more aggressive than girls. Over time, children's belief that people of the opposite gender are different—and somewhat mysterious—translates into heterosexual desire. However, some children see themselves as more similar to children of the opposite gender. For example, boys who do not like rough-and-tumble play or sports but like to play with dolls or other "girls' toys" might grow up feeling different from other boys. Similarly, girls who prefer "boys' sports" frequently feel awkward around other girls. According to Bem, the best predictor of sexual orientation is the degree to which children are gender-conforming or nonconforming; children who fit in sometimes but not others are likely to become bisexual.

Advocates of Bem's theory point out that it is supported by earlier studies showing that 66 percent of gay men (compared to 10 percent of heterosexual men) did not enjoy activities typical of their own gender. Critics point out that Bem's theory does not take into account the fact that what is defined as gender-appropriate behavior differs widely across cultures and over time. For example, thirty years ago, girls who wanted to play soccer might have been viewed as tomboys with few female friends, whereas today, many girls—and boys—play soccer, and their sports participation does not single them out as different from others of their gender. Bem's theory also does not explain the stages in the process of taking on a homosexual identity or how labeling by others may influence people's perceptions of themselves as homosexual, heterosexual, or bisexual.

Symbolic Interactionist Perspectives

In contrast to biological and psychological perspectives, symbolic interactionist perspectives view heterosexual and homosexual conduct as learned behavior and focus on the process by which individuals come to identify themselves as gay, lesbian, bisexual, or straight. According to symbolic interactionists, most people acquire the status of *heterosexual* without being consciously aware of it because heterosexuality is the established norm and they do not have to struggle over their identity. But the same is not true of people who identify themselves as *homosexual* or *bisexual*. In fact, some sociologists suggest that sexual orientation is a master status for many gay men, lesbians, and bisexuals (Schur, 1965). **A *master status* is the most significant status a person possesses because it largely determines how individuals view themselves and how they are treated by others.** Master status based on sexual orientation is particularly significant when it is linked to other subordinate racial-ethnic group statuses. For example, working-class gay Latinos are more hesitant than white, middle-class gay men to come out to their families because of cultural norms pertaining to *machismo* (masculinity) and the

Individuals seem to accept their identities as lesbian, gay, or bisexual in stages. Initially there is identity confusion. But seeking out others who are open about their sexual orientation and experimenting sexually can eventually lead to acceptance.

fear that relatives will withdraw the support that is essential for surviving at the subordinate end of race and class hierarchies (see Almaguer, 1995).

Symbolic interactionists have identified several stages in the process of accepting a lesbian, gay, or bisexual identity (Weinberg et al., 1994). First, people experience identity confusion—a situation in which they feel different from other people and struggle with admitting that they are attracted to individuals of the same sex. For example, someone who identified himself as a fourteen-year-old boy posted the following note on an Internet newsgroup:

> I feel like my life is over. Am I gay? God, I hope not. I walk around going, "God, I hope not." I walk around going, "Do I like him?" "Do I like her?" "How would it feel to do it with him/her?" WHY DOES THIS HAVE TO HAPPEN TO ME!! The funny thing is, I absolutely detest everything about sex with men, and relationships with men. But somehow, I feel attracted to them anyway!! (Gabriel, 1995b:1)

In the past, many gay and lesbian people had nowhere to turn in their quest for answers and support from others; today, many use the Internet and other forms of global communication to connect with others who share their concerns (Gabriel, 1995b).

The second stage in establishing a lesbian or gay identity is seeking out others who are openly lesbian or gay and perhaps engaging in sexual experimentation or making other forays into the homosexual subculture. In the third stage, people attempt to integrate their self-concept and acceptance of a label such as "homosexual," "gay," or "lesbian" by pursuing a way of life that conforms to their definition of what those labels mean (Coleman, 1981/2; Ponse, 1978; Cass, 1984). Like most "stage" theories, however, not all people go through these stages. Even those who do might not go through each stage in the same way, and some move back and forth between stages (Weinberg et al., 1994).

Studies on how people come to accept their sexual identity as gay, bisexual, or lesbian show the significance of labeling and how it can create barriers to full participation in American society. However, these studies typically are based on a relatively narrow selection of people, which makes it difficult to generalize the findings to larger populations. That is, respondents who openly identify themselves as gay or bisexual might not be characteristic of the larger homosexual or bisexual population (Weinberg et al., 1994).

Functionalist and Conflict Perspectives

Unlike the symbolic interactionist approach, which focuses primarily on how individuals come to identify themselves as homosexual, bisexual, or heterosexual, functionalist perspectives focus on the relationship between social structure and sexual orientation. To functionalists, social norms and laws are established to preserve social institutions and maintain stability in society. From this perspective, then, many societies punish homosexual conduct because it violates the social norms established by those societies and thus undermines the stability of the societies. Sociologist David P. Aday, Jr., provides an overview of this perspective:

> Marriage and family are structural arrangements that contribute to the continuity of our contemporary society.... [Homosexuality undermines] arrangements that currently operate to replace societal members in an orderly way—that is, the arrangement has survival value....If homosexual conduct were allowed to exist unchallenged and unpunished, then it might in time undermine norms and laws that underpin monogamous marital sex, at least some of which results in the production of offspring to repopulate the society....The punishment of homosexual conduct, from ridicule and discrimination to imprisonment, reinforces expectations about heterosexual and marital sex and defines the boundaries of society. (Aday, 1990:25)

■ *Does this photo tend to support or reject some functionalist analysts' assumption that gay or lesbian families destroy "family values" in this country? Why or why not?*

The functionalist perspective explains why some people do not believe that homosexual conduct or marriages between lesbian or gay couples should be protected legally. It also explains why some religious and political leaders call for a renewal of "family values" in this country.

Critics suggest that the functionalist approach supports the status quo and ignores a need for new definitions of marriage and family. If marriage is understood to be the decision of two people to live together in a partnership—to be a family—then the intention or the capacity to have children should not be a condition. These critics say that nothing but custom mandates that marital partners must be of different genders (Nava and Dawidoff, 1994).

Whereas the functionalist approach focuses on how existing social arrangements create a balance in society, the conflict approach focuses on *tensions* in society and *differences* in interests and power among opposing groups. From this perspective, people who hold the greatest power are able to have their own attitudes, beliefs, and values—about sexual orientation, in this case—represented and enforced while others are not (Aday, 1990). Therefore norms pertaining to *compulsory heterosexuality* reflect the beliefs of dominant group members who hold high-level positions in the federal and state government, the military, and other social institutions. However, critics assert that the conflict approach fails to recognize that some people who have wealth and power are gay or lesbian yet take no action to reduce discrimination based on sexual orientation.

According to Karl Marx, conflicts over values are an essential element of social life, and less-powerful people often challenge the laws imposed on them by those in positions of power. For example, adverse decisions by state courts and the U.S. Supreme Court often result in increased political activism by gay and lesbian rights groups. In recent years, more openly lesbian and gay people can be found in public office as elected or appointed officials, in the medical and legal professions, as educators and business leaders, and in all walks of life. However, regardless of their location in the power structure, most gay men, lesbians, and bisexuals remain acutely aware that many social barriers have not been lifted and there has not been a major shift in people's attitudes toward homosexuality and bisexuality.

With rapid Internet communications, lesbians and gay men around the world keep informed about political decisions that may adversely affect them. Many coalitions have been formed to organize gay pride marches and protests around the world. For example, the International Lesbian and Gay Association reports that more than three hundred lesbian and gay groups exist in more than fifty nations (Hendriks et al., 1993).

IS THERE A SOLUTION TO INEQUALITY BASED ON SEXUAL ORIENTATION?

As we have emphasized in previous chapters, how people view a social problem is related to how they believe the problem should be reduced or solved. Inequality based on sexual orientation is no exception because there are many divergent views and policies related to sexual orientation, and some people have very strong feelings about this issue.

Functionalist/Conservative Solutions to the Problem

According to functionalist and conservative perspectives, social norms and laws exist to protect the family and maintain stability in society. Given this, sexual orientation becomes a social issue: Gay activists' demands for equal rights, including the reversal of sodomy laws and legal recognition of same-sex marriage, become major threats to the stability of society. Organizations established to protect "traditional marriage" have been active in advocating passage of a constitutional amendment banning same-sex marriage (see Box 6.3, p. 117).

Recently, conservative political leaders and media analysts have blamed same-sex marriages for destabilizing families because they are thought to detach procreation from the institution of marriage in the public's view. As a result of this belief, some functionalist theorists and conservative politicians argue that members of the LGBT community are not in need of protection by the government in regard to issues of equal rights or antigay discrimination laws. Family values and morality are often indicated as key reasons why public policies should not be changed to take into account gay rights issues. In a survey of public attitudes about the acceptance of lesbians, gays, and bisexuals, for example, about 23 percent of the people surveyed indicated that "more acceptance is bad for the country," and many stated that "morality" was one reason for their concern (Kaiser Family Foundation, 2000).

In sum, many functionalist and conservative analysts view gays, lesbians, bisexuals, and transgendered persons as part of the *problem* rather than as part of the *solution* for bringing about stability to families and society in the twenty-first century. They support policies such as "Don't Ask, Don't Tell" in the military and other efforts to encourage members of the LGBT community to change their sexual orientation. They believe that homosexuality is dysfunctional for society in that it does not contribute to society's need for new members, and it undermines social norms and laws that preserve the family unity and maintain stability in society.

Conflict/Liberal Solutions to the Problem

Conflict theorists believe that prejudice and discrimination based on sexual orientation are embedded in the social structure of society and are reinforced by those who hold the greatest power and thus are able to perpetuate their own attitudes, beliefs and values about what constitutes "normal" sexual conduct. From this perspective, homophobia is similar to racism, sexism, and ageism, and the overt and covert discrimination that gays and lesbians experience is similar to the discrimination experienced by people of color, all women, and older people.

According to the conflict approach, the best way to reduce inequality based on sexual orientation is to repeal laws prohibiting sexual acts between consenting adults and to pass laws that ban all forms of discrimination against people who are lesbian, gay, bisexual, or transgendered. However, to gain equality rights, conflict and liberal analysts acknowledge that activism and continued zeal is necessary: People must continue to demand social change, and some brief gains are quickly lost if individuals and organizations do not continually follow-up on the actions of antigay activists. These advocates often point out that public awareness of inequality based on sexual orientation might have been much slower in coming, and the Gay Liberation Movement might not have occurred for many years, had it not been for a group of gay activists who clashed with New York City Police in 1969. The angry response by militant gay activists caused the police to stop raiding the Stonewall Inn and other gay bars and clubs and brought into existence the Gay Liberation Movement. Today, more than 3,000 organizations seek equal rights and protections for gays, lesbians, bisexuals, and transgendered persons, and these groups represent a wide cross section of the American population.

In sum, conflict and liberal political analysts believe that political activism is important because members of the LGBT community need to have a "voice" in political decisions and to be treated in the same manner as any other person in the United States. They should be granted the same rights as heterosexual individuals with regard to issues such as marriage, inheritance, adoption and custody of children, and health care benefits. However, these analysts also suggest that gays, lesbians, bisexuals, and transgendered persons should not be the only ones responsible for reducing or eliminating inequality based on sexual orientation:

> It all comes down to this: Are people equal in this society by virtue of their citizenship, or not? If the answer is no, then we will be saying that equality does not exist in America anymore but has been replaced by tiers of citizenship, and that what tier you occupy depends on whether people like you or not. And if we accept this, then we will have repudiated the constitutional principles of liberty and equality upon which America was founded.... (Nava and Dawidoff, 1994:167)

Symbolic Interactionist Solutions to the Problem

From a symbolic interactionist perspective, homosexual conduct is learned behavior, and people go through stages in establishing a lesbian or gay identity. Society should therefore be more tolerant of people as they come to accept their sexual identity. Legal and social barriers that prevent people who are gay, lesbian, bisexual, or transgendered from fully participating in society should be removed, thus making the complex psychological and social process of coming out to friends, family, and coworkers easier for those who choose to do so.

If we apply a symbolic interactionist approach to reducing inequality based on sexual orientation, we might look at ways in which society could make it easier for people to accept an identity as gay, lesbian, bisexual or transgendered. It is difficult for individuals to accept a master status based on sexual orientation when that status is stigmatized by others in society. Although many people do not overtly stigmatize other individuals or ridicule them to their face, labeling continues in the United States as long as high-profile comedians and ordinary people tell "jokes" about sexual orientation and freely use slang terms to refer to individuals based on their real or imagined sexual orientation. Young people might be socialized, for example, not to use derogatory terms that are related to sexual orientation when they are "putting down" their friends. If symbolic interactionists are correct in their assessment of the importance of labeling in determining how people perceive of themselves and others, then the manner in which individuals refer to each other, even when "just joking," should be a topic for sensitivity training and for socialization throughout the life course.

In sum, although there is more acceptance of gays and lesbians today compared to a few years ago, much remains to be done in regard to eliminating prejudice and discrimination, including verbal abuse and sometimes physical violence, based on sexual orientation. Policy issues identified as important by members of the LGBT community are far from being resolved in the United States, and gains typically are measured one state at a time. Yet even these gains are frequently temporary. What the future holds for social inequality based on sexual orientation is unclear; however, it is apparent that the public and many policymakers remain divided on questions associated with homosexuality and the policy issues that are associated with sexual orientation.

SUMMARY

■ *What criteria do sociologists use to study sexual orientation?*

Sociologists define sexual orientation as a preference for emotional-sexual relationships with persons of the same sex (homosexuality), the opposite sex (heterosexuality), or both (bisexuality). Recent studies have used three criteria for classifying people as homosexual or bisexual: (1) sexual attraction to persons of one's own gender, (2) sexual involvement with one or more persons of one's own gender, and (3) self-identification as a gay man, lesbian, or bisexual.

■ *How do religion and law influence people's beliefs about homosexuality?*

Most major religions regard homosexuality as a sin. Contemporary religious fundamentalists denounce homosexual conduct as a sign of great moral decay and societal chaos. Throughout American history, moral and religious teachings have been intertwined with laws that criminalize homosexual conduct. Some states have sodomy laws or other laws pertaining to "deviant sexual conduct," "crimes against nature," or "unnatural intercourse" whereby people can be imprisoned for oral or anal intercourse.

■ *How does cohabitation differ from domestic partnership?*

In cohabitation, same-sex or opposite-sex partners live together without being legally married. Many gay or lesbian couples cohabit in this country because they cannot enter into legally recognized marital relationships. However, some cities and states have given legal recognition to domestic partnerships—household partnerships in which unmarried couples live together in a committed, sexually intimate relationship and are granted the same rights and benefits as those accorded to married couples. Domestic partnership agreements benefit some couples by providing health insurance coverage and other benefits that were not previously afforded them.

■ *What types of discrimination do gay and lesbian people experience?*

Although lesbians and gay men experience discrimination in most aspects of daily life, some of the principal areas are (1) child custody and adoption, (2) housing, (3) medical care, (4) occupations, and (5) the military. In each of these areas, gains have been made over the past three decades. However, discrimination against lesbians and gay men remains among the most blatant of all forms of prejudice and discrimination experienced by members of subordinate groups.

■ *How have changes in the definition of hate crimes affected gay men and lesbians?*

Before the early 1990s, hate crimes against gay men and lesbians were not acknowledged. The enactment of the Hate Crime Statistics Act of 1990 enabled hate crimes to be classified on the basis of sexual orientation, race, ethnicity, religion, or other characteristics that are devalued or "hated." Hate crimes against gays and lesbians appear to be most prevalent where homophobic attitudes are tolerated or overlooked.

■ *How do biologists and psychologists explain sexual orientation?*

Biologists suggest that sexual orientation might be determined by a person's genetic inheritance. Researchers have identified an area (but not the specific gene) on the X chromosome that might carry the predisposition for homosexuality. Until fairly recently, psychologists associated homosexuality with maladjustment or mental illness. Today, however, social psychologists believe that genetic and social factors combine to produce sexual orientation. According to Bem's theory, the best predictor of sexual orientation is the degree to which children are gender-conforming or nonconforming; children who fit in sometimes but not at other times are likely to become bisexual.

■ *How do symbolic interactionists explain problems associated with sexual orientation?*

According to symbolic interactionists, most people acquire the status of heterosexual without being consciously aware of it. For lesbians, gay men, and bisexuals, however, sexual orientation can be a master status because it largely determines how individuals view themselves and how they are treated by others. Symbolic interactionists identify several stages in the process of accepting the identity of lesbian, gay, or bisexual: (1) experiencing identity confusion, (2) seeking out others who are openly lesbian or gay and sometimes engaging in sexual experimentation, and (3) attempting to integrate self-concept and acceptance of a label such as "homosexual," "gay," or "lesbian."

■ *How do functionalists explain problems associated with sexual orientation?*

Functionalists focus on how social norms and laws are established to preserve social institutions, such as the family, and to maintain stability in society. They also analyze reasons why societies find it necessary to punish sexual conduct that violates social norms prohibiting nonmarital sex and same-sex sexual relations. According to functionalists, homosexual conduct is punished because it undermines social institutions and jeopardizes the society.

■ *How do conflict theorists explain problems associated with sexual orientation?*

Conflict theorists believe that the group in power imposes its own attitudes, beliefs, and values about sexual orientation on everyone else. Thus norms enforcing compulsory heterosexuality reflect the beliefs of dominant-group members in the federal and state governments, the military, and other social institutions. According to conflict theorists, social change can occur only if people demand that laws be changed to bring about greater equality for gay men and lesbians.

■ *How have gay rights advocates sought to reduce inequality based on sexual orientation?*

Beginning with the Gay Liberation Movement in the 1960s, advocates have argued that lesbians and gay men are citizens and entitled to the same rights and protections that other citizens enjoy, including the right to equal employment and housing, legally sanctioned marriage, and protection from harassment and hate crimes. Some analysts suggest that future social change depends on the continued vigilance of gay and lesbian advocacy organizations.

KEY TERMS

deviance, p. 112
domestic partnership, p. 115
homophobia, p. 112
master status, p. 122
sexuality, p. 111
sexual orientation, p. 110

QUESTIONS FOR CRITICAL THINKING

1. How is homophobia similar to racism, sexism, and ageism? How is it different?
2. As a sociologist, how would you study the problem of discrimination against lesbians and gay men? What are the strengths and weaknesses of using survey research, interviews, and observations to study discrimination based on sexual orientation?
3. Some people think that state laws should be changed to give legal recognition to same-sex marriage. How would you find out what students at your college or university believe about this issue? If student organizations for gay men and lesbians exist on your campus, how might you find out about members' beliefs on this topic? Do you think their responses would differ from those of a cross section of the student population? Why or why not?
4. In Chapters 2 through 6, we have examined inequality and discrimination as it relates to class, race/ethnicity, gender, age, and sexual orientation. If you could do one thing to reduce these problems, what would it be? What resources would be needed to implement your plan?

Chapter 7

Prostitution, Pornography, and the Sex Industry

THINKING SOCIOLOGICALLY

- Why are prostitution and pornography referred to as the sex industry? What factors have contributed to the growth of the global sex industry?
- Is prostitution a legitimate career choice or is it a form of social deviance? How do sociological perspectives explain the persistence of prostitution worldwide?
- Does the recent availability of pornography on cell phones and portable DVD players raise new questions about the ability of society to control pornography if individuals choose to view it?

I was a minister's daughter. As far as I was concerned, prostitution was the last thing in the entire world I would think of.... Then I met my man. That's how I got into it.... They meet you. They're nice to you. They take you out. It's like you think you're meeting a normal guy and falling in love.... Some of them, they tell you right up front that you have to work for them. My man told me after two weeks. He said he cared for me, he liked me, and he felt deeply, but this is what he does and the only way I could be with him is by coming out here and working. He drove me around here. He said, "See those girls? They have furs, diamonds, houses. They have everything." I fell for it. My first day, I made $100. One hundred dollars! I couldn't believe it! After a while, you're not thinking about the sex. There's no intimacy. You don't[care] about your date. If he dropped dead, fine. Just leave your wallet behind.

—Nadia, a nineteen-year-old prostitute in New Youk City (Kasindorf, 1988:56)

To some, like Nadia, sex work is a career choice- with willing buyers and sellers, a purely economic exchange-that is no more or less degrading than any other profession (McWilliams, 1996). Certainly in this country, it is a thriving multibillion-dollar industry that includes prostitution, the adult film and video trade, printed pornography, escort services, massage parlors, and strip and table dancing clubs. However, prostitution and other types of sex work have always been controversial; not all social scientists even agree on whether or not the sex industry is a social problem. To better understand the controversy over prostitution, pornography, and other sex work, let's look at what constitutes deviant behavior.

DEVIANCE, THE SEX INDUSTRY, AND SOCIAL PROBLEMS

In Chapter 6, *deviance* was defined as a behavior, belief, or condition that violates social norms. To learn about deviance, sociologists ask such questions as the following: Why are some types of behavior considered deviant while others are not? Who determines what is deviant? Whose interests are served by stigmatizing some people as deviants but not others?

Sociologists generally take one of three approaches in studying deviance. The first approach assumes that deviance is *objectively given:* A deviant is any person who does not conform to established social norms—specifically, folkways, mores, and laws. Folkways are informal norms or everyday customs that may be violated without serious consequences. Contemporary U.S. folkways include eating certain foods with silverware and shaking hands when introduced to someone. In comparison, mores are strongly held norms that have moral and ethical connotations. College football players who scalp (sell at inflated prices) the free game tickets they receive from their school for their family members and friends behave unethically and violate social mores. Laws are formal, standardized norms that are enacted by legislatures and enforced by formal sanctions such as fines and imprisonment. Laws may be either civil or criminal. *Civil law* deals with disputes between people or groups, such as an argument between a landlord and a tenant over the provisions of an apartment lease. *Criminal law* deals with public safety and well-being and defines the behaviors that constitute a ***crime*—a behavior that violates criminal law and is punishable by a fine, a jail term, or other negative sanctions.** Crimes range from relatively minor offenses, such as traffic violations, to major offenses, such as murder.

If deviance is considered to be objectively given, then prostitution and pornography are viewed as violations of deeply held convictions (folkways or mores) about good taste or morality or as significant departures from existing criminal laws (Smith and Pollack, 1994). To limit the amount of deviance and criminal behavior in society, in this view, societies employ social control mechanisms. ***Social control* refers to the systematic practices developed by social groups to encourage conformity and discourage deviance.** Social control can be either internal or external. Internal social control occurs through socialization: People learn to adhere to the norms of social groups and the larger society. Internal social control mechanisms are strengthened by external mechanisms such as the criminal justice system, which enforces laws whether or not individuals choose to adhere to them.

The second approach to studying deviance considers it to be *socially constructed:* A behavior, belief, or condition is deviant because it is labeled as such (Goode, 1996; Rubington and Weinberg, 1996). Sociologist Howard S. Becker (1963:8) summed up this approach when he wrote, "Social groups create deviance by making rules whose infraction constitutes deviance, and by applying those rules to particular people and labeling them as *outsiders.*" According to Becker and other interactionists, deviance is not a quality of any act the person commits; rather, a deviant is one to whom the label of deviant has been successfully applied. Thus street prostitutes who openly solicit customers ("johns") are more likely to be labeled deviant than are women and men who work for high-priced escort services, even though their actions are essentially the same.

The third approach assumes that deviance is rooted in *the social structure of society,* particularly in power relations. In fact, according to this approach, deviance is defined—initially and disproportionately—by the most powerful members of the dominant class, racial, and gender groups. Rule makers and rule enforcers protect the power and privilege of dominant-group members, often at the expense of subordinate-group members. Thus prostitutes are more likely than their customers or pimps to be apprehended and punished for their alleged sexual deviance.

What is sexual deviance? Although all societies have social norms regulating sexual conduct, not all societies regulate it in the same way. In the United States alone, definitions of what is sexually deviant have varied from time to time, from place to place, and from group to group. Traditionally, at least four types of sexual conduct between heterosexual partners have been regarded as deviant: (1) premarital sex or fornication—sexual relations between two people who are not married to each other; (2) extramarital sex or adultery—sexual relations between a married person and a partner other than her or his spouse; (3) promiscuous sex—casual sexual relations with many partners; and (4) underage sex or statutory rape—sexual relations with children below the age of consent as defined by state law, usually about age fourteen, fifteen, or sixteen. Prostitution crosses several lines of *proscribed* (prohibited) sexual conduct and is viewed as deviance because it involves promiscuous behavior between two (or more) people, who might be married to other people, and sometimes involves underage sex. Despite changes in prescribed rules of sexual conduct during the twentieth century, the United States is one of the few highly industrialized nations that still defines prostitution as a crime.

PROSTITUTION IN GLOBAL PERSPECTIVE

Narrowly defined, ***prostitution* is the sale of sexual services (of oneself or another) for money or goods and without emotional attachment.** More broadly defined, systems of prostitution refer to any industry in which women's and/or children's—and sometimes men's—bodies are bought, sold, or traded for sexual use and abuse (Giobbe, 1994). According to this definition, systems of prostitution include pornography, live sex shows, peep shows, international sexual slavery, and prostitution as narrowly defined. The vast majority of prostitutes around the globe are women and children. A certain amount of male prostitution does exist, although most boys and men in the sex industry engage in sexual encounters with other males (see McNamara, 1994; Browne and Minichiello, 1995; Snell, 1995).

The World's Oldest Profession?

Prostitution has been referred to as the "world's oldest profession" because references to it can be found throughout recorded history. Still, over the past 4,000 years, prostitution has been neither totally accepted nor completely condemned. For example, although prostitution was widely accepted in ancient Greece, where upper-class prostitutes were admired and frequently became the companions of powerful Greek citizens, the prostitutes themselves were refused the status of wife—the ultimate affirmation of legitimacy for women in Greek society—and were negatively compared with so-called virtuous women in a "bad woman–good woman" dichotomy (see Bullough and Bullough, 1987; Roberts, 1992; Jolin, 1994).

In other eras, attitudes and beliefs about prostitution have ranged from generally tolerant to strongly averse. Such early Christian leaders as St. Augustine and St. Thomas Aquinas argued that prostitution was evil but encouraged tolerance toward it. According to Aquinas, prostitution served a basic need that, if unmet, would result in greater harm than prostitution itself. Later Christian leaders, such as Martin Luther in sixteenth-century Europe, believed that prostitution should be abolished on moral grounds (Otis, 1985; Jolin, 1994).

In the nineteenth-century feminist movement, women for the first time voiced their opinions about prostitution. Some believed that prostitution led to promiscuity and moral degeneracy in men and should therefore be eradicated. Others believed that prostitution should be legitimized as a valid expression of female sexuality outside of marriage. Recently, some advocates have suggested that prostitution should be viewed as a legitimate career choice for women (prostitute as sex worker), but others have argued that prostitution is rooted in global gender inequality (prostitute as victim of oppression).

The Global Sex Industry

The past three decades have seen the industrialization, normalization, and globalization of prostitution. Although *industrialization* typically refers to the mass production of manufactured goods and services for exchange in the market, sociologist Kathleen Barry (1995:122) suggests that this term should also apply to commercialized sex manufactured within the human self. Prostitution becomes *normalized* when sex work is treated as merely a form of entertainment and there are no legal impediments to promoting it as a commodity. The *globalization* of prostitution refers to the process by which the sex industry has become increasingly global in scope (e.g., international conglomerates of hotel chains, airlines, bars, sex clubs, massage parlors, brothels, and credit card companies that have an economic interest in the global sex industry), which has occurred as people's political, economic, and cultural lives have become linked globally (Barry, 1995; Davidson, 1996). For evidence of this globalization, one has only to look at recent investigations by journalists and sociologists of the use of child prostitutes in the sex tourism industry (see Box 7.1 on page 132).

The demand for prostitution is greatest when large numbers of men are congregated for extended periods of time in the military or on business far from home. A connection between wartime rape and increased prostitution has been documented for the Vietnam War and more recently for the wars in El Salvador and Bosnia. A network television news report in 2002 found numerous bars near U.S. military bases in South Korea—bars that were off-limits to local residents—where women who allegedly were forced into prostitution by the bar owners engage in paid sex with U.S. soldiers (Macintyre, 2002).

Although recent research has indicated that the global sex industry, especially prostitution, contributes to the transmission of HIV, the virus that causes AIDS, many agencies and governments have not come to grips with the problem. For example, the Japanese Foundation for AIDS Prevention, an organization affiliated with the Japanese government, launched a poster campaign featuring a grinning, middle-aged man wearing a business suit and displaying his passport, with a caption reading, "Have a nice trip! But be careful of AIDS." The Japanese government is obviously aware that many businessmen participate in sex tourism abroad (Sachs, 1994), but the poster gives a mixed message rather than a strong warning.

The global sex industry reflects the economic disparity between the poorest regions of the world—where women and children may be bought, sold, or traded like any other commodity—and the richest regions, such as Europe and North America, where many of the global sex industry's consumers reside (see Bauerlein, 1995; Davidson, 1996). However, some women in the sex trade hope to attain a better life by maintaining ties with customers from whom they receive money and who might help them qualify for visas that allow them to move to another country where they think they will find a better life. Often they are sadly disappointed, as was the case for "Carmen," a sex worker in Sosúa, a small town on the north coast of the Dominican Republic. Carmen had a Belgian client who sent money to her, but when she ceased to hear from him, she wrote the following letter:

> Dear______________,
> I have been thinking of you every day and have been waiting for a fax to hear how you are. I got your money wire, thanks. But I still want to see you. Please send me a fax at the following number…and, if possible, a fax number where I can reach you.
>
> I miss you very much and think of you all the time. I love you very much.
>
> I want to hear from you. I hope you come to visit again very soon.
>
> Many kisses,
> Carmen

Carmen never heard from this client again (Brennan, 2002:162). According to sociologists Barbara Ehrenreich and Arlie Russell Hochschild (2002:9–10), although many women in low-income nations hope for a better life through prostitution, the men who seek them out as sexual partners typically are looking for something far different, namely a short-term encounter with a woman who embodies "the traditional feminine qualities of nurturance, docility, and eagerness to please.…[Some] men seek in the 'exotic Orient' or 'hot-blooded tropics' a woman from the imagined past."

Social Problems in Global Perspective

Box 7.1

Economic Development or Childhood Sexual Slavery?

> I worked for two escort agencies when I was first started in the sex trade, and both were closed down. I was terrified when the police raided the apartment that served as a booking office for the second agency. Those of us who were not arrested endured petty racist comments from the officers for about two hours.
>
> I chose to work for an escort service because I was young, starting out in a precarious industry, alone in the city and, like those hapless customers who are arrested in street sweeps, without connections. Working for an escort service was a way to earn my living and keep a roof over my head. But when the chance to work for a madam with a steady supply of reliable clients arose, I was relieved…
>
> Escort services are risky. When they are closed by the authorities, people's lives are turned upside down. Many of us don't recover. As one call girl told me when I was looking for a safer way to work, "If you get busted, I don't want to know you." Nobody wants to work with you if you've been in visible trouble, nor is just after a raid the best time in your life to start looking for a more conventional job. A conviction will sink you chances of getting hired. (Quan, 2008: A27)
>
> —*Tracy Quan, a former New York City "call girl," explains how she got started in the sex industry and why she always had concerns about her safety when working for an escort service.*

To some, like Tracy, sex work is a career choice—with willing buyers and sellers, a purely economic exchange—that is no more or less degrading than any other profession (McWilliams, 1996). Certainly sex work in the United States is a thriving multibillion-dollar industry that includes prostitution, the adult film and video trade, printed pornography, escort services, massage parlors, and strip and table dancing clubs. However, prostitution and other types of sex work have always been controversial; not all social scientists even agree on whether or not the sex industry is a social problem. To better understand the controversy over prostitution, pornography, and other sex work, let's look at what constitutes deviant behavior.

Although it is impossible to know exactly how many child prostitutes there are in the world, recent estimates suggest that as many as 1 million girls and boys age seventeen and younger engage in prostitution in Asia alone. Initially, social analysts believed that the end of the Vietnam War and economic development would end child prostitution in Asian cities such as Shanghai, Hong Kong, and Hanoi, where brothels have existed for many years. But this has not happened. Instead, sex tourism has emerged as a form of economic development, and fear of contracting AIDS has dramatically increased child prostitution in some nations. Brothel owners purchase girls as young as age twelve and force them to become house prostitutes. Girls who try to escape are caught, severely beaten, and sometimes starved. While imprisoned in the brothel, they are forced to have sex with many customers each night (Kristof, 1996b).

In Thailand, a large sex industry services Thai men and foreigners. Most of the prostitutes are younger than fifteen years old. In impoverished areas, young girls can no longer

Health Aspects of Prostitution for Women

Although some people view prostitution as nothing more than a job or as a way to make money when few other economic alternatives exist, prostitution should be classified as a hazardous occupation because of its negative physical and psychological effects. Studies of global sexual exploitation have documented that prostitution gravely impairs women's health and constitutes a form of violence (Raymond 1999). Frequently, women engaged in prostitution suffer physical injuries—such as bruises, broken bones, black eyes, and concussions—similar to those suffered by women who are victims of domestic violence. Although few studies have examined the physical effects of prostitution on male prostitutes, it is likely that boys and men are also vulnerable to physical abuse by individuals who pay for their sexual services.

Along with physical violence, women employed in the global sex industry are vulnerable to numerous health risks, including sexually transmitted diseases such as HIV/AIDS, gonorrhea, herpes, and syphilis. They also have a high risk of chronic gynecological problems such as pelvic pain and pelvic inflammatory disease. Pregnancy and pregnancy-related complications constitute another significant concern for girls and women in prostitution (Willis, 2000).

Research shows that emotional health is another serious issue associated with prostitution. Some psychologists have found that many prostitutes suffer from what they refer to as a "combat disorder" that is similar to the post-traumatic stress disorders and combat fatigue that veterans of war may experience. In one study, for example, researchers determined that prostitutes—as young as twelve and as old as sixty-one years of age—in San Francisco and six major cities in Europe, Asia, and Africa had sustained recurrent physical or sexual assaults

Box 7.1 (continued)

These prostitutes are waiting for potential customers outside a bar in Bangkok, Thailand's downtown red-light district. What global, social, and economic factors contribute to the growing number of girls and young women working in the sex industry worldwide?

earn a living in agriculture, and their opportunities in the labor market are limited to extremely low-wage production and service jobs—often assembly-line work for transnational corporations. In contrast, sex work offers a rate of pay that, though still very low, can be 25 times higher than the wages for seamstresses or domestics. Sex-based tourism in Thailand is estimated at $4 billion a year. In fact, because many foreign visitors consider sex the country's chief attraction, on the macroeconomic level sex is now part of the economy of international domination.

Analysts have suggested that the prostitution industry has become more thoroughly capitalistic and globalized than ever before. From this point of view, advocates of social change suggest that sex workers should be thought of as working people who are entitled to human rights and workers' rights (see Kempadoo and Doezema, 1998).

Questions to Consider

1. How is the global sex industry linked to the international division of labor and other forms of globalization?
2. Do human rights and international governmental organizations (such as the United Nations) have a responsibility to intervene in cases of child sexual slavery?
3. What can we learn about the status of females in many countries based on information about the sex industry and sex tourism?

in the course of their work and that many of them suffered from psychiatric problems as a result (Zuger, 1998). Other studies have identified various emotional consequences of prostitution, including depression, anxiety, eating disorders, and alcohol and drug abuse (Raymond, 1999).

In contrast to some Hollywood films that offer a romanticized view of prostitution (such as the film *Pretty Woman,* starring Julia Roberts), it appears that many girls and women view themselves as being trapped in the global sex industry and that some are concerned about the physical and psychological consequences of their work.

PROSTITUTION IN THE UNITED STATES

Trafficking in women and children is as great a problem in the United States as it is in low-income nations. In recent years, organized prostitution networks have been identified in urban, suburban, and rural areas of the country. Newspaper accounts over the past decade have described thousands of incidents in which immigrant women have been forced to have sex with many men to pay off their passage to the United States. Women and children from Asia and Mexico have been among the most frequently exploited by smugglers. Today, the U.S. mail-order bride industry is a multimillion-dollar business that markets women from low-income nations as "brides" to men in the United States and other Western nations (*Factbook on Global Sexual Exploitation,* 1999).

The Nature of Prostitution

Clearly, not all prostitutes are alike: Life experiences, family backgrounds, years of formal education, locales of operation, types of customers, and methods of doing business vary widely. Even with these differences, however, sociologists have identified five levels or tiers of prostitution, ranging from escort prostitutes to street prostitutes and women exchanging sex for drugs in crack houses.

Top-tier prostitutes typically are referred to as *escorts* or *call girls* and *call boys.* They are considered the upper echelon in prostitution because they tend to earn higher fees and have more selectivity in their working conditions and customers than do other prostitutes (see Macy, 1996). Escort prostitutes typically have more years of formal education than other types of prostitutes do. Most of them do not think of themselves as prostitutes. Many dress nicely—and often conservatively—so that they do not call undue attention to themselves at luxury hotels, clubs, and apartment buildings. Sydney Biddle Barrows (1986:69), the former owner of a well-known New York escort service, explains:

> While good looks were generally important [for escort prostitutes], I was more concerned with the right look. Men have always responded to the way I dress, and I decided that the elegant, classic look that worked for me would also work for the girls.... Quite a few of the new girls had no money and nothing appropriate to wear, so I would either lend them something of mine or take them to Saks and charge whatever they needed on my credit card. They would pay me back from their future earnings.

Escort prostitutes work "on call," going out to see customers who are referred to them by their escort service, pimp, or other procurers such as hotel concierges and taxi drivers who receive a percentage of the prostitute's fees. Although their work is not as visible as that of other prostitutes, they face some of the same hazards, including abusive customers and sexually transmitted diseases.

The second tier of prostitutes comprises hustlers, strippers, and table dancers who engage in prostitution on the side. People in this tier work out of nightclubs, bars, and strip joints primarily. The hustlers are sometimes referred to as *bar girls* or *bar boys* because they are supposed to pressure (hustle) customers to buy drinks. Most hustlers are not paid by the bar but earn their livelihood by negotiating sexual favors with potential customers, who often are lonely and want someone to talk to as well as to have sex with (Devereaux, 1987).

The third tier is made up of *house girls* who work in brothels (houses of prostitution) run by a madam or a pimp who collects up to half of the fees earned by the women. Customers choose "dates" from women lined up in a parlor or receiving room. House prostitutes are not allowed to engage in "dirty hustling" (winking, running one's tongue over one's lips, or shaking a leg) or to turn down a customer (Devereaux, 1987). Because prostitution is illegal in most states, houses of prostitution typically operate as body-painting studios, massage parlors, or other businesses. The only legal brothels in the United States are located in eleven counties in Nevada where prostitution has been decriminalized. However, the state of Nevada requires house prostitutes to register, be fingerprinted, pay a state business fee, and provide up-to-date medical certification that they are free of sexually transmitted diseases.

Near the bottom tier of prostitution are *streetwalkers,* who publicly solicit customers and charge by the "trick." Most street prostitutes work a specific location and defend it from other prostitutes, as Nadia (whom we met earlier) explains:

> I only work this corner, 'cause this is the first-class street.... Even here, you know there's always the chance you're going with someone who might want to kill you. My [pimp] drives around to make sure I'm okay, but not every day. So you're always alert. You watch your date's every move. You're sexy, you're smiling, you're teasing, everything, but you're watching their every move. You're always listening to their conversation so you can know what they're leading up to. Then you're okay. (quoted in Kasindorf, 1988:56)

Nadia and other streetwalkers derive status and some degree of protection from their pimps. However, researchers have also documented the exploitative and sometimes violent nature of the pimp–prostitute relationship.

The very bottom tier of prostitution is occupied by women who are addicted to crack cocaine and engage in crack-for-sex exchanges (Fullilove et al., 1992). Researchers have found that many crack-addicted women perform unprotected oral sex on men in crack houses in exchange for hits of crack. According to one study,

> Some men will enter a crack house, purchase enough rocks for two people for several hours, and then make it clear to every woman in the house what he has in mind.... [There] seems to be an expectation [in the crack house] that if a man wants to have sex with a woman, she will not oppose the offer. The expectations are implicit. Everyone involved—the house owner, the male user/customer, and the female user/prostitute are all aware of what is expected. (Inciardi et al., 1993b:74–75)

Although less research has been done on prostitution tiers in male prostitution, the tiers appear to be similar to those of female prostitution except that most customers are of the same gender as the prostitute. For example, in her report on escort services, journalist Marianna Macy (1996:249) found that some male escorts exist but that "Men normally go see men." Some male prostitutes work as hustlers in bars and nightclubs, where they typically wear blue jeans, leather jackets, and boots, seeking to project a strong heterosexual image. Sexual orientation is frequently an issue with male prostitutes, some of whom do not define themselves as gay and limit the types of sexual acts they are willing to perform. Others view sex strictly as an economic exchange by defining work-related sex as "not real sex" (Browne and Minichiello, 1995).

The Extent of Prostitution

Estimates of the number of working prostitutes in the United States range from 100,000 to more than 500,000, but accurate estimates are impossible to get for several reasons (Reynolds, 1986). First, there is the question of how prostitution is defined. Second, because of its illegal nature, much prostitution is not reported. Third, arrest records—which are almost the only source of official information on prostitution—do not reflect the extent of prostitution. Because they visibly solicit customers, streetwalkers are more likely to be apprehended, tried, and convicted of prostitution than are prostitutes working for exclusive escort services. Finally, many people drift into and out of prostitution, considering it temporary work between full-time jobs or as part-time work while attending school (Potterat et al., 1990). Recent statistics on prostitution arrests provide limited information about many aspects of prostitution; however, it is possible to gain some idea about who is most likely to be arrested for prostitution-related offenses. As shown in Box 7.2 on page 136, women are much more likely to be arrested for prostitution in any given year than are men. However, there has been an increase in the number of men arrested for prostitution-related offenses.

Prostitution and Age, Class, and Race

Although some prostitutes are as young as age thirteen or fourteen, the vast majority are between the ages of seventeen and twenty-four. The peak earning age appears to be about twenty-two (Clinard and Meier, 1989; DePasquale, 1999). In contrast, the typical male customer is middle-aged, white, and married, although some teenage and college-age males also hire prostitutes

(National Victims Resource Center, 1991). Often, the age difference between teenage prostitutes and older customers is striking, as a woman who was forced into prostitution at age thirteen by a pimp explains:

> The men who bought me—the tricks—knew I was an adolescent. Most of them were in their 50s and 60s. They had daughters and granddaughters my age. They knew a child's face when they looked into it.... It was even clearer that I was sexually inexperienced. So they showed me pornography to teach me and ignored my tears as they positioned my body like the women in the pictures, and used me. (Giobbe, 1993:38)

Although a small percentage of teenagers enter prostitution through coercion, most are runaways who have left home because of sexual abuse or other family problems. Some teen prostitutes are "throwaways"—thrown out of their homes by parents or other family members (Snell, 1995; Vissing, 1996). Regardless of their prior history, many teens become prostitutes because prostitution is the best—or only—job they can get.

Social class is directly linked to prostitution: Lower-income and poverty-level women and men are far more likely to become prostitutes than are more affluent people (Miller, 1986). Some people with little formal education and few job skills view prostitution as an economic necessity. As one woman stated, "I make good money [as a prostitute]. That's why I do it; if I worked at McDonald's for minimum wage, then I'd feel degraded" (quoted in McWilliams, 1996:340). However, women working for exclusive escort services are more likely to have attended college and come from

Social Problems and Statistics

Box 7.2

the middle or upper-middle class. For example, Heidi Fleiss, the so-called Hollywood madam, is the daughter of a prominent California physician.

Race is also an important factor in prostitution. Sociologist Patricia Hill Collins (1991) suggests that African-American women are affected by the widespread image of black women as sexually promiscuous and therefore potential prostitutes. Collins traces the roots of this stereotype to the era of slavery when black women—and black men and children—were at the mercy of white male slave owners and their sexual desires. According to Collins (1991:175), prostitution exists within a "complex web of political and economic relationships whereby sexuality is conceptualized along intersecting axes of race and gender." Today, prostitution remains linked to the ongoing economic, political, and social exploitation of people of color, especially women. At the same time, since 1971, there has been a significant reversal in the racial composition of people who are arrested for prostitution and commercialized vice, which includes keeping a brothel, procuring (pimping), and transporting women for immoral purposes (see Figure 7.2).

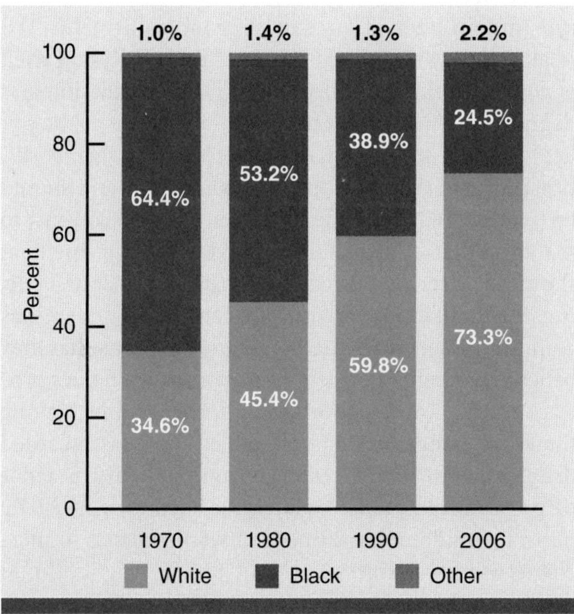

■ *Figure 7.2* ***Percent distribution of prostitution arrests by race, 1970–2006***

Sources: FBI, 2004, U.S. Census Bureau, 2008.

SOCIOLOGICAL PERSPECTIVES ON PROSTITUTION

Sociologists use a variety of perspectives to examine prostitution as a social problem. Functionalists focus on how deviance, including prostitution, serves important functions in society. Interactionists investigate microlevel concerns, such as how and why people become prostitutes and how the stigmatization affects their self-esteem. Conflict perspectives seek to explain how the powerful enact their moral beliefs into law and how prostitution is related to capitalism and/or patriarchy.

The Functionalist Perspective

Functionalists believe that the presence of a certain amount of deviance in society contributes to its overall stability. According to early sociologist Emile Durkheim, deviance clarifies social norms and helps societies to maintain social control over people's behavior. By punishing those who engage in deviant behavior such as prostitution, the society reaffirms its commitment to its sexual norms and creates loyalty to the society as people bind together to oppose the behavior.

According to sociologist Kingsley Davis (1937), in societies that have restrictive norms governing sexual conduct, including the United States, prostitution will always exist because it serves important functions. First, it provides quick, impersonal sexual gratification that does not require emotional attachment or a continuing relationship with another person (Freund et al., 1991). Second, prostitution provides a sexual outlet for men who do not have ongoing sexual relationships because they are not married or have heavy work schedules. Third, prostitution provides people with the opportunity to engage in sexual practices—such as multiple sex partners, fellatio (oral stimulation of the male genitalia), cunnilingus (oral stimulation of the female genitalia), anal intercourse, or sadomasochism (S&M), including the use of such devices as handcuffs, whips, and chains—that regular sex partners or spouses might view as immoral or distasteful. Fourth, prostitution protects the family as a social institution by making a distinction between "bad girls" or "bad boys"—with whom one engages in promiscuous sexual behavior—and "good girls" and "good boys"—with whom one establishes a family. Finally, prostitution benefits the economy by providing jobs for people who have limited formal education and job skills.

The Symbolic Interactionist Perspective

Why do people become prostitutes? Do some prostitutes like their work? Symbolic interactionists investigate questions such as these by using a social psychological framework, for example, by examining people's lived experiences. Here is an excerpt from an interview with a prostitute named Dolores:

> I set my own schedule. I set my own limits and made my own rules, and I didn't have to answer to anyone. I learned a lot about myself: what I would and would not do for money, and what I was willing to do for the right amount of money.... I didn't have to see anyone I didn't want to see. If a man was too boring or too rough or too crude or took too much time, I didn't have to see him again. I loved it. (French, 1988:180)

Dolores's remarks suggest that some people become prostitutes because it provides them with greater autonomy and more career options than they otherwise would have. These reasons fit with sociologist Howard Becker's (1963) suggestion that entering a deviant career is similar in many ways to entering any other occupation. The primary difference is the labeling that goes with a deviant career. Public labeling of people as deviant and their acceptance or rejection of that label are crucial factors in determining whether or not a person stays in a deviant career. Some people are more willing than others to accept the label "deviant" or might believe that they have no other option.

Why do men seek out prostitutes? Research by symbolic interactionists suggests that some young men seek out prostitutes to fulfill what they believe is a rite of passage from boyhood to manhood. Consider, for example, John's comments after several trips to a house of prostitution:

> We went back to school, Mike and I, after going to that first whorehouse. We were probably the only two guys in the class that had done it. We were celebrities. We had crowds around us when we'd tell them all the details, how great it was, what studs we were.... My reaction to all this was it wasn't really very exciting. After all the talk you hear about it, all the writing, all the pictures, all the taboos about sex, I thought, "For this? This is what it was about?"... It wasn't something bad; it just wasn't nearly as exciting as I thought it would be. But we thought, "This is a good chance to learn," so we went back several times.... I can remember up to eleven.... I always thought I'd keep count all my life; that was part of what being a man was all about. (quoted in Raphael, 1988:74–75)

Social analysts suggest that the need of men of all ages to validate their sexual prowess or reaffirm their masculinity is an important factor in their seeking out prostitutes (Raphael, 1988). Symbolic interactionist perspectives such as these highlight how people define social realities—such as the importance of sexual prowess or masculinity—in light of competing and often contradictory values they have learned through socialization.

The Conflict Perspective

Conflict perspectives on prostitution highlight the relationship between power in society and sex work: The laws that make prostitution illegal are created by powerful dominant-group members who seek to maintain cultural dominance by criminalizing sexual conduct that they consider immoral or in bad taste (Barry, 1995).

Conflict analysts using a liberal feminist framework believe that prostitution should be decriminalized—meaning that laws making prostitution a crime should be repealed. These analysts argue that prostitution is a ***victimless-crime*—a crime that many people believe has no real victim because it involves willing participants in an economic exchange.** Therefore sex workers should not be harassed by police and the courts. According to Margo St. James, a former prostitute and founder of an activist group called COYOTE (Call Off Your Old Tired Ethics), "The profession itself is not abusive; it's the illegality; it's the humiliation and degradation that is dealt to them at the hands of the police" (quoted in McWilliams, 1996:340). In other words, prostitution is sex work in the sex industry and should be treated as a labor issue. However, in sharp contrast to the idea that prostitution is a victimless crime that should be decriminalized and treated as a labor issue, organizers of anti-prostitution campaigns in various communities have pointed out various factors that they believe are tangible evidence that prostitution does produce harm to a neighborhood's quality of life. Among these are dangerous paraphernalia such as discarded drug syringes, which often accompany the practice of prostitution; public health risks such as HIV/AIDS; harm to children; harassment of women; costs to merchants whose businesses are disrupted; neighborhood decline; and invasion of the neighborhood by outsiders such as johns, addicts, and pimps (Weitzer, 2000).

Conflict perspectives using Marxist feminist and radical feminist frameworks suggest that women become prostitutes because of structural factors such as economic inequality and patriarchy. Capitalism and patriarchy foster economic inequality between women and men and force women to view their bodies as simply commodities: "When a man has bought a woman's body for his use as if it were like any other commodity...the sex act itself provides acknowledgment of patriarchal right. When women's bodies are on sale as commodities in the capitalist market...men gain public acknowledgment as women's sexual masters" (Pateman, 1994:132).

According to Marxist feminists, the only way to eliminate prostitution is to reduce disparities in income levels between women and men and eliminate poverty. However, radical feminists believe that prostitution will not be eliminated until patriarchy is ended.

Conflict theorists who focus on the interrelationship of race, class, and gender in examining social problems suggest that criminalizing prostitution uniquely affects poor women, especially poor women of color, who are overrepresented among street prostitutes. According to these theorists, white male supremacy, which traditionally preserves the best-paying jobs for men, makes women of color particularly vulnerable to recruitment or coercion into prostitution. As one woman explains, "As a Black coming up in Indiana in the steel mill industry up there, they hired men. All the men got jobs in the mills there; very few women...but there were lots of jobs for you in strip joints, dancing, or even down at some of the restaurants and bars outside of the steel mills for when the guys came in" (quoted in Giobbe, 1994:122).

Analysts using this framework also note that discrimination in law enforcement uniquely affects women of color. For example, law enforcement officials target street prostitutes and other sex workers, particularly when political elites decide to crack down on "deviant" behavior such as prostitution and pornography (Barry, 1995).

PORNOGRAPHY

Nina Hartley, founder of the Pink Ladies club, a group of women in the pornography industry, wrote of herself (1994:176–177):

> "A feminist porno star?" Right, tell me another one, I can hear some feminists saying...why porno? Simple—I'm an exhibitionist with a cause: to make sexually graphic (hard core) erotica, and today's porno is the only game in town....As I examine my life, I uncover the myriad influences that led me to conclude that it was perfectly natural for me to choose a career in adult films....I stripped once a week while getting my bachelor's degree in nursing, magna cum laude....I went into full time [adult] movie work immediately following graduation.

***Pornography* is the graphic depiction of sexual behavior through pictures and/or words—including by electronic or other data retrieval systems—in a manner that is intended to be sexually arousing.** Although Hartley claims to be a feminist porn star, many social analysts, as Hartley herself notes, believe that this is a contradiction in terms. Most of these analysts believe that pornography is a pressing social problem. But what kind of social problem is it? Religious groups typically construe pornography as a social problem because they say that it is obscene. On the other hand, social analysts, particularly feminists, usually frame the problem in terms of patriarchy—male oppression of women (Leong, 1991). Thus, the specific nature of pornography as a social problem is not clear-cut, as sociologist Wai-Teng Leong (1991:91) explains:

> Some religious groups preach that pornography propagates perverse sexualities and its proliferation portends the poverty of morality. Some women promulgate the view that pornography preserves and promotes patriarchal power. Some other women claim that pornography in popular music leads to all kinds of teenage pathology. On the other hand, producers of pornography argue that their products have the positive potential of catharsis, channeling off sexual desires into masturbatory fantasies. And many people who purchase pornography consume it in the privacy of their homes and cannot comprehend why a private matter should become a public problem.

Adding to the confusion over the nature of pornography as a social problem is the difficulty social scientists have in determining what constitutes pornography. Over time, public attitudes change regarding what should be tolerated and what should be banned because of ***obscenity*—the legal term for pornographic materials that are offensive by generally accepted standards of decency.** Who decides what is obscene? According to what criteria? In *Miller v. California* (1973), the U.S. Supreme Court held that material can be considered legally obscene only if it meets three criteria: (1) The material as a whole appeals to prurient interests (lustful ideas or desires); (2) the material depicts sexual conduct in a patently offensive way as defined by state or federal law; and (3) the work as a whole lacks serious literary, artistic, political, or scientific value (Russell, 1993). But according to some analysts, including Leong (1991), the Court's decision has contributed to the social construction of pornography as a social problem.

The Social Construction of Pornography as a Social Problem

The social construction of pornography as a social problem involves both a cognitive framework and a moral framework. The cognitive framework refers to the reality or factualness of the situation that constitutes the "problem." In regard to pornographic materials, one cognitive framework might be based on the assumption that pornography *actually affects* people's actions or attitudes; an opposing cognitive framework might be based on the assumption that pornography is a fantasy mechanism that allows people to express the forbidden without actually engaging in forbidden behavior (Kipnis, 1996). The moral framework refers to arguments as to whether something is immoral or unjust. In the case of pornography, moral condemnation arises from the belief that graphic representations of sexuality are degrading, violent, and sinful. From this perspective, pornography is less about sex than about violating taboos in society. The moral framework often distinguishes between pornography and ***erotica*—materials that depict consensual sexual activities that are sought by and pleasurable to all parties involved.** According to sociologist Diana E. H. Russell (1993), materials can be considered erotic—rather than obscene—only if they show respect for all human beings and are free of sexism, racism, and homophobia. Contemporary erotica might include romance novels that describe two consenting adults participating in sexual intercourse (see Snitow, 1994). On the other hand, materials depicting violent assault or the sexual exploitation of children would be considered pornographic or obscene. However, the distinction appears to be highly subjective, as feminist scholar Ellen Willis (1981:222) notes: "Attempts to sort out good erotica from bad porn inevitably come down to 'What turns me on is erotic: what turns you on is pornographic.'"

Even in the age of high-tech, Internet pornography, many people seek out sexually-oriented magazines, videos, and other X-rated merchandise in settings such as the one shown here. Why do many people believe that places of business such as this harm not only individuals and their families but also the larger community?

The Nature and Extent of Pornography

As part of the multibillion-dollar sex industry, pornography is profitable to many people, including investors, filmmakers, and owners of stores that distribute such materials. *Hard-core* pornography is material that explicitly depicts sexual acts and/or genitals. In contrast, *soft-core* pornography is suggestive but does not depict actual intercourse or genitals.

Computer telecommunications has become one of the most prevalent ways that pornographic images are made available to people. In the comfort of one's own home or office, an individual can find vast amounts of sexually explicit materials on "X-rated" cable television channels, Internet news groups that specialize in adult chat areas and graphics exchanges, and various sexually oriented websites.

It is estimated that the porn film industry alone is a $10 billion-per-year enterprise, a figure that is greater than all of Hollywood's annual box office receipts and does not include revenues from porn magazines, Internet sites, cable adult channels, and the sale of sexual devices (McNeil, Osborne, and Pavia, 2005). Some individuals in the pornography industry gain wealth from their activities: For top actors at the high end of the pay scale, hourly earnings can be quite high and the work is often glamorously portrayed. Typically, female workers earn about 50 percent more than the men. Although a woman's earnings depend on her looks, a man's career is based more on his ability to perform sexually (Abbott, 2000). Consequently, some men in the porno film industry believe that they are being exploited, as was the case of "Ron," who suggests that profits do not extend to all actors in the films:

> You'd have to go a long way to find an industry with worse labor practices. They work people very hard; they pay them very little, really, for what they do.... As a

porn performer, you're putting up with a couple of days of hard, even abusive, behavior that compromises your ability to do anything else in your life ever again, because the piece of evidence of your past misbehavior continues to exist.... But after you've done porn films, you can't do anything else. You can't even do commercials....Another thing. There's an endless appetite for new faces and new bodies, which means they work [actors] to death for about six months or a year, put out twenty to thirty videos with them. And then they can't get work any more. New ones have come along. The audience is sick of looking at the old ones and wants to see new ones. (quoted in Stoller, 1991:209–210)

According to some social analysts, pornography is a prime example of the principle of supply and demand. As long as demand remains high, pornographers will continue to market their goods and services and find new ways to use technology. According to Walter Kendrick, a scholar whose research focuses on pornography:

> Pornographers have been the most inventive and resourceful users of whatever medium comes along because they and their audience have always wanted innovations. Pornographers are excluded from the mainstream channels, so they look around for something new, and the audience has a desire to try any innovation that gives them greater realism or immediacy. (quoted in Tierney, 1994:H18)

Each new development in technology changes the meaning of pornography and brings new demands for regulation or censorship. Today, interactive media presentations and pornography on the Internet are widely believed to be a far more powerful influence on people, especially children, than the printed word is (see Box 7.3).

Social Problems and Social Policy

Box 7.3

The Issue of Real versus Virtual Actors in Internet Child Pornography

> Prior to the invention of the Internet, consumers and distributors of child pornography had to know each other or have connections to exchange materials. Underground networks facilitated the trade of photographs or videos through the mail or in person. Currently, however, subscribers...can simply download graphic images through their modems to be able to view and print images.
>
> The anonymity available on the Internet hinders the detection of child pornography. A user can create any identity and transmit a message from California, through New Zealand, and then to Arkansas, making it impossible to determine the origin. Furthermore, "anonymous remailers" enable a user to re-route outgoing messages by removing the source address, assigning an anonymous identification code number with the remailer's address, and forwarding it to the final destination. (Simon, 1999:7)

According to the legal analyst quoted above, the Internet has changed the manner in which pornography can be created, distributed, and accessed. Similarly, computers have made it possible for software programmers to create products that show sexually explicit visual depictions of children (and adults) without using actual people. These computer simulations have produced new questions about what forms of pornography are legal to distribute on the Internet. Initially, when "virtual" actors—computer-generated images—were used by child pornographers, many antipornography advocates argued that virtual child pornography was no different from any other form of child pornography, including that which involved actual children. When some child pornographers claiming to use only virtual actors were apprehended by law enforcement officials, these pornographers stated that their products should be exempt from regulations governing child pornography on the Internet because their pictures and films did not show real children.

How has social policy shaped the manner in which we look at the issue of real versus virtual child pornography? Initially, the U.S. Congress shaped social policy when it passed the Child Pornography Prevention Act (CPPA) in 1996. According to this act, it was illegal to send or receive depictions of what appear to be minors (persons below age eighteen) engaging in sexually explicit conduct. According to the CPPA, child pornography included sexual depictions that allowed observers to believe that they were actually seeing minors engaged in sexual conduct. Thus possession of any type of child pornography would be a criminal offense if the material has been transported in interstate commerce, which includes being sent over the Internet.

(continued)

Box 7.3 (continued)

However, this is not where the social policy story ended. Next, the issue was argued before the U.S. Supreme Court, and the majority of the justices struck down the CPPA, ruling that virtual child pornography must be distinguished from child pornography that involves actual actors. The Court made this ruling on the basis of the argument that virtual pornography neither shows a real crime being committed nor involves a real victim (Ashcroft v. Free Speech Coalition, 2002). The Court's decision remains highly controversial. Advocates for the elimination of child pornography in any form on the Internet assert that their efforts to curb such activities have been seriously hampered owing to the Court's distinction between real and virtual pornography. Supporters of laws such as CPPA argue that the necessity of protecting children from being victimized by child pornographers should outweigh any restrictions that the law places on freedom of speech.

By contrast, those who agree with the Supreme Court's decision state that freedom of speech is a more important right to be protected than providing law enforcement officials with the restrictive tools to prosecute those who make, distribute, or use virtual child pornography because, in the final analysis, there is no real, living person to be protected in virtual pornography—only a computer-generated image that has no constitutional rights.

What distinctions can and perhaps should be drawn between images that are generated by computer software programs as compared with those made with actual child actors? Do you believe that the judges of the U.S. Supreme Court will change their view on this issue in the future? Why or why not?

Research on Pornography

During the past three decades, two presidential commissions have examined pornography and reached contradictory conclusions. The 1970 U.S. Commission on Pornography and Obscenity found no conclusive links between pornography and sex crimes or antisocial behavior. However, the 1986 Attorney General's Commission on Pornography (known as the Meese Commission) concluded that pornography is dangerous, causes sex crimes, increases aggression in males, inspires sexism against women, and encourages *pedophilia* (adults engaging in sexual intercourse with children). Although some members strongly disagreed, the Meese Commission concluded that sexually explicit materials should be further restricted and obscenity laws should be more stringently enforced.

Sociologists do not agree on the extent to which pornography that depicts excessive sex, violence, and the domination of one person by another affects behavior. More than 80 percent of X-rated films in one study included scenes showing women dominated and exploited by men. The vast majority of these films portrayed physical aggression against women, and about half explicitly depicted rape (Cowan et al., 1988; Cowan and O'Brien, 1990). Explicit violence is also part of many videos in the adult section of video stores (see Duncan, 1991). Nevertheless, studies have not established that watching such films and videos contributes to aggressive or violent behavior in viewers, and most people therefore do not support efforts to censor adults' access to pornographic material.

Pornography and Age, Gender, Class, and Race

Because viewing pornography is a secretive activity, data on the consumers of various forms are limited. Some studies have found that the typical customer of an adult bookstore is a white, relatively well-educated, married, middle-class man between the ages of twenty-five and sixty-six. Other studies have found that younger and more educated adults express more accepting attitudes toward pornography than do older, less educated adults (Lottes, 1993).

Overall, men watch more sexually explicit material and hold more favorable attitudes toward it than women do. Some analysts attribute this difference to gender role socialization. In a society in which men are socialized to be sexual initiators and often fear rejection, pornography is satisfying because it typically shows a willing female partner. In contrast, women have been socialized to respond negatively to material showing nude bodies and male pleasure that may occur at the expense of a woman's sense of safety and dignity (see Reiss, 1986). However, in recent years, more women have become consumers of *Playgirl* magazine, erotic novels, and videos such as those by Candida Royalle, a former porn star, that are made specifically for women (see Lottes, 1993; Macy, 1996).

In general, women are more vocal than men in opposing pornography. According to sociologist Michael Kimmel (1990), men are relatively silent for several reasons: embarrassment or guilt for having enjoyed pornography, anger at women's interference in male privilege, lack of interest in what they perceive to be a nonissue, fear that speaking out will lead to questions about their masculinity, reluctance to talk openly about their sexual feelings, and confusion about "what it means to be a 'real man' in contemporary society" (Kimmel, 1987:121).

According to film scholar Laura Kipnis (1996), much of the sentiment against pornography is rooted in class-based elitism: Opposition to pornography is a form of snobbery related to maintaining class distinctions in society. From this perspective, rejecting pornography amounts to rejecting all that is vulgar, trashy, and lower class. Although Kipnis does not suggest that all consumers of pornography are lower class, she believes that members of the upper classes typically view pornography consumers as lower-class people who might imitate the images they see. Similarly, women who appear in pornography or consume it are seen as brainwashed or unenlightened people who lack "class."

In another class analysis of pornography, philosopher Alan Soble (1986) linked men's use of pornography with their feelings of boredom and powerlessness, which are the result of capitalist work relations, the nature of labor, and the centralization of economics and politics. For these men, pornography becomes a diversion—a means of escaping from the dull, predictable world of work. Soble suggests that consumers of pornography use the material to construct fantasies and gain a sense of control; it gives men the opportunity—otherwise rarely available—to organize the world and conduct its events according to their own wishes and tastes. In Soble's eyes, pornography consumption is not an expression of men's power as much as it is an expression of their lack of power (Soble, 1986).

In other research, sociologists Alice Mayall and Diana E. H. Russell (1993) have detailed how different racial-ethnic groups are portrayed in pornography. Examining materials in a heterosexual pornography store, the researchers found that skin color is a highly salient issue: White women were featured in 92 percent of the pornography, perhaps because they fulfill traditional stereotypes equating female beauty with white skin and Caucasian features (Mayall and Russell, 1993).

People of color were more likely to be found in materials featuring rape, bondage and sadomasochism, anal sex, sex with children, and sex between women. Among women of color, African-American women were most frequently featured, followed by Asian or Asian-American women, and Latinas. African American men who consume pornography have a choice of buying magazines portraying only whites, white men with African-American women, or African-American men with white women. The researchers were unable to determine whether these options were based on the preferences of consumers or those of the makers of pornography (Mayall and Russell, 1993). Sociologist Patricia Hill Collins (1991) suggests that racism in pornography can be traced to the oppression of black women in slavery: African-American women were depicted as animals and used as sex objects for the pleasure of white men. Others have noted that at the same time that the white man was exploiting the black woman, he was obsessive about protecting the white woman from the black man (Gardner, 1994).

IS THERE A SOLUTION TO PROBLEMS ASSOCIATED WITH PROSTITUTION, PORNOGRAPHY, AND THE SEX INDUSTRY?

Despite some efforts to reduce or eliminate prostitution, pornography, and other components of the sex industry, this type of behavior has received little attention in recent years because of a national focus on problems in the economy, the war in Iraq, and other social issues that are considered by many to be more pressing concerns. At the local level, law enforcement officials in areas where prostitution is illegal tend to deal with individual occurrences on a case-by-case basis of whether the behavior is viewed as a public nuisance and how many complaints are received about the people involved. Similarly, pornography seldom raises a stir until the subjects involved are children or the person disseminating pornographic images is in a position of authority, such as a minister, teacher, or college professor, who is held to standards of high moral conduct. Overall, however, enough people tend to view prostitution, pornography, and other services provided by the sex industry as detrimental to society and as a threat to young people that these types of activities remain subject to prosecution when charges are brought against the individuals involved. How might the various theoretical and political perspectives that we have examined offer solutions to these problems?

Sexually explicit sites on the Internet are available to many students through their university Internet accounts. Should colleges and universities be able to restrict students' access to computer pornography? Why or why not?

Functionalist/Conservative Solutions

As you will recall, some functionalist theorists have suggested that some segments of the sex industry, such as prostitution, serve an important function in society because they offer sexual gratification and sexual outlets to people who otherwise have none and might engage in more harmful or illegal activities if these seemingly legitimate avenues of relief were not available to them. However, while some functionalist and conservative analysts acknowledge that the sex industry may produce goods and services that serve as a "safety valve" for some, many believe that these goods and services can be a "trigger" for others. For this reason, a solution to the problems produced by the sex industry is regulation and control. Prostitution and pornography must be carefully controlled, particularly so that children are shielded from these activities and materials. Cities and states where prostitution is legal and pornography is tolerated, for example, often pass ordinances regarding where brothels, X-rated video stores, and similar establishments can be located. Areas typically banned include sites that are near schools, churches, and some residential neighborhoods. To reduce or solve problems associated with such businesses, local law enforcement officials may more closely monitor the area and regulate workers in the industry, including frequent inspections of businesses or requirements that health permits be on display. For workers in the sex industry, practices such as these are often described as "harassment"; however, law enforcement officials, "legitimate" business owners, local residents, and others often see these activities as keeping matters under control and protecting the community's children.

From a *religious conservative* point of view, however, prostitution and pornography are threats to the moral values of society, particularly family values. The presence of prostitution and pornography in a society encourages people to have sexual intercourse outside marriage and to engage in deviant sexual behavior. Both visible prostitutes, in the form of streetwalkers and brothel workers, and invisible prostitutes, such as those who advertise their services on the Internet, are a threat to the moral well-being of society and must be dealt with as such. In regard to pornographic materials, sexually explicit and violent materials should be censored or eliminated outright to protect families and societal values. However, as some critics have pointed out, the controversy over censorship may be rapidly becoming obsolete in a world linked by the Internet and other rapid sources of communication. In such a world, whose community standards should be applied in determining whether materials are obscene? Censorship is a very complicated proposition in the global marketplace.

Conflict/Liberal Solutions

People who advocate a conflict or liberal point of view regarding prostitution and/or pornography emphasize the relationship between power in society and sex work. Laws controlling prostitution and pornography are created by powerful dominant-group members who seek to maintain cultural dominance by criminalizing conduct that they believe to be immoral or in bad taste. For some of these individuals, many aspects of the sex industry are nothing more than victimless crime, and the way to solve the "problem" of prostitution and pornography is to decriminalize these activities and let consenting adults do what they want to as long as it does not harm other people. From this perspective, until other social problems, such as poverty, racism, and sexism, are reduced or solved, there will always be prostitution because it serves as a way to earn money. Similarly, as long as there is a high demand for pornographic materials and people are willing to pay for them, other individuals will be willing to provide them. Critics argue, however, that there is no such thing as a victimless crime. In regard to prostitution, for example, they point out that most women in prostitution, including many who work for "high end" escort services, were sexually abused as children or that they went into the escort business because of economic hardship and the prevalence of racism in the United States (Farley and Malarek, 2008: A27).

Among the conflict/liberal approaches to dealing with prostitution, pornography, and other aspects of the sex industry are those feminist analysts who believe these activities demean and exploit women. According to this approach, pornography is sexist in its portrayal of women, emphasizes male dominance and female submission, and encourages the valuing of women according to their ability to please men, and, therefore, should be done away with. However, not all feminists agree that this is how to solve the problem. Some believe that pornography and prostitution should both be abolished while others believe that we should focus instead on eliminating structural factors that contribute to women's economic inequality and their oppression under patriarchy rather than initially trying to eliminate the sex industry. Other feminists primarily focus on pornography as a form of sexual discrimination and see this problem as a civil rights issue. From this perspective, communities should pass antipornography ordinances so that individuals who are victimized by pornography would be able to sue the pornographers who produced the goods for damages (see Russell, 1993). In sharp contrast, anticensorship feminists do not believe that any single factor such as pornography causes women's subordination. Focusing on pornography as the primary source of sexual oppression, they say, "downplays the sexism and misogyny at work within all of our most respectable social institutions and practices, whether judicial, legal, familial, occupational, religious, scientific, or cultural" (Segal, 1990:32). Therefore pornography should not be censored because open discussions about sexuality and sexual practices promote women's sexual freedom and their right to express themselves (Willis, 1983; Kaminer, 1990).

Symbolic Interactionist Solutions

Since symbolic interactionists focus on the process of interaction, this perspective primarily might offer solutions to issues relating to prostitution and the sex industry based on people who are engaged in sex work or those who create, produce, and distribute pornography. What kinds of perceptions do individuals in the sex industry have regarding themselves? What kinds of perceptions do the consumers of goods and services provided by the sex industry have of themselves? The answers to these kinds of questions might help us to gain a better understanding of why demands for these types of services may remain strong over time as well as why the supply of prostitutes, pornographic materials, and other sex industry products may also remain constant or increase during specific eras.

According to most symbolic interactionists, people view sex work—including prostitution and pornography—through the lens of their own mores and philosophical beliefs. Prostitution and pornography have gone through a process whereby they have been *socially constructed* as social problems by individuals in some sectors of American society, but not necessarily others, based on individual and collective cognitive and moral frameworks that are used to evaluate these goods and services (as discussed previously in this chapter). From this approach, what might have been identified in the past as "deviant" sexual behavior may now be thought of as relatively normative as it has become more widely accepted in popular culture and everyday life. Similarly, the line between "adult entertainment" and "hard-core pornography" may become blurred as people become more tolerant of certain kinds of language or behavior than in the past. An example is the greater acceptance by larger segments of the U.S. population of soft-core pornography in publications such as *Playboy Magazine* and in the E! Network reality series, *The Girls Next Door,* which features the much younger, live-in girlfriends of *Playboy* founder, Hugh Hefner.

As some analysts have pointed out, however, the symbolic interactionist perspective is most useful when it is intertwined with what we know about inequalities based on race, class, gender, age, and other social attributes. To gain a better understanding of why people participate in certain kinds of behavior or hold specific beliefs, we must understand where they are located within global hierarchies based on class, gender, or race/ethnicity. For example, in a forum on the topic "Should Prostitution Be Legalized?" University of Chicago Professor of Law and Ethics Martha Nussbaum made this surprising comparison:

> The difference between the sex worker and the professor, who takes money for the use of a particular intimate part of her body, namely her mind, is not the difference between a "good woman" and a "bad woman." It is, usually, the difference between a prosperous well-educated woman and a poor woman with few employment options. (quoted in *The Chronicle of Higher Education,* 2008: B4)

This statement captures both the symbolic interactionists' emphasis on how issues are socially constructed and the larger picture of how inequality and discrimination are an integral component of why people engage in certain kinds of activities.

To reduce problems associated with the sex industry by applying a symbolic interactionist approach, we need to find out more about how people perceive of their actions and what social meanings they attach to their experiences in the sex industry. Do individuals involved in the sex industry have different perspectives on the *self* than those who are not? How does their *self-esteem* compare with individuals who are not involved in, or consumers of, the services offered by prostitutes, pornographers, or other sex workers? According to some symbolic interactionist analysts, for example, the widely-used explanation that states that many sex workers suffer from poor self-esteem has major limitations in helping us to gain a better understanding of this issue or to identify ways in which prostitution and pornography might be dealt with as social problems in society. As opposed to the notion that "sex workers suffer from low self-esteem," some researchers have concluded that high self-esteem is closely linked to deviant or antisocial behavior such as may be found in some components of the sex industry. If this assumption is correct, it will be impossible to reduce or eliminate the problems associated with prostitution or pornography by merely viewing people who are engaged in this kind of work as being individuals who suffer from "low self-esteem."

By focusing on the micro relations of social life, symbolic interactionist approaches identify social issues and suggest possible resolutions to those issues that are labeled as being *a problem in need of a solution;* this perspective thus helps us to look more closely at how the people's interactions add up to larger social concerns. This approach also keeps us from overlooking certain important issues that "big picture" approaches, such as functionalist and conflict theories or conservative and liberal political perspectives, tend to ignore or miss altogether.

SUMMARY

■ *How do sociologists view deviance?*

Some sociologists view deviance as objectively given: Social problems such as prostitution and pornography are violations of folkways, mores, or laws. Others view deviance as socially constructed: A behavior, belief, or condition is deviant because it is labeled as such. Still others believe that deviance is rooted in the social structure of society: People who are in positions of power maintain their cultural dominance by defining as deviant the behaviors that they consider immoral, distasteful, or threatening to them.

■ *What kinds of behavior have traditionally been defined as sexual deviance in the United States?*

Four types of sexual conduct among heterosexual partners have traditionally been regarded as deviant: premarital sex (fornication), extramarital sex (adultery), promiscuous sex (casual sexual relations with many partners), and underage sex (statutory rape).

■ *What is prostitution and how has it changed in recent years?*

Prostitution is the sale of sexual services (one's own or another's) for money or goods and without emotional attachment. According to some social analysts, prostitution has recently become industrialized, normalized, and globalized. The industrialization of prostitution refers to commercialized sex as a product that is manufactured within the human self. Normalization is the process whereby sex work comes to be treated as a form of entertainment with no legal impediments to promoting it as a commodity. The globalization of prostitution refers to the process by which the sex industry has increasingly become global in scope.

■ *What levels, or tiers, of prostitution have sociologists identified?*

Sociologists have identified several categories:

Escort prostitutes (call girls or call boys) earn higher fees and can be more selective in their working conditions and customers than other prostitutes. Hustlers (bar girls or bar boys) work out of nightclubs, bars, and strip joints, where they solicit their customers. House prostitutes (house girls) work in brothels, and a substantial portion of their earnings goes to the house madam or pimp. Street prostitutes (streetwalkers) publicly solicit customers and charge by the "trick." At the very bottom of the tiers are those who exchange sex for crack cocaine.

■ *How do functionalists view prostitution?*

Functionalists point out that prostitution, like other forms of deviance, is functional for society. Prostitution continues because it provides people with (1) quick, impersonal sexual gratification without emotional attachment; (2) a sexual outlet for those who have no ongoing sexual relationships; (3) the opportunity to engage in nontraditional sexual practices; (4) protection for the family as a social institution; and (5) jobs for low-skilled people.

■ *How do symbolic interactionists view prostitution?*

Symbolic interactionists believe that prostitution, like other forms of deviance, is socially constructed. Entering a deviant career such as prostitution is like entering any other occupation, but public labeling—and the individual's acceptance or rejection of that label—determines whether a person stays in a deviant career.

■ *How do conflict theorists view prostitution?*

There are several conflict perspectives on prostitution. Liberal feminists consider prostitution a victimless crime, involving a willing buyer and a willing seller, that should be decriminalized. Marxist feminists see prostitution as being linked to the capitalist economy. Radical feminists trace the roots of prostitution to patriarchy in society. Conflict theorists who focus on the intersection of race, class, and gender believe that the criminalization of prostitution is a form of discrimination against poor women, particularly poor women of color.

■ *Does pornography differ from obscenity and erotica?*

Sometimes it is difficult to distinguish among these categories, but pornography usually refers to the graphic depiction of sexual behavior through pictures and/or words, including delivery by electronic or other data retrieval systems, in a manner that is intended to be sexually arousing. Obscenity is the legal term for pornographic materials that are offensive by generally accepted standards of decency. Erotica refers to material depicting consensual sexual activities that are sought by and pleasurable to all parties involved.

■ *Has pornography changed in recent years?*

Yes, technological innovations have greatly increased the variety of pornographic materials available as well as their methods of distribution. According to some analysts, as long as the desire for such materials is high, the multibillion-dollar pornography industry will continue to produce and market goods and services, adapting to new technologies as they become available.

■ *Does research indicate that pornography contributes to sexual violence?*

No conclusive answer has been found to this question. Some studies have found that hard-core pornography is associated with aggression in males and sexual violence in society, but other studies have found no conclusive evidence that pornography contributes to sexual violence. However, most feminist scholars suggest that pornography exploits all women and sometimes men and children.

■ *How do people react to the censorship of pornography?*

Reactions to the censorship of pornography are varied. People with a liberal view of pornography believe that it is a safety valve for society and that censorship, not pornography, is the social problem. Religious conservatives consider pornography a threat to moral values and encourage censorship of some materials. Antipornography feminists view pornography as a primary source of male oppression and violence against women and argue for its restriction or elimination. Anticensorship feminists believe that some pornography is bad but that censorship is worse because it suppresses free speech.

KEY TERMS

crime, p 130
erotica, p 140
obscenity, p 139
pornography, p 139
prostitution, p 130
social control, p 130
victimless crime, p 138

QUESTIONS FOR CRITICAL THINKING

1. Suppose you are going to participate in a class debate on decriminalizing prostitution. What arguments would you present in favor of decriminalization? What arguments would you present against decriminalization?
2. Are prostitution and pornography the result of sexism, racism, homophobia, and class-based inequality? Why or why not?
3. On the basis of the text discussion of pornography, obscenity, and erotica, find examples from the mainstream media (including films, music videos, talk shows, and fashion ads in magazines) that might fit each category.
4. Peter McWilliams suggests that the problem with censorship can be summed up in two words: Who decides? Who do you think should decide what materials, if any, should be censored as pornographic or obscene? Besides deciding what's acceptable and what isn't, who should decide on the punishment for violating these standards?

Chapter 8

Alcohol and Other Drugs

THINKING SOCIOLOGICALLY

- Is there a relationship between alcohol and drug use and class, gender, age, and race?
- What major health and legal problems are associated with abuse of alcohol and other drugs?
- What drug and alcohol prevention strategies and treatment programs are most widely used to help reduce this social problem?

It's days like today when I just have to stop and be thankful I didn't get myself killed in college. This is a tragic story [of a student's alcohol-related death] and one that happens far too often and comes close to happening enough to make any parent shudder.

I'm 23 now, and I've learned to have a glass of wine with dinner and be content. Two short years ago, I tried to do 21-on-21 with the full support of all my friends. I still have the picture of my arm signed 21 times by all the people who bought me drinks. Lucky for me, the bar we chose was stingy with alcohol and most of my drinks contained less than a half a shot. Still I managed to throw up halfway through the night and "rally" by going right back out to keep drinking.

This night was not an anomaly in my college drinking experience. I made some bad choices, but I think it's important for parents to be aware that many colleges today have a culture of binge drinking that goes beyond being young and stupid.

I was a serious student—graduating with a 3.9 GPA from a prestigious liberal arts college before going on to medical school. But looking back on how I spent those four years and how many times I encouraged a friend to have "just one more drink" I can't help but feel like I was part of all that is wrong with college culture these days.

—"Liz" responds with her own experiences (in a blog) to a* New York Times *article describing the death of Jesse Drews, a college student who attempted to quickly consume 21 alcoholic drinks in celebration of his 21st birthday (see Parker-Pope, 2008:A1).

When many people think about death from an alcohol overdose, they typically believe that such events primarily involve routine alcohol abusers or hardcore alcoholics. This is not always the case, however: One-time or occasional drinkers, such as Jesse Drews who went out for one night of "fun," may be seriously harmed or killed by a single alcohol-related incident. In the case of Drews, one night of drinking to celebrate his twenty-first birthday with two college friends resulted in his death. In a popular ritual known as "21-on-21," some young people attempt to drink at least 21 shots of liquor as part of their twenty-first birthday coming-of-age ritual. After Drews allegedly consumed between 10 and 12 shots of alcohol, his friends took him home because of his inebriated condition. His parents found him unresponsive in the early morning hours, and Drews was later pronounced dead, a result of an alcohol overdose (Parker-Pope, 2008). Tragedies such as this have led a number of parents and advocates for "responsible drinking" to create organizations that will inform people about the dangers associated with excessive alcohol consumption and to encourage them to become responsible drinkers if they are going to drink at all. In this chapter, we examine some of the problems associated with alcohol abuse and with the consumption of other kinds of drugs.

DRUG USE AND ABUSE

What is a drug? There are many answers to this question, so the definition is not always consistent or clear. For our purposes, a ***drug* is any substance—other than food or water—that when taken into the body alters its functioning in some way.** Drugs are used for either therapeutic or recreational purposes. Therapeutic use occurs when a person takes a drug for a specific purpose such as reducing a fever or controlling an epileptic seizure. Sometimes, individuals who take prescription drugs for therapeutic purposes cross the line to drug abuse. Recreational drug use occurs when a person takes a drug for no other purpose than achieving some pleasurable feeling or psychological state. Alcohol and tobacco (nicotine) are licit (legal) drugs that are used for recreational purposes; heroin and cocaine are illicit (illegal) recreational drugs (Levinthal, 2007). Licit drugs, which include such substances as vitamins, aspirin, alcohol, tobacco, and prescription drugs, are legal to manufacture, sell, possess, and use. Illicit drugs such as marijuana, cocaine, heroin, and LSD (lysergic acid diethylamide) are socially defined as deviant, and using them is criminal behavior and hence a social problem. We live in a society that is saturated with both licit and illicit drugs, some of which are difficult to obtain, others of which are as available as drugs at the local convenience store.

Defining Drug Abuse

What is drug abuse? *Drug abuse* is the excessive or inappropriate use of a drug that results in some form of physical, mental, or social impairment. A more difficult question to answer is "What constitutes drug abuse?" When looked at from this perspective, drug abuse has both objective and subjective components. The *objective component* is physical, psychological, or social evidence that harm has been done to individuals, families, communities, or the entire society by the use of a drug. The *subjective component* refers to people's perceptions about the consequences of using a drug and the social action they believe should be taken to remedy the problem.

Sometimes when people talk about drug abuse, the subjective component—the perception of consequences—overrides the objective component. Consider, for example, the subjective and objective components underlying our society's view of the use of marijuana. The subjective component of marijuana use is the

Signe Wilkinson, Cartoonists & Writers Syndicate/cartoonweb.com

general belief that marijuana is harmful and therefore should not be legal, even though there is little evidence that marijuana use is detrimental to health. The subjective component of alcohol use is the general belief that it is harmless and acceptable, even though there is considerable evidence that it impairs more people and produces greater costs to individuals and society than does marijuana use. Therefore, the use of alcohol is legal.

Drug Addiction

The term ***drug addiction (or drug dependency)*** **refers to a psychological and/or physiological need for a drug to maintain a sense of well-being and avoid withdrawal symptoms.** Drug dependency has two essential characteristics: tolerance and withdrawal. ***Tolerance*** **occurs when larger doses of a drug are required over time to produce the same physical or psychological effect that was originally achieved by a smaller dose.** Tolerance is a matter of degree: Some drugs produce immediate and profound levels of tolerance, whereas others produce only mild tolerance. For example, when a person first drinks a five-ounce cup of coffee, containing about 100 milligrams of caffeine, the stimulant effect is usually quite pronounced. After that person drinks the same amount of coffee over a period of several days or weeks, the effect is greatly diminished, and a second or third cup of coffee (for a total of 200 to 300 milligrams of caffeine) becomes necessary to duplicate the earlier feeling (Levinthal, 2007). ***Withdrawal*** **refers to a variety of physical and/or psychological symptoms that habitual drug users experience when they discontinue drug use.** For example, people who suddenly terminate their alcohol intake after long-term, heavy drinking experience various physical symptoms ranging from insomnia to DTs (*delirium tremens,* or mental confusion often accompanied by sweating and tremor) and psychological symptoms such as a reduced sense of self-worth.

ALCOHOL USE AND ABUSE

The use of alcohol—ranging from communion wine in religious ceremonies to beer, wine, and liquor at business and social gatherings—is considered an accepted part of the dominant culture in the United States. *Alcohol* and *alcoholic beverages* are terms that refer to the three major forms in which ethyl alcohol (ethanol) is consumed: *wine,* which is made from fermentation of fruits and contains between 12 and 14 percent ethyl alcohol; *beer,* which is brewed from grains and hops and usually contains 3 to 6 percent alcohol; and *liquor,* which includes whiskey, gin, vodka, and other distilled spirits and usually contains 40 percent (80 proof) to 50 percent (100 proof) alcohol. In the United States, adults consume an average of 2.4 gallons of wine, 21.3 gallons of beer, and 1.4 gallons of liquor a year. In fact, adults consume more alcoholic beverages (25.0 gallons) on average than milk (21.0 gallons) (U.S. Census Bureau, 2008). But statistics on average alcohol consumption do not indicate how much *each* person drinks during a given year. Some people do not drink at all, and others drink heavily. Among those who drink, 10 percent account for roughly half the total alcohol consumption in this country (Levinthal, 2007).

Many people do not think of alcohol as a drug because it can be purchased legally—and without a prescription—by adults. It is, however, a psychoactive drug that is classified as a *depressant* because it lowers the activity level of the central nervous system. The impairment of judgment and thinking that is associated with being drunk is the result of alcohol depressing the brain's functions. Alcohol also affects mood and behavior. One to two drinks often bring a release from tensions and inhibitions. Three to four drinks affect self-control—including reaction time and coordination of hands, arms, and legs—and judgment, muddling the person's reasoning ability. Five to six drinks affect sensory perception, and the person might show signs of intoxication such as staggering, belligerence, or depression. At seven to eight drinks, the drinker is obviously intoxicated and may go into a stupor. Nine or more drinks affect vital centers, and the drinker can become comatose or even die. Of course, factors such as body weight, physical build, and recent food and fluid consumption must be taken into account in estimating the rate of alcohol absorption in the body.

Although negative short-term effects of drinking are usually overcome, chronic heavy drinking or alcoholism can cause permanent damage to the brain or other parts of the body. Social scientists divide long-term drinking patterns into four general categories. *Social drinkers* consume alcoholic beverages primarily on social occasions; they drink occasionally or even relatively frequently. *Heavy drinkers* are more frequent drinkers who typically consume greater quantities of alcohol when they drink and are more likely to become intoxicated. *Acute alcoholics* have trouble controlling their use of alcohol and plan their schedule around drinking. *Chronic alcoholics* have lost control over their drinking and tend to engage in compulsive behavior such as hiding liquor bottles and sneaking drinks when they are not being observed. Film and television portrayals of alcohol use and abuse sometimes are framed to glamorize this behavior, but other times the stories are framed in such a manner that reveals the problems that chronic alcohol abuse creates for individuals and their families.

Alcohol Consumption and Class, Gender, Age, and Race

Although people in all social classes consume alcohol, income and class differences are associated with alcohol use. For example, studies show that people who earn more than $50,000 a year tend to drink expensive special or imported beers and more wine than liquor, whereas those who earn less than $20,000 tend to consume less expensive domestic beers and drink more beer than wine or liquor (Levinthal, 2007). The relationship between social class and rates of alcohol abuse is not as clear. Some studies show that people in the middle and upper classes are *less* likely to be heavy drinkers or have high rates of alcoholism; however, other studies show that alcohol consumption and abuse tend to be *higher* in the middle and upper classes than in the lower class. In any case, more affluent people typically have greater resources and more privacy than lower-income individuals have and can often protect themselves from the label "drunk" or "alcoholic." A member of the upper-middle or upper class who drinks to excess at the country club is less visible to the public and less likely to be negatively sanctioned by law enforcement officials—unless the person drives while under the influence—than is a lower-income or poverty-level person who sits on a public sidewalk drinking beer or wine.

Gender, age, and race are also associated with drinking behavior. More men than women drink, and men are more likely than women to be labeled as problem drinkers or alcoholics. Women who drink alcoholic beverages tend to be lighter drinkers than men, who are more likely to consume alcohol daily and experience negative personal and social consequences from drinking. However, drinking patterns in the teen years are similar for males and females.

In one national survey, 43.4 percent of all respondents between the ages of twelve and seventeen reported that they had tried alcohol at least once, and 17.6 percent reported that they were current users (U.S. Census Bureau, 2008). Some researchers have found adolescent drinking is associated with declining academic achievement and increasing emotional distress, although this varies with the extent to which young people drink within the peer context (Crosnoe, Muller, and Frank, 2004). According to the Census Bureau (2008), the vast majority of persons in the eighteen to twenty-five age category have tried alcohol at least once, and over 60 percent are current users. Among first-year college students, about half of the respondents in a national survey reported that they consumed alcohol frequently or occasionally (see Figure 8.1). Young adults—particularly men—between the ages of twenty-one and thirty are at greater risk of alcohol abuse if they remain single or become divorced than they are if they marry or remain married and become parents (Chilcoat and Breslau, 1996).

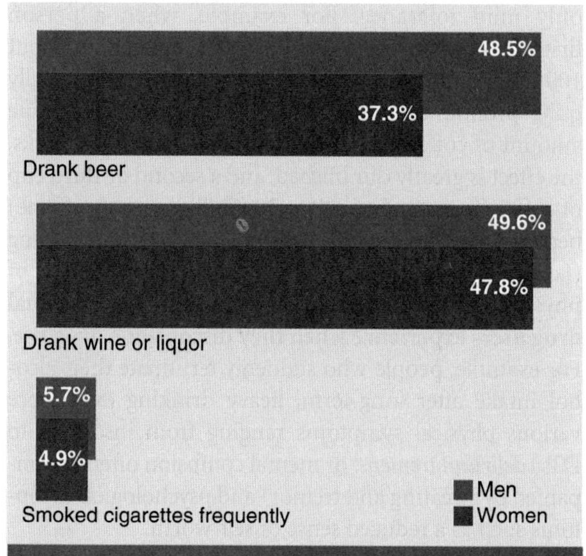

Figure 8.1 ***Alcohol consumption and smoking among first-year college students. Based on survey responses of 271,441 freshmen entering four-year institutions in the fall of 2006***

Source: Chronicle of Higher Education, 2007.

Social Problems in the Media

Box 8.1

TV Shows and the Framing of Alcohol Use

> It was open bar 3 o'clock on, every day, for three months. It's a very stressful situation to have so many cameras on you. It takes a lot of getting used to. So there's a relaxation factor that alcohol can assist with. Like any situation in which people are drinking socially, it's easy to keep drinking with them.
>
> *—Dave Kerpen, a cast member of the now-defunct reality dating show* Paradise Hotel, *discusses why he consumed eight alcoholic drinks during his first night on the show (Fletcher, 2006).*

> I'm a little bit concerned about this season's bachelor, Matt, and his relationship chooser. Last week, Matt and the bachelorettes frolicked in Las Vegas while consuming far too much alcohol. In fact, alcohol consumption has been a main feature in many of this season's scenarios. It seemed that all Matt got in return for the free-flowing champagne and martinis was a drunken, overly dramatic encounter with Shayne, this season's Drama Queen. Surprisingly, he gave her a rose [and in the season finale, proposed to her].
>
> *—Nina Atwood (2008), a counselor and self-identified "dating and relationship coach," discusses her concern about the extent to which reality shows such as* The Bachelor *rely on excessive alcohol consumption to create romantic sparks among the show's participants.*

Many reality shows on television feature alcohol consumption with mixed results. If we think about how social drinking is framed on these programs, it is easy to identify at least three frames. One is the "social drinking is fun" framework, which carries the message that participants who regularly—and sometimes excessively—consume alcoholic beverages know how to enjoy life, fit in with a group, and maybe even be selected as the "best" marriage partner on series such as ABC's *The Bachelor* and *The Bachelorette.* When the "social drinking is fun" framework is used, drinking is represented as a glamorous and pleasurable activity: Champagne sparkles in fine, crystal glasses, and vibrant toasts are made by expensively-dressed participants who engage in animated conversation, thereby sending the message to viewers that it would be fun to be part of the good life, and having a drink might be the place to start.

The second framework used on some reality TV series that show extensive alcohol consumption is the "Excessive drinking makes me talk silly and act stupid, but I really know better." Participants on MTV's *Real World* series routinely consume large amounts of alcohol, become embroiled in heated arguments, and sometime participate in fights or small-scale vandalism. As an MTV spokesperson stated, "Drinking is never glorified [in *The Real World*]; consequences are shown" (Fletcher, 2006). However, even when participants went to excess, the cameras continued to roll, giving audiences a voyeuristic view of people acting poorly. According to the executive producer of *Average Joe,* a former reality series, "Alcohol is the socially accepted drug of choice for our culture. So when you see people abuse it on a reality television show, maybe we should be looking at the problem of alcohol abuse and not the reality show. Alcohol's the problem; we're just showing it" (quoted in Fletcher, 2006).

The third framing method used to show excessive alcohol consumption on some television entertainment news shows is the "rehab as a revolving door" approach that has been popularized in coverage of hard-partying celebrities such as Paris Hilton, Britney Spears, and Lindsay Lohan. Celebrity "news" programs, such as *E News* and ABC TV's *Entertainment Tonight,* carry "glamour" stories about heavy consumption of alcohol by high-profile individuals and then follow up with stories about their "stints" in rehab. Some shows report on celebrities who briefly enter rehab and come out miraculously cured; others show the revolving door effect as the same individuals are readmitted on numerous occasions to gain sobriety. Celebrities entering rehab are shown arriving in expensive vehicles, wearing designer clothing and sunglasses, and being whisked into the facility. Meanwhile, photographers are yelling their names and shooting the least flattering photos they can get to sell to celebrity TV news shows and magazines. At the bottom line, it becomes difficult to find reality shows or celebrity news programs that do not feature alcohol consumption.

Questions to Consider

1. Does it matter how alcohol consumption and abuse are shown on television?
2. What media frames do you think are most often used on television and in films to show the problems associated with excessive alcohol consumption and other forms of drug abuse?
3. Are portrayals of alcohol consumption and illegal drug use different when done by male and female participants? By people from different racial, ethnic, or national groups? How about by people from the upper, middle, and lower classes?

Most research on race and alcohol consumption has focused on male drinking patterns; studies show that young African-American males as a category are less likely than their white counterparts to abuse alcohol, but later in life this pattern is reversed. After age thirty, African-American men have higher rates of heavy drinking and alcoholism than white males have. Some analysts attribute this difference to structural inequalities that uniquely affect men of color, such as high rates of unemployment in central cities, racial discrimination in employment practices, and inadequate housing conditions (Herd, 1988). Low-income Native-American men living on government-controlled reservations are especially vulnerable to chronic alcohol abuse and alcoholism. Some studies show that factors such as physical health, marital status, religious orientation, and previous life experiences apparently play a role in consumption of alcoholic beverages by Latinas and African-American women (Taylor and Jackson, 1990). However, Latinas and African-American women who have higher levels of income and education typically consume alcohol more frequently than do their counterparts with lower incomes and education levels (Parker et al., 1995).

Alcohol-Related Social Problems

Alcohol consumption in the United States has been declining across lines of class, gender, race, and age over the past two decades. Nevertheless, chronic alcohol abuse and alcoholism are linked to many social problems. Here we will examine health problems, workplace and driving accidents, and family problems.

Health Problems

Although not all heavy drinkers and chronic alcohol abusers exhibit the major health problems that are typically associated with alcoholism, their risk of them is greatly increased. For alcoholics, the long-term health effects include *nutritional deficiencies* as a result of poor eating habits. Chronic heavy drinking contributes to high caloric consumption but low nutritional intake. Alcoholism is also associated with fluctuations in blood sugar levels that can cause adult-onset diabetes. Structural loss of brain tissue may produce *alcoholic dementia,* which is characterized by difficulties in problem solving, remembering information, and organizing facts about one's identity and surroundings (Levinthal, 2007).

Chronic alcohol abuse is also linked to *cardiovascular problems* such as inflammation and enlargement of the heart muscle, poor blood circulation, reduced heart contractions, fatty accumulations in the heart and arteries, high blood pressure, and cerebrovascular disorders such as stroke (Levinthal, 2007). However, studies show that moderate alcohol consumption—such as a glass of wine a day—might improve body circulation, lower cholesterol levels, and reduce the risk of certain forms of heart disease.

Over time, chronic alcohol abuse also contributes to irreversible changes in the liver that are associated with *alcoholic cirrhosis,* a progressive development of scar tissue in the liver that chokes off blood vessels and destroys liver cells by interfering with their use of oxygen. Alcoholic cirrhosis is the ninth most frequent cause of death in the United States, and most deaths from it occur between ages forty and sixty-five (U.S. Census Bureau, 2008). Given all the possible health problems, perhaps it is not surprising that alcoholics typically have a shorter life expectancy—often by as much as ten to twelve years—than that of nondrinkers or occasional drinkers who consume moderate amounts of alcohol.

Abuse of alcohol and other drugs by a pregnant woman can damage the fetus. The greatest risk of ***fetal alcohol syndrome (FAS)*****—a condition characterized by mental retardation and craniofacial malformations that may affect the child of an alcoholic mother**—occurs during the first three months of pregnancy. Binge drinking during the third week of gestation has been linked particularly with this syndrome because that is when crucial craniofacial formation and brain growth take place in the fetus.

Alcohol in the Workplace

A study by the National Institute on Alcohol Abuse and Alcoholism found that lost productivity and time spent in treatment programs as a result of alcoholism cost about $100 billion annually in the United States (Pedersen-Pietersen, 1997). Other job-related problems that are associated with drinking include absenteeism, tardiness, and workplace accidents. Excessive alcohol consumption impairs the sensorimotor skills necessary to operate machinery, heavy equipment, and motor vehicles. Numerous studies have shown a relationship between alcohol—and other drugs—and many workplace injuries or fatalities (Macdonald, 1995). On the basis of Bureau of Labor Statistics reports of more than 1,300 fatal occupational accidents, researchers have concluded that alcohol, cocaine, and marijuana are the three leading substances involved in workplace injuries and deaths (Marine and Jack, 1994).

Driving and Drinking

Drivers who have been drinking often do not realize how much alcohol they have consumed or what effects it has on their driving ability. As a result, many people drive dangerously even when they are not legally drunk, which in most states requires a minimum blood alcohol level of 0.08 or 0.10 and is referred to as driving while intoxicated (DWI) or driving under the influence (DUI). Alcohol-related driving accidents occur, for example, when drivers lose control of their vehicles or fail to see a red traffic light, or a car or pedestrian in the street, or a sharp curve in the road; they also occur when a pedestrian who has had too much to drink is killed after being struck by a motor vehicle. Alcohol has been implicated in about 40 percent of all fatal accidents involving a motor vehicle in the United States. In fatal motor vehicle accidents in which the driver was between sixteen and twenty years of age, the driver had a blood alcohol level of 0.08 or more in 19 percent of the accidents; the percentage of drunk drivers in such fatalities increases dramatically for persons in the twenty-one to twenty-four age group (see Figure 8.2).

As high as these figures are, the exact size of the problem is unknown because only 68 percent of the drivers killed in automobile crashes are tested for alcohol, and only 24 percent of the drivers who survive accidents in which someone else dies are tested (Wald, 1996b). Moreover, despite the efforts to educate people about the hazards of drinking and driving made by some alcoholic beverage manufacturers and groups such as Mothers Against Drunk Driving, public interest in the issue appears to be declining.

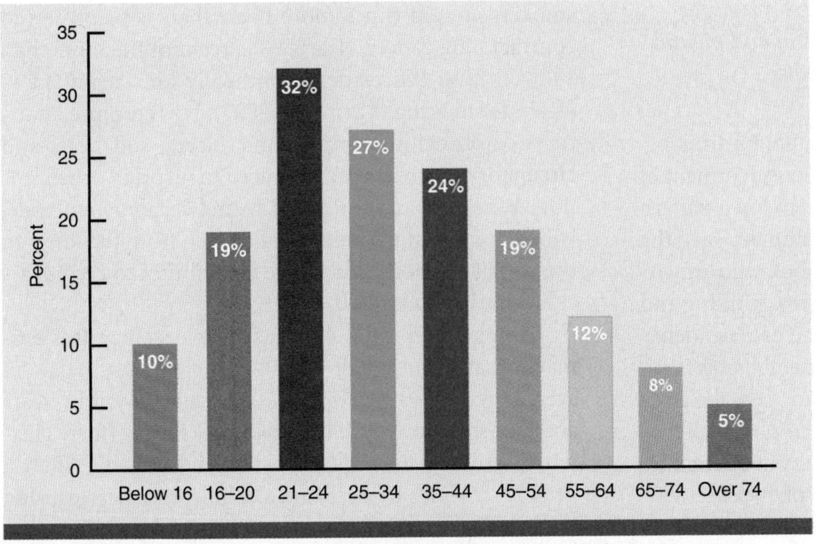

Family Problems

Chronic alcohol abuse or alcoholism makes it difficult for a person to maintain social relationships and have a stable family life. For every person who has a problem with alcohol, an average of at least four other people are directly affected on a daily basis (Levinthal, 2007). Domestic abuse and violence in families are frequently associated with heavy drinking and alcohol abuse by one or more family members. Growing up in a family that is affected by alcohol can have a profound impact on children. The extent to which alcohol abuse affects other family members depends on the degree of alcoholism and the type of alcoholic. Some alcoholic parents are violent and abusive; others are quiet and sullen or withdrawn. To outsiders, the family of an alcoholic might appear to be normal, but family members might feel as though they have an "elephant in the living room," as journalist Joyce Maynard (1994:80–81) explains:

> I grew up in an alcoholic household. But as difficult as it was dealing with my father's drinking, the greater pain for me was the secret keeping. Adult children of alcoholics refer to the phenomenon as "the elephant in the living room": You have a huge, inescapable fact about your life that affects everything in your home, but nobody mentions it, although everybody's behavior is altered to accommodate or deal with it.... Our family squeezed past the elephant in the living room, felt his breath on our faces, and rearranged furniture to make room for him. I hid liquor bottles if a friend was coming over. To prevent my father from driving, I even stashed away the keys to his car. But I never uttered a word, and neither did the rest of my family, about what was behind those actions.... It wasn't until I became an adult myself that I recognized the unhealthiness of our family's conspiracy of silence.

As Maynard suggests, family members of alcoholics frequently become enablers—people who adjust their behavior to accommodate an alcoholic. Enabling often

■ *Figure 8.2* ***Percentage of drivers involved in fatal crashes with blood alcohol levels of 0.08 or higher, 2003, by age group***

Source: National Center for Statistics and Analysis, 2004.

Alcohol abuse and domestic violence are major problems in many families. In a society that glamorizes alcohol consumption, it is difficult for some people to understand the physical and mental harm that excessive drinking may cause.

takes the form of lying to cover up the alcoholic's drinking, absenteeism from work, and/or discourteous treatment of others. Enabling leads many families to develop a pattern of ***codependency*****—a reciprocal relationship between the alcoholic and one or more nonalcoholics who unwittingly aid and abet the alcoholic's excessive drinking and resulting behavior** (Jung, 1994). When codependency occurs, the spouse or another family member takes on many of the alcoholic's responsibilities and keeps the alcoholic person from experiencing the full impact of his or her actions. Children who grow up in alcoholic families tend to have higher than normal rates of hyperactivity, antisocial behavior, low academic achievement, and cognitive impairment (Levinthal, 2007). However, although the statistical risks of becoming an alcoholic increase if one's parent has been an alcoholic, most children of alcoholics (as many as 59 percent) do not become alcoholics themselves (Sher, 1991).

TOBACCO (NICOTINE) USE AS A SOCIAL PROBLEM

The nicotine in tobacco is a toxic, dependency-producing psychoactive drug that is more addictive than heroin. It is categorized as a *stimulant* because it stimulates central nervous system receptors, activating the release of adrenaline, which raises blood pressure, speeds up the heartbeat, and gives the user a sense of alertness. Some people claim that nicotine reduces their appetite, helps them to lose weight, and produces a sense of calmness and relaxation. Perhaps these physical and psychological effects of nicotine dependency help to explain why about one in every five U.S. adults over the age of seventeen smokes and about 70 percent of all smokers have more than fifteen cigarettes a day.

Although the overall proportion of smokers in the general population has declined somewhat since the 1964 Surgeon General's warning that smoking is linked to cancer and other serious diseases, tobacco is still responsible for about one in every five deaths in this country. People who smoke cigarettes, cigars, or pipes have a greater likelihood of developing lung cancer and cancer of the larynx, mouth, and esophagus than nonsmokers do because nicotine is ingested into the bloodstream through the lungs and soft tissues of the mouth (National Institute on Drug Abuse, 1999). In fact, smokers are ten times more likely than nonsmokers to contract lung cancer. Nearly 90 percent of the more than 140,000 lung cancer deaths annually are attributed to cigarette smoking (Levinthal, 2007). Furthermore, many cases of bronchitis, emphysema, ulcers, and heart and circulatory disorders can be traced to nicotine consumption. When tobacco burns, it forms carbon monoxide, which disrupts the transport of oxygen from the lungs to the rest of the body and hence contributes to cardiovascular disease (Levinthal, 2007).

Smoking typically shortens life expectancy. It is estimated that about a half a pack (ten cigarettes) a day on average reduces a person's life expectancy by four years and that smoking more than two packs a day (forty cigarettes) reduces life expectancy by eight years. When a person uses both tobacco and alcohol, the cancer-causing effects of tobacco are exacerbated (Levinthal, 2007).

Even people who never light up a cigarette are harmed by ***environmental tobacco smoke*****—the smoke in the air as a result of other people's tobacco smoking** (Levinthal, 2007). When someone smokes a cigarette, about 75 percent of the nicotine ends up in the air. Researchers have found that nonsmokers who carpool or work with heavy smokers are more affected by environmental smoke than are nonsmokers who are only occasionally exposed to it. Therefore smoking has been banned in many public and private facilities throughout the country.

Not surprisingly, cigarette smoking adversely affects infants and children. Infants who are born to women who smoke typically have lower than average birth weights and sometimes slower rates of physical and mental growth. When a pregnant woman smokes, blood vessels constrict, which reduces the amount of oxygen reaching the fetus. Carbon monoxide transmitted from the mother's blood to the fetus interferes with the distribution of oxygen that does reach the fetus (DiFranza and Lew, 1995). Children who grow up in households in which one or both parents smoke are more apt to suffer from frequent ear infections, upper respiratory infections such as bronchitis and sinusitis, allergies, asthma, and other health problems than are children whose parents do not smoke.

Today, about 4.1 million teenagers smoke, and many report that they started in the sixth or seventh grade. The National Institute on Drug Abuse reports that about 12 percent of eighth-graders say that they smoke. About 19 percent of high school seniors report that they smoke on a daily basis, and about 10 percent indicate that they smoke as many as half a pack of cigarettes a day. Like smokers of all ages, high school-age smokers differ from nonsmokers on the basis of educational level and socioeconomic status. High school seniors who are not planning to attend college are three times more likely to smoke half a pack a day than are college-bound seniors. Those who drop out of high school are four times more likely to smoke cigarettes daily than are those who remain in high school through graduation. College students have lower rates of smoking than do individuals of the same age who are not attending college (Levinthal, 2007).

In recent years, young people have been targeted by marketing of smokeless tobacco products such as chewing tobacco and moist snuff, which is placed between the cheek and the gum. White teenage boys and young adult males, particularly in the South and West, are the primary consumers of these products. However, because oral smokeless tobacco is absorbed through the membranes of the mouth into the bloodstream, it increases the risk of cancer of the tongue, cheeks, gums, and esophagus. Most habitual snuff users have leukoplakia—a white, thick precancerous patch that is visible on tissues in the mouth—and erythroplakia—a red precancerous spot inside the mouth and nasal cavity.

Why do so many people use nicotine if it is so dangerous? Several reasons have been suggested. First, nicotine creates a high level of dependency, so once a person has begun to use tobacco regularly, the withdrawal symptoms may be strong enough to make the person light up another cigarette. Some researchers have found that the majority of people who smoke recognize that smoking is bad for them and would like to quit but cannot. Second, sophisticated marketing campaigns associate smoking with desirable cultural attributes such as achieving maturity, gaining wealth and happiness, or being thin and sexy. Although cigarette manufacturers are no longer allowed to advertise their products on radio or television, other venues are open to them. More than $15 billion dollars are spent annually on magazine and newspaper advertising, billboards, sponsorship of sports events, price discounts, and other forms of cigarette promotions (FTC, 2005). Some cigarette ad campaigns appear to specifically target young people, and they appear to work. Researchers have found that 86 percent of all children who smoke prefer heavily advertised brands such as Marlboro, Camel, or Newport.

Efforts by the U.S. government in the late 1990s to regulate the tobacco industry appear to have failed, at least for now. Attempts to pass legislation under which tobacco products would have become more regulated and less readily available to the public were defeated in Congress. Some advocates of tobacco regulation believe that it will be extremely difficult to get legislation passed as long as tobacco companies remain a major source of campaign contributions.

PRESCRIPTION DRUGS, OVER-THE-COUNTER DRUGS, AND CAFFEINE

When most people think of drug abuse, they picture unscrupulous drug dealers in dark alleys selling illegal drugs. But legal drugs also can be abused. Legal drugs fall into two categories: *prescription drugs,* which are dispensed only by a registered pharmacist on the authority of a licensed physician or dentist, and *over-the-counter (OTC) drugs,* which are available off the shelf and are restricted only by the customer's ability to pay.

Prescription Drugs

Pain medication is probably the prescription drug that is most frequently abused. Although millions of people benefit from *narcotics*—natural or synthetic opiates such as morphine (brand names Duramorph and Roxanol), propoxyphene (Darvon), and codeine—that relieve pain, suppress coughing, control chronic diarrhea, and reduce heroin withdrawal symptoms, there are risks of short-term abuse and long-term psychological and physical dependence. Over time, users develop tolerance for the drug they are taking and must continue to increase dosages to obtain the same effect that was derived from the lower dose. Drug dependency that results from physician-supervised treatment for a recognized medical disorder is called *iatrogenic addiction.* Iatrogenic addiction is most likely to occur with long-term use and/or high dosages of a prescription drug; it most often affects people from the middle or upper class who have no previous history of drug abuse or addiction (Levinthal, 2007).

Two widely prescribed drugs that have been the subject of controversy regarding their use and abuse are methylphenidate (Ritalin) and fluoxetine (Prozac). Ritalin is a stimulant that is prescribed for children who are diagnosed with *attention deficit hyperactivity disorder* (ADHD) or *attention deficit disorder (ADD).* According to the American Psychiatric Association, these disorders are characterized by emotionality, behavioral hyperactivity, short attention span, distractibility, impulsiveness, and perceptual and learning disabilities. Although some children are probably correctly diagnosed with this disorder, one survey has concluded that Ritalin is overprescribed. In the United States, 3 to 5 percent of all schoolchildren take Ritalin. Boys are three times more likely than girls to be diagnosed with ADHD or ADD, and it is estimated that 10 to 12 percent of boys between the ages of six and fourteen take or have taken the drug (Crossette, 1996). Advocates believe that children with normal to above-average intelligence who are performing poorly in school can benefit from Ritalin, which has proven to be safe for more than forty years. But critics argue that many parents, doctors, and teachers see Ritalin as a quick fix for dealing with troublesome children and note that the drug typically is prescribed to be taken *only* during the school year (Crossette, 1996).

Another controversial prescription drug is Prozac, an antidepressant. Introduced in 1987 as a breakthrough medication for clinical depression, Prozac has become a "cure-all for the blues," a far milder form of depression. Advocates believe that the more than 4.5 million prescriptions for Prozac that are filled annually enhance the quality of life for many people, freeing them from depression and suicidal thoughts. But the long-term side effects of the drug are unknown, and there is some evidence that Prozac is associated with intense, violent suicidal thoughts in some patients. Both Prozac and Ritalin are approved by the U.S. Food and Drug Administration (FDA) and are considered safe and effective if taken as directed (Angier, 1990; Kramer, 1993). Prozac is the only antidepressant approved for use with adolescents, and an official with the American Psychiatric Association estimates that 1.5 million kids are taking Prozac or similar medications each year (Helms, 2005). Use of Prozac by adolescents became a major controversy when a young man taking the drug shot and killed nine people at his school before taking his own life. As a result, the FDA ordered that prominent warnings be placed on all antidepressants noting that they carry an increased risk of suicidal thinking and behavior in children (Helms, 2005).

Abuse of prescription drugs among teenagers has become an increasing problem in another way as well: Some young people use *legal* medicines *illegally,* even having "pharming parties" where they trade drugs from their families' medicine cabinets with each other. Columbia University's National Center on Addiction and Substance Abuse estimates that about 2.3 million youths between the ages of twelve and seventeen take legal medications illegally each year. Compounding the problem of taking painkillers, antianxiety medicines, and ADHD and ADD drugs without proper medical supervision is the fact that many young people combine the drugs with alcohol. Ironically, the problem of taking legal drugs illegally is exacerbated by the fact that it is easier for young people to acquire prescription drugs in their own homes than it is to get illegal ones (Banta, 2005).

Over-the-Counter Drugs

A fine line exists between prescription and over-the-counter (OTC) drugs. Today, both types of drugs are advertised directly to the consumer in the electronic and print media with suggestions to "ask your doctor or pharmacist about [our product]." Some drugs are available both by prescription and over the counter, depending on their strength and dosage. For example, medications for acid reflux and stomach ulcers (e.g., Zantac and Tagamet) that are now sold over the counter were previously available only by prescription.

Widely used OTC drugs include analgesics, sleep aids, and cough and cold remedies. Abuse of aspirin and other analgesics can cause gastric bleeding, problems with blood clotting, complications in surgery patients and pregnant women in labor and delivery, and Reye's syndrome (a potentially life-threatening condition that can arise when children with flu, chicken pox, or other viral infections are given aspirin). Overdoses of analgesics such as acetaminophen (e.g., Tylenol and Anacin-3), aspirin, and ibuprofen (e.g., Motrin and Advil) have been linked to cases of attempted suicide, especially by white females between the ages of six and seventeen years. Few of these suicide attempts have resulted in death except when the analgesics were combined with alcohol or other drugs (Levinthal, 2007). Like analgesics, sleep aids are dangerous when combined with alcohol or some cough and cold remedies because they are depressants that slow down the central nervous system. Even cough and cold medications alone have side effects, such as drowsiness, that can be hazardous if users attempt to drive a car or operate heavy machinery. To counteract drowsiness, some drug companies add caffeine to their product.

Caffeine

Although it is a relatively safe drug, caffeine is a dependency-producing psychoactive stimulant (Gilbert, 1986). Caffeine is an ingredient in coffee, tea, chocolate, soft drinks, and stimulants such as NoDoz and Vivarin. Most people ingest caffeine because they like the feeling of mental alertness and reduced fatigue that it produces. Because caffeine blocks the brain's production of adenosine, a brain chemical that calms the brain's arousal centers, it has a "wake up"effect on people (Medpagetoday.com, 2005). However, the extent to which caffeine actually improves human performance is widely debated. Caffeine may improve concentration when a person is performing boring or repetitive tasks, but it has little effect on the performance of complex tasks such as critical thinking and decision making (Curatolo and Robertson, 1983; Dews, 1984). The short-term effects of caffeine include dilated peripheral blood vessels, constricted blood vessels in the head, and a slightly elevated heart rate (Levinthal, 2007). Long-term effects of heavy caffeine use (more than three cups of coffee or five cups of tea per day) include increased risk of heart attack and osteoporosis—the loss of bone density and increased brittleness associated with fractures and broken bones (Kiel et al., 1990). Overall, some people believe that the social problems associated with the abuse of caffeine and prescription and OTC drugs are relatively minor when compared with the social problems associated with illegal drugs.

ILLEGAL DRUG USE AND ABUSE

Are some drugs inherently bad and hence classified as illegal? What constitutes an illegal drug is a matter of social and legal definitions and therefore is subject to change over time. During the nineteenth and early twentieth centuries, people in the United States had fairly easy access to drugs that are currently illegal for general use. In the early 1800s, neither doctors nor pharmacists had to be state licensed. Patent medicines, which sometimes contained such ingredients as opium, morphine, heroin, cocaine, and alcohol, could be purchased in stores, through mail-order advertisements, and from medicine wagons run by people who called themselves doctors and provided free entertainment to attract crowds (Young, 1961). Over time, because of the rapidly growing number of narcotics addicts, prescriptions became required for some drugs. Some forms of drug use were criminalized because of their association with specific minority groups. For example, opium could legally be consumed in cough syrup, but smoking the same amount of opium was declared illegal in 1908 because opium smoking was a favorite pastime of the Chinese workers who were building railroads in the western United States (James and Johnson, 1996). Other forms of opium use were regulated when Congress passed the Harrison Narcotics Act in 1914.

The Harrison Act required anyone who produced or distributed drugs to register with the federal government, keep a record of all transactions, and pay a tax on habit-forming drugs such as heroin, opium, and morphine; it also required that certain drugs be purchased only from physicians (James and Johnson, 1996). However, the Harrison Act and drug-related legislation that has followed it have not been able to eliminate illegal drug use in this country (Bertram et al., 1996). Today, the most widely used illegal drugs are marijuana, stimulants such as cocaine and amphetamines, depressants such as barbiturates, narcotics such as heroin, and hallucinogens such as LSD.

Marijuana

Marijuana is the most extensively used illicit drug in the United States: About one in three people over the age of twelve has tried marijuana at least once. It is ingested by smoking a hand-rolled cigarette known as a *reefer* or a *joint* or through a pipe or other smoking implement. Potent marijuana—marijuana with high levels of the plant's primary psychoactive chemical, delta-9 tetrahydrocannabinol (THC)—has existed for many years, but potency has increased in recent years because of indoor gardens in the United States. Indoor crops have levels of THC up to four times as high as that in plants grown outdoors and in other nations (Navarro, 1996).

Although most marijuana users are between the ages of eighteen and twenty-five, use by teens between the ages of twelve and seventeen has more than doubled over the past decade, and almost 8 percent of persons between the ages of fourteen and fifteen have used marijuana during the past month (Substance Abuse and Mental Health Services Administration, 2001). Many teenage users report that marijuana is as easy to acquire as alcohol or cigarettes are. According to one teenager, "It is so popular, so well known, it is around everywhere. Nobody is afraid of the consequences of selling it or buying it.... It is really easy to get" (quoted in Friend, 1996:2A). Many young people buy the drug from friends who grow their own plants.

Marijuana is both a central nervous system depressant and a stimulant. In low to moderate doses, the drug produces mild sedation; in high doses, it produces a sense of well-being, euphoria, and sometimes hallucinations. Marijuana slightly increases blood pressure and heart rate and greatly lowers blood glucose levels, causing extreme hunger. The human body manufactures a chemical that closely resembles THC, and specific receptors in the brain are designed to receive it. Marijuana use disrupts these receptors, impairing motor activity, concentration, and short-term memory (Cowley, 1997). As a result, complex motor tasks such as driving a car or operating heavy machinery are dangerous for a person who is under the influence of marijuana. Some studies show that heavy marijuana use can impair concentration and recall in high school and college students (Wren, 1996b). Users become apathetic and lose their motivation to perform competently or achieve long-range goals such as completing their education. Overall, the short-term effects of marijuana are typically milder than the short-term effects of drugs such as cocaine.

High doses of marijuana smoked during pregnancy can disrupt the development of a fetus and result in lower than average birth weight, congenital abnormalities, premature delivery, and neurological disturbances (Levinthal, 2007). Furthermore, some studies have found an increased risk of cancer and other lung problems associated with inhaling because marijuana smokers are believed to inhale more deeply than tobacco users.

Over the past decade, medical uses of marijuana have been widely debated. In 1985, the Food and Drug Administration approved a synthetic version of THC, called Marinol, for prescription use to ease the nausea and vomiting that are common side effects of chemotherapy in cancer patients. Marinol is now also used to help AIDS patients regain their appetites (Cowley, 1997). Although recent reports by the Institute of Medicine have confirmed the medical merits of marijuana, the study did not give blanket approval of marijuana as a medicine (Kalb, 1999), and thus the debate over what to do about this widely used—but still controlled—substance continues (see Box 8.2).

Stimulants

Cocaine and amphetamines are among the major stimulants that are abused in the United States. Both are popular because they increase alertness and give people a temporary sense of well-being. It is quite another matter when a user becomes dependent on one of them and experiences withdrawal symptoms.

Cocaine and Crack

Cocaine is an extremely potent and dependency-producing drug derived from the small leaves of the coca plant, which grows in several Latin American countries. In the nineteenth century, cocaine was introduced in the United States as a local anesthetic in medical practice and a mood-enhancer in patent medicines. It was an ingredient in Coca-Cola from the 1880s to the early 1900s (Miller, 1994). Today, cocaine is the third most widely used psychoactive drug after alcohol and marijuana. Cocaine

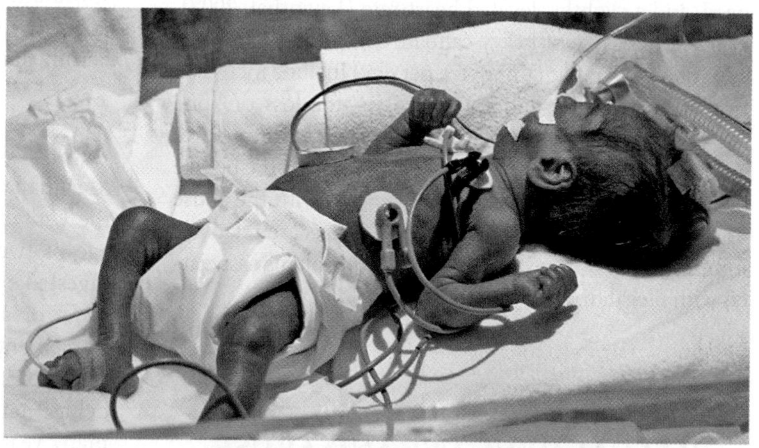

One devastating effect of drug abuse in the United States is the number of "crack babies who are born." Some of these infants suffer severe withdrawal symptoms at birth and have ongoing developmental problems.

Social Problems and Social Policy

Box 8.2

The Battle over Marijuana: Medicalization or Legalization

> Perhaps the most persuasive argument for medicinal marijuana I've encountered came two years ago, when the California Assembly was debating a medical-marijuana bill. One GOP assemblyman said he had had a great deal of trouble with the issue. But when a relative was dying a few years before, the family had used marijuana to help her nausea. That story helped the bill pass. Wouldn't it be awful if people changed their minds only after someone close to them had died?
>
> —*Marcus Conant (1997:26), a doctor at the University of California, San Francisco, who has treated more than 5,000 HIV-positive patients.*

> [Until adequate testing is done on marijuana]... it is inconceivable to allow anyone of any age to have uncontrolled use of marijuana for any alleged illness—without a doctor's examination or even a prescription.... Can you think of any other untested, homemade, mind-altering medicine that you self-dose, and that uses a burning carcinogen as a delivery vehicle?
>
> —*Barry R. McCaffrey (1997:27), a retired army general and former director of the Office of National Drug Control Policy, Washington, D.C.*

As these statements suggest, the controversy over marijuana is far from resolved. Advocates of *legalization* suggest that marijuana use should no longer be subject to legal control. Some states have adopted some form of decriminalization for the possession of small amounts—usually less than one ounce or so—of marijuana. Other states have passed medical-marijuana laws that permit use of the drug under specific medical circumstances. Advocates of these laws believe that doctors should be allowed to prescribe marijuana or that the federal government should lift the ban on the medical use of this drug altogether. Advocates of medical legalization believe that marijuana's benefits in treating certain medical conditions far outweigh its possible adverse consequences. For example, marijuana can help to control glaucoma, an eye disease that eventually produces blindness. It also can forestall AIDS-related complications, ease the nausea brought on by cancer chemotherapy, and counter some of the symptoms of epilepsy and multiple sclerosis (Cloud, 2002). Advocates envision a physician-controlled, prescription-based system or a legalized regulatory system something like the one that is in place now for alcohol and tobacco. If marijuana were treated as a legal substance, it could be subject to restrictions on advertising, content, purchase age, and other regulations for production, distribution, and sale.

In sharp contrast, federal drug enforcement officials and other opponents of medical-marijuana laws or legalization argue that the medical benefits of marijuana are modest at best and the drug is useless or dangerous at worst. Negative effects of marijuana identified in various studies include changes in brain chemistry that can affect memory and attention spans and that can lead to difficulty in concentration and in learning new, complex information. Marijuana also increases heart rate and blood pressure, irritates lungs, an decreases blood flow to the arms and legs, and can reduce sexual performance (Cloud, 2002). Opponents believe that medical-marijuana laws or legalization would increase the general level of use and open the door for legalization of drugs such as cocaine, heroin, amphetamines, and hallucinogens.

The debate over legalization of marijuana is far from over. At the time of this writing, eleven states (Alaska, California, Colorado, Hawaii, Maine, Maryland, Montana, Nevada, Oregon, Vermont, and Washington) have passed laws allowing the use of marijuana for medical purposes, and several state have decriminalized its recreational use so that the fine for possession of marijuana in limited amounts is about the equivalent of a traffic ticket. However, that does not mean that a person cannot be prosecuted in those states: In 2005, the U.S. Supreme Court ruled that medical marijuana users could be federally prosecuted because federal drug laws take precedence over state drug laws—and under federal law, marijuana is a *controlled substance,* which makes distribution of the drug a crime, even if it is being used for medicinal purposes.

The Supreme Court ruling left it up to Congress to decide whether or not to allow individual states to legalize the medical (or other) use of marijuana. Should Congress allow states to set their own policies regarding the legalization of marijuana to treat certain diseases? Should marijuana use for medical purposes be legalized? What do you think?

typically comes in two forms: powder and crack. In its powdered form, users typically sniff, or "snort," the drug into their nostrils or inject it intravenously. Crack is a hardened, potent form of cocaine that is smoked by users. When an increase in the use of crack became noticeable, it resulted in an intensification of the "war on drugs" that had been implemented by the Reagan administration in 1982 (Beckett, Nyrop, Pfingst, and Bowen, 2005).

About 23 million people over the age of twelve in this country report that they have used cocaine at least once, and about 1.7 million acknowledge having used it during the past month (Substance Abuse and Mental Health Services Administration, 2001). According to recent research, more males than females use cocaine, and the majority of users are in their twenties. In the mid-1980s, extensive media coverage of the hazards of cocaine use resulted in decreased usage by middle-class white high school and college students; however, an upswing in use occurred among young subordinate-group members living in lower–income sections of larger cities. Statistics show that African-Americans have much higher rates of cocaine use; however, one sociological study in Seattle found that high arrest rates for crack cocaine possession among African-American and Latino/a users could be attributed to the fact that law enforcement officials focused their efforts on subordinate-group users of crack cocaine. According to the researchers:

> Indeed, law enforcement's focus on black and Latino individuals and on the drug most strongly associated with "blackness" suggests that law enforcement policies and practices are predicated on the assumption that the drug problem is, in fact, a black and Latino one, and that crack, the drug most strongly associated with urban blacks, is "the worst." (Beckett, Nyrop, Pfingst, and Bowen, 2005:435)

In addition to law enforcement's focus on crack cocaine and subordinate-group populations, lack of economic opportunity contributes to the growth of the drug business in depressed, inner-city economies. For some central city residents living in poverty, with no hope of gainful employment, cocaine is a major source of revenue and an entry point for other drug-related crime. Here's how one fourteen-year-old male in Miami, Florida, described his involvement in the drug business (quoted in Inciardi et al., 1993a:86–87):

> I was sort of a scout, a lookout, for Mr. George. That was the name of the man who delivered the stuff [cocaine] to the places that sold it.... I was 11, an' Mr. George had a kid like me probably on every block.... I'd be in my front yard, see, watchin' for the cops. Mr. George would drive by my house...a few times. I'd watch and see if he was being followed. If everything looked OK, I'd go over to his car an' he'd give me the stuff, and tell me where to take it, or who to give it to. Sometimes he'd just give me a key an' say somethin' like "blue Pontiac 75/25." That would mean that near the corner of 75th Street and 25th Avenue there'd be a blue Pontiac. The stuff, and instructions, or maybe something else, would be in the trunk. Mr. George was real careful. When I'd drop it off I'd collect the money too.... For each job I'd get $10.

This young man's experience is not unique; studies indicate that selling drugs such as cocaine, crack, and heroin is the fastest-growing means of economic survival for men in locations ranging from Miami to Harlem (New York City) and Los Angeles (Bourgeois, 1995).

The effects of cocaine on the human body depend on how pure the dose is and what effect the user expects. Most cocaine users experience a powerful high, or "rush," in which blood pressure rises and heart rate and respiration increase dramatically. Reactions vary in length and intensity, depending on whether the drug is injected, smoked, or snorted. When the drug wears off, users become increasingly agitated and depressed. Some users become extremely depressed and suicidal; others develop such a powerful craving that they easily become addicted to the drug (Gawin and Ellinwood, 1988). Occasionally, cocaine use results in sudden death by triggering an irregular heart rhythm.

People who use cocaine over extended periods of time have higher rates of infection, heart disturbance, internal bleeding, hypertension, cardiac arrest, stroke, hemorrhaging, and other neurological and cardiovascular disorders than nonusers do. Although these problems often develop gradually as cocaine use continues, some users experience the problems after a single dose. Intravenous cocaine users who share contaminated needles and syringes are also at risk for AIDS. The risk of contracting AIDS is especially high in crack houses, where women addicts often engage in prostitution (see Chapter 7) to acquire drugs.

Cocaine use is extremely hazardous during pregnancy. Children born to crack-addicted mothers usually suffer painful withdrawal symptoms at birth and later show deficits in cognitive skills, judgment, and behavior controls. "Crack babies" must often be cared for at public expense in hospitals and other facilities because their mothers cannot meet the children's basic needs or provide nurturance. But social scientist Philippe Bourgeois suggests that blame for the problem cannot be placed on the women alone. Many mothers of crack babies desperately seek meaning in their lives and refuse to sacrifice themselves to the impossible task of raising healthy children in the inner city. Instead, Bourgeois blames the problem on patriarchal definitions of "family" and the dysfunctional public sector that relegates the responsibility for nurturing and supporting children almost exclusively to women. For change to occur, fathers and the larger society must share the women's burden (Bourgeois, 1995).

Amphetamines

Like cocaine, amphetamines ("uppers") stimulate the central nervous system. Amphetamines in the form of diet pills and pep formulas are legal substances when they are prescribed by a physician, but many people, believing that they cannot lose weight or have enough energy without the pills, become physically and/or psychologically dependent on them. Speed freaks—heavy users who inject massive doses of amphetamines several times a day—often do "runs," staying awake for extended periods of time, eating very little, and engaging in bizarre behavior such as counting cornflakes in a cereal box or pasting postage stamps on the wall before "crashing" and sleeping for several days (Goode, 1989). Recent concern about amphetamine abuse has focused on a smokable form called ICE that contains a high percentage of the pure drug and produces effects that last from four to twenty-four hours (Lauderback and Waldorf, 1993). Chronic amphetamine abuse can result in *amphetamine psychosis,* which is characterized by paranoia, hallucinations, and violent tendencies that may persist for weeks after use of the drug has been discontinued. Overdosing on amphetamines can produce coma, brain damage, and even death.

Depressants

Many people who abuse stimulants also abuse depressants—drugs, including alcohol, that depress the central nervous system and may have some pain-killing properties. The most commonly used depressants are barbiturates (e.g., Nembutal and Seconal) and antianxiety drugs or tranquilizers (e.g., Librium, Valium, and Miltown). Relatively low oral doses of depressants produce a relaxing and mildly disinhibiting effect; higher doses result in sedation. Users can develop both physical addiction to and psychological dependence on these depressants. Users sometimes use depressants for *potentiation*—the interaction that takes place when two drugs are mixed together to produce a far greater effect than the effect of either drug administered separately. Heroin users, for example, will sometimes combine heroin and barbiturates in hopes of prolonging their high and extending their heroin supply (Levinthal, 2007).

Recently, Rohypnol and GHB (gamma hydroxybutyrate), also known as "Grievous Bodily Harm" or "Liquid X," have been topics of discussion on college campuses. Rohypnol is used as an anesthetic and sleep aid in other countries, but it is not approved for use in the United States. Before it was banned by the FDA in 1990, GHB was sold in health food stores and used by body builders to increase muscle growth. Currently, GHB is manufactured illegally, and some people acquire the recipe on the Internet. Rohypnol and GHB are popular among young people because they are inexpensive ("lunch money") drugs and produce a "floaty" state, a mild euphoria, increased sociability, and lowered inhibitions. For some people, Rohypnol works like a powerful sleeping pill. Jenny Altick was a college student when she tried the drug: "I'd just pass out. . . . it seemed like a very safe thing to take. It wasn't like acid or something that was totally chemical and bad. If you're thinking about trying coke [cocaine], you've heard how bad it is. There's that little thing in your head. But this one, no one had heard about it. It was one of those new things everyone was doing" (quoted in Bonnin, 1997:E1). For other users, however, the consequences are more dire. Rohypnol is known as the "date rape drug" because a number of women have reported that they were raped after an acquaintance secretly slipped the drug into their drink. The combination of alcohol and Rohypnol or GHB has also been linked to automobile accidents and deaths from overdoses, which occur because it is difficult to judge how much intoxication will result when depressants are mixed with alcohol (Bonnin, 1997).

Narcotics

Narcotics or opiates are available in several forms: natural substances (e.g., opium, morphine, and codeine); opiate derivatives, which are created by making slight changes in the chemical composition of morphine (e.g., heroin and Percodan); and synthetic drugs, which produce opiatelike effects but are not chemically related to morphine (e.g., Darvon and Demerol). Because heroin is the most widely abused narcotic, we will focus primarily on its effects.

Who uses heroin? Young people are among the heaviest heroin users; however, only about 1 percent of people between eighteen and twenty-nine years of age have ever used the drug. Some people who try the drug experience adverse side effects such as nausea and vomiting and never use it again; others become addicted. Current estimates of the number of U.S. heroin abusers range from 300,000 to 700,000. Most studies conclude that the typical heroin abuser is a young male, often a subordinate-group member, under age thirty, who lives in a low-income area of a large urban center such as New York City (Levinthal, 2007).

What effect does heroin have on the body? Most heroin users inject the drug intravenously—a practice known as *mainlining* or *shooting*—which produces a tingling sensation and feeling of euphoria that is typically followed by a state of drowsiness or lethargy. Heroin users quickly develop a tolerance for the drug and must increase the dosage continually to achieve the same effect. Heroin and other opiates are highly addictive; users experience intense cravings for the drug and have physical symptoms such as diarrhea and dehydration if the drug is withdrawn.

What are the long-term effects of heroin? Although some users experience no long-term physical problems, there are serious risks involved in heroin use. In high doses, heroin produces extreme respiratory depression, coma, and even death. Because the potency of street heroin is unknown, overdosing is always a possibility. Street heroin also tends to be diluted with other ingredients that produce adverse reactions in some users. Shooting up with contaminated needles can lead to hepatitis or AIDS. Heroin use also has been linked more directly to crime than have some other types of drug use. Because hard-core users have difficulty holding a job yet need a continual supply of the drug, they often turn to robbery, burglary, shoplifting, pimping, prostitution, or working for the underground drug industry (Johnson et al., 1985).

Hallucinogens

Hallucinogens or psychedelics are drugs that produce illusions and hallucinations. Mescaline (peyote), lysergic acid diethylamide (LSD), phencyclidine (PCP), and methylenedioxy methanphetamine (MDMA) produce mild to profound psychological effects, depending on the dosage. Mescaline or peyote—the earliest hallucinogen used in North America—was consumed during ancient Native-American religious celebrations.

In the 1960s, LSD became a well-known hallucinogen because of Dr. Timothy Leary's widely publicized advice, "Turn on, tune in, drop out." LSD is one of the most powerful of the psychoactive drugs; a tiny dose (10 micrograms) of the odorless, tasteless, and colorless drug can produce dramatic, highly unpredictable psychological effects for up to twelve hours. These effects are often referred to as a *psychedelic trip*, and users report experiences ranging from the beautiful (a good trip) to the frightening and extremely depressing (a bad trip). Consequently, some LSD users take the drug only with the companionship of others who are familiar with the drug's effects. However, some studies have found that there is a possibility of *flashbacks* in which the user reexperiences the effects of the drug as much as a year after it was taken. Most long-term psychiatric problems associated with the drug involve people who are unaware that they have been given LSD, who show unstable personality characteristics before taking the drug, or who experience it under hostile or threatening circumstances (Levinthal, 2007).

Among the most recent hallucinogens are PCP ("angel dust") and MDMA ("Ecstasy"). PCP can be taken orally, intravenously, or by inhalation, but it is most often smoked. Initially, PCP was used as an anesthetic in surgical procedures, but it was removed from production when patients who received it showed signs of agitation, intense anxiety, hallucinations, and disorientation. Production then went underground, and PCP became a relatively inexpensive street drug that some dealers pass off as a more expensive drug such as LSD to unknowing customers.

In the mid-1980s, MDMA ("Ecstasy") hit the street market. Manufactured in clandestine labs by inexperienced chemists, Ecstasy, or "E," is a "designer drug" that is derived from amphetamines and has hallucinogenic effects. Users claim that it produces a state of relaxation, insight, euphoria, and heightened awareness without the side effects of LSD. Ecstasy has a high abuse potential and no recognized medical use (Milkman and Sunderwirth, 1987). It is far easier to explain *what* some of the major drugs taken in contemporary societies are than it is to explain *why* many people abuse drugs.

EXPLANATIONS OF DRUG ABUSE

Why do people abuse drugs? Various explanations have been given. Some focus on biological factors; others emphasize environmental influences. Social scientists believe that drug abuse is associated with continuous and cumulative influences from the time of conception throughout the life course. Thus to answer the question of why people abuse drugs, we must examine the intertwining biological, psychological, and sociological factors that affect people's behavior.

Biological Explanations

Some biological explanations of alcohol and other drug addiction focus on genetic factors. Some studies of alcoholism have found that children who have an alcoholic birth parent have a higher than normal risk of becoming alcoholics themselves, even if they are adopted at birth and reared by nonalcoholic parents. These studies suggest that the child of an alcoholic parent inherits a biological predisposition (or vulnerability) to problem drinking or alcoholism. For example, the child might inherit increased sensitivity to alcohol as indicated by impaired enzyme production, brain function, and physiological responsivity during alcohol intake. The child also might inherit cognitive or learning impairments (e.g., hyperactivity, attention deficit disorder, or language delay) or psychological features (e.g., impulsivity, sensation seeking, anxiety, or aggressiveness) that increase the risk of alcohol abuse by exaggerating the rewarding biological and psychological properties of alcohol (Levinthal, 2007).

Other biological studies focus on the relationship between the brain and drug addiction. These studies have found convincing evidence that drugs such as alcohol, heroin, and cocaine act directly on the brain mechanisms that are responsible for reward and punishment. As the drugs stimulate the areas of the brain that create the sensation of pleasure and suppress the perception of pain, the user receives reinforcement to engage in further drug-taking behavior. According to these findings, then, drugs that provide an immediate rush or intense euphoria (e.g., cocaine and heroin) are more likely to be abused than are drugs that do not. Similarly, drugs that produce pleasant but rapidly dissipating effects (e.g., alcohol) tend to encourage users to take additional doses to maintain the pleasurable effects. Biological explanations provide some insights into drug abuse, but biological factors alone do not fully explain alcoholism and other drug dependency.

Currently, researchers are studying the genetics of alcoholism and drug dependency to assess the extent to which drug abuse is related to biological factors as opposed to the social environment in which a person lives. Does our genetic makeup play a role in alcoholism and dependency on other drugs? Some scientists have found that genetic markers such as the dopamine D2 receptor are present more often in alcoholics than in nonalcoholics. In animal studies that do not include human beings, this receptor has been associated with brain functions that are related to reward, reinforcement, and motivation to act in a specific manner. Although human genome research might hold promise for identifying genes related to drug dependency, researchers currently have not identified one specific gene that is linked to alcohol-related behavior. It is believed that more than one gene is responsible for vulnerability to drug abuse and that other factors, including psychological influences and the social setting in which a person lives, may play a more significant role in determining an individual's vulnerability to drug addiction.

Psychological Explanations

Psychological explanations of drug abuse focus on either personality disorders or the effects of social learning and reinforcement on drug-taking behavior. Some studies have found that personality disorders—antisocial personality, psychopathy, impulsivity, affective disorder, and anxiety, among others—are more common among drug abusers than among nonabusers (Shedler and Block, 1990). Hyperactivity, learning disabilities, and behavioral disorders in childhood are also associated with a greater risk of substance abuse in adolescence or young adulthood. When people have low self-esteem or lack motivation, their desire to get away from problems is intensified, and drugs often provide the most available option for escape.

Social psychologists explain drug behavior in terms of social learning. According to *social learning theory,* drug and alcohol use and abuse are behaviors that are acquired and sustained through a learning process. Learning takes place through instrumental conditioning (positive reinforcement or punishment) and modeling (imitation) of other people's behavior. Every person learns attitudes, orientations, and general information about drug use from family members, friends, and significant others, so he or she comes to associate positive consequences (positive reinforcement) and negative consequences (punishment) with drug use. Therefore, whether the person abstains from, takes, or abuses drugs depends on the past, present, and anticipated rewards and punishments he or she associates with abstinence, use, or abuse. In a nutshell, the more an individual defines drug behavior as good, or at least excusable, the more that person is likely to use drugs.

Sociological Explanations

The social psychological perspective on drug abuse and the symbolic interactionist perspective overlap. In contrast, functionalists focus on how drug use and abuse fulfills a function in society, and conflict theorists emphasize the role of powerful elites in determining what constitutes legal or illegal drug use.

The Symbolic Interactionist Perspective

Like social psychologists, sociologists who use a symbolic interactionist framework believe that drug behavior is learned behavior that is strongly influenced by families, peers, and other people. In other words, individuals are more likely to use or abuse drugs if they have frequent, intense, and long-lasting interactions with people who use or abuse drugs. For example, some children learn to abuse alcohol or other drugs by watching their parents drink excessively or use illegal drugs. Other young people learn about drug use from their peer group. In his classic study of marijuana users, sociologist Howard S. Becker (1963) concluded that drug users not only learn how to "do" drugs from other users but also what pleasurable reactions they should expect to have from drug use.

People also are more prone to accept attitudes and behaviors that are favorable to drug use if they spend time with members of a ***drug subculture*****—a group of people whose attitudes, beliefs, and behaviors pertaining to drug use differ significantly from those of most people in the larger society.** Over time, people in heavy drinking or drug subcultures tend to become closer to others within their subculture and more distant from people outside the subculture. Given this, participants in hard-core drug subcultures quit taking drugs or drinking excessively only when something brings about a dramatic change in their attitudes, beliefs, and values regarding drugs. Although it is widely believed that most addicts could change their behavior if they chose to do so, according to labeling theory, it is particularly difficult for individuals to discontinue alcohol and other drug abuse once they have been labeled "alcoholics" or "drug addicts." Because of the prevailing ideology that alcoholism and drug addiction are personal problems rather than social problems, individuals tend to be held solely responsible for their behavior.

The Functionalist Perspective

Why does the level of drug abuse remain high in the United States? Functionalists point out that social institutions such as the family, education, and religion, which previously kept deviant behavior in check, have become fragmented and somewhat disorganized. Because they have, it is now necessary to use formal mechanisms of social control to prohibit people from taking illegal drugs or driving under the influence of alcohol or other drugs. External controls in the form of law enforcement are also required to discourage people from growing, manufacturing, or importing illegal substances. Functionalists believe that activities in society continue because they serve important societal functions. Prescription and over-the-counter drugs, for example, are functional for patients because they ease pain, cure illness, and sometimes enhance or extend life. They are functional for doctors because they provide a means for treating illness and help to justify the doctor's fee. They are functional for pharmacists because they provide a source of employment; without pills to dispense, there would be no need for pharmacists. But dysfunctions also occur with prescription drugs: Patients can experience adverse side effects or develop a psychological dependence on the drug; doctors, pharmacists, and drug companies might be sued because they manufactured, prescribed, or sold a drug that is alleged to cause bodily harm to users.

Illicit drugs also have functions and dysfunctions. On the one hand, illicit drug use creates and perpetuates jobs at all levels of the criminal justice system, the federal government, and social service agencies that deal with problems of alcoholism and drug addiction. What, for example, would employees at the Drug Enforcement Administration (DEA), the principal federal narcotics control agency, do if the United States did not have an array of illicit drugs that are defined as the "drug problem"? On the other hand, the dysfunctions of illicit drug use extend throughout society. At the individual level, addictive drugs such as heroin, cocaine, and barbiturates create severe physical and mental health problems as well as economic crises for addicts, their families, and acquaintances. At the societal level, drug abuse contributes to lost productivity, human potential and life, and money. Billions of dollars in taxpayers' money that might be used for education or preventive health care are spent making and enforcing drug laws and dealing with drug-related crime and the spread of AIDS by addicts who shoot up with contaminated needles. Addiction to illegal drugs, the abuse of legal drugs, and the abuse of alcohol and tobacco exacerbate the loss of human potential and undermine the stability of society.

The Conflict Perspective

According to conflict theorists, people in positions of economic and political power make the sale, use, and possession of drugs abused by the poor and the powerless illegal. We mentioned earlier that opium smoking was outlawed because it was associated with the Chinese. Similarly, marijuana smoking, which was associated primarily with

Mexican workers who were brought to the United States during the 1920s to work in some fields and factories, was restricted by the Marijuana Tax Act of 1937. Although the name of this legislation suggests that its purpose was to raise tax revenues, the intent was to criminalize marijuana and provide a mechanism for driving Mexican workers back across the border so that they would not be a threat to U.S.-born workers who couldn't find jobs during the Great Depression. As middle- and upper-middle-class, college-educated people took up marijuana smoking in the 1950s and 1960s, many states reduced the penalties for its use. In sum, restricting the drugs that members of a subordinate racial-ethnic group use is one method of suppressing the group and limiting its ability to threaten dominant-group members or gain upward mobility in society. Whether a drug is legal or illegal is determined by those who control the nation's political and legal apparatus.

Conflict theorists also point out that powerful corporate interests perpetuate the use and abuse of legal drugs. Corporations that manufacture, market, and sell alcohol, tobacco, and pharmaceuticals reap huge profits from products that exact a heavy toll on the personal health and well-being of abusers, their families and communities, and the larger society. Recent congressional hearings on the tobacco industry's alleged manipulation of nicotine levels to make cigarette smoking more addictive have helped to highlight this point. However, by contributing millions of dollars each year to election campaigns, these corporations position themselves to manipulate political decisions that could affect them. Members of Congress who control most tobacco-related regulations typically receive large campaign contributions from political action committees funded by the tobacco industry and often represent districts where tobacco companies are among the largest employers. Using their wealth and political clout, elites in tobacco companies have spent years vigorously fighting measures, including those that would classify and regulate tobacco as a drug, affecting the industry's more than $50 billion annual revenue (Kluger, 1996).

IS THERE A SOLUTION TO PROBLEMS ASSOCIATED WITH ALCOHOL AND DRUG ABUSE?

How to prevent abuse of alcohol and other drugs and how to treat drug-related problems after they arise are controversial issues in contemporary society. What kinds of drug abuse prevention programs are available? Will future treatment programs for alcoholics and drug addicts differ from the ones that are available today?

Prevention Programs

Drug and alcohol prevention programs can be divided into three major categories: primary, secondary, and tertiary prevention. *Primary prevention* refers to programs that seek to prevent drug problems before they begin. Most primary prevention programs focus on people who have had little or no previous experience with drugs. In contrast, *secondary prevention* programs seek to limit the extent of drug abuse, prevent the spread of drug abuse to substances beyond those already experienced, and teach strategies for the responsible use of licit drugs such as alcohol (Levinthal, 2007). For example, a program directed at college students who already consume alcohol might focus on how to drink responsibly by

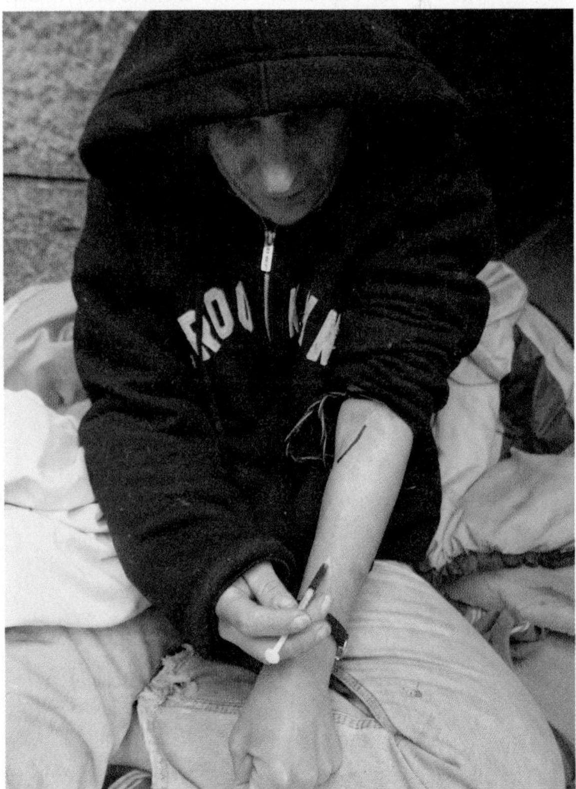

This woman may be playing double jeopardy with her life. The purity of street drugs often is in doubt, and shooting up with contaminated needles is a significant source of new AIDS cases in the United States.

emphasizing the dangers of drinking and driving. Finally, *tertiary prevention* programs seek to limit relapses by individuals recovering from alcoholism or drug addiction. The purpose of tertiary prevention is to ensure that people who have entered treatment for some form of drug abuse become free of drugs and remain that way.

In the United States, a variety of primary and secondary prevention strategies have been employed, including (1) reduction in the availability of drugs, (2) punishment of drug addicts, (3) scare tactics and negative education, (4) objective information approaches, (5) promotional campaigns, and (6) self-esteem enhancement and affective education (Levinthal, 2005). We'll look at each in more detail.

In an attempt to reduce the supply and availability of drugs, U.S. law enforcement agencies have expended vast resources to control the domestic production, sale, and consumption of illicit drugs, but their efforts have removed only a small fraction of drugs (Wren, 1996a). The U.S. government has also tried to reduce the influx of drugs from other countries. However, estimates of global retail sales of illicit drugs range from $180 billion to more than $300 billion annually, making the underground drug economy one of the most expansive commercial activities in the world. In North America and Europe alone, the combined sales of heroin, cocaine, and marijuana add up to about $122 billion annually (Stares, 1996). Despite drug laws and an array of sanctions against drug trafficking, drug use and abuse have not been significantly deterred in the United States or elsewhere. Map 8.1 shows the volume of drugs that continue to arrive in the United States from other nations. Efforts to punish offenders of U.S. drug laws have clogged the criminal justice system and overcrowded prisons without noticeably reducing the sale and consumption of illegal drugs in this country. In fact, scare tactics and negative education programs have not fared much better; they turn students off and do not achieve their desired goal. In fact, scare tactics appear to pique some students' curiosity about drugs rather than deter their use. Objective information programs often begin in kindergarten and progress through grade 12. Using texts, curriculum guides, videos, and other materials, teachers impart factual information about drugs to students, but as with scare tactics, students

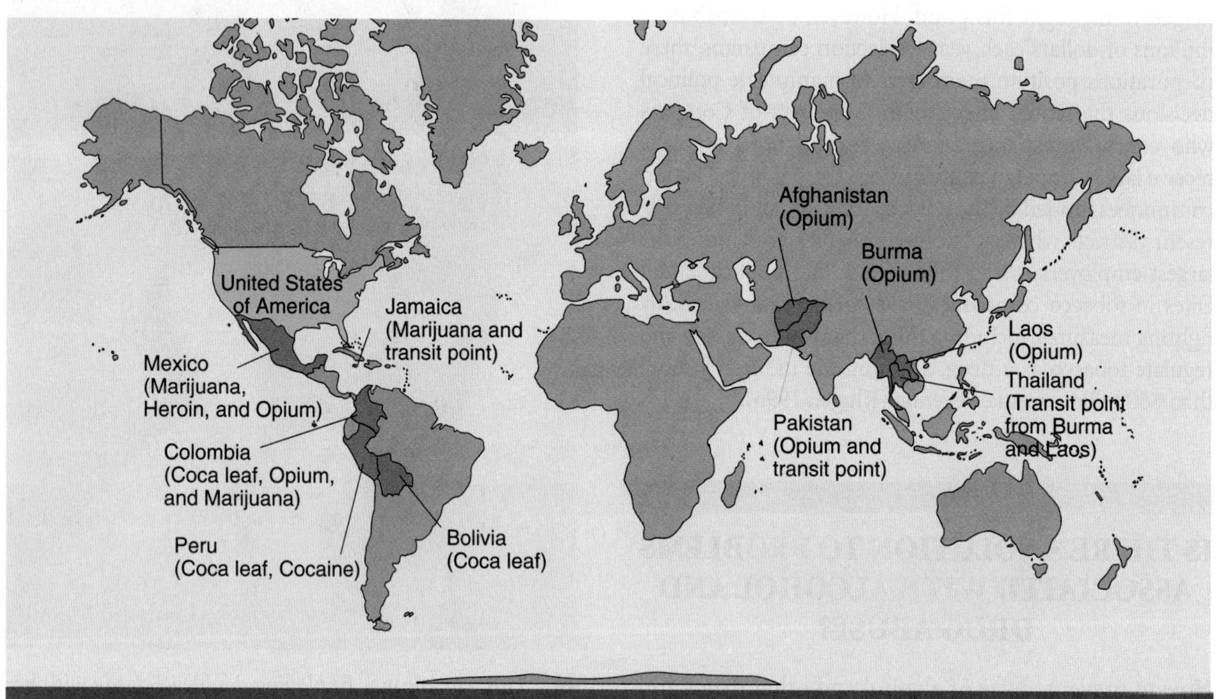

■ ***Map 8.1* Main sources of illegal drugs imported into the United States.**

Sources: U.S. Department of State, 2008.

sometimes become more—instead of less—interested in drug experimentation. "Just Say No" and other "magic bullet" promotional campaigns for preventing drug abuse have also had limited success in deterring drug use. An eighteen-year-old student who smoked his first marijuana joint at age thirteen explains why he thinks these programs are ineffective: "When someone tells you not to do it, that makes you want to do it even more" (Kolata, 1996a:A12). Self-esteem enhancement and affective education programs focus on the underlying emotional and attitudinal factors that are involved in drug abuse while building character through teaching positive social values and attitudes. These programs are most effective when they are incorporated into more comprehensive prevention programs.

If the purpose of prevention programs is to reduce actual drug-taking behavior, what types of programs have the greatest likelihood of success? Many social analysts suggest that family- and school-based primary and secondary prevention programs are the most effective. Previously, some prevention programs focused on high school students, but today elementary schools are among the first lines of attack because drug-taking behavior now starts at younger ages. Nearly 75 percent of U.S. public schools have a program known as DARE (Drug Abuse Resistance Education), which is taught by specially trained police officers who teach children how to resist drugs. Critics suggest that police officers, whom many young people view as authority figures, are not the best people to teach adolescents that drug use is not cool. Critics also note that one-shot programs that are forced on students might not prevent drug abuse. Children who have been through the DARE program are no less likely to smoke, drink, or use other drugs than are children who have not been through the program (Kolata, 1996a).

Prevention programs for the future that look hopeful emphasize *life skills training.* The Life Skills Training Program developed by Gilbert Botvin at Cornell Medical School consists of a fifteen-session curriculum directed toward seventh-grade students. Booster sessions are offered in the eighth and ninth grades. The program provides information on the short-term consequences of alcohol or other drug use and teaches participants critical thinking skills, independent decision making, ways to reduce anxiety and resist peer pressure to take drugs, and ways of gaining a sense of personal control and self-esteem (Botvin and Tortu, 1988). Unlike programs that primarily tell students to stay off drugs, life skills training attempts to give students the tools they need to stay drug free. Although the short-term effects of life skills programs are impressive, according to social scientist Charles F. Levinthal, they erode over time (2007). Still, Levinthal believes that we can learn important lessons from prevention strategies that have failed in the past, lessons that we can use to create better approaches in the future.

Future prevention programs will be family-, school-, and community-based. They will offer alternative activities and outlets to drug use. These programs, like other drug abuse prevention efforts, will take into account issues that affect people differently depending on their race/ethnicity, religion, or other factors. Reaching across lines of race, class, and gender, the next generation of drug abuse prevention programs will use cable television channels to make people aware of the effects of drugs on the human body and how to get help in dealing with alcoholism and drug addiction. The Internet will become a vital source of information. Current World Wide Web sites provide an array of information on drugs and offer unique features such as an on-line dictionary of street drug slang. Future prevention programs provide cause for optimism but only if social structural factors change. If illegal drugs continue to flow into the United States, and television, other mass media, and advertising continue to glamorize smoking, drinking, and other drug use, the future of preventive programs is bleak. Without social change, efforts will be directed toward apprehension and incarceration of drug offenders and treatment programs for drug addicts and alcoholics, not toward primary or secondary prevention strategies.

Treatment Programs

Tertiary prevention programs are programs that aim to ensure that people who have sought help for some form of drug abuse remain drug free. It follows from the biological and social learning explanations for substance abuse and alcohol addiction that treatment must deal with the body's physiological and psychological responses. Therefore, *alcohol and drug treatment* involves the use of activities designed to eliminate physical and psychological addiction and to prevent relapse—returning to abuse and/or addiction. Most treatment programs are based on a medical model or therapeutic community.

The Medical Treatment Model

The *medical treatment model* considers drug abuse and alcoholism to be medical problems that must be resolved by medical treatment by medical officials. Treatment might take the form of *aversion therapy* or *behavioral conditioning.* For example, drugs such as Cyclazocine and Naloxone are given to heroin and opiate addicts to prevent the euphoric feeling that they associate with taking the drugs. Supposedly, when the pleasure is gone, the person will no longer abuse the drug. Some heroin addicts also receive methadone detoxification to alleviate withdrawal symptoms associated with stopping heroin use. Over a one- to three-week period, the patient receives decreasing doses of methadone, a synthetic opium derivative that blocks the desire for heroin but does not have its negative side effects.

Antabuse is used in the treatment of alcoholism. After the person has been detoxified and no alcohol remains in the bloodstream, Antabuse is administered along with small quantities of alcohol for several consecutive days. Because this combination produces negative effects such as nausea and vomiting, the individual eventually develops an aversion to drinking, which becomes associated with uncomfortable physical symptoms. Although the medical treatment model works for some people, it is criticized for focusing on the physiological effects of alcohol and drug dependency and not dealing with the psychological and sociological aspects of dependency.

The Therapeutic Community

When substance abusers are perceived to have an underlying psychological problem, treatment generally involves counseling, rehabilitation, and/or the therapeutic community. Counseling often employs rehabilitated alcoholics or addicts who encourage participants to take more responsibility for their lives so that they can function better in the community. Some counseling and rehabilitation programs take place on an outpatient basis or as day treatment; others involve residential treatment. *Outpatient programs* allow drug abusers to remain at home and continue working while attending regular group and individual meetings. *Day treatment* takes place in a hospital setting where the abuser participates in day-long treatment groups and individual counseling sessions and returns home in the evening. The *therapeutic community approach* is based on the idea that drug abuse is best treated by intensive individual and group counseling in either a residential or a nonresidential setting. Residential treatment takes place in a special house or dormitory where alcoholics or drug addicts remain for periods of time ranging from several months to several years. One of the most widely known residential treatment centers is the Betty Ford Clinic in California; many others exist throughout the country. Residents in these programs receive therapy and try to establish new behavior patterns outside of their drinking or drug abuse environments (Bertram et al., 1996).

Perhaps the best-known nonresidential therapeutic community is Alcoholics Anonymous (AA), founded in 1935, and its offshoot, Narcotics Anonymous (NA). Both AA and NA provide members with support in their efforts to overcome drug dependence and addiction. AA was established in 1935 by two alcoholics who were seeking a way of returning to sober life. Today, the organization has more than 30,000 chapters with more than 600,000 members. Members use only their first names to ensure anonymity, and recovering alcoholics serve as sponsors and counselors for others. AA and NA are based on a twelve-step program that requires members to acknowledge that they are alcoholics or drug addicts who must have the help of a higher power (usually identified as God) and other people to remain sober or drug free. Other programs continue to be developed to aid alcohol- and drug-addicted individuals. Some are organized around religious principles, such as Mothers Against Methamphetamine, while others focus on individual willpower (see Box 8.3).

All the approaches for reducing alcohol and drug abuse that we have discussed can help certain individuals, but none address what to do about social structural factors that contribute to the drug problem. Because drug- and alcohol-related problems and their solutions are part of deeper social issues and struggles, they cannot be dealt with in isolation, as social scientist Philippe Bourgeois (1995:319, 327) explains:

> Drugs are not the root of the problems... they are the expression of deeper, structural dilemmas. Self-destructive addiction is merely the medium for desperate people to internalize their frustrations, resistance, and powerlessness. In other words, we can safely ignore the drug hysterias that periodically sweep through the United States. Instead we should focus our ethical concerns and political energies on the contradictions posed by the persistence of inner-city poverty in the midst of extraordinary opulence. In the same vein, we

Critical Thinking and You

Box 8.3

Calling on a Higher Power or Using Self-Reliance? Alcohol and Drug Abuse Programs

> "That's my younger brother Jim," Dr. Mary Holley tells a group of two dozen drug addicts, pointing to a photo of a hollow-eyed young man projected on the wall. "Three weeks after that picture was taken, he found a gun at my uncle's house and blew his brains out because he couldn't stand it anymore." (quoted in Schindehette and Truesdell, 2005:101)

With these words Dr. Mary Holley, an obstetrician, hoped to catch the attention of people who, like her brother, were addicted to crystal meth. After researching the damage that meth causes to the brain, Holley started Mothers Against Methamphetamine (MAMa) to help spread the word about the dangers of this drug and to help addicts recover. MAMa is based on two key principles: (1) that addicts need help from other people to overcome their addiction and, perhaps even more important, (2) that addicts need help from God or a "power greater than themselves" to overcome their addiction. Because of her religious beliefs, Holley views drug addiction as "primarily a spiritual disease, not a social disease" (Poovey, 2004). MAMa's approach is similar to Alcoholics Anonymous (AA) and Narcotics Anonymous (NA) in that the founders of these programs emphasized that addicts need the help of a higher power and of other people, especially in a one-on-one, individualized approach where one recovering alcoholic or drug addict helps other recovering drinkers or drug addicts.

Over the years, there have been controversies as to the extent to which religion should play a part in AA and NA meetings—where direct references are made to reliance on God in the Twelve Step recovery program. Part of the debate has centered around people who were ordered to attend AA meetings after being convicted of drunk driving and who believed that they should not be required to do something that involves religion (Gelman, 1991). However, AA leaders state that the belief in God or a "power greater than themselves" is a fundamental principle of their organization and that this is a necessary belief if addicts are to be successful in their recovery.

Secular alcohol and drug recovery groups (those that use no religious references) have been organized by addicted individuals who found that existing programs did not meet their needs. Among these secular programs are Rational Recovery (RR), Secular Organization for Sobriety (SOS), and Women for Sobriety (WFS), all of which focus on individual willpower and the importance of taking responsibility for one's own actions to overcome addiction. Group support is also important, but members are not required to acknowledge God or to "confess" their problems to other members. The ideas of individual willpower and group support, for example, are expressed in the motto of Women for Sobriety (2005): "We are capable and competent, caring and compassionate, always willing to help another; bonded together in overcoming addictions."

MAMa, AA, and NA represent one approach to dealing with a social problem at the individual level; RR, SOS, and WFS represent another. Consider the following questions in thinking about these divergent approaches to dealing with alcohol and drug abuse.

Questions for Critical Thinking

1. What are the advantages of bringing religion into recovery programs? What problems might be associated with this approach?
2. Is there a difference in a person voluntarily attending meetings of an organization such as AA as compared to being ordered to attend by a judge? If so, what are the key distinctions?
3. If you were asked to design a recovery program, would you more closely follow the approach of AA or of the secular organizations? Why?

> need to recognize and dismantle the class- and ethnic-based apartheids that riddle the U.S. landscape. . . . Any long-term paths out of the quagmire will have to address the structural and political economic roots, as well as the ideological and cultural roots of social marginalization. The first step out of the impasse, however, requires a fundamental ethical and political reevaluation of basic socioeconomic models and human values.

If the United States sets out to reduce inequalities in all areas of social life, perhaps the drug problem will be alleviated as well. What do you think it would take to make this happen?

SUMMARY

■ *What are the major patterns of drinking?*

Social scientists divide long-term drinking patterns into four categories: (1) Social drinkers consume alcoholic beverages primarily on social occasions and drink either occasionally or relatively frequently; (2) heavy drinkers are more frequent drinkers who typically consume greater quantities of alcohol when they drink and are more likely to become intoxicated; (3) acute alcoholics have trouble controlling their use of alcohol and plan their schedule around drinking; and (4) chronic alcoholics have lost control over their drinking and tend to engage in compulsive behavior such as hiding liquor bottles.

■ *What are the major hazards associated with tobacco use?*

Nicotine is a toxic, dependency-producing drug that is responsible for about one in every five deaths in the United States. People who smoke have a greater likelihood of developing cardiovascular disease, lung cancer, and/or cancer of the larynx, mouth, and esophagus. Even those who do not smoke may be subjected to the hazard of environmental tobacco smoke—the smoke in the air as a result of other people's tobacco smoking. Infants born to women who smoke typically have lower than average birth weights and sometimes have slower rates of physical and mental growth.

■ *What problems are associated with use of prescription and over-the-counter drugs?*

Some prescription drugs have the potential for short-term abuse and long-term psychological and physical dependence. This form of dependency is known as iatrogenic addiction—drug dependency that results from physician-supervised treatment for a recognized medical disorder. Over-the-counter drugs, which are widely advertised and readily available, may be dangerous when combined with alcohol or other drugs.

■ *What categories of people are most likely to use marijuana?*

Most marijuana users are between the ages of eighteen and twenty-five; however, use by twelve- to seventeen-year-olds more than doubled in the 1990s. More men than women smoke marijuana; however, teenage girls are slightly more likely than boys to have used marijuana at least once.

■ *In the United States, what are the major stimulant drugs?*

Cocaine and amphetamines are the major stimulant drugs that are abused in the United States. Cocaine is an extremely potent and dependency-producing stimulant drug. Amphetamines can be obtained legally in the form of diet pills and pep formulas when they are prescribed by a physician.

■ *What are depressants and what health-related risk do they pose?*

As the name indicates, depressants depress the central nervous system; they also may have some pain-killing properties. The most common depressants are barbiturates and antianxiety drugs or tranquilizers. Users may develop both physical addiction and psychological dependency on these drugs. There is also the risk of potentiation—the drug interaction that takes place when two drugs are mixed together and the combination produces a far greater effect than that of either drug administered separately.

■ *What other drugs are widely abused in the United States?*

Narcotics or opiates, including natural substances (e.g., opium, morphine, and codeine), opiate derivatives (e.g., heroin and Percodan), and synthetic drugs with opiatelike effects (e.g., Darvon and Demerol) are frequently abused. Hallucinogens or psychedelics such as mescaline (peyote), lysergic acid diethylamide (LSD), phencyclidine (PCP), and MDMA (Ecstasy) are also widely abused.

■ *How do biological and psychological perspectives view alcohol and drug addiction?*

Biological explanations of alcohol and drug addiction focus on inherited biological factors and on the effects of drugs on the human brain. Psychological explanations of drug abuse focus on personality disorders and the effects of social learning and reinforcement on people's drug-taking behavior.

■ *How do sociological perspectives view alcohol and drug addiction?*

Symbolic interactionists believe that drug use and abuse are learned behaviors that are strongly influenced by families, peers, and others who serve as role models. People are more prone to accept attitudes and behaviors that are favorable to drug use if they spend time with members of a drug subculture. Functionalists believe that drug-related problems have increased as social institutions such as the family, education, and religion have become fragmented and somewhat disorganized. However, use of alcohol and other drugs serves important functions even though some aspects of their use are dysfunctional for society. According to conflict theorists, people in positions of economic and political power are responsible for making the sale, use, and possession of some drugs illegal. Conflict theorists also point out that powerful corporate interests perpetuate the use and abuse of alcohol, tobacco, and other legal drugs.

■ *What is the purpose of prevention and treatment programs?*

Primary prevention programs seek to prevent drug problems before they begin. Secondary prevention programs seek to limit the extent of drug abuse, prevent the spread of drug abuse to other substances beyond the drugs already experienced, and teach strategies for the responsible use of licit drugs such as alcohol. Tertiary prevention programs seek to limit relapses by individuals recovering from alcoholism or drug addiction. They may be based on either a medical model or the therapeutic community. The best-known therapeutic community is Alcoholics Anonymous (AA).

■ *What other factors must be taken into account in efforts to reduce the drug problem?*

Alcoholism and drug abuse are intertwined with other social problems such as dramatic changes in the economic and technological bases of the society, the growing gap between the rich and poor, and inequalities based on race/ethnicity and gender.

KEY TERMS

codependency, p. 156
drug, p. 150
drug addiction (or drug dependency), p. 151
drug subculture, p. 166
environmental tobacco smoke, p. 156
fetal alcohol syndrome (FAS), p. 154
tolerance, p. 151
withdrawal, p. 151

QUESTIONS FOR CRITICAL THINKING

1. Does public tolerance of alcohol and tobacco lead to increased use of these drugs? Why do many people view the use of alcohol and tobacco differently from the use of illicit drugs?
2. If stimulants, depressants, and hallucinogens have such potentially hazardous side effects, why do so many people use these drugs? If drug enforcement policies were more stringently enforced, would there be less drug abuse in this country?
3. As a sociologist, how would you propose to deal with the drug problem in the United States? If you were called on to revamp existing drug laws and policies, what, if any, changes would you make in them?
4. How have changes in technology affected the problem of alcohol and drug abuse over the past century? How have changes in the global economy affected drug-related problems in this country and others?

Chapter 9

Crime and Criminal Justice

THINKING SOCIOLOGICALLY

- What do you think of when you hear the word *crime*? Do the media influence how we think about crime?
- Is there a relationship between class and violent crime? Property crime? Corporate crime?
- How do structural explanations of crime differ from those based on a biological or psychological approach?

In a trial involving the alleged smuggling of hundreds of illegal immigrants from Mexico to work in U.S. chicken-processing plants, prosecutors played excerpts from a secretly recorded conversation between an undercover FBI agent, who posed as a smuggler, and the manager of a Tyson Foods plant, who was seeking to hire undocumented workers:

FEDERAL AGENT: *[After explaining that he was a friend of a mutual friend]. He said you wanted to talk to me?*

CHICKEN-PLANT MANAGER: *Yeah, about help.... Now I'm going to need quite a few.... Starting on the 29th, a Monday, we are going to start. How many can I get, and how often can you do it?*

FEDERAL AGENT: *Well, it's not a problem. I think [the mutual friend] told me that you wanted 10?*

CHICKEN-PLANT MANAGER: *Well, 10 at a time. But over the period of the next three or four months... I'm going to replace somewhere between 300 and 400 people, maybe 500. I'm going to need a lot.*

FEDERAL AGENT:*... I can give you what you need.*

CHICKEN-PLANT MANAGER: *Now let me ask you this. Do these people have a photo ID and a Social Security card?*

FEDERAL AGENT: *No.... These people come from Mexico. I pick them up at Del Rio. That's in Texas, after they cross the river, and then we take them over there, and they get their cards. [The mutual friend] gets them their cards, I guess.*

CHICKEN-PLANT MANAGER: *I need to talk to him about that.*

FEDERAL AGENT: *About the cards?*

CHICKEN-PLANT MANAGER: *Yes, some of them that's got the INS card [issued by the U.S. Immigration and Naturalization Service], and if they put it in a computer... if it's not any good... something happens, and we have to lay them off. But if they just have got a regular photo ID from anywhere and a Social Security card, then we don't have to do that.*

—Quoted in Bartlett and Steele, 2004

As a crime, the smuggling of illegal immigrants into the United States typically involves not only helping them get into the country but also securing fake paperwork for them. Based on the recording from the Tyson case, it would appear that the chicken-plant manager was aware of what he was doing and committed a crime. However, a larger issue arises in criminal cases such as this: Are corporate executives responsible for criminal activity involving their employees and plants? In this case, Tyson and five managers were charged with conspiring to smuggle illegal immigrants into the United States to work on the production lines of the company. However, Tyson representatives stated that the charges against the company were "absolutely false. In reality, the specific charges are limited to a few managers who were acting outside of company policy at five of our 57 poultry-processing plants" (quoted in Bartlett and Steele, 2004). Eventually, two managers pleaded guilty, but the corporation and the other three managers were acquitted on all charges (Bartlett and Steele, 2004). According to prosecutors, the plant managers believed that their actions were necessary because they were unable to find cheap legal labor to work in the factories where slaughtered chickens are processed and prepared for sale in grocery stores and restaurants throughout the nation (Poovey, 2003).

As was true in this case, crimes involving importing and hiring illegal immigrants typically focus on *individual* behavior and not on the part that *corporations* play in recruiting workers. Law enforcement officials can fine corporations that encourage the hiring of illegal workers, but eventually the ones with the "dirty hands"—the ones who get punished—are those employees who carry out the practices of the organization.

From one sociological perspective, crime is rooted in *the social structure of society*, particularly in power relations. As described in Chapter 7, a *structural approach* to understanding deviance and crime makes us aware that the most powerful members of the dominant racial, class, and gender groups have economic, political, and social power that often protects them from being apprehended and punished. There are exceptions, of course, such as in cases involving high-ranking officials of several corporations that were found guilty of various types of corporate fraud in recent years. In this chapter, we examine crimes that are committed by people at all levels of society, ranging from perpetrators of garden-variety street crimes to CEOs who improperly use millions of dollars in corporate money.

CRIME AS A SOCIAL PROBLEM

Many people in the United States fear crime and are somewhat obsessed with it even though they have no direct daily exposure to criminal behavior. Their information about crime comes from the news media and sometimes from watching real-crime television shows such as *America's Most Wanted* or fictionalized crime stories such as *CSI* or *Law and Order* on television. Media coverage of crime is extensive and might in fact contribute to our widespread perception that crime has increased dramatically in this country. The truth, however, is rather different: The rate of serious and violent crime generally has fallen during the last ten years (FBI, 2007). That is not to say that crime isn't a problem. Crime statistics tell only part of the story. Crime is a significant social problem because it endangers people's lives, property, and sense of well-being. About 35 million people annually are victims of crimes in the United States, and 100 billion tax dollars are spent annually on law enforcement and the administration of justice (Donziger, 1996). Even individuals who are not directly victimized by crime are harmed because they have to pay increased taxes to fight it (Barlow and Kauzlarich, 2002).

Problems with Official Statistics

Over the past two decades, sophisticated computer-based information systems have not only improved rates of detection, apprehension, and conviction of offenders but also have provided immediate access to millions of bits of information about crime, suspects, and offenders (Barlow and Kauzlarich, 2002). The leading source of information on crimes reported in the United States is the Uniform Crime Report (UCR). It is published annually by the Federal Bureau of Investigation and is based on data provided by federal, state, and local law enforcement agencies. The UCR tracks three categories of reported crimes: violent crimes, property crimes, and other offenses. Violent crimes include murder, rape, robbery, and aggravated assault. Examples of property crimes are burglary (breaking into private property to commit a serious crime), motor vehicle theft, arson, and larceny (theft of property worth $50 or more). The UCR also includes a "Crime Clock" (see Figure 9.1), showing how often (on average) certain crimes are committed in this country. In 2006, for example, a murder occurred in the United States on an average of once every 31 minutes, a robbery every minute, and a forcible rape every six minutes (FBI, 2007). During the same year, there were about 10.4 million arrests for all criminal offenses (excluding traffic violations). Because these statistics are highly publicized, it is easy to see why people are concerned for their personal safety, their property, and their very lives.

How accurate are these crime statistics? Any answer to this question must take into account the fact that legal definitions of some offenses vary from jurisdiction to jurisdiction and that the statistics reflect only crimes that are reported to law enforcement agencies or that police officers see occur. According to the UCR, overall rates of crime (number of crimes per 100,000 people), which increased sharply between 1987 and 1991, have (except during 2001) decreased annually since then. This downward trend probably reflects several factors, including a shift in population. The percentage of the U.S. population under age twenty-six—the age group that is most likely to commit crimes—began to decline in 1992. The FBI is in the process of replacing the UCR with a more comprehensive system called the National Incident-Based Reporting System (NIBRS). This system will keep more detailed information about offenders and allow sophisticated statistical analysis, but it too will be limited to data on reported crimes.

Because the number of crimes that are reported is not necessarily the number of crimes that are *committed*, the Bureau of Justice Statistics conducts an annual National Crime Victimization Survey (NCVS) of 100,000 randomly selected households to identify crime victims, whether the crime was reported or not (see Chapter 1). These surveys indicate that the number of crimes that are committed is substantially higher than the number that is reported. However, the NCVS has limitations too: (1) Responses are based on recall, and some people don't remember specifically when a

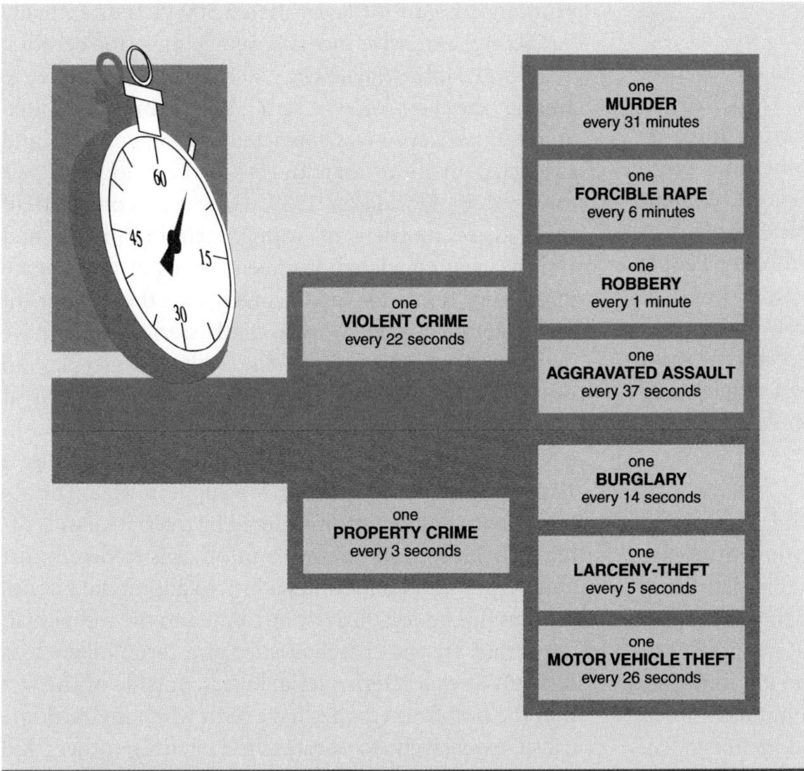

■ *Figure 9.1* ***Crime clock, 2006***
The crime clock should be viewed with care. Being the most aggregate representation of UCR data, it is designed to convey the annual reported crime experience by showing the relative frequency of occurrence of certain offenses. This mode of display should not be taken to imply a regularity in the commission of the offense; rather, it represents the annual ratio of crime to fixed time intervals.

Source: FBI, 2008.

crime occurred; (2) for various reasons, respondents might not be truthful; and (3) the surveys focus on theft and assault and do not measure workplace crimes such as embezzlement or bribery (Vito and Holmes, 1994).

Defining Crime and Delinquency

Crime is behavior that violates the criminal law and is punishable by fine, jail term, or other negative sanctions. In the United States, criminal laws can be enacted at the local, state, and federal levels. As a result, some laws apply uniformly throughout the states while others vary from state to state or apply only in the local jurisdiction where they were passed. Whether the law that is broken is federal, state, or local, there are two components to every crime: the act itself and *criminal intent*, expressed in the concept of *mens rea*, meaning "guilty mind." An individual's intent in committing a crime can range from willful conduct (hiring someone to kill one's spouse) to an unintentional act of negligence that is defined as a crime (leaving a small child unattended in a locked automobile in extremely hot weather, resulting in the child's death). Criminal law is divided into two major categories: misdemeanors and felonies. ***Misdemeanors* are relatively minor crimes that are punishable by a fine or less than a year in jail.** Examples include public drunkenness, shoplifting, and traffic violations. ***Felonies* are more serious crimes, such as murder, rape, or aggravated assault, that are punishable by more than a year's imprisonment or even death.** Children and adolescents below a certain age (usually eighteen) who commit illegal or antisocial acts usually are not charged with criminal conduct but are adjudicated as *delinquent* by a juvenile court judge. However, when older juveniles are charged with violent crimes, it is becoming increasingly common to *certify* or *waive* them to adult court.

TYPES OF CRIMES

To make the study of crime—a large and complex subject—manageable, sociologists and criminologists categorize types of crime. In this section, we will look at six categories of crime: violent crime, property crime, occupational crime, corporate crime, organized crime, and juvenile delinquency.

Violent Crime

In the United States, a violent crime occurs an average of once every twenty-three seconds (FBI, 2007). ***Violent crime* consists of actions involving force or the threat of force against others and includes murder, rape, robbery, and aggravated assault.** Violent crimes are committed against people; nonviolent crimes are usually committed against property. People tend to fear violent crime more than other kinds of crime because victims are often physically injured or even killed and because violent crime receives the most sustained attention from law enforcement officials and the media (see Parker, 1995; Warr, 2000).

Murder

The UCR defines ***murder* as the unlawful, intentional killing of one person by another.** (Killing in self-defense or during wartime is not murder.) By this definition, murder involves not only an unlawful act but also *malice aforethought*—the *intention* of doing a wrongful act. A person who buys a gun, makes a plan to kill someone, and carries out the plan has probably committed murder. In contrast, *manslaughter* is the unlawful, *unintentional* killing of one person by another. An intoxicated person who shoots a gun into the air probably holds no malice toward the bystander who is killed by a stray bullet. Sometimes a person's intentions are clear, but many times they are not, and the lines between intentional, unintentional, and accidental homicides are often blurred.

***Mass murder* is the killing of four or more people at one time and in one place by the same person.** Based on this definition, there is no shortage of examples of mass murder in the United States. Among the recent mass murders that have received the most media coverage are the 2007 Westroads Mall (Omaha, Nebraska) shooting in which Robert A. Hawkins killed eight people before committing suicide, and the 2008 Northern Illinois University (DeKalb, Illinois) lecture-hall shooting in which the perpetrator, Steven Kazmierczak, killed five people and wounded eighteen others. According to criminologists, mass murderers tend to kill in the areas where they live. They are likely to be males, problem drinkers, and collectors of firearms and other weapons, which they often hide (Dietz, 1986). Some recent mass murderers have been disgruntled employees or former employees who seek out supervisors and coworkers in the workplace; a number of these violent eruptions have occurred in post offices and other business establishments.

***Serial murder* is the killing of three or more people over more than a month by the same person.** Serial murders account for fewer than 5,000 victims annually but receive extensive media coverage. In prior decades, Ted Bundy, John Wayne Gacy, and Jeffrey Dahmer were among the best-known serial killers in the United States. Bundy, who was convicted of three murders and suspected in more than thirty-six other killings, was executed in Florida in 1989. Gacy was convicted of thirty-three murders of young men in Illinois, and Dahmer was convicted of fifteen counts of first-degree intentional homicide in Wisconsin after the murders of many young males. More recently, serial killers have included Angel Resendiz ("The Railway Killer"), who wandered the country on trains, allegedly killing at many as 24 people nationwide, and Robert L. Yates, Jr. ("The Prostitute Killer"), who murdered at least 12 prostitutes in the Spokane, Washington, area. The actual number of victims murdered by a serial killer is often difficult for law enforcement officials to determine, and perpetrators sometimes admit to additional killings that cannot be conclusively attributed to the individual.

What are the characteristics of a serial killer? It is difficult to characterize serial killers, outside of the fact that the best-known ones have been white males. Some travel extensively to locate their victims; others kill near where they live. One study identified four basic types of serial killers: (1) *visionaries*, who kill because they hear a voice or have a vision that commands them to commit the murderous acts; (2) *missionaries*, who take it on themselves to rid the community or the world of what they believe is an undesirable type of person; (3) *hedonists*, who obtain personal or sexual gratification from violence; and (4) *power/control seekers*, who achieve gratification from the complete possession of the victim (Holmes, 1988).

Nature and extent of the problem Statistics on murder are among the most accurate official crime statistics available. Murders rarely go unreported, and suspects are usually apprehended and charged; in 2006, there were 17,034 murders that were reported to law enforcement authorities in the United States (FBI, 2007). Although annual rates vary slightly, murder follows certain patterns in terms of gender, age, race, and region of the country. Men make up the vast majority of murder victims and offenders. Of the 13,000 to 18,000 murders that are reported annually in this country, about 80 percent of the victims and 90 percent of the offenders are male. Males kill other males in about 86 percent of cases. Females kill 14 percent of the male victims, often because the females believe that they are in a life-threatening situation.

Age patterns are clearly evident in murder rates. Almost 90 percent of all murder victims are eighteen years of age or older; nearly half of these are between ages twenty and thirty-five. Murder arrest rates per 100,000 for youths age ten through seventeen have decreased significantly over the past twelve years. According to one analyst, the decrease is due to "some of the glamour of being a thug, walking around with a gun... [being gone]...because people 13, 14, and 15 years old have seen so many of their friends or relatives being killed or going to prison" (Butterfield, 1996:A9).

Most murders are intraracial. More than half of all murder victims in the United States are African American, and more than 90 percent of them are killed by other African Americans. Similarly, about 80 percent of white murder victims are killed by other white people (FBI, 2007). Murder takes a greater toll on young African-American males than on any other group in society. Race and class factors are often intertwined: Poor people are much more likely to kill and to be killed than are members of the middle and upper classes, and a higher proportion of people of color live below the U.S. poverty level because of racial discrimination and generations of inequality in education and employment.

Large metropolitan areas of the nation have a murder rate of about 10 victims per 100,000 residents; rural counties and cities outside metropolitan areas have a rate of about 5 per 100,000 (FBI, 2007). However, the incidence of murder is unevenly distributed within cities. Many suburbs have extremely low rates of murder compared to those of city centers. In the United States overall, murder is most likely to occur in the Southern states. Not only is the South the most populous region, it also views the possession and use of guns and other weapons more positively than most other regions.

In the past, most murder victims knew their killers, but this pattern seems to be gradually changing. Today, slightly more than half of all murder victims know their assailants. About 15 percent are related to their assailants, and 35.9 percent are acquainted with them well enough to at least engage in an argument. Of the remaining victims, 13.9 percent are murdered by strangers, and in about 35.2 percent of cases, the relationship between victim and offender is unknown (see Figure 9.2). This pattern does differ somewhat when we look at gender differences in victimization. Among female murder victims, almost 25 percent are slain by a husband or boyfriend, whereas only 3 percent of male victims are killed by a wife or girlfriend (FBI, 2007).

Across the nation, guns are used in approximately 67 percent of all murders annually—a fact that leads to ongoing political debate over gun control, especially of handguns. The death rate from guns among African-American males aged fifteen to nineteen is about 153 per 100,000 as contrasted with about 28 per 100,000 among their white peers. Cutting or stabbing instruments are used in slightly more than 13 percent of murders, and hands, fists, and feet are used as murder weapons about 6 percent of the time (FBI, 2007).

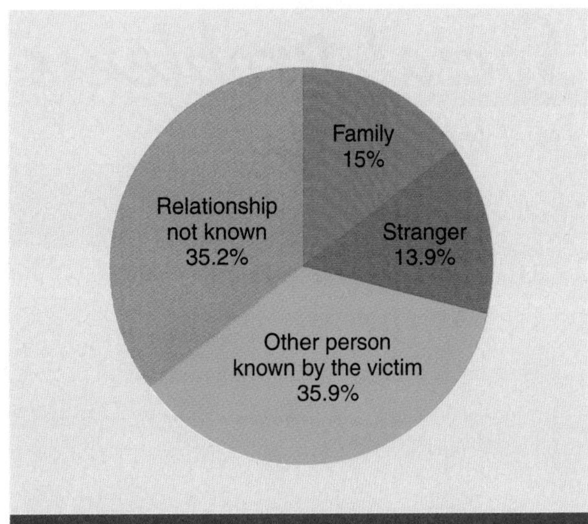

■ *Figure 9.2* ***Murder by relationship of victim and offender, 2006***

Source: FBI, 2008.

Social responses to murder Even though most murders are not random, many people have a deep and persistent fear of strangers. According to one analyst,

> We have responded [in various ways to the threat of murder]. Some of us by minimizing our time in public space for fear of encountering the random menace; many by purchasing a range of weapons, locks, bolts, alarms, and insurance; parents, by acting as virtual bodyguards for our children; governments, by dispensing crime prevention advice which promotes individual responsibility for keeping crime at bay. But has this reduced our fear? Or contributed to our greater security? Clearly not. (Stanko, 1990:viii)

Individual responses are intensified by media coverage of violent personal crimes, especially murder. The special newsworthiness of murder is discussed in Box 9.1 on page 180.

At state and federal levels, the government has responded to the public's fear of murder by increasing expenditures on fear reduction programs and crime prevention programs that supposedly will help

Social Problems in the Media

Box 9.1

Murder in the Media: Framing News Stories to Get Attention

"If it ain't a homicide, then I'm not interested."

—*A newspaper reporter as he leafed through the morning police blotter reports (Chermak, 1995:55)*

"Do you have any bodies for me?"

—*A reporter making her daily calls to police divisions, hospitals, and the coroner's office (Chermak, 1995:55)*

Crime is a major category of news reported in the media. Why are newspaper reporters and television journalists so interested in covering murders? Violent crime, especially murder, provides a unique opportunity for the media to frame news stories in a way that immediately catches the attention of readers and viewers who may consider themselves to be immune to the typical news story. Although journalists frame stories about murder in a variety of ways, two are prevalent: (1) "How bad is it?" framing, and (2) "Can you believe this?" framing.

"How bad is it?" framing typically emphasizes the seriousness of the situation, including how *unsuspecting individuals* became *homicide victims* simply by being in the wrong place at the wrong time. In other words, anyone can become a victim of a homicide: Look what happened to these "innocent bystanders," a favorite phrase of journalists. At the bottom line, murder is newsworthy, but some murders are more newsworthy than others: The answer to the question, "How bad is it?" must be "Real bad!"

The second media framing device, "Can you believe this?" framing, emphasizes some odd or unique characteristic of the victim, the perpetrator, or both. Certain characteristics may make a victim's murder more newsworthy. Age is very important. Children and the elderly are considered special groups within society and therefore get special media attention. Children are innocents, and the elderly are believed to deserve a peaceful life; when such people are murdered, the public thinks that the system has let them down.

Other characteristics of victims and perpetrators also are important in "Can you believe this?" framing. Among these are the victim's occupation. When a criminal justice professional—especially a police officer—is murdered, or someone in the helping professions (e.g., a nurse, doctor, teacher, or social worker), the case gets a great deal of attention. Murder victims from the suburbs are more newsworthy than residents of the inner city; because educated, middle-class people are less often victimized, they may hold an important position, and more of the media audience can relate to them. Moreover, reporters get better human interest stories from the survivors: "[People] are so fatalistic in the inner city; it is almost like they expected it to happen" (Chermak, 1995:68). Sometimes reporters are afraid to go to inner-city neighborhoods to interview friends and relatives of the victim. Murder in the suburbs, especially a wealthy suburb, also gets more attention because educated and affluent residents have contacts in the media.

Characteristics of perpetrators, as well as victims, can increase the "Can you believe this?" factor. Age is important if the perpetrator is young. If the perpetrator is a politician or in the criminal justice system, the story immediately becomes important because these people are believed to have betrayed the public trust. As with victims, occupation is also important. A perpetrator who is a doctor, teacher, or priest—a guardian of life—is very newsworthy. In certain cases, it is the relationship between the victim and the defendant that makes a murder newsworthy, as when a parent murders a child.

Questions to Consider

1. Are you surprised by how the media frame stories about murder?
2. What criteria do you think journalists should use to determine whether a homicide is newsworthy or not?
3. What media framing approaches can you identify from news reports of crime in your city?

people to make their homes and neighborhoods safe. Lawmakers and enforcers continue to seek longer prison sentences, often without possibility of parole, for anyone who is convicted of murder (especially mass or serial murder).

Rape

Many people think of rape as a sexually motivated crime, but it is actually an act of violence in which sex is used as a weapon against a powerless victim (Vito and Holmes, 1994). Although both men and women can be victimized by rape, the legal definition of ***forcible rape*** **is the act of forcing sexual intercourse on an adult of legal age against her will.** Sexual assaults or attempts to commit rape by force or threat of force are included in FBI statistics on this crime. Unlike murder or other violent crimes, the age of the victim is a central issue in charging a person with rape. ***Statutory rape*** **refers to sexual intercourse with a person who is under the legal age of consent as established by state law** (some states now use the term *illegal intercourse* instead of *statutory rape*). In most states, the legal age of consent is between ages sixteen and eighteen. A few states have attempted to include male victims of sexual assault in definitions of rape. However, criminologists estimate that (excluding men who are raped in prison) only about 1 percent of reported rape victims are men.

Acquaintance rape **is forcible sexual activity that meets the legal definition of rape and involves people who first meet in a social setting** (Sanday, 1996). Some scholars prefer this definition because it encompasses dates and casual acquaintances but excludes spouses (marital rape) and relatives (incest). The phrase was coined to distinguish forced, nonconsensual sex between people who know one another from forced, nonconsensual sex between strangers, but both are rape.

Acquaintance rape is often associated with alcohol or other drug consumption, especially among college students. We probably know much less about the actual number of acquaintance rapes than we do about the number of stranger rapes because victims are less likely to report sexual attacks by people they know. A study by the National Victim Center (1992) found that most rapes involve people who are at least acquaintances, and these rapes have the lowest probability of being reported to the police. It is estimated that fewer than 20 percent of the victims of acquaintance rape report the crime to the police, and 69 percent of the victims believe that others will blame them for having caused the rape (Martin, 1992).

On college campuses, acquaintance rape sometimes takes the form of gang or party rape. Unlike individual acquaintance rape, gang rape is used as a reinforcing mechanism for membership in the group of men (Warshaw, 1994). In fact, men who rape in groups might never commit individual rape. As they participate in gang rape, they experience a special bonding with each other and use rape to prove their sexual ability to other group members and thereby enhance their status among members.

Nature and extent of the problem Statistics on rape are misleading at best because rape is often not reported. According to national victimization studies, however, since the 1950s, on average, one in five women in the United States has been the victim of forced sex at some time during her life (Sanday, 1996). Some women are victimized more than once. Although some women do not report that they have been raped because they believe that nothing will be done about it, arrests have been made in more than half the forcible rapes reported to law enforcement officials in recent years (FBI, 2007).

Like murder, rape follows certain patterns in terms of gender, age, race, and region of the country. Because of the definition that law enforcement officials use, rape is gender specific; that is, the victims of forcible rape are always female, and men make up the vast majority of offenders. Occasionally, women are charged as accomplices to male companions. Of the approximately 95,000 rapes reported annually, almost 90 percent of the victims were raped, and the remaining 10 percent were the victims of attempted rape or sexual assaults (FBI, 2007).

Rape is committed by men of every class, race, ethnicity, and cultural background and across a wide range of age and educational levels (Fairstein, 1995). Although there is no single profile of a rapist, most rapists tend to be under age twenty-five; their typical victims are also under twenty-five, white, divorced or separated, poor, and unemployed or in school (Vito and Holmes, 1994). In most reported rapes, the victim is under eighteen years of age. Although females of all ages are raped, the rate of victimization drops off sharply after age thirty-four.

Offenders and victims are usually of the same race and class. Although numerically more white women are raped than African-American women and more white men commit rape than African-American men, the probabilities of being a rape victim or an offender are significantly higher for African Americans than for whites (FBI, 2007). Moreover, in an intersection of class and race, young poor women of color who live in city centers are much more likely to be rape victims than other women generally are.

The rate of reported rape varies geographically; the most populous Southern states account for almost 35 percent of the total each year, followed by states in the Midwest, the West, and the Northeast. Across all regions, the rate of rape is approximately 65 victims per 100,000 females in large metropolitan areas, 75 per 100,000 in cities outside metropolitan areas, and 45 per 100,000 females in rural areas. Although most regions have experienced recent declines in reported rape (ranging from 1.9 percent in the West to 3.5 percent in the Midwest), the primary decrease has been in the metropolitan areas of these regions (FBI, 2007).

Social responses to rape As the discrepancies between official statistics and victimization studies indicate, societal attitudes toward rape primarily affect the victims of rape. Many rapes are never reported. The extremely traumatic nature of the crime prevents some victims from coming forward. They might believe that if they don't think about it or talk about it, the experience will "go away." Often, the fear generated by the attack is carried over into a fear that the attacker might try to get even or attack again if the crime is reported. This is a particularly significant issue for women who are still in proximity to their attacker. Suppose the attacker is in the same college class or works at the same place as the victim. How can the woman file a report without disrupting her whole life? Many women also fear how they will be treated by the police and, in the event of a criminal trial, by prosecutors and defense attorneys. Many victims also fear publicity for themselves and their families (Sanday, 1996).

Gang Violence and Hate Crimes

Gang violence includes murder, rape, robbery, and aggravated assault. Typically, gangs are composed primarily of young males of the same race or ethnicity. Some gangs are basically peer groups that hang out together, but others are well organized and violent. In recent years, gang activity and gang-related violence have increased significantly not only in large metropolitan areas but also in smaller cities and suburbs. Incidents involving gang violence are among the most frequently mentioned memories of some students in Chicago's public high schools:

> One day in the halls the gangs came up to me and asked what I was doing. They said if I were in a gang they would kill me right there.... Another time a car came up to me and [they] started shooting.
>
> The gangs killed one of my best friends. In high school, I always feel afraid because the gangs hang around the school and try to recruit the current students. (quoted in Hutchison and Kyle, 1993)

This group portrait of the 18th Street gang in California shows members standing in front of a mural and flashing their gang's signs. What factors do you think are most important in determining whether or not a person will join a gang?

Sociologists Jack Levin and Jack McDevitt (1993) suggest that gangs look for opportunities to violently attack "outgroup" members because they are seeking a thrill and view their victims as vulnerable. When violent attacks are made because of a person's race, religion, skin color, disability, sexual orientation, national origin, or ancestry, they are considered to be *hate crimes* (see Chapter 1).

Of course, not all hate crimes are committed by gang members. Consider the case of Joseph Paul Franklin, for example, who believed that it was his mission to rid the United States of African Americans and Jews. He has been convicted of bombing a Jewish synagogue and killing several interracial couples, and he has expressed no remorse for his actions:

> In his confession to the police, after he detailed every step of the synagogue attack, Franklin was asked if there was anything he'd like to say. He stared thoughtfully over the top of his glasses. There was a long silence. "I can't think of anything," he answered. Then he was asked if he felt any remorse. There was another silence. "I can't say that I do," he said. He paused again, then added, "The only thing I'm sorry about is that it's not legal."
>
> "What's not legal?"
>
> Franklin answered as if he'd just been asked the time of day: "Killing Jews." (Gladwell, 1997:132)

When people with beliefs and attitudes like this join violent gangs or paramilitary groups, they can perpetrate devastating acts of violence, terrorism, and even war.

Social responses to gang violence and hate crimes For many years now, the threat of gang violence—particularly such seemingly random events as drive-by shootings—has contributed to a climate of fear in low-income and poverty-level areas of city centers. People living in smaller cities and suburban areas often believed that gang violence was not their problem. As gangs have spread and become increasingly violent, however, it has become apparent that no one is immune. Therefore, the demand for harsher penalties for youthful offenders, who often are under the jurisdiction of juvenile courts and not the adult criminal justice system, has grown. In some urban areas, law enforcement officials have been slow to deal with hate crimes perpetrated by gang members against recent immigrants to the United States and against people of color.

Intervention by law enforcement officials and the criminal justice system has had only limited success in dealing with the structural problems—lack of educational opportunities and jobs, inadequate housing, and racial and ethnic discrimination—that accompany much gang behavior. The best solution seems to come from former gang members and former felons who band together to help break the cycle of crime and hopelessness that they believe produces gang violence. For example, the Alliance of Concerned Men of Washington, D.C., a collection of middle-aged former felons, substance abusers, and inmates, mediated a truce between two factions of a gang that had been terrorizing a southeast Washington neighborhood. Members of the alliance not only reduced gang violence in the city but also helped gang members to find jobs, giving them hope that they would be able to reach their eighteenth birthdays (Janofsky, 1997).

Property Crime

***Property crime* is the taking of money or property from another without force, the threat of force, or the destruction of property.** Burglary, larceny-theft, motor vehicle theft, and arson are examples of property crimes. According to victimization surveys, the most frequent property crime is *burglary*—the unlawful or forcible entry or attempted entry of a residence or business with the intent to commit a serious crime. The burglar illegally enters by, for example, breaking a window or slashing a screen (forcible entry) or through an open window or unlocked door (unlawful entry). Burglaries usually involve theft. Although burglary is normally a crime against property, it is more serious than most nonviolent crimes because it carries the possibility of violent confrontation and the psychological sense of intrusion that is associated with violent crime. To fully grasp the possibility of violent confrontation, consider the following explanations by two burglars of the pressures—both internal and external—that motivate them to commit burglary:

> Usually what I'll do is a burglary, maybe two or three if I have to, and then this will help me get over the rough spot.... Once I get it straightened out, I just go with the flow... the only time I would go and commit a burglary is if I needed the money at that point in time. That would be strictly to pay the light bill, gas bill, rent. (Dan Whiting, quoted in Wright and Decker, 1994:37)

> You ever had an urge before? Maybe a cigarette urge or a food urge, where you eat that and you got to have more and more? That's how that crack is. You smoke it and it hits you [in the back of the throat] and you got to have more. I'll smoke that sixteenth up and get through, it's like I never had none. I got to have more. Therefore, I gots to go do another burglary and gets some more money. (Richard Jackson, quoted in Wright and Decker, 1994:39)

According to victimization surveys, African Americans and Latinos/as have a higher than average risk of being burglarized than whites do. Risk of victimization is also much higher for families with incomes under $7,500 living in rental property or in city centers. In contrast, people who live in well-maintained residences with security systems on well-lit streets or cul-de-sacs are less likely to be victimized (Vito and Holmes, 1994). The UCR does not accurately represent the number of burglaries committed because people tend to report them only when very valuable goods are taken.

The most frequently reported index crime is *larceny-theft*—unlawfully taking or attempting to take property (with the exception of motor vehicles) from another person. Larceny-theft includes purse snatching and pickpocketing. Although most people who are arrested for larceny-theft are white, African-Americans are overrepresented in arrests for this type of crime given the proportion of the total population that is African-American. The average age of arrest for larceny-theft is twenty-five, and many offenders are under the influence of alcohol or other drugs at the time of their arrest (Gentry, 1995).

Statistics on auto theft are more accurate than those for many other crimes because insurance companies require claimants to report the theft to police. Analysts have identified four basic motives for auto theft: (1) joyriding—the vehicle is stolen for the fun of riding around in it and perhaps showing off to friends; (2) transportation—the vehicle is stolen for personal use; (3) as an aid in the commission of another crime; and (4) profit—the vehicle is sold or taken to a "chop shop," where it is dismantled for parts, which are then sold separately (Barlow, 1996). Middle-class youths tend to steal cars for fun and joyriding; urban lower-class minority youths are responsible for most auto thefts for economic profit.

Shoplifting accounts for billions of dollars in losses to retail business each year. For some stores, the annual loss can be as high as 2–5 percent of the total value of inventory (Vito and Holmes, 1994). Early criminologists found that shoplifters fell into three categories: the *snitch*—someone with no criminal record who systematically pilfers goods for personal use or to sell; the *booster* or *heel*—the professional criminal who steals goods to sell to fences or pawnshops; and the *kleptomaniac*—someone who steals for reasons other than monetary gain (e.g., for sexual arousal) (Holmes, 1983). Most experts think that shoplifting is committed primarily by amateurs across lines of race, class, gender, and age (Barlow and Kauzlarich, 2002).

The last type of nonviolent property crime that we will examine is *identity theft*—using another individual's personal information (such as a bank account, credit card account, driver's license, or Social Security number) to commit fraud or theft. A lost or stolen wallet or purse can provide a potential offender with all the identification necessary to open up charge accounts in the victim's name and run up large bills before the individual becomes aware of what has happened. Thieves can also obtain personal information by stealing incoming or outgoing mail, such as credit card and bank statements. Personal information can also be stolen by people with legitimate access to personal data (airline or hotel reservationists or department or grocery store personnel, for example) or by computer hackers. Today, identity theft is a serious and growing problem—both in the United States and around the world—due in part to the vast amounts of personal information about people that is stored on computers, but also due to the increasing sophistication of the criminals who obtain and misuse that information (see Box 9.2).

Identity theft is extremely difficult on the victim. Sometimes, it takes several years for the victim to get his or her credit and finances back to normal. One recent survey of identity-theft victims found that more than half reported that they still had not restored their credit and resolved their cases after more than a year of trying to do so (*Austin American-Statesman*, 2005:C1).

Occupational (White-Collar) Crime

***Occupational (white-collar) crime* refers to illegal activities committed by people in the course of their employment or normal business activity.** When sociologist Edwin H. Sutherland (1949) first introduced the term *white-collar crime*, he was referring to such acts as employee theft, fraud (obtaining money or property

Social Problems in Global Perspective

Box 9.2

Who Am I? Identity Theft in the Global Village

Item: Linda Trevino, who lives in a Chicago suburb, applied for a job last year at a local Target department store, and was denied. The reason? She already worked there—or rather, her Social Security number already worked there. Follow-up investigation revealed the same Social Security number had been used to obtain work at 37 other employers, mostly by illegal immigrants trying to satisfy government requirements to get a job. (Sullivan, 2005)

Item: Al Qaeda cells use identity theft to raise money. Imam Samudra, the terrorist who masterminded the bombing in Bali that killed more than two hundred people in 2002, wrote a jailhouse manifesto about funding terrorism through identity theft and computer fraud. (Weisman, 2005)

Item: On-line banking customers in South Africa were shocked when a perpetrator gained unauthorized access by means of so-called "spyware" to the personal computer of an Absa [Bank] customer's banking particulars and used the identity of that customer to transfer money from the victim's account to his own account.... [The] Absa incident should [be] a wake-up call for all those who, in this electronic age, so carelessly assume that our identity is our own exclusive right and is immune from criminal abuse. (Watney, 2004:20)

As these news items suggest, identity theft is a growing problem not only in the United States (where about 10 million

Although we hear more about property and violent crimes, occupational (white-collar) crimes are also an all-too-familiar occurrence in our nation. Richard "Dickie" Scruggs, shown here as he entered the Jackson, Mississippi courthouse, was convicted for his role in a judicial bribery scheme to ensure that each of his clients received a favorable ruling in certain judges' courts.

under false pretenses), embezzlement (theft from an employer), and soliciting bribes or kickbacks. Of the many occupational crimes committed by people in their workplaces, few get reported and prosecuted by law enforcement officials. In 2000, federal prosecutors charged 8,766 persons with white-collar crimes, convicting almost 80 percent of those persons and obtaining prison sentences for about 4,000 of them. But that total includes people accused of almost every type of fraud, ranging from bankruptcy and insurance fraud to postal theft and counterfeiting, as well as the cases of securities fraud that made the headlines; and of the almost 160,000 inmates serving sentences in federal prisons in 2001, fewer than 1 percent were serving time for white-collar crimes (Leaf, 2002). In recent years, some forms of white-collar crime have made headlines as a result of the huge amounts of money involved and the effect that they have had on the nation's economy; these crimes are often referred to as *corporate crime*.

Corporate Crime

***Corporate crime* refers to illegal acts committed by corporate employees on behalf of the corporation and with its support**. Examples include antitrust violations (seeking an illegal advantage over competitors); deceptive advertising; infringements on patents, copyrights, and trademarks; unlawful labor practices involving the exploitation or surveillance of employees; price fixing; and financial fraud, including securities fraud, tax evasion, and insider trading. These crimes arise from deliberate decisions by corporate personnel to profit at the expense of competitors, consumers, employees, and the general public. In recent years, criminal charges were filed against high-ranking executives at WorldCom (parent company of what then was the nation's second-largest long-distance telephone company) and Enron (an energy-trading

Box 9.2 (continued)

Americans are victimized annually) but in nations around the world. Newspapers and television reports inform us almost daily that hackers have stolen another million credit card numbers from an ill-protected database or that financial group insiders have hawked credit card and account information to outsiders who have committed a flurry of costly crimes (Levy and Stone, 2005). Instant computer communications and the Internet have made it easier for identity theft to occur on a large scale, and organized crime groups in Eastern Europe, Nigeria, and Somalia are known to operate large identity theft divisions because the profits are so great and the risks are so low.

Identity theft costs U.S. consumers and businesses more than 53 billion dollars per year (Young, 2005). Compared with bank robberies and other kinds of garden-variety theft, the nature and extent of this problem is only now being fully understood. Hopefully, however, some progress is being made in reducing this problem as we become more aware of its existence. As one analyst noted, "International problems require international solutions. The good news is that progress is being made. A joint effort of law enforcement agencies in the United States, the United Kingdom, Canada, Bulgaria, Belarus, Poland, Sweden, the Ukraine, and the Netherlands led to the arrest... of twenty-eight identity thieves who operated an on-line global clearinghouse for stolen credit card numbers used by thousands of criminals throughout the world" (Weisman, 2005). Although efforts such as this are just a beginning, at least we are starting to look at this social problem from a global perspective rather than from the viewpoint that individuals who are not careful are the ones whose identities are stolen and that they have no one to blame but themselves.

conglomerate that previously had been one of the nation's largest corporations) for allegedly fraudulently overstating those entities' financial situation by billions of dollars. However, these were not isolated cases; high-ranking former officers of Adelphia Communications and Tyco International were convicted of looting those companies of many millions of dollars for their own use. Still other cases of corporate crime included the conviction of biopharmaceutical company ImClone's CEO, Sam Waskal, for selling shares of that company's stock on the basis of insider information that the price of the company's stock was going to fall drastically as a result of a negative public announcement by the government.

Corporate crime has both direct and indirect economic effects. Direct economic losses from corporate crime are immense in comparison to the money lost in street property crime. For example, losses from twenty years of street crime are estimated to be less than half of the losses from the savings and loan (S&L) failures that occurred in the 1980s (Friedrichs, 1996). Some of these failures involved bank fraud and other crimes. Failed S&Ls cost U.S. taxpayers hundreds of billions of dollars (Pizzo et al., 1991).

The indirect costs of corporate crime include higher taxes, increased cost of goods and services, higher insurance rates, massive losses by investors, and an overall loss of faith by the public in the economy. Loss of retirement benefits has been a key concern of many employees of corporations whose officials have increased their personal wealth without regard for the effects that their criminal actions may have on employees and everyday citizens. The retirement plans of millions of U.S. citizens, for example, lost billions of dollars in recent years as a result of securities fraud (Leaf, 2002). And although personal injury and loss of life are usually associated with homicides and conventional street crimes, deaths resulting from such corporate crimes as deliberately polluting the air and water, manufacturing defective products, or selling unsafe foods and drugs far exceed the number of homicides each year.

Organized Crime

Organized crime **is a business operation that supplies illegal goods and services for profit.** These illegal enterprises include drug trafficking, prostitution, gambling, loan-sharking, money laundering, and large-scale theft such as truck hijackings (Simon, 1996). No single entity controls the entire range of corrupt and illegal enterprises in the United States (Chambliss, 1988). Instead, there are many groups—syndicated crime networks—that can thrive because there is great demand for illegal goods and services. Sometimes these groups form alliances with businesspeople, law enforcement officials, and politicians. Some law enforcement and government officials are corrupted through bribery, campaign contributions, and favors that are intended to buy them off. Known linkages between legitimate businesses and organized crime exist in banking, hotels and motels, real estate, garbage collection, vending machines, construction, delivery and long-distance hauling, garment manufacture, insurance, stocks and bonds, vacation resorts, and funeral parlors (National Council on Crime and Delinquency, 1969). Syndicated crime networks operate at all levels of society and even globally.

Juvenile Delinquency

Juvenile delinquency **involves a violation of law or the commission of a status offense by a young person under a specific age.** Many behaviors that are identified as juvenile delinquency are not criminal acts per se but status offenses—acts that are illegal because of the age of the offender—such as cutting school, buying and consuming alcoholic beverages, or running away from home. In most states, the age range for juvenile delinquency is from seven to seventeen. Older offenders are considered adults and are tried in a criminal court.

How prevalent is juvenile crime? People under age eighteen account for about 16 percent of all arrests in the United States. About 17 percent of people arrested in 2006 for violent crimes were under the age of eighteen. In that year, people under age eighteen were responsible for 16 percent of the violent crime arrests and 26 percent of the property crime arrests. More than 23 percent of the people arrested for robbery and 28 percent of the people arrested for larceny-theft were under age eighteen (FBI, 2007). Note that these are arrest figures and do not necessarily reflect the true nature and extent of crime and status violations among juvenile offenders.

Juveniles who are apprehended are processed by the juvenile justice system, which is based on the assumption that young people can do better if they are placed in the right setting and receive guidance. Thus unlike adult offenders, whose cases are heard in criminal courts, most juveniles' cases are heard in juvenile courts or by specially designated juvenile judges. Unfortunately, most juvenile correction facilities or "training schools" hold large numbers of young people in overcrowded conditions and provide only limited counseling and educational opportunities for rehabilitation (Donziger, 1996).

WHO COMMITS CRIMES?

The most significant factor in any study of delinquency and crime arrest rates is gender. Men are more likely than women to commit major property crimes (for example, robbery and larceny-theft), whereas women are more likely than men to be involved in minor property crimes (for example, larceny and fraud) and in prostitution offenses. Men have higher arrest rates than women for violent crimes such as homicide, aggravated assault, robbery, and burglary; women are most often arrested for such nonviolent crimes as shoplifting, passing bad checks, credit card fraud, and employee pilferage. Although a considerable number of arrests and convictions for larceny and theft occur among women, men still account for the vast majority of these arrests and convictions. Criminologists estimate that 12–15 percent of all homicides in this country are committed by women. Most of these are linked to domestic violence and self-defense (Harlow, 1991; Belknap, 1996).

Although there are significant gender differences in the types of crimes committed, there are also commonalities. First, for both sexes, the most common offenses are driving under the influence of alcohol or drugs (DUI), larceny, and minor or criminal mischief. These three categories account for about 47 percent of all male arrests and about 49 percent of all female arrests. Second, liquor law violations (such as underage drinking), simple assault, and disorderly conduct are middle-range offenses for both men and women. Third, the rate of arrests for murder, arson, and embezzlement are relatively low for both men and women.

Age is also an important factor in any study of delinquency and crime arrest rates. The proportion of the population that is involved in serious crimes, such as homicide, rape, and robbery, tends to peak during the teenage years or early adulthood and then decline with age. Several reasons have been advanced for age–crime patterns, including differential access to legitimate or ***illegitimate opportunity structures*****—circumstances that allow people to acquire through illegitimate activities what they cannot achieve legitimately**—at various ages; differences in social factors such as peer influences; physiological factors such as the effects of aging on strength, speed, and aggression; and building up deviant networks that make it possible for people such as bookies or fences to commit less visible crimes (Steffensmeier and Allan, 2000).

Although individuals from all social classes commit crimes, some kinds of crimes are more associated with lower or upper socioeconomic status. People from lower socioeconomic backgrounds are more likely to be arrested for violent and property crimes; people from the upper classes generally commit white-collar or corporate crimes. Moreover, the majority of crimes committed by doctors, lawyers, accountants, and other professionals are ignored because of the prestige associated with these professions. Friends and neighbors assume that these people are law-abiding citizens, and law enforcement officials are not likely to scrutinize their behavior.

When we examine the intersection of race and class in arrest data, we see that low-income African Americans are overrepresented. In 2006, whites accounted for 68 percent of all property crime arrests and 58 percent of all violent crime arrests; African Americans accounted for 29 percent of property crime arrests and 39 percent of violent crime arrests (FBI, 2008). However, African Americans make up slightly over 13 percent of the U.S. population. Compared with the arrest rates for African Americans, arrest rates for whites are higher for nonviolent property crimes such as fraud and larceny-theft but lower for violent crimes such as robbery and murder.

Having considered who commits crimes, let's look at who the victims are. Most people fear the violent stranger, but the vast majority of murders are committed by family members, friends, neighbors, or coworkers. In slightly fewer than half the cases, the murderers are members of the victim's family or acquaintances. As we have already noted, most murder is intraracial. That is, whites most often murder whites (86 percent of the time), and African Americans most often murder African Americans (94 percent of the time) (see Table 9.1).

According to the NCVS, men are the most frequent victims of crimes of violence and theft, although women are more fearful of crime, particularly crime directed toward them, such as forcible rape (Warr, 2000). The elderly also tend to be more fearful of crime but are the least likely to be victimized. Young men of color between the ages of twelve and twenty-four have the highest rates of criminal victimization (Karmen, 2000).

TABLE 9.1 Percentage of all Homicides by Race of Killers and Victims, 2006

Victims	Killers		
	White	Black	Other/Unknown
White	86%	8.8%	5.2%
Black	4%	94%	2%

Source: FBI, 2008.

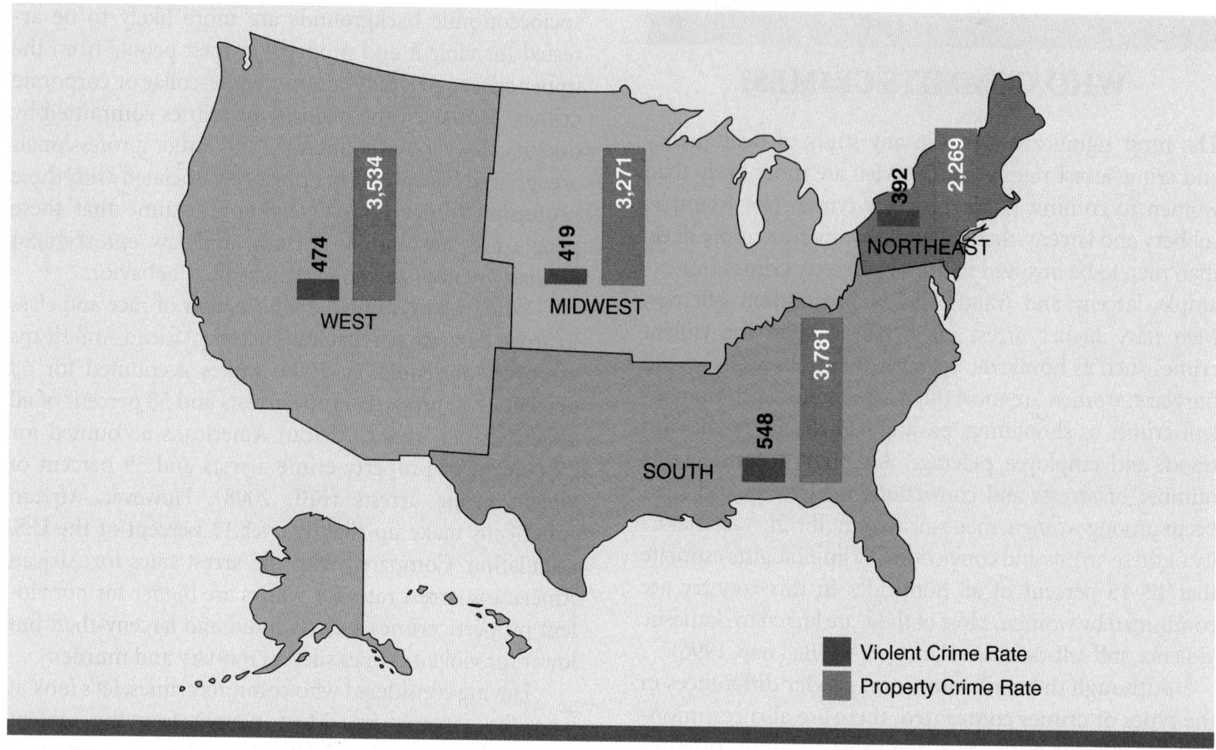

■ Map 9.1 ***Violent and property crime by region, 2006 (per 100,000 inhabitants).***
Source: FBI, 2008.

The NCVS data on robbery victims indicates that males are robbed at more than twice the rate of females. African Americans are more than three times as likely to be robbed as whites. Young people have a much greater likelihood of being robbed than middle-aged and older people do. People from lower-income families are more likely to be robbed than are those from higher-income families (Karmen, 2000). Risk of being a crime victim varies by region of the country, too. Risk of violent crime or property crime is greatest in the Western states and the South (see Map 9.1).

BIOLOGICAL AND PSYCHOLOGICAL EXPLANATIONS OF CRIME

As with other social problems, crime and delinquency have been explained in biological, psychological, and sociological terms. Most biological and psychological explanations assume that criminal behavior is an inherent or acquired individual trait with genetic, biological, or psychological roots. Sociological perspectives, in contrast, focus on external factors.

Biological Explanations

One of the earliest biological explanations of criminality came from the *positivist school*, which created physical typologies that were used to classify and study criminals (Barlow and Kauzlarich, 2002). The biological approach of Cesare Lombroso, a nineteenth-century Italian physicist, is probably the best known. Lombroso suggested that some people were born criminals or *atavists*—biological throwbacks to an earlier stage of evolution—and could be recognized by their low foreheads and smaller than normal human cranial capacities. A later theory, also based on physical traits, that received some attention for a time was proposed by physician William Sheldon (1949). According to Sheldon's *somatotype theory*, *mesomorphs*—people who are muscular, gregarious, aggressive, and assertive—are more prone to delinquency and criminal behavior than are *endomorphs*—people who are fat, soft, round, and extroverted—or *ectomorphs*—people who are thin, wiry, sensitive, and introverted.

Contemporary biological approaches based on genetics have attempted to link higher rates of aggression in men to levels of testosterone or chromosomal abnormality (an extra Y chromosome). But this research has produced no consistent findings, and social scientists argue that the differences in aggression could be due to gender-role socialization of men and women rather than to biological factors (Katz and Chambliss, 1995).

Other contemporary biological approaches suggest that violence is a natural and inevitable part of human behavior that can be controlled only by social organization. Some scientists, however, say that violence is neither natural nor inevitable but is the result of traumatic brain injury or some combination of brain injury and other factors. Although most people with brain injuries are not violent, injuries to certain parts of the brain or injuries in combination with an abusive childhood or psychotic symptoms (e.g., paranoia) can affect an individual's ability to conform to societal norms.

The cortex of the brain—particularly the frontal lobes—is most closely associated with violent behavior. It is the cortex that modifies impulses, allowing us to use good judgment, make decisions, and organize behavior; it also facilitates learning and adherence to rules of conduct (Gladwell, 1997). Using various neurological and psychiatric examinations, medical experts try to determine whether violent offenders have frontal-lobe impairment, were abused as children, or have any psychological disorders. These factors, especially in combination, make people prone to violent behavior because they have fewer inhibitions.

Psychological Explanations

Like biological explanations of delinquency and crime, psychological explanations focus on individual characteristics. Some researchers have used personality inventories in hopes of identifying abnormal personality traits in individuals who have committed crimes or engaged in delinquent behavior. Other researchers have investigated the effects of social learning and positive reinforcement (e.g., rewards such as money or special attention) and negative reinforcement (e.g., the withdrawal of reward or lack of attention) on delinquent and criminal behavior.

The most enduring psychological explanations of delinquency and crime seem to be the ones that bridge the biological explanations by linking intelligence and crime. Since the introduction of IQ (intelligence quotient) tests in the early 1900s, some analysts have suggested that people with lower intelligence scores are more likely to commit crimes than are people with higher intelligence scores. However, both the validity of IQ tests and the assertion that low intelligence causes delinquency or crime have come under great scrutiny and much criticism (see Hirschi and Hindelang, 1977).

Of course, some social analysts do acknowledge the possibility of a relationship between low intelligence and delinquency or crime. These analysts note that low intelligence might indirectly promote delinquency because it affects school performance. Similarly, less intelligent offenders might commit more obvious crimes and be more likely to be apprehended by law enforcement officials (Vito and Holmes, 1994).

One psychological explanation of violent crime focuses on *aggression*—behavior that is intended to hurt someone, either physically or verbally—that results from frustration (Weiten and Lloyd, 1994). According to the *frustration-aggression hypothesis*, people who are frustrated in their efforts to achieve a highly desired goal become aggressive toward others (Dollard et al., 1939). The object of the aggression becomes a *scapegoat*, a substitute for the actual source of frustration who can be blamed, especially if that person or group is incapable of resisting the hostility or aggression (see Chapter 3).

Explaining violence in biological and/or psychological terms suggests responses that are based on some type of psychiatric or other medical intervention. After all, if violent behavior is associated with specific neurological problems, it can be diagnosed like any other neurological illness and treated with drugs, including, possibly, anticonvulsants, antidepressants, and antihypertensive medications that act on the cortex to moderate violent behavior.

SOCIOLOGICAL EXPLANATIONS OF CRIME

Unlike biological and psychological explanations that focus on individual behavior, sociological explanations focus on those aspects of society that might contribute to delinquent or criminal behavior.

The Functionalist Perspective

Although there are numerous functionalist perspectives on crime and delinquency, we will focus on two perspectives: strain theory and control theory as illustrated in social bond theory.

Functionalist explanations for why people commit crimes can be traced to Emile Durkheim, who believed that the macrolevel structure of a society produces social pressures that result in high rates of deviance and crime. Durkheim introduced the concept of *anomie* to describe a social condition that engenders feelings of futility in people because of weak, absent, or conflicting social norms. According to Durkheim (1964/1895), deviance and crime are most likely to occur when anomie is present in a society. On the basis of Durkheim's theory, sociologist Robert Merton (1938, 1968) developed strain theory to explain why some people conform to group norms while others do not. ***Strain theory* is the proposition that people feel strain when they are exposed to cultural goals that they cannot reach because they do not have access to a culturally approved means of achieving those goals.** When some people are denied legitimate access to cultural goals such as success, money, or other material possessions, they seek to acquire these things through deviant—and sometimes criminal—means.

Merton identified five ways in which people respond to cultural goals: conformity, innovation, ritualism, retreatism, and rebellion (see Table 9.2). *Conformity* occurs when people accept the culturally approved goals and pursue them through the approved means. People who choose conformity work hard and save their money to achieve success. Someone who is blocked from achieving a high level of education or a lucrative career typically conforms by taking a lower-paying job and attending school part-time, joining the military, or trying alternative (but legal) avenues, such as playing the lottery. People who choose *innovation* accept society's goals but use illegitimate means to achieve them. Innovations for acquiring material possessions include shoplifting, theft, burglary, cheating on income taxes, embezzling money, and other kinds of occupational crime. *Ritualism* occurs when people give up on societal goals but still adhere to socially approved means for achieving them. People who cannot obtain expensive material possessions or wealth seek to maintain the respect of others by being "hard workers" or "good citizens" to an extreme degree. *Retreatism* occurs when people abandon both the approved goals and the approved means of achieving them. Retreatists include hard-core drug addicts and some middle- or upper-income people who reject conventional trappings of success and the means to acquire them, choosing to "drop out" instead. *Rebellion* occurs when people reject both the approved goals and the approved means for achieving them and advocate an alternative set of goals and means. Rebels might use violence (such as vandalism or rioting) or nonviolent tactics (such as civil disobedience) to change society and its cultural beliefs, or they might withdraw from mainstream society, like the Amish, to live their own style of life.

Another functionalist perspective—control theory—seeks to answer the question "Why do people *not* engage in deviant behavior?" According to control theory, people are constantly pulled and pushed toward deviant behavior. Environmental factors (pulls), such as adverse

TABLE 9.2 Merton's Strain Theory

Mode of Adaptation	Method of Adaptation	Agrees with Cultural Goal	Follows Institutional Means
Conformity	Accepts culturally approved goals; pursues them through culturally approved means	Yes	Yes
Innovation	Accepts culturally approved goals; adopts disapproved means of achieving them	Yes	No
Ritualism	Abandons society's goals but continues to conform to approved means	No	Yes
Retreatism	Abandons both approved goals and the approved means to achieve them	No	No
Rebellion	Challenges both the approved goals and the approved means to achieve them	No—seeks to replace	No—seeks to replace

Source: Adapted froim Merton (1968).

living conditions, poverty, and lack of educational opportunity, draw people toward criminal behavior while, at the same time, internal pressures (pushes), such as feelings of hostility or aggressiveness, make people not want to act according to dominant values and norms (Reckless, 1967). If this is true, why doesn't everyone who is poor or has a limited education commit crimes? According to control theorists, people who do not turn to crime or delinquent behavior have *outer containments*—supportive family and friends, reasonable social expectations, and supervision by others—or *inner containments*—self-control, a sense of responsibility, and resistance to diversions.

The best-known control theory is ***social bond theory*—the proposition that criminal behavior is most likely to occur when a person's ties to society are weakened or broken**. According to Travis Hirschi (1969), who proposed this theory, social bonding consists of (1) *attachment* to other people, (2) *commitment* to conformity, (3) *involvement* in conventional activities, and (4) *belief* in the legitimacy of conventional values and norms. When a person's social bonds are weak and when peers promote antisocial values and violent behavior, the probability of delinquency and crime increases (Massey and Krohn, 1986).

When analyzing violent crime, some functionalists believe that a sense of anomie is the root cause. Others believe that violence increases when social institutions such as the family, schools, and religious organizations weaken and the primary mechanisms of social control in people's everyday lives become external—law enforcement and the criminal justice system.

Several other functionalist perspectives on violence were discussed in Chapter 1. The *subculture of violence hypothesis* notes that violence is part of the normative expectations governing everyday behavior among young males in the lower classes (Wolfgang and Ferracuti, 1967). These violent subcultures are most likely to develop when young people, particularly males, have few legitimate opportunities available in their segment of society and when subcultural values accept and encourage violent behavior.

According to the *lifestyle-routine activity approach*, the patterns and timing of people's daily movements and activities as they go about obtaining the necessities of life—such as food, shelter, companionship, and entertainment—are the keys to understanding violent personal crimes and other types of crime in our society (Cohen and Felson, 1979). In other words, changes in social institutions, such as more families in which both parents (or the sole parent) work outside the home or shopping hours being extended into the night, put some people at greater risk of being victims of violent crime than others (Parker, 1995).

Functionalist explanations contribute to our understanding of crime by emphasizing that individuals who engage in such behavior are not biologically or psychologically impaired but are responding to social and economic conditions in society. However, functionalists are not without their critics. Strain theory might point out that people from low-income and poverty-level backgrounds are prevented from achieving success goals through legitimate channels, but it is still criticized for focusing almost exclusively on crimes committed by the lower classes and ignoring crimes committed by people in the middle and upper classes. Critics of social bond theory say that it is limited in its ability to explain more serious forms of delinquency and crime (Krohn, 2000).

The Conflict Perspective

Conflict theorists explain criminal behavior in terms of power differentials and/or economic inequality in society. One approach focuses on how authority and power relationships can contribute to some people—but not others—becoming criminals. According to Austin Turk (1966, 1971), crime is not a *behavior* but a *status* that is acquired when people with the authority to create and enforce legal rules apply those rules to others.

A second conflict approach focuses on the relationship between economic inequality and crime. Having roots in the work of Karl Marx, the *radical-critical conflict approach* argues that social institutions (such as law, politics, and education) create a superstructure that legitimizes the class structure and maintains capitalists' superior position. In fact, say these theorists, the crimes people commit are based on their class position. Thus crimes committed by low-income people typically involve taking things by force or physical stealth, whereas white-collar crime usually involves nonphysical means such as paper transactions or computer fraud. Some critical theorists believe that affluent people commit crimes because they are greedy and continually want more than they have, whereas poor people commit street crimes such as robbery and theft to survive (Bonger, 1969/1916). Finally, some conflict explanations are based on feminist scholarship and focus on why women commit crimes or engage in delinquent behavior. Scholars who use a *liberal feminist* framework believe that women's delinquency or crime is a rational response to gender discrimination in society. They attribute crimes such as prostitution and shoplifting to women's lack of educational and job opportunities and stereotypical expectations about roles women should have in society (Daly and Chesney-Lind, 1988). Scholars who espouse radical feminism believe that patriarchy contributes to crimes such as prostitution, because, according to society's sexual double standard, it is acceptable for a man to pay for sex but unacceptable for a woman to accept money for such services. A third school of feminist thought, *socialist feminism*, believes that women are exploited by capitalism and patriarchy. Because most females have relatively low-wage jobs and few economic resources, crimes such as prostitution and shoplifting become a means of earning money and acquiring consumer products. Feminist scholars of color, however, point out that none of the feminist theories include race/ethnicity in their analyses. As a result, some recent studies have focused on the relationship between crime and the simultaneous effects of race, class, and gender (Arnold, 1990).

In sum, the conflict approach is useful for pointing out how inequalities of power, class, race, and gender can contribute to criminal or delinquent behavior. Nevertheless, critics say that conflict theorists have not shown that powerful political and economic elites manipulate law making and enforcement for their own benefit. Rather, say these critics, people of all classes share a consensus that acts such as murder, rape, and armed robbery are bad (Klockars, 1979).

The Symbolic Interactionist Perspective

Symbolic interactionists emphasize that criminal behavior is learned through everyday interaction with others. We will examine two major symbolic interactionist theories: differential association theory and labeling theory. ***Differential association theory* states that individuals have a greater tendency to deviate from societal norms when they frequently associate with people who tend toward deviance rather than conformity.** According to sociologist Edwin Sutherland (1939), who formulated this theory, people learn not only the techniques of deviant behavior from people with whom they associate but also the motives, drives, rationalizations, and attitudes. Former gang member Nathan McCall (1994:93–94) describes such a learning process in his own life:

> Sometimes I picked up hustling ideas at the 7 Eleven, which was like a criminal union hall: Crapshooters, shoplifters, stickup men, burglars, everybody stopped off at the store from time to time. While hanging there one day, I ran into Holt.... He had a pocketful of cash, even though he had quit school and was unemployed. I asked him, "Yo, man, what you been into?" "Me and my partner kick in cribs and make a killin'. You oughta come go with us sometimes...." I hooked school one day, went with them, and pulled my first B&E [breaking and entering].... After I learned the ropes, Shell Shock [another gang member] and I branched out, doing B&Es on our own. We learned to get in and out of houses in no time flat.

As McCall's description indicates, criminal activity often occurs within the context of frequent, intense, and long-lasting interactions with people who violate the law. When more factors favor violating the law than not, the person is likely to become a criminal. Although differential association theory contributes to our knowledge of how deviant behavior reflects the individual's learned techniques, values, attitudes, motives, and rationalizations, critics note that many individuals who are regularly exposed to people who break the law still conform most of the time. Many critics think that the theory does not adequately take into account possible connections between social inequality and criminal behavior.

Labeling theory, which was mentioned briefly in Chapter 1, takes quite a different approach from differential association theory. According to ***labeling theory*, delinquents and criminals are people who have been successfully labeled as such by others.** No behavior is inherently delinquent or criminal; it is defined as such by a social audience (Erikson, 1962). According to sociologist Howard Becker (1963), labeling is often done by

Many children around the world (including this young boy in Leicestershire, England, UK) love to play with toy guns. How might functionalists, conflict theorists, and symbolic interactionists explain this social phenomenon?

moral entrepreneurs—people who use their own views of right and wrong to establish rules and label others "deviant." Furthermore, the process of labeling is directly related to the power and status of the people who do the labeling and those who are being labeled. In support of this theory, one study of juvenile offenders has found that youths from lower-income families were more likely to be arrested and indicted than were middle-class juveniles who did the same things (Sampson, 1986). Sociologists have also noted that the criminal justice system generally considers such factors as the offender's family life, educational achievement (or lack thereof), and social class in determining how to deal with juvenile offenders. According to one study, the individuals who are most likely to be apprehended, labeled delinquent, and prosecuted are people of color who are young, male, unemployed, and undereducated and who live in urban high-crime areas (Vito and Holmes, 1994).

Sociologist Edwin Lemert (1951) expanded labeling theory by distinguishing between primary and secondary deviance. ***Primary deviance* is the initial act of rule breaking** in which the individual does not internalize the delinquent or criminal self-concept. ***Secondary deviance* occurs when a person who has been labeled a deviant accepts that new identity and continues the deviant behavior.** The concept of secondary deviance is important to labeling theory because it suggests that when people accept a negative label or stigma that has been applied to them, the label can actually contribute to the behavior it was meant to control. In other words, secondary deviance occurs if a person is labeled a juvenile delinquent, accepts that label, and then continues to engage in delinquent behavior. Labeling theory is useful for making us aware of how social control and personal identity are intertwined. Critics, however, do not think that labeling theory explains what causes the original acts that constitute primary deviance, nor do they think that it adequately explains why some people accept deviant labels and others do not (Cavender, 1995).

Using functionalist, conflict, or symbolic interactionist perspectives, it is increasingly difficult to determine what types of criminal behavior may be learned through ideas that are set forth in video games, television programs, and movies. Scholars have begun to systematically study the popularity of video games, for example, that provide opportunities for seemingly law-abiding individuals to live vicariously by committing a series of crimes, including rape and murder within the context of the video game.

THE CRIMINAL JUSTICE SYSTEM

The term *criminal justice system* is misleading because it implies that law enforcement agencies and courts constitute one large, integrated system when actually they are a collection of somewhat interrelated, semiautonomous bureaucracies (Sheley, 2000). The ***criminal justice system* is the network of organizations—including the police, courts, jails, and prisons—involved in law enforcement and the administration of justice** (Donziger, 1996). Originally, the criminal justice system was created to help solve the problem of social disorder and crime. Today, however, some social analysts wonder whether the criminal justice system is part of the problem. Most cite two reasons for concern: (1) The criminal justice system fails in its mission to prevent, control, or rehabilitate offenders; and (2) unequal justice occurs because officials discriminate against people on the basis of race, class, gender, age, sexual orientation, or other devalued characteristics. We'll examine both issues in greater depth. First, though, let's look at each component of the justice system, starting with the police.

The Police

The police are the most visible link in the criminal justice system because they determine how to apply the law to control crime and maintain order. The police in the United States arrest and jail about 11 million people each year. Four factors seem to influence the occurrence of an arrest: (1) the nature of the alleged offense or problem; (2) the quality of available evidence; (3) the age, race, and sex of the alleged offender; and (4) the level of deference shown to police officers (Mastrofski, 2000). Given these factors, law enforcement officials have fairly wide *discretion*—use of personal judgment regarding whether and how to proceed in a given situation—in deciding who will be stopped and searched and which homes and businesses will be entered and for what purposes (Donziger, 1996). Because they must often make these decisions in a dangerous environment, sociologist Jerome Skolnick (1975) argues, police officers develop a sense of suspicion, social isolation, and solidarity. A New York City police officer describes this feeling:

> Guys...will eat you alive, even with the uniform on. They can sense fear, smell it like a dog smells it. Some of

> the mopes will come right out and tell you you're nothing, and you don't want that, oh no. If you're going to do this job, wear this uniform, you definitely don't want that. If it gets around that you're soft, that without your nightstick and gun you can't fight, that's bad. If you allow someone to smoke a joint in front of you or curse you out, word will spread throughout the neighborhood like a disease. You're a beat cop, out here every day, alone, so you set standards right away. (Norman, 1993:64)

Most officers feel that they must demand respect on the streets, but they also know that they must answer to their superiors, who expect them to handle situations "by the book."

The problem of discretion is most acute in the decision to use deadly force. Generally, deadly force is allowed only when a suspect is engaged in a felony, is fleeing the scene of a felony, or is resisting arrest and has endangered someone's life (Barlow, 1996). But police officers' lives are often on the line in confrontations with suspects, and sometimes the officers have less firepower than the individuals they are attempting to apprehend. In a Los Angeles bank robbery, for example, the robbers were wielding AK-47 automatic rifles and using 100-round ammunition drums and 30-round clips from which they were firing steel-jacketed bullets capable of penetrating the police officers' body armor (Story, 1997).

People of color often have a negative image of police because they believe that they receive differential treatment from the police (Anderson, 1990; Cose, 1993; Mann, 1993). Some analysts think that studies of police shootings lend credence to this belief. Rates of police shootings vary widely from one jurisdiction to another, but the percentage of shooting incidents involving African-American suspects is disproportionately high. African Americans are from five to thirteen times more likely than whites to be killed by police officers (Mann, 1993). Historically, criminal justice personnel at all levels have been white and male. The composition might be slowly changing, but white Americans still make up more than 80 percent of all police officers (U.S. Census Bureau, 2008).

In the past, women were largely excluded from law enforcement because of stereotypical beliefs that they were not physically and psychologically strong enough for the work. Today, however, women account for slightly more than 12 percent of all police officers (U.S. Census Bureau, 2008). Still, research shows that although more females have entered police work, they sometimes receive lower evaluations from male administrators than male officers do even when objective measures show that the female officers are equally effective on patrol (Reid, 1987).

How can police departments become more effective in reducing crime as a social problem? According to some analysts, police departments with entrenched problems must first reform their own agencies and win the respect of the communities they serve. One way to do this is to be sure that police departments reflect the racial and ethnic composition of the communities they serve. It is difficult for an all-white police force to build trust in a primarily African-American neighborhood (Donziger, 1996). Greater representation of women in police departments might reduce complaints that domestic violence, child abuse, and other family-related problems are sometimes minimized or ignored by police officers.

Some police departments have begun community policing as a way of reducing crime. Community policing involves integrating officers into the communities they serve—getting them out of their patrol cars and into a proactive role, recognizing problems, and working with neighborhood citizens to find solutions. In cities where community policing has been implemented, crime rates appear to have dropped; however, it should be noted that there has also been a general trend toward fewer crimes, especially violent crimes, in some cities where community policing is not employed (Donziger, 1996).

The Courts

Criminal courts are responsible for determining the guilt or innocence of people who have been accused of committing a crime. In theory, justice is determined in an adversarial process: A prosecutor (an attorney who represents the state) argues that the accused is guilty, and a defense attorney argues that the accused is innocent. In reality, judges have a great deal of discretion. Working with prosecutors, they decide who will be released, who will be held for further hearings, and—in many instances—what sentences will be imposed on people who are convicted.

Because courts have the capacity to try only a small fraction of criminal cases, prosecuting attorneys also have considerable discretion in deciding when to prosecute and when to negotiate a plea bargain with a defense attorney. About 90 percent of criminal cases are never tried in court; they are resolved by ***plea bargaining*****—a process whereby the prosecution negotiates a reduced sentence in exchange for a guilty plea.** In other words, defendants (especially those who are poor and cannot afford to pay an attorney) plead guilty to a lesser crime in return for not being tried for the more serious crime for which they were arrested. As cases are sifted and sorted through the legal machinery, steady attrition occurs. At each stage, various officials determine what alternatives will be available for the cases that remain in the system (Hills, 1971). Now that many jurisdictions specify mandatory minimum sentences, offenders typically spend a longer time in prison. In fact, mandatory sentencing guidelines have removed sentencing power from judges and juries and transferred it to prosecutors, who determine what charges will be brought against the defendant. Unless the defendant is found not guilty, the judge must sentence him or her according to the statutory prescription for the offense regardless of any facts that might have led a different prosecutor to charge differently or of any mitigating circumstances in the case.

Punishment and the Prisons

***Punishment* is any action designed to deprive a person of things of value (including liberty) because of an offense the person is thought to have committed** (Barlow, 2002). Punishment is seen as serving four functions:

1. *Retribution* imposes a penalty on the offender. Retribution is based on the premise that the punishment should fit the crime: The greater the degree of social harm, the more the offender should be punished. An individual who murders, for example, should be punished more severely than one who steals an automobile.
2. *Social protection* results from restricting offenders so that they cannot continue to commit crimes.
3. *Rehabilitation* seeks to return offenders to the community as law-abiding citizens. However, the few rehabilitation programs that exist in prisons are seriously understaffed and underfunded. Often, the job skills (such as agricultural work) that are taught in prison do not transfer to the outside world, and offenders are not given help in finding work that fits the skills they might have once they are released.
4. *Deterrence* seeks to reduce criminal activity by instilling a fear of punishment. Criminologists debate, though, whether imprisonment has a deterrent effect, given that 30–50 percent of those who are released from prison commit further crimes.

"My client pleads great wealth."

Today, more than one in 100 American adults are behind bars, and the prison population nationwide is approximately 1.6 million people (Liptak, 2008). Moreover, another 723,000 people are in local jails where they will spend at least one night of incarceration. Although incarceration rates have risen overall in recent years, the rate for minorities (with the exception of Asian Americans, who are the least likely to be incarcerated) is disproportionately higher than for whites. For example, one in 15 adult African-American males is behind bars, and one in 36 adult Latino men is incarcerated.

According to the text, punishment serves four functions: retribution, social protection, rehabilitation, and deterrence. Which of these functions is shown in this photo?

Overall, the rate of incarceration for African Americans is six times greater rate than whites: 1,947 per 100,000 African Americans as compared to 306 per 100,000 white Americans. Nearly half of all prison admissions are African Americans, even though the majority of violent crime nationwide is committed by whites (FBI, 2008).

Jail and prison conditions often do little to rehabilitate offenders. In fact, three out of four inmates are housed in such overcrowded facilities that two people often live in a space only slightly larger than a walk-in closet. Some inmates suffer physical abuse by prison officials or other inmates. States spent $44 billion in tax dollars on corrections in 2007, a 127 percent increase when adjusted for inflation over the $10.6 billion that was spent in 1987; thus, as one analyst suggested, "Getting tough on crime has gotten tough on taxpayers" (Liptak, 2008:A14).

Because of plea bargains, credit for "good time" served, and overcrowded prison conditions, most convicted criminals do not serve their full sentences. They are released on either probation (close supervision of their everyday lives in lieu of serving time) or parole (early release from prison). About 4.7 million people are currently on probation or parole (U.S. Census Bureau, 2008). If offenders violate the conditions of their probation or parole, they can be returned to prison to serve their full sentence. Some courts use shaming penalties—named for punishments that were used by the seventeenth-century Puritans—with probationers or as alternatives to incarceration. Shaming penalties typically take the form of a message to the community, just as the public stocks did in the seventeenth century. For example, as a condition of his probation, one Illinois man had to put this sign at the end of his driveway: "Warning. A Violent Felon Lives Here. Travel at Your Own Risk" (Hoffman, 1997:A1). Drunk drivers might get special license plates; men who have been convicted of soliciting prostitutes might be identified in the media or on billboards; and shoplifters have been required to walk in front of the stores from which they stole, carrying signs admitting their guilt. Because these sentences are usually the result of a guilty plea, they cannot be appealed except under very special circumstances (Hoffman, 1997).

Aside from their deterrent effect, shaming penalties are a way of avoiding the high cost of incarceration, another taxpayer burden. The average cost of building a new cell in a state prison is more than $55,000, and the cost per prisoner averages almost $24,000 per year, excluding food and medical services. However, spending varies widely from state to state, as evidenced by the fact that Rhode Island spent an average of $45,000 per prisoner in 2005, as compared to $13,000 in Louisiana. Increasing numbers of older prisoners add to the costs because they often have chronic health conditions that require long-term medical care. The $24,000 average per prisoner actually comes closer to $70,000 a year for elderly state prison inmates.

The Death Penalty

In 2007, 42 persons in 10 states were executed with the majority (26) being in Texas. Of persons executed in that year, 28 were white, 14 were African-American, and all were men (U.S. Bureau of Justice Statistics, 2008).

About 4,700 people have been executed in the United States since 1930, when the federal government began collecting data on executions (U.S. Bureau of Justice Statistics, 2008). The death penalty—or *capital punishment*—is a highly controversial issue. Removal—not just expulsion—from one's group is considered the ultimate form of punishment. In the United States, capital punishment is considered an appropriate and justifiable response to very serious crimes.

In 1972, the U.S. Supreme Court ruled (in *Furman v. Georgia*) that *arbitrary* application of the death penalty violates the Eighth Amendment to the Constitution but that the death penalty itself is not unconstitutional. In other words, determining who receives the death penalty and who receives a prison term for similar offenses should not be done on a lotterylike basis (Bowers, 1984). To be constitutional, the death penalty must be imposed for reasons other than the race/ethnicity, gender, and social class of the offender.

Opponents of capital punishment argue that the death penalty is discriminatory because people of color, especially African Americans and poor people, are at greater risk of receiving a death sentence than are their white, more affluent counterparts (Smith, 2000). In fact, the former slave states are more likely to execute criminals than are other states, and African Americans are eight to ten times more likely to be sentenced to death for crimes such as homicidal rape than are whites (non-Latinos/as) who commit the same offense (Marquart et al., 1994).

People who have lost relatives and friends because of a crime often see the death penalty as justifiable compensation—"an eye for an eye." Others fear that innocent individuals will be executed for crimes they did not commit. However controversial the death penalty is, it is likely to remain in place well into the twenty-first century because many political leaders and U.S. Supreme Court justices have expressed support for it.

Is the solution to our "crime problem" to build more prisons and execute more people? Only about 20 percent of all crimes result in arrest, only half of these lead to a conviction, and fewer than 5 percent of convictions result in a jail term. The "lock 'em up and throw away the key" approach has little chance of succeeding. As for individuals who commit occupational and corporate crime, the percentage that enters the criminal justice system is so minimal that prison is relatively useless as a deterrent to others. Furthermore, the high rate of recidivism strongly suggests that the rehabilitative efforts of our existing correctional facilities are sadly lacking. One thing is clear: The existing criminal justice system cannot solve the crime problem. Some people believe that the way to reduce street crime, at least, is to short-circuit criminal behavior (see Box 9.3).

Is equal justice under the law possible? As long as racism, sexism, classism, and ageism exist in our society, equal justice under the law might not be possible for all people. However, that does not keep it from being a goal that citizens and the criminal justice system can strive to reach.

Social Problems and Social Policy

Box 9.3

Crime Prevention or the Prison-Industrial Complex?

> I know something serious has happened when I wake up well before dawn to discover two guards wearing armored vests and riot helmets taking a head count.... It's apparent that the prison is on "full lockdown status." At the minimum, we will be locked in our cells twenty-four hours a day for the next several days.... The experienced prisoner knows to be prepared for a few weeks of complete isolation.
>
> —*Quoted in Hopkins, 1997:66*

With these words, author Evans D. Hopkins describes the day at the Nottoway Correctional Center in Virginia when two correctional officers and two nurses were taken hostage by three prisoners after a botched escape attempt. On that day, officials declared a lockdown that ultimately lasted four and a half months.

Although some politicians and social analysts believe that building more prisons and giving long sentences to offenders is the way to reduce the crime problem in the United States, others think that we should spend our money and energy on crime prevention instead. According to *prevention ideology*, the best way to reduce delinquency and crime is early intervention and prevention (Bynum and Thompson, 1996). Prevention typically takes three avenues: (1) early childhood and youth socialization that contributes to law-abiding behavior; (2) attacking the roots of delinquency and crime—poverty, unemployment, racism, sexism, drug abuse, and other problems discussed in this book; and (3) specific programs or services that intervene before individuals who have already engaged in delinquent or criminal behavior become immersed in deviant subcultures.

Current U.S. social policy is not based on prevention but consists of programs that include hiring more police officers, strengthening and enforcing gun control laws, and implementing the "three strikes" law, which requires a mandatory life sentence without parole for an individual who is convicted of a third felony. In fact, recent studies show that the government and private security companies spend nearly the same amount on crime control each year as the Pentagon spends on national defense (Donziger, 1996). The "war on crime"

(continued)

Box 9.3 (continued)

approach has contributed to the growth of a prison-industrial complex—a network of private companies, the government, and politicians—that greatly influences crime policy. In the past, most money spent on crime control went to public prisons; today, many state and local governments contract with private companies to build and operate correctional facilities, generating an annual revenue to these companies of more than $250 million. Other private enterprises also benefit from the prison-industrial complex, including investment houses that underwrite jail and prison construction and companies that provide food service, transportation, and health care for the facilities. Still other companies benefit from the sale of protective vests for guards, security systems, closed-circuit television systems, and other surveillance apparatus. Some analysts suggest that the prison-industrial complex, with its interlocking financial and political interests, has good reason to support the "war on crime" instead of developing social policies that prevent delinquency and crime before they happen (Donziger, 1996).

Does living in a prison environment with full lockdown status, as Hopkins describes, turn inmates into law-abiding citizens when they are released? What strategies can you suggest for rehabilitating prisoners? For preventing crime before it occurs?

IS THERE A SOLUTION TO THE CRIME PROBLEM?

Since most efforts to reduce or eliminate crime in the United States rely at least partly on the political system and on law enforcement officials, many people look to elected officials and community volunteers for answers on how to deal with the crime problem.

Functionalist/Conservative Solutions

Some functionalist approaches suggest that it is important to identify the social pressures that result in high rates of deviance and crime if we are to reduce the number of crimes that are committed. According to this perspective, when there is a vast disparity between what people would like to have and what they think they can reasonably attain, there is a greater likelihood that crimes will be committed. Based on this approach, one way to reduce crime is through community policing, an organizational strategy among law enforcement agencies that focuses on addressing the causes of crime and reducing the fear of crime and social disorder by using problem-solving tactics and police-community partnerships (COPS, 2008). According to Herman Goldstein, a founder of the problem-oriented approach, more careful analysis of what's going on in communities and a better understanding of the types of crimes that are being committed will make it possible for law enforcement officials and community residents to implement new and more effective strategies for dealing with the problem. In sum, learning about current problems in order to prevent them from occurring again in the future is the key to this approach (COPS, 2008). However, some critics view this as a form of social control and surveillance by law enforcement officials, which they believe is wrongfully applied more often in low-income and minority neighborhoods than in urban enclaves and affluent suburbs.

Similar to functionalist approaches to reducing crime, conservative political analysts typically focus on how to strengthen neighborhoods, communities, and society through the maintenance of a moral order that is rooted in strong families, social and religious organizations, and other community networks. Some conservative analysts emphasize the importance of "get-tough" policies that result in more "law and order" as an effective means of reducing crime, and they suggest that laws must be enforced and criminal penalties imposed on those who violate the rules. Some conservative analysts support "three strikes" laws passed by various states that mandate that a person who receives a third conviction of a serious crime must be sentenced to life in prison without possibility of parole.

Conflict/Liberal Solutions

From a conflict approach, it would be necessary to reduce power differentials and/or economic inequality in society in order to solve the problem of crime. According to conflict theorists using a Marxist approach, although some consensus may exist across class lines that certain types of crime, such as murder, rape, and armed robbery, are bad, other crimes primarily may be viewed as a threat to members of the capitalist class who desire to maximize their wealth and power in society. In other words, people who have few opportunities to gain a good education or to get a job that pays a living wage are more likely to commit property crimes to help them get by than are those who have greater opportunities. Of course, this explanation does not deal satisfactorily with the issue of why some wealthy people commit property crimes or engage in fraudulent behavior within major corporations.

Some branches of conflict theorizing and liberal political analysis look at race as an important variable that must be addressed when we think about how to reduce crime. From this approach, if crime is to be reduced, racism must also be reduced. Members of racial and ethnic groups that have been the objects of prejudice and discrimination across generations have not had the same opportunities as dominant group members, and once they are accused of committing a crime, the criminal justice system becomes a revolving door that offers no legitimate exit because they have a "record" and few employers are willing to hire them.

In recent years, advocates using conflict and/or liberal assumptions about reducing crime have suggested that a start to solving the problem of the relationship between race and crime might be for the police, the courts, and other branches of the criminal justice system to treat people in different classes and racial/ethic groups more fairly and more equally. For example, allegations against police officers pertaining to excessive injuries or brutality toward detainees have frequently been lodged against white officers who were in the process of investigating crimes where the alleged perpetrators were persons of color.

Liberal political analysts believe that an important way to eliminate crime in the United States is to empower people. They suggest doing this by greatly improving our public schools; having city, state, and national economic development programs that expand job opportunities for all people; and using public dollars to create better, safer housing where people do not feel threatened in their own homes. Critics of this approach point out that, particularly in tough economic times, suggestions such as these for reducing or eliminating crime have little chance of succeeding, first because there is no money for such programs, and second, because the private sector, not the government, should be responsible for the creation of jobs, housing, and other needed goods and services in society.

Symbolic Interactionist Solutions

As with the solution to other types of social problems, symbolic interactionists make us aware that any behavior that is learned, including criminal behavior, can be unlearned. As a result, the way to reduce crime is teach people the importance of law-abiding behavior and to engage in other endeavors that help to modify and eliminate criminal behavior in society. People who have frequent, intense, and long-lasting interactions with individuals who violate the law, for example, are more likely to violate the law themselves. Finding a means to keep children and young people away from individuals who commit crimes by getting them out of schools and neighborhoods known for high crime rates may help some individuals break out of a cycle of criminal behavior, incarceration, and more criminal behavior. However, applying this individualistic approach does little for solving the larger crime problem in society even if it helps some individuals avoid crime and gain new opportunities. Consider, for example, an elite private school in New York City or another large urban area that provides scholarships for promising low-income students, often from predominantly minority neighborhoods, so that they can get a good education and eventually enroll in a prestigious Ivy League university such as Harvard, Yale, or Princeton. Success stories such as these are frequently printed in major newspapers and posted on the Internet; however, some critics argue that this is elitism ("We know best for a few well-chosen individuals") rather than making a genuine effort to help disadvantaged youths achieve their American Dream.

Finally, symbolic interactionists who use a social constructionist approach point out that different people have different realities about what causes crime, and thus it is necessary to listen to diverse voices to find out how we might reduce or eliminate crime. Based on a social construction of reality approach, for example, the presence of guns is a key factor in why some crimes are committed. As a result, taking illegal handguns off the street has been identified as a viable way to reduce crime in cities such as New York and Boston where illegal firearms have widely been seized and destroyed. If the assumption is correct that guns contribute to crime rates, then the solution is to have far fewer guns in people's hands, particularly those individuals who have a prior criminal record (see Baker, 2008).

Since the 2001 terrorist attacks in this country and more recent ones in other nations, the United States government has attempted to balance the need to protect its citizens against violence and crime with its responsibility to protect individual rights. The government is responsible for upholding the democratic principle that any individual accused of a crime is "innocent until proven guilty." However, many are concerned that this principle is being violated, particularly along lines of race, class, and nationality, and that what some people see as a *solution* to our crime problem, such as greater surveillance and social control, ultimately may not be a solution at all but instead may contribute to our crime *problem* as greater surveillance is placed on law-abiding citizens while individuals who perpetrate the most dangerous crimes largely remain undetected. Hopefully, we will gain a better grasp on how to reduce or solve crime in the future.

SUMMARY

■ *Why is it difficult to study crime and delinquency?*

Studying crime, criminals, and juvenile delinquency is difficult because it involves complex human behavior, and many criminals and victims hide their involvement. There also are problems inherent in using official sources of data such as the Uniform Crime Report because they reflect crimes that are reported rather than crimes that are committed and they do not provide detailed information about offenders.

■ *How does violent crime differ from property crime?*

Violent crime consists of actions involving force or the threat of force against others and includes murder, rape, robbery, and aggravated assault. Property crime consists of taking money or property from another without force, the threat of force, or the destruction of property.

■ *Why is rape as a violent crime not well understood, and how is this lack of understanding reflected in our social response to rape?*

First, many people think that rape is a sexually motivated crime, but it is actually an act of violence in which sex is used as a weapon against a powerless victim. Moreover, statistics on rape are misleading at best because rape is often not reported. Many reasons keep victims from coming forward. Some victims may be so traumatized that they just want to forget about it. Others fear that their attacker will try to get even. Many also fear how they will be treated by the police and, in the event of a trial, by prosecutors and defense attorneys.

■ *What is occupational crime?*

Occupational (white-collar) crime refers to illegal activities committed by people in the course of their employment or normal business activity. Occupational crime includes computer and other high-tech crimes, as well as more traditional crimes such as employee theft, fraud (obtaining money or property under false pretenses), embezzlement (theft from an employer), soliciting bribes or kickbacks, and insider trading of securities.

■ *How does occupational crime differ from corporate crime?*

Occupational crimes are illegal activities committed by people in the course of their employment or normal business activity. Corporate crimes are illegal acts committed by corporate employees on behalf of the corporation and with its support.

■ *What is organized crime and why does it flourish in the United States?*

Organized crime is a business operation that supplies illegal goods and services for profit. These illegal enterprises include drug trafficking, prostitution, gambling, loan-sharking, money laundering, and large-scale theft. Organized crime thrives because there is great demand for illegal goods and services.

■ *How does juvenile delinquency differ from adult crime?*

Juvenile delinquency refers to a violation of law or the commission of a status offense by people who are younger than a specific age. Many behaviors that are identified as juvenile delinquency are not criminal acts per se but status offenses—acts that are illegal because of the age of the offender—such as cutting school or purchasing and consuming alcoholic beverages. Juvenile hearings take place in juvenile courts or before juvenile judges, whereas adult offenders are tried in criminal courts.

■ *Who is most likely to be arrested for a crime in the United States?*

Men are more likely to be arrested than are women. Teenagers and young adults are most likely to be arrested for serious crimes such as homicide, rape, and robbery. Although individuals from all social classes commit crimes, people from lower socioeconomic backgrounds are more likely to be arrested for violent and property crimes, whereas people from the upper classes generally commit white-collar or elite crimes. Low-income African Americans are overrepresented in arrest data.

■ *How do functionalists explain crime?*

Functionalists use several theories to explain crime. According to strain theory, people are socialized to desire cultural goals, but many people do not have institutionalized means to achieve the goals and therefore engage in criminal activity. Control perspectives, such as social bond theory, suggest that delinquency and crime are most likely to occur when a person's ties to society are weakened or broken.

■ *How do conflict theorists explain crime?*

Conflict theorists explain criminal behavior in terms of power differentials and/or economic inequality in society. One approach focuses on the relationship between authority and power and crime; another focuses on the relationship between economic inequality and crime. Feminist approaches offer several explanations of why women commit crimes: gender discrimination, patriarchy, and a combination of capitalism and patriarchy.

■ *How do symbolic interactionists explain crime?*

Symbolic interactionists emphasize that criminal behavior is learned through everyday interaction with others. According to differential association theory, individuals have a greater tendency to deviate from societal norms when they frequently associate with people who are more likely to deviate than conform. Labeling theory says that delinquents and criminals are those people who have been successfully labeled by others as such.

■ *What are the components of the criminal justice system?*

The criminal justice system is a network of organizations involved in law enforcement, including the police, the courts, and the prisons. The police are the most visible link in the criminal justice system because they are responsible for initially arresting and jailing people. Criminal courts are responsible for determining the guilt or innocence of people who have been accused of committing a crime. Imprisonment, probation, and parole are mechanisms of punishment based on retribution, social protection, rehabilitation, and deterrence.

■ *Why is the death penalty controversial?*

The death penalty—or capital punishment—is a highly controversial issue because removal from the group is considered the ultimate punishment. Some people believe that it is an appropriate and justifiable response to very serious crimes; others view this practice as discriminatory because people of color—especially African Americans—and poor people are at greater risk of receiving a death sentence than are their white, more affluent counterparts.

KEY TERMS

acquaintance rape, p. 181
corporate crime, p. 185
criminal justice system, p. 193
differential association theory, p. 192
felony p. 177
forcible rape, p. 181
illegitimate opportunity structures, p. 187
juvenile delinquency, p. 186
labeling theory, p. 192
mass murder, p. 178
misdemeanor, p. 177
murder, p. 178
occupational (white-collar) crime, p. 184
organized crime, p. 186
plea bargaining, p. 194
primary deviance, p. 193
property crime, p. 183
punishment, p. 195
secondary deviance, p. 193
serial murder, p. 178
social bond theory, p. 191
statutory rape, p. 181
strain theory, p. 190
violent crime, p. 178

QUESTIONS FOR CRITICAL THINKING

1. Why doesn't the United States use all of its technological know-how to place known criminals and potential offenders under constant surveillance so that the crime rate can be really reduced?
2. If most of the crimes that are committed are property crimes, why do so many people fear that they will be the victims of violent crime?
3. Does the functionalist, conflict, or symbolic interactionist perspective best explain why people commit corporate crimes? Organized crimes? Explain your answer.
4. If money were no object, how would you reorganize the criminal justice system so that it would deal more equitably with all people in this country?
5. What approach do you believe might be most effective in reducing crime in the United States?

Chapter 10

Health Care: Problems of Physical and Mental Illness

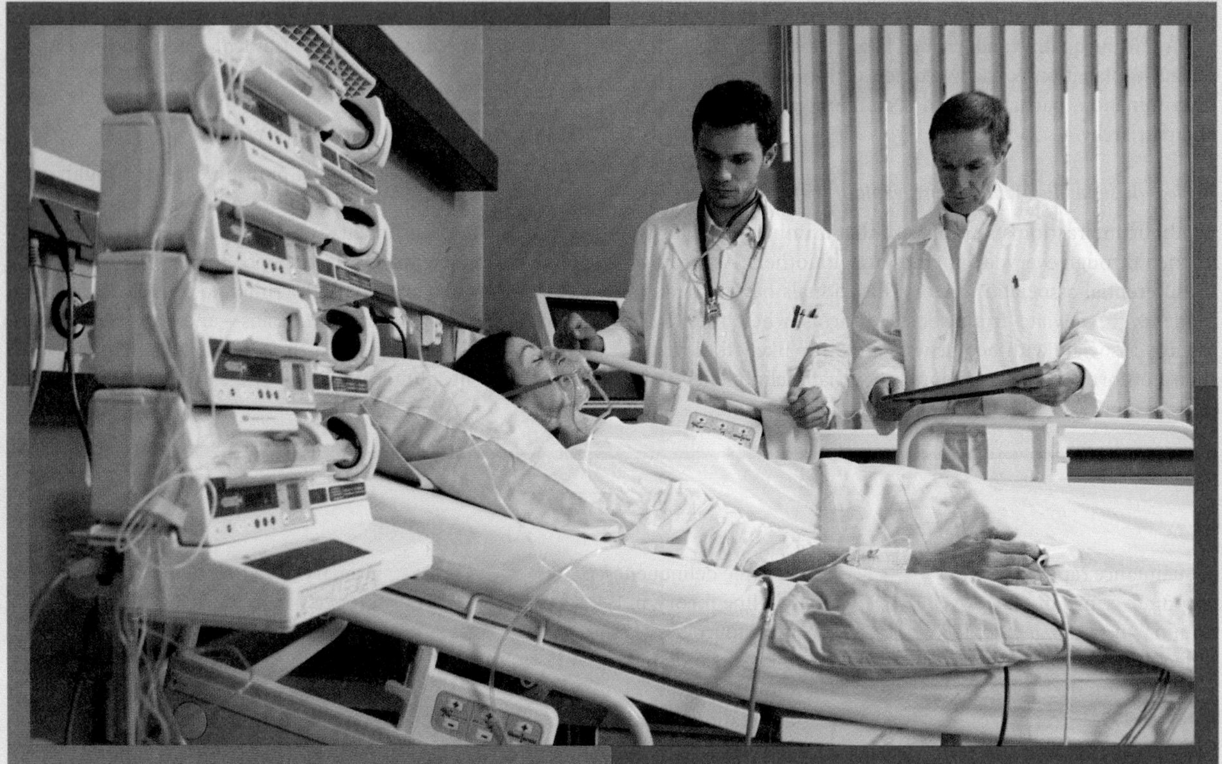

THINKING SOCIOLOGICALLY

- What are some of the most pressing health problems in the United States and other high-income nations? In low-income nations?
- Why are people more likely to discuss a physical illness with others as compared with a mental illness?
- How is health care paid for in the United States? What effect does this have on the care people receive?

*I am a family man, husband to a lovely and funny woman, a loose cannon named Meredith [Vieira]. Anyone who watches [*The Today Show *on NBC TV] knows her well.... I am the father of three gorgeous children with their own view of the world. Ben, Gabe, and Lily are forces to be reckoned with.... There is a powerful circumstance with which all of us must reckon, however. My health sucks, a condition that has become everybody's problem. Illness is a family affair.*

For thirty years, I have done battle with multiple sclerosis (MS). The disease touches everything I do and affects my body from head to toe. Chronic illness occupies a lowly position in the hierarchy of suffering but takes a toll. By the end of the millennium, I was suddenly clashing with another fierce adversary. Twice in one year, firefights with colon cancer erupted, further compromising the quality of my life.

I have become a magnet for trouble, an aficionado of living on the edge, a most dangerous place for any individual to hang out. The experience has taught me extraordinary lessons about living. Once, I did not know the verb cope. *Now I know it all too well.*

—In his autobiographical book,* Blindsided, *former television news producer Richard M. Cohen (2004:xiv–xv) explains how he learned to cope with MS, a chronic illness that left him legally blind and with limited use of his vocal cords, arms, and legs.

As a highly respected media professional, Richard M. Cohen found his life greatly changed when MS and cancer played havoc with his well-being. However, his story makes us aware that, for those suffering from long-term illness, the struggle for emotional health runs as deep as the disease itself. People with MS, colon cancer, and other diseases have found inspiration in his words: He shows that illness can be more than a *personal problem* involving a single individual. Illness often is a shared problem involving families, entire communities, and the nation as a whole. Thus, illness is a *social problem* that requires the attention of the entire nation to provide appropriate treatment, to fund research for new drugs and cures, and to create an environment that is accessible for those who need special accommodations in buildings, on city streets, and in public transportation. MS and colon cancer are only two of the many diseases that affect individuals, families, communities, and the health-care industry in the United States and other countries. This chapter examines health-care problems, including both physical and mental illness, and current problems in providing health services in this country.

HEALTH CARE AS A SOCIAL PROBLEM

According to the World Health Organization (1946:3), *health* is a state of complete physical, mental, and social well-being. In other words, health is not only a biological issue; it is also a social issue. Many people think that there is a positive relationship between the amount of money a society spends on health care and the overall physical, mental, and social well-being of its people. After all, physical and mental health are intertwined: Physical illness can cause emotional problems; mental illness can produce physical symptoms. According to this belief, spending a great deal of money on health care should result in physical, mental, and social well-being. If this is true, however, people in the United States should be among the healthiest and most fit in the world. We spend more than one and one-half trillion dollars—the equivalent of $3,800 per person—on health care each year. The health service industry accounts for more than 14 percent of the gross domestic product, a proportion that has increased substantially since the 1960s (U.S. Census Bureau, 2008). Table 10.1 shows the increase in health service expenditures between 1990 and 2005.

However, although we, as individuals, pay more for health services than do people in other high-income nations, our expenditures do not translate into improved life expectancy for everyone. ***Life expectancy* is an estimate of the average lifetime of people born in a specific year.** During the past 100 years, overall life expectancy has increased in the United States. The life expectancy of individuals born in 2005, for example, is 77.8 years, compared to only 47.3 years for people born in 1900. But today's life expectancy statistics vary by sex and race. Overall, females born in 2005 can expect to live about 80.4 years, compared to 75.2 years for males. African-American males born in 2005, however, have a life expectancy of only 69.5 years, compared to 76.5 years for African-American females (Centers for Disease Control and Prevention, 2007).

In high-income nations, life expectancy has increased as a nation's infant mortality rate has decreased. The ***infant mortality rate* is the number of deaths of infants under one year of age per 1,000 live births in a given year.** The infant mortality rate is an important indication of a society's level of preventive

TABLE 10.1 National Health Expenditures, by Type: 1990–2005

Type of Expenditure*	1990	1995	2000	2005
Total	696.0	990.2	1,309.4	1,987.7
Annual percent change	11.8	5.7	7.1	6.9
Percent of gross domestic product	12.0	13.4	13.3	16.0
Private expenditures	413.5	533.6	714.9	1,085.0
Health services and supplies	401.9	521.1	697.3	1,013.5
Out-of-pocket payments	137.3	146.5	192.6	249.4
Insurance premiums	233.5	329.7	449.3	694.4
Other	31.1	44.9	55.3	69.8
Medical research	1.0	1.4	3.4	3.7
Public expenditures	282.5	456.6	594.6	902.7
Percent federal of public	68.2	70.6	70.0	71.3
Health services and supplies	267.7	436.5	564.2	847.3
Medicare	110.2	183.1	225.1	324.0
Public assistance medical payments	78.7	149.5	209.3	324.9
Temporary disability insurance	0.1	0.1	–	0.1
Workers' compensation (medical)	17.5	21.9	25.3	33.5
Defense Dept. hospital, medical	10.4	12.1	14.0	26.1
Maternal, child health programs	1.8	2.2	2.7	2.6
Public health activities	20.2	31.4	45.8	56.6
Veterans' hospital, medical care	11.3	15.4	19.1	30.2
Medical vocational rehabilitation	0.5	0.7	0.8	0.5
State and local hospitals	13.1	14.1	13.4	19.2
Other	3.8	6.0	8.8	11.6
Medical research	11.7	15.7	25.4	36.3
Medical structures and equipment	9.2	11.5	14.7	19.1

*In billions of dollars, except percentages, excludes Puerto Rico and island areas.

Source: U.S. Census Bureau, 2008.

(prenatal) medical care, maternal nutrition, childbirth procedures, and care for infants. For all our expenditures in health care, however, infant mortality in the United States is considerably higher than it is in a number of other high-income nations (see Table 10.2). Perhaps the single most important cause of infant mortality is lack of prenatal care. Drinking, smoking, taking drugs, and maternal malnutrition all contribute. Divergent infant mortality rates for African Americans and whites indicate another problem: unequal access to health care. Even with today's high-tech medicine, the infant mortality rate for African-American infants is twice as high as the rate for white infants. In 2004, for example, the U.S. mortality rate for African-American infants was 13.2 per 1,000 live births compared to 5.7 per 1,000 live births for white infants (National Center for Health Statistics, 2007).

Acute and Chronic Diseases and Disability

Life expectancy in the United States and other developed nations has increased largely because vaccinations and improved nutrition, sanitation, and personal hygiene have virtually eliminated many acute diseases, including measles, polio, cholera, tetanus, typhoid, and malaria. ***Acute diseases*** **are illnesses that strike suddenly and cause dramatic incapacitation and sometimes death** (Weitz, 2007). Acute diseases that are still common in the United States are chicken pox and influenza. Recently, too, multi-drug-resistant strains of tuberculosis, Lyme disease, and HIV (the virus that causes AIDS) have become pressing health problems.

With the overall decline in death from acute illnesses in high-income nations, however, has come a

TABLE 10.2 Infant Mortality Rates in Selected Countries (2006)

Country or Area	Rate	Country or Area	Rate
United States	6.4	Iraq	48.6
Afghanistan	160.2	Italy	5.8
Algeria	29.9	Japan	2.8
Argentina	14.7	Kenya	59.0
Australia	4.6	Korea, North	23.3
Bangladesh	60.8	Korea, South	6.2
Brazil	28.6	Mexico	20.3
Burma	52.3	Netherlands	5.0
Canada	4.7	Pakistan	70.8
Chile	8.6	Peru	30.9
China	23.1	Philippines	22.8
Colombia	20.8	Poland	7.2
Egypt	30.7	Russia	11.3
Ethiopia	93.6	Saudi Arabia	12.8
France	3.4	Spain	4.4
Germany	4.1	Syria	28.6
Guatemala	30.8	Taiwan	5.6
India	37.1	Thailand	19.5
Indonesia	33.3	United Kingdom	5.1
Iran	39.3		

Rate = number of deaths of children under one year of age per 1,000 live births in a calendar year.

Source: U.S. Census Bureau, 2008.

corresponding increase in ***chronic diseases*, illnesses that are long term or lifelong and that develop gradually or are present from birth** (Weitz, 2007). Chronic diseases are caused by various biological, social, and environmental factors. Worldwide, some of these factors are the same, and some are different (see Box 10.1). According to some social analysts, we can attribute many chronic diseases in our society to the *manufacturers of illness*, groups that promote illness-causing behavior and social conditions, such as smoking (McKinlay, 1994). The effect of chronic diseases on life expectancy varies because some chronic diseases are progressive (e.g., emphysema worsens over time), whereas others are constant (e.g., paralysis after a stroke); also, some are fatal (lung cancer), but others are not (arthritis and sinusitis).

Some chronic diseases produce disabilities that significantly increase health-care costs for individuals and for society. Disability can be defined in several ways. Medical professionals tend to define it in terms of organically based impairments—that is, the problem is entirely within the body. However, disability rights advocates believe that disability is a physical or health condition that stigmatizes or causes discrimination. Perhaps the best way to define disability is, as medical sociologist Rose Weitz (2007) has said, in terms of both physical and social factors: ***Disability* is a restricted or total lack of ability to perform certain activities as a result of physical limitations or the interplay of these limitations, social responses, and the social environment.** An estimated 54 million people in the United States have one or more physical or mental disabilities, and the number continues to increase for several reasons. First, with advances in medical technology, many people who in the past would have died from an accident or illness now survive with an impairment. Second, as people live longer, they are more likely to experience chronic diseases (such as arthritis) that can have disabling consequences. Third, people born with serious disabilities are

Social Problems in Global Perspective

Box 10.1

Global Enemies of Health: The Double Burden of Low-Income Nations

> The world is living dangerously—either because it has little choice, or because it is making the wrong choices.
>
> —*Dr. Gro Harlem Brundtland, Director-General, World Health Organization (World Health Organization, 2002:163)*

Recently, the annual report of the World Health Organization (WHO) listed these top ten selected risks to health around the globe:

1. Underweight
2. Unsafe sex
3. High blood pressure
4. Tobacco consumption
5. Alcohol consumption
6. Unsafe water, sanitation, and hygiene
7. Iron deficiency
8. Indoor smoke from solid fuels
9. High cholesterol
10. Obesity

Some of the items on this list are typically associated with poverty, such as unsafe water, poor sanitation and hygiene, iron deficiency, and being underweight. According to WHO, "in poor countries today there are 170 million underweight children, over three million of whom will die this year as a result" (World Health Organization, 2002:x). The problem of being underweight is most prevalent among children who are five years of age or younger, and it is estimated that being underweight was a contributing factor in 60 percent of all child deaths in low-income nations in 2002.

By contrast, other items on this list—such as high cholesterol, high blood pressure, and obesity—are typically associated with wealthy societies. WHO estimates that there are more than one billion adults worldwide who are overweight, of whom at least 300 million are "clinically obese." In North America and Western Europe combined, for example, about 500,000 people die annually from obesity-related diseases. Thus, obesity is a health problem because it can contribute to more likely to survive infancy because of medical technology. (Estimates suggest that fewer than 15 percent of people with a disability today were born with it; accidents, disease, violence, and war account for most disabilities in this country.) For many people with chronic illness and disability, life takes on a different meaning. Knowing that they probably will not live out the full life expectancy for people in their age category, they come to treasure each moment. Today, some of the most tragic instances of life cut short occur because of AIDS.

The AIDS Crisis

AIDS—acquired immune deficiency syndrome—has reached crisis proportions in the United States and other nations. AIDS is caused by infection with a virus called human immunodeficiency virus (HIV), which is passed from one person to another through blood-to-blood and sexual contact.

How is AIDS transmitted? AIDS is transmitted primarily through bodily fluids, such as semen (through oral, anal, or vaginal sex with someone who is infected with HIV) or blood (usually by sharing drug needles and syringes with an infected person). It can also be

Progress has been made in curbing the progression of HIV in some affected individuals. However, AIDS remains a pressing social problem that is largely addressed through the efforts of activists and protesters such as the ones shown here, who are participating in a rally outside New York's United Nations building on the 25th anniversary of the AIDS pandemic.

Box 10.1 (continued)

premature death, but it is even more likely to produce chronic disease and disability.

However, in recent years, obesity, diabetes, and heart disease have become significant health problems in many lower-income nations as well. The dividing line between the health problems of people in high-income nations and those in low-income nations is not as clear as we might initially think. Although a significant number of people in some low-income nations are underweight and lack proper nutrition, many more people around the globe are consuming foods that contribute to health problems such as high blood pressure and high cholesterol. WHO attributes the problem of obesity to a change in global dietary patterns worldwide as more people are consuming larger amounts of industrially processed fatty, salty, and sugary foods. According to Dr. Brundtland, "In the slums of today's mega-cities, we are seeing noncommunicable diseases caused by unhealthy diets and habits, side by side with undernutrition" (World Health Organization, 2002:x). Some social analysts believe that a contributing factor to the growth in the rates of obesity is the global spread of processed (as compared to freshly produced) foods and the proliferation of fast-food restaurants.

Ironically, we are faced with dual and seemingly competing problems in regard to global nutrition: Some individuals are chronically underweight and in peril because of the lack of food, whereas others are chronically overweight and in peril because of either too much food intake or too much of the wrong kinds of foods. We cannot ignore this problem if, in fact, 22 million of the world's children under age six are overweight or obese, and in some parts of the African continent, fatness and obesity afflict more children than malnutrition does.

Throughout the world, individuals, governments, and corporations will need to cooperate if we are to reduce the problems associated with being underweight or being obese. Similarly, prevention will be essential for reducing health risks, and education is the first step in that direction.

Questions for Critical Thinking

1. Can you think of ways in which individuals, corporations, and governmental agencies might combat enemies of health around the world?
2. What part does food play in contributing to health problems?
3. Have U.S. corporations contributed to nutrition problems in other nations? Why or why not?

transmitted by blood transfusions (although testing donated blood for the presence of HIV has made this rare in high-income nations) and by infected mothers before or during birth or while breast-feeding. AIDS is *not* transmitted by routine contact such as a handshake or hugging a person who has the disease or by using eating utensils that a person with AIDS has used.

How many people have been diagnosed with HIV/AIDS in the United States? An estimated 1,039,000 to 1,185,000 persons in this country were living with HIV/AIDS in 2003, the most recent year for which data are available. Each year, between 35,000 and 40,000 new cases of HIV/AIDS are diagnosed in adults, adolescents, and children. Males accounted for almost three quarters (73 percent) of all new diagnoses among adolescents and adults in 2006, and the majority of these cases were attributed to male-to-male sexual contact. Especially jarring is the fact that, although African Americans make up about 13 percent of the population, they constitute almost half (49 percent) of all new HIV/AIDS cases each year. Age is another pressing concern: Persons between the ages of 25 and 44 accounted for 58 percent of all new cases diagnosed in 2006 (Centers for Disease Control, 2008).

The U.S. Centers for Disease Control (2008) estimates that more than 500,000 people in the United States have died from AIDS-related complications over the past 25 years. Advances in treatments have slowed the progression of HIV infection to AIDS and significantly reduced the number of deaths among persons with AIDS. However, we should note that people do not die of AIDS; they die because HIV gradually destroys their immune systems by attacking the white blood cells, making them vulnerable to diseases such as pneumonia, tuberculosis, yeast infection, Kaposi's sarcoma, and other forms of cancer.

Is there a cure for AIDS? Thus far, there is no cure for AIDS. However, newer anti-HIV medications can be used to control the reproduction of the virus and slow the progression of HIV-related disease. Highly Active Antiretroviral Therapy, which combines three or more anti-HIV medications in a daily regimen, has led to dramatic improvements in the health of many people with HIV; however, once HIV develops into AIDS, it eventually is fatal.

Not all social scientists agree on how AIDS will ultimately affect life expectancy, mortality rates, or the health-care industry in the United States. Treatment for AIDS-related illnesses, perhaps even more than that for other chronic diseases, is complex and costly and typically requires lengthy stays in a hospital or hospice. The incidence of AIDS, the number of AIDS patients, and the cost of caring for AIDS patients are highest and most concentrated in city centers, where clinics, hospitals, and other medical facilities are overcrowded, underfunded, and understaffed. Some analysts estimate that more people in the United States will die from AIDS-related illnesses in the future than have died in all the wars fought by this nation. Unfortunately, the AIDS problem in the United States is only a small part of the global picture of devastation caused by this disease.

MENTAL ILLNESS AS A SOCIAL PROBLEM

Mental illness is a social problem because of the number of people it affects, the difficulty of defining and identifying mental disorders, and the ways in which mental illness is treated. Although most social scientists use the terms *mental illness* and *mental disorder* interchangeably, many medical professionals distinguish between a *mental disorder*—a condition that makes it difficult or impossible for a person to cope with everyday life—and *mental illness*—a condition that requires extensive treatment with medication, psychotherapy, and sometimes hospitalization. The most widely accepted classification of mental disorders is the American Psychiatric Association's (1994) *Diagnostic and Statistical Manual of Mental Disorders IV* (DSM-IV) (see Figure 10.1 on page 209). The DSM is now in its fourth edition, and with each revision, its list of disorders has changed and grown. Listings change partly because of new scientific findings, which permit more precise descriptions that are more useful than are broad terms covering a wide range of behaviors, and partly because of changes in how we view mental disorders culturally. When the next edition (DSM-V) is published in 2012, the listings will probably differ somewhat from those found in Figure 10.1.

How many people are affected by mental disorders? About 57.7 million people, or one in four adults, in the United States suffer from a diagnosable mental disorder. Many of these illnesses began in childhood or adolescence, with the most common problems being anxiety disorder, mood disorders, impulse-control disorders, and substance abuse disorders. Even though mental disorders are widespread in the population, people who are suffering from a serious mental illness—such as schizophrenia, bipolar affective disorder, and major depression—accounted for about 6 percent or 1 in 17

1. Disorders first evident in infancy, childhood, or adolescence	These disorders include mental retardation, attention-deficit hyperactivity, anorexia nervosa, bulimia nervosa, and stuttering.
2. Organic mental disorders	Psychological or behavioral disorders associated with dysfunctions of the brain caused by aging, disease, or brain damage.
3. Substance-related disorders	Disorders resulting from abuse of alcohol and/or other drugs such as barbiturates, cocaine, or amphetamines.
4. Schizophrenia and other psychotic disorders	Disorders with symptoms such as delusions or hallucinations.
5. Mood disorders	Emotional disorders such as major depression and bipolar (manic-depressive) disorder.
6. Anxiety disorders	Disorders characterized by anxiety that is manifest in phobias, panic attacks, or obsessive-compulsive disorder.
7. Somatoform disorders	Psychological problems that present themselves as symptoms of physical disease such as hypochondria.
8. Dissociative disorders	Problems involving a splitting or dissociation of normal consciousness such as amnesia and multiple personality.
9. Eating or sleeping disorders	Includes such problems as anorexia and bulimia or insomnia and other problems associated with sleep.
10. Impulse control disorders	Symptoms include the inability to control undesirable impulses such as kleptomania, pyromania, and pathological gambling.
11. Personality disorders	Maladaptive personality traits that are generally resistant to treatment such as paranoid and antisocial personality types.

■ Figure 10.1 ***Mental disorders identified by the American Psychiatric Association***

Source: Adapted from American Psychiatric Association, 1994.

adults in the United States (National Institute of Mental Health, 2008).

Mental disorders are very costly to the nation. Direct costs associated with mental disorders include the price of medication, clinic visits, and hospital visits. However, there are many indirect costs as well. These include the lost earnings of individuals, the costs associated with homelessness and incarceration, and other indirect costs that exist but are difficult to document (National Institute of Mental Health, 2008).

Treatment of Mental Illness

Even though statistics indicate that people with mental disorders usually do not seek professional treatment, the leading cause of hospitalization for men between the ages of fifteen and forty-four and the second leading cause (after childbirth) for women in that age group is mental disorders, particularly disorders related to substance abuse (U.S. Census Bureau, 2008). However, the vast majority of people with lifetime disorders eventually do receive treatment for their condition even though they may delay as much as six to eight years before making treatment contact for mood disorders and 9 to 23 years for anxiety disorders (Wang and others, 2005).

People who do seek professional help are treated with medication and psychotherapy to help them understand the underlying reasons for their problem. Sometimes they are treated in psychiatric wards of local hospitals or in private psychiatric hospitals. Because medication is used so routinely today, we tend to forget that institutionalization used to be the most common treatment for severe mental illness. In fact, it was the development of psychoactive drugs that made possible the deinstitutionalization movement of the 1960s.

Deinstitutionalization **is the practice of discharging patients from mental hospitals into the community.** Although deinstitutionalization was originally devised as a solution to the problem of warehousing mentally ill patients in large, prisonlike mental hospitals in the first half of the twentieth century, many social scientists now view deinstitutionalization as a problem. To understand how this solution evolved into a problem, one must understand the state of mental health care in the United States in the 1950s and 1960s. Involuntary (i.e., without a patient's consent) commitment allowed many patients to be warehoused in state mental hospitals for extended periods of time with only minimal and sometimes abusive custodial care. According to sociologist Erving Goffman (1961), mental hospitals are a classic example of a ***total institution*****—a place where people are isolated from the rest of society for a period of time and come under the complete control of the officials who run the institution.** Patients are stripped of their individual identities—or depersonalized—by being required to wear institutional clothing and to follow a strict regimen of activities, meals, and sleeping hours. The deinstitutionalization movement sought to release patients from the hospitals so that they could live at home and go about their daily activities. Professionals believed that the patients' mental disorders could be controlled with medication and treatment through community-based mental health services. Other advocates hoped that it would remove the stigma attached to hospitalization for mental illness. This stigma is described by Susanna Kaysen (1993:123–124), who, at age eighteen, was committed to a private mental hospital for two years:

> The hospital had an address, 115 Mill Street....
>
> In Massachusetts, 115 Mill Street is a famous address. Applying for a job, leasing an apartment, getting a driver's license: all problematic....
>
> "You're living at One fifteen Mill Street?" asked [one prospective employer].... "And how long have you been living there?"
>
> "Oh, a while." I gestured at the past with one hand.
>
> "And I guess you haven't been working for a while?" He leaned back, enjoying himself.
>
> "No," I said. "I've been thinking things over."
>
> I didn't get the job.
>
> As I left the shop my glance met his, and he gave me a look of such terrible intimacy that I cringed. I know what you are, said his look.... In the world's terms... all of us [at the hospital] were tainted.

Mental illness is depicted in films such as A Beautiful Mind, *in which actor Russell Crowe plays the schizophrenic genius John Forbes Nash. Some films make us more aware of the actual problems associated with mental illness, but others sensationalize or trivialize this important social problem.*

Although deinstitutionalization had worthwhile goals—protection of civil rights, more humane and less costly treatment—in too many cases, it simply moved people out of mental hospitals into the streets and jails. Many social analysts believe that the movement was actually triggered by changes in public health insurance. With the introduction of Medicare and Medicaid in 1965, states were more than willing to move patients from state-funded mental hospitals to nursing homes that would be paid for largely by federal government funding (Weitz, 2007). Today, critics of deinstitutionalization argue that it exacerbated long-term problems associated with treating mental illness. Often, the mental problems were never treated. As John A. Chiles, professor of psychiatry at the University of Texas Health Science Center in San Antonio, writes:

> Some people [with schizophrenia] never find their way into the system. If they do, it's often into the legal system through petty crime. One local patient attempted a bank robbery while pointing a paintbrush at the teller. "Give me some money," he demanded. "How about $6.25?" asked the skeptical teller. "OK," he agreed. He was apprehended outside the bank and charged with armed robbery. There are more schizophrenics in the Bexar County Jail than there are in the San Antonio State Hospital. And this is similar to many cities across the country. (quoted in Lawrence, 1996:20)

If schizophrenia and other serious mental illnesses do not lead to jail, they often result in homelessness. One study concluded that as many as 30 percent of homeless people were previously patients in mental hospitals and about 80 percent have some diagnosable mental disorder (Searight and Searight, 1988). However, it is difficult to determine which came first—the mental disorder or homelessness. If you or I were homeless, for instance, what are the chances that we might develop mental health problems if we tried to survive on the streets or in and out of shelters and city jails? In any case, social scientists and homeless advocates agree that most homeless shelters and other community services cannot adequately meet the needs of people known as "the homeless mentally ill" (see Torrey, 1988).

Although involuntary commitment to mental hospitals has always been controversial, it remains the primary method by which police officers, judges, social workers, and other officials deal with people—particularly the homeless—whom they have reason to believe are mentally ill and imminently dangerous to themselves and others (Monahan, 1992). However, it should be recognized that involuntary commitment is a social control mechanism, used to keep people with a history of mental illness off the streets so that they cannot engage in violent crime. It does little—if anything—to treat the medical and social conditions that contribute to mental disorders (Catalano and McConnell, 1996). Given this, state mental hospitals tend to function as revolving doors to poverty-level board and care homes, nursing homes, or homelessness; patients who can pay for private psychiatric facilities through private insurance coverage or Medicare are not part of this cycle (Brown, 1985).

Race, Class, Gender, and Mental Disorders

Studies of race-, class-, and gender-based differences in mental disorders show that some of these factors are more important than others. Although there are no significant differences in diagnosable mental illness between African Americans and white Americans (the two groups that are most often compared), studies of racism show interesting implications for mental health. For example, in a study of the effects of racism on the everyday lives of middle-class African Americans, social scientists Joe R. Feagin and Melvin P. Sikes (1994) found that repeated personal encounters with racial hostility deeply affect the psychological well-being of most African Americans, regardless of their level of education or social class. In a subsequent study, Feagin and Hernán Vera (1995) found that white Americans also pay a high psychic cost for the prevalence of racism because it contradicts deeply held beliefs about the American dream and equality under the law. In earlier work on the effects of discrimination on mental well-being, social psychologist Thomas Pettigrew (1981) suggested that about 15 percent of whites have such high levels of racial prejudice that they tend to exhibit symptoms of serious mental illness. According to Pettigrew, racism in all its forms constitutes a "mentally unhealthy" situation in which people do not achieve their full potential.

Only a few studies have focused on mental disorders among racial-ethnic groups such as Mexican immigrants and Mexican Americans, and they have yielded contradictory results. One study found that strong extended (intergenerational) families, which are emphasized in Mexican culture, provide social support and sources of self-esteem, even if the individuals have low levels of education and income (Mirowsky and Ross, 1980). Another study found the opposite: that maintaining a strong connection to Mexican culture, rather than adopting an Anglo (white/non-Latino/a) culture, is not the primary consideration in whether or not Mexican Americans develop mental disorders (Burnham et al., 1987).

Still another study from a national survey of people of Mexican origin found that "dark and Indian-looking Chicano men" in the United States are more likely to develop depression than are "lighter, European-looking Chicanos and their dark-skinned female counterparts" (Codina and Montalvo, 1994). This study also found that women and men who lose their fluency in Spanish while living in the United States experience more depression than do those who remain fluent in the language and keep closer ties to their culture (Codina and Montalvo, 1994), findings that support the Mirowsky and Ross study.

Most researchers agree that social class is related to mental illness. For example, one study that examined the relationship between mental disorders, race, and class (as measured by socioeconomic status—a combined measure of income, occupation, and education) found that as social class improves for both white Americans and African Americans, the rate of mental disorders decreases (Williams et al., 1992). However, although researchers agree that there is a relationship between class and mental disorders, they do not agree on whether lower social class status causes mental illness or mental illness causes lower social class status (Weitz, 2007). Analysts using the *social stress framework* to examine schizophrenia—the disorder that is most consistently linked to class—believe that stresses associated with lower-class life lead to greater mental disorders. In contrast, analysts using the *social drift framework* argue that mental disorders cause people to drift downward in class position. To support their argument, they note that individuals who are diagnosed with schizophrenia typically hold lower-class jobs, that is, lower than would be expected on the basis of their family backgrounds (Eaton, 1980; Weitz, 2007).

Gender also appears to be a factor in mental illness. Researchers have consistently found that the rate of diagnosable depression is about twice as high for women as for men, that this gender difference typically emerges in puberty (Cleary, 1987), and that the incident rate rises as women and men enter adulthood and live out their unequal statuses (Mirowsky, 1996). Although women have higher rates of minor depression and other disorders that cause psychological distress, men have higher rates of personality disorders (for example, compulsive gambling or drinking) as well as higher rates of maladaptive personality traits such as antisocial behavior (Link and Dohrenwend, 1989; Weitz, 2007). Some analysts suggest that the difference in types of mental disorders is linked to gender-role socialization, which instills aggressiveness in men and learned helplessness in women. According to the *learned helplessness theory*, people become depressed when they think they have no control over their lives (Seligman, 1975). Because this theory emphasizes that people think they have no control, it assumes a *subjective perception* and therefore implies that women contribute to their own helplessness. But feminist analysts argue that the powerlessness in many women's lives is an *objective condition* (Jack, 1993). Support for the feminist view comes from numerous studies indicating that women in high-income, high-status jobs usually have higher levels of psychological well-being and fewer symptoms of mental disorders regardless of their marital status (Horowitz, 1982; Angel and Angel, 1993).

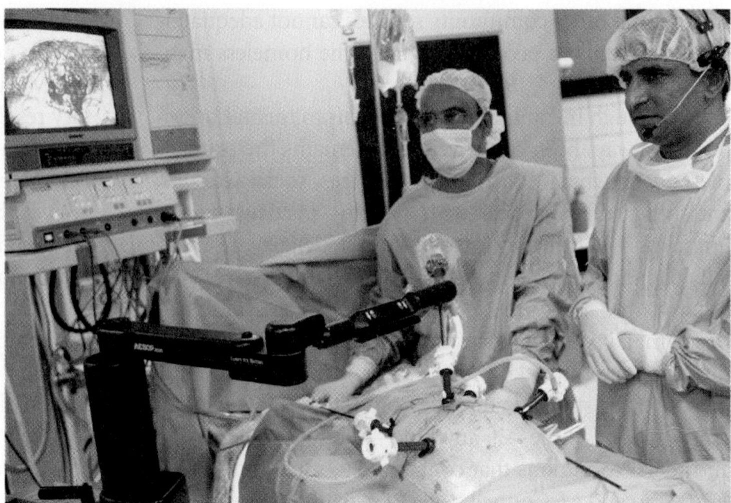

Robotic surgery, which can filter out a doctor's tiny hand tremor, is an example of contemporary high-tech medicine. However, the high cost of some medical equipment is a factor in the crisis in health care in the United States today.

Although numerous studies have been done on women with mild depression, women with serious mental illnesses have been nearly ignored (Mowbray et al., 1992). Furthermore, mental disorders in women have often been misdiagnosed, and on many occasions, physical illnesses have been confused with psychiatric problems (see Busfield, 1996; Lerman, 1996; Klonoff, 1997). It is generally agreed that additional studies of women's diversity across lines of race, class, age, religion, and other factors are necessary before we can accurately assess the relationship between gender and mental illness and how women are treated in the mental health-care industry (Gatz, 1995).

THE CRISIS IN U.S. HEALTH CARE

What is the most crucial problem facing people in the United States regarding health care? Some analysts believe that it is the fact that the United States is only one of two high-income nations that does not have some form of universal health coverage for all citizens. The other is the Union of South Africa. Although no system of health care in the world fully meets the medical needs of all residents living in a country, health care in the United States has been especially criticized because its costs are far higher than in any other advanced nation regardless of whether we measure these costs in regard to the total dollars that are spent on health care, what percentage health-care costs are of the total economy, or on a per capita basis. This issue brings us to a crucial question in regard to health care expenditures and who should pay for them (see Box 10.2). However, although we can examine the strengths and limitations of how health-care systems are funded and operate in nations such as Sweden, Britain, and Canada, it is important to realize that accurate comparisons between health care in these nations and the United States are difficult to make because the social policies and populations of these countries vary widely.

Health-Care Organization, Rising Costs, and Unequal Access

Medical care in the United States is provided on a fee-for-service basis: Patients are billed individually for each service they receive, including treatment by doctors, laboratory work, hospital visits, prescriptions, and other health-related services. Fee-for-service is an expensive way of delivering health care because there are few restrictions on the fees charged by doctors, hospitals, and other medical providers. Because the United States is a wealthy nation, we have been willing to spend more on health care than other nations. According to a report in the *New York Times* (2007:WK9), for example:

> We are richer than other countries and so willing to spend more. But authoritative analyses have found that we spend well above what mere wealth would predict. This is mostly because we pay hospitals and doctors more than most other countries do. We rely more on costly specialists, who overuse advanced technologies, like CT scans and M.R.I. machines, and who resort to costly surgical or medical procedures a lot more than doctors in other countries do.

Another problem in regard to overspending is the manner in which incentives from some insurance plans may encourage patients and doctors to overutilize expensive medical services and procedures.

Private Health Insurance

Costly to begin with, fee-for-service health care became even more so with the development of the health insurance industry. During the Great Depression of the 1930s, the American Hospital Association, fearing that many hospitals would go bankrupt because patients could not pay their hospital bills, founded Blue Cross—a nonprofit company—to sell health insurance to people so that they could pay their hospital bills. Shortly thereafter, the American Medical Association established Blue Shield to provide coverage for physicians' bills. Under Blue Cross/Blue Shield and other private insurance programs, patients do not pay doctors and hospitals directly. Instead, they pay premiums into a fund that in turn pays doctors and hospitals for each treatment a patient receives as long as the services are covered and the patient has paid the annual deductible.

According to medical sociologist Paul Starr (1982), the main reason for medical inflation in this country is third-party fee-for-service because it gives doctors and hospitals an incentive to increase provision of medical services. That is, the more services they provide, the more fees they charge and the more money they make. At the same time, patients have no incentive to limit their visits

Social Problems and Social Policy

Box 10.2

Who Pays for Health Care? A Brief Look at Canada, the United Kingdom, and Sweden

We often hear complaints about health care in the United States, where it is a well-known fact that we spend more on health care than any other high-income nation. However, despite that expenditure, we have a lower life expectancy and higher infant-mortality rates than countries that spend less than half as much, and we have many people who go without health care because it is too expensive.

Who should pay for health care? Some people believe that it is not up to a nation to take care of everyone, but others believe health care should be available for all. In other words, they advocate a *universal health-care system* like those found in Canada, the United Kingdom, and Sweden. In Canada's single-payer system, for example, citizens never see a medical bill or an insurance form or pay for a prescription because the national health insurance system pays all medical costs directly. Hospitals get a yearly budget, and doctors bill the provincial governments (equivalent to our state governments), which administer the health-care system, on a fee-for-service basis. Fees are negotiated annually between doctors and the provincial government. Individuals choose any primary-care doctor they wish, but they need a referral to a specialist. Overall, Canadians have better access to health care than U.S. citizens do and, as a result, they make more visits to the doctor, are hospitalized more often and for longer periods of time, and have higher immunization rates. By international standards, Canadians are healthier, have longer life expectancies, and a lower infant mortality rate than do U.S. citizens. Is there any fly in this ointment? Well, one. The cost of health care is skyrocketing, and Canada—like the United States—must find ways to control costs. Efforts continue to find ways to reduce spending for hospitals, drugs, and doctors' services, which account for the bulk of health spending (Canadian Institute for Health Information, 2004). Because Canada has a dual system in which doctors also may operate a private practice where they offer patients medical care on a fee-for-service basis, one way to reduce costs would be to encourage more patients to go the private insurance route.

The United Kingdom (Britain) also has a dual system, but most patients are covered through the National Health System

(continued)

Box 2.3 (continued)

(NHS), which is funded by general taxation and national insurance contributions. NHS pays for hospital stays, physicians' services, and prescription drugs, but this system has been extensively criticized because of its heavy backlog, including long waiting times for appointments, doctor visits, emergency services, and surgery partly brought about by lack of sufficient doctors and nurses and inadequate medical facilities. In 2000, the British government launched a ten-year reform program to overhaul the health system. Although recent reports suggest that improvements have been made, one criticism persists: "If you are old or poor you are unlikely to get the level of service you deserve. The fact remains those who shout the loudest get the best care" (Triggle, 2005). Among those patients who receive the quickest and perhaps best care in the U.K. are those individuals (approximately 12 percent of the population) who have private health insurance.

Sweden, our final country for comparison, has a health-care system that covers all residents of Sweden regardless of nationality. National health insurance is financed through taxes, and county councils own and operate hospitals, employ physicians, and run the majority of general practices and outpatient facilities. Although most physicians are salaried employees of the government, some work in private practice and are paid by the counties on a fee-for-service basis. Like other countries, Sweden faces numerous problems with its health-care system, including how to motivate doctors who are paid the same amount regardless of how many patients they see and how to deal with sharply rising costs as the country's population ages and as more people are diagnosed with chronic problems such as allergies, obesity, and psychosomatic problems (Swedish Institute, 2003). Although the level of health in Sweden is high, some analysts believe that Sweden (which has a population about equal to that of New York City) is going to be hard pressed to continue this level of coverage in the future.

As we look at other nations, we see that similar problems are present in health care. Perhaps one approach to the health-care problem in the United States is to continue to look at our own structure and ask, "Where does the money go?" According to recent reports, in the United States, "15 percent of premiums paid to private insurers goes not to health care but for administrative expenses," which means that bureaucratic paperwork, including the costs of assessing risk, rating premiums, designing benefit packages and reviews, and paying or refusing to pay claims, eats up a significant portion of the dollars that go into private health insurance plans. By contrast, similar administrative costs for public insurance programs (Medicare and Medicaid, for example) are about 4 percent (Krugman, 2005b). Of course, this is only one of many factors (discussed in this chapter) that contribute to the spiraling cost of U.S. medical treatment, but it deserves further study.

Having a high quality of health care available for all people in the United States is clearly an important long-term goal for many; however, in the short term, we may need to ask how we are spending money in what we cannot accurately refer to as a health-care system. The phrase, "follow the money" has become a popular rallying cry for many groups; perhaps health care is also a social problem where this approach might be useful.

Questions for Critical Thinking

1. Why do most countries with national health plans have a dual system of medical service? What might the presence of "private" patients and "private" plans tell us about social inequality in those nations?
2. Thinking about your own experiences with doctors, hospitals, and other medically related settings, what are you learning in your sociology course that might help you to evaluate the treatment (from a nonmedical standpoint) that you received?
3. When people in the United States are trying to reduce or solve a social problem, what might we gain by analyzing how other countries deal with a similar problem? What are the limitations of such an approach?

to doctors or hospitals because they have already paid their premiums and feel entitled to medical care (Starr, 1982).

Health-care costs began to spiral with the expansion of medical insurance programs in the 1960s. At that time, third-party providers (public and private insurers) began picking up large portions of doctor and hospital bills for insured patients. Recently, in an effort to reduce the demand for health-care services and medical costs, many insurance companies have established an option known as *preferred provider organizations* (PPOs), with such names as HealthSelect (a Blue Cross/Blue Shield entity). In a PPO, doctors work out of their own offices on a fee-for-service basis but contract with an insurance company to provide care for insured patients. The doctors agree to charge set fees for particular services; these fees may be higher or lower than those for other patients who are not covered by the PPO. This model of health-care delivery shares certain commonalities with the health maintenance organization (HMO) and managed care models.

Like other private insurance plans, HMOs emerged during the Great Depression as a means of providing workers with health coverage at a reasonable rate by keeping costs down. A ***health maintenance organization* (HMO) provides, for a fixed monthly fee, total heath care with an emphasis on prevention to avoid costly treatment later.** The doctors do not work on a fee-for-service basis, and patients are encouraged to get regular checkups and to practice good health habits (exercise and eat right). As long as patients use only the doctors and hospitals that are affiliated with their HMO, they pay no fees, or only small copayments, beyond their insurance premium (Anders, 1996). Believing that the HMO model could be a source of high profits because of its emphasis on prevention, many for-profit corporations moved into the HMO business in the 1980s (Anders, 1996). However, research has shown that preventive care is good for the individual's health but does not necessarily save money. Early detection of diabetes or high cholesterol, for example, often means a lifetime of costly treatments and drugs. Indeed, some health experts have suggested that for-profit HMOs are unlikely to provide top-notch early detection and prevention programs because of the costs—especially future costs—involved (Rosenthal, 1997). Some critics have even charged that some HMOs require their physicians to withhold vital information from their patients if it is going to cost the HMO money to provide the needed procedure or hospitalization (Gray, 1996). Recently, some HMOs have responded to such criticism (and threats of lawsuits) by allowing doctors and patients greater participation in the HMO's process of determining treatment.

Another approach to controlling health-care costs is known as ***managed care*—a term that is used to refer to any system of cost containment that closely monitors and controls health care providers' decisions about medical procedures, diagnostic tests, and other services that should be provided to patients** (Weitz, 2007). In most managed care programs, patients choose a primary-care physician from a list of participating doctors. When patients need medical services, they first contact the primary-care physician; then, if a specialist is needed for treatment, the primary-care physician refers the patient to a specialist who participates in the program. Doctors must get approval before they perform certain procedures or admit a patient to the hospital. If they do not, the insurance company has the prerogative of not covering part of the cost. Although managed care does contain some medical care costs, many physicians are opposed to it and to HMOs. As one doctor explains (Williams, 1997:A19):

> I was a physician for more than 20 years. Now I am a provider. "Provider" is the term used by health maintenance organizations to refer to physicians and other health-care professionals. They attempt to suppress the very word "physician," and for good reason: It has connotations of expertise, authority and respect, which are incompatible with the managed-care agenda.... I have a busy and previously successful internal medicine practice. An hour of my time is now worth approximately 60 percent of its value several years ago. I work more than 60 hours a week. My current personal income, after office expenses, works out to less than $35 per hour. I know many internists who are doing no better. I find myself very discouraged and sometimes rather angry.... It is the apparent intent of those who drive managed care that medicine be reduced to a commodity, and a cheap commodity at that, to be bought, sold and manipulated solely for the financial benefit of their industry. I believe this portends very serious problems ahead, not only for the profession but for the future of patient care and the well-being of the population at large.

Not only are physicians' revenues reduced under managed care, but so are revenues to hospitals, which means that hospitals can no longer afford to treat uninsured patients who come through their doors seeking treatment for everything from flu to heart disease. In the past, hospitals passed much of the cost of treating uninsured patients to paying patients, but managed care has cut out any margin for doing this (Preston, 1996). Finally, despite cost containment measures, health care continues to be a significant expenditure in the United States because of the for-profit structure of much medical care, the fragmented health care provided by government-funded insurance programs, and the spiraling cost of high-tech medicine. In recent years, new medical technologies have added millions of dollars to hospital budgets even as the basic health-care needs of many people have not been met.

Public Health Insurance

Today, of the total U.S. health-care bill, patients pay slightly less than 20 percent; insurance companies pay about 36 percent, and the government pays more than 45 percent (U.S. Census Bureau, 2008). Although private health insurance companies were well established by the 1950s and almost all working people and their immediate families had hospitalization insurance, those who did not work—the elderly and the poor—were often uninsured. Federal legislation extending health-care coverage to the elderly and the poor was not passed until the 1960s. From its inception, federally funded health-care assistance was a two-tiered system: a medical entitlement program for older people (Medicare) and a medical welfare system for the poor (Medicaid). Medicare is a program that covers most people age 65 and over who are eligible for Social Security or who buy into the program by paying a monthly premium. The largest single insurance program in the country, Medicare is made up of two separate programs: Part A, a hospital insurance program, and Part B, a supplementary medical insurance program. Although Medicare provides coverage for many older people who otherwise would have no health insurance, there are large gaps in its coverage, and elderly near-poor individuals often find it difficult to pay the required deductibles (an initial specified amount that the patient pays before the insurance begins payments) and copayments (shared costs). Also, Medicare provides only limited coverage for costly and sometimes long-term expenses such as posthospital nursing services, home health care, nursing homes, and hospice services.

Unlike Medicare coverage, which is based primarily on age, Medicaid provides medical, hospital, and long-term care for people who are poor and either aged, blind, disabled, or pregnant. Also, whereas Medicare is funded by people's payments into the Social Security system, Medicaid is funded by federal and state governments. As a result, many people view Medicaid as a welfare program and Medicare as an entitlement program—people are assumed to have earned medical coverage through years of hard work and paying into the system. Perceptions aside, both Medicare and Medicaid, like other forms of health insurance, dramatically expand the resources for supplying and financing medical services, especially for people with chronic disabling illnesses that extend over months or years. Analysts therefore suggest that these programs are extremely costly to the public because they provide no incentive for keeping costs down or managing resources. For example, many hospitals use Medicare funds to build new buildings, buy the latest high-tech equipment, and pay nonmedical personnel in marketing and fundraising positions. Some physicians abuse the system by operating "Medicaid mills" that charge excessive fees for unnecessary tests and treatments.

During the past twenty years, the growing number of Medicaid recipients with AIDS has increased Medicaid costs. These costs have been driven still higher by AIDS patients, who, upon losing their jobs, also lose their company-provided private insurance coverage and therefore seek Medicaid. It seems likely that Medicare costs will also increase in the future as more people over age fifty are being diagnosed with AIDS.

The Uninsured and the Underinsured

Despite public and private insurance programs, more than one-third of all U.S. citizens are without health insurance or had difficulty getting or paying for medical care at some time in the last year. The problem of being uninsured cuts across income lines (see Box 10.3). An estimated 47 million people in the United States had no health insurance in 2006—an increase of about 2.2 million people since 2005 (DeNavas-Walt, Proctor, and Smith, 2007). About 12 percent of children under 18 years of age were uninsured in 2006. For children living in poverty, the percentage of uninsured was even higher: Almost 20 percent of children in homes below the official poverty line were without health insurance of any kind (DeNavas-Walt, Proctor, and Smith, 2007). About 70 percent of the uninsured said that they had been employed some of the time they were without health insurance. Jobs in agriculture, personal services, construction, business and repair services, retail, self-employment, and recreation and entertainment have higher-than-average percentages of uninsured employees. One study has found that some corporations are cutting medical benefits for rank-and-file employees or moving them into managed care programs that strictly limit benefits while company executives continue to have health plans that provide full coverage for office visits and hospitalization for monthly premiums of less than $10 and no annual deductible or out-of-pocket expenses (Myerson, 1996). The bitter reality of being uninsured was best expressed by Tommy Markham, who at age forty-eight was disabled by a stroke: "You could be damn near dying, and the first thing they ask is 'Do you have insurance?'" (Abraham, 1993:3).

Social Problems and Statistics

Box 10.3

Families Without Health Insurance

Sometimes, it is easy to get confused when the media report on statistics released by organizations such as the U.S. Census Bureau because it is not clear what the statistics actually represent.

What is health insurance coverage? The Census Bureau classifies health insurance coverage as private coverage or government coverage. Private health insurance is provided through an employer or a union or purchased by an individual from a private company. Government health insurance includes federal programs such as Medicare, Medicaid, and military health insurance, as well as the State Children's Health Insurance Program (SCHIP) and individual state health plans. By contrast, individuals are considered to be uninsured if they were not covered by any type of health insurance *at any time* during the given calendar year in which the data were reported.

What does it mean when the media recently reported that 15 percent of households were without health insurance in 2006 (the latest year for which data were available)? Does this mean that the problem of lack of insurance is evenly distributed across the nation? No, we must have additional data to determine the distribution of households without health insurance in the United States. For example, the percentage of households without health insurance varies widely based on family income: The likelihood of being covered by health insurance rises with income. Consider the following difference statistics: Among families with incomes of $75,000 or more, only about 7 percent were without health insurance at any time during 2006 while more than 27 percent of people in families with incomes of $25,000 or less were without health insurance. Figure 10.2 shows the percentage of households within an income bracket that were without health insurance.

Regardless of how you view the statistics, the lack of health insurance is a social problem, since more than 15 percent of all households in the United States in 2006 were not covered by any type of health insurance for some period of time in that year. The number of households without health insurance increased to about 47 million people in 2006 as compared to 44.8 million who were uninsured in 2005.

Questions for Consideration:

1. What do you think should be done to reduce the health insurance problem in the United States?
2. Should we assume that people have better health and receive better quality health care because they have a higher income? Why or why not?

Source: DeNavas-Walt, Proctor, and Smith, 2007.

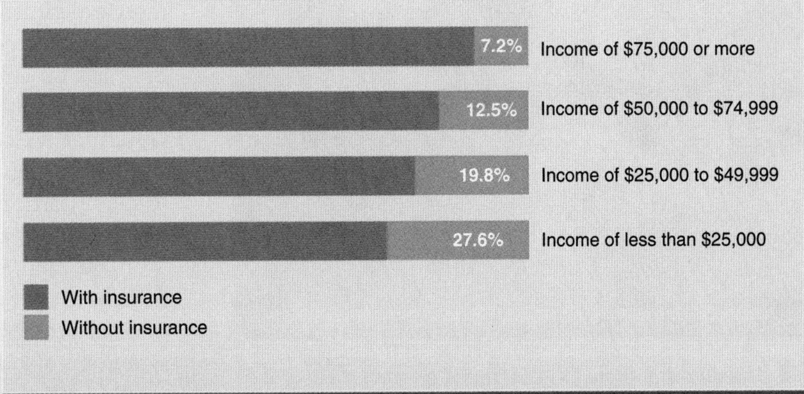

■ Figure 10.2 **Percentages of households without health insurance, 2006, by income**

Source: DeNavas-Walt, Proctor, and Smith, 2007.

Race, Class, Gender, and Health Care

Just as deinstitutionalization was initially seen as the solution to mental health care and is now viewed by many as the problem, health insurance plans were initially considered a solution but have now become a problem, especially when they perpetuate unequal access to health care because of race, class, or gender. According to a large federal study, even when people are covered by Medicare or Medicaid, the care they receive and their overall life expectancies are influenced by their race and income. Among other things, people of color across class lines and low-income whites typically receive less preventive care and less optimal management of chronic diseases than others (Leary, 1996). Under Medicaid, the poorest people sometimes receive the fewest services because of limitations placed on eligibility and the way in which payment of fees to doctors is structured. For example, many doctors are unwilling to work in a city center for a Medicaid reimbursement of $20 a visit. Even with private health insurance, people living in city centers where there are high levels of poverty and crime or in remote rural areas have difficulty getting medical treatment because most doctors prefer to locate their practices in "safe" areas, particularly ones with a patient base that will produce a high income.

Like race and class, gender is an important factor in health care. Numerous researchers have found pervasive gender inequality in health care in the United States (Nechas and Foley, 1994; Rosser, 1994). The long-term exclusion of women from medicine continues to have a detrimental impact on their health in this country and elsewhere. Women are underrepresented in the medical profession, representatively less research is done on health-care issues specifically pertaining to them, and women have differential access to medical treatment.

Inequalities in health care based on race, class, and gender, are often very evident in settings such as this dental clinic, which was set up in a school to provide temporary health services to disadvantaged people. How might we better meet the medical and dental needs of all people in this country?

Although more women have become physicians in recent years, about 80 percent of medical doctors in the United States today are men. The underrepresentation of women in medicine can be traced back to 1910 and the publication of the Flexner Report, a study on the state of medical education in the United States commissioned by the American Medical Association and the Carnegie Foundation. According to educator Abraham Flexner (1910), the only way to make the practice of medicine more scientific was to make medical education more rigorous, and the way to accomplish this was to close a number of medical schools. Flexner's plan was implemented, but not in an even-handed way: Only one of the three women's medical schools and two schools for African Americans survived. As a result, white women and people of color were largely excluded from medical education for the first half of the twentieth century. Until the civil rights movement and the women's movements of the 1960s and early 1970s, virtually all physicians were white, male, and upper- or upper-middle class. However, women made up 49 percent of medical students in 2005–06, providing a strong indication that the percentage of women in the medical profession will continue to rise over the next decade (Magrane and Lang, 2005).

Although the more equitable gender enrollments in medical schools are welcome and long overdue, there is still a male-centered focus on human health and health-care delivery in both medical school and medical practice. Funding for research on women's health issues and diseases is lacking, and women have been excluded from most experimental drugs trials, which are conducted to determine the positive and negative effects that a specific drug has on a given category of patients. Many clinical studies virtually ignore women. In 2001, a study by the Government Accounting Office concluded that the U.S. Food and Drug Administration was not effectively monitoring research data to determine how sex differences affect drug safety and effectiveness.

The failure to include women in research contributes to their differential treatment for certain kinds of medical problems. For example, women with the same symptoms of kidney failure as men are much less likely to receive an organ transplant. Similarly, far fewer women than men with an abnormal heart scan are referred for a procedure known as cardiac catheterization to remedy the problem. Without adequate studies, diseases in women may go unrecognized, be misdiagnosed, or be attributed to a nonphysical factor. According to medical sociologists, both male and female doctors need more training in health issues pertaining to women so that they can treat the majority of the U.S. population.

SOCIOLOGICAL EXPLANATIONS AND SOLUTIONS

What are the primary causes of health-care problems in the United States? How can health-care problems be reduced or eliminated? The answers that social scientists give to these questions depend on their theoretical framework. Analysts approaching these questions from a functionalist perspective focus on how illness affects the smooth operation of society and on the functions medicine serves as a social institution. Some sociologists using a conflict perspective focus on how a capitalist economy affects health and health-care delivery; others look at inequalities of race, class, and gender. Finally, sociologists who use a symbolic interactionist framework look at the social and cultural factors affecting communication between doctors and patients.

The Functionalist Perspective

The functionalist perspective views illness as a threat to a smoothly functioning society because it is necessary for all people to fulfill their appropriate social roles. According to this view, when people become ill, they cannot fulfill their everyday responsibilities to family, employer, or the larger society and instead adopt the *sick role*—patterns of behavior expected from individuals who are ill. Sociologist Talcott Parsons (1951) identified four role expectations of the sick role: (1) sick people are not responsible for their incapacity; (2) they are exempted from their usual role and task obligations; (3) they must want to leave the sick role and get well; and (4) they are obligated to seek and comply with the advice of a medical professional. In other words, illness is a form of deviance that must be controlled. According to Parsons, physicians are the logical agents of social control. By certifying that a person is physically or mentally ill and by specifying how the ill person should behave, doctors use their professional authority to monitor people with illnesses, thereby granting them only a temporary reprieve from their usual social roles and responsibilities. Today, however, the dramatic increase in chronic illness and the disorganization in the delivery system for medical services mean that many people have less access to doctors and doctors have less control over those aspects of patients' lives that can increase their chances of becoming ill. Patients thus end up incurring large medical bills and being unproductive in society.

Functionalists believe that the problems in U.S. health care are due to macrolevel changes, such as the development of high-tech medicine, overspecialization of doctors, erosion of health-insurance coverage, and increased demand for health care by consumers. Since World War II, functionalists say, the rapid growth of medical knowledge has produced a glut of information, new technologies, and greatly improved surgical techniques. To remain competitive in the face of this new technology and the demand for it, hospitals operating in the same city have often purchased the same extremely expensive equipment. The costs of the equipment are passed on to consumers in the form of higher medical bills and insurance premiums. In the same way that hospitals believe they must have all the latest technology, most medical students have come to believe that they have to specialize—rather than enter general or family practice—to build a large patient base and thereby increase their income and prestige. Thus both doctors and hospitals have begun to view health care as a commodity and to provide a far wider array of services (treatment for substance abuse, day care for the mentally ill, and elective procedures such as cosmetic surgery) to sell to consumers (potential patients). At the same time, most individuals have come to view health care as a right to which they are entitled. As both the supply of and demand for medical treatment have grown, lobbying organizations such as the American Medical Association and the American Hospital Association and business, labor, and consumer (especially the elderly) groups have entered into battle with Congress over the extent to which federal and state government should regulate health care.

What solutions might emerge from a functionalist approach to problems associated with health care? Although functionalists agree that the high cost of health care and disorganization in the U.S. health-care industry is clearly dysfunctional for both individuals and society, they do not agree on what should be done. Some believe that the whole health-care system should be reorganized; others think that cost containment is the best answer. Some conservative analysts have suggested, for example, that there must be more careful coordination of the care of chronically ill patients, who account for the largest portion of the nation's health-care expenditures. Cost-cutting measures should also be extended to hospital services, physicians' fees, drug prices, and overuse of advanced technologies such as CT scans and M.R.I. machines.

In addition to cost-cutting measures that would make health consumers conscious of the costs of their care, some analysts believe that it is important to foster competition among health plans in an effort to reduce costs and provide better services. Other analysts favor managed care, such as HMOs, believing that they will continue to bring down costs and improve the quality of health services; however, managed care in the past has been unpopular with many doctors and patients alike because they believed that this approach hampered the delivery of high-quality health care that was tailored to the individual patient.

The Conflict Perspective

The conflict approach is based on the assumption that problems in health-care delivery are rooted in the capitalist economy, which views medicine as a commodity that is produced and sold by the medical-industrial complex. The ***medical-industrial complex*** **encompasses both local physicians and hospitals as well as global health-related industries such as the pharmaceutical and medical supply companies that deliver health care today.** Although wealthy patients and patients with good insurance might receive high-quality care in the medical-industrial complex structure, low-income and poverty-level people often do without. In this view, physicians hold a legal monopoly over medicine and benefit from the existing structure because they can charge inflated fees. Similarly, hospitals, clinics, and other medical facilities control how health care is delivered and what various services will cost patients.

In the twenty-first century, health care delivery takes place in large medical complexes such as the one shown here. According to conflict theorists, medical centers are only one component of the much larger medical-industrial complex that generates billions of dollars in revenue annually.

Three factors will inevitably perpetuate inequalities of U.S. health care: (1) high health-care costs due to advanced medical services and the use of expensive medications and technology; (2) abuse of existing systems by some health-care professionals, particularly those who overcharge patients, provide unnecessary services, or charge for expensive services that were never rendered; and (3) the aging population that will continue to increase sharply and place greater strain on Medicare, Medicaid, and other health resources (Bagby, 1997). As one woman explained to her granddaughter, "Your generation is giving my generation a free ride and the sooner we stop it the better. There is no way on earth to eliminate the [federal] debt without touching entitlements" such as Medicare (Bagby, 1997:21).

What solutions might arise if we apply a conflict/liberal approach to analyzing health care issues? As strange as it may seen, some conflict/liberal thinkers agree with the functionalist/conservative analysts who believe that managed care and other cost-containment strategies might be helpful in solving some health-care problems. However, conflict/liberal theorists focus primary on managed care and other cost-containment methods as ways of reducing the control of physicians over patients and others in the medical-industrial complex, such as nurses, medical technicians, or other hospital and clinical personnel.

Conflict theorists are quick to point out that cost-containment efforts such as managed care are nothing more than a bandage being placed on the hemorrhaging cost of health care. This approach, say conflict theorists, does not deal with the larger systemic problem of how health care is delivered in a capitalist economy where medical care is a commodity like a pair of shoes or other items and services an individual might purchase in the marketplace.

For this reason, some conflict theorists believe that problems in health care will be reduced in the United States only when large-scale race-, class-, and gender-based inequalities in this nation are adequately addressed and reduced. As long as societal conditions—environmental pollution, lack of affordable housing, high levels of stress associated with working conditions or unemployment, inadequate nutrition, and lack of early diagnosis for diseases such as breast cancer and heart disease—affect people differentially based on their race, class, and gender, health care will be unequal. Most conflict theorists believe that short of a dramatic change in the nation's political economy, the primary way to deal with health care is to treat it as a common good that should be provided and regulated by the government just as highways, schools, courts, and national defense are (Shweder, 1997).

The Symbolic Interactionist Perspective

Symbolic interactionists believe that many problems pertaining to health and illness in our society are linked to social and cultural factors that influence how people define physical illness and mental illness. According to symbolic interactionists, we socially construct "health" and "illness" and how both should be treated. As a result, both medical and nonmedical "experts" play a role in determining what constitutes physical and mental illnesses and how these illnesses should be treated by society. For example, in 1997, under the Americans with Disabilities Act, the Equal Employment Opportunity Commission established guidelines requiring that employers take "reasonable steps" to accommodate employees with mental illnesses—the same requirement that previously applied only to people with physical disabilities (Stolberg, 1997). What exactly does "reasonable steps" mean? According to one analyst, "That could mean anything from a flexible schedule for an anxious person, to a desk near a window for a person who grows depressed with too little light, to a quiet work space for a schizophrenic" (Stolberg, 1997:E1).

Symbolic interactionists also examine how doctors and patients interact in health-care settings. For example, medical schools provide future doctors with knowledge and skills that laypeople do not have. Given this competence gap, some physicians do not think that it is necessary—or possible—to communicate certain kinds of medical information to patients. Some hesitate to communicate the diagnosis of a fatal illness or, more often, might simply not explain why they are prescribing certain medications or what side effects or drug interactions could occur.

One way to solve this communication problem, according to symbolic interactionists, is to increase the number of family practice doctors, because these doctors usually focus on patient care and communication, not just the scientific and technological aspects of health care. Another way is to emphasize prevention and work with patients on behaviors to practice and avoid if they want to stay healthy. A third way to change health care is to limit the bureaucracies in mental hospitals where individuals are labeled by their diagnosis and not viewed as people with specific emotional and physical needs to be met. Finally, symbolic interactionists say, more public health campaigns are needed to make people aware of issues in health care and health-care reform, and perhaps those campaigns need to emphasize what it is like to be unable to afford necessary health care. Consider, for example, the Patten family. Leo Patten has emphysema from smoking and breathing foul air in the factories where he worked as a machinist. Elma Patten has had heart bypass surgery, a mastectomy, a hysterectomy, and two wrist operations for a repetitive motion injury related to her work (Kilborn, 1993). After decades of middle-class security, the Pattens have dwindling savings and fear that another medical setback will drive them out of their $65,000 home and onto the welfare rolls. According to Elma Patten, "A person keeps their nose to the grindstone, works hard, pays their bills on time. Then when your health goes bad they kick you into a corner" (Kilborn, 1993:4A14). The Pattens wonder whether they will be able to pay their doctor, whom they like because she communicates with them. However, the Pattens' future—like that of many people with chronic illnesses—is caught up in political and economic issues about health-care delivery that will apparently remain with us for decades.

In a nutshell, what are some symbolic interactionist solutions to the health-care problem? As previously stated, some analysts who use a symbolic interactionist approach focus on the doctor–patient relationship as being problematic. According to these analysts, the doctor–patient relationship should be demystified so that the physician does not have all of the social power in the encounter. Then better communication must be encouraged between health-care providers and the patients who are the recipients of their services. These theorists argue that if patients were given the information and resources they need for prevention, self-treatment, and home care, the need and demand for expensive medical care would be greatly reduced (Stewart, 1995). For example, if patients received more information and encouragement from their doctors in regard to preventive measures that might improve their health, patients might become more concerned about weight control, exercise, going to a physician for regular checkups, and eliminating habits such as smoking and excessive alcohol consumption that are potentially detrimental to their health.

Because of the emphasis on interpersonal communications in many symbolic interactionist approaches to health care, some other solutions deal with disease management after a patient has been diagnosed with a chronic condition such as heart disease, diabetes, or cancer. Those patients who believe that they can successfully communicate with their physicians and other health-care providers are more likely to comply with health-related directives they have been given regarding a treatment regime, taking proper dosages of medications in a timely fashion, and routinely scheduling physical exams and other tests as needed or recommended. By contrast, those patients who do not have a good understanding of what their doctors have told them to do, or who receive an inadequate explanation about the importance of following a medical regime, will more often fail to follow the doctor's directions.

Symbolic interactionist views on the doctor–patient relationship are faced with a different set of challenges today because of newer technologies. Some physicians and nurses now routinely interact with established patients through e-mail communications as a personal solution to larger, potential communication problems, particularly as doctors and other members of their medical staff typically see more patients per hour and per day than in the past: Patients can e-mail the doctor's office to get a prescription refilled, to ask a question, or to report such medical information as their blood pressure or glucose level if requested by the physician. However, there are new problems built into using e-mail as a form of communication between doctors and patients because it sometimes is crucial for the doctor, nurse, or another health-care professional to see the patient in order to diagnose a condition, prescribe the most appropriate medication, or determine if other health-related problems are present.

In the past, most patients relied primarily on doctors for heath-related information. Today, many people receive medical information from the media and the Internet. Thousands of websites are devoted to health and medical information, ranging from potentially life-saving research in top medical journals to alternative therapies such as herbal preparations and colonic irrigation (Fisher, 1996; Kolata, 1996c). Many computer bulletin boards, chat rooms, and Usenet newsgroups have emerged to support people with diseases such as AIDS and multiple sclerosis (Kantrowitz, 1993). Whether this proliferation of information helps to demystify doctor–patient relationships remains to be seen, and as has been previously discussed, applying symbolic interactionist perspectives to problems does not address larger, systemic problems in the larger system of health care in the United States.

In the 2008 presidential election, candidates spoke to the issue of how they would revise the existing health-care delivery system if elected; however, it remains to be seen what, if any, real changes will be made as we enter the second decade of the twenty-first century. Without proper planning, the United States will not have a fully functioning health-care system. Instead, we have many individual components—ranging from doctors in private practice to for-profit HMOs, pharmaceutical companies, and insurance companies—each with its own agenda for health-care delivery. Also, health care must shift its focus from acute diseases to prevention and to a closer analysis of those problems that are associated with chronic illness and disability because these are most costly for individuals and society.

SUMMARY

■ *Why is health care a social problem?*

Health care is a social problem because, according to the World Health Organization, health is a state of complete physical, mental, and social well-being. In other words, health is a social issue. Although people in the United States pay more for health services than people in other high-income nations, our expenditures do not translate into improved life expectancy for everyone.

■ *What kinds of health problems cause most of today's high health-care costs?*

Because acute illnesses (e.g., measles, polio) are largely under control with vaccinations and improved public health practices, most health problems today are chronic diseases (e.g., arthritis, diabetes, heart disease) or disabilities (e.g., back injuries, hearing or vision problems, mental retardation), which require long-term treatment. Medical advances mean that many people who are born with serious disabilities survive, as do many who would have died from acute illnesses or accidents in earlier times. As more people survive and live longer, more are likely to experience chronic illnesses and disabilities.

■ *Why is AIDS considered a health crisis in the United States and other nations?*

First, the number of cases is rising annually. Second, many people infected worldwide are infected through heterosexual intercourse; it is not a disease that is restricted to any single group. Third, there is no cure; once HIV develops into AIDS, it is fatal. Fourth, treatment is complex and costly and typically requires lengthy stays in a hospital or hospice. Finally, numerous ethical issues (e.g., issues relating to testing) have yet to be resolved.

■ *Why is mental illness a social problem?*

Mental illness is a social problem because of the number of people it affects, the difficulty in defining and identifying mental disorders, and the ways in which it is treated. Deinstitutionalization—discharging mental patients from hospitals into the community—was considered a solution to the problem of warehousing patients, but it has created new problems.

■ *Historically, what kinds of health care have been available in the United States?*

Originally, there was fee-for-service care in which patients paid directly for treatment they received from doctors and hospitals. The Great Depression brought about third-party fee-for-service care: Patients pay premiums to private or public health insurance companies that in turn pay the doctors and hospitals. Both of these health-care structures are expensive because there are few restrictions on fees charged by health-care providers.

■ *What other types of private health-care insurance are available in the United States?*

Some insurance companies now offer preferred provider organizations (PPOs) in which doctors contract to treat insured patients for set fees; these fees may be higher or lower than the fees for other patients who are not enrolled in the PPO. For a set monthly fee a health maintenance organization (HMO) provides total care with an emphasis on prevention; patients must use the doctors and hospitals affiliated with the HMO. Managed care refers to any system of cost containment that closely monitors and controls health-care providers' decisions about what medical tests, procedures, and other services should be provided to patients; a patient's primary-care physician must get approval to send the patient to a specialist or order hospitalization and costly tests or procedures. Since many for-profit companies have entered health care, there is some concern that quality of care is sacrificed to cost containment.

■ *What is the difference between Medicare and Medicaid?*

Medicare is public health insurance for people age sixty-five and over that is funded by Social Security payments. Medicaid is public health insurance for people who are poor and either aged, blind, disabled, or pregnant; it is funded by federal and state governments. Both programs are considered costly to the public because there are no incentives to keep costs down.

■ *How do race, class, and gender affect health care?*

Research shows that people of color across class lines and low-income whites typically receive less preventive care and less optimal management of chronic diseases than others do. Women have been underrepresented in the medical profession (though that is changing); medical training, practice, and research are male-centered; and women receive differential treatment for certain kinds of medical problems.

■ *What are the sociological explanations for health-care problems?*

Functionalists consider the sick role a form of deviance that medicine as an institution controlled until recently. Today, however, the supply of and demand for health care means that patients incur large medical bills and are unproductive to society. Some functionalists believe that the whole health system must be reorganized; others think that managed care is the best answer. Some conflict theorists believe that our health problems are rooted in capitalism and the medical-industrial complex; others believe that only when race-, class-, and gender-based inequalities are reduced will inequalities in health care be reduced. Symbolic interactionists believe that communication problems between doctors and patients create many of our health problems and that people must, among other things, become more involved in health-care issues and health-care reform.

KEY TERMS

acute diseases, p. 205
chronic diseases, p. 206
deinstitutionalization, p. 209
disability, p. 206
health maintenance organization (HMO), p. 215
infant mortality rate, p. 204
life expectancy, p. 204
managed care, p. 215
medical-industrial complex, p. 220
total institution, p. 209

QUESTIONS FOR CRITICAL THINKING

1. Because the United States takes pride in its technological and social standing in the world, people are usually surprised to learn that our infant mortality rate is higher than the rates in most other high-income countries. Why is it and what do you think individuals can do at the community level to save these young lives?
2. In what ways are race, class, and gender intertwined with mental disorders? Consider causes and treatments.
3. Reread the doctor's statement on page 215. Do you agree that managed care is detrimental to patient care, or do you side with conflict theorists who believe that doctors uphold the fee-for-service system because it allows them to inflate the cost of treatment? Is there a middle ground?
4. Do you think the U.S. health-care system needs reforming? If so, what would you propose?

Chapter 11

The Changing Family

THINKING SOCIOLOGICALLY

- Why do some people believe that the family as a social institution is in a state of decline?
- How are family problems linked to larger issues of social inequality in society?
- Does extensive media coverage of high-profile domestic violence cases make us more aware of the causes and consequences of this pressing social problem?

Since the divorce what's been hard is worrying about paying the bills—having enough money for food for my son. I don't even get to think about buying him new sneakers.

—A thirty-five-year-old white secretary, who was married for sixteen years and had one child, talks about her financial worries (Kurz, 1995:90)

I could do bad by myself.... If we got married and he's working, then he lose his job. I'm going to stand by him and everything. I don't want to marry nobody that don't have nothing going for themselves.... I don't see no future.... I could do bad by myself.

—Renee, an African-American woman, explains why she did not want to marry her current companion (Jarrett, 1997:353).

The collection agencies call at least 20 times a day. For a little quiet, Diane McLeod stashes her phone in the dishwasher.... Separated and living with her 20-year-old son, she worked two jobs so she could afford her small, two-bedroom ranch house in suburban Philadelphia, the Kia she drove to work and the handbags and knickknacks she liked. Then last year, back-to-back medical emergencies helped push her over the edge. She could no longer afford either her home payments or her credit card bills. Then she lost her job. Now her home is in foreclosure and her credit profile is in ruins.

—Journalist Gretchen Morgenson (2008: A1) describes the plight of Diane McLeod, a woman who was deeply in debt and about to lose her home.

Many people today experience family-related problems similar to those described by these individuals. The economic hardships associated with single parenthood and divorce are particularly problematic for women. Thinking about these issues from a sociological perspective, we may conclude that family-related problems are a challenge not only to the individuals such as these but also to our entire society. Let's take a closer look at contemporary families and some problems many of them face.

THE NATURE OF FAMILIES

What is a family? For many years, this question has generated heated debate. Although some analysts using a functionalist/conservative approach typically state that any definition of the family must emphasize tradition and stability, other analysts argue that any useful definition of families must take into account diversity and social change. Traditionally, family has been defined as a group of people who are related to one another by blood, marriage, or adoption and who live together, form an economic unit, and bear and raise children (Benokraitis, 2008). According to this definition, families are created through childbearing, and it is the parent–child relationship that links generations. Today, however, the traditional definition of family is often modified to incorporate diverse living arrangements and relationships such as single-parent households, cohabiting unmarried couples, domestic partnerships of lesbian or gay couples, and several generations of family members (grandparent, parent, and child) living under the same roof. To encompass these arrangements, we will use the following definition as we look at family-related social problems: ***Families*** **are relationships in which people live together with commitment, form an economic unit and care for any young, and consider the group critical to their identity** (Benokraitis, 2008; Lamanna and Riedmann, 2009).

Changing Family Structure and Patterns

The basis of the traditional family structure is ***kinship*****, a social network of people based on common ancestry, marriage, or adoption.** Kinship is very important in preindustrial societies because it serves as an efficient means of producing and distributing food and goods (e.g., clothing, materials for building shelter) and transferring property and power from one generation to the next. In many preindustrial societies the primary kinship unit is the ***extended family*****—a family unit composed of relatives in addition to parents and children, all of whom live in the same household.** Extended families typically include grandparents, uncles, aunts, and/or other relatives in addition to parents and children. When the growing and harvesting of crops are the basis of economic production, extended families mean that large numbers of people participate in food production, which can be essential to survival. Living together also enables family members to share other resources, such as shelter and transportation. Though extended families are not common in the United States, they are in some countries in Latin America, Africa, Asia, and parts of Eastern and Southern Europe.

With industrialization, other social institutions begin to fulfill kinship system functions. The production and distribution of goods and services, for example, largely shifts to the economic sector. The form of kinship that is most typical in industrialized nations is the ***nuclear family*****—a family unit composed of one or two parents and their dependent children that lives apart from other relatives.** The nuclear family in an industrialized society functions primarily to regulate sexual activity, socialize children, and provide family members with affection and companionship. Although many people view the two-parent nuclear family as the ideal family, today, married couples with children under age eighteen now occupy fewer than one in every four U.S. families (U.S. Census Bureau, 2008). This is a significant decrease since 1970, when two out of five families (40 percent) were two-parent households. Sociologists attribute the decrease to a greater number of births among unmarried women, a trend toward postponing or forgoing marriage and childbearing, and high rates of separation and divorce. It is also possible that marriage with children has become the province of people who are college-educated and affluent, while the working class and poor have steered away from marriage and opted to live together and raise children without being married. Does this mean that the future of the U.S. family is in doubt? We turn to that issue now.

Are U.S. Families in Decline?

Will the family as a social institution disappear in the future? Families are not necessarily in decline, but some new patterns have emerged:

- Compared with previous decades, fewer people are currently married. In 2009, slightly less than half (49 percent) of U.S. households contained a married couple. By contrast, about 71 percent of households in 1970 contained a married couple (see Figure 11.1).
- Marriage rates have declined across all income categories; however, rates have declined the most among lower income individuals.
- People with college degrees are more likely to marry than non–college-educated individuals. Dual-income families are the norm among college-educated persons.
- However, college-educated women often postpone marriage, choosing to live with a partner for a period of time before marriage.
- For many people, cohabitation has become an intermediate step between singlehood and marriage. Some cohabitation is by gay and lesbian domestic partners who reside in states where they are not permitted by law to marry.
- More people are living alone today because they either never married or experienced divorce or the death of a spouse.
- There are more single-parent households than in the past. One of the largest increases has been in the number of single-father households.

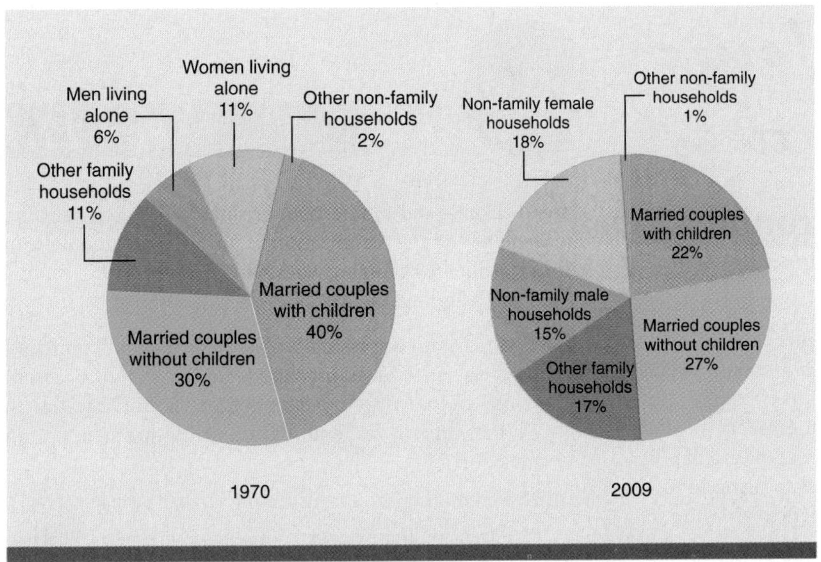

■ ***Figure 11.1*** ***U. S. households by type, 1970 and 2009***

Source: U.S. Census Bureau, 2009. (1-Year Estimates)

If we examine these trends in marriage and family relations, it does not necessarily mean that the family as a social institution is declining: It is simply changing. Based on a social change perspective, we can conclude that families are becoming more complex and diverse; however, they are not necessarily in a state of irreversible decline. According to sociologist Andrew Cherlin (1992), the family will last as a social institution precisely because it can adapt to social change and modify its form. And, the United States is not alone in seeing the structure of the family undergo profound change: Around the world, in both rich and poor nations, new patterns are emerging in regard to single-parent households, divorce rates, and other factors that affect families (see Box 11.1 on page 228).

Changing Views on Marriage and Families

Are our views relatively consistent regarding marriage and families over time? The answer to this question is both "yes" and "no." The term *marriage* refers to a legally recognized and/or socially approved arrangement between two individuals that carries certain rights and obligations and usually involves sexual activity. In the United States, the only legal form of marriage is ***monogamy*****—a marriage between one woman and one man.** The marriage rate (number of marriages per 1,000 population) in the United States is about 7.5 percent annually (U. S. Census Bureau, 2008). In recent years, several states have changed their laws to allow for the marriage of same sex couples; however, at the federal level such laws have not been changed.

Getting married was once a cultural imperative. There was "something wrong" with a person who didn't marry. But since the 1970s, people's attitudes toward marriage and the family have changed as other aspects of society have changed. Cultural guidelines on marriage and childbearing have changed as our society has experienced a broader cultural shift toward autonomy and personal growth. In the 1970s, according to Cherlin (1992:127), "Family life became a matter of personal choice in which individuals made decisions based on a calculus of self-interest and self-fulfillment. Marriage was still desirable, but no one any longer had to be married to be a proper member of society." Marriage also became much less of an economic necessity for women in the 1970s because of new job opportunities and rising incomes. Although women's wages remained low in comparison to men's during this time, their wages rose in absolute terms (Cherlin, 1992). Today, our perspectives have greatly changed on women in the workplace, and their earnings are crucial to the economic well-being of many families.

Of course, we cannot discuss marriage without also taking into consideration the high rate of divorce in the United States. Over the past 105 years, the U.S. divorce rate (the number of divorces per 1,000 population) shifted from a low of 0.7 in 1900 to an all-time high of 5.3 in 1981, and then leveled off at 3.6 in 2005 (U.S. Census Bureau, 2008). Though many people believe that marriage should last "until death do us part," others feel that marriage is a commitment "for as long as love allows." Through a pattern of marriage, divorce, and remarriage, many people reaffirm their commitment to the institution of marriage but not to the individual they initially married. This pattern of successive marriages, in which a person has several spouses over a lifetime but is legally married to only

Social Problems in Global Perspective

Box 11.1

The Changing Family Around the World

> Ms. Polyakovskaya lives with her 6-month-old baby, relying on friends and baby-sitters to watch Aleksandr when she is at work. The father, an unmarried journalist, has never seen his child. Her 6-year-old son, Simeon, is being raised by his grandmother and great-grandmother in Kiev. Ms. Polyakovskaya says she hopes to bring him to Moscow, but cannot even afford train fare to visit him.
>
> She loves her job covering music and ballet, but it is ill paid. In her bare one-room apartment, she sleeps on a tiny, fold-out couch next to the baby's crib. An ironing board serves as a desk. But like many women raising children alone, she said she does not want to marry again.
>
> "My life is difficult," she said, "but God, if I had to come home from work and clean, cook and iron for a husband who keeps telling me I am doing it wrong, it would be even worse."
>
> —*Yelena Polyakovskaya, age thirty-two, a television reporter in Russia (Stanley, 1995)*

Yelena Polyakovskaya is one of a growing number of women in Russia raising her family without a husband. Approximately 15 to 20 percent of Russian families are single-parent households. This is a lower figure than in the United States (with about 27 percent single-parent households), but in Russia, single mothers span all social strata; in the United States, single-parent households are largely in the poorest urban areas (Stanley, 1995). In Japan, single-parenthood because of abandonment or divorce is rare, but a practice called *tanshin hunin* has the same effect. When middle-managers are transferred, they go without their families so that their children don't have to change schools. When possible, the fathers commute home on weekends, but the mothers are essentially single parents (O'Connell, 1994).

Increasing single-parenthood is just one worldwide trend. According to Judith Bruce, author of a report published by the Population Council, a nonprofit group in New York, "trends like unwed motherhood, rising divorce rates, smaller households and the feminization of poverty are not unique to America, but are occurring worldwide" (Lewin, 1995). Among the report's findings are the following:

- Divorce rates are rising. In many developed countries, divorce rates have increased substantially in recent years; in less developed countries, about one-fourth of first marriages end by the time women are in their forties.
- Unwed motherhood is increasing virtually everywhere.
- Children in single-parent households are more likely to be poor than are children in two-parent households, especially when the parent is the mother (often termed the feminization of poverty).
- Though the reason varies from country to country, more women are entering the work force and taking increasing economic responsibility for children. In Bangladesh, for example, where older husbands take young wives, when a husband dies, the wife must find work to support their children. In Asia, if a father who migrates for better work opportunities stops sending money, the mother must support the family herself. In sub-Saharan Africa, a woman's husband might go on to another polygamous marriage and support those children instead (Lewin, 1995).

The fact that families around the world are changing in similar ways shows that there is nothing inevitable about the form of the family or the roles of women and men even within a single society. The fact of so much change in the most basic unit of society also poses important questions for the future.

Questions for Critical Thinking

1. Is the basic problem in family life really inequality between women and men?
2. Would shared responsibilities in the home and equal opportunities in the workplace create better families?
3. Can some general principles for social policies be developed, given vastly different societal conditions? What do you think?

one partner at a time, is referred to as *serial monogamy.* Some social analysts consider serial monogamy a natural adaptation to other social changes in society; others think that it is detrimental to individuals and to society and serves as further evidence of deeply embedded problems in the family as a social institution. One thing is certain, however, much greater diversity exists in intimate relationships and families in this nation.

DIVERSITY IN INTIMATE RELATIONSHIPS AND FAMILIES

Greater diversity in intimate relationships and families in the United States has come about because of dramatic increases in (1) singlehood, (2) postponing marriage, (3) living together without marriage (cohabitation and domestic partnerships), (4) dual-earner marriages, and (5) one-parent families.

Singlehood

Although some will eventually marry, there are about 78 million men and women in the United States who have never been married. The proportion of the U.S. population that has never been married has continued to grow since the 1960s. Some people choose singlehood over marriage because it means greater freedom from commitments to another person. Others choose it because of more career opportunities (especially for women), the availability of sexual partners without marriage, the belief that the single lifestyle is full of excitement, and the desire for self-sufficiency and freedom to change and experiment. Though some analysts think that individuals who prefer to remain single hold more individualistic values and are less family-oriented than are people who choose to marry, sociologist Peter Stein (1981) has found otherwise: Many singles still feel a strong need for intimacy, sharing, and continuity and, as a result, develop relationships with other singles, valuing friends and personal growth more highly than marriage and children.

Singlehood is an important period in the life of many people. Being single is often idealized by the media, as in the HBO series Entourage, *where these characters are shown going out together for a night on the town.*

Some people are single not by choice but by necessity. Because of macrolevel factors such as war and structural changes in the economy, such as recession and high rates of unemployment, many young working-class people cannot afford to marry and set up their own households. Indeed, some college graduates have found that they cannot earn enough money to set up households separate from those of their parents.

Although the unmarried population has increased across racial and ethnic categories, African Americans and Latinos are less likely than their white (non-Hispanic) counterparts to have never married. The proportion of never-married singles varies significantly by racial and ethnic group. Among males age fifteen and over, about 47 percent of African Americans have never been married, compared to about 41 percent of Latinos and 29 percent of whites. Among women age fifteen and over, about 43 percent of African Americans have never married, compared to almost 31 percent of Latinas and 22 percent of whites (U.S. Census Bureau, 2008). If these figures seem to be unusually high, it is important to note that the U.S. Census Bureau, the agency that accumulates and disseminates such statistics, has recently shifted downward from age eighteen to age fifteen when calculating these data for never-married persons. However, still striking is the lower marriage rate among African Americans when compared to Latinos/as, and whites (non-Hispanic). Trends that may contribute to these rates include:

1. Young African-American men have higher rates of mortality than young African-American women do.
2. More African-American women are college-educated and tend to make more money than African-American men do.
3. Some African-American men have less to offer to potential female partners in a marriage because they have experienced discrimination, have had limited educational opportunities, and now have few job prospects.
4. Reported rates of homosexuality are higher among African-American men than those in other racial/ethnic categories. Homosexuality rates among African-Americans men are also higher than for women.
5. More African-American men than African– American women marry members of other racial-ethnic groups.

The numbers of singles have also increased among Latinos/as because this population is comprised of individuals who are younger than those in the non-Latino (non-Hispanic) population and many of them have not reached an age when marriage is considered to be appropriate among family and friends. Latinas/os who are in the process of migrating from one nation to another or from one region to another seeking employment opportunities may postpone marriage until they can create a stable economic situation for themselves and their family.

Among older singles who want to marry for the first time or to remarry after divorce or widowhood, men have an advantage over women because of the double-standard of aging that affects women and men differently, and the pool of eligible persons seeking marriage is made up of more women than men.

Postponing Marriage

Young people today are less eager to get married than they were two decades ago; many are remaining single into their late twenties. The median age at which men first get married is 27.5 years, and the median age for women is 25.1 years (U.S. Census Bureau, 2008). Although the age at which people marry for the first time has been rising steadily since the 1950s, it has accelerated since the 1970s. Between 1970 and today, the proportion of women aged twenty-five to twenty-nine who have never married has tripled.

Why are more people postponing first marriages? Although some reasons are the same as those for staying single, sociologists suggest four key factors: (1) economic uncertainty, (2) women's increasing participation in the labor force, (3) sexual relationships outside marriage having become more socially acceptable and contraception having become more effective, (4) as a result of rising divorce rates, less eagerness to get married and thus risk getting divorced. Likewise, a significant increase in cohabitation and domestic partnerships contributes to the percentage of people who are counted as single or postponing marriage.

Cohabitation and Domestic Partnerships

The popularity of cohabitation has increased in the past two decades. ***Cohabitation* is two adults living together in a sexual relationship without being legally married.** It is not known how many people actually cohabit because the U.S. Census Bureau refers to couples who live together simply as "unmarried couple households" and does not ask about emotional or sexual involvement. According to Census Bureau data, however, the heterosexual couples who are most likely to cohabit are under age forty-five and have been married before or are older individuals who do not want to lose financial benefits (such as retirement benefits) that are contingent on not remarrying. Among younger people, employed couples are more likely to cohabit than college students are.

For some couples, cohabitation is a form of trial marriage and constitutes an intermediate stage between dating and marriage. In a major study by the National Center for Health Statistics, researchers found that a majority of cohabitation relationships lasting more than three years eventually culminated in marriage, although the results varied on the basis of many factors including race, ethnicity, age, education, and level of income (Bramlett and Mosher, 2002).

According to anthropologist Margaret Mead (1966), dating patterns in the United States do not adequately prepare people for marriage and parenting responsibilities. Mead proposed a two-stage marriage process, each with its own ceremony and responsibilities. In the first stage, the individual marriage, two people would make a serious commitment to each other but agree not to have children during this stage. In the second stage, the parental marriage, the couple would decide to have children and to share responsibility for their upbringing. Unlike cohabitation, Mead's two stages of marriage would both be legally binding.

Does cohabitation contribute to marital success? The evidence is mixed. Some studies show that cohabitation has little or no effect on marital adjustment, emotional closeness, satisfaction, and intimacy (Watson and DeMeo, 1987). Other studies indicate that couples who cohabit first are more likely to divorce than those who do not (Bennett, Blanc, and Bloom, 1988). Apparently, partners in this study who had cohabited were less satisfied with their marriages and less committed to the institution of marriage than were those who had not lived together before marrying. The researchers theorized that cohabitation might contribute to people's individualistic attitudes and values while making them more aware that alternatives to marriage exist (Axinn and Thornton, 1992; Thomson and Colella, 1992).

Many gay and lesbian couples consider themselves married and living in a lifelong commitment. Because the law in most states does not allow them to marry legally, they establish *domestic partnerships* (see Chapter 6). To make their commitment public, some couples exchange rings and vows under the auspices of churches such as the Metropolitan Community Church (the national gay church) and even some mainstream churches. One reason people prefer legal marriage to domestic partnerships is that employee health insurance coverage and other benefits are offered to legal spouses, although today some employers offer similar benefits to domestic partners.

Dual-Earner Marriages

More than 50 percent of all marriages in the United States are ***dual-earner marriages*—marriages in which both spouses are in the labor force.** Over half of all employed women hold full-time, year-round jobs, and in a change from the past, there are more married women with young children in the paid labor force today than there were in the past. In 2006, 60 percent of all women with a child under age three were in the paid workforce (U.S. Census Bureau, 2008).

Many married women who are employed outside the household face hours of domestic work and child care when they go home. Sociologist Arlie Hochschild (1989) refers to women's dual workdays as the ***second shift*—the domestic work that many employed women perform at home after completing their work day on the job.** According to Hochschild, the unpaid housework that women do on the second shift (see Chapter 4) amounts to an extra month of work each year. In households with small children or many children, the amount of housework increases (Hartmann, 1981). Across race and class, numerous studies confirm that domestic work remains primarily women's work (Gerstel and Gross, 1995) even though some middle- and upper-middle-class fathers have become increasingly involved in parenting in recent decades.

This is an increasingly familiar sight in many U.S. neighborhoods where both parents are employed outside the household and have child care responsibilities at home as well. How might our nation be more responsive to the needs of parents in dual-earner marriages and their children?

In recent years, more husbands have come to share some of the household and child-care responsibilities, especially when the wife's earnings are essential to family finances. But even when husbands assume some of the household responsibilities, they typically spend much less time in these activities than do their wives. Women and men perform different household tasks, and the deadlines for their work vary widely. Recurring tasks that have specific times for completion (such as bathing a child or cooking a meal) tend to be the women's responsibility, whereas men are more likely to do the periodic tasks that have no highly structured schedule (such as mowing the lawn or changing the oil in the car) (Hochschild, 1989).

Couples with more egalitarian ideas about women's and men's roles tend to share more equally in food preparation, housework, and child care (Wright, Shire, Hwang, Dolan, and Baxter, 1992). An *egalitarian family* is one in which the partners share power and authority equally. As women have gained new educational and employment opportunities, a trend toward more egalitarian relationships has become evident in the United States. Some degree of economic independence makes it possible for women to delay marriage or to terminate a problematic marriage (O'Connell, 1994). For some men, the shift to a more egalitarian household occurs gradually, as the following quotation indicates:

> It was me taking the initiative, and also Connie pushing, saying, "Gee, there's so much that has to be done." At first I said, "But I'm supposed to be the breadwinner," not realizing she's also the breadwinner. I was being a little blind to what was going on, but I got tired of waiting for my wife to come home to start cooking, so one day I surprised the hell out [of] her and myself and the kids, and I had supper waiting on the table for her. (Gerson, 1993:170)

Problems associated with providing economic support for the family and rearing children are even more pressing in many one-parent households.

Comparing Two-Parent and One-Parent Households

When the mother and father in a two-parent household truly share parenting, children have the benefit of two primary caregivers. Some researchers have found that when fathers take an active part in raising the children, the effect is beneficial for all family members. Fathers find increased contact with their children provides more opportunities for personal and emotional gratification (Coltrane, 1989).

However, living in a two-parent family does not guarantee children a happy childhood. Children whose parents argue constantly, are alcoholics, or abuse them have a worse family experience than do children in a single-parent family where there is a supportive environment. Women who are employed full-time and are single parents probably have the greatest burden of all. These women must fulfill their paid employment duties and meet the needs of their children and the household, often with little help from ex-husbands or relatives.

How prevalent are one-parent households? The percentage of households headed by single parents has remained at about nine percent from 1994 through 2006, the last year for which data are available. There were 12.9 million one-parent families in 2006, and single mothers headed up 10.4 million of those, as compared with 2.5 million single-father families. About 42 percent of all white children and 86 percent of all African-American children spend part of their childhood in a household headed by a single mother who is divorced, separated, never-married, or widowed (Garfinkel and McLanahan, 1986).

What effect does a one-parent household have on children? According to one study based on six nationally representative data sets of more than 25,000 children from various racial and social class backgrounds, children growing up with only one biological parent are at risk for serious problems, including poor academic achievement, dropping out of school, drug and alcohol abuse, teen pregnancy, early marriage, and divorce (McLanahan and Sandefur, 1994). Obviously, living in a one-parent family does not necessarily cause these problems. Factors such as poverty, discrimination, unsafe neighborhoods, and high crime rates must also be considered. In fact, other researchers have found some benefits to growing up in a one-parent family (Lauer and Lauer, 1991). For example, children in one-parent families are often less pressured to conform to rigid gender roles. Rather than having chores assigned by gender, as is common in two-parent families, single-parent children typically take on a wider variety of tasks and activities. Many single-parent children also show high levels of maturity and self-sufficiency earlier because they have to help out at a younger age than do children in other families (Lauer and Lauer, 1991).

What about the fathers of children in one-parent households headed by women? Although some fathers remain involved in their children's lives, others become "Disneyland daddies"—occasionally taking their children out for recreational activities or buying them presents on birthdays and holidays. Personal choice, workplace demands on time and energy, location of the ex-wife's residence, and limitations placed on visitation by custody arrangements are all factors that affect how often absentee fathers visit their children. As more parents are receiving joint custody of their children, it appears that joint custody can minimize the disruption of divorce in a child's life if the ex-spouses cooperate with each other and live in relatively close geographical proximity. Ex-spouses who constantly argue or live far away from each other can create serious problems for "commuter" children, as author David Sheff (1995:64) describes:

> My son began commuting between his two homes at age 4. . . . The commuter flights between San Francisco and Los Angeles were the only times a parent wasn't lording over him, so he was able to order Coca-Cola, verboten at home. . . . But such benefits were insignificant when contrasted with his preflight nightmares about plane crashes. . . . Like so many divorcing couples, we divided the china and art and our young son. . . . First he was ferried back and forth between our homes across town, and then, when his mother moved to Lo.s Angeles, across the state. For the eight years since, he has been one of the thousands of American children with two homes, two beds, two sets of clothes and toys, and two toothbrushes.

The transition from a two-parent family to a one-parent family is only one of many child-related family issues that many people today must deal with, as we discuss in the next section.

CHILD-RELATED FAMILY ISSUES

One of the major issues facing many individuals and families today is reproductive freedom, a term that implies both the desire of individuals to have a child and the desire *not to have* one. As sociologists Leslie King and Madonna Harrington Meyer (1997:8) explain,

> The average woman is fertile, and therefore must attempt to control her reproductivity, for one-half of her life. For most women, it is the preoccupation with preventing births that consumes their health-care dollars and energies; for a small minority, it is the preoccupation with achieving a birth that dominates. The ability to control

fertility is, to a great extent, linked to access to various forms of reproductive health services, including contraceptives and infertility treatments. Yet, in the United States, insurance coverage of contraceptive and infertility treatments is fragmented.

Reproductive Freedom, Contraception, and Abortion

Reproductive freedom has been a controversial issue throughout much of U.S. history. In the nineteenth century, the government instituted formal, legal policies to ensure that some people would not produce children. By incarcerating "wayward girls" and limiting their right to marry and by passing laws that permitted the sterilization of the poor, the criminal, or the "feebleminded," political leaders attempted to prevent people who were thought to be "unfit" from reproducing (Luker, 1996). Today, say some researchers, the government discourages births among the poor by mandating the coverage of contraceptives for women on Medicaid (King and Harrington Meyer, 1997).

The introduction of new drugs raises new questions about issues such as women's reproductive rights versus the availability of abortion. This ad promotes RU-486, the controversial abortion pill, which has become available in the United States in recent years.

Contraceptive devices such as condoms and diaphragms were widely available and relatively technologically sophisticated in the first half of the nineteenth century. By the 1850s, however, the government had begun to establish policies limiting their availability to prevent a drop in the birth rate among white Americans (Luker, 1996). Abortion became illegal in most states by 1900. Physicians—among others—had begun to crusade against abortion in the 1800s because most procedures were done by people (such as barbers) who had no medical training. Some physicians apparently believed that if these abortionists could be stopped, physicians would become the arbiters of whether or not women should have abortions. The ban on abortion and the limited availability of contraceptives did not prevent wealthy women from practicing birth control or procuring an abortion (Luker, 1996).

It was not until the introduction of the birth control pill in 1960 that women gained almost complete control of their fertility. The "Pill" quickly became the most popular contraceptive among married women in the United States. During this time and into the early 1970s, public opinion about women's reproductive freedom began to change somewhat. In 1971, the U.S. Supreme Court upheld women's right to privacy in reproductive matters in *Griswold v. Connecticut.* The Court ruled that laws prohibiting the use of contraception by married couples violated the constitutional right to privacy. In subsequent cases, the Court included unmarried adults and minors in this protection.

Many U.S. women spend about 90 percent of their fertile years trying to avoid pregnancy (Gold and Richards, 1994). An estimated 60 percent of all women between the ages of fifteen and forty-four are using contraceptives at any specific time. Unplanned pregnancies, then, are usually the result of not using contraceptives or using contraceptives that do not work or are not used as intended. Of the 6.4 million pregnancies in the United States each year, about 3.6 million (56 percent) are unintended, and about 2.8 million (44 percent) are intended (Gold and Richards, 1994). In the 2000s, poor women are getting pregnant unintentionally at considerably higher rates than they were in the mid-1990s. They are also giving birth to more unplanned children and having more abortions. By contrast, unplanned pregnancies among middle- and upper-income women have declined substantially. Sociologists attribute this change to the fact that state and federal reproductive health programs have been cut back substantially and that those programs that still exist now have more restrictions placed on the kinds of services they may provide to clients. For example, many programs now focus on abstinence rather than contraception, and many clients are unwilling to accept this restriction on their sexual conduct.

Money may also be a factor in regard to birth control: The most effective forms are the most expensive. Many oral contraceptives cost from $40 to $50 per month, for an annual cost of about $500 to $600 a year.

Over the past three decades, the roles that government, religious organizations, physicians, and the legal establishment should play in reproductive decisions continue to be highly controversial in this country. Perhaps the most significant legal action involving reproductive rights was the Supreme Court decision in *Roe v. Wade* (1973) that women have a constitutionally protected right to choose abortion, and the state cannot unduly interfere with or prohibit that right. The court distinguished among trimesters of pregnancy in its ruling. During the first three months, decisions about the pregnancy are strictly private—made by women in consultation with their physicians; in the second trimester, the state may impose some restrictions but only to safeguard women's health; in the third trimester, the state may prohibit abortion—because of the fetus's viability (ability to survive outside a woman's womb)—except when necessary to preserve the woman's life or health.

Although the Court has not overturned *Roe v. Wade,* subsequent laws and decisions have eroded some of women's reproductive rights and made abortions more difficult to obtain, particularly for poor women and unmarried pregnant teenagers. For example, in 1993, the Supreme Court ruled that requiring a minor to get written permission from both parents for an abortion did not constitute an "undue burden" for a fourteen- or fifteen-year-old girl. And in 2003, Congress enacted a law banning partial birth (late term) abortions.

Opposition to abortion has resulted in violence against physicians and the personnel of clinics where abortions are performed, which has caused a number of facilities to close. In response, in 1993, Congress passed the Freedom of Access to Clinic Entrances Act, making it a federal offense to attack an abortion clinic or obstruct clients from going to one. Nevertheless, antiabortion activists continue to try to make it difficult for women to have abortions. Some social analysts fear that if abortion is restricted, women will once again seek abortions in "back rooms," as they did in the era of illegal abortions (see Miller, 1993; Messer and May, 1994). In recent years, the French abortion pill RU-486, which was approved in 2000 for use in the United States by the Food and Drug Administration, has become an increasingly popular alternative to abortions and allows women to make abortion-related decisions in private, as compared to the necessity of visiting public clinics where they may be confronted by protesters. According to one recent report, "At a time when the overall number of abortions has been steadily declining, RU-486-induced abortions have been rising by 22 percent a year and now account for 14 percent of the total—and more than one in five early abortions performed by the ninth week of pregnancy" (Stein, 2008: A1).

At the microlevel, abortion is a solution for some pregnant women and their families but a problem for others, particularly when they face religious or family opposition. At the macrolevel, abortion is both a problem and a solution when activists try to influence the making and enforcement of laws pertaining to women's reproductive rights and the control of new reproductive technologies.

Infertility and New Reproductive Technologies

Infertility is defined as an inability to conceive after a year of unprotected sexual relations. Today, infertility affects nearly 5 million U.S. couples, or one in twelve couples in which the wife is between the ages of fifteen and forty-four. In 40 percent of the cases, the woman is infertile, and in another 40 percent it is the man; 20 percent of the time, the cause is impossible to determine (Gabriel, 1996).

Sexually transmitted diseases are a leading cause of infertility: Each year, 100,000 to 150,000 women become infertile as a result of a sexually transmitted disease that develops into pelvic inflammatory disease (Gold and Richards, 1994). There are also some women—both married and unmarried—who would like to have a child but cannot because of disabilities. Still other women in lesbian relationships would like to be parents. Some analysts point out that a growing number of prospective parents delay childbearing into their thirties and forties when it might be more difficult for them to conceive.

About 50 percent of infertile couples who seek treatment can be helped by conventional, relatively low-tech treatments such as fertility drugs, artificial insemination, and surgery to unblock fallopian tubes. The other 50 percent require advanced technology, sometimes called assisted reproductive technology (ART). Many middle- and upper-income couples, for example, receive in vitro fertilization (IVF), which costs between $9,000 and $12,000 per cycle (see Table 11.1). Often

TABLE 11.1 Forms of Assisted Reproductive Technology

Name	Description
In vitro fertilization (IVF)	Eggs that were produced as a result of administering fertility drugs are removed from the woman's body and fertilized by sperm in a laboratory dish. The embryos that result from this process are transferred to the woman's uterus.
Micromanipulation	Viewing the process through a microscope, a specialist manipulates egg and sperm in a laboratory dish to improve the chances of a pregnancy.
Cryopreserved embryo transfer (CPE)	Embryos that were frozen after a previous assisted reproductive technology procedure are thawed and then transferred to the uterus.
Egg donation	Eggs are removed from a donor's uterus, fertilized in a laboratory dish, and transferred to an infertile woman's uterus.
Surrogacy	An embryo is implanted in the uterus of a woman who is paid to carry the fetus until birth. The egg may come from either the legal or the surrogate mother, and the sperm may come either from the legal father or a donor.

Source: Gabriel, 1996.

the first attempt is unsuccessful, and couples may pay for second and third cycles of the drug before pregnancy occurs or they become discouraged and terminate the treatments.

Despite the popularity of such treatments and the growth of fertility clinics, many couples are still unable to become parents. For couples like Michael and Stephanie Plaut, who have spent three years and thousands of dollars trying to have a baby through IVF and other procedures, every unsuccessful attempt is traumatic. Journalist Felicia Lee (1996:A1) has documented the trauma the couple undergoes: "Michael Plaut answered the telephone... [and the] call confirmed his worst fear: the pregnancy test was negative. The Plauts sobbed, held each other and then had a glass of Scotch. 'It's like we're in a period of mourning,' Mrs. Plaut said. 'You just get to the point where you want this to be over.'" Couples like the Plauts, who have their hopes raised by the new reproductive technologies only to find that they do not work for them, often form support groups. Many couples finally decide to remain childless, but some adopt one or more children.

Adoption

Adoption is a legal process through which the rights and duties of parenting are transferred from a child's biological and/or legal parents to new legal parents. The adopted child has all the rights of a biological child. In most adoptions, a new birth certificate is issued, and the child has no further contact with the biological parents, although some states have right-to-know laws under which adoptive parents must grant the biological parents visitation rights.

Matching children who are available for adoption with prospective adoptive parents can be difficult. The children often have specific needs, and prospective parents often specify the kind of children they want to adopt. Because many prospective parents do not want to adopt children who are nonwhite (most prospective parents are white), are older, or have disabilities or diseases, children who are available for adoption often move from foster home to foster home (Zelizer, 1985).

Prospective parents frequently want infants, but fewer infants are available for adoption than in the past because better means of contraception exist, abortion is more readily available, and more unmarried teenage parents are deciding to keep their babies. Some teenagers, however, believe that adoption is the best way to solve the problem of early childbearing. Christina, one of many teenagers facing the realities of an early pregnancy and lack of resources to meet the child's needs, explained her decision this way:

> I know I can't keep my baby. I can't give it all the things a baby needs and I sure can't dump it on my parents because they can't afford to take care of their own family.

> I've decided to give it up for adoption. I think it's better for the baby to give it up to parents who can't have a baby themselves. I think that I'm really doing a favor to my baby, although I'm always going to wonder what it looks like and what it's doing. (Luker, 1996:163)

Teen Pregnancies and Unmarried Motherhood

The birth rate among teenagers is higher in the United States than in any other high-income nation. Although the pregnancy rate among *all* female teenagers had decreased over the past three decades, the birth rate for teenagers increased in 2006 for the first time since 1991, and child-bearing among unmarried women reached the highest level on record. The birth rate for females aged 15 to 19 rose by 3 percent in 2006 over the previous year, to 41.9 live births per 1,000 as compared to 40.5 in 2005. After 14 years of decreasing birth rates among teenagers, analysts have been unable to determine the specific causes of this increase and to assess whether it is a permanent change or merely a temporary fluctuation.

Although a popular myth claims that most births to unmarried teenagers occur in the city centers of large urban areas, the greatest number of teens giving birth occurs in the South and in less urbanized areas (see Map 11.1). Increases in teen birth rates in 2006 were largest among African-American girls (with an increase of 5 percent) while the rate increased by 3 percent for white (non-Hispanic) and 2 percent for Latina teens. Among the key factors behind this statistic are the poverty and lack of employment opportunity for African-American males, as we discussed in Chapter 3.

According to social analysts, the outcome of teen pregnancies is problematic because teenage mothers are typically unskilled at parenting, are likely to drop out of school, and have no social support other than relatives. Family support is extremely important to unmarried pregnant teens because emotional and

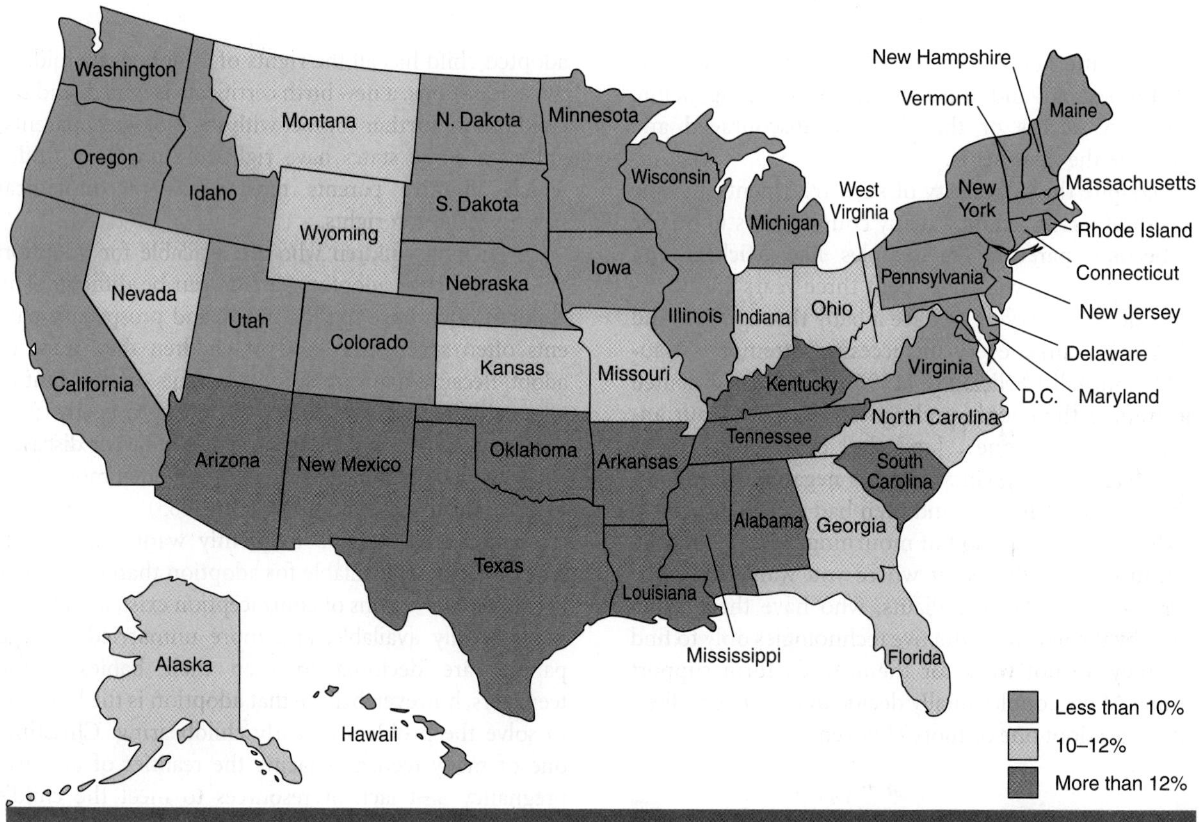

■ *Map 11.1* ***Births to teenage mothers as a percentage of all births, by state, 2005***

Source: U.S. Census Bureau, 2008.

financial support from the fathers of their children is often lacking. Without this support, teen mothers rely on their own mothers and grandmothers to help with childrearing. As a result, many unmarried teenage mothers do not make the same transition from the family of orientation to the family of procreation that most people make when they become parents. The ***family of orientation*** **is the family into which a person is born and in which early socialization takes place.** When teenage mothers and their children live with their grandmothers or other relatives, they do not establish the separate family unit known as a ***family of procreation*—the family that a person forms by having or adopting children, which married couples with young children create.**

The picture for the children of teenage mothers without parental support is especially bleak because few of these mothers have adequate parenting skills or knowledge of child development. Children of unwed teenage mothers tend to have severely limited educational and employment opportunities and a high likelihood of living in poverty (Benokraitis, 2008). In addition, about 43 percent of the teenagers who first give birth between the ages of fifteen and nineteen have a second child within three years (Benokraitis, 2008). The future of these children is in even greater jeopardy today because of the 1996 welfare reform law that reduces assistance to single mothers with young children, especially unmarried mothers under age eighteen (see Chapter 2).

Teenagers are not the only ones having children without getting married these days. Unmarried girls and women accounted for 38.5 percent of all U.S. births in 2006. Among African Americans, they accounted for 70.7 percent of births; among Latinas, 49.9 percent; and among whites, 26.6 percent (U.S. Census Bureau, 2008). According to demographer Charles Westoff, increasing birth rates among unmarried girls and women reflect "the declining significance of marriage as a social obligation or a social necessity for reproduction. Increasing proportions of white women who have not been married are deciding that having a child is more important than any kind of disapproval they might face" (quoted in Connell, 1995). With less of a social stigma attached to unmarried pregnancy, fewer women seem to be seeking abortion and are deciding instead to raise the child themselves whether the pregnancy was planned or not.

DIVORCE AND REMARRIAGE

Divorce is the legal process of dissolving a marriage that allows former spouses to remarry if they so choose. Have you heard such statements as "One out of every two marriages ends in divorce"? Statistics might initially appear to bear out this statement, but it is really more complex than that (see Box 11.2 on page 238).

Divorce laws in many states once required the partner seeking the divorce to prove misconduct on the part of the other spouse. Under today's *no-fault divorce laws,* however, proof of blameworthiness is no longer necessary, and most divorces are granted on the grounds of *irreconcilable differences,* which means that a breakdown has occurred in the marital relationship and neither partner is to be specifically blamed.

With or without blame, divorce usually has a dramatic economic and emotional impact on family members. An estimated 60 percent of divorcing couples have one or more children. By age sixteen, about one out of every three white children and two out of every three African-American children experience divorce in their families (Kurz, 1995). Indeed, some children experience more than one divorce during their childhood because one or both of their parents may remarry and subsequently divorce again.

The process of getting a divorce typically creates great tension in former marital partners. Many couples air their grievances against each other in front of a judge or in a courtroom full of people, further adding to their stress.

Social Problems and Statistics

Box 11.2

Divorce changes relationships not only for the couple and children involved, but also for other relatives. Some grandparents feel that they are the big losers. Grandparents who wish to see their grandchildren have to keep in touch with the parent who has custody, but if the grandparents are in-laws, they are less likely to be welcomed and might be seen as taking the "other side" simply because they are the parents of the ex-spouse. Recently, some grandparents have sued for custody of minor grandchildren. For the most part, these suits have not been successful except when there has been some question about the emotional stability of the biological parents or the suitability of a foster-care arrangement.

Most people who divorce remarry. In fact, in more than 40 percent of all marriages, either the bride, the groom, or both have previously been married. Among individuals who divorce before age thirty-five, about half remarry within three years of their first divorce (Bramlett and Mosher, 2002). Most divorced people marry others who have been divorced, though remarriage rates vary by gender and age. At all ages, a greater proportion of men than women remarry, often relatively soon after the divorce. Among women, the older a woman is at the time of divorce, the lower is her likelihood of remarrying. Women who have not graduated from high school and have young children tend to remarry relatively quickly. Women with a college degree and without children are less likely to remarry.

Divorce and remarriage often creates complex family relationships. ***Blended families* are families that consist of a husband and wife, children from previous marriages, and children (if any) from the new marriage.** At least initially, stress in blended families may be fairly high because of rivalry among the children and hostilities directed toward stepparents or babies born into the family. In some cases, when parents divorce and marry other partners, the children become part of a *binuclear family,* living with one biological parent and a stepparent part of the time and with the other biological parent and another stepparent the rest of the time.

As sociologist Andrew Cherlin (1992) points out, the norms governing divorce and remarriage are ambiguous, so people must make decisions about family life (such as who should be invited to a birthday celebration or a wedding) on the basis of their own feelings about the people involved. But in spite of the problems, many blended families succeed.

DOMESTIC VIOLENCE

The term *domestic violence* obscures the fact that most victims of domestic violence are women and children. Women are more likely to be assaulted, injured, or raped by their male partners than by any other type of assailant. Children are extremely vulnerable to abuse and violence because of their age and their economic and social dependence on their parents or other adult caregivers.

Child Abuse

According to the 1974 Federal Child Abuse Prevention and Treatment Act, child abuse and neglect is the physical or mental injury, sexual abuse, or negligent treatment of a child under the age of eighteen by a person who is responsible for the child's welfare. Most of us, when we hear the words *child abuse,* think in terms of physical injury or sexual abuse, but the most frequent form of child maltreatment is *child neglect*—not meeting a child's basic needs for emotional warmth and security, adequate shelter, food, health care, education, clothing, and protection. We will focus primarily on physical injury and sexual abuse because these actions are classified as violent personal crimes. In the past, children in the United States were considered the property of their parents and could be punished or ignored as the parents wished. With passage of the Social Security Act in the 1930s, however, children became legally protected even from their own parents. Still, many physical injuries to children are intentionally inflicted by parents and other caregivers. Parental violence can, in fact, lead to the *battered child syndrome,* a psychological disorder in which a child experiences low self-esteem and sometimes clinical depression associated with former or current abuse perpetrated by a biological or custodial parent (Kempe et al., 1962).

The physical abuse of children in the United States is a serious social problem that remains largely hidden unless an incident results in the death or serious injury of a child. Some researchers have found that children are most likely to be assaulted in their own homes if their parents were abused, neglected, or deprived as children and if their parents are socially isolated as adults. Parents who lack a support network and suddenly face a crisis tend to make their children the targets of their frustration and sometimes their aggression (Kempe and Kempe, 1978). Other researchers have found that abusive parents characteristically feel unloved and unworthy and totally unprepared to cope with their circumstances (Tower, 1996).

The signs of physical abuse include bruises, particularly on the back of the legs, upper arms and chest, neck, head, or genitals. Fractures in infants under twelve months of age are a strong indication of abuse, as are head injuries and burns, especially cigarette burns. Most physicians and emergency room personnel are trained to identify signs of child abuse so that parents or guardians can be reported to the appropriate authorities. In fact, reporting of suspected child abuse has improved significantly in recent years because of increased training, awareness, and legislation, including the Federal Child Abuse Prevention and Treatment Act of 1974, which established that reports of suspected abuse would be investigated promptly and fully. In the past, even when physicians suspected abuse, they often chose to treat the child but not to report the incident, believing that abuse would be too difficult to prove (Tower, 1996).

One of the most disturbing forms of physical abuse of children is sexual abuse. Unfortunately, there is a lack of consensus on how to define sexual abuse. In one study, child sexual abuse was defined in terms of three actions: intrusion, molestation with genital contact or other forms of fondling, and inadequate supervision of a child's sexual activity (see Tower, 1996). Another study included all behaviors ranging from "sexual overtures" to sexual intercourse occurring between a child age thirteen or under and someone five or more years older or between adolescents aged thirteen to sixteen and someone ten or more years older (Finkelhor, 1984).

Although it is difficult to estimate the incidence and prevalence of sexual abuse, it appears that between 10 and 15 percent of girls and boys experience some form of sexual contact as children (Finkelhor, 1984). At all ages, females are more likely than males to be victims of sexual abuse as well as incest—sexual relations between individuals who are so closely related that they are forbidden to marry by law. Males are more likely to experience assault in public places by strangers or nonrelatives; girls are more likely to experience long-term victimization by relatives or family acquaintances in their own home. Both male and female victims are more likely to be abused by male offenders, and offenders are known to their victims in the vast majority of cases (Knudsen, 1992).

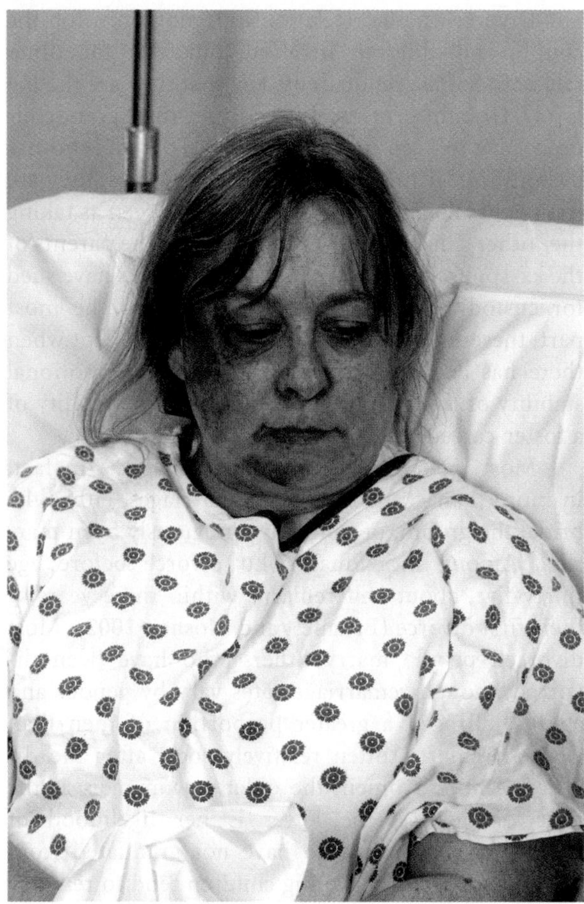

Domestic violence is a hidden problem in some families. Although the woman pictured here is receiving medical attention for her injuries, many victims do not come forward to report abuse because they fear that they may be battered again or be blamed by others for their problem.

Spouse Abuse

From the days of early Rome to current times, spouse abuse has been acknowledged to exist, but until recently, it was largely ignored or tolerated. Today, it is estimated that as many as 5 million spouses, primarily wives, are abused each year. Women are much more likely than men to be victims of domestic violence of all types. The U.S. Attorney General's office estimates that at least 94 percent of all cases of spouse abuse involve a man beating a woman. In fact, physical abuse by husbands or boyfriends is the single most common source of injury among women (Murphy-Milano, 1996). Injuries sustained by victims of spouse abuse are as serious as, or more serious than, the injuries incurred in 90 percent of all rapes, robberies, and other aggravated assaults. Spouse abuse ranges in intensity from slapping, kicking, and hitting with a closed fist to inflicting critical injuries or death (Straus et al., 1980). Spouse abuse occurs across lines of race, class, region, religion, and other factors. Charlotte Fedders, for example, was abused by her husband, John Fedders, a powerful young lawyer in the Reagan administration:

> I was in the bathroom sitting on a closed toilet, bathing two of the boys in the tub. John came home, went upstairs, and saw my note [that she had written a check for $80 to a marriage counselor]. He came into the bathroom and started beating me with his fists and pulling on my hair. I turned away to protect myself, and he beat me on my back. I managed to get out and run into Luke's [an older son] room, because I didn't think that he'd hit me in front of Luke. But he ran after me. I can remember crouching in the corner. He beat my neck and shoulder and back. Then he chased me into our bedroom. He yelled at one point, "I don't give a . . . if I kill you." It was one of the worst beatings John ever gave me. And I hadn't done anything but written a check. (Fedders and Elliott, 1987:158–159)

Although Fedders had the financial means to divorce her husband and to go on to become an advocate for battered women, many abused women come from low-income backgrounds and have few options. Unfortunately, many of these women end up victims of homicide. Women are more than three times as likely to be killed by a spouse than men are, with the exception of African-American husbands, who are at greater risk of being killed by their spouses than are African-American wives or white spouses of either gender. Moreover, the risk of being killed by one's spouse is greater for individuals in interracial marriages than it is for those who marry within their race (Mercy and Saltzman, 1989). When women kill their spouses, it is often because they have been physically and sexually abused over a long period of time and see themselves as hopelessly trapped in a dangerous relationship.

Related to the issue of spouse abuse is marital rape. In *marital rape,* a husband forces sexual intercourse on his resisting wife. The federal criminal code and most state laws now identify marital rape as a crime. Analysts have identified three types of marital rape: (1) battering rape, in which sexual violence is part of a larger pattern of abuse; (2) nonbattering rape, in which the husband and wife do not agree over when, where, and whether or not to have sex; and (3) obsessive rape, which involves male sexual obsessions, sometimes related to use of pornography or force to become aroused (Finkelhor and Yllo, 1985). Many victims of spouse abuse and/or marital rape fear that if they try to leave the abusive spouse, they will endanger themselves and their children. Studies have shown that women who have been severely sexually assaulted by their husbands and do not have adequate support services for victims of domestic violence where they live are the most likely to kill their spouses (Browne and Williams, 1987).

Social Responses to Domestic Violence

High-profile cases of domestic violence, often involving celebrities or professional athletes, call our attention to the problem of domestic abuse, but on a day-to-day basis many people who are aware of such violence do not report it because they do not want to become involved in what they see as a "private matter."

Historically, in the United States, an *ideology of nonintervention*—a strong reluctance on the part of outsiders to interfere in family matters—has led people and police officers to ignore or tolerate domestic violence (Lauer, 1995). Unfortunately, the pattern of violence that ultimately results in a homicide is eerily similar in many cases of domestic abuse, and in most of those cases, death might have been prevented by earlier intervention. Positive changes are now being made in how law enforcement officials handle domestic violence calls—changes that are long overdue. As with other social problems we have examined, the causes, effects, and possible solutions for domestic violence and other family-related problems depend on the theoretical framework the analyst uses.

SOCIOLOGICAL EXPLANATIONS AND SOLUTIONS

What purposes do families serve in contemporary societies? Do families create problems for society or solve them? How can we reduce family-related social problems in the twenty-first century? Different theoretical perspectives provide us with divergent answers and solutions. Functionalists believe that the family fulfills important functions for individuals at the microlevel and for the entire society at the macrolevel. Conflict and feminist theorists, on the other hand, consider families to be a primary source of inequality—and sometimes abuse and violence—in society. Taking a microlevel approach, symbolic interactionists analyze family-related social problems in terms of socialization and social interactions among family members.

Functionalist Perspectives

Functionalists emphasize the importance of the family in maintaining the stability of society and the well-being of individuals. According to Emile Durkheim, marriage is a microcosmic replica of the larger society; both marriage and society involve a mental and moral fusion of physically distinct individuals (Lehmann, 1994). Durkheim also believed that a division of labor contributed to greater efficiency in marriage and families (and all areas of life). In his study of family life in the United States, Talcott Parsons (1955) also viewed a division of labor as important. He saw the husband in an ideal nuclear family as fulfilling an instrumental role—meeting the family's economic needs, making important decisions, and providing leadership—and the wife as fulfilling an expressive role—running the household, caring for children, and meeting family members' emotional needs.

Using Durkheim's and Parsons's work as a basis for their model of the family, contemporary functionalists believe that a division of labor makes it possible for families to fulfill a number of functions that no other social institution in high-income nations can perform as efficiently and effectively:

1. *Regulating sexual behavior and reproduction.* Families are expected to regulate the sexual activity of their members and thus control reproduction so that it occurs within specific boundaries. Sexual regulation of family members by the family is supposed to protect the principle of legitimacy—the belief that all children should have a socially and legally recognized father (Malinowski, 1964).
2. *Socializing and educating children.* Parents and other relatives are responsible for teaching children the values and norms of their culture.
3. *Providing economic and psychological support.* Families are responsible for providing for their members' physical (food, shelter) and emotional needs.
4. *Providing social status.* Families confer social status on their members, including ascribed statuses such as race, ethnicity, nationality, class, and religious affiliation, although some of these statuses can change later in life.

Considering their view of the family, functionalists believe that problems in the family are a social crisis. The functional family provides both social order and economic stability by providing for the survival and development of children; the physical and emotional health of adults; and the care of the sick, injured, elderly, and disabled. The family is also the front line for reinforcing society's norms and values. Functionalists consider the family to be part of the solution to many problems faced by people in contemporary societies. In this view, dysfunctions in families are problems that threaten the well-being of individuals, groups, and nations.

Functionalists believe that changes in other social institutions, such as the economy, religion, education, law, medicine, and the government, contribute to family-related problems. For example, some functionalists think that changing the law to recognize no-fault divorce contributes to higher rates of divorce and dramatically increases the number of single-parent households, which do not provide children with the nurturance and guidance they get in a two-parent home (Popenoe, 1996).

Functionalist/Conservative Solutions

Based on a functionalist/conservative approach, a central way to reduce or eliminate family problems is through strengthening relationships and family ties, not reducing or diminishing them through practices such as cohabitation or divorce. Some functionalists and individuals applying a conservative political perspective suggest that marriage is protective, particularly for women because it provide the necessary stability and pledge of endurance that is required to maintain a healthy intimate relationship. Marriage, from this approach, should be seen as a lifelong commitment in which both partners meet their responsibilities to each other and seek to uphold the stability and protective nature of the family.

Conservative political solutions to reducing family problems include making divorces more difficult to obtain by revisiting state laws such as "no fault divorce" that make it relatively easy for either partner to dissolve a marriage. Similarly, parents should be held accountable through laws that protect children by making parents responsible for their financial, social, and moral well-being. So-called dead-beat-Dads who do not pay child support payments should be more harshly dealt with so that all parents realize that they must take care of the children they produce.

In sum, functionalist/conservative perspectives on family problems emphasize the importance of keeping families together and reducing the ills that are created by domestic violence, abortion, and divorce. According to some analysts using this approach, divorce contributes to other social problems such as poverty, depression and mental illness, and poor health. Therefore, it is important to reinforce families so that we may reduce or eliminate other social problems in society.

Conflict and Feminist Perspectives

Most conflict and feminist analysts believe that functionalist views on family problems are idealized and inadequate. Rather than operating harmoniously and for the benefit of all members, families are sources of social inequality and conflict over values, goals, and access to resources and power.

Conflict theorists who focus on class relations in capitalist economies compare family members to workers in a factory. Women are dominated by men in the home just as workers are dominated by managers and capitalists in factories (Engels, 1972). As wives and mothers, women contribute to capitalism by producing the next generation of workers and providing the existing labor force with food, clean clothes, and emotional support. Not only does women's work in the family benefit the capitalist class, it also reinforces women's subordination because the work is unpaid and often devalued. In support of this view, conflict theorists note that women who work solely in their own homes for many years usually do not have health insurance or a retirement plan apart from sharing in their husbands' employment benefits.

Many feminist theorists, however, think that male dominance and female subordination began long before capitalism and the private ownership of property arose as an economic system (Mann, 1994). They see women's subordination as being rooted in patriarchy, particularly in men's control over women's labor power. At the same time that women's labor in the home is directed by men, it is undervalued, which allows men to benefit from their status as the family breadwinner (Firestone, 1970; Goode, 1982). In one study, sociologist Jane Riblett Wilkie (1993) found that most men are reluctant to relinquish their status as family breadwinner. Although only 15 percent of the families in the United States are supported solely by a male breadwinner, many men continue to construct their ideal of masculinity on the basis of this role. It is acceptable for wives to enter the paid workforce if their role is simply to earn money; they should not, however, challenge the ideal roles of male breadwinner and female homemaker.

Conflict and Feminist Solutions

Both conflict and feminist theorists think that family problems derive from inequality—not just within the family, but in the political, social, and economic arenas of the larger society as well (Aulette, 1994). In fact, pervasive societal inequality leads to one of the most tragic family problems: wife battering. According to these theorists, wife battering and other forms of domestic violence might even be conscious strategies that men use to control women and perpetuate gender inequality (Kurz, 1989). Almost 30 percent of all female murder victims are killed by current or former husbands or boyfriends, whereas only 3 percent of all male murder victims are killed by current or former wives or girlfriends. In a study of women killed in New York City from 1990 through 1994, researchers found that one-third of the women killed by their husbands were married but not living with their spouses at the time of their deaths, a finding that suggests that these women were trying to leave the relationships at the time (Belluck, 1997).

In sum, family problems can be reduced or eliminated from a conflict or feminist perspective if we become aware of the true roots of oppression and do something about them. Laws must be strengthened not so much to maintain the strength of family ties but rather to aggressively pursue individuals who take advantage of or harm those with whom they share close domestic partnerships or marital ties. Problems associated with unplanned pregnancies and births among unmarried teenagers must be addressed head on, for example, by providing current and non-threatening information about the most effective means of contraception rather than trying to persuade hormone-driven teens that abstinence is the only way. Using this approach, people are empowered to make their own decisions about partnerships, marriage, family planning, and other issues that may produce problems in families and intimate relationships.

Symbolic Interactionist Perspectives

Some symbolic interactionists view the family communication process as integral to understanding the diverse roles that family members play; therefore these analysts examine how husbands, wives, and children act out their roles and react to the parts played by others. Although societies differ widely on the rules and norms that shape family and kin relationships, people are socialized to accept their society's form of the family as the acceptable norm. According to sociologists Peter Berger and Hansfried Kellner (1964), marital partners develop a shared reality through their interactions with each other. Although newlyweds bring separate identities to a marriage, over time they construct a shared reality as a couple. In the process, the partners redefine their past identities to be consistent with their new realities. Symbolic interactionists say that the process of developing a shared reality is continuous and occurs not only in the family, but also in any group in which the couple participates together. In cases of separation and divorce, the process is reversed: Couples may start with a shared reality but once again become individuals with separate realities in the process of uncoupling their relationship.

How do symbolic interactionists explain problems in a family? Some look at the subjective meanings and interpretations people give to their everyday lives. According to sociologist Jessie Bernard (1982), women and men experience marriage differently. While the husband might see his marriage very positively, the wife might feel less positive about her marriage. The reverse can also be true. Evidence for the different realities of marriage comes from research that shows that husbands and wives often give very different accounts of the same event (Safilios-Rothschild, 1969).

Still other symbolic interactionists view family problems in terms of partners' unrealistic expectations about love and marriage, which can lead to marital dissatisfaction and sometimes divorce. These analysts note that our culture emphasizes romantic love—a deep and vital emotion based on significant need satisfaction, caring for and acceptance of another person, and the development of an intimate relationship (Lamanna and Riedmann, 2009). Indeed, most couples in the United States get married because they are in love, but being a "nation of lovers" doesn't mean that men and women have the same ideas about what constitutes romantic love. According to sociologist Francesca Cancian (1990), women tend to express their feelings verbally, whereas men tend to express their love through nonverbal actions such as fixing dinner or doing household repairs. Women might not always interpret these actions as signs of love. One man complained (Rubin, 1976:146), "What does she want? Proof? She's got it, hasn't she? Would I be knocking myself out to get things for her—like to keep up this house—if I didn't love her? Why does a man do things like that if not because he loves his wife and kids? I swear, I can't figure what she wants." His wife replied, "It's not enough that he supports us and takes care of us. I appreciate that, but I want him to share things with me. I need for him to tell me his feelings."

Symbolic Interactionist Solutions

Families and intimate relationships have changed dramatically during the past one hundred years as other interaction patterns in society have also changed. Some analysts believe that we expect too much of the family and our intimate relationships with others: We expect people to make us happy rather than realizing that we too must work at happiness in the relationship. According to symbolic interactionists, problems in marriages may be reduced if people become aware of the different realities they have about marriage and family life. Through better communication with each other, family members can work toward making the home a more positive place in which to live.

Dealing with negative communication patterns must be coupled with reducing partners' unrealistic expectations about love and marriage. Many of these expectations are fostered by media representations of "ideal love," "dream weddings," and "the perfect life." However, if problems in families are to be reduced at the macrolevel of society, symbolic interactionists believe that we must start at the microlevel to bring about this change. Through modifying people's everyday perceptions about intimate relationships and family life, we can begin to change larger patterns of belief in society about what is realistic and what is not in dealing with the dilemmas that face families today, ranging from interpersonal communication problems and work dilemmas to economic hardships and lack of time for family life in a more constructive manner. However, one thing is certain: We must be willing to accept change, but many changes continue to occur in individual families and in the family as a social institution in the United States and other nations.

As we have seen in this chapter, because of these changes, some people believe that the family as we know it is doomed. Some analysts think that returning to traditional family values can save this important social institution and create a more stable society. Another point of view, however, comes from sociologist Lillian Rubin (1994), who suggests that clinging to a traditional image of families is hypocritical in light of our society's failure to support the family, whether through family allowances or decent public-sponsored child-care facilities (see Box 11.3).

Although many people demonstrate their faith in the future of the family as a social institution by their own choices, a macrolevel societal commitment to the family is also needed, as sociologist Demie Kurz (1995:232) states:

> As a society we should make a commitment to helping all families—traditional nuclear families, two-parent, two-earner families, and single-parent families—and to providing adequately for their members, particularly their children. To help families we must reduce female and

male poverty, making special efforts to end institutionalized discrimination against minorities. We must also promote equality between men and women in the family. This includes creating new conceptions of what it means to be a father and what it means to be a partner in a marriage and share family life and household work. It also means taking decisive steps to end violence toward women and children. Although the costs of creating humane and just social policies are high, the cost of failing to promote the welfare of family members is far higher.

Social Problems and Social Policy

Box 11.3

Paying for Child Care? "It Takes a Village..."

> Child care is the largest expense I have. It exceeds everything. It's higher than rent, higher than food. It's higher than everything we have.
>
> —*Elizabeth Pokorny (CBS News, 2004)*

Although Elizabeth Pokorny is an accountant and her husband is a mechanic, she is worried about the high cost of child care, and she has good reason to be. Quality day care costs the Pokorny family about $1,000 a month, which is more than they can realistically afford, even on their combined incomes. Paying for child care is an even greater burden for a family with just one paycheck.

Who should pay for child care? Some people believe that it should be the parents' responsibility—that parents should not have children whom they cannot afford to raise. Other people believe that paying for child care should be the responsibility of the government. However, the U.S. government does not compare favorably with other high-income nations in this regard. At most, our government provides 25 to 30 percent of the cost of child care for three- to six-year-olds. By contrast, in most other high-income nations, the government provides most of the child-care costs for children above two years of age—France provides 100 percent, for example, and Denmark, Finland, and Sweden provide about 80 percent of the cost (The Future of Children, 2001).

Shouldn't the "village" concept be at work here—doesn't society have a responsibility to the children who represent that nation's future? For our government to contribute more to the cost of child care, we as a people would need to view child care as a national concern that is critical to meeting two of our nation's priorities: helping families work and making sure that all children enter school ready to learn (Children's Defense Fund, 2003). But we don't view it as a national concern, especially compared with homeland security, war, and Social Security.

Some analysts believe that employers should be the ones to pay the cost of child care because they benefit the most from the hours that their workers spend on the job. From this standpoint, subsidizing child care for employees' children is a

(continued)

Why is high-quality, affordable day care a pressing problem in our society? How can we more effectively meet the needs of both children and their parents?

Box 11.3 (continued)

good investment: Without safe, reliable, affordable care for their children, employees find it more difficult to be productive workers, and the cost of quality child care is a concern not only for families in low-income brackets, but also for many middle-class families who are feeling the squeeze of high gas prices, food costs, and rent or home-mortgage payments. However, it appears that few employers are willing or able to provide real help with child care in the twenty-first century. Many employers complain of sharply rising health-care costs for their employees and believe that global competition is cutting into their earnings, thus making funding of child care for their employees a luxury that the employers simply cannot afford.

In other words, we have not as yet embraced the "village" concept. We have not, as a nation, accepted the fact that we all have a responsibility to the children who represent this nation's future.

Questions to Consider

1. Are financial constraints at various levels of government and in corporate America so great that these social institutions simply cannot afford to invest in the nation's future by putting more money into child care? Are we spending money for things that are less important than our children to the future of the nation?
2. Should we rethink our national priorities in regard to the government funding of child care if we truly believe that we want to "Leave No Child Behind"?
3. Even if we have no children of our own, do we have a responsibility to the nation's children? Or are children the sole responsibility of their families, regardless of the parents' ability to pay for proper care and education for the children? What do you think?

SUMMARY

■ *What is a family?*

A family is a relationship in which people live together with commitment, form an economic unit, care for any young, and consider the group critical to their identity. This definition modifies the traditional definition to account for today's greater diversity in living arrangements and relationships in families.

■ *Are U.S. families in decline?*

Not at all, say analysts who take a social change perspective. Families are becoming more complex and diverse, adapting to other changes in society. For one thing, marriage is no longer a cultural imperative; for another, many people reaffirm their belief in the institution through serial monogamy, a succession of marriages over a lifetime.

■ *What are the sociological perspectives on family-related problems?*

Functionalists believe that the family provides social order and economic stability; the family is the solution to many societal problems, and dysfunctional families threaten the well-being of individuals and the whole of society. Conflict and feminist theorists see the family as a problem in society, not a solution; they believe that the family is a major source of inequality in society. Symbolic interactionists view the family first in terms of socialization. Some speak of the shared reality of marriage; some view family problems in terms of the subjective meanings that people give to their everyday lives; and some cite partners' unrealistic expectations about love and marriage.

■ *What characterizes singlehood in the United States today?*

The proportion of the U.S. population that has never married has continued to grow since the 1960s. Some people remain single by choice, others by necessity; many working-class young people cannot afford to marry and set up a household.

■ *Why do young people postpone marriage today?*

Four factors are important: The changing job structure in the United States leads to economic uncertainty; more women are in the labor force; sexual relationships outside of marriage are more socially acceptable than before; and young people observing the rising divorce rate may be cautious about jumping into marriage.

■ *Does cohabitation usually lead to a successful marriage? What is a domestic partnership?*

According to one recent study, only about 50 percent of cohabiting couples marry, and evidence on whether those marriages succeed is mixed. Some studies show little or no effect; others show that partners who cohabit are more likely to divorce than partners who do not. A domestic partnership is a household partnership in which an unmarried couple lives together in a committed, sexually intimate relationship and is granted the same rights and benefits as married heterosexual couples.

■ *What does research show about dual-earner marriages?*

More than 50 percent of all marriages in the United States are dual-earner marriages, that is, marriages in which both spouses are in the labor force. Many women in these marriages do the domestic work at home after completing their workday jobs, though there seems to be a trend toward more egalitarian families.

■ *Is a two-parent family always preferable to a one-parent family?*

If the parents argue constantly, are alcoholics, or abuse the children, a supportive single-parent family would be preferable. However, growing up in a single-parent household poses serious risks to a child that are complicated by other factors, such as poverty, discrimination, unsafe neighborhoods, and high crime rates.

■ *Why is reproductive freedom such a controversial issue?*

Reproductive freedom implies the desire to have or not to have a child, and the roles that religious organizations, physicians, and the legal establishment should play in controlling a woman's fertility continue to be debated. Contraception, abortion, and the new reproductive technologies all raise personal and—when activists on either side get involved—societal issues.

■ *Are teen pregnancies increasing or declining?*

Teen pregnancies have decreased over the past thirty years, but the teenage birth rate is higher in the United States than in any other high-income nation. Recently, there has been an increase in births among unwed teenage mothers, particularly among African-American teens.

■ *Who gets divorced, and do most people remarry?*

Many factors affect who gets divorced (e.g., marrying during the teen years or having limited economic resources), and these factors are interrelated with class, race, and age, so it is very difficult to determine any kind of statistical likelihood of divorce. Most people do remarry, and divorce and remarriage leads to complex family relationships, such as blended families.

KEY TERMS

blended family, p. 239
cohabitation, p. 230
dual-earner marriages, p. 231
extended family, p. 226
family, p. 226
family of orientation, p. 237
family of procreation, p. 237
kinship, p. 226
monogamy, p. 227
nuclear family, p. 226
second shift, p. 231

QUESTIONS FOR CRITICAL THINKING

1. Sociologist Andrew Cherlin says that the family is a highly adaptable social institution, but we can minimize the costs of change in the family unit by modifying other social institutions of daily life, such as the economy and workplace. What specific suggestions can you give for modifications in these and other areas?
2. What do you think of Margaret Mead's proposal of a two-stage marriage? What problems might it forestall? Would it create any new ones?
3. What suggestions can you offer to help offset the potentially detrimental effects of single-parent households, especially when the parent is a woman who is employed full-time?
4. How do you think changing trends in American families will affect families and intimate relationships in the future?

Chapter 12

Problems in Education

THINKING SOCIOLOGICALLY

- What factors have contributed to your success in school? Have you also experienced problems that caused you to fall short of some of your objectives?
- Major sociological perspectives differ on problems related to education. What are the major causes, effects, and possible solutions for problems in today's schools according to each of these approaches?
- How do race, class, and gender affect people's educational opportunities?

When we were in junior high school, my friend Rich and I made a map of the school lunch tables according to popularity. This was easy to do, because kids only ate lunch with others of about the same popularity. We graded them from A to E. "A" tables were full of football players and cheerleaders and so on. "E" tables contained the kinds with mild cases of Down's syndrome, which in the language of the time we called "retards."

We sat at a "D" table, as low as you could get without looking physically different. We were not being especially candid to grade ourselves as D.... Everyone in the school knew exactly how popular everyone else was, including us.... I know a lot of people who were nerds in school, and they all tell the same story: there is a strong correlation between being smart and being a nerd, and an even stronger inverse correlation between being a nerd and being popular. Being smart seems to make you unpopular.... And that, I think, is the root of the problem. Nerds serve two masters. They want to be popular, certainly, but they want even more to be smart. And popularity is not something you can do in your spare time, not in the fiercely competitive environment of an American secondary [middle and high] school.... Merely understanding the situation [nerds are in] should make it less painful. Nerds aren't losers. They're just playing a different game, and a game much closer to the one played in the real world....

—Paul Graham (Ph.D. in Computer Science from Harvard, designer of ARC language, and creator of Yahoo Store) describes in his recent book,* Hackers & Painters: Big Ideas from the Computer Age *(2004), how he and other "nerds" have become successful as adults, an accomplishment that he does not attribute to American public schools.

Most of us have memories about our junior high and high school years that include where we thought we fit in to the student pecking order. Often this hierarchy or pecking order was symbolized by the people we ate with and where we sat at lunch because this was one brief period in the school day when we were allowed to make personal choices about our interactions with other people. Individuals like Paul Graham remember the school hierarchy as being based on athletic ability, personal appearance, and one's general popularity while others remember their cafeteria as having enclaves where students "chose" to sit with others from their own racial or ethnic category (see Tatum, 2003). At the individual (micro) level, some people realize that their school's social environment did not mesh with their personal interests and aptitudes while others describe their school years as being among the best in their lives. At the societal (macro) level, sociologists who study ***education*—the social institution responsible for transmitting knowledge, skills, and cultural values in a formally organized structure**—are particularly interested in factors that contribute to the success of schools and problems that cause them to fall short of their ideals and objectives. Today, we have a wide gap between the ideals of U.S. education and the realities of daily life in many schools. As a result, many business and political leaders, parents, teachers, students, and other concerned citizens identify a number of problems with U.S. education. In this chapter, we examine contemporary problems in education and assess how these problems are intertwined with other social problems in the United States and worldwide. We'll begin with an overview of sociological perspectives on problems in education.

SOCIOLOGICAL PERSPECTIVES ON EDUCATION

The way in which a sociologist studies education depends on the theoretical perspective he or she takes. Functionalists, for example, believe that schools should promote good citizenship and upward mobility and that problems in education are related to social disorganization, rapid social change, and the organizational structure of schools. Conflict theorists believe that schools perpetuate inequality and that problems in education are the result of bias based on race, class, and gender. Meanwhile, interactionists focus on microlevel problems in schools, such as how communication and teachers' expectations affect students' levels of achievement and dropout rates.

Functionalist Perspectives

Functionalists believe that education is one of the most important social institutions because it contributes to the smooth functioning of society and provides individuals with opportunities for personal fulfillment and upward social mobility. According to functionalists, when problems occur, they can usually be traced to the failure of educational institutions—schools, colleges, universities—to fulfill one of their manifest functions. ***Manifest functions* are open, stated, and intended goals or consequences of activities within an organization or institution.** Although the most obvious manifest function of education is the teaching of academic subjects (reading, writing, mathematics, science, and history), education has at least five major manifest functions in society:

Socialization. From kindergarten through college, schools teach students the student role, specific academic subjects, and political socialization. In kindergarten, children learn the appropriate attitudes and behavior for the student role (Ballantine and Hammack, 2009). In primary and secondary schools, students are taught specific subject matter that is appropriate to their age, skill level, and previous educational experience. At the college level, students expand their knowledge and seek out new areas of study. Throughout, students learn the democratic process.

Transmission of culture. Schools transmit cultural norms and values to each new generation and play a major role in assimilation, the process whereby recent immigrants learn dominant cultural values, attitudes, and behavior so that they can be productive members of society.

Social control. Although controversy exists over whose values should be taught, schools are responsible for teaching values such as discipline, respect, obedience, punctuality, and perseverance. Schools teach conformity by encouraging young people to be good students, conscientious future workers, and law-abiding citizens.

Social placement. Schools are responsible for identifying the most qualified people to fill available positions in society. Students are often channeled into programs on the basis of their individual ability and academic achievement. Graduates receive the appropriate credentials for entering the paid labor force

Change and innovation. Schools are a source of change and innovation. To meet the needs of student populations at particular times, new programs—such as AIDS education, computer education, and multicultural studies—are created. College and university faculty members are expected to conduct research and publish new knowledge that benefits the overall society. A major goal of change and innovation in education is to reduce social problems.

In addition to these manifest functions, education fulfills a number of ***latent functions*—hidden, unstated, and sometimes unintended consequences of activities in an organization or institution.** Consider, for example, these latent functions of education: Compulsory school attendance keeps children and teenagers off the streets (and, by implication, out of trouble) and out of the full-time job market for a number of years (controlling the flow of workers). High schools and colleges serve as matchmaking institutions where people often meet future marriage partners. By bringing people of similar ages, racial and ethnic groups, and social class backgrounds together, schools establish social networks.

Functionalists acknowledge many dysfunctions in education, but one seems overriding today: Our public schools are not adequately preparing students for jobs and global competition. In comparative rankings of students across countries on standardized reading, mathematics, and science tests, U.S. students are lagging. For example, in the 2003 Trends in International Mathematics and Science Study, a comprehensive study of science and math achievement by students in forty-five countries, U.S. students barely ranked in the top

10 nations in science and the top 15 nations in math. Countries that outperformed the United States in math included Singapore, where all students are tracked individually and expected to perform, and Japan, where teachers are generally better trained and prepared than their U.S. counterparts. However, the Japanese recently have become concerned about a decline in students' scores on standardized math and reading tests, a decline that has affected how many parents view public schools and children's needs for additional tutoring (see Box 12.1). Despite these concerns, Japan remains well ahead of the United States with regard to students' scores on math, reading, and science exams. When the results of the latest study are released late in 2008, it will be interesting to see if these scores have changed significantly across various nations.

Social Problems in Global Perspective

Box 12.1

Cramming for Success in Japan and South Korea

> It's no secret that the Japanese have long been obsessed with education. Students flock to shrines to write prayers on wooden tablets asking for good grades. The lure of top schools is so strong that even kindergartners sometimes study for months before entrance exams, and students who fail college entrance tests are known to spend a year or two polishing their skills for another shot. For years that obsession has paid off in global leadership in innovation and design for Japan. These days, though, the country is losing its edge.
>
> *—Business journalists Ian Rowley and Hiroko Tashiro (2005) describe the emphasis placed on education in Japan as a prelude to explaining why cram schools have become a billion-dollar industry.*

> The students here were forsaking all the pleasures of teenage life. No cell phones allowed, no fashion magazines, no television, no Internet. No dating, no concerts, no earrings, no manicures—no acting their age. All these are mere distractions from an overriding goal... to clear the fearsome hurdle that can decide their future—the national college entrance examination.
>
> *—Journalist Choe Sang-Hun (2008) of the* New York Times *explains the "boot camp" atmosphere of a cram school in Yongin, South Korea, to show how much importance parents and students place on getting high marks on the exam that determines whether students will be admitted into a top-notch university.*

Cram schools or *juku* have been around for many years in nations such as Japan and South Korea; however, they are growing in popularity as the need to excel on standardized entrance examinations for college has become increasingly important to many families. What are cram schools or *juku*? *Juku,* or cram schools, are afternoon, evening, and weekend tutoring schools where students receive additional instruction in academic subjects, while specifically focusing on how to score high on standardized exams. At Jongro Yongin Campus, students are miles away from any kind of transportation and they do nothing but cram from 6:30 A.M. to past midnight, seven days a week. To attend cram school or *juku,* major family commitments are required: Money from parents and time from young people. In Japan, for example, Atsuki Yamamoto's parents pay $9,200 a year for him to attend Nichinoken four evenings a week from 5 P.M. to 9 P.M. and take exams every Sunday to prepare for entrance exams at elite junior high schools. The Yamamotos hope that, if Atsuki is admitted to an elite private junior high school, he will later be accepted at a top high school and, eventually, a prestigious university (Rowley and Tashiro, 2005). In South Korea, Park Hong-ki spends $1,936 a month for his son's tuition at Jongro and admits that, "It's a big financial burden for me" (Sang-Hun, 2008). The Yamamotos in Japan and the Hong-kis in South Korea are not alone in their hopes and aspirations for their children, as evidenced by the popularity of cram schools in these Southeast Asian nations.

In Japan and South Korea, education is everything to many people: The job you get depends on the university you attended, which depends on the high school you went to, which in turn depends on your elementary school, which, finally, depends on where you went to preschool. Thus, the sooner a child begins cramming, the better: Three- and four-year-olds prepare for preschool entrance exams by sitting at little desks in a ninety-minute class designed to improve performance on IQ tests (WuDunn, 1996). Even at this young age, the competition to attend the better schools is so strong that children may see each other as rivals rather than as classmates. According to one Japanese headmaster, "Preparation for entrance exams makes students turn everyone into rivals, so they come to find pleasure in another's failure.... What is most important for human society

(continued)

Box 12.1 (continued)

[compassion] is not nurtured in Japan" (WuDunn, 1996). In South Korea, many top government posts are filled with individuals who graduated from Korea University, considered to be one of the nation's most prestigious universities.

Recently, cram schools in Japan have increased in popularity not only with parents but also with business investors. Of the more than 50,000 *juku* in Japan, many are owned by national corporations that advertise extensively and earn about ten billion dollars in profits each year. According to business journalists, "Japan's new insecurity over its age-old obsession [education], it seems, is good for business" (Rowley and Tashiro, 2005). Perhaps the same could also be said for the growing cram school business in South Korea.

Questions to Consider

1. How does the emphasis on high test scores and educational achievement in Japan and South Korea compare with the major educational concerns in U.S. education?
2. Do children in nations such as Japan and South Korea pay too high a price for educational achievement? Why or why not?
3. What might U.S. students gain from intensive educational programs such as those found in a cram school? What problems might these students encounter in such a high-pressure environment?

Functionalist and conservative efforts to improve education were introduced during the first term of the Bush Administration. To reform education, President George W. Bush signed into law the No Child Left Behind Act of 2001. By changing the federal government's role in kindergarten through twelfth grade and by asking schools to be accountable for students' learning, proponents of this law hope to improve education for the nation's children. Several critical steps are set forth to produce a more "accountable" education system:

- States will create a set of standards—beginning with math and reading—for what all children should know at the end of each grade in school; other standards will be developed over a period of time.
- States must test every student's progress toward meeting those standards.
- States, individual school districts, and each school will be expected to make yearly progress toward meeting the standards.
- School districts must report results regarding the progress of individual schools toward meeting these standards.
- Schools and districts that do not make adequate progress will be held accountable and could lose funding and pupils; in some cases, parents can move their children from low-performing schools to schools that are meeting the standards.

It is unclear how effective some of these changes have been in bringing about higher-quality education for students and producing better graduation rates across class and racial/ethnic categories as discussed later in the chapter.

Conflict Perspectives

Sociologists using a conflict framework for analyzing problems in education believe that schools—which are supposed to reduce social inequalities in society—actually perpetuate inequalities based on class, race, and gender (Apple, 1982). In fact, conflict theorists such as Pierre Bourdieu argue that education *reproduces* existing class relationships (see Bourdieu and Passeron, 1990). According to Bourdieu, students have differing amounts of *cultural capital* that they learn at home and bring with them to the classroom (see Chapter 2). Children from middle- and upper-income homes have considerable cultural capital because their parents have taught them about books, art, music, and other forms of culture. According to Bourdieu, children from low-income and poverty-level families have not had the same opportunities to acquire cultural capital. Some social analysts believe that it is students' cultural capital, rather than their "natural" intelligence or aptitude, that is measured on the standardized tests used for tracking. Thus test results unfairly limit some students' academic choices and career opportunities (Oakes, 1985).

Other sociologists using the conflict framework focus on problems associated with the hidden curriculum, a term coined by sociologist John C. Holt (1964) in his study of why children fail. The ***hidden curriculum*** **refers to how certain cultural values and attitudes, such as conformity and obedience to authority, are transmitted through implied demands in the everyday rules and routines of schools** (Snyder, 1971). These conflict theorists suggest that elites use a hidden curriculum that teaches students to be obedient and patriotic—values that uphold the status quo in society and turn students into compliant workers—to manipulate the masses and maintain their power in society (Bowles and Gintis, 1976).

Although students from all social classes experience the hidden curriculum to some degree, working-class and poverty-level students are the most adversely affected (Ballantine and Hammack, 2009). When middle-class teachers teach students from lower-class backgrounds, for example, the classrooms are very structured, and the teachers have low expectations about the students' academic achievement (Alexander et al., 1987). In one study of five elementary schools with students from different class backgrounds, researchers found significant differences in how knowledge was transmitted despite similar curricula (Anyon, 1980). Schools for working-class students emphasize procedures and rote memorization without much decision making, choice, or explanation of why something is done a particular way. In contrast, schools for middle-class students stress the processes that are involved in getting the right answer. Elite schools develop students' analytical powers and critical-thinking skills, teaching them how to apply abstract principles to problem solving. These schools also emphasize creative activities so that students can express their own ideas and apply them to different areas of study. Compare the following comments from students in high-track and low-track classes who were asked what they learned in a particular class (Oakes, 1985:86–89):

> "I want to be a lawyer and debate has taught me to dig for answers and get involved. I can express myself." (High-Track English).
>
> "To understand concepts and ideas and experiment with them. Also to work independently." (High-Track Science).
>
> "To behave in class." (Low-Track English).
>
> "To be a better listener in class." (Low-Track English).
>
> "I have learned that I should do my questions for the book when he asks me to." (Low-Track Science).

As these comments show, the hidden curriculum teaches working-class and poverty-level students that they are expected to arrive on time, follow bureaucratic rules, take orders from others, and experience high levels of boredom without complaining (Ballantine and Hammack, 2009). The limitations on what and how these students are taught mean that many of them do not get any higher education and therefore never receive the credentials to enter high-paying professions (Bowles and Gintis, 1976). Our society emphasizes *credentialism*—a process of social selection that gives class advantage and social status to people who possess academic qualifications (Collins, 1979). Credentialism is closely related to *meritocracy*—a social system in which status is assumed to be acquired through individual ability and effort (Young, 1994). People who acquire the appropriate credentials for a job are assumed to have gained the position through what they know, not who they are or who they know. According to conflict theorists, however, the hidden curriculum determines in advance that credentials will stay in the hands of the elites, so the United States is not a meritocracy even if it calls itself one.

Symbolic Interactionist Perspectives

Whereas functionalists examine the relationship between the functions of education and problems in schools and conflict theorists focus on how education perpetuates inequality, symbolic interactionists study classroom dynamics and how practices such as labeling affect students' self-concept and aspirations.

Symbolic interactionists believe that education is an integral part of the socialization process. Through the formal structure of schools and interpersonal relationships with peers and teachers, students develop a concept of self that lasts long beyond their schooling. Overall, social interactions in school can be either positive or negative. When students learn, develop, and function effectively, their experience is positive. For many students, however, the school environment and peer group interactions leave them discouraged and unhappy. When students who might do better with some assistance from teachers and peers are instead labeled "losers," they might come to view themselves as losers and thus set the stage for *self-fulfilling* prophecies. As was noted in Chapter 1, a self-fulfilling prophecy occurs when an unsubstantiated belief or prediction results in behavior that makes the original false belief come true.

Standardized tests can also lead to labeling, self-fulfilling prophecies, and low self-esteem. In fact, say symbolic interactionists, standardized tests such as IQ (intelligence quotient) tests particularly disadvantage racial, ethnic, and language minorities in the United States (see Haney, 1993). IQ testing first became an issue in the United States in the early 1900s when immigrants from countries such as Italy, Poland, and Russia typically scored lower than immigrants from Northern Europe did. As a result, teachers did not expect them to do as well as children from families with Northern European backgrounds and therefore did not encourage them or help them overcome educational obstacles

(Feagin, Baker, and Feagin, 2006). In time, these ethnic groups became stigmatized as less intelligent.

Today, the debate over intelligence continues, but the focus has shifted to African Americans. In their highly controversial book *The Bell Curve: Intelligence and Class Structure in American Life,* Richard J. Herrnstein and Charles Murray (1994) argue that intelligence is genetically inherited and people cannot be "smarter" than they are born to be, regardless of their environment or education. According to Herrnstein and Murray, certain racial-ethnic groups differ in average IQ and are likely to differ in "intelligence genes" as well. To bolster their arguments, Herrnstein and Murray point out that on average, people living in Asia score higher on IQ tests than white Americans and that African Americans score 15 points lower on average than white Americans.

Many scholars have refuted Herrnstein and Murray's conclusions, but the idea of inherited mental inferiority tends to take on a life of its own when there are people who want to believe that such differences exist (Duster, 1995; Hauser, 1995; Taylor, 1995). Thus on the basis of IQ testing and psychological evaluations, many minority students, particularly boys, are designated *learning disabled* and placed in special education programs. African Americans and Hispanics are overrepresented in special education programs, based on their percentage in the overall U.S. population: Although white (non-Hispanic) students between the ages of 6 through 21 represent nearly 62 percent of all students served by special education programs, African-American (non-Hispanic) students account for 21 percent of all students while Hispanic students make up about 15 percent (U.S. Department of Education, 2008). Earlier studies in California and Texas show that many African-American and Mexican-American children are placed in special education classes on the basis of IQ scores and other tests when their real problems are cultural influences and lack of English language skills and understanding (Brooks and South, 1996). Some analysts believe that a relatively large number of students are initially placed in special education classes because they do not know how to read or because they show evidence of having one or more behavioral problems.

According to symbolic interactionists, labels such as *learning-disabled* stigmatize students, *marginalize* them—put them at the lower or outer limits of a group—in their interactions with parents, teachers, and other students, and lead to self-fulfilling prophecies (Carrier, 1986; Coles, 1987). Possibly as a result as many as 70 percent of special education students may either drop out of school or are expelled (U. S. Department of Education, 2008).

Labeling students *gifted and talented* might also result in self-fulfilling prophecies. Students who are identified as having above-average intellectual ability, academic aptitude, creative or productive thinking, or leadership skills might achieve at a higher level because of the label. However, this is not always the case. Afraid that their academic achievement will make them unpopular, high-achieving students can become victims of *anti-intellectualism*—hostility toward people who are assumed to have great mental ability or toward subject matter that is thought to require significant intellectual ability or knowledge. For many years, white students have been overrepresented in gifted-and-talented programs while students of color are underrepresented (National Center for Educational Statistics, 2006). As one social scientist stated, if students are not given equal opportunities for gifted education, it is "a mythology that schools represent the great equalizing force in society . . . [and] . . . every child has an equal chance at success and achievement" (Sapon-Shevin, 1993:43–44).

PROBLEMS IN U.S. EDUCATION

Although we have already identified a variety of problems in education, other issues must be addressed in planning for the future of this country. These issues include the problem of illiteracy; the impact of high rates of immigration on educational systems; race, class, and gender inequalities in educational opportunities; and growing concerns about violence in schools.

What Can Be Done about Illiteracy?

In her memoir, *Life Is Not a Fairy Tale,* Fantasia Barrino, one of the *American Idol* winners, explained that she is functionally illiterate and that she had to fake her way through portions of the televised talent show that required her to read lines. The story of her life was dictated to a freelance writer, but she committed herself to learning how to read because she wants to be able to read to her daughter. Moreover, Fantasia Barrino's situation is not an isolated case. Today, one in four U.S. adults is ***functionally illiterate*—unable to read and/or write at the skill level necessary for carrying out everyday tasks.** Illiteracy is much higher for minority-group members than for U.S.-born whites; 16 percent of white adults are illiterate, compared to 44 percent of adult African Americans and 56 percent of adult Latinos/as. This may be partly due to larger, underlying social problems, such as poverty, which contribute to

Illiteracy is a social problem that we may be able to reduce with adequate time and resources. Various organizations seek to reduce illiteracy by offering classes to help children and adults learn how to read and write.

deep and widespread social inequality among minority-group members and their children.

Estimates range from 40–44 million people in the U.S. adult population who have been identified as functionally illiterate. Many people who are functionally illiterate have graduated from high school but still cannot read at the sixth-grade level (Kaplan, 1993).

Some social analysts believe that illiteracy will not be as big a problem in the future because new technologies will make reading and writing as we know it obsolete. These analysts note that the Information Age increasingly depends on communication by computers, not on basic reading and math computation skills. Still other educators and community leaders believe that illiteracy can be overcome through televised instruction in basic skills and courses on the Internet. However, not all social analysts believe that technology is the answer: Knowing how to read the printed word remains the access route to every other form of intellectual information (Kozol, 1986). People need basic literacy skills before they can benefit from computers and other information technologies. Business and industry are now playing a role in solving the problem; it is estimated that employers spend over $60 billion annually to educate functionally illiterate workers in the effort to increase their skill levels and productivity.

Some critics say that the illiteracy problem is largely an immigration problem. Recent immigrants to this country continue to speak their own languages rather than learn English. However, high rates of illiteracy should not necessarily be blamed on U.S. immigration policies because many persons who have lived in this country since birth have this problem (Kozol, 1986).

Immigration and Increasing Diversity in Schools

Debates over the role of schools in educating immigrants for life in the United States are not new. In fact, high rates of immigration—along with the rapid growth of industrial capitalism and the factory system during the Industrial Revolution—brought about the free public school movement in the second half of the nineteenth century. Many immigrants arriving in U.S. cities during this time spoke no English and could neither read nor write. Because of the belief that democracy requires an educated citizenry, schools were charged with the responsibility of "Americanizing" immigrants and their children. Workers needed basic reading, writing, and arithmetic skills to get jobs in factories and offices. Initially, an eighth-grade education was considered sufficient for many jobs, but soon a high school diploma became a prerequisite for most jobs above the level of the manual laborer. Schooling during this era was designed primarily to give people the means to become self-supporting. Educational systems were supposed to turn out workers who had the knowledge and skills needed to enter the labor market and produce profits for managers and owners.

In the second half of the twentieth century, this country again experienced high rates of immigration from many nations around the world, and many of the newcomers were school-age children (Portes and MacLeod, 1996). In the twenty-first century, some recent groups of immigrants are well educated, but most have limited formal education and few job skills. Today, about 20 percent of U.S. residents age five and older speak a language other than English at home (see Table 12.1 on page 256). Because we use language to communicate with others, develop a sense of personal identity, and acquire knowledge and skills necessary for survival, schools must cope with language differences among students.

Although most recent immigrants rely on public schools to educate their children, some supplement school efforts with additional educational opportunities. For example, some Asian- and Pacific-American parents have established weekend cram schools, which are similar to the *juku* in Japan, *buxiban* in China, and *hagwon* in Korea. Students spend a full day on subjects such as math and English and get specialized help in building study skills and learning test-taking strategies. Their parents are willing to sacrifice so that the children will not experience language and cultural barriers that limit opportunities (Dunn, 1995).

TABLE 12.1 Principal Languages Spoken at Home (United States)

Language Used at Home	Persons Five Years Old and Over Who Speak It
English only	216,176,000
Spanish	32,184,000
Chinese	2,300,000
French	1,383,000
Tagalog	1,142,000
Vietnamese	1,120,000
German	1,377,000
Korean	812,000
Russian	802,000
Italian	984,000
Arabic	662,000
Portuguese	608,000
Polish	687,000
French Creole	462,000
Gujarathi	303,000
Hindi	458,000
Japanese	549,000
Persian	326,000
Greek	462,000
Urdu	324,000
Serbo/Croation	271,000
Armenian	207,000
Hebrew	203,000
Mon-Khmer (Cambodian)	190,000
Navaho	173,000
Yiddish	189,000
[Other Native North American languages]	137,000

Source: U.S. Census Bureau, 2008.

How best to educate children of recent immigrants with lower levels of education and income is a pressing problem in states that have high levels of immigration, such as California, Texas, Illinois, and New York. Some school districts establish transitional programs for newcomers, six months to four years of classes taught in English and in the student's native language. Some schools offer bilingual education in as many as ten languages in major subjects such as math, science, and social studies. Preliminary studies of newcomer programs show that many children not only learn English and about U.S. culture but also get help in overcoming traumatic experiences and educational deficits suffered in their country of origin.

Although some school officials believe that newcomer programs are the most efficient way to bring together students who speak the same language and teachers who can communicate with them, others consider them a form of segregation because recent immigrants are isolated from the mainstream. Segregation is also still a problem for many students who were born in the United States.

Educational Opportunities and Race, Class, and Gender

Most research on access to educational opportunities for minority students has focused on how racially segregated schools affect student performance and self-esteem. Indeed, some fifty years after the 1954 Supreme Court ruling in *Brown v. The Board of Education of*

Urban high schools face many challenges today. One pressing concern is how to provide the best educational opportunities for a highly diverse group of students.

Topeka, Kansas, which stated that "separate but equal" schools are unconstitutional because they are inherently unequal, racial segregation appears to be increasing in education rather than decreasing (Brooks and South, 1996). Progress in bringing about racial *desegregation* (the abolition of legally sanctioned racial-ethnic segregation) and *integration,* which, for schools, involves taking specific action to change the racial or class composition of the student body, has been extremely slow for African Americans because segregated schools mirror race- and class-based residential segregation. Today, students of color make up the vast majority of the student body in some urban school districts, whereas middle- and upper-class white students make up the majority of the student body in private urban schools or suburban public schools. According to sociologists, schools in which racial and ethnic minorities are in the majority typically have high teacher-student ratios (more students per teacher), inexperienced teachers who are sometimes less qualified, lower expectations of students, and high dropout rates (Feagin, Baker, and Feagin, 2006).

What are the future educational prospects for African Americans, Latinas/os, and other students of color? On the one hand, although racial segregation is still prevalent in some areas of the country, the education gap appears to be narrowing between whites and African Americans; young African Americans are earning high school diplomas at about the same rate as their white counterparts (Holmes, 1996b). On the other hand, the President's Advisory Commission on Educational Excellence for Hispanic Americans concluded that segregation of Latina/o students in poorly funded schools contributes to Latino/a students' low educational attainments (Shannon, 1996). Latino/a students are more likely than white (Anglo) students to attend schools in which racial and ethnic minorities make up the majority of the student body, and there are few Latino/a teachers to serve as role models and mentors. Although Latina/o youth accounted for almost one fifth (20 percent) of the public school students in 2006, fewer than 10 percent of public school teachers were Latinos/as (U.S. Department of Education, 2008). In fact, the faculty of most public schools usually does not reflect the racial-ethnic or gender composition of the student body. Both Latinas/os and African Americans are underrepresented among teachers, administrators, and school board members in most systems. More than 80 percent of public school teachers are white (roughly the same proportion as twenty years ago), and nearly 75 percent are women.

Moreover, fewer Latina/o children than white (Anglo) children have had an opportunity to attend preschool programs such as Head Start. The average Latino/a child's school-readiness skills—such as identifying colors and shapes—are less well developed than those of the average white (Anglo) child. As children move through high school and college, the dropout rate for Latinas/os between eighteen and twenty-four years of age grows dramatically: In 2005, it was 32 percent (U.S. Census Bureau, 2008). The percentage of Latinos/as who have not finished high school has been higher than the percentage of whites (Anglos) and African Americans over the past three decades (see Figure 12.1 on page 258).

One explanation for the high dropout rate comes from a comprehensive study of Latino/a high school graduates in Texas. Researchers found that high dropout rates were more closely linked to practices in schools and attitudes within the community than to individual or family problems (Romo and Falbo, 1996). Across lines of race and ethnicity, students from poor families are three to four times more likely to become school dropouts than are students from affluent families.

Another explanation for high dropout rates, particularly among students of color, is that students may be "pushed out" of school because low-achieving students are viewed as bringing down standardized test scores, which are used to evaluate not only students but also teachers and administrators. Media reports may further contribute to the emphasis placed on standardized tests as a means of "passing" or "failing" students, teachers, and schools (see Box 12.2 on page 259).

Even racially integrated schools often re-create segregation in the classroom when tracking or ability grouping is used (Mickelson and Smith, 1995). ***Tracking* is the practice of assigning students to specific courses and educational programs on the basis of their test scores, previous grades, or both.** Lower-level courses and special education classes are disproportionately filled with children of color, while gifted-and-talented programs and honors courses are more likely to be filled with white and Asian- and Pacific-American students (McLarin, 1994). Moreover, even though roughly as many African Americans as whites are earning high school diplomas today, African-American and white students do not achieve at the same level, and achievement differences increase with every year of schooling. The achievement gap between African-American and white first-graders is less than the gap between white and African-American

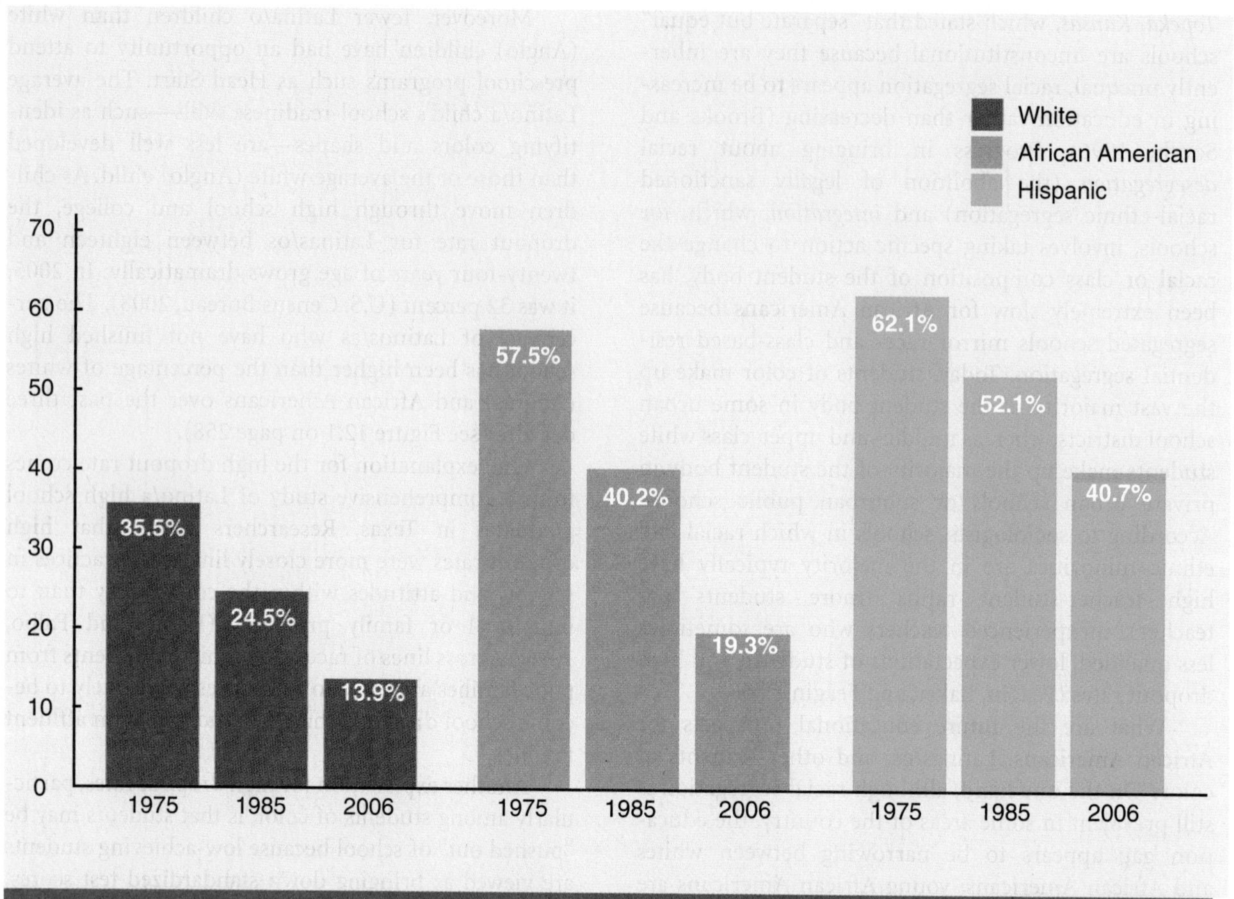

■ *Figure 12.1* ***Percentage of persons not completing high school by race and Hispanic origin, 1975, 1985, and 2006***

Source: U.S. Census Bureau, 2008.

twelfth-graders. According to some researchers, schools typically reinforce—rather than reduce—the effects of race and class inequalities in society (Mickelson and Smith, 1995).

How does gender bias in schools negatively affect female students? Contemporary gender bias has its roots in historical assumptions about the divergent roles of women and men in society, including the belief that males should be educated for the public sphere (i.e., work and civic involvement) and females for the private sphere (i.e., home and childrearing). An extensive national survey on gender and self-esteem by the American Association of University Women (1992) found that young women and young men are treated differently in our educational system. First, teachers pay less attention to girls than to boys. In observing thirty physical science and chemistry classes, researchers found that teachers encouraged boys to talk in class and to volunteer for demonstrations and experiments more often than girls; girls were more likely to be observers and to be self-conscious and quiet (Jones and Wheatley, 1990). Many teachers also encourage boys to be problem solvers by asking them more complicated questions than they ask girls. In addition, reading materials may use language in biased ways (e.g., using masculine pronouns throughout), or they may stereotype women or ignore them. Finally, because boys tend to be more boisterous than girls, classroom activities are geared to holding boys' interest. Thus through teacher reactions and classroom reading materials, female students come to learn that they are less

Social Problems in the Media

Box 12.2

Report Card Framing: Does Education Get an "A" or an "F"?

> The news from American high schools is not good. The most recent test results from the National Assessment of Educational Progress, commonly known as the national report card, finds that American 12th graders are actually performing worse in reading than 12th graders did in 1992, when a comparable exam was given. In addition, 12th-grade performance in reading has been distressingly flat since 2002, even though the states were supposed to be improving the quality of teaching to comply with the No Child Left Behind education act.
>
> —*Editorial,* New York Times *(February 27, 2007)*

Media reports such as this one showing the latest results of a national exam given to students in U.S. schools are routinely found in newspapers, on Internet websites, and on television news broadcasts. In most cases, bad test scores receive more attention than good scores in media accounts. In fact, the media often use test scores to "grade" students and schools in much the same way that educators use report cards to inform students and their parents about how students are doing in school.

Some sociologists who study the media use the terminology *report card framing* to refer to this type of coverage. As previously discussed, media framing refers to the manner in which reporters and other journalists organize information before they present it to an audience. For reporters on the "education beat," for example, part of that organization involves determining how to report on nationwide student testing and what slant to give the story regarding the positive or negative evaluation of those grades. As a result, *report card framing* refers to how the media give students, teachers, and schools "passing" or "failing" grades based on the results of standardized test scores. This type of framing assumes that such scores are a good measure of the academic achievements of students and the quality of teachers and schools. This framing does not take into account students' diverse family backgrounds in regard to class, race/ethnicity, nationality, region, and urban, suburban, or rural residential location. It also does not consider whether standardized exams may be biased against students who come from backgrounds that are different from those who prepare the questions on standardized exams. Similarly, report card framing assumes that tests are the best way to determine how well teachers teach and how well the educational system in our country functions.

Questions to Consider

1. Should journalists and other members of the media expand their reporting on education to cover a wider array of issues than just the results of standardized examinations?
2. To what extent do standardized test scores capture what is really happening in the classroom? Do they show what is most important in the learning process for students?
3. What other issues do you believe might be equally, or more, important for the media to cover in regard to schools and problems in education today?

important than male students. Over time, differential treatment undermines females' self-esteem and discourages them from taking courses—such as mathematics and science—that are dominated by male teachers and students (Raffalli, 1994). Some analysts believe that schools are "gender-sorting machines" that steer girls and young women into outdated female roles and contribute to permanently low self-esteem (Schrof, 1993). At best, low self-esteem is associated with reduced expectations for the future and less self-confidence; at worst, it is associated with depression and sometimes even attempted suicide (American Association of University Women, 1992; Orenstein, 1994).

In recent years, some improvements have occurred in girls and young women's educational opportunities. More females are now enrolled in advanced placement and honors courses and in academic areas, such as math and science, which previously have been the province of boys and young men. Schools increasingly have been encouraged to foster the development of all students regardless of their

To overcome gender bias in schools, some parents are now enrolling their children in same-sex schools such as this New York City public school that enrolls only girls.

gender, race, or class; however, many factors make it difficult for this already hard-pressed social institution to meet the needs and demands of highly diverse student populations.

School Violence

About 16 students are murdered at U.S. schools each year, but fortunately, this number is lower late in the first decade of the twenty-first century than it was in the 1990s (Stobbe, 2008). In collecting data on school violence, the Centers for Disease Control and Prevention include killings that occur at elementary, middle, or high schools, on school-sponsored trips, or while students are on their way to or from school. Between 1999 and 2006, the total number of such deaths was 116 throughout the nation. Even though the numbers and rates are somewhat lower than in the past, violence and the threat of violence remain a serious problem in many schools. Today, some school buildings look like fortresses or prisons with high fences, bright spotlights at night, and armed security guards. Many schools have installed metal detectors at entrances, and some search students for weapons, drugs, and other contraband as they enter. Consider this journalist's description of how one school district is attempting to reduce violence (Applebome, 1995a:A1):

> The sprawling new brick building next to the Dallas County Probation Department has 37 surveillance cameras, six metal detectors, five full-time police officers and a security-conscious configuration based on the principles of crime prevention through environmental design. It is not the Big House. It is a schoolhouse: Dallas's $41 million state-of-the-art Townview Magnet Center.

Most educational analysts acknowledge that technology alone will not rid schools of violence and crime. Organizations such as the American Federation of Teachers have called for enhancing safety in schools by requiring higher student standards of conduct and achievement and giving teachers and administrators the authority to remove disruptive students. Some school districts now require students to wear uniforms in an effort to reduce violence and crime because it was assumed that, if all students are required to dress alike, young people are less likely to be killed for their sneakers, jewelry, or designer clothes (Mathis, 1996).

Teachers, too, may be the victims of violence on school premises. One study found that about 5,000

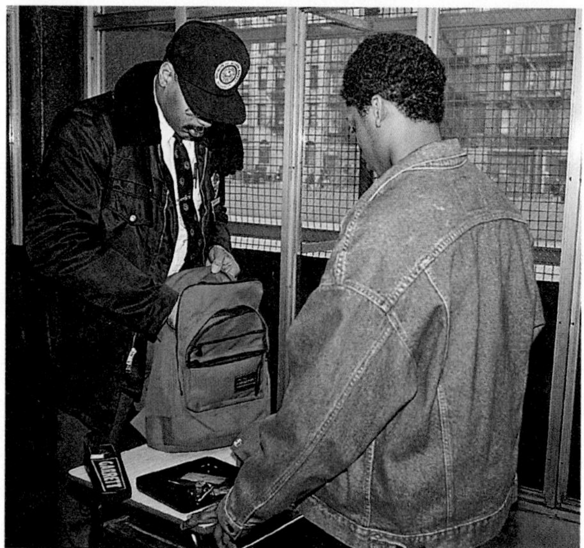

Prison, airport, or school? Security guards and metal detectors have become an increasingly visible scene in many social institutions, including schools throughout the United States. Do such measures deter school violence? Why or why not?

teachers are attacked or assaulted at schools each month; about 1,000 of the victims require medical attention (Applebome, 1995a). According to a spokesperson for one teacher's organization, "In the long run, we will not solve the problems of the schools by turning them into fortresses. But for the short term, we're going to have to cope with problems that are not immediately going away" (Applebome, 1995a:B8). Providing safety at school for students and teachers alike is only one crisis facing school districts that are burdened with shrinking budgets, decaying buildings, and heightened demands for services.

PROBLEMS IN SCHOOL FINANCING

Because financing affects all other aspects of schooling, perhaps it is the biggest problem in education today. Although many people believe that the federal government makes significant contributions to public education, most funds come from state legislative appropriations and local property taxes. State and local governments contribute less than 45 percent each toward total education expenses, and the federal government pays the remaining 6 percent, largely for special programs for students who are disadvantaged (e.g., Head Start) or have disabilities. In recent years, however, major industries in city centers have either gone out of business or relocated, resulting in the erosion of property tax revenues. In some cities and regions, this problem has been made worse by the move of middle- and upper-income families to suburban areas that have their own property tax. Without the funds from property taxes, schools in the city centers cannot purchase the latest textbooks and computer technology that today's students need. In other cities and regions, more affluent families are remaining in, or returning to, city centers to reside in luxury apartments, lofts, and other residences for the upper classes. Cities with revitalized downtown and uptown areas may have less trouble paying for the education of school-aged children; however, the prevailing belief in most urban school districts is that these organizations are strapped for cash and being required to do "more and more with less and less."

At the same time that educational funds are growing more scarce, a record number of students are enrolled in the nation's schools: nearly 74 million in 2006. Unfortunately, many schools are overcrowded and in need of major repairs. A report on New York City's public schools, for example, noted that one school in the borough of Queens was so overcrowded that science classes were held in a boys' shower room off the gymnasium (Applebome, 1996). This same report found that many buildings had crumbling brickwork, rotting window frames, and rusted steel beams that were about as resistant to stress as a chocolate chip cookie (Applebome, 1995b). According to the U.S. General Accounting Office, at least $140 billion is needed for building repairs and upgrades in the nation's schools.

Is there a way to resolve problems of unequal funding among the states, among school districts within states, and among schools within school districts? In recent years, the federal courts have held some states accountable for the unequal funding that has resulted in "rich" and "poor" school districts. However, most proposals to improve educational funding have been limited in scope and seem to benefit some groups at the expense of others. One plan—a voucher system—would give students and their families a specified sum of government money to purchase education at the school of their choice. Advocates of the voucher system say that the U.S. Department of Education should be eliminated and federal funds should be given to the states in the form of block grants that would then be dispersed as vouchers, approximately $1,000 per student regardless of family income. These advocates argue that schools would have to provide better-quality instruction at lower costs because they would be competing for students. However, critics say that the voucher system would offer only a limited number of students better opportunities and would not resolve the larger problem of underfunded schools. They note that a fully operational voucher system might mark the end of public education in this country. As the debate over solutions goes on, some parents have formed organizations, such as Parents for Public Schools, to support public education and build alliances among parents from different races and economic backgrounds. Some of these organizations focus on raising bond issues; others organize public rallies to call attention to problems in education (Applebome, 1997).

Some analysts believe that the problem of underfunding could be solved by significantly reducing expenditures for administration and other noninstructional activities and using that money in the classroom. More than 33 cents of every dollar spent on public education goes for support services rather than education. Support services include such things as administrative costs, libraries, buses, sporting events, and repairs to existing buildings. However, problems in education are not limited to the elementary and secondary levels; higher education has its problems, too.

PROBLEMS IN HIGHER EDUCATION

Higher education serves several important functions in society: the transmission of specialized knowledge and skills, production of new information and technologies, and preparation of the next generation of professionals and scholars. Over the past decade, however, many public colleges and universities have come under increasing financial pressure as appropriations by state legislatures and federal funding have been cut. In response, some schools have intensified their fund-raising efforts, pursuing corporations, nonprofit foundations, and alumni. To remain solvent, many of these schools have also had to increase tuition and student fees.

The Soaring Cost of a College Education

Increases in average yearly tuition for four-year colleges continue to be higher than the rate of inflation. Although public community colleges and state colleges and universities typically have lower tuition rates than private colleges because they are funded primarily by tax dollars, some have grown too expensive for low-income students, particularly with the decline in scholarship funds and grants. Many students today must take out student loans and go into debt to attend college. Although some students find part-time jobs, their earnings make only a small dent in the cost of tuition and books. Students from more affluent families with two parents present are more likely to attend private colleges, where annual costs range from an average of $15,000 annually to more than $35,000.

Some social analysts maintain that a college education is still a bargain because students receive instruction, a room, and three meals a day, as well as athletic facilities, counseling, job placement help, and other services. But social scientists applying a conflict framework to the problem of soaring college costs say that the high cost of a college education reproduces the existing class system: Some students lack access to higher education because they do not have adequate financial resources, and those who attend college are stratified according to their ability to pay. The type of college that students attend, for instance, is frequently chosen on the basis of financial considerations. A 2002 study found that 40 percent of Latino/as are enrolled in two-year and community colleges as compared to 25 percent of white and African American students between the ages of 18 and 24. According to the report, two-year institutions typically offer a number of advantages that help to explain this difference: As a rule, tuition is lower, degree programs are often designed to accommodate part-time students, and many classes are offered in the evenings to assist part-time students. Also, because community colleges are often located near residential areas, students can attend college while living at home (Fry, 2002). Cost and location are therefore major factors in decisions about college education.

The Continuing Debate over Affirmative Action

For many years, affirmative action programs in higher education—programs that take race, ethnicity, and gender into consideration for admissions, financial aid, scholarships, fellowships, and faculty hiring—have been the subject of debate among academics and nonacademics alike. The legal battle over affirmative action heated up with the 1978 U.S. Supreme Court decision in *Bakke v. The University of California at Davis.* In that case, Allan Bakke, a white male, sued the University of California at Davis, claiming that its policy of allocating 16 of 100 places in the first-year class to members of underrepresented minority groups was discriminatory. Bakke claimed that he had been denied admission to the university's medical school even though his grade point average and Medical College Admissions Test score were higher than those of some minority applicants who were admitted under the university's affirmative action program. Although the Court ruled that Bakke should be admitted to the medical school, it left the door open for schools to increase diversity in their student population.

The affirmative action controversy intensified in the 1990s. In 1995, the regents of the University of California adopted a policy discontinuing any special consideration of "race, religion, sex, color, ethnicity, or national origin" in admissions criteria, and voters in California passed Proposition 209, which is a sweeping prohibition of affirmative action. In 1996, the U.S. Fifth Circuit Court of Appeals ruled in *Hopwood v. State of Texas* that affirmative action programs in public education—even if they were intended to achieve a more diverse student body or to eliminate the present effects of past discrimination—unconstitutionally discriminated against whites. As a result of these and other similar events, it appeared that programs designed to increase minority-group enrollment at institutions of higher education might become a thing of the past.

In 2003, however, the U.S. Supreme Court ruled in *Grutter v. Bollinger* (involving admissions policies of the University of Michigan's law school) and *Gratz v. Bollinger* (involving the undergraduate admissions policies of the same university) that race can be a factor for universities in shaping their admissions programs, as long as it is within carefully defined limits. Some analysts believe that these two cases were a victory for affirmative action; other analysts believe that the effect of these decisions will be limited in scope.

In the twenty-first century, organizations such as the American Association of University Women continue to be advocates for continuing and expanding affirmative action programs in the belief that equity is still an issue. According to affirmative action advocates, greater opportunities in education and the workplace are still very important for women and people of color because discriminatory policies and covert practices often work against them. From this approach, having affirmative action programs in place also serves as a preventive measure: Making people aware that it is important to be committed to equal opportunity for all people and to diversity in education and jobs may help to reduce or eliminate potential problems of bias before they occur.

ARE THERE SOLUTIONS TO EDUCATIONAL PROBLEMS?

During the twenty-first century, we must not underestimate the importance of education as a social institution. It is a powerful and influential force that imparts the values, beliefs, and knowledge that are necessary for the social reproduction of individual personalities and entire cultures (Bourdieu and Passeron, 1990). But in what direction should this tremendous social force move? As a nation, we have learned that spending more money on education does not guarantee that the many pressing problems facing this social institution will be solved (see Box 12.3 on page 264). On the other hand, it is essential that schools be funded at a level where they can meet the needs of growing and increasingly diverse student populations. Equally important to funding issues are factors such as the quality of instruction received by students, the safety of the school environment, and the opportunity for each student to reach his or her academic and social potential. Various theoretical approaches and political perspectives provide different solutions to the educational problems that we face today.

Functionalist/Conservative Solutions

Functionalist approaches emphasize the importance of the manifest functions of education and making certain that these functions are fulfilled in contemporary schools. From this approach, greater emphasis should be placed on teaching students the basics and making certain that they have the job skills that will make it possible for them to become contributing members of the U.S. workforce. Problems such as functional illiteracy, school violence, unprepared or ineffective teachers, and school discipline issues must be dealt with so that test scores are improved and a higher percentage of students not only graduate from high school but also attend college. Functionalists typically believe that when dysfunctions exist in the nation's educational system, improvements will occur only when more stringent academic requirements are implemented for students. To make this possible, teachers must receive more rigorous training and evaluation, and high expectations must

Social Problems and Statistics

Box 12.3

Does Spending More Money Guarantee a Better Education?

When political leaders and other policy makers debate problems in education, they often use statistics to back up their arguments. Statistics show that some problems—such as large class size or inadequate school facilities—might be reduced if more money were spent on education. However, statistics also show that simply spending more money does not guarantee better outcomes for children's education. Figure 12.2 shows, for example, that although federal discretionary spending on education more than doubled between 1990 and 2004, this additional expenditure has not improved reading scores overall. Consider the following facts regarding education in the United States:

- Fewer than one-third of the nation's fourth-graders read proficiently.
- Reading performance has not improved in more than fifteen years.
- Fewer than 20 percent of the nation's twelfth-graders score proficiently in math.
- Among the industrialized nations, U.S. twelfth-graders rank near the bottom in science and math (No Child Left Behind, 2002).

On the basis of these data, should we assume that less money should be spent on education? Definitely not! However, statistics do show that money alone isn't always the answer to social concerns. What other factors contribute to low reading scores? How might some of these problems be reduced or eliminated?

be held for all students to help them reach grade-level or above achievement in all subjects they are studying.

Conservative political leaders in various states have emphasized that one possible solution to educational problems is to increase support for struggling students and underperforming schools by requiring school districts to use federal funds that have been set aside for tutoring and school choice. At the national level, there has been much discussion about rewarding the best teachers and encouraging them to take jobs in underperforming schools by providing them with additional pay and other incentives for assuming these positions. At the bottom line, the focus of functionalist/conservative approaches to solving educational problems in the United States is to make schools more competitive and to ensure that students graduate from high school prepared for jobs in the twenty-first century global marketplace. Strengthening math and science education, for example, is a key way in which political leaders believe that U.S. schools can become more competitive. Some analysts believe that continuing the policies established by the No Child Left Behind law is the best way to achieve greater competitiveness; however, others argue that this approach has either been "too little, too late," or that it has been shown to be ineffective in reducing the nation's educational problems. And, they would find no complaint from many conflict theorists or liberal political analysts who also believe that the U.S. educational system is fraught with problems that policies such as No Child Left Behind have done little to remedy.

Conflict/Liberal Solutions

To address major problems in schools such as class-based social reproduction, tracking, and the hidden curriculum, many conflict theorists believe that major restructuring must occur in public education. In fact, key issues that contribute to vast educational inequality in this country are the divide that exists between public and private schools, between "rich" and "poor" public school districts, and inequalities that exist among schools within one district. Although exclusive private schools provide an outstanding education for children from the upper classes to prepare them for future leadership positions, these schools often serve to the detriment of children from low-income and poverty-level families because the resources of the

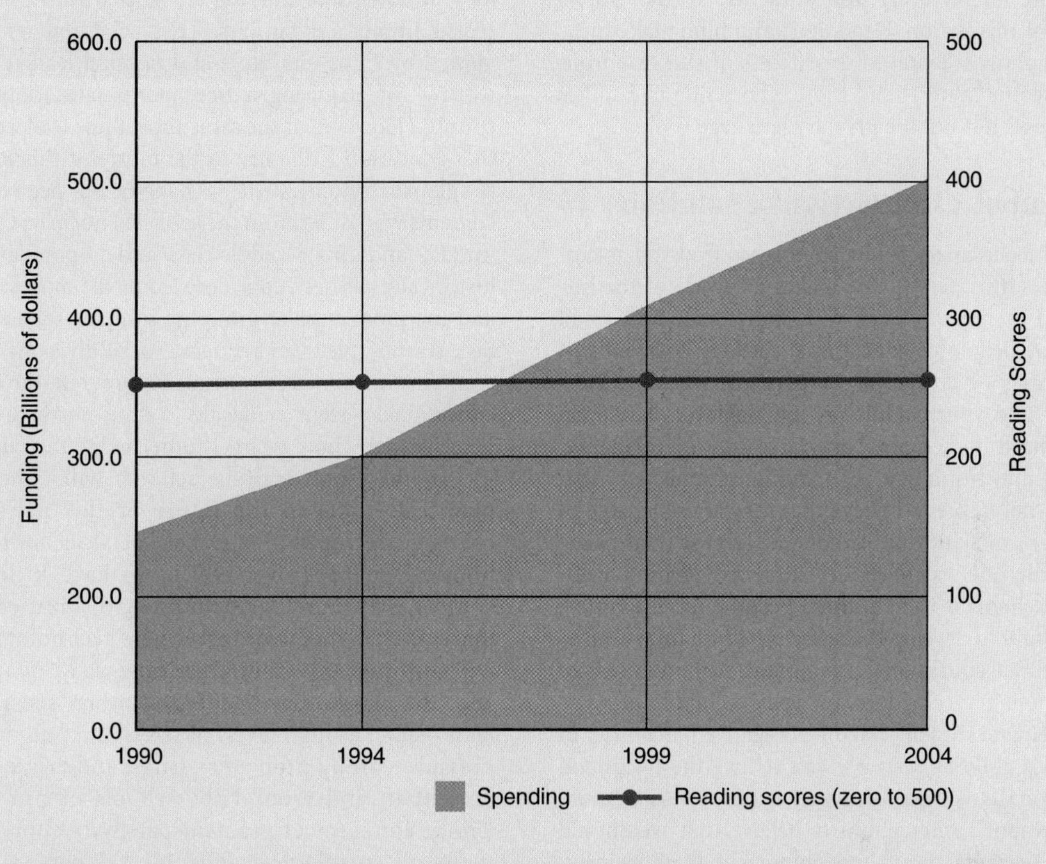

■ *Figure 12.2* **Education Spending and Reading Scores,* 1990-2004**

Source: U.S. Department of Education, 2004, 2005.

*Reading scores are for thirteen-year-olds.

affluent do not flow into the frequently overcrowded, outdated, and "underachieving" schools that are attended by children of members of the working class and the poor. In public school districts, great disparities in school funding must be done away with so that students have more equal educational opportunities. Students who would benefit from enrichment programs, special programs, or bilingual education should be provided with these necessary resources regardless of their parents' socioeconomic status, race/ethnicity, or country of origin.

Liberal political leaders typically believe that legislation must be passed or continually reaffirmed to fight race discrimination and gender and sexual inequality in schools. These are viewed as continuing problems that are not solved simply by the passage of one measure, such as Title IX of the Educational Amendments of

1972, but instead require continued vigilance across the decades. The same is true in regard to the funding of education: Increased government funding for public schools is crucial if we are to produce greater equality and more opportunity for students in the public schools of this nation. Head Start and bilingual education programs are vital to the success of students from lower-income families and those who reside in families where English is not the primary language spoken.

Symbolic Interactionist Solutions

Since symbolic interactionist approaches focus on micro-level issues, this perspective makes us aware of the importance of how we deal with individuals and small groups of people in educational settings. Problems in schools may be created or perpetuated when we label children and young adults as low achievers based on standardized test scores or classroom performance. Labeling may result in a self-fulfilling prophecy for students if they come to believe that they are incapable of learning or of achieving at the same level as their peers. As a result, one way to reduce students' learning problems in schools is to help them become more effective learners and to develop the self-confidence they need to reach greater educational attainment. Although fear of failure alone typically does not cause a child to be a less than adequate student, having a negative perception of one's own abilities certainly can reduce the likelihood that he or she will perform well in school. As a result, some symbolic interactionists believe that we should educate teachers about how important their expectations are when it comes to the student's achievement level. If teachers encourage their students, help them become higher achievers, and make them feel successful, those students often will act like higher achievers and come to expect more of themselves.

Applying the symbolic interactionist approach to viewing problems in education, we might take a closer look at how some children are labeled who come from recent immigrant families. These children tend to be viewed by some educators and political leaders as "unworthy" of acquiring a free, public education in this country. However, at the same time, these leaders suggest that education is the key to the future of this nation in the global economy. Perhaps changing our perspective on students who differ from the so-called norm of the white, middle- and upper-middle class student population that historically has been considered to be the most successful and the most popular grouping in many schools might be a starting place for reducing social divisions that become insurmountable as students progress through the educational system or decide to drop out because they perceive that school is largely unrelated to their life.

In the final analysis, schools will continue to play a key role in the future of this nation, and changes are inevitable. Other social, economic and political changes over which we have little or no control are occurring, including globalization of the marketplace and workforce, new technologies that will continually revolutionize how we work and play, and the day-to-day reality of other social problems—such as high levels of stress and bullying, peer pressure, family problems, drugs, and crime—being present in and around the schools of our nation. Unlike some social problems, analysts applying virtually all sociological and political perspectives to the problems found in schools believe that change must occur: They simply disagree on what those changes should be.

SUMMARY

■ *What is education?*

Education is the social institution responsible for transmitting knowledge, skills, and cultural values in a formally organized structure.

■ *What is the functionalist perspective on education?*

Functionalists believe that education contributes to the smooth functioning of society when it fulfills its manifest functions—the open, stated, and intended goals or consequences of its activities. Education has at least five major manifest functions: socialization, transmission of culture, social control, social placement, and change and innovation. Schools also fulfill a number of latent functions—hidden, unstated, and sometimes unintended consequences of its activities.

■ *What is the conflict perspective on education?*

Conflict theorists believe that schools, which are supposed to reduce inequality in society, actually perpetuate inequalities based on class, race, and gender. The sociologist Pierre Bourdieu, for example, says that children from low-income and poverty-level families come to school with less cultural capital (values, beliefs, attitudes, and competencies in language and culture) than middle- and upper-income children have. Conflict theorists also think that elites manipulate the masses and maintain their power in society through a hidden curriculum that teaches students to be obedient and patriotic and thus perpetuates the status quo in society.

■ *What is the symbolic interactionist perspective on education?*

Symbolic interactionists study classroom dynamics and how practices such as labeling affect students' self-concept and aspirations. If students are labeled "learning disabled" for example, the label might become a self-fulfilling prophecy, that is, an unsubstantiated belief or prediction that results in behavior that makes the false belief come true. A student who is erroneously labeled "learning disabled" might stop trying, and teachers might lower their expectations, with the result that the student doesn't succeed in the long run.

■ *What is illiteracy and what can be done about it?*

Functional illiteracy is being unable to read and/or write at the skill level necessary for carrying out everyday tasks. On the national level, the United States attempted to solve the illiteracy problem by passing the No Child Left Behind Act, but the results of implementing this law have been mixed. When the economic climate of the nation is better, leaders in business and industry are more likely to establish programs to educate functionally illiterate workers; however, their efforts are more limited in difficult economic times. Volunteer organizations that teach basic reading skills to young people and adults have been successful in helping more people learn to read, write, and engage in such important daily activities as balancing a checkbook.

■ *Why are high rates of immigration a problem for U.S. schools?*

Though some immigrants are well educated, most have limited formal education and few job skills. Also, many immigrants are children, so schools must cope with language differences among students. Some school districts offer transitional newcomer programs with bilingual instruction, but critics say that these programs are a form of segregation.

■ *How do race, class, and gender affect educational opportunities?*

The Supreme Court outlawed segregation in 1954, but segregated schools still exist because segregated schools mirror race- and class-based residential segregation. Schools in which racial and ethnic minorities are in the majority typically have high teacher-student ratios, less qualified teachers, lower expectations of students, and high dropout rates. Despite such disadvantages, young African Americans are earning high school diplomas at the same rate as white Americans. Latino/a students face many educational obstacles, including few school-readiness programs (such as Head Start), few Latino/a teachers as role models, and high dropout rates. An extensive survey on gender shows that teachers treat boys and girls differently in the classroom, so females' self-esteem and life expectations suffer.

■ *How has violence affected our schools?*

Many schools now look like fortresses and use metal detectors and security guards to screen entering students. To lessen the possibility of students being killed for shoes, jewelry, or designer clothes, some school districts now require students to wear uniforms.

■ *What is the crisis in school financing?*

Most educational funds come from state legislative appropriations and local property taxes, but the eroding tax base in city centers leaves schools underfunded. At the same time, record numbers of students are entering the public school system, and many schools are overcrowded and need major repairs. One proposed solution is the voucher system, whereby families are given vouchers to "buy" education at the school of their choice. Critics say that this plan would offer only a limited number of students better opportunities and wouldn't solve the funding problem.

■ *What are the major problems in higher education?*

The soaring cost of a college education is a major problem because, say conflict theorists, it reproduces the existing class system: Those who attend college are stratified according to their ability to pay. There is also the question of affirmative action. Should race, ethnicity, and gender be taken into consideration for admissions, financial aid, scholarships, and faculty hiring? While the debate continues, one thing is certain: Minority enrollments have dropped in many schools that have reduced or eliminated affirmative action programs either voluntarily or as the result of a court order.

■ *What are the urgent educational problems of the twenty-first century?*

To compete in the global economy, we must come to terms with illiteracy in our adult population and we must provide all children with safe, high-quality education. Some experts say that the best way to achieve both goals is through holding schools and school districts accountable for the education their students receive.

KEY TERMS

education, p. 249
functionally illiterate, p. 254
hidden curriculum, p. 252
latent functions, p. 250
manifest functions, p. 250
tracking, p. 257

QUESTIONS FOR CRITICAL THINKING

1. Are you for or against school uniforms? What psychological effects of uniforms might improve student behavior and academic performance? What are the drawbacks to school uniforms?
2. What creative solutions can you propose for the school financial crisis? That is, if the federal government doesn't increase its contribution and voters resist increased taxes, where can state legislatures find more money for education?
3. Should we think of more innovative ways in schools to educate students who come from diverse family backgrounds and other nations of the world? Or should students be expected to quickly accept the language and cultural patterns that are prevalent in their school?

Chapter 13

Problems in Politics and the Global Economy

THINKING SOCIOLOGICALLY

- Do the rich actually get richer while the poor get poorer? What part does the political economy play in the distribution of wealth in the United States?
- How is uneven economic development related to problems in the global economy?
- "Politics is a rich man's game." Based on this chapter, do you agree or disagree with this statement?

In our free society, it is left to each of us to make our own way in the world—and our jobs, businesses, savings, pensions, farms, and homes are the work of years.... Take these away, and a million dreams are undone.... Economic policy is not just some academic exercise, and we in Washington are not just passive spectators. We have a responsibility to act—and if I am elected president I intend to act quickly and decisively. We need reforms that promote growth and opportunity. We need rules that assure fairness and punish wrongdoing in the market. We need tax policies that respect the wage-earners and job creators who make this economy run, and help them to succeed in a global economy. In all of this, it will not be enough to simply dust off the economic policies of four, eight, or twenty-eight years ago. We have our own work to do. We have our own challenges to meet.

—John McCain (2008), speaking during his campaign for president of the United States in 2008, describes why he believes that, if elected president, he should be actively involved in economic policy decisions that affect the lives of millions of Americans.

I've often said that this election is a defining moment in our history. On major issues like the war in Iraq or the warming of our planet, the decisions we make in November and over the next few years will shape a generation, if not a century. Nowhere is that more true than when it comes to our economy.... Gas prices are out of control. Food prices are soaring.... College is becoming less affordable. And we've seen more foreclosures than at any time since the Great Depression.... So we have a choice to make in this election.... We can choose to remain on the path that has led our economy into so much trouble, or we can reclaim the idea that here in this country, you can make it if you try. In the end, that's all most Americans are asking for.... You don't expect government to solve all your problems.... But what you do expect is a government that isn't run by the special interests. What you do expect is that if you're willing to work hard, you should be able to find a job that pays a decent wage, that you shouldn't go bankrupt when you get sick, that you should be able to send your children to college even if you're not rich, and that you should be able to retire with dignity and security. That's what you should expect. And that's why I'm running for president of the United States....

—Barack Obama (2008), President of the United States, made this statement while running as a Democratic Party candidate, to explain his belief that political leaders must be involved in economic policy making.

In every national political election, the candidates speak about the importance of the U.S. economy, the woes that the typical American faces in the current economic climate, and why it is important for political leaders to make every effort to bring about fundamental changes in the economy. The interrelationship between politics and economics is shown in the above excerpts from statements made by two candidates running for the U.S. presidency in 2008. Will these candidates—or others following after them in the future—be able to bring about meaningful changes that will actually improve the lives of Americans and solidify the position of the United States in the global economy? It is difficult to say; however, in the past—like the present—economic issues tend to weigh heavily on people's minds and to be identified as a major social problem when enough people have the perception that they are not better off now than they were four years ago or eight years ago, when previous political leaders were elected to office.

Across lines of race/ethnicity, class, and gender in the United States, economic issues remain a top concern for many people. In most cases, people see their economic fate as being linked not only to local, national, and global economic conditions, but also to decisions that political leaders make that may affect their financial livelihood and economic situation. In this chapter we examine politics and the economy together because they are deeply interrelated.

Politics **is the social institution through which power is acquired and exercised by certain individuals and groups.** Although political decisions typically are made on a nation-by-nation basis, many of these decisions affect the lives and economic status of people in other nations as well. The ***economy*** **is the social institution that ensures that a society will be maintained through its production, distribution, and consumption of goods and services.** Because of the extent to which politics and the economy are related in high-income, industrialized nations such as the United States, some sociologists believe that it is more accurate to refer to the "political economy" as one entity—a combined social institution where the players, rules, and games often overlap. The ***political economy*** **refers to the interdependent workings and interests of political and economic systems.** To gain a better understanding of how the political economy works, it is important to take a closer look at various types of economic systems, the global economy, and the role of governments and corporations in shaping economic conditions around the world.

THREE MAJOR MODERN ECONOMIC SYSTEMS

There are three major modern economic systems: capitalism, socialism, and mixed economies. Of course, there is no such thing as "pure" capitalism or "pure" socialism, but each is characterized by several key tenets that distinguish it as an approach to producing and distributing goods and services in a society.

Capitalism

Capitalism **is an economic system characterized by private ownership of the means of production, from which personal profits can be derived through market competition and without government intervention.** There are four distinctive features of "ideal" capitalism: private ownership of the means of production, pursuit of personal profit, competition, and lack of government intervention.

First, capitalism is based on the right of individuals to own various kinds of property, including those that produce income (e.g., factories and businesses). In a capitalist economy, individuals and corporations not only own income-producing property, but they also have the right to "buy" people's labor.

Second, capitalism is based on the belief that people should be able to maximize their individual gain through personal profit, which is supposed to benefit everyone, not just the capitalists. The idea that "rising tides lift all boats" is central to the pursuit of personal profit being a major tenet of capitalism: the belief is that, if some businesses have high profits, these profits will benefit not only the capitalists who own those businesses, but also their workers and the general public, which will benefit from increased public expenditures for things that everyone uses, such as roads and schools.

Third, capitalism is based on competition, which is supposed to prevent any one business from making excessive profits. For example, when companies are competing for customers, they must offer innovative goods and services at competitive prices. The need to do this, it is argued, prevents excessive profits. One twenty-first century economic problem is the extent to which competition has been reduced or eliminated in many economic sectors by the business practices of major corporations.

Finally, capitalism is based on a lack of government intervention in the marketplace. According to this *laissez-faire* (meaning "leave alone") policy, also called *free enterprise,* competition in a free marketplace should be the force that regulates prices and establishes workers' wages, rather than the government doing so.

Socialism

As compared to capitalism, ***socialism*** **is characterized by public ownership of the means of production, the pursuit of collective goals, and centralized decision making.** Under socialism, there are governmental limits on the right of individuals and corporations to own productive property. In a truly socialist economy, the means of production are owned and controlled by a collectivity or by the state, not by private individuals or corporations. Unlike capitalist economies, in which the primary motivation for economic activity is personal profit, the primary motivation in a socialist economy is supposed to be the collective good of all citizens. Although socialist economies typically have less economic inequality than the United States, there has been a move in many nations toward *privatization,* a process in which resources are converted from state ownership to private ownership, and the government maintains an active role in developing, recognizing, and protecting private property rights. Struggles over privatization continue today in formerly socialist countries such as Turkey where its largest steel maker, a state-controlled company, was put up for sale in 2005. At that time, the Turkish state owned 46 percent of the company's shares, controlled the board, and appointed the senior management. Through privatization of the steel maker, political leaders hoped to realize a profit that would help to pay down the country's budget deficit and attract foreign investors, who previously had been put off by extensive governmental regulations (Landler, 2005). As more socialist countries shift toward a capitalist model, it is important to reflect on how Karl Marx viewed socialism as an answer to the problems produced by capitalism.

Highly critical of the growing economic inequality that emerged as capitalism flourished in the 1800s, the early economist and social thinker Karl Marx argued that socialism could serve as an intermediate stage on the way to an ideal communist society in which the means of production and all goods would be owned by everyone. Under communism, Marx said, people would contribute according to their abilities and receive according to their needs. Moreover, government would no longer be necessary, since government existed only to serve the interests of the capitalist class. Problems of economic and political instability, low standards of living, and other internal issues have plagued the former Soviet Union, Cuba, and other nations that have tried to establish socialist and communist economic systems.

Mixed Economies

No economy is purely capitalist or purely socialist; most are mixtures of both. A ***mixed economy*** **combines elements of both capitalism (a market economy) and socialism (a command economy).** In one type of mixed economy, *state capitalism,* the government is involved in the dealings of privately owned companies, including having a strong role in setting the rules, policies, and objectives of the businesses. Countries such as Japan and Singapore in Asia and Saudi Arabia in the Middle East are examples of state capitalism; however, the outcomes are quite different. In Asia, greater government involvement may have resulted in greater good for more individuals, but in Saudi Arabia, it appears to have only made a few people extremely wealthy.

Some Western European nations, including Sweden, Great Britain, and France, have an economic and political system known as *democratic socialism,* in which private ownership of some of the means of production is combined with governmental distribution of some essential goods and services and free elections. In these nations, the government is heavily involved in providing services such as medical care, child care, and transportation for all residents. For this reason, some analysts refer to these economies as *welfare capitalism* to highlight the fact that privately owned companies coexist with extensive governmental programs that provide certain essential services to everyone without cost or at a greatly reduced cost.

PROBLEMS IN THE GLOBAL ECONOMY

The global financial crisis that occurred in 2008 demonstrated how closely connected problems in the U.S economy are with those of other nations. When U.S. financial institutions were in crisis, the economic well-being of many other nations was also in question because it has widely been assumed that high-income nations with advanced economic development would continue to set the pace of global economies.

Not all nations are at the same stage of economic development, however, and this creates a widely stratified global economy in which some countries are very wealthy, some are much less wealthy, and still others are very poor. As we discussed in Chapter 2, we refer to these as high-income, middle-income, and low-income nations. How these nations are classified is related to their level of economic development and the amount of national and personal income in the country. This development can be traced back to the economic organization of societies in the past.

Inequality Based on Uneven Economic Development

Depending on the major type of economic production, a society can be classified as having a preindustrial, industrial, or postindustrial economy. In preindustrial economies, most workers engage in ***primary sector production*****—the extraction of raw materials and natural resources from the environment.** In this type of economy, materials and resources are used without much processing. Today, extracting gold and silver from mines in Indonesia is an example of primary sector production.

By comparison with preindustrial economies, most workers in industrial economies are engaged in ***secondary sector production*—the processing of raw materials (from the primary sector) into finished products.** Work in industrial economies is much more specialized, repetitious, and bureaucratically organized than in preindustrial economies. Assembly-line work, now done on a global basis, is an example. Here is Ben Hamper's (1991:88–89) description of his first day working on the rivet line at a truck and bus manufacturing plant here in the United States:

> The Rivet Line was the starting point for all that went on during the three-day snake trail needed to assemble a truck. The complex birth procedure began right here. It started with a couple of long black rails. As the rails were hoisted onto crawling pedestals, the workers began riveting them together and affixing them with various attachments. There weren't any screws or bolts to be seen. Just rivets. Thousands upon thousands of dull gray rivets. They resembled mushrooms....I looked around at [other workers] who would soon be my neighbors. I'd seen happier faces on burn victims.

Although computers and other technology have changed the nature of the production process, factory work is often specialized, repetitious, heavily supervised, and full of rules for workers to follow, whether these assembly plants are located in the United States, China, or other nations in today's global economy.

Unlike preindustrial and industrial economies, postindustrial economies are characterized by ***tertiary sector production*,** which means that **workers provide services rather than goods as their primary source of livelihood.** Tertiary sector production includes work in such areas as fast-food service, transportation, communication, education, real estate, advertising, sports, and entertainment. Inequality typically increases in postindustrial economies where people in high-tech, high-wage jobs often thrive financially and have business connections throughout the world while, at the same time, workers in low-tech, low-wage jobs in the service sector (such as fast-food servers or hotel cleaning personnel) may have a hard time paying their basic bills and may feel very isolated from the economic mainstream of their own society. Although the United States still has a primary production and manufacturing sector, the service sector is the most rapidly growing component of our economy. For this reason, some sociologists refer to the United States as an advanced industrial society, which is characterized by greater dependence on an international division of labor (Hodson and Sullivan, 2008). In the United States, corporations rely on workers throughout the world to produce goods and services for paying customers in this country and elsewhere.

Industrial and postindustrial economies often blend in the twenty-first century workplace. Shown here is a clean room (a factory-type setting) at a computer hard-drive manufacturing plant where products are made for use in the communication and information technology sectors.

At one end of the international division of labor is low-wage labor. For example, along the U.S.–Mexican border, some U.S. corporations run *maquiladora* plants—factories in Mexico where components manufactured in the United States are assembled into finished goods and shipped back to the United States for sale. In countries such as Mexico, where the economy is less robust, it is possible to find workers who are willing and able to work for lower wages and fewer benefits than the typical worker in a high-income nation. At the other end of the international division of labor are workers in countries such as Ireland and India, where U.S. corporations are able to find well-educated workers who view jobs in fields such as insurance claims processing, reading of certain types of medical tests, and filling out tax returns for U.S. workers to be a source of economic stability and upward mobility. As a result, what may be viewed as a problem in the global economy for some in the United States, namely the shifting of jobs from this country to other nations, may be viewed as a solution in those countries where young workers see their employment opportunities expanding and no longer feel a need to move elsewhere to work. Transnational corporations headquartered in high-income nations have had a major influence on economies and governments worldwide.

Transnational Corporations and the Lack of Accountability

Today, the most important corporate structure is the ***transnational corporation*—a large-scale business organization that is headquartered in one country but operates in many countries, which has the legal power (separate from individual owners or shareholders) to enter into contracts, buy and sell property, and engage in other business activity.** Some transnational corporations constitute a type of international monopoly capitalism that transcends the boundaries and legal controls of any one nation. The largest transnationals are headquartered in the United States, Japan, Korea, other industrializing Asian nations, and Germany. Currently, transnational corporations account for more than 25 percent of total world production. Not all large U.S. corporations that do business abroad are transnational; for example, General Motors doesn't qualify because only about one-third of its assets and one-third of its sales are outside the United States, and most of these are in other high-income nations such as Australia, Canada, and various European countries. Examples of true transnational corporations are Asea Brown Boveri, a Swiss-Swedish engineering group, and Philips, a Dutch electronics firm. Both have 85 percent of their sales outside the country in which they are headquartered (Waters, 1995). Transnationals dominate in petrochemicals, motor vehicles, consumer electronics, tires, pharmaceuticals, tobacco, soft drinks, fast food, financial consulting, and luxury hotels (Waters, 1995).

The shareholders in transnational corporations live throughout the world. Although corporate executives often own a great number of shares, most shareholders have little control over where plants are located, how much employees are paid, or how the environment is protected.

Because transnational corporations are big and powerful, they play a significant role in the economies and governments of many countries. At the same time, by their very nature, they lack accountability to any government or any regulatory agency. Because transnationals do not depend on any one country for labor, capital, or technology, they can locate their operations in countries where political and business leaders accept their practices and few other employment opportunities exist. For example, when Nike workers went on strike in Indonesia, Nike subcontracted to Korean entrepreneurs operating assembly plants in Vietnam, where employees work for bare-bones wages and, according to media coverage, plant managers physically abuse some of the women. Although many workers in low-income nations earn less than a living wage from transnational corporations, the products they make are often sold for hundreds of times the cost of raw materials and labor. Designer clothing and athletic shoes are two examples of this kind of exploitation. Young women working in Nike factories in Indonesia and Vietnam, for example, go barefoot and cannot afford to buy the shoes they assemble (Goodman, 1996).

Still another concern is that transnational corporations foster global consumerism that inevitably changes local cultures and encourages a "shop till you drop" mentality through extensive advertising and strategic placement of their business operations around the world. McDonald's golden arches and Coca-Cola signs can be seen from Times Square in New York to Red Square in Moscow, and the malls of China might be mistaken for those located anywhere except that they are much larger (see Box 13.1).

PROBLEMS IN THE U.S. ECONOMY

Although an economic boom occurred late in the twentieth century, corporate wealth became increasingly concentrated. Economic concentration refers to the extent to which a few individuals or corporations control the vast majority of all economic resources in a country. Concentration of wealth is a social problem when it works to society's detriment, particularly when people are unable to use the democratic process to control the actions of the corporations.

Concentration of Wealth

The concentration of wealth in the United States can be traced through several stages. In the earliest stage (1850–1890), most investment capital was individually owned. Before the Civil War, about 200 families controlled all major trade and financial organizations. By the 1890s, even fewer—including such notables as Andrew Carnegie, Cornelius Vanderbilt, and John D. Rockefeller—controlled most of the investment capital in this country (Feagin, Baker, and Feagin, 2006).

In early monopoly capitalism (1890–1940), ownership and control of capital shifted from individuals to corporations. As monopoly capitalism grew, a few corporations gained control over major U.S. industries, including the oil, sugar, and grain industries. A ***monopoly* exists when a single firm controls an industry and accounts**

Social Problems in Global Perspective

Box 13.1

The Malling of China: Transnational Corporations and Global Consumerism

> We like this place a lot. They have a lot of fun things to do. They have shopping and even rides. So we like it and yes, we'll come back again.
>
> —*Shopper Ruth Tong, explaining why her family likes the South China Mall (Barboza, 2005:C7)*

> And, considering its description, what's not to like about this mall?
>
> South China Mall is a $400 million fantasy land: 150 acres of palm-tree-lined shopping plazas, theme parks, hotels, water fountains, pyramids, bridges, and giant windmills. Trying to exceed even some of the over-the-top casino extravaganzas in Las Vegas, it has a 1.3 mile artificial river circling the complex, which includes a district modeled on the world's seven "famous water cities," and an 85-foot replica of the Arc de Triomphe.
>
> —*(Barboza, 2005:C7)*

The recent Olympic Games in Beijing made many Americans more aware of commonalities (as well as differences) in the lifestyles and popular culture of citizens in China as compared with those in the United States. However, for a number of years, interesting parallels have existed in regard to consumerism in these two nations.

Thousands of miles away from the United States, shoppers at the South China Mall can find a replica of Los Angeles's "Hollywood" sign, a giant Imax theater complex that looks like it came straight out of Southern California, a Teletubbies theme park, and a food court that features McDonalds, Pizza Hut, and other global food chains.

Is the malling of China a problem? On the positive side, consumerism is rapidly growing in China, and that means economic development for the country and new opportunities not only for developers but also for large corporations to sell more of their soft drinks, food, toys, media products, clothing, cosmetics, and other products in a fast-growing retail market. Although the annual income per person in China is about the equivalent of $1,100, more people are coming to the malls in hopes of enjoying the good life through consumerism and entertainment. In the past, China was referred to as a nation of savers; today, capitalists hope that this country will become a nation of tireless shoppers (Barboza, 2005).

As China shifts from an economy with limited merchandise and few shopping options, its more affluent citizens may join the nearly two billion people worldwide who belong to the *consumer class,* described as "the group of people characterized by diets of highly processed food, desire for bigger houses, more and bigger cars, higher levels of debt, and lifestyles devoted to the accumulation of nonessential goods" (Mayell, 2004). Unlike the past, when most consumers lived in high-income, developed nations, almost 50 percent of all global consumers today live in developing countries such as China and India (each of which has a population in excess of one billion people) where corporations have the best opportunities for market expansion.

On the negative side of the "malling" issue, locally owned businesses, including a number of small shops, department stores, and open-air food markets in the major cities of China, are rapidly disappearing. Some critics believe that the loss of local, indigenous businesses, coupled with the invasion by

(continued)

The $400 million South China Mall, shown here, currently is the world's largest shopping mall with more than 7.1 million square feet of shopping, dining, and entertaining space for the millions of customers who visit each year.

Box 13.1 (continued)

transnational corporate retail and food operations, produces *global homogenization*—the loss of cultural practices and distinctive features of a society (Ritzer, 1995:173). Others reply that this exaggerates the problem, because along with homogenizing comes differentiating: If something can be sold in one locale, it can be sold in any locale (Waters, 1995:142). In other words, we are all enriched by global consumerism. The British may eat Big Macs instead of fish and chips, but Americans now eat fish and chips—and we drink Perrier mineral water, buy Chanel perfume, and drive Volvos, Toyotas, Volkswagens, and Hyundais. We import from other cultures just as other countries import American culture. Shopping mall developers and transnational corporations are simply giving consumers what they want. If they were not meeting consumer demands, the argument goes, then the shopping malls would close and people would refuse to eat at the sign of the golden arches or wear the latest fad, such as faded torn jeans sold as new merchandise. And perhaps they have a point: No one forced Ruth Tong (mentioned above) to visit the South China Mall with her husband and young son. When she arrived, she liked what she saw, and she plans to return—just like the mall's developers are hoping that she, and tens of thousands of others like her, will do!

Questions for Consideration

1. Is global consumerism a problem? If so, are corporations responsible for the problem?
2. How is rising consumption related to job creation and economic stability in a country?
3. What effect does over-consumption have on the global environment and an individual's health and happiness?

Is this sight a familiar one to you? In stores throughout the world, consumers increasingly are using their credit cards to make purchases of basic necessities such as food and clothing. What are the risks of excessive credit card debt? What are some risks associated with a high national debt and staggering amounts of consumer debt?

for all sales in a specific market. In early monopoly capitalism, some stockholders derived massive profits from such companies as American Tobacco Company, Westinghouse Electric Corporation, F. W. Woolworth, and Sears, which held near-monopolies on specific goods and services (Hodson and Sullivan, 2008).

In advanced monopoly capitalism (between 1940 and the present), ownership and control of major industrial and business sectors became increasingly concentrated. After World War II, there was a dramatic increase in ***oligopoly*****—a situation in which a small number of companies or suppliers control an entire industry or service.** Today, a few large corporations use their economic resources—through campaign contributions, PACs, and lobbying—to influence the outcome of government decisions that affect their operations. Smaller corporations have only limited power and resources to bring about political change or keep the largest corporations from dominating the economy.

Today, mergers often occur across industries. In this way, corporations gain near-monopoly control over all aspects of the production and distribution of a product because they acquire both the companies that supply the raw materials and the companies that are the outlets for the product. For example, an oil company might hold leases on the land where the oil is pumped out of the ground, own the refineries that convert the oil into gasoline, and own the individual gasoline stations that sell the product to the public. Corporations that have control both within and across industries and are formed by a series of mergers and acquisitions across industries are referred to as conglomerates—combinations of businesses in different commercial areas, all of which are owned by one holding company. Media ownership is a case in point (see Chapter 14).

Further complicating corporate structures are *interlocking corporate directorates*—members of the board of directors of one corporation who also sit on the board of one or more other corporations. Although the Clayton Antitrust Act of 1914 made it illegal for a person to sit on the boards of directors of two corporations that are in direct competition with each other at the same time, a person may serve simultaneously on the board of a financial institution (a bank, for example) and the board of a commercial corporation (a computer-manufacturing company or a furniture store chain, for example) that borrows money from the bank. Directors of competing corporations also may serve together on the board of a third corporation that is not in direct competition with the other two. The problem with such interlocking directorates is that they diminish competition by producing interdependence. People serving on multiple boards are in a position to forge cooperative arrangements that benefit their corporations but not necessarily the general public. When several corporations are controlled by the same financial interests, they are more likely to cooperate with one another than to compete. The directors of some of these corporations are highly paid for their services: Annual compensation for board members of some top corporations is well over a million dollars with stock and stock options. Many directors serve on the boards of several companies, receiving lucrative salaries and benefits from each of them.

The National Debt and Consumer Debt

The national debt—the U.S. total public debt—is a major concern in the twenty-first century. The national debt is the amount of money owed by the federal government to creditors who hold U.S. debt instruments. In other words, the *national debt* consists of the total amount of money the federal government has borrowed over the years from U.S. citizens and foreign lenders to finance overspending. As of August 2008, the total U.S. federal debt was approximately $9.6 trillion, or about $32,000 per U.S. resident. This figure does not include other promises that the government will disburse future funds for Social Security, Medicare, and Medicaid.

Throughout U.S. history, this nation has had public debt, and for many years, this debt has continued to grow. However, after decades of the federal government spending more money each year than it was making, in the late 1990s, a period of economic expansion occurred and slower growth in some spending areas made it possible for the government to produce a surplus of more than $100 billion a year (between 1999 and 2001). But, as the nation entered the twenty-first century, a combination of tax cuts and increased spending as a result of terrorism and war (among other factors) resulted in a growing budget deficit that increased from $318 billion in 2005 to approximately $410 billion in 2008 (Congressional Budget Office, 2008). As a result, the national government remains deeply in debt. When asked to provide a visual image of the amount of our national debt, one political analyst stated, "If you laid the debt out in dollars from end to end, it would reach out into space four times the distance between the earth and the sun" (Bagby, 1997:47). What would it take to pay off the debt? Consider this: "If Congress paid down the deficit at a dollar every second, it would take more than 130,000 years, or roughly the amount of time that has passed since the Ice Age, to pay down the present debt" (Bagby, 1997:47).

National debt is only one major problem we face; another is the amount of consumer debt in this country. Like the federal government, many individuals and families in this country are deeply in debt. Consumer debt has grown significantly since the 1980s, and in 2008, it had reached more than $2.52 trillion. Even more worrisome to analysts was the fact that the ratio of consumer debt to income has increased. Two factors contribute to high rates of consumer debt. The first is the instability of economic life in modern society; unemployment and underemployment are commonplace. The second factor is the

Corporations in the military-industrial complex produce weapons systems such as the F-22 Raptors shown here. What are the benefits of spending billions of dollars on advanced military equipment such as this? What are the economic and non-economic costs?

availability of credit and the extent to which credit card companies and other lenders extend credit beyond people's ability to repay. Recent increases in consumer debt have largely been attributed to heavier use of revolving credit, primarily credit cards, in which consumers, at best, paid only their minimum balance rather than the total amount charged to a card in a given month. Some people run up credit card charges that are greatly out of proportion to their income; others cannot pay off the charges they initially believed they could afford when their income is interrupted or drops. For example, "Sally Bowman" (a pseudonym) ran up $20,000 in charges, a sum that was more than half her total yearly income:

> It all started when I graduated from college and took a low-paying job. . . . I didn't want to live like a student so I used credit cards to buy myself furniture and eat dinners out. I wasn't extravagant, I just didn't want to deprive myself. . . . When I got a new card with a $5,000 credit limit, it felt like someone just handed me $5,000. . . . The reality has been that I got in the hole financially. (Tyson, 1993:E1; cited in Ritzer, 1995:67)

Having a high level of consumer debt is a personal problem for people like "Sally Bowman," but it is also a public issue, particularly when credit card issuers give fifth, sixth, or seventh credit cards to people who are already so far in debt that they cannot pay the interest, much less the principal, on their cards.

In recent years, many homeowners who have been having trouble juggling their credit card debts have turned to home equity loans as a means of reducing their bills. Home equity loans consist of borrowing money from a mortgage company and pledging the equity in your home (the difference between what you previously owed and the value of the residence) as collateral for the new debt. For a number of years, large numbers of U.S. homeowners refinanced their residential mortgages through Fannie Mae, one of the nation's largest mortgage companies, only to see the housing boom in their region of the country evaporate, or to have other unexpected events occur (such as loss of a job or a medical emergency), which resulted in foreclosure on their home. Fannie Mae and Freddie Mac are buyers of home mortgages, and they are stockholder-owned corporations that are a critical part of the nation's housing finance system, owning or guaranteeing more than half of all home mortgages outstanding. However, in 2008, Fannie Mae and Freddie Mac were placed under federal control as the United States government took over these massive corporations because they recorded combined losses of about $14 billion and had a history of accounting scandals, questionable management practices, and maintaining inadequate capital reserves. The bailout and recapitalization of Fannie Mae and Freddie Mac was only the beginning of what became a major financial crisis: the U.S. housing market continued to experience a meltdown with homeowners seeing the value of their residences decline sharply in some areas of the country. In addition, the market lost confidence in government-sponsored mortgage entities, and numerous mortgage companies and banks were either bought out by other financial institutions or were bailed out by the federal government. This institutional crisis then spread around the globe and to individuals in this country who were heavily in debt. Many of these persons have filed for bankruptcy and lost their homes to foreclosure. Where this major economic crisis will end is unknown at this time.

Can consumer debt be reduced? According to sociologist George Ritzer, both consumers and lenders must become more responsible if consumer debt is to be reduced. Ritzer (1995:71) is particularly critical of banks and credit card companies that entice students in high school or college to become accustomed to buying on credit, saying that it lures many people into a "lifetime of imprudence and indebtedness." He believes that the government should restrain credit card companies by limiting the profits they can make and by restricting mail and telephone campaigns offering incentives to accept new credit cards (Ritzer, 1995). But many people are adamantly opposed to any kind of government intervention in the marketplace, whether it relates to credit cards or anything else. Of course, what some refer to as "government intervention" is viewed by others as corporate welfare.

Corporate Welfare

Corporate welfare occurs when the government helps industries and private corporations in their economic pursuits. Corporate welfare is not new in the United States. Between 1850 and 1900, corporations received government assistance in the form of public subsidies and protection from competition. To encourage westward expansion, the federal government gave large tracts of land to privately owned railroads. Antitrust laws that were originally intended to break up monopolies were used against labor unions that supported workers' interests (Parenti, 1988). Tariffs, patents, and trademarks all serve to protect corporations from competition.

Today, government intervention includes billions of dollars in subsidies to farmers through crop subsidy programs, tax credits for corporations, and large subsidies or loan guarantees to auto makers, aircraft companies, railroads, and others. In 2006, the federal government spent $92 billion in direct and indirect subsidies to businesses and private-sector corporate entities. Some corporations that received millions in taxpayer-funded benefits included Boeing, Xerox, IBM, Motorola, Dow Chemical and General Electric. Overall, most corporations have gained much more than they have lost as a result of government involvement in the economy.

Why do we have corporate welfare programs today? Some can be traced back to the Great Depression in the 1930s, when programs were initiated to bail out companies and stabilize the U.S. economy. Today, for example, billions of dollars in federal subsidies are given to the shipbuilding industry to protect it from foreign competition and to appease maritime unions that want to salvage high-paying jobs for workers. However, even existing ships have difficulty making a profit, so it hardly makes sense to build new ones. Some analysts say that the subsidies continue because of lobbying efforts and political contributions by labor unions and the shipbuilding industry (Tumulty, 1996). As a result, many members of Congress find it is easier to cut back on domestic spending, including Medicare and Medicaid, than to cut corporate handouts (Tumulty, 1996). Obviously, they do not refer to these programs as corporate welfare or corporate handouts, but rather by names that make the programs sound more deserving. The words used can be very important in the political process (see Box 13.2).

PROBLEMS IN POLITICAL PARTICIPATION AROUND THE WORLD

Social scientists distinguish between politics and government: *Politics* as previously defined, is the social institution through which power is acquired and exercised by some people and groups. The essential component of politics is *power*—the ability of people to achieve their goals despite opposition from others (see Chapter 2). People who hold positions of power achieve their goals because they have control over other people; those who lack power carry out the wishes of others. Powerful people get others to acquiesce to their demands by using persuasion, authority, or force.

In contemporary societies, the primary political system is ***government*—a formal organization that has legal and political authority to regulate relationships among people in a society and between the society and others outside its borders.** The government (sometimes called the state) includes all levels of bureaucratized political activity such as executive, central, and local administrations; the legislature; the courts; and the armed forces and police.

Political participation varies widely because political freedom is uneven worldwide. Although people in the United States might take elections as a given and decide not to participate even when they have the freedom to do so, people in seventy-three nations with 42 percent of the world's population do not have the opportunity to participate in free and fair elections (United Nations Development Programme, 2007), and 106 governments still restrict many of the civil and political freedoms of their citizens. Although democratization occurred in more nations late in the twentieth century, early in the twenty-first century new concerns arose regarding the extent to which a larger percentage of the world's population would actually have political freedom. Nations with "limited" democracies often have minimal political participation because citizens have little trust in their government and are disaffected from politics. Voter turnout typically is extremely light in countries that are dominated by a single powerful political party or group. How governments go about their business and the extent to which individuals have the basic right to choose their political leaders and form of government, or the right to change them, is one of the bedrock issues facing the global community today. These global issues remain a concern to many people in the United States and elsewhere around the world.

PROBLEMS IN U.S. POLITICS

The United States is a ***democracy*, a political system in which the people hold the ruling power either directly or through elected representatives.** In a *direct participatory democracy,* citizens meet regularly to debate and decide issues of the day. Ancient Athens was a direct democracy, as was colonial New England with its town meetings. Even today, many New England towns use the town meeting. However, even in its beginnings, the United States was not a direct democracy. The framers of the Constitution believed that decisions should be made by representatives of the people. To ensure that no single group could control the government, they established a *separation of powers* among the legislative, executive, and judicial branches of government and a *system of checks and balances,* giving each branch some degree of involvement in the activities of the others.

In countries that have some form of *representative democracy,* such as the United States, citizens elect representatives who are responsible for conveying the concerns

Critical Thinking and You

Box 13.2

Are You a Conservative or a Liberal? The Language of the Political Economy

The American Heritage Dictionary of the English Language (2000) defines *conservatism* and *liberalism* as follows:

Conservatism:

1. The inclination, especially in politics, to maintain the existing or traditional order.
2. A political philosophy or attitude emphasizing respect for traditional institutions (such as family, education, and religion), distrust of too much government involvement in business and everyday life, and opposition to sudden change in the established order.

A conservative is one who favors traditional views and values. A conservative is a supporter of political conservatism.

Liberalism:

1. The state or quality of being liberal.
2. A political theory founded on the natural goodness of humans and the autonomy of the individual and favoring civil and political liberties, government by law with the consent of the governed, and protection from arbitrary authority.

A liberal is one who is open to new ideas for progress, favors proposals for reform, and is tolerant of the ideas and behavior of others.

This sounds simple enough, doesn't it? However, politicians, scholars, and everyday people constantly argue about the meaning of these words as they seek to determine where individuals fit on the political spectrum, a continuum that represents the wide range of political attitudes. Linguistics scholar George Lakoff (2002) raises a number of interesting points that might assist us in our critical thinking about our views on the political economy. According to Lakoff, conservatives and liberals not only choose different topics on which to focus their attention, but they also use different words to discuss these topics:

> Here are some words and phrases used over and over in conservative discourse: character, virtue, discipline, tough it out, get tough, tough love, strong, self-reliance, individual responsibility, backbone, standards, authority, heritage, competition, earn, hard work, enterprise, property rights, rewards, freedom, intrusion, interference, meddling, punishment, human nature, traditional, common sense, dependency, self-indulgent, elite, quotas, breakdown, corrupt, decay, rot, degenerate, deviant, lifestyle.

Lakoff asks us to think about the following questions: What unifies this collection of words? Why do conservatives choose the words they do? What do these words mean to conservatives? Now, let's look at Lakoff's list of words that are favorites among liberals:

> Liberals talk about: social forces, social responsibility, free expression, human rights, equal rights, concern, care, help, health, safety, nutrition, basic human dignity, oppression, diversity, deprivation, alienation, big corporations, corporate welfare, ecology, ecosystem, biodiversity, pollution, and so on.

Obviously, we cannot easily sort everyone into either the conservative or liberal school of thought based on their choice of words. In fact, people move around somewhat on the political spectrum: Individuals may have more liberal attitudes on some social issues and more conservative attitudes on others.

Where does this discussion leave you? Do you most often use the language of liberalism or of conservativism? Are you a middle-of-the-road-type person when it comes to political issues? What words do you most often use in discussing political and economic issues? Think about your attitudes on the following topics and state what, if anything, you believe the government should do about the following: Abortion; death penalty; government funds for victims of floods, earthquakes, fires, and other natural disasters; health care as a commodity; health care as a right; increasing/decreasing budgets for the military, prisons, and homeland security; increasing/decreasing spending for regulatory agencies that control businesses and seek to protect the environment; and welfare for the chronically poor and homeless. These are only a few of the social concerns that face our nation today. Listen to local, state, and national political leaders: What language do they use? Do their actions reveal attitudes that are conservative, liberal, or somewhere in between as they confront social problems and seek to reduce or eliminate them?

and interests of those they represent. If these representatives are not responsive to the wishes of the people, voters can unseat them through elections. This is not to say that representative democracy is equally accessible to all people in a nation. The framers of the U.S. Constitution, for example, gave the right to vote only to white males who owned property. Eventually, nonlandowners were given the vote, then African-American men, and finally, in 1920, women. Today, democratic participation is at least theoretically available to all U.S. citizens age eighteen and over.

Unfortunately, today voter apathy and influence-buying through campaign contributions threaten to undermine the principles on which our government is based. We'll look at voter apathy first.

Voter Apathy and the Gender Gap

Although there were predictions that record voter turnout might occur in the 2008 presidential election, the turnout (62 percent of registered voters) was roughly the same as in 2004 when 61 percent of registered voters cast ballots in the election. However, increases were seen in voter turnout by young people, Latinos/as, and African American voters. Looking back, however, the general trend in voter participation in the United States has not been positive for the democratic process.

In previous elections for the U.S. Senate and House of Representatives, fewer than 40 percent (39.3 percent) of eligible voters participated in the election. Slightly over 50 percent of the voting-age population (age 18 and older) voted in the 2000 and 2004 presidential elections. The 2004 election was one in which the winning candidate (George W. Bush) received only slightly more than one-half of all votes cast.

When elections can be that close, what causes voter apathy? According to studies by the Pew Research Center for the People and the Press, many people do not vote because they see no reason for change, others are turned off by excessive polling by media and other groups (people see no point to voting if the outcomes are predictable), and still others either disagree with negative advertising by candidates and parties or believe that the issues raised by the candidates are not important or will have no effect on their personal economic situation.

Along with voter apathy, the emergence and persistence of the ***gender gap*****—the difference between a candidate's number of votes from women and men**—is a dominant feature of U.S. politics today. Political analysts first noticed a gender gap in the early 1980s, but the gap grew wider and more apparent in subsequent elections. In 1980, the gender gap was about eight points (men were 8 percent more likely than women to support Ronald Reagan for president). In 2004, the gap increased to eleven points (women were 11 percent more likely than men to vote for John Kerry than for George W. Bush). In 2008, a sizable gender gap was evident in the presidential election results. Women strongly preferred Obama (56 percent) to McCain (43 percent) while men split their votes about evenly, with Obama receiving 49 percent of the votes to 48 percent for McCain. The gender gap for 2008 was 7 percentage points, which was virtually identical to the 7–point gap in 2004.

Why is there a gender gap? Most analysts agree that the gap is rooted in how women and men view economic and social issues, such as welfare reform, abortion, child care, and education, and what they believe the nation's priorities should be. Voter apathy and an increase in the gender gap have received substantial attention in recent years but nothing like the scrutiny given to allegations of political influence-buying by large campaign contributors.

Politics and Money in Political Campaigns

Presidential and congressional candidates and their supporters raise and spend millions of dollars every two years on the elections for national political positions. Where does all the money go? The cost of running for political office has skyrocketed. The costs of advertising and media time, staff, direct-mail operations, telephone banks, computers, consultants, travel expenses, office rentals, and many other campaign expenses have increased dramatically over the past two decades. Unless a candidate has private resources, contributions can determine the success or failure of his or her bid for election or reelection.

Certain kinds of campaign contributions are specifically prohibited by law: Corporate contributions to presidential and congressional candidates have been illegal since 1907, and contributions from labor unions were outlawed in 1943. In 1974, Congress passed a law limiting an individual's total contribution to federal candidates to $25,000 a year and no more than $1,000 per candidate. In 2002, these limits were raised to $2,000 per candidate and no more than $95,000 in any two-year period. However, these individual limits can be sidestepped by bundling, which occurs when a donor collects contributions from family members, business associates, and others and then "bundles" them together and sends them to a candidate. For example, during the 2000 presidential election, supporters of Republican candidate George W. Bush included a group of volunteer fundraisers referred to as the "pioneers," each of whom pledged to raise at least $100,000 which would be bundled as hard money contributions and given to Bush's campaign for use in getting him elected (Nyhart, 2001).

Federal law also limits individual contributions to a political action committee to a maximum of $5,000. ***Political action committees (PACs)*** **are special-interest groups that fund campaigns to help elect (or defeat) candidates based on their positions on specific**

TABLE 13.1 The Ten Largest U.S. Political Contributors, 2008

American Federation of State, County, and Municipal Employees	$39,632,103
AT&T Inc	$39,502,961
National Association of Realtors	$32,879,706
Goldman Sachs	$29,322,212
American Association for Justice	$29,106,889
International Brotherhood of Electrical Workers	$28,480,884
National Education Association	$28,153,159
Laborers Union	$26,708,339
Service Employees International Union	$26,562,163
Carpenters & Joiners Union	$25,745,082

Source: Center for Responsive Politics, 2008.

issues. PACs were originally organized by unions to get around the laws that prohibited union gifts. Today, there are thousands of PACs representing businesses, labor unions, and various single-issue groups (such as gays and lesbians and environmental groups). Over the years, many of these PACs contribute millions of dollars toward their favorite political causes (see Table 13.1 on page 282).

Finally, federal law limits contributions made to political parties for campaigning to $28,500, but until 2002, there was no limit on contributions made for the purpose of party-building, such as distributing "vote Democratic" or "vote Republican" bumper stickers or organizing get-out-the-vote drives. However, both the Democratic and Republican parties used these contributions to pay for administrative expenses and overhead, thus freeing up other party money to support candidates. This *soft-money loophole*—contributing to a political party instead of to a specific candidate—became a major issue, and the same law that increased contribution limits in 2002 allegedly closed this loophole (see Box 13.3 on page 283).

What agency monitors campaign contributions and how effective has this agency been? The Federal Election Commission—the enforcement agency that monitors campaign contributions—is considered "one of the most toothless agencies in Washington" (Cohn, 1997). Violations, when discovered, are typically not punished until some time after an election is over. As a result, a very small percentage of the U.S. population is contributing extraordinarily large amounts to get their candidates elected. Is this sort of influence-buying a recent phenomenon? According to journalist Kevin Phillips (1995), influence-buying has been going on for some time in this country, and most political candidates and elected officials do not refuse such contributions.

Although the general public realizes that special-interest groups and lobbyists often have undue influence on political decisions and the outcome of elections, most people believe that they are powerless to do anything about it. When respondents in a Gallup Poll survey were asked, "Would you say the government is pretty much run by a few big interests looking out for themselves or that it is run for the benefit of all the people?" 76 percent said that they believed big interests ran the country, only 18 percent believed the government operates for the benefit of all, and 6 percent had no opinion (Golay and Rollyson, 1996).

Government by Special-Interest Groups

What happens when special-interest groups have a major influence on how the government is run? Some special-interest groups exert their influence on single issues such as the environment, gun control, abortion, or legislation that affects a particular occupation (e.g., the American Medical Association) or business (e.g., the National Restaurant Association). During the 2002 elections, two of the best-funded and most politically active special-interest groups were the United Seniors Association, which was heavily backed by pharmaceutical companies and spent almost $9 million for television ads, and the AFL-CIO, which spent about $3.5 million in support of candidates who took a pro-labor stance (CNN.com, 2002a).

Other special-interest groups represent specific industries and make contributions to candidates who will protect their interests and profits. One strong lobby is the sugar industry, which makes major contributions to members of Congress in hopes of maintaining price

Social Problems and Social Policy

Box 13.3

"He Who Pays the Piper, Calls the Piper's Tune?" Passing Campaign Finance Reform

> [T]he money flowing into the coffers of political candidates and political parties is staggering. It comes from corporations, wealthy individuals, political action committees, and other interest groups—all with agendas that often are at odds with what is good for average Americans.
>
> *—Donald L. Bartlett and James B. Steele of the* Philadelphia Inquirer *(1996)*

Prior to the passage of the Bipartisan Campaign Reform Act of 2002 (the McCain-Feingold bill), millions of dollars in "soft money" was used to buy television advertising in political elections. This expenditure was a major concern for people who believe the old saying that, if you pay the piper, you should be able to hear the tune you want to hear played. Special-interest groups and wealthy individual contributors with legislation pending before Congress often had a similar expectation that if you gave money to a candidate, it was not unreasonable to expect political favors in return.

Does the Campaign Reform Act change the ability to buy influence? Primarily, this law bans "soft money" contributions—the unregulated donations to national political parties by individuals, corporations, and unions that are supposed to be earmarked for use by the political party itself and are not to be used to support the races of individual candidates. Under the act, political parties at the state and local levels are able to collect money, but the maximum allowable donation is smaller than in the past, and there will be greater regulation of how the funds are used. For example, an individual may contribute no more than $2,000 each to political candidates in any primary or general election, for a total of no more than $95,000 in total gifts. Political action committees are restricted to donations of no more than $5,000 to any one candidate and $15,000 to any one political party but with no overall limit as to how much can be given in gifts.

Does the law work? Since the act doubled the allowable amount of "hard money" (direct contributions) that can be given to individual candidates, special-interest groups have shifted their focus to individual contributors, encouraging them to give money directly to political candidates and parties while clearly making the special-interest group's viewpoints known on social issues and pending legislation (such as bills regarding gun control, right to die, the environment, and Medicare). Although opponents have strenuously challenged the Bipartisan Campaign Reform Act in the courts, primarily arguing that the act violated their free speech, the U.S. Supreme Court upheld the new law.

Do you think that a social policy change such as the Bipartisan Campaign Reform Act can bring about a change in the way that special interests affect U.S. politics? What other changes in ideology and social policy might be necessary before the U.S. Congress and state legislatures more clearly reflect the opinions of their constituents rather than the more narrow focus on certain topics by special-interest groups and political action committees?

supports, special loans, and protective restrictions on imports that help to prop up the price of sugar. For a number of years, the federal government has guaranteed a price floor for sugar and has limited the sugar supply by placing quotas on domestic production and strict limitations on imports by imposing quotas and tariffs. As a result, Florida sugar companies and their wealthy owners have derived great benefit from special-interest groups that represent their interests at the expense of consumers. However, "Big Sugar," as it is commonly referred to, lost some of its clout because the North American Free Trade Agreement allows for Mexican sugar to enter the United States without any quotas or duties, which may result in a flood of imports.

Of course, not everyone is represented by a PAC or a special-interest group. As one senator pointed out, "There aren't any Poor PACs or Food Stamp PACs or Nutrition PACs or Medicare PACs" (quoted in Greenberg and Page, 1993:240). Conversely, "big business" interest groups wield disproportionate power in U.S. politics, undermining the democratic process (Lindblom, 1977; Domhoff, 1978).

Government by Bureaucracy

Special-interest groups wield tremendous political power, but so does the federal bureaucracy. The federal bureaucracy, or ***permanent government*****, refers to the top-tier civil service bureaucrats who have a strong power base**

and play a major role in developing and implementing government policies and procedures. The federal government played a relatively limited role in everyday life in the nineteenth century, but its role grew during the Great Depression in the 1930s. When faced with high rates of unemployment and persistent poverty, people demanded that the government do something. Public welfare was instituted, security markets were regulated, and programs for labor-management relations were set in place. With better technology and demands that the government "do something" about the problems facing society, government has continued to grow. In fact, since 1960, the federal government has grown faster than any other segment of the U.S. economy. Today, more than 3 million people are employed by the federal bureaucracy, in which much of the actual functioning of the government takes place.

Sociologists point out that bureaucratic power in any sphere tends to take on a life of its own over time, and this is evident in the U.S. government. Despite efforts by presidents, White House staffs, and various presidential cabinets, neither Republican nor Democratic administrations have been able to establish control over the federal bureaucracy (Dye and Zeigler, 2009). In fact, many federal bureaucrats have seen a number of presidents come and go. The vast majority of top-echelon positions have been held by white men for many years. Rising to the top of the bureaucracy can take as long as twenty years, and few white women and people of color have reached these positions.

The government bureaucracy is able to perpetuate itself and expand because many of its employees possess highly specialized knowledge and skills and cannot easily be replaced. As the issues facing the United States have grown in number and complexity, offices and agencies have been established to create rules, policies, and procedures for dealing with such things as nuclear power, environmental protection, and drug safety. These government bureaucracies announce about twenty rules or regulations for every one law passed by Congress (Dye and Zeigler, 2009). Today, public policy is increasingly made by agencies rather than elected officials. The agencies receive little direction from Congress or the president, and although their actions are subject to challenge in the courts, most agencies are highly autonomous.

The federal budget is the central ingredient in the bureaucracy. Preparing the annual federal budget is a major undertaking for the president and the Office of Management and Budget, one of the most important agencies in Washington. Getting the budget approved by Congress is an even more monumental task. However, as Dye and Zeigler (2009) point out, even with the highly publicized wrangling over the budget by the president and Congress, the final congressional appropriations usually are within 2 to 3 percent of the budget that the president originally proposed.

As powerful as the federal bureaucracy has become, it is not immune to special-interest groups. Special-interest groups can help an agency to get more operating money. Although the president has budgetary authority over the bureaucracy, any agency that believes that it did not get its fair share can raise a public outcry by contacting friendly interest groups and congressional subcommittees. This outcry can force the president to restore funding to the agency or prod Congress into appropriating money that was not requested by the president, who might go along with the appropriation to avoid a confrontation. Special-interest groups also influence the bureaucracy through the military-industrial complex.

The Military-Industrial Complex

The term ***military-industrial complex*** **refers to the interdependence of the military establishment and private military contractors.** The complex is actually a three-way arrangement involving one or more private interest groups (usually corporations that manufacture weapons or other military-related goods), members of Congress who serve on congressional committees or subcommittees that appropriate money for military programs, and a bureaucratic agency (such as the Defense Department). Often, a revolving door of money, influence, and jobs is involved: Military contractors who receive contracts from the Defense Department also serve on advisory committees that recommend what weapons should be ordered. Many people move from job to job, serving in the military, then in the Defense Department, then in military industries (Feagin, Baker, and Feagin, 2006).

In the 1970s, sociologist C. Wright Mills (1976) stated that the relationship between the military and private industry was problematic and could result in a "permanent war economy" or "military economy" in this country. But economist John Kenneth Galbraith (1985) argued that government expenditures for weapons and jet fighters stimulate the private sector of the economy, creating jobs and encouraging spending. In other words, military spending by Congress is not an economic burden but a source of economic development. It also enriches those corporations that build jet fighters and other warplanes, such as Boeing and Lockheed Martin. According to one executive who has spent much of his career involved in building jet fighters for the U.S. military, getting a $1 trillion Pentagon contract for a new generation of jet fighters is of utmost importance to his company: "It's the Super Bowl. It's winner takes all. It's the huge plum. It's the airplane program of the century. If you don't win this program, you're a has-been in tactical aircraft" (quoted in Shenon, 1996a:A1).

The 2007 federal budget allocated $439.3 billion for defense spending (a 6.9 percent increase over the preceding year), but that amount did not include $170 billion allocated for military operations in Afghanistan and Iraq or other funds allocated by the budget for other costs of the war against terror. The budget included additional funds to train "first responders" (firefighting, law enforcement, and emergency medical personnel) regarding how to respond to potential future threats. Buried within the budget, as usual, were funds for numerous projects that would bring jobs and tax money to the home districts of influential members of Congress, a practice referred to as *pork barreling.*

The United States will always have an active military-industrial complex because of our emphasis on *militarism*—a societal focus on military ideals and an aggressive preparedness for war. The belief in militarism is maintained and reinforced by values such as patriotism, courage, reverence, loyalty, obedience, and faith in authority, as sociologist Cynthia H. Enloe (1987:542–543) explains:

> Military expenditures, militaristic values, and military authority now influence the flow of foreign trade and determine which countries will or will not receive agricultural assistance. They shape the design and marketing of children's toys and games and of adult fashions and entertainment. Military definitions of progress and security dominate the economic fate of entire geographic regions. The military's ways of doing business open or shut access to information and technology for entire social groups. Finally, military mythologies of valor and safety influence the sense of self-esteem and well-being of millions of people.

SOCIOLOGICAL PERSPECTIVES ON THE POLITICAL ECONOMY

Politics and the economy are so intertwined in the United States that many social scientists speak of the two as a single entity: the political economy. At issue for most social scientists is whether political and economic power are concentrated in the hands of the few or distributed among the many in this country. Functionalists adopt a pluralistic model of power, whereas conflict theorists adopt an elitist model.

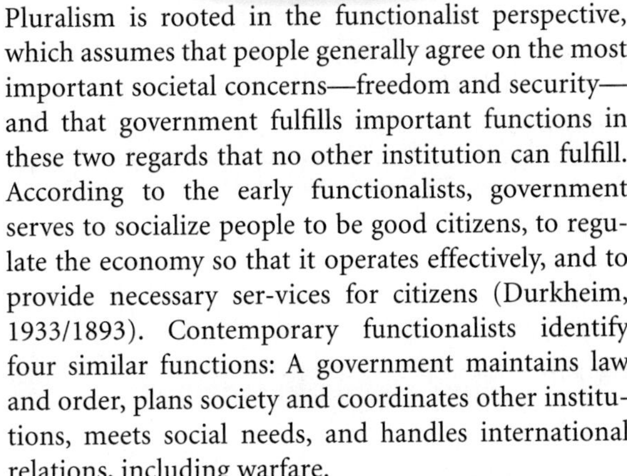

The Functionalist Perspective

Pluralism is rooted in the functionalist perspective, which assumes that people generally agree on the most important societal concerns—freedom and security—and that government fulfills important functions in these two regards that no other institution can fulfill. According to the early functionalists, government serves to socialize people to be good citizens, to regulate the economy so that it operates effectively, and to provide necessary ser-vices for citizens (Durkheim, 1933/1893). Contemporary functionalists identify four similar functions: A government maintains law and order, plans society and coordinates other institutions, meets social needs, and handles international relations, including warfare.

But what happens when people do not agree on specific issues or concerns? Functionalists say that divergent viewpoints lead to political pluralism; that is, when competing interests or viewpoints arise, government arbitrates. Thus, according to the ***pluralist model*, power is widely dispersed throughout many competing interest groups in our political system** (Dahl, 1961). In the pluralist model, (1) political leaders make decisions on behalf of the people through a process of bargaining, accommodation, and compromise; (2) leadership groups (such as business, labor, law, and consumer organizations) serve as watchdogs to protect ordinary people from the abuses of any one group; (3) ordinary people influence public policy through voting and participating in special-interest groups; (4) power is widely dispersed in society (the same groups aren't equally influential in all arenas); and (5) public policy reflects a balance among competing interest groups, not the majority-group's view (Dye and Zeigler, 2009).

How might a social analyst who uses a functionalist framework address problems in politics and the economy? Such an analyst might begin by saying that since dysfunctions are inevitable in any social institution, it is important to sort out and remedy the specific elements of the system that are creating the problems. It should not be necessary to restructure or replace the entire system. Consider, for example, government regulations: Some regulations are good, and some are bad. The trick, functionalists say, is to keep the good ones and get rid of the bad. Too often, the U.S. government moves between two extremes: overregulation of business and society or seeking to end most, if not all, regulation. As social analysts Donald L. Barlett and James B. Steele (1996:214) suggest, "We must preserve the rules that assure the quality of American life: the food you eat, the medicines you take, the air you breathe and the water you drink. They have evolved over a century." Barlett and Steele go on to say, however, that demanding that U.S.-owned companies comply with regulations that are not required of their competitors in foreign countries creates an uneven playing field. Hence a tariff should be imposed on imported products equal to the amount of money that U.S. businesses must spend to comply with government regulations (Barlett and Steele, 1996). This perspective is based on the belief that a certain amount of government intervention in the economy is appropriate but that too much—or the wrong kind—is detrimental.

The Conflict Perspective

Most conflict theorists believe that democracy is an ideal, not a reality, in our society today because the government primarily benefits the wealthy and the politically powerful, especially business elites. In fact, according to conflict theorists, economic and political elites use the powers of the government to impose their will on the masses. According to the ***elite model*****, power in political systems is concentrated in the hands of a small group, whereas the masses are relatively powerless.** In the elite model, (1) elites possess the greatest wealth, education, status, and other resources and make the most important decisions in society; (2) elites generally agree on the basic values and goals for the society; (3) power is highly concentrated at the top of a pyramid-shaped social hierarchy, and those at the top set public policy for everyone; (4) public policy reflects the values and preferences of the elite, not of ordinary people; and (5) elites use the media to shape the political attitudes of ordinary people (Dye and Zeigler, 2003).

According to sociologist C. Wright Mills (1959a), the United States is ruled by a ***power elite*****, which at the top is composed of business leaders, the executive branch of the federal government, and the military (especially the "top brass" at the Pentagon).** The corporate rich—the highest-paid CEOs of major corporations—are the most powerful because they have the unique ability to parlay their vast economic resources into political power. The next most powerful level is occupied by Congress, special-interest groups, and local opinion leaders. The lowest (and widest) level of the pyramid is occupied by ordinary people, the unorganized masses who are relatively powerless and vulnerable to economic and political exploitation.

Individuals in the power elite have similar class backgrounds and interests and interact on a regular basis. Through a revolving door of influence, they tend to shift back and forth between and among business, government, and military sectors. It is not unusual for people who have served in the president's cabinet to become directors of major corporations that do business with the government, for powerful businesspeople to serve in the cabinet, or for former military leaders to become important businesspeople. Through such political and economic alliances, people in the power elite can influence many important decisions, including how federal tax money will be spent and to whom lucrative subsidies and government contracts are awarded.

In his analysis of the political economy, sociologist G. William Domhoff (1978) speaks of a ruling class, which is made up of the corporate rich, a relatively fixed group of privileged people who wield power over political processes and serve capitalist interests. The corporate rich influence the political process in three ways: (1) by financing campaigns of candidates who favor their causes; (2) by using PACs and loophole contributions to obtain favors, tax breaks, and favorable regulatory rulings; and (3) by gaining appointment to governmental advisory committees, presidential commissions, and other governmental positions. For example, some members of the ruling class influence international politics through their involvement in banking, business services, and law firms that have a strong interest in overseas sales, investments, or raw materials extraction (Domhoff, 1990).

Some analysts who take a conflict perspective say that the only way to overcome problems in politics and the economy is to change the entire system. Our present system exploits poor whites, people of color, women of all colors, people with disabilities, and others who consider themselves disenfranchised from the political and economic mainstream of society. Other conflict theorists think that we can solve many problems by curbing the abuses of capitalism and the market economy and thereby reducing the power of political and economic elites. Political scientist Benjamin R. Barber believes that we cannot rely on the capitalist (market) economy to look after common interests:

> It is the job of civil society and democratic government and not of the market to look after common interests and make sure that those who profit from the common planet pay its common proprietors their fair share. When governments abdicate in favor of markets, they are declaring nolo contendere [no contest] in an arena in which they are supposed to be primary challengers, bartering away the rights of their people along the way.... Markets simply are not designed to do the things democratic polities do. They enjoin private

> rather than public modes of discourse, allowing us as consumers to speak via our currencies of consumption to producers of material goods, but ignoring us as citizens speaking to one another about such things as the social consequences of our private market choices.... They advance individualistic rather than social goals.... Having created the conditions that make markets possible, democracy must also do all the things that markets undo or cannot do. It must educate citizens so that they can use their markets wisely and contain market abuses well. (Barber, 1996:242)

ARE THERE SOLUTIONS TO PROBLEMS IN POLITICS AND THE ECONOMY?

A number of key factors will establish the future course of politics, both in the United States and in other nations. The level of economic growth will have a significant effect on the amount of money that high-income nations will be able to invest in domestic programs (such as education, the environment, health care, and elder care) and in alleviating international problems (such as growing economic inequality within and among nations, the spread of HIV/AIDS and other diseases, and political upheavals and wars). However, political decisions also will be crucial in determining where money is spent and how much is allocated for war, international programs, and domestic programs.

In the United States, the future of our well-being is, at least to some extent, in the hands of our political leaders, whom—at least in most instances—we have elected. Our future is also in the hands of powerful economic leaders, such as corporate decision makers whom we did not elect. Some political leaders and corporate officers appear to seek the common good; however, others have proven themselves to be unworthy of our trust, as revealed in numerous media headlines and articles. As discussed in the next chapter, the media provide us with most of the information we have about the current political and economic issues that confront us today and in the future.

SUMMARY

■ *What kind of economic system does the United States have?*

The United States has a capitalist economy. Ideally, capitalism is characterized by private ownership of the means of production, pursuit of personal profit, competition, and lack of government intervention.

■ *How are societies classified by their predominant type of work?*

Societies are classified as preindustrial, industrial, or postindustrial. Preindustrial societies engage in primary sector production—the extraction of raw materials and natural resources from the environment. Industrial societies engage in secondary sector production—the processing of raw materials (from the primary sector). Postindustrial societies engage in tertiary sector production—providing services rather than goods.

■ *What are transnational corporations, and why do they pose social problems?*

Transnational corporations are large-scale business organizations that are headquartered in one country but operate in many countries. Transnationals lack accountability to any government or regulatory agency. They are not dependent on any one country for labor, capital, or technology. They can play important roles in the economies and governments of countries that need them as employers and accept their practices.

■ *Why is the national debt a serious problem? How is consumer debt a public issue?*

When we increase the national debt, we are borrowing from future generations, which will leave them with higher taxes, fewer benefits, and a lower rate of economic growth. Consumer debt becomes a public issue when people cannot repay their credit card loans.

■ *What is corporate welfare?*

Corporate welfare occurs when the government helps industries and private corporations in their economic pursuits. Many subsidies that were originally put in place to help stabilize the economy continue unnecessarily because of labor union and PAC lobbying and campaign contributions.

■ *Why is voter apathy a problem? What is the gender gap?*

Voter apathy undermines the basis on which representative democracy is built; if large numbers of people don't vote, the interests of only a few are represented. The gender gap is the difference between a candidate's number of votes from women and men. More than ever today, women and men seem to view economic and social issues differently.

■ *Why have campaign contributions been an issue in recent elections?*

Campaign contributions are regulated, but individuals, unions, and corporations have circumvented the law through the soft-money loophole—contributing to a political party instead of to a specific candidate—and through political action committees. Political action committees (PACs) are special-interest groups that fund campaigns to help elect (or defeat) candidates on the basis of their positions on specific issues. Because running for office is expensive, contributions can make the difference between a candidate's success or defeat. Although recent legislation has made soft-money contributions in some elections illegal, the effects of that law on U.S. elections is not yet known.

■ *What is the military-industrial complex?*

The military-industrial complex refers to the interdependence of the military establishment and private military contractors. The military-industrial complex can be a revolving door of money, influence, and jobs.

■ *What are the sociological perspectives on the political economy?*

The functionalists use a pluralist model, believing that power is widely dispersed through many competing interest groups in our political system. Functionalists therefore believe that problems can be solved by identifying dysfunctional elements and correcting them. Conflict theorists use an elite model, believing that power in political systems is concentrated in the hands of a small group, whereas the masses are relatively powerless. Sociologist C. Wright Mills used the term *power elite* for this small group of top business leaders, the executive branch of the federal government, and the "top brass" of the military.

KEY TERMS

capitalism, p. 271
democracy, p. 280
economy, p. 271
elite model, p. 286
gender gap, p. 281
government, p. 279
military-industrial complex, p. 284
mixed economy, p. 272
monopoly, p. 276
oligopoly, p. 276
permanent government, p. 282
pluralist model, p. 285
political action committees (PACs), p. 281
political economy, p. 271
politics, p. 271
power elite, p. 286
primary sector production, p. 272
secondary sector production, p. 273
socialism, p. 271
tertiary sector production, p. 273
transnational corporation, p. 274

QUESTIONS FOR CRITICAL THINKING

1. Imagine that you are given unlimited funds and resources to reverse the trend in voter apathy. What would you do at the local level? What would you do at the state and national levels to bring about change?
2. How would you respond to the Gallup Poll survey question, "Would you say the government is pretty much run by a few big interests looking out for themselves or that it is run for the benefit of all the people?" Explain your answer.
3. Do you favor or oppose the proposal made by sociologist George Ritzer that the federal government should restrain credit card companies? Do you agree with his means—limiting profit and restricting incentives for accepting new credit cards? What other approaches would you suggest?

Chapter 14

Problems in the Media

THINKING SOCIOLOGICALLY

- How do new technologies continue to make the media more important in all aspects of contemporary life?
- Why are today's media industries known as "Big Media"?
- Do the media—either intentionally or unintentionally—perpetuate race, class, and gender stereotypes that may influence our thinking about people outside our own social groupings?

Pakistan:

Did you notice the time? Has it been five hours (or more!) since you've been watching movie clip after movie clip on YouTube? Or maybe you were just randomly searching people's profiles on Facebook or chatting on MSN with old fifth grade companions that you last met more than two decades ago, all in the name of good old "socializing" of course.

From "virtual window shopping" on E-Bay to reading tons of often low quality Internet literature in search of an inspiration to blog, compulsive webaholics have been known to spend hours on end on these and other such largely trivial activities, often disguising their struggles with Internet addiction with flashy terms like "research" and "entertainment." Yes, Internet addiction is our own worse nightmare.

—Zainub Razvi (2007) describes how he and many others in Pakistan have become addicted to the Internet in his "Confessions of Webaholics."

United States:

Dear readers,

While I was at the beach, I realized that I, Amanda Hirsch, am an Internet Addict.... It started out innocently enough. I thought I wanted a tech holiday.... But there I was, surrounded by ocean and sand, and a little voice inside me said, darkly, "give me my blogs." (I wanted to check the dozen or so blogs I read on a regular basis—a subset of the longer list of blogs to which I subscribe.)

My inner dialogue proceeded as follows:

"No! You're at the beach. You should relax."

"But—"

"No. Don't open that can of worms. You'll get sucked in and miss this beautiful day."

"But what if I really want to read blogs? Why is that so different than reading a novel? It's not like I'll be surfing aimlessly."...

Then, approximately 15 minutes later:

"Oh, it was so much fun to read my blogs, I think I'll read a little email.... "

"I know, I know, it sounds bad. But I won't check work messages—just emails from friends."

And so it began....

—Amanda Hirsch (2008), a freelance Web consultant, explains how reading blogs and emails and surfing the Internet had become a difficult habit for her to break, even when she allegedly was taking a day off for leisure activities.

From Pakistan to the United States, few forms of mass media have become so widely used and popular as quickly as the Internet with its vast amounts of information, communication options, and games to play. The Internet provides us with a vast invisible community, and it sometimes provides us with an opportunity to become a part of what is going on, not just to sit by as a passive observer as when we are watching television. As one analyst suggested, "We feel strangely connected to the unseen multitudes, including people we actually know and millions we've never met. At the same time we feel safe in our isolated electronic cocoons; we know we won't encounter bodily harm (other than a little long-term muscular atrophy)" (Bayan, 2001). Despite all the Internet has to offer as a form of media, however, it also has a potentially addictive effect on people. Whether spending large amounts of time on the Internet should or should not be considered an addiction in the medical usage of the term is a topic of widespread debate, but the American Medical Association officially stopped short of terming Internet and video game addiction as a form of mental illness (Razvi, 2007). Although individuals who "withdraw" from Internet use are not going to have physical symptoms as do those who cease to use alcohol or tobacco, some heavy Internet users believe that they would experience severe psychological effects from being disconnected from information, communications, and entertainment on the World Wide Web.

Today, the Internet is only one of a myriad of media sources that vie for our time and attention and garner billions of dollars for some of the owners of global media conglomerates. In this chapter, we examine social problems related to the political economy of media industries, potential effects the media might have on viewers and readers, and how sociological perspectives inform our thinking on media-related problems.

THE IMPORTANCE OF THE MEDIA IN CONTEMPORARY LIFE

The media play a vital role in the daily lives of many people. Whether we realize their existence or try to ignore their influence, various forms of the media are with us constantly. What constitutes the media? Media is the plural of medium, which refers to any device that transmits a message. Thus, as we noted in Chapter 4, the media include newspapers, magazines, television, and movies among other things. When sociologists refer to the media (or mass media), however, they are usually speaking of the ***media industries*****—major businesses that own or own interests in radio and television production and broadcasting; motion pictures, movie theaters, and music companies; newspaper, periodical (magazine), and book publishing; and Internet services and content providers that influence people and cultures worldwide.** To understand how pervasive media industries are in our daily lives, consider one day in the life of Scott Schatzkamer, a college student who reported that one morning he awakened to the sound of an AM/FM adult-contemporary radio station and, during the day and evening, watched ESPN's *SportsCenter* (owned by Disney), read part of Time Warner's *Sports Illustrated*, listened to a radio station owned by Disney, played Electronic Arts' Madden NFL 2000 on his fraternity's Sony PlayStation, checked his e-mail several times on AOL, logged on to ESPN.com for sports scores, read assignments in *General Chemistry* (published by Houghton Mifflin) and *Psychology in Perspective* (published by Pearson), and watched a baseball game on News Corporation's Fox Network (Heilbrunn, 2000). During the course of Scott's day, he was under the influence of numerous forms of media provided by a number of media outlets, some of which share corporate ownership at the top. Recent estimates show that the average person in the United States spends more than one-half of his or her waking hours in some media-related activity. Indeed, today, many people spend more time in media-related activities (see Table 14.1) than they do in any other single endeavor, including sleeping, working, eating, or talking with friends and family (Biagi, 2009).

Is this time well spent? Most analysts and media scholars agree that the media industries that emerged in the twentieth century are one of the most significant social institutions at work in the United States and many other nations. They facilitate human communication and provide news and entertainment. By doing so, however, they have a powerful influence on all other social institutions, including education, health-care delivery, religion, families, and politics. Some aspects of this influence are positive, but other aspects might be negative. Some critics who are concerned about possible negative influences note that we are experiencing a media glut and increasing commercialization of all aspects of life (Biagi, 2009). For example, commercialization of the Internet and the rise of the World Wide

TABLE 14.1 How Much Time Do People Spend with Mass Media?

It is estimated that the average U.S. adult age 18 and older (except as noted) spent the following number of hours with various forms of media in 2007.

Type of Media	Number of Hours
Television (including pay cable)	1,659
Radio	821
Recorded music*	189
Consumer-online Internet access	184
Daily newspapers	172
Home video games*	124
Books	108
Magazines	73
Home video	63

*Includes people age twelve and older

Source: U.S. Census Bureau, 2008.

Web in the 1990s has magnified the number of media messages and products that confront people who use computers and online services (McChesney, 2004). Other critics question the effects of contemporary media ownership on U.S. democracy (McChesney, 2004). They point out that radio, television, newspapers, and the Internet are the main sources of news and entertainment for most people; therefore, it is important to know who owns the media and to assess the quality of the information that is disseminated (Biagi, 2009; McChesney, 2004).

THE POLITICAL ECONOMY OF MEDIA INDUSTRIES

How did the contemporary media industries come to be known as "Big Media"? The answer seems to lie in one word: *technology*. Technology, in the form of motion pictures, radio, and television, increased competition and broadened markets in the twentieth century. Before that, newspapers and books had been the primary means of disseminating information and entertainment to large numbers of people simultaneously. The companies that were involved in these forms of media were usually small and focused on a single output: Newspapers were produced by companies whose only business was newspapers, and books were published by companies whose only business was books (Biagi, 2009). However, at least two factors limited the market for the information and entertainment provided by the newspaper and publishing industries: the length of time it took to get the product to consumers and the consumer's literacy. Radio, by contrast, offered consumers immediate access to information and entertainment from coast to coast. Introduced in 1920, radio promptly became a competitor to the newspaper and publishing industries. Simply by turning a knob, consumers could listen to the latest news (sometimes even as it happened), hear the latest song, laugh with their favorite comedian, or thrill to the adventures of their favorite detective. Consumers and corporate executives alike believed that radio's dominance in the media industries could not be shaken. However, in the 1950s, a new technology emerged to threaten the newspaper and radio industries: television. Television had all the advantages of radio and one more: moving images. Now consumers could not only listen to the world around them, they could also watch it.

Media Ownership and Control

Just as technology played a significant role in the development of the media industries, it has played a significant role in the changes that have occurred within these industries.

Consider, for a moment, the effects that fiber-optic cable, broadcast satellites, and computers have had on these industries. The introduction of cable television, for example, brought about a significant shift in media ownership. The development of more sophisticated space satellites in the 1970s made it possible for cable television systems to become interconnected throughout the United States and contributed to the success of cable networks such as Home Box Office (HBO) and Cable News Network (CNN), for which viewers pay a monthly fee. Having a variety of cable channels to watch increased the number of cable TV subscribers, resulting in more broadcast stations being built and the creation of additional cable channels. At the same time, the dramatic increase in cable television viewers drastically reduced the audience share previously held by the "Big Three" television networks—NBC, CBS, and ABC (Budd, Craig, and Steinman, 1999)—and led to rapid changes in the ownership and control of these networks. Within a few months in the mid-1980s, the three major networks, which had seemed indomitable, all changed ownership through purchases, takeovers, and mergers.

Although these changes seemed to have occurred overnight, some analysts point out that since the 1960s, media ownership has become increasingly more concentrated, and the trend has been for a few megacorporations to own most media businesses and for companies to own more than one form of the media business (Biagi, 2009). Still, as a result of the changes in the "Big Three," a few megacorporations gained a great deal of control over all aspects of the television industry, from program production to distribution to the audience. In their never-ending search for profit, these corporations also consolidated their holdings in other sectors of the media, ranging from film and music production to books and magazine publishing. They also acquired interests in technologies such as computers and direct broadcasting from satellite. In 2000, America Online (AOL) and Time Warner entered into the largest media merger up to that date. Why would the largest worldwide media company, Time Warner, agree to join AOL? The answer lies in access to the Internet, which is central to the contemporary music, publishing, and television industries (Hansell, 2000). Through the merger, AOL's 22 million subscribers were linked to Time Warner's cable television systems, which had about 13 million customers. Analysts describe these types of mergers in the media industries as convergence, meaning that a melding of the communications, computer, and electronics industries has occurred. Convergence in the media industry has led to media concentration. ***Media concentration* refers to the tendency of the media industries to cluster together in groups with the goal of enhancing profitability** (Biagi, 2009). Figure 14.1 shows some of the top media industries.

As this definition suggests, profit is the driving force in media concentration. According to media scholar Shirley Biagi (2009), media companies are owned by people who want to make money. Since profits in this sector are high compared with profits in the manufacturing sector, businesspeople view investments in the media industries positively. Thus far, corporate megamergers have led to the following changes in the media industries (based on Biagi, 2009):

1. *Concentration of ownership within one industry.* For example, ten chains own newspapers that represent more than 51 percent of the daily circulation in the United States. Among the top ten are the Gannett Company, Knight-Ridder, Newhouse, News Corp., the New York Times Company, Cox Enterprises, and the Tribune Company. These chains control more than 300 daily newspapers. Each firm is ranked among the 1000 largest firms in the world and does well over $1 billion in business per year (Biagi, 2009; McChesney, 2004; Asher, 2000).
2. *Cross-media ownership.* Cross-media ownership occurs when media companies own more than one type of media property. Today, a single giant media corporation might own newspapers, magazines,

NEWS CORP.	TIME WARNER	NBC UNIVERSAL	WALT DISNEY
British Sky Broadcasting	America Online (AOL)	Bravo	ABC Radio Network
Dow Jones Newswires and Indexes	Cartoon Network	CNBC	ABC Television Network
Fox Broadcasting Company	Cinemax	MSNBC	ABC radio and television stations
Fox Television Network	CNN	NBC Studios	Club Penguin
Fox Television Stations	CW Television Network	NBC Television Network	*Discovery Magazine*
FX Network	*Fortune Magazine*	SciFi Channel	Disney Channel
HarperCollins Publishing	HBO	*SciFi Magazine*	Disneyland and DisneyWorld parks and resorts
History Channel	*In Style Magazine*	Telemundo Television	ESPN Sports Network
My Space Records	New Line Cinema	Universal Pictures	Hyperion Books
National Geographic Channel	*People Magazine*	Universal Studios Theme Parks	Miramax Films
Twentieth Century Fox Films	TBS Superstation	USA Network	Disney Stores
New York Post	*Time Magazine*		Walt Disney Studios
Wall Street Journal	UBU Productions		
	Warner Bros. Entertainment		

■ *Figure 14.1* ***"Big Media" conglomerates***

radio, television stations, and numerous cable television channels. Even among smaller media corporations, cross-media ownership is common.

3. *Conglomerate ownership*. Conglomerates occur when a single corporation owns companies that operate in different business sectors. General Electric, one of the leading electronics and manufacturing firms in the United States, owns 80 percent of the stock of NBC Universal, a media conglomerate that owns NBC Television Network, NBC Studios, more than a dozen local NBC television stations, and MSNBC.
4. *Vertical integration*. Vertical integration occurs when the corporations that make the media content also control the distribution channels. Walt Disney Company, for example, owns film and television production companies (Miramax Films and ABC Entertainment Television Group), which supply programming for its television network (ABC), which helps to promote cable channels that are owned in part by Disney (ESPN, Lifetime TV and E! Entertainment TV). These in turn have ties with Hyperion, the Disney book-publishing unit.

Supporters of convergence believe that much can be gained by these corporate strategies and speak of synergy. The term *synergy* is often used to describe the process that is used in capitalizing on a product to make all the profit possible. Media analysts believe that synergy is created, for example, when a corporation acquires ownership of both a production studio and a television network. Theoretically, the products that are made by one branch of the company may be distributed and sold by the other branch of the company in a more efficient and profitable manner than they would if separate companies were involved. Rupert Murdoch's News Corporation is a good example of synergy. News Corporation produced the television program *X-Files*, aired it over its Fox network as well as its worldwide television channels, and now shows reruns on twenty-two Fox television stations and the FX cable network. *X-Files* books and other related merchandise were created and sold through subsidiaries of News Corporation. An *X-Files* movie was made by Twentieth Century Fox, which is also owned by News Corporation.

Most people in the media industries do not see consolidation as a problem. However, some media executives have acknowledged that the close link between their sectors can lead to conflicts of interest or accusations of collusion. Michael Eisner, former chairman of Disney, has stated that he believes that ABC News (which is owned by Disney) should not cover Disney.

Problems Associated with Convergence

As Table 14.2 indicates, concentration and conglomeration are profitable for investors and media executives. In 2007, forty-six members of the *Forbes* list of the 400 wealthiest people in the United States had gained their wealth from media and entertainment (*Forbes*, 2007).

TABLE 14.2 Selected Media Moguls and Their Wealth

Name	Key Media Business	Estimated Wealth
Ann Cox	Chambers Cox Enterprises	12.6 billion
Michael Bloomberg	Bloomberg	11.5 billion
John Kluge	Metromedia	9.5 billion
Rupert Murdoch	News corp	8.8 billion
Donald Newhouse	Publishing	8.5 billion
Samuel Newhouse, Jr.	Publishing	8.5 billion
Sumner Redstone	Viacom	7.6 billion
James Kennedy	Cox Enterprises	6.3 billion
Blair Parry-Okedon	Cox Enterprises	6.3 billion
David Geffen	movies, music	6.0 billion

Source: The Forbes 400: A Billion Dollars Is No Longer Enough. Retrieved July 5, 2008. Online; http://www.forbes.com/2007/09/19/richest-americans-forbes-lists-richlist07-cx_mm_0920rich_land.html

How many product placements do you see in this scene from the film Talladega Nights: The Ballad of Ricky Bobby? *Why are corporations willing to pay large amounts of money for such product placements?*

However, many analysts believe that convergence has reduced the amount of *message pluralism*, the broad and diverse representation of opinion and culture that is available to the public (Biagi, 2009). As one media scholar has noted, as a result of convergence,

> media fare is even more closely linked to the needs and concerns of a handful of enormous and powerful corporations, with annual revenues approaching the [Gross Domestic Product] of a small nation. These firms are run by wealthy managers and billionaires with clear stakes in the outcome of the most fundamental political issues, and their interests are often distinct from those of the vast majority of humanity. By any known theory of democracy, such a concentration of economic, cultural, and political power into so few hands—and mostly unaccountable hands at that—is absurd and unacceptable. On the other hand, media fare is subjected to an ever-greater commercialization as the dominant firms use their market power to squeeze the greatest possible profit from their products. (McChesney, 1999:29–30)

Commercialization and branding have found their way to the Internet, which, even as it is hailed as a new source of news and entertainment that is relatively free from corporate constraints, has experienced criticism similar to the criticism leveled at more established forms of media (see Box 14.1 on page 296).

Among the problems that analysts believe have been brought about by convergence are (1) the decline of journalism as a public service profession, (2) constant pressure for all journalistic endeavors to be immediately profitable, (3) a significant decrease in the quantity and quality of international news available to U.S. audiences, (4) the quashing of public debate about the power of the media industries and how they deal with important social issues, and (5) a dramatic increase in the influence of powerful Washington lobbyists who represent the interests of the media conglomerates (McChesney, 2004; Phillips, 1999). Because the reach of the media industries is worldwide, these concerns are not limited to the United States.

GLOBAL MEDIA ISSUES

To understand the effect transnational media corporations may have on other nations of the world, consider this: Seven major media conglomerates—Time Warner Inc., Walt Disney Company, Viacom, Inc., News Corporation, CBS Corporation, Cox Enterprises, and NBC Universal—control most of the publishing, recording, television, film, and mega–theme park business in the high-income nations of the world. Of these, Time Warner and Disney have the largest media and entertainment operations. Time Warner has more than 200 subsidiaries worldwide. The corporation owns controlling interest not only in CNN (Cable News Network) in the United States but also CNN International, which broadcasts in several languages to more than 200 nations (McChesney, 2004).

Perhaps it should not be surprising that advertising by transnational corporations has fueled the rise of commercial television, and consequently the profitability of media conglomerates, around the world. For example, more than half of the advertising on the ABN-CNBC Asia network is for transnational corporations, most of which are U.S.-based businesses (McChesney, 2004). As international agreements over trade, such as NAFTA (the North American Free Trade Agreement), and GATT (the General Agreement on Tariffs and Trade), have come into effect, companies in fields such as oil production, aerospace engineering, and agribusiness have used transnational media corporations to improve their communication base and extend their international operations (Schiller, 1996). All in all, then, the global economy has proved profitable for media conglomerates. It has been estimated that about 60 percent of all the revenues generated by U.S. film and television production companies are made in nations other than the United States.

Among analysts, however, there is growing concern about the amount of control a few media giants have over the world's information. Some have predicted that major

Social Problems in the Media

Box 14.1

media conglomerates will soon control about 90 percent of all global information (Kilbourne, 1999). These same few giant media companies are rapidly gaining ownership and control of both the hardware and the software that will make it possible for them to fully control messages and images appearing in any format (Schiller, 1996; Kilbourne, 1999). This prediction is particularly alarming to those who are already critical of how the media giants depict other nations (see Box 14.2).

Although global media industries obviously provide news and entertainment to people who otherwise might not know what is going on in the world, according to media

Social Problems in Global Perspective

Box 14.2

Skewed Depictions of China in the Media?

> Do Chinese enterprises and companies continue to sell fake pet food, pharmaceuticals, tires, toothpaste, and toys around the world?
>
> Did China clean up its environmental problems just long enough for the Olympic Games to be held?
>
> Is corruption a major problem in China?
>
> Has China stepped up persecution of Buddhist monks with mass detentions in Tibet?

These are only a few of the headline stories aired on television, published in newspapers, and written on web blogs during the 2008 Summer Olympic Games in China. These questions raised the issue among some analysts about whether media coverage of China was accurate or if it provided a skewed depiction of that nation.

Is the U.S. media biased in its coverage of China? Some analysts believe that media coverage of China is unduly critical and reflects an underlying bias held by some American televisions news anchors, journalists, and bloggers who argue that the old mold of the repressive Communist Party cannot be broken and that censorship and social problems remain rampant in that nation. They cited, for example, the fact that the Chinese government placed a ban during the 2008 Beijing Olympics on live television broadcasts from Tiananmen Square—the location where Chinese troops rushed in and killed pro-democracy protesters in 1989. Did hosting the Games in China and having 24/7 media coverage of the events and surrounding activities demonstrate that the country now has greater openness? Or did Chinese Communist Party officials hope to make their nation *appear* to be more open than in the past (Associated Press, 2008)?

In response to that question, other analysts stated that media coverage of China has been relatively balanced in how it shows the state of life in that country. According to this perspective, discussions in the media about the "Greening of China," for example, are accurate in that leaders have continued to welcome clean energy technology to their nation; however, they are overcome by problems that make it difficult to bring about this change. Party leaders would like for Western companies to come in and help develop products and services that will produce a cleaner environment in the future. China would also like to break its addiction to oil, develop a stronger tourism industry, and have a "cleaner, knowledge-based, service/financial economy" (Friedman, 2008: WK10).

One American journalist writing from Guangzhou, China, may have summed up the reality of depictions of China in the media when he stated that, on issues such as the development of wind power, "It's a good news/bad news story." Perhaps this statement can be generalized to other types of coverage of that nation as well. The journalist, *New York Times* columnist, and best-selling book author Thomas L. Friedman (2008:WK10) summed up how he might write a "Postcard from South China" about his "summer vacation" observations:

> Dear Mom and Dad, this place is so much more interesting than it looks from abroad. I met wind and solar companies eager for Western investment and Chinese college students who were organizing a boycott of an Indonesian paper company for despoiling their forest. An "Institute of Civil Society" has quietly opened at the local Sun Yat-sen University. The Communist Party is trying to break the old mold without breaking its hold. It's quite a drama. Can't wait to come back next summer and see how they're doing. . . .

As Friedman suggests, nations that are in the midst of change, with plenty of resistance to that change simultaneously being present, are difficult for media analysts to accurately describe: Do you focus primarily on the positive? Do you emphasize the negative? Is it possible to balance both perspectives? These are the questions that media commentators must face on a global basis as they attempt to describe politics and social life, with all of its attendant strengths and weaknesses, in the widely diverse nations of the world. (For an additional discussion of media coverage in China, see Box 14.3, "Critical Thinking and You" on page 305.)

critic Robert McChesney (1999), they also contribute to the development of "neoliberal" democracies in those nations in which people have the formal right to vote but the wealthy actually hold political and economic power:

> The global commercial media system is radical, in the sense that it will respect no tradition or custom, on balance, if it stands in the way of significantly increased profits. But it ultimately is politically conservative, because the media giants are significant beneficiaries of the current global social structure, and any upheaval in property or social relations, particularly to the extent it reduced the power of business and lessened inequality, would possibly—no, probably—jeopardize their positions. (McChesney, 1999:100).

Many critics also worry that the U.S.-based giants undermine traditional cultural values and beliefs, replacing them with U.S. values, particularly those supporting materialism and consumerism. According to media critic Jean Kilbourne (1999:55), "Although the conglomerates are transnational, the culture they sell is American.... Today we export a popular culture that promotes escapism, consumerism, violence, and greed." Kilbourne (1999:56) provides this example:

> In 1980 the Gwich'in tribe of Alaska got television, and therefore massive advertising for the first time. Satellite dishes, video games, and VCRs were not far behind. Before this, the Gwich'in lived much the way their ancestors had for a thousand generations. Within ten years, the young members of the tribe were so drawn by television they no longer had time to learn ancient hunting methods, their parents' language, or their oral history. Legends told around campfires could not compete with *Beverly Hills 90210*. Beaded moccasins gave way to Nike sneakers, sled dogs to gas-powered skimobiles, and "tundra tea" to Folger's instant coffee.

As Kilbourne and other media scholars point out, for the first time in history, people are hearing most stories of life not from their parents, schools, churches, or friends, but from transnational media conglomerates that have something to sell. If it is true that the media are a crucial influence in shaping and creating global cultural perceptions, then all of us must give careful consideration to the images and information offered to us.

Children and young people often watch violent scenes such as this on television. Social scientists are interested in how such images influence a person's attitudes about violence throughout life.

POTENTIAL MEDIA EFFECTS

Today, as we have said, the global media industries are the primary source of news and entertainment for many people. Although these industries probably have greater influence over some people than others, media analysts suggest that all of us are more profoundly—and often negatively—influenced by media messages than we realize. In at least two areas—the portrayal of aggression and violence and the presentation of race, class, and gender stereotypes—the influence might be negative.

Aggression, Violence, and the Media

Should we be concerned about how—and the extent to which—the media depict aggressive and/or violent behavior? A number of media analysts assert that the need of media industries to capture public interest and thus increase the size of their markets has contributed to the use of violence or incidences of violence as a means of selling newspapers, television programs, movies, heavy metal and rap music, and other media-related commodities. According to an extensive study that was conducted by the Center for Communications and Social Policy at the University of California at Santa Barbara, violent television shows made up 60 percent of all television programming during the three years of the study. Moreover, that percentage continued to increase over the course of the study (Stern, 1998). A comprehensive economic analysis of television programming led one researcher to conclude that violent fare emerges as a logical extension of commercial broadcasting. Although television executives claim that their programs reflect audience desires, they do so in a commercially exploitable manner (Hamilton, 1998). In other words, when audiences say that they want to see justice triumph, television executives make sure that justice does triumph in their programs—but only after several violent fights or shootings that hold viewers in their seats even during commercials.

What effect does the depiction of violence have on audiences? There is no definitive answer to this question. Most scholars do not believe that the media *cause* aggressive behavior in people. Although there have been some studies that have shown a relationship between at least short-term aggressive behavior and media depictions of violence, other studies have suggested that the media might actually prevent acts of violence by providing people with an outlet for pent-up feelings and emotions. According to the *cathartic effect hypothesis*, television shows, videos, motion pictures, and other forms of media offer people a vicarious outlet for their feelings of aggression and thus may reduce the amount of violence engaged in by the media consumer. Believing that research does not support this hypothesis, other analysts have suggested that continual depictions of violence tend to desensitize viewers and create values that contribute to aggressive behavior and feelings of fear and frustration (Gerbner, 1995). These analysts point out that depictions of violence do not require the use of language; thus global audiences are drawn to violence because it needs no translation. Over time, however, desensitization makes it necessary for films and television programming to become even more violent to attract the potential audience's attention. This theory might help to explain the recent popularity of animal documentaries showing "kill sequences" and blood fights among animals (McElvogue, 1997). At a minimum, constant exposure to violence-laden media content might contribute to an individual's feelings of fear and a need for greater security and protection in everyday life.

According to media scholar Jean Kilbourne, one of the many ways in which the media perpetuate violence against women is through advertising. Kilbourne (1999) analyzed tens of thousands of advertisements to determine what effect they might have on viewers. According to Kilbourne, "The poses and postures of advertising are often borrowed from pornography, as are many of the themes, such as bondage, sadomasochism, and the sexual exploitation of children" (Kilbourne, 1999:271). She points out that advertisements showing women as dead or in the process of being killed are particularly popular themes among perfume advertisers. Advertising in other nations can be even more explicit. An Italian version of *Vogue* showed a man aiming a gun at a nude woman who was wrapped in plastic and had a leather briefcase covering her face (Kilbourne, 1999).

Media advertising also tends to treat women as sexual objects. To sell products, advertisements frequently show women in compromised positions or as the victims of rape or other violence and thus contribute to the ongoing subordination of women. Such depictions may also suggest that forcing sex on a woman is an acceptable norm, as Kilbourne (1999:273) points out:

> Men are also encouraged [by advertisements] to never take no for an answer. Ad after ad implies that girls and women don't really mean "no" when they say it, that women are only teasing when they resist men's advances. "NO" says an ad showing a man leaning over a woman against a wall. Is she screaming or laughing? Oh, it's an ad for deodorant and the second word, in very small print, is "sweat." Sometimes it's "all in good fun," as in the ad for Possession shirts and shorts featuring a man ripping the clothes off a woman who seems to be having a good time. And sometimes it is more sinister. A perfume ad running in several teen magazines features a very young woman, with eyes blackened by makeup or perhaps something else, and the copy, "Apply generously to your neck so he can smell the scent as you shake your head 'no.'" In other words, he'll understand that we don't really mean it and he can respond to the scent like any other animal.

As studies continue on the relationship between violence in the media and in everyday life, we will no doubt learn more about the causes and consequences of extensive media violence in society.

Racial and Ethnic Stereotyping

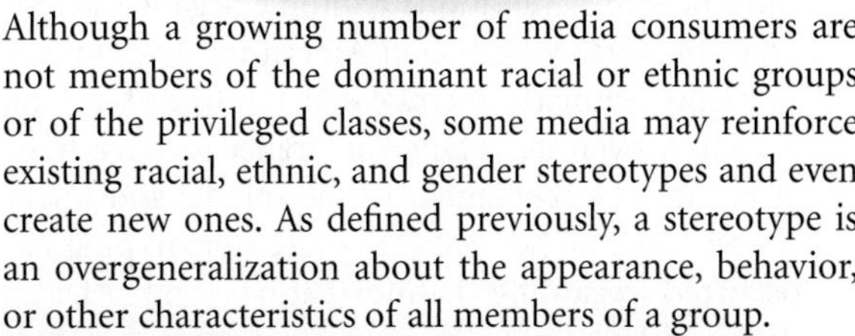

Although a growing number of media consumers are not members of the dominant racial or ethnic groups or of the privileged classes, some media may reinforce existing racial, ethnic, and gender stereotypes and even create new ones. As defined previously, a stereotype is an overgeneralization about the appearance, behavior, or other characteristics of all members of a group.

Numerous media scholars have documented the long history of stereotyping of racial and ethnic subordinate groups in film, television programming, and other media forms. Studies have examined the effects of stereotyping on people's perceptions of groups ranging from Italian Americans and Jewish Americans to African Americans, Latinos/Latinas, Asian and Pacific Americans, and Arab Americans.

No matter which racial or ethnic group is depicted, stereotyping often involves one or more of the following:

1. *Perpetuating images that appear to be positive in nature and thus flattering to members of a specific racial or ethnic group but which convey a negative undertone.* For example, some stereotypes attribute a superior trait or ability, such as being "naturally" better at activities such as music and sports or mathematics and science, to members of one racial or ethnic category. Exaggerating African Americans' proficiency at sports or Asian Americans' ability to do math are among the continuing one-dimensional characterizations of many films and television shows, including several recent reality series.
2. *Exaggerating the physical appearance of subordinate-group members or suggesting that all people in a specific category "look alike" or "act alike."* Statements by subordinate-group characters in various forms of media entertainment, such as "Well, you know how all of us _____s are!" supposedly are inoffensive because they are spoken by a person from that racial or ethnic category, and some analysts see nothing wrong with this, believing that such comments are not meant to be taken seriously. However, constant repetition of the same "humorous" comments may influence our perceptions about people.
3. *Creating racial or ethnic characters who have undesirable attributes, ranging from laziness and unwillingness to work to a lack of education or intelligence and lower class attitudes and behavior.* Italian-American media-watch groups such as the National Italian American Foundation have argued that shows such as *The Sopranos* (a fictionalized TV entertainment show now in syndication) reinforce negative stereotypes by portraying Italian Americans as criminals or bigots. Similarly, members of the white working class have been stereotyped as "trailer park trash" or as lacking the refinement of the middle and upper classes. Overall, however, far more stereotyping has occurred regarding Latinos/Latinas and African Americans.
4. *Using statements and visual images that link subordinate racial or ethnic group members to illegal actions, such as terrorism, gang or organized crime activity, prostitution, and drug dealing.* In the aftermath of the 9/11 (2001) terrorist attacks in the United States and the 7/7 (2005) attacks in London, Arab and Muslim stereotypes have been considered "fair game" by many television comedians and entertainment writers. However, this is not an entirely new occurrence: For many years Hollywood films—many of which are now shown on classic movie cable channels—have portrayed Arabs in a negative manner, often as violent, religious fanatics or as outlandish sheiks or seductive belly dancers, leaving audiences to think of Arabs as being "all alike" even though persons in this category come from more than twenty-two different countries.

Why does racial and ethnic stereotyping persist in the entertainment media? Negative stereotyping continues to exist in shows and films for several reasons. Offensive material, including the use of negative stereotypes, offensive language, and inappropriate behavior, often produces controversy, which brings more media coverage and sometimes turns an average or mediocre television show or film into an overnight success. Similarly, racial stereotyping is frequently used for comic effect or to create stock characters. Media entertainment writers, editors, and producers heavily rely on readily recognizable stock characters who make it possible for audiences to give little thought to who the person is or what he or she is really like so that the plot on a sitcom or the "games" on a reality TV show can begin. In reality television, conflict among the contenders (such as to become Donald Trump's next apprentice or to win the big prize after numerous ordeals on *Survivor*) is heavily edited before the programs are aired. By selecting contestants with divergent attributes, such as race/ethnicity, age, gender, or education level, and by emphasizing those differences during filming, it is easier to incite conflict among the contenders that can be further edited to create greater controversy and generate audience interest.

Obviously, stereotypes sometimes are unintentional. However, when media creators and producers become aware of the negative effects that stereotypical depictions may have on subordinate-group members, particularly children, will they continue to perpetuate these images? Perhaps as the media industries and those who use them to advertise their goods begin to view nonwhite racial and ethnic groups around the globe as viable consumers of their products, greater concern will be shown over stereotypical images.

Gender Stereotyping

According to scholars who have conducted studies of gender stereotypes in the contemporary media, such stereotyping may result, at least in part, from the underrepresentation of women as producers, directors, and executives in the largest media industries. Regardless of the cause, some studies of television and film have shown the following gender stereotypes of women:

1. *The intertwining of gender and age bias as it uniquely affects women.* Gender-specific age bias is apparent in the casting of many female characters. Older men and significantly younger women are often cast in leading roles in films, causing some women actors to ask "where are the roles for older women in Hollywood?"
2. *The perpetuation of traditional roles for women and the maintenance of cultural stereotypes about the importance of beauty, thinness, and femininity for getting and keeping a man.* Female characters who do not live up to the gendered expectations associated with femininity are overtly or subtly punished for their conduct. ABC's *Desperate Housewives* is both a satiric portrayal of housewives living in suburbia and a reaffirmation of beliefs about how white, affluent women should look and behave, particularly if they want to get and keep a husband.
3. *Impulsive conduct by women holding professional positions.* When television shows portray professional women, the women are often shown as engaging in compulsive behavior such as constantly purchasing very expensive designer shoes, smoking or drinking alcohol excessively, and having other bizarre habits. Men are not exempted from such portrayals, but they are more likely to be shown as displaying professional competence in the workplace.
4. *Women in positions of power as abusing their positions.* Prior to the 1990s, most female characters were depicted in lower-status occupations or in roles that were clearly subordinate to those of men. Although more female characters on prime-time television shows and in film today are lawyers or judges than in the past, these characters are often shown as "seducers, harassers, and wimps in black robes" (Goodman, 1999:AR 47). When female characters are not seducing men, they are often depicted as "bitches" or "bimbos." On *Judge Judy*, Judy Sheindlin, a former family court judge in New York, berates and demeans people appearing in her court (Goodman, 1999).
5. *Women overwhelmed by their work or seemingly having few job responsibilities even when they are employed full-time.* The imbalance between the portrayal of female characters as either having so much work to do that they cannot complete it all or the depiction of them as having an important occupation but spending little time actually doing the work tends to convey the message that women are less than adequate in many careers and occupations. In the ABC series, *Brothers & Sisters*, for example, Kitty Walker (played by Calista Flockhart) is the Communications Director for her husband's presidential campaign; however, rather than being portrayed as busily working on behalf of his election (which would be the typical role of a Communications Director), she is routinely shown engaging in activities such as getting dance lessons or selecting one of the multiple wedding dresses she selected during a single season of the series.

Although the depiction of women characters in television programs, films, and other forms of media has improved significantly in recent decades, much remains to be done if women are to be shown in the wide diversity of occupations and endeavors in which real-life women participate on a daily basis.

Although "Judge Judy" Sheindlin's remarks are sometimes tempered with humor, she often berates the people who appear in her TV courtroom. Why are "outspoken women" often evaluated more harshly than "firm, decisive men"?

It should be noted that, although the nature of male stereotypes is somewhat different, men have not been exempt from gender stereotyping in the media. Among the most frequently employed stereotypes of male characters are men depicted primarily as jokers, jocks, strong silent types, big shots, action heroes, or buffoons. For example, working-class men frequently are portrayed as buffoons who are dumb, immature, irresponsible, or lacking in common sense. These male characters are the object of jokes and are often shown as being sloppy in appearance, ignorant, and sometimes racist (Kendall, 2005).

SOCIOLOGICAL PERSPECTIVES ON MEDIA-RELATED PROBLEMS

Just as they do in regard to other social issues, symbolic interactionist, functionalist, and conflict approaches to media-related problems start with differing assumptions about these problems.

The Symbolic Interactionist Perspective

Perhaps the earliest symbolic interactionist theory concerning the media's effect on individuals and groups was the *hypodermic needle theory*, which suggested that audiences were made up of passive individuals who were equally susceptible to the messages of the media. However, a World War II study of military personnel who were shown movies that were designed to portray the enemy as evil and to increase morale among soldiers concluded that most of the subjects showed little change in their morale level. On the basis of these findings, researchers suggested an alternative explanation: the theory of limited effects. **The *theory of limited effects* states that the media have a minimal effect on the attitudes and perceptions of individuals.** According to this theory, people are not always selective about what they watch or read, but they gather different messages from the media, and many people carefully evaluate the information they gain. This theory notes that when people are interested in and informed about an issue, they are less likely to be influenced by what members of the media report. Those who are poorly informed or have no personal information about a particular topic or issue are likely to be affected by what other people, including reporters and journalists, say about the social concern.

A similar theory, known as *use and gratification theory*, suggests that people are active audience participants who make conscious decisions about what they will watch, listen to, and read and where they will surf on the Internet. However, this theory assumes that people using different media have specific wishes or desires and will choose media sources that gratify their desires. In other words, people use the media to entertain and inform themselves but are aware of the limitations the media have in their coverage of topics and the forms of entertainment.

Another symbolic interactionist theory, mentioned in previous chapters, is ***social learning theory*, which is based on the assumption that people are likely to act out the behavior they see in role models and media sources.** To support this theory, social psychologist Albert Bandura conducted a series of experiments on aggression in children (Bandura and Walters, 1977). For the experiment, children were divided into four groups. One group watched a film of a man attacking and beating a large, inflatable doll and being rewarded for his behavior. The second group saw a similar film, except that in this version the man was punished for attacking the doll. The third group was shown a version in which the man was neither rewarded nor punished for his behavior. The final group was not shown any film. Before the experiment, researchers believed that the children who saw the man rewarded for hitting the doll would be the most likely to show aggressive behavior toward the doll. However, this did not prove to be true. Regardless of which version of the film they saw, children who were prone to aggression before the film tended to act aggressively toward the doll, but other children did not. As a result, the researchers concluded that many factors other than the media influenced aggressive behavior in children, including their relationship with their parents, how much formal education their parents possessed, and the personality of the children.

More recent theories have sought to explain the effects of media on individuals by emphasizing the part that viewers, listeners, and readers play in shaping the media. According to the *audience relations approach*, people use their own cultural understandings to interpret what they hear and see in the media. Factors involved in the audience relations approach include how much previous knowledge individuals have about a topic and the availability of other sources of information. This viewpoint is somewhat in keeping with functionalist approaches, which highlight the important contemporary functions of the media.

The Functionalist Perspective

Functionalist approaches to examining the media often focus on the functional—and sometimes dysfunctional—effects the media have on society. Functionalists point out that the media serve several important functions in contemporary societies.

- First, the media provide news and information, including warnings about potential disasters such as an approaching hurricane.
- Second, the media facilitate public discourse regarding social issues and policies such as welfare reform.
- Third, the media pass on cultural traditions and historical perspectives, particularly to recent immigrants and children (Lasswell, 1969).
- Fourth, the media are a source of entertainment, providing people with leisure-time activities (Biagi, 2009).
- Finally, the media confer status on individuals and organizations by frequently reporting on their actions or showing their faces and mentioning their names. According to sociologist Joshua Gamson (1994:186), becoming a media celebrity is a means of gaining power, privilege, and mobility: "Audiences recognize this when they seek brushes with it and when they fantasize about the freedom of fame and its riches and about the distinction of popularity and attention."

As Gamson notes, some people become celebrities because the media confer that status on them. In other words, as the popular saying goes, "Some people are famous for being famous." For example, most people in the United States knew nothing about the Kardashian family until the American reality-based television series *Keeping Up With the Kardashians* was introduced on E! The daily ups and downs of the Kardashian/Jenner family constitute the entire storyline for this continuing series. Kris Jenner, the mother, was married in real life to the late Robert Kardashian, who became famous as one of the defense attorneys in the highly-televised O. J. Simpson murder trial. She is currently married to Bruce Jenner, an Olympics champion in the 1970s. The older daughters in the Kardashian/Jenner family own a women's boutique, named DASH, and the son dates actress/singer Adrienne Bailon. Synopses of two episodes show the extent to which the idea of "famous for being famous" may apply here: "Khloe attends acting class; Kris hires a fashion consultant for Bruce" and "Kris injures her knee training to be a cheerleader; Kourtney, Kim, and Khloe teach their younger sisters about puberty."

Although the media are a source of entertainment for many, functionalist theorists state that the media are

Most of the world would not have heard of the Kardashians if they had not starred in E! Television Network's reality series, Keeping Up With the Kardashians. *Shown here are the mother and stepfather, Kris and Bruce Jenner, of the Kardashian sisters, Khloe, Kourtney, and Kim. Do you think the comment, "Famous for being famous" might apply here? Why or why not?*

dysfunctional when they contribute to a reduction in social stability or weaken other social institutions such as the family, education, politics, and religion. For example, television has brought about significant changes in family interaction patterns, as one media scholar explains:

> The most pervasive effect of television—aside from its content—may be its very existence, its readily available, commanding, and often addictive presence in our homes, its ability to reduce hundreds of millions of citizens to passive spectators for major portions of their waking hours. Television minimizes interactions between persons within families and communities. One writer I know only half-jokingly claims, "I watch television as a way of getting to know my husband and children." Another associate, who spent years in Western agrarian regions, relates how a farmer once told her: "Folks used to get together a lot. Now with television, we see less of each other." (Parenti, 1998:188)

Over time, the media not only change how people interact with each other, but also can have a profound influence on individuals' perceptions of one another and their impressions of the world. When dysfunctions occur, the problems should be addressed for the benefit of individuals, families, and the larger society. Some functionalist approaches suggest that individuals and families are responsible for social change in regard to the media. Analysts who favor this approach suggest that rather than changing the nature of television programming, parents should monitor their children's television watching, and schools should offer media education for parents and children to make them aware of the classic persuasion and propaganda techniques often used in programming and advertising (Minow and LaMay, 1999).

The Conflict Perspective

Conflict theorists typically link the media industries with the capitalist economy. In this approach, members of the capitalist class own and control the media, which, along with other dominant social institutions, instruct people in the values, beliefs, and attitudes that they should have (Curran, Gurevitch, and Woollacott, 1982). According to this perspective, the *process of legitimization* takes place as media consumers are continually provided with information that supports the validity of existing class relations. As a result, members of the working class are lulled into a sense of complacency in which they focus more on entertainment and consumption than on questioning existing economic and social relations. This perspective is sometimes referred to as ***hegemony theory*****—the view that the media are instruments of social control and are used by members of the ruling classes to create "false consciousness" in the working classes.** Although there are various conflict approaches, most view ownership and economic control of the media as a key factor in determining what kinds of messages are disseminated around the globe. Media analysts such as Michael Parenti (1998:149) believe that media bias is inevitable as transnational media industries become concentrated in the hands of a few megacorporations:

> Media bias usually does not occur in random fashion; rather, it moves in the same overall direction again and again, favoring management over labor, corporations over corporate critics, affluent whites over inner-city poor, officialdom over protestors, the two-party monopoly over leftist third parties, privatization and free-market "reforms" over public-sector development, U.S. domination of the Third World over revolutionary or populist social change, investor globalization over nation-state democracy, national security policy over critics of that policy, and conservative commentators and columnists...over progressive or populist ones.

According to Parenti, the built-in biases of the media reflect the dominant ideology that supports the privileged position of members of the capitalist class. Parenti (1998) lists a number of ways in which media manipulation occurs: (1) Sponsors control broadcasting decisions; (2) information might be suppressed by omitting certain details of a story or the entire story, particularly if the story could have a negative effect on a person or organization to whom members of the media feel beholden; (3) a story might be attacked or the reporting may not present a balanced view of the diverse viewpoints involved; (4) negative labels that subsume a large number of people, for example, "Islamic terrorists," "inner-city gangs," might be used; and (5) stories might be framed to convey positive or negative connotations through the use of visual effects, placement, and other means. Like other conflict theorists, Parenti (1998:157) believes that the media tell people what to think before they have had a chance to think about an issue for themselves: "When we understand that news selectivity is likely to favor those who have power, position, and wealth, we move from a liberal complaint about the press's sloppy performance to

Spiderman *movies made in the United States have captured the attention of audiences around the world. Shown here on a cinema wall in Beijing is an ad for* Spiderman 3. *Are films such as this popular worldwide because of the universality of their appeal to audiences or is this a reflection of the aggressive marketing practices of major media conglomerates?*

a radical analysis of how the media serve the ruling circles all too well with much skill and craft."

In an era marked by increased concentration of all forms of media, including the Internet and the World Wide Web, conflict perspectives on media ownership and control raise important questions in the United States and around the world (see Box 14.3). Although people who are engaged in political dissent and social activism, such as the U.S. environmental movement, have been able to marshal the media on their behalf, the media often implicitly support the status quo because of their own corporate interests and the need to maintain and enhance advertising revenues.

Regardless of which theoretical perspective on the media industries most closely resembles our own thinking, each of us should take a closer look at the ideas, images, and advertisements that bombard us daily. Although most of us may believe that we are not affected by the constant stream of advertisements that we encounter, we should realize, as media scholar Jean Kilbourne (1999:27) states, "The fact is that much of advertising's power comes from this belief that advertising does not affect us. The most effective kind of propaganda is that which is not recognized as propaganda." Although individuals alone cannot solve the problems associated with the media industries, they can become more aware of the pervasive impact of television, films, newspapers, the Internet, and other forms of mass communication.

Critical Thinking and You — Box 14.3

Media Ownership: Can Business and Personal Ties Create a Disservice to Audiences?

- Mr. [Rupert] Murdoch has flattered Communist Party leaders and done business with their children.
- His Fox News network helped China's leading state broadcaster develop a news Web site.
- He joined hands with the Communist Youth League, a power base in the ruling party, in a risky television venture, his China managers and advisers say. (Kahn, 2007).

These statements about how Rupert Murdoch has attempted to break into the Chinese media market with his News Corporation indicate that conflict perspectives on media ownership and control may have some validity in assessing the kinds of coverage we receive about nations such as China. Media analysts have suggested that he has cooperated with China's censors and state broadcasters, that he has cultivated political ties that he hopes will keep him from having regulatory interference in regard to his business ventures, and he has often gone on the record as supporting the politics of Chinese leaders (Kahn, 2007).

As a result of Mr. Murdoch's efforts, he has been the guest of a variety of Chinese political leaders on numerous occasions. Murdock's television channels provide more programming in China than any other foreign media group. These channels include not only news but also movies, music videos, and sports. In recent years, News Corporation has also developed a partnership with China Mobile, the state-owned company that is the world's largest mobile communications operator, in hopes of providing media content to mobile-phone users. He and his wife own a residence in Beijing, and she has extensive business connections in the nation as well. Are business and personal ties such as those of Rupert Murdoch just a matter of good business and personal preferences, or do they affect the media coverage of nations such as China?

Questions for Critical Thinking

1. Should media owners become involved in the politics of a nation? Does it matter whether this involvement occurs in the United States or in a foreign country?
2. If you analyze the possible effects of Rupert Murdoch's relationships with political leaders in China, do you believe that his involvement with Communist Party leaders will influence how his company, News Corporation, frames news stories about that nation? Why or why not?
3. How might it be possible to provide the "fairest" news coverage of various nations around the world?

ARE THERE SOLUTIONS TO MEDIA-RELATED PROBLEMS?

Problems associated with the media will continue well into this century, and many of the issues will probably become even more complex. For example, it has been suggested that the Internet and e-commerce will affect all aspects of life, particularly in high-income nations such as the United States. Some analysts have suggested that U.S. cities will lose more of their tax base to untaxed Internet commerce, bringing about a need to restructure relations between cities, states, and the federal government (Friedman, 2000). Indeed, the ability of a single government to control the activities of transnational media industries may be weakened as globalization continues to occur. Thus according to journalist Thomas L. Friedman (2000:A31), a world of global communications means that many issues that were once considered the domain of individual nations and governments will have to be rethought:

> Issues such as freedom of speech and libel are going to have to be rethought as the Internet makes everyone a potential publisher in cyberspace—but with no censor or editor in charge. Privacy protection is going to have to be rethought in a world where for $39 web sites will search out anyone's assets and home address for you. And our safety nets are going to have to be rethought in a world in which access to the Internet is going to be viewed as a human right, essential for basic survival—especially as governments move more services to the web.

In the years to come, new communication technology will undoubtedly continue to change our lives. Although new forms of media offer many potential benefits, they also raise serious concerns about social life as many of us know it.

SUMMARY

■ *What are the media industries? How much time do individuals spend in media-related activities?*

According to social scientists, the media industries are media businesses that influence people and cultures worldwide and own interests in radio and television production and broadcasting; motion pictures, movie theaters, and music companies; newspaper, periodical (magazine), and book publishing; and Internet services and content providers. Today, many people spend more time in media-related activities than they do in any other single endeavor, including sleeping, working, eating, or talking with friends and family; therefore some analysts believe that the media have a major influence on how people think, feel, and act.

■ *What part does technology play in how various media industries change over time?*

For many years, newspapers were the primary source of news. However, new technologies brought about radio as the media phenomenon of the 1920s and television as the phenomenon of the 1950s. With the introduction of communications technologies such as computers, fiber-optic cable, and broadcast satellites, the media industries continue to change rapidly.

■ *How has media ownership changed?*

Although there once were a variety of independent companies that produced books, records, television programs, and films, there are now large corporate conglomerates that own more than one form of the media business.

■ *What is convergence? How does it relate to media concentration?*

Convergence refers to a melding of the communications, computer, and electronics industries that gives a few huge corporations control over an increasing proportion of all media sources. Convergence contributes to greater concentration in the media. Media concentration refers to the tendency of the media industries to cluster together in groups.

■ *What forms can media concentration take?*

Media concentration can take several forms: (1) within one industry (such as newspaper chains); (2) cross-media ownership, in which media companies own more than one type of media property (such as newspaper chains and television stations); (3) conglomerate ownership, in which corporations own media properties but also own other businesses; and (4) vertical integration, in which the corporations that make the media content also control the distribution channels (such as film and television production companies, television networks, and movie theaters).

■ *Why do some people favor media convergence whereas others do not?*

Supporters believe that much can be gained from the synergy created by media convergence because it makes it possible to take a media brand and capitalize on it. This process is clearly profitable for investors and media executives; however, media critics believe that convergence limits the news and entertainment that the public receives by reducing message pluralism. Other problems include (1) the decline of journalism as a public service profession, (2) constant pressure for all journalistic endeavors to be immediately profitable, (3) a significant decrease in the quantity and quality of international news available to U.S. audiences, (4) the quashing of public debate about the power of the media industries and how they deal with important social issues, and (5) a dramatic increase in the influence of powerful Washington lobbyists representing the interests of the media giants.

■ *What potential problems are associated with global media concentration?*

A few large media conglomerates are rapidly gaining control over most of the publishing, recording, television, film, and mega–theme park business worldwide. One major problem is the extent to which a few media giants have almost complete control over the world's information. Some people in other nations have been critical of how the media conglomerates depict nations around the globe and the influence, often negative, that they have on the politics and culture of other nations.

■ *Why are some media critics concerned about depictions of violence in the media?*

Although most scholars do not believe that the media cause aggressive behavior in people, a number of media analysts assert that the media's need to capture public interest has contributed to the gratuitous use of violence as a means of selling newspapers, television programming, movie tickets, heavy metal and rap music, and other media-related commodities. According to a recent study, violent television shows made up 60 percent of all television programming. Some studies have shown a relationship between short-term aggressive behavior and media depictions of violence; however, others have suggested that the media may prevent acts of violence by providing people with an outlet for pent-up feelings and emotions.

■ *What forms of media communication typically show violence against women?*

According to media scholar Jean Kilbourne, advertising, which often uses semipornographic images and themes such as bondage, sadomasochism, and the sexual exploitation of children to sell products, is one of the ways in which the media perpetuate violence against women. The media also contribute to the view of women as sexual objects that do not need to be taken seriously.

■ *What is a stereotype and how can the media perpetuate stereotypes about racial and ethnic groups?*

A stereotype is an overgeneralization about the appearance, behavior, or other characteristics of all members of a group. The media can perpetuate stereotypes by casting some groups as having superior traits such as being "naturally" better at music and sports or mathematics and science and then using the "model minority" image to question why some people succeed while others do not. Other media stereotyping includes exaggerating people's physical appearance, suggesting that all people in a specific category "look alike," creating racial or ethnic characters who have undesirable attributes, and using statements and visual images that continually link subordinate racial or ethnic group members to illegal actions.

■ *Why is gender stereotyping pervasive in the media? What major forms does this problem take?*

Underrepresentation of women among producers, directors, and executives in the largest media industries might be a factor in the more limited range of roles available to women in television programs and films. First, gender-specific age bias is apparent in the casting of many female characters. Second, television shows and films often perpetuate traditional roles for women and maintain cultural stereotypes of femininity.

■ *How do symbolic interactionists explain the influence of the media on individuals?*

According to the theory of limited effects, the media have a minimal effect on individuals' attitudes and perceptions. The use and gratification theory suggests that people are active audience participants who make conscious decisions about what they will watch, listen to, and read and where they will surf on the Internet. However, social learning theory is based on the assumption that people are likely to act out the behavior they see in role models and media sources. The audience relations approach states that people interpret what they hear and see in the media by using their own cultural understandings as a mental filtering device.

■ *How do functionalist and conflict perspectives on the media differ?*

According to some functionalist analysts, the media fulfill several important functions in contemporary societies, including providing news and information, facilitating public discourse on social issues and policies, passing on cultural traditions and historical perspectives, and entertaining people. In contrast, conflict theorists assert that members of the capitalist class (either intentionally or unintentionally) use the media to provide information that supports the validity of existing class relations. Hegemony theory states that the media are an instrument of social control that is used by members of the ruling classes to create false consciousness in the working classes.

KEY TERMS

hegemony theory, p. 304
media concentration, p. 293
media industries, p. 291
social learning theory, p. 302
theory of limited effects, p. 302

QUESTIONS FOR CRITICAL THINKING

1. Why is media concentration a potentially greater social problem than concentration in other industries?
2. If you were an owner or large shareholder in a major media company, how might you view synergy? What negative effects might synergy have on those who are in your reading, listening, viewing, and/or Internet audiences?
3. Is continued consolidation in the media a serious threat to democracy? Should we be concerned about the ability of some companies to "buy" political influence? Why or why not?

Chapter 15

Population, Global Inequality, and the Environmental Crisis

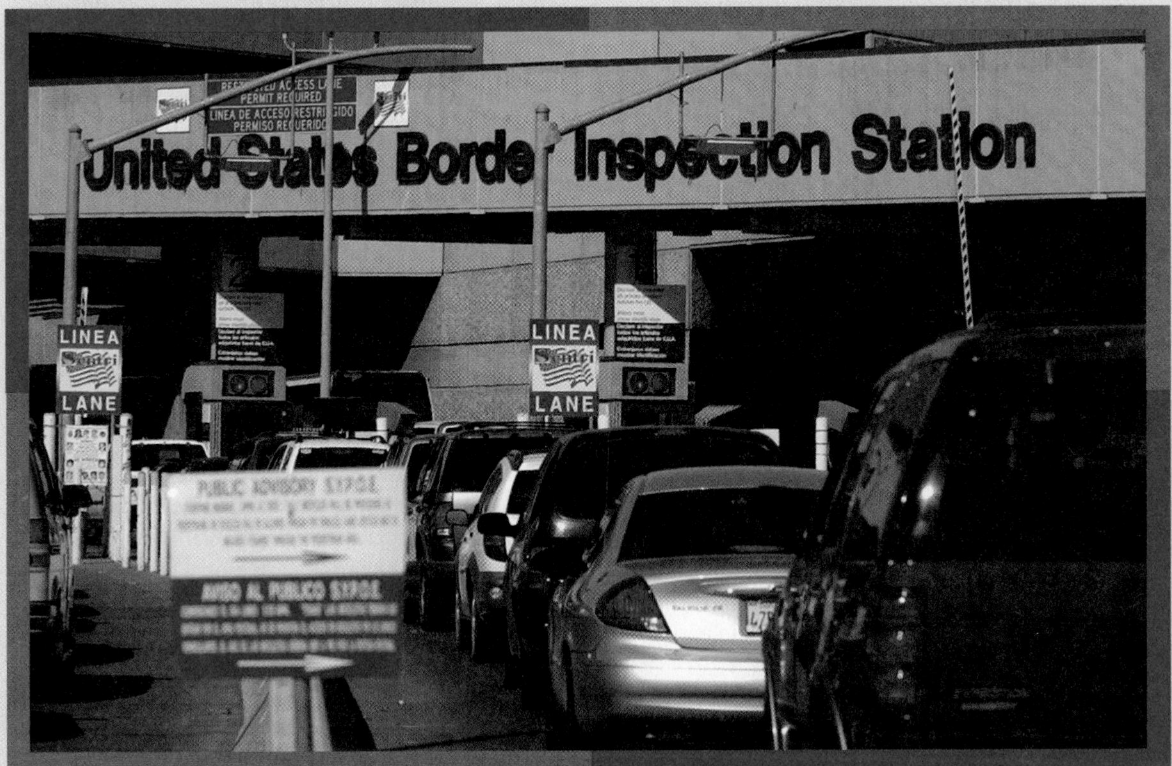

THINKING SOCIOLOGICALLY

- If fertility and mortality also affect population growth, why is immigration typically described as *the* driving force behind changes in the size, composition, and distribution of the U.S. population?
- How are wealth and material comfort in high-income nations related to depletion of the earth's resources and pollution of the environment?
- What does the environmental justice framework add to our knowledge of contemporary environmental problems? Would functionalists typically agree with this perspective?

America has a problem and the world has a problem. America's problem is that it has lost its way in recent years—partly because of 9/11 and partly because of the bad habits that we have let build up over the last three decades, bad habits that have weakened our society's ability and willingness to take on big challenges.

The world also has a problem: It is getting hot, flat, and crowded. *That is, global warming, the stunning rise of middle classes all over the world, and rapid population growth have converged in a way that could make our planet dangerously unstable....*

I am convinced that the best way for America to solve its big problem—the best way for America to get its "groove" back—is for us to take the lead in solving the world's big problem. In a world that is getting hot, flat, and crowded, the task of creating the tools, systems, energy sources, and ethics that will allow the planet to grow in cleaner, more sustainable ways is going to be the biggest challenge of our lifetime.

But this challenge is actually an opportunity for America. If we take it on, it will revive America at home, reconnect America abroad, and retool America for tomorrow.

***—In his recent book,* Hot, Flat, and Crowded, *journalist Thomas L. Friedman (2008:5–6) calls for people in the United States to lead the way in a worldwide effort to replace wasteful, inefficient energy practices with a strategy for clean energy, energy efficiency, and conservation that he refers to as* Code Green.**

Clearly, many individuals share Thomas Friedman's (2008:11) concerns about the future given current worldwide patterns of rapid population growth; the massive number of new consumers who walk onto "the global economic playing field with their own versions of the America dream" and create a massive demand for "things" that devour energy, natural resources, land, and water while emitting climate-changing greenhouse gases; and global warming. In this chapter, we will look first at the problem of global overpopulation as it is influenced by fertility, mortality, and immigration. Then we turn to the relationship between population and the environment, focusing on the environmental crisis of the twenty-first century.

GLOBAL OVERPOPULATION

During the past fifty-five years, the world's population has more than doubled, growing from 2.5 billion in 1950 to over 6.72 billion in the 2000s. At this rate, the world population will double again in the next fifty years. Even today, more than 1 billion of the world's people do not have enough food and lack basic health care. Will the earth's resources be able to support such a population? This is an urgent question and one for which we need answers.

Population Growth

Growth rates vary among nations; high-income nations (for example, the United States) have a lower population growth rate than low-income nations do, especially those in Africa, Asia, and Latin America. A *population* is all the people living in a specified geographic area. In some nations, the population growth rate is negative; that is, fewer people are added to the population through birth and immigration than are lost through death and emigration. Current estimates suggest that countries such as Italy, Romania, Russia, and Spain will shrink in population over the next fifty years (Sanger, 2000).

***Demography* is the study of the size, composition, and distribution of populations.** Global population changes are important because they have a powerful influence on social, economic, and political structures both within societies and between societies. For example, the population growth imbalance between high-income and middle- and low-income nations is a potential source of global conflict, particularly if world hunger and environmental destruction increase. Three primary factors affect the rate of population growth in any nation or area: fertility (births), mortality (deaths), and migration (movement between geographic areas). We will look at each in turn.

Fertility

***Fertility* refers to the number of children born to an individual or a population.** The most basic measure of fertility is the *crude birth rate*—the number of live births per 1,000 people in a population in a given year. In 2005, there were 4.1 million live births in the United States, yielding a crude birth rate of 14 per 1,000. This rate was down slightly from 16.6 per 1,000 in 1990 (National Center for Health Statistics, 2007a). The crude birth rate is used to gauge fertility because it is based on the entire population and does not take into account the variables that affect fertility, such as age, marital status, and race/ethnicity.

The level of fertility in a society is associated with social, as well as biological, factors. For example, countries that have high rates of infant and child mortality often have high birth rates. By having many children, parents in these nations are more likely to see a few of them survive to adulthood. In nations without social security systems to provide old-age insurance, parents often view children as an "insurance plan" for their old age. In patriarchal societies, having many children—especially sons—is proof of manliness. Finally, in cultures in which religion dictates that children are God-given and family planning is forbidden because it "interferes with God's will," many more children are usually born (Hauchler and Kennedy, 1994).

Although men obviously are important in the reproductive process, the measure of fertility focuses on women because pregnancy and childbirth are more easily quantified than biological fatherhood. One factor in determining how many children will be born in a given year is the number of women of childbearing age (usually between the ages of fifteen and forty-five) who live in the society. Other biological factors that affect fertility include the general health and nutrition level of women of childbearing age. However, on the basis of biological capability alone, most women could produce twenty or more children during their childbearing years. In industrialized nations, therefore, many people limit their biological capabilities by practicing abstinence, refraining from sexual intercourse before a certain age, using contraceptives, being sterilized, or having one or more abortions over the course of their reproductive years. Fertility rates also are affected by the number of partners who are available for sex and/or marriage, the number of women of childbearing age in the workforce, and government policies regarding families.

Mortality

Birth rates are one factor in population growth; another is a decline in ***mortality*—the number of deaths that occur in a specific population.** The simplest measure of mortality is the *crude death rate*—the number of deaths per 1,000 people in a population in a given year. In 2005, there were 2.4 million deaths in the U.S. population, which yields a crude death rate of 8.5 deaths per 1,000 (National Center for Health Statistics, 2007b). In many nations, mortality rates have declined dramatically as diseases, such as malaria, polio, cholera, tetanus, typhoid, and measles, have been virtually eliminated by vaccinations and improved sanitation and personal hygiene (Weeks, 2005).

In addition to measuring the crude death rate, demographers often measure the *infant mortality rate*—the number of deaths of infants under one year of age per 1,000 live births in a given year. In general, infant mortality has declined worldwide over the past two decades because many major childhood and communicable diseases are now under control. Still, infant mortality rates vary widely between nations. In high-income nations, the average was 6 deaths per 1,000 live births in 2006 (Japan had a low of 4 deaths per 1,000 live births), in sharp contrast to about 76 deaths per 1,000 live births in southern Asia and about 105 deaths per 1,000 live births in sub-Saharan Africa (United Nations Development Programme, 2007).

In any nation, the infant mortality rate is an important reflection of a society's level of preventive (prenatal) medical care, maternal nutrition, childbirth procedures, and neonatal care for infants. In the United States, differential levels of access to these services are reflected in the gap between infant mortality rates for African Americans and whites. In 2004, for example, mortality for African-American infants was 14 deaths per 1,000 live births, compared to 6 per 1,000 live births for white infants (National Center for Health Statistics, 2007b).

Demographers also study *life expectancy,* the estimated average lifetime of people born in a specific year. For example, in 2006, the life expectancy at birth for a person born in the United States was 77.8 years, compared to 82 years in Japan and less than 50.0 years in the African nations of Burundi, Chad, Rwanda, and Uganda (United Nations Development Programme, 2007). Life expectancy varies not only by nation but also by sex. Females born in the United States in 2005 have a life expectancy of about 80 years, whereas males born in that year have a life expectancy of about 74 years. Life expectancy also varies by race. African-American men, for example, have a life expectancy at birth of about 69 years, compared to 75 years for white males (National Center for Health Statistics, 2007b).

Migration

***Migration* is the movement of people from one geographic area to another for the purpose of changing residency.** Migration takes two forms: *immigration*—the movement of people *into* a geographic area to take up residency—and *emigration*—the movement of people *out of* a geographic area to take up residency elsewhere. Today, more than 35 million people live outside their countries of origin.

In the early 1990s, about 1 million people were entering the United States each year, but this number decreased to about 900,000 annually because of more restrictive U.S. immigration policies and stricter enforcement after 2001. However, it should be noted that official immigration statistics do not reflect the actual number of immigrants who arrive in this country. The U.S. Citizenship and Immigration Service records only legal immigration based on entry visas and change-of-immigration-status forms. Some people who enter the country as temporary visitors, coming for pleasure or business, as students, or as temporary workers or trainees do not leave when their stated purpose has been achieved and their permits expire.

Approximately 48,000 refugees are also admitted to this country annually as permanent residents. According to the 1951 United Nations Convention on Refugees, the term *refugee* applies solely to those who leave their countries because of persecution for reasons of race, religion, nationality, membership in a particular social group, or political opinion (Kane, 1995). People who leave home to escape famine, for example, do not officially qualify as refugees.

The largest proportion of immigrants entering the United States each year arrive illegally. Many come from Mexico, El Salvador, Guatemala, Poland, Haiti, the Bahamas, and Nicaragua (U.S. Census Bureau, 2008). Government officials estimate that between 4 million and 10 million people annually enter this country illegally (U.S. Census Bureau, 2008). Of course, it is not known how many of them return to their countries of origin or how many people enter, leave, and reenter, as is often done by undocumented workers who come and go between the United States and Mexico or Canada.

Many immigrants come to the United States because it offers them greater job opportunities and freedom from the political, religious, sexual, or racial/ethnic oppression of their home countries. For example, researchers have found that many women migrate to this country from the Dominican Republic to improve their economic position and to escape a repressive patriarchal environment. When both husband and wife migrate from the Dominican Republic, the wife is more likely to remain in this country than the husband because she finds that working gives her more economic security and power at home. Many husbands save their money and return to the Dominican Republic (Grasmuck and Pessar, 1991).

To determine the effects of immigration and emigration, demographers compute the *crude net migration rate*—the net number of migrants (total in-migrants minus total out-migrants) per 1,000 people in a population in a given year. Currently, the net migration rate in the United States is about 2.9 per 1,000 population, which means that between two and three more people per 1,000 population enter this country than leave it each year (based on U.S. Census Bureau, 2008).

Many nations face the challenges and opportunities offered by the migration of people worldwide (see Box 15.1).

The Impact of Population Growth

What is the effect of population growth on a society? Population growth affects ***population composition*—the biological and social characteristics of a population, including such attributes as age, sex, race, marital status, education, occupation, income, and size of household.** In the United States, for example, the age distribution of the population is associated with the demand for community resources such as elementary and secondary schools,

Social Problems in Global Perspective

Box 15.1

International Migration: Problem or Solution?

> "We cannot bear all the misery in the world!" This simple slogan has long been proclaimed in most industrialized countries. The misery to which they refer is that endured by the millions of people who come knocking on the doors of the richest countries to obtain a small piece of the development cake to which they have hitherto been denied. However, while misery is a very sad reality, the spectre of invasions en masse by foreign nationals seeking to grab nations' riches is no more than a deceptive fantasy blithely dreamt up by reactionary forces and extremists bent on stirring up the xenophobic sentiments which they have long cashed in on at the ballot box....
>
> The fact that migrant workers are used as scapegoats remains a sad reality. As soon as economic or political crises are upon us...the spotlight unfailingly shines on immigrant workers.
>
> *—Manuel Simón Velasco (2002), director of the International Labor Organization (an agency of the United Nations) Bureau for Workers' Activities, explains how the world's political leaders often use the issue of international migration to stir up voters' sentiments and to provide a ready scapegoat for current social problems.*

For years, many nations have strictly limited immigration; however, anti-immigrant sentiment does not bode well in the future for nations that have aging populations and declining birth rates. According to the United Nations, migrants follow the flow of jobs, and in countries with severely shrunken labor forces and increasing ranks of older retirees, immigrants may be part of the solution to population concerns rather than part of the "problem" as they have been perceived in the past.

Today, many European countries (as well as the United States, Canada, and Japan) are faced with populations that will have more older people and fewer babies than ever before. If these nations want to maintain the social services and economic structures that many residents have become accustomed to, it will be necessary for them to "lower their borders" and accept even more change in the racial and ethnic composition of their populations. According to United Nations estimates, unless Europeans are willing to work until the age of seventy-seven, the countries of Europe will have to add more than 1 million immigrants a year, four times the level of immigration in the previous decade, to produce the needed supply of workers. If things remain as they are, by 2050 the European population will be only 660 million, down from 730 million at the beginning of the 2000s (Velasco, 2002). Overall, the countries of the European Union will need to allow the immigration of about 35 million people to maintain their populations at the level of the 1990s.

As the pressure from overpopulation builds in some nations, and the United States, Canada, and some European countries have increasingly "aging" populations, demographers believe that the flow of migrant workers, both "legal" and "illegal," will increase dramatically around the world. Many immigration-related challenges remain, however, and perhaps the greatest of these is the perpetual threat of terrorism, which is typically attributed first to immigrants whether this is true or not. Recent bombings in the United States, the United Kingdom, Spain, and other countries have produced new waves of anti-immigration sentiment and an increase in hate crimes perpetrated against people based on preconceived notions about their racial group, ethnicity, religion, or nationality.

While some nations continue to look to the past to determine what should be done about immigration in the future, spokespersons for organizations such as the United Nations believe that political leaders and citizens must acknowledge that their countries face either a declining and aging population or a future that is built by immigrants.

Questions to Consider

1. To what extent is it possible for a nation to control its borders? What part does geography play in border control? What part does politics play?
2. How might functionalist and conflict theorists differ in their explanations of the causes and consequences of international migration?
3. What do you think will be the future of immigration in the United States? Will our concerns about terrorism overshadow the ever-present demand for low-wage workers in this country?

libraries, health care and recreational facilities, employment opportunities, and age-appropriate housing.

What are the effects of rapid population growth on individuals? According to Population Action International's Human Suffering Index (HSI), the countries that have the highest rates of growth also have the most human suffering. For example, twenty of the twenty-seven countries listed in the "extreme human suffering" category are in Africa, the fastest-growing region in the world (*Human Suffering Index,* 1992). The HSI also shows that while many people in poverty-stricken regions die from hunger and malnutrition each year, people in the most high-income nations spend billions of dollars annually on diet products and exercise gear because they think they are overfed and overweight.

What are the consequences of global population growth? Not all social analysts agree on the answer to this question. As you will discover in the sections that follow, some analysts warn that the earth is a finite system that cannot support its rapidly growing population. Others believe that capitalism—if freed from government intervention—could develop innovative solutions to such problems as hunger and pollution. Still others argue that capitalism is part of the problem, not part of the solution.

The Malthusian Perspective

Rapid population growth and overpopulation are not new problems. Causes and solutions have been debated for more than two centuries. In 1798, for example, Thomas Malthus, an English clergyman and economist, published *An Essay on Population.* Malthus (1965/1798) argued that the global population, if left unchecked, would exceed the available food supply. The population would increase in a geometric (exponential) progression (2, 4, 8, 16,...), but the food supply would increase only by an arithmetic progression (1, 2, 3, 4,...). Thus the population would surpass the food supply, ending population growth and perhaps eliminating the world population (Weeks, 2005). Disaster, according to Malthus, could be averted only by positive checks (e.g., famine, disease, and war) or preventive checks (e.g., sexual abstinence before marriage and postponement of marriage for as long as possible) to limit people's fertility.

The Neo-Malthusian Perspective

Today, *neo-Malthusians* (or "new Malthusians") speak of the "population explosion" and "population bomb" to emphasize the urgent need to reduce global population growth. Among the best known neo-Malthusians are biologists Paul Ehrlich and Anne H. Ehrlich, who believe that world population growth is following the exponential growth pattern that Malthus described (Ehrlich and Ehrlich, 1991:15):

> Exponential growth occurs in populations because children... remain in the population and themselves have children. A key feature of exponential growth is that it often seems to start slow and finish fast. A classic example... is the pond weed that doubles each day... to cover the entire pond in thirty days. The question is, how much of the pond will be covered in twenty-nine days? The answer, of course, is that just half of the pond will be covered in twenty-nine days. The weed will then double once more and cover the entire pond the next day. As this example indicates, exponential growth contains the potential for big surprises.

To neo-Malthusians, the earth is a dying planet with too many people in relation to the available food supply. Overpopulation and rapid population growth exacerbate global environmental problems ranging from global warming and rainforest destruction to famine and epidemics such as AIDS.

Demographic Transition Theory

According to ***demographic transition theory,* some societies move from high birth and death rates to relatively low birth and death rates as a result of technological development.** The demographic transition takes place in four stages. The *preindustrial stage* is characterized by little population growth: High birth rates are offset by high death rates. This period is followed by the *transitional* or *early industrial stage,* which is characterized by significant population growth as the birth rate remains high but the death rate declines because of new technologies that improve health, sanitation, and nutrition. Today, large parts of Africa, Asia, and Latin America are in this second stage. The third stage is *advanced industrialization and urbanization:* The birth rate declines as people control their fertility with various forms of contraception, and the death rate declines as medicine and other health-care technologies control acute and chronic diseases. Finally, in the *postindustrial stage,* the population grows very slowly, if at all. In this stage, a decreasing birth rate is coupled with a stable death rate.

Proponents of demographic transition theory believe that technology can overcome the dire predictions of Malthus and the neo-Malthusians. Critics point out that not all nations go through all the stages or in the manner outlined. They think that demographic transition theory explains development in Western societies but not necessarily that in others. As an example, they cite China, which reduced its birth rate because of the government's mandated one-child-per-family policy, but has received extensive criticism after the nation lost many children to a natural disaster.

World Hunger

Food shortages, chronic hunger, and malnutrition are the consequences of rapid population growth, particularly in middle-income nations. More than 35 million people in middle-income nations experience continuous hunger or *chronic malnourishment*—inadequate food to provide the minimum energy necessary for doing light work over a period of time (ELCA World Hunger, 2005). Chronic malnutrition contributes to childhood health problems such as anemia (a blood condition that produces weakness and a lack of energy and can result in child mortality or impaired mental functioning), stunting (impaired physical growth or development), and being underweight (United Nations Development Programme, 2004). In pregnant women, malnutrition increases the risk of anemia, infection, birth complications, and lack of breast milk (see Figure 15.1 on page 316). In contrast, improvements in nutrition significantly reduce health risks and the spread of some communicable illnesses (Hauchler and Kennedy, 1994).

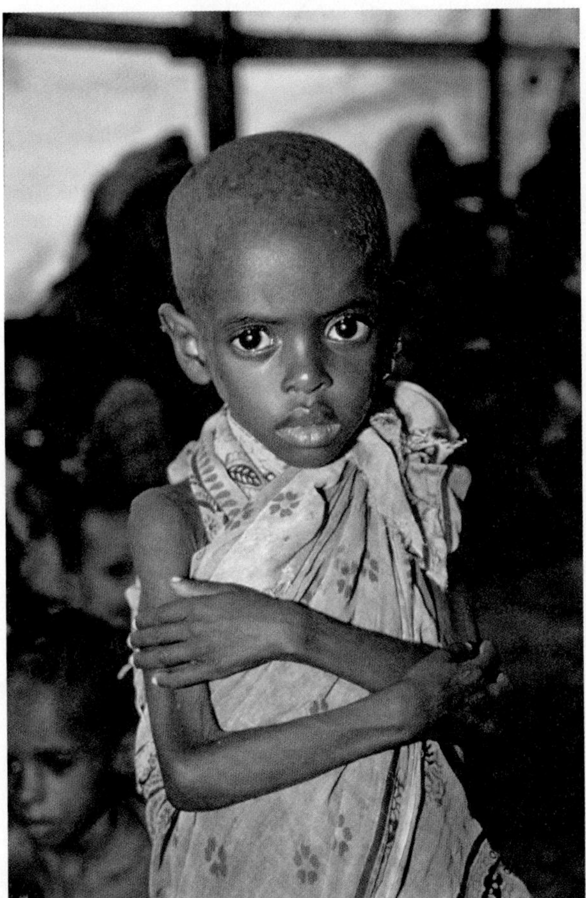

Starving children in nations such as Somalia raise important questions about Malthusian and neo-Malthusian perspectives. Is world hunger primarily a consequence of overpopulation or are other political and economic factors also important?

What efforts are being made to reduce global food shortages and world hunger? Organizations such as the United Nations, the World Health Organization, and the International Red Cross have programs in place, but the most far-reaching initiatives are known as the green revolution and the biotechnological revolution.

The Green Revolution

The *green revolution* refers to dramatic increases in agricultural production that have been made possible by high-yield "miracle" crops. In the 1940s, researchers at the International Maize and Wheat Improvement Center started the green revolution by developing high-yield varieties of wheat, which increased world grain production. The new dwarf-type wheat, which produces more stalks, has dramatically increased the wheat yield in countries such as India and Pakistan since the 1960s. Researchers have also developed a high-yield dwarf rice with twice as many grains per plant, greatly improving the rice output in India, Pakistan, the Philippines, Indonesia, and Vietnam (Weeks, 2005).

How successful has the green revolution been in reducing world hunger? During the 1970s, the green revolution helped to increase the global food supply at a somewhat faster pace than the global population grew, but in the 1980s and 1990s, agricultural production slowed considerably. Also, although the new miracle crops have increased food production in Latin America and Asia, they have not really benefited Africa (Kennedy, 1993).

They have not done so for several reasons. For one thing, the fertilizers, pesticides, and irrigation systems that are needed to produce them are very costly and are beyond the budgets of most middle- and low-income nations. Furthermore, the fertilizers

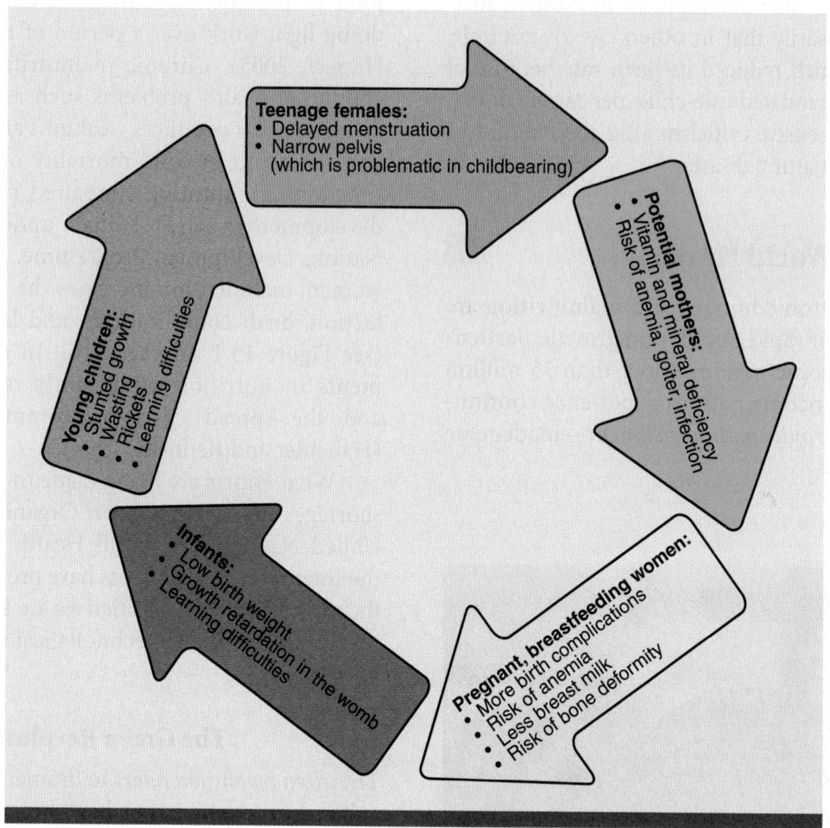

■ **Figure 15.1** **The circle of malnutrition**

Source: Based on United Nations, 1995.

and pesticides often constitute health hazards and become a source of surface water and groundwater pollution (Weeks, 2005). Moreover, for the green revolution to eliminate hunger and malnutrition, the social organization of life in many middle- and low-income nations would have to change significantly. People would have to adopt the Western methods of farming on which the green revolution was built, and they would have to be willing to produce a single crop in very high volume. But reliance on a single crop can lead to nutritional deficiencies if other varieties of food are not available. Even with these drawbacks, however, the green revolution continues. Researchers recently developed high-yield sorghum, yams, and other crops that can be grown successfully in the nations of Africa where some of the greatest food shortages exist (Weeks, 2005).

The Biotechnological Revolution

A second approach to reducing global food shortages, known as the *biotechnological revolution,* encompasses any technique for improving plants or animals or using microorganisms in innovative ways. Using growth hormone to increase milk output in cows is one technique. Scientists are also exploring ways to genetically alter the reproductive cells of fish, poultry, sheep, and pigs to speed up conventional breeding times. Scientists have already genetically altered microorganisms in several ways. Researchers have found, for example, that it is possible to spray frost-sensitive plants, such as strawberries, with a strain of bacteria that will protect the plants against up to 80 percent of frost damage.

Some scientists believe that the biotechnological revolution can close the gap between worldwide food production and rapid population growth, but the new technology is not without problems. First, giving growth hormones to animals can make their meat unfit for human consumption. Hogs that get growth hormones are prone to gastric ulcers, arthritis, dermatitis, and other diseases (Kennedy, 1993). Second, the cost of biotechnological innovations is beyond the budgets of most middle- and low-income nations. Third, the new biotechnologies are developed for use with conventional (Western) farming methods (Hauchler and Kennedy, 1994). Fourth, genetic erosion (by breeding or gene manipulation) might eventually make the people of the world reliant on only a few varieties of plants and animals for their entire food supply and thus vulnerable to famine as the result of a single pest or disease. Finally, environmental accidents, such as the unintentional release of genetically manipulated microorganisms, pose a potential hazard.

Increasing the food supply is one way of coping with a rapidly growing world population—but hardly the only way. Some people believe that we can forestall the problem by controlling fertility.

CONTROLLING FERTILITY

The global population increase since 1900 has been unprecedented, and an additional three billion young people will soon enter their reproductive years (United Nations Development Programme, 2002). Although demographers know that limiting fertility is the best way to slow down population growth, they also know that the issue is fraught with controversy. Consider the three preconditions that demographer Ansley Coale (1973) believes are necessary before there can be a sustained decline in a society's fertility:

- *People must accept calculated choice as a valid element in marital fertility.* If people believe that a supernatural power controls human reproduction, it is unlikely that they will risk offending that deity by trying to limit fertility. On the other hand, the more worldly-wise people are, the more likely they are to believe they have the right to control reproduction.
- *People must see advantages to reduced fertility.* People must have some reason to want to limit fertility. Otherwise, natural attraction will lead to unprotected sexual intercourse and perhaps numerous children.
- *People must know about and master effective techniques of birth control.* The means for limiting family size must be available, and people must know how to use them successfully.

Although Coale believes that all three preconditions must be met to limit fertility effectively, most government policies focus only on the third: family planning measures (Weeks, 2005).

Family Planning

Family planning programs provide birth control information, contraceptive devices, sometimes sterilization and abortion procedures, and health services. The earliest programs were based on the assumption that women have large families because they do not know how to prevent pregnancy or they lack access to birth control devices. Though we know today that other issues are involved, most programs are still based on this assumption. They do little, for example, to influence a couple's desire to have children and appear not to realize that in some middle- and low-income nations, women are not free to make their own decisions about reproduction. There is overwhelming evidence that women want only the number of children that they can care for adequately (United Nations Development Programme, 2007). At the same time, however, many of these women are socialized to accept the ideal of the perfect mother, so motherhood confers social status and a sense of personal achievement. Children are considered a gift and a blessing, providing women with affection that they might not otherwise receive and securing the mother's position in the kinship group and the larger society (O'Connell, 1994).

Critics of family planning programs argue that most policies are developed by political leaders in high-income nations who are motivated by race and class issues rather than by a genuine concern about world hunger or overpopulation. They say that high-income nations—such as England, France, and the United States—encourage births among middle- and upper-income white women in their own countries but advocate depopulation policies in low-income regions such as sub-Saharan Africa, where most residents are people of color (O'Connell, 1994). For example, the French government is promoting larger families because of a rapidly aging population, a low

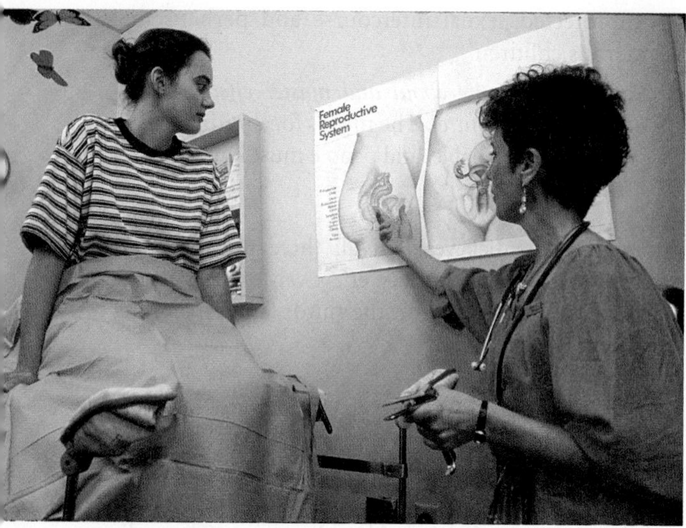

Organizations such as Planned Parenthood work to make people aware of the importance of limiting the number of children that they have. What factors contribute to people's choices in regard to controlling fertility?

fertility rate, and a national concern that the country is losing its identity because of high immigration rates (Weeks, 2005).

Zero Population Growth

With *zero population growth*, there is a totally stable population, one that neither grows nor decreases from year to year because births, deaths, and migration are in perfect balance (Weeks, 2005). For example, the population growth rate would be zero if a nation had no immigration or emigration and the birth rate and the death rate were the same (Ehrlich and Ehrlich, 1991).

The United States is nearing zero population growth because of several factors: (1) A high proportion of women and men in the labor force find satisfaction and rewards outside of family life; (2) birth control is inexpensive and readily available; (3) the trend is toward later marriage (see Chapter 11); (4) the cost of raising a child from birth to adulthood is rising rapidly; and (5) schools and public service campaigns make teenagers more aware of how to control fertility (United Nations Development Programme, 2002). Near-zero population growth is one characteristic of the U.S. population; another is a rapidly changing population.

IMMIGRATION AND ITS CONSEQUENCES

High rates of immigration are changing the composition of the U.S. population. In 2006, approximately 35 million people—or 12 percent of the total U.S. population—came here from other nations (U.S. Census Bureau, 2007c). In fact, the proportion of U.S. immigrants is at its highest point since the early 1940s. In 1944, immigration accounted for 30 percent of that year's increase in the U.S. population and contributed to the growth of large urban centers such as New York, Los Angeles, and Miami. On a global basis, immigration and internal migration are causing urban populations to grow faster than the total population (see Map 15.1). Because most cities do not have the capacity to deal with existing residents, much less significant increases in the number of those residents, especially those with limited education and economic wherewithal, immigration and internal migration often lead to patterns of urban squalor and high levels of stress in daily living.

What are the consequences of today's high rate of immigration to the United States as a whole? Not all social analysts agree on the answer to this question. Some believe that immigrants cost U.S. taxpayers billions of dollars each year (see Huddle, 1993), although the cost varies widely from state to state. One study estimated that households in California pay about $5,028 per capita in state and local taxes to cover services such as education, welfare, public health, and police protection for immigrants, whereas New Jersey residents pay about $230 a year for immigrant services (Serrin, 1997). But a study conducted by the National Academy of Sciences found that immigration also produces substantial economic benefits for the United States. In fact, immigrants might contribute as much as $15 billion a year to the economic output of this country. This same study pointed out that low-skilled, U.S.-born workers can lose jobs because of competition from immigrant workers.

The National Academy of Sciences study also found the following:

- If immigration to the United States continues at the present rate, it will account for more than two-thirds of the expected population growth in the next fifty years.
- The wage gap between immigrants and U.S.-born workers will grow wider because many recent immigrants are arriving from poorer nations where the

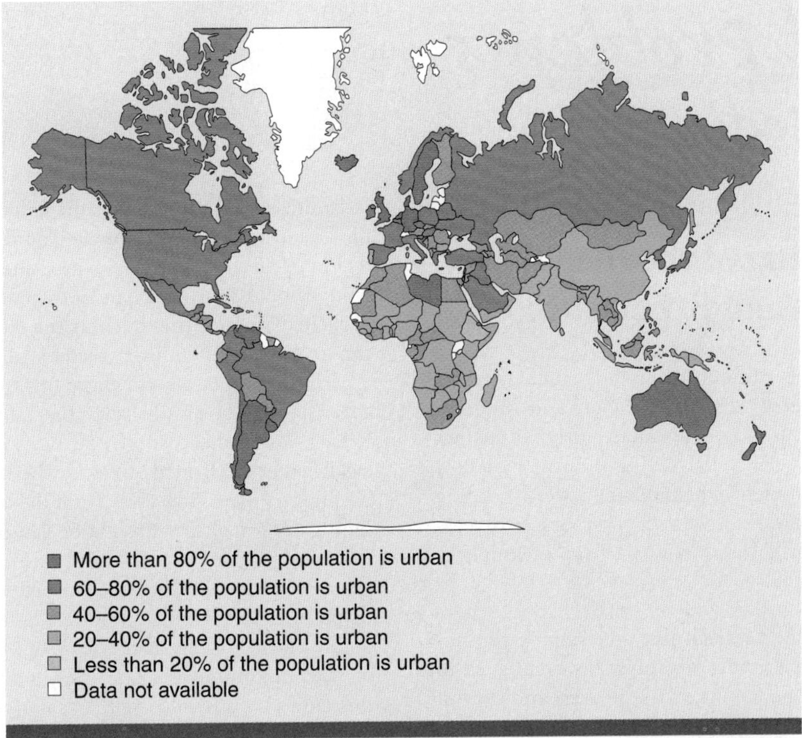

■ *Map 15.1* ***Urban population as a percent of total national population***

Source: U.S. Census Bureau, 2008.

average levels of education, wages, and skills are far below those of the United States.

- Immigration has contributed to an increase in the number of high school dropouts in the United States, and this increase has lowered the wages of high school dropouts by about 5 percent.

Clearly, the costs and benefits of immigration are widely argued about by various political, economic, and social analysts. Some economists believe that the entry of large numbers of immigrant workers into the country provides a great benefit to everyone because existing land, capital, and technology can be used more efficiently, and the standard of living can rise for many people. These economists also argue that, rather than being a drain on the U. S. economy, immigrant workers add to this nation's coffers by paying property taxes, sales taxes, Social Security taxes, and income taxes. In sharp contrast, however, other economists conclude that immigrant workers are a liability because they use public services, such as public education, government assistance, and fire and police protection, far in excess of what they pay in taxes (Thoma, 2006).

Some social analysts believe that any discussion of the costs and benefits of immigration should distinguish between legal and illegal immigration. From this perspective, illegal immigration differs from legal immigration because illegal immigrants are more likely to have low job-skill levels, which means that they are typically employed in agriculture, construction, household work, lawn mowing and landscaping, fast-food and hotel service, and lower-level manufacturing jobs. Because of the nature of these jobs and the relationships between employers and recent illegal immigrants, those who benefit the most from the presence of illegal immigrants are the employers who hire these workers and the consumers who use their services.

Members of the media have played an active role in disseminating information, as well as generating controversy, on problems associated with international immigration (see Box 15.2 on page 320). But stemming the flow of immigrants appears to be a virtually impossible task for any one nation, as does alleviating the problem of environmental degradation.

Social Problems in the Media

Box 15.2

POPULATION AND THE ENVIRONMENT

Although it is popularly believed that most environmental problems arise from rapid growth in middle- and low-income nations, this isn't the case. Many scientists believe that high-income nations present a much greater threat to the earth's ecosystems. An *ecosystem* is "all the populations of plants and animal species that live and interact in a given area at a particular time, as well as the chemical and physical factors that make up the nonliving environment" (Cable and Cable, 1995:124). Thus an ocean is an ecosystem; a tropical rainforest is an ecosystem; and on a much smaller scale, a house on a lot is an ecosystem. When all of the earth's ecosystems are put together, they make up the *biosphere.*

Ecosystems do not have an infinite ability to support population growth or environmental depletion or destruction. In fact, some scientists believe that many of the world's ecosystems have already exceeded their *carrying capacity*—the maximum population that an ecosystem can support without eventually being degraded or destroyed. According to biologists Paul Ehrlich and Anne H. Ehrlich (1991), a baby born in the United States will have twice the destructive impact on the earth's ecosystems and services as a baby born in Sweden, 140 times the impact of a baby born in Bangladesh or Kenya, and 280 times the impact of a baby born in Chad, Rwanda, Haiti, or Nepal. How did the Ehrlichs reach such a conclusion? They developed a formula for determining the impact that human beings have on their environment: $I = P \times A \times T$, or Impact = Population × Affluence × Technology. Thus the size of the population, its level of affluence, and the technology available in the society are major contributing factors to ***environmental degradation*—disruptions to the environment that have negative consequences for ecosystems** (Cable and Cable, 1995). Environmental degradation involves both removing natural resources from the environment and adding to environmental problems through pollution.

In the United States, environmental degradation increases as people try to maintain the high levels of wealth and material comfort to which they have become accustomed. They consume the earth's resources and pollute its environment with automobiles, airplanes, speedboats, computers, television sets, year-round air conditioning and heating, and other amenities that are far beyond the grasp of most of the world's people. Although these products are made possible by high levels of industrial production and economic growth, economic growth often depletes and destroys the environment.

Economic Growth and Environmental Degradation

During most of the twentieth century, economic growth in the United States was based on increased output in the manufacturing sector. The environment is affected at all phases of the manufacturing process, from mining and transportation to manufacturing and waste disposal. As you will recall from Chapter 13, industrial production involves extracting raw materials—natural resources—from the environment, usually through mining. Mining depletes mineral resources and fossil fuel reserves—coal, oil, and natural gas. Mining also disturbs ecosystems, particularly surface mining, which strips bare the land, destroying natural vegetation and wildlife habitats. Other problems typically follow, including erosion of the land by wind and water and runoff of acids, silt, and toxic substances into nearby surface water and groundwater, which leads to the pollution of rivers and streams with toxic compounds that kill fish and other aquatic life (Cable and Cable, 1995).

The environmental impact of mining doesn't stop when the raw materials have been mined. Now the raw materials must be transported to a plant or factory, where workers will transform them into manufactured products. Transporting requires the use of energy, particularly the burning of fossil fuels, which contributes to air pollution because motor vehicles produce carbon monoxide, nitrogen oxides, and photochemical pollutants. Each of these pollutants is associated with various illnesses, including heart and respiratory disease and cancer. The manufacturing process further depletes fossil fuels and contributes to air pollution. People who work in or live near facilities that pollute the environment are often harmed by the manufacturing process because of the solid or toxic wastes.

Many analysts believe that we cannot continue this pattern of environmental degradation. Future economic development—in the United States and globally—will require drastic changes in the structure of industry, especially in the energy, transportation, chemical, and agricultural sectors of the economy (Hauchler and Kennedy, 1994). If we don't make changes, environmental degradation constitutes a major threat to the well-being of all human beings and ecosystems on the earth. Let's look now at some

"I'm rather fortunate. I have no parents, so Medicare is no problem, and I have no children, so the environment is no problem."

specific kinds of environmental degradation: air pollution; problems with water, soil, and forests; and solid, toxic, and nuclear waste.

Air Pollution

Nature performs many *ecosystem services*–valuable, practical functions that help to preserve ecosystems. For example, if the atmosphere is not overburdened, it can maintain a proper balance between carbon dioxide and oxygen, as well as providing ozone for protection against ultraviolet radiation (see Table 15.1). However, air pollution interferes with many ecosystem services. The carbon dioxide that pollutes the air we breathe keeps the sun's heat from radiating back into space, thereby causing the earth to heat up (the greenhouse effect, discussed in the next section). Other air pollutants deplete the upper atmosphere ozone layer—a gaseous layer 30 miles above Earth's surface—that shields the earth from ultraviolet radiation (Petersen, 1994). Ozone depletion can make life unsustainable by killing the organic life that produces food and oxygen.

The drastic increase in air pollution that began in the twentieth century has placed an undue burden on the atmosphere's ecosystem services (Stevens, 1997). Beginning with the Industrial Revolution in the late nineteenth and early twentieth centuries, more and more pollutants have been emitted into the atmosphere by households, industries, and automobile traffic. The result is constantly increasing amounts of carbon dioxide, carbon monoxide, nitrogen oxide, and sulfur oxide, as well as heavy metals such as lead, zinc, and copper in our air (Hauchler and Kennedy, 1994). Today, 85 percent of the air pollution in urban areas can be

TABLE 15.1 What the Natural World Does for Us (If We Don't Mess It Up Too Much)

Food production	Produces fish, game, and crops—even without our help.
Raw materials	Produces (without our help) the raw materials from which humans create things.
Genetic resources	On its own, creates the ability for crops, vegetation, and animals to survive.
Pollination	Without our help, plants and animals naturally reproduce.
Biological control	Somehow, most species of plants and animals survive for millions of years without our help.
Climate regulation	Unless we mess it up, nature has created an ozone layer that protects all plant and animal life from the sun's ultraviolet radiation.
Water regulation	If we don't mess with it, the world's water supply keeps reproducing and distributing itself.
Gas regulation	If we don't mess it up too badly, nature keeps carbon dioxide and oxygen in balance—a balance that is necessary for life.
Recreation	Just think of the wonderful sights and recreation that nature has created.

Source: Stevens, 1997.

attributed to the internal combustion engines that are used in automobiles and other vehicles (U.S. Census Bureau, 2008). Although laws have reduced the amount of pollution from automobiles and industries in the United States, more than 40 percent of the population resides in areas where air pollutants still exceed acceptable levels (Hauchler and Kennedy, 1994).

Air pollution affects all life and ecosystems on the planet. Air pollution in the form of acid rain destroys forests, streams and lakes, and other ecosystems. ***Acid rain* is rainfall containing large concentrations of sulfuric and nitric acids (primarily from the burning of fuel and car and truck exhausts).** In Germany, for example, acid rain is believed to have damaged more than half the trees—up to 80 percent in some regions (Hauchler and Kennedy, 1994). Efforts to reduce acid rain in the United States have been blocked by the automobile industry; companies that mine, haul, and sell high-sulfur coal; and coal miners. Fortunately, new industries are less dependent on burning coal than are older factories in the industrial Northeast and Midwest states (Petersen, 1994).

Air pollution is a pressing problem in many nations, but nowhere more so than in Mexico City, where daylight hours often look like this photo. How is air pollution related to people's health and life expectancy?

In the past, air pollution in middle- and low-income nations was attributed primarily to the fight for survival and economic development, whereas most air pollution in high-income nations was attributed to relatively luxurious lifestyles. However, distinctions between air pollution in high-income and middle- and low-income nations are growing weaker, even though the United States and other Western industrial nations account for about 68 percent of the carbon monoxide in the atmosphere (World Resources Institute, 1992). Automobile ownership, once considered a luxury, is rising rapidly in urban centers in middle-income nations such as Mexico, Brazil, Taiwan, Indonesia, and China. Mexico City, known as the smog capital of the world, has more than three hundred days a year when the air quality fails to meet World Health Organization standards (Energy Information Administration, 2004). Affluent Mexican residents buy bottled oxygen at the drugstore; the less affluent buy quick shots of oxygen at street-corner kiosks. Cities such as Bombay, Lagos, Shanghai, and Jakarta have also seen significant increases in the number of automobiles, bringing corresponding rises in air pollution and traffic problems.

Some efforts are being made to curb fossil fuel pollution. In the United States, antipollution laws have brought about changes in how automobiles are made and the fuels they consume. Cars are now equipped with catalytic converters and other antipollution devices, and leaded gasoline (a major offender) has been phased out. However, although some middle-income nations are requiring antipollution devices on new vehicles, many leaded gas-burning cars—often used cars from the United States—are still a significant source of air pollution.

Industrial air pollution has been reduced in some regions of the United States, but pollution controls are often expensive, and many corporations try to find ways to avoid making costly plant conversions. Some move their plants to middle- and low-income nations that have less stringent environmental regulations; others try to avoid antipollution guidelines through government waivers, sometimes known as pollution credits. The federal Clean Air Act of 1990 created these credits to reward state agencies and companies that kept their emissions below federal governmental limits. Recently, however, New York State used its accumulated credits to lure heavily polluting corporations to the state. Essentially, then, the pollution credits that the state earned for reducing its own pollution emissions would allow these corporations to pollute in return for moving to the state and paying New York taxes (Hernandez, 1997). Environmental activists ask why the state should subsidize polluters in the name of economic development and at the expense of people's health and the environment (Hernandez, 1997).

The Greenhouse Effect

Emissions from traffic and industry not only add to general air pollution but also contribute to the ***greenhouse effect*—an environmental condition caused by excessive quantities of carbon dioxide, water vapor, methane, and nitrous oxide in the atmosphere.** When carbon dioxide molecules build up in the earth's atmosphere, they act like the glass roof of a greenhouse, allowing sunlight to reach the earth's surface but preventing the escape of solar infrared radiation (heat) back into space. The heat that cannot escape is reflected, causing the earth's surface temperature to rise. Some scientists believe that the earth will have a temperature increase of as much as five degrees over the next hundred years. In fact, if current rates of emission into the atmosphere remain unchanged, temperature increases might eventually bring about catastrophic consequences.

One consequence could be significant changes in weather patterns and climate. Changes in weather patterns could bring increased evaporation, creating new deserts and decreasing regional water reserves. Changes in air circulation and climatic conditions could result in more frequent hurricanes, flooding, tidal waves, and droughts. Vegetation zones could shift, and forests in the northern hemisphere might die off.

Not all scientists believe that the greenhouse effect exists or that its effects will be this disastrous. However, studies show a marked retreat of glaciers and the beginning of a shift in vegetation, and one possible cause is the greenhouse effect (Hauchler and Kennedy, 1994).

To reduce greenhouse gases, political and economic leaders in high-income nations want middle- and low-income nations to lower their birth rates so that the total number of people contributing to the problem does not rise. But leaders in these nations think that high-income nations should institute stringent restrictions on consumption and pollution in their own countries and use some of their resources to help other countries with economic development. Then, they say, it may be possible to significantly reduce their birth rates (Hauchler and Kennedy, 1994).

Depletion of the Ozone Layer

In 1992, a hole the size of North America was reported in the ozone layer over Antarctica, and the size of the hole has been increasing ever since then (United Nations Environmental Program, 2002). Ozone is vital to life on earth because it is the only gas in the atmosphere that can absorb the sun's dangerous ultraviolet radiation. A thinning ozone layer increases risk of skin cancer, damages marine life, and lowers crop yields. Since adoption of the Montreal Protocol in 1987, production of the main chlorofluorocarbons (CFCs) that were depleting the ozone layer has been reduced by 85 percent, and the ozone layer is expected to recover by 2065.

Problems with Water, Soil, and Forests

Water, soil, and forests (vegetation) are interdependent crucial resources that face increasing degradation or destruction because of pollution. As a result of climate changes, waste, pollution, and rapid depletion, the earth's drinking water is endangered, and its fertile land is being lost.

Water Shortages and Pollution

Water depletion and pollution are serious problems in the United States. However, these problems are not limited to the United States. Although approximately 70 percent of the earth's surface is covered by water, most water is not drinkable: 97 percent is saltwater, 2 percent is in ice caps and glaciers, and most of the remaining 1 percent is so far underground that it is beyond human reach. The primary sources of water for use and consumption are rainfall, streams, lakes, rivers, and aquifers (accessible underground water supplies). About half of the world's rivers are seriously depleted and polluted (United Nations Environmental Program, 2002).

Because of the current rate of world population growth and existing climatic conditions, water scarcity is increasing throughout the world. About eighty countries, comprising 40 percent of the world's population, are suffering serious water shortages. If the greenhouse effect brings about changes in the climate, many countries in Africa may experience serious water shortages that will be further exacerbated by the growing problem of water pollution.

Where does the water go? The largest amount (about 70 percent) is used for crop irrigation; in some African and Asian countries, as much as 85 percent of the available water is used in agriculture. The second largest use of water is in industry (23 to 25 percent). Industrial use of water depends on the level of development in a country and the structure of its economy. For example, high-income nations use as much as 60 percent of their water for industry, whereas a middle- or low-income nation might use less than 10 percent. A mere 8 percent of all available water is used for domestic or private household use. Affluent people in high-income nations use far more water (up to 1,000 quarts per person per day) than do families living in African villages, where water must often be carried several miles. Diseases related to the lack of safe drinking water cause over 4 million deaths annually (United Nations Environmental Program, 2002).

Water pollution seriously diminishes the available supply of water. Water can be polluted in a variety of ways. Most often, the cause is unpurified or insufficiently treated sewage from households and industry discharged into groundwater or surface water or pesticides and mineral fertilizers leached from farmland. The pollutants range from nitrates and phosphates to metals, salts, and pathogenic microorganisms.

The paper-manufacturing industry is a major water polluter. Dioxin and other chlorinated organic compounds used in manufacturing paper products are emitted into the streams below paper mills. People can become seriously ill from drinking the polluted water or eating contaminated fish. Environmental activists believe that paper mills should be required to convert to totally closed systems in which there are no chemical discharges into nearby water. Converting is costly, but a few paper mills are leading the way in the United States. Mills in Canada and Europe are required to use closed systems (Cushman, 1997). But not all water pollution comes from industry. Agriculture, especially as practiced by transnational corporations that are engaged in agribusiness, also pollutes water. Fertilizers and pesticides containing hazardous toxic chemicals that seriously impair water quality are used extensively and often leach into water supplies.

Soil Depletion and Desertification

About 11 percent of the earth's surface is used for growing crops, 32 percent is forest, and 24 percent is used to graze animals. Each year, however, many acres of usable land are lost through erosion and contamination. *Deforestation*—excessive removal of trees—usually results in serious erosion. Since the 1992 Earth Summit in Rio de Janeiro, high-income nations have made an effort to protect forests. Unfortunately, prior industrialization in the United States and other high-income nations has already taken a serious toll on forests, and the pattern is continuing in some middle- and low-income nations as they become more industrialized. In the United States, logging in the national forest system, especially in the Pacific Northwest, is an issue. Environmentalists say that logging increases landslides, floods, and changes in rivers and streams, which devastate fish stocks. Furthermore, when road building, which is necessary to get to the trees in the forest, is combined with cutting all the timber in an area (clear-cutting), the damage is even greater. More water flows down slopes, and when roads wash out, rocks and soil fall onto lower slopes and into streambeds.

Today, many regions are losing an increasing amount of useable land as a result of ***desertification*—the process by which usable land is turned into desert because of overgrazing, harmful agricultural practices, or deforestation.** It is estimated that desertification destroys as many as 15 million acres of land a year. An additional 50 million acres of crop and pasture land become inefficient each year because of excessive application of herbicides and pesticides, insufficient crop rotation, and intensified agricultural production (United Nations Environmental Program, 2002).

Although desertification takes place in both high-income and middle- and low-income nations, its effects are particularly devastating in middle- and low-income nations. When a country is already hard hit by rapid population growth, virtually any loss of land or crops is potentially devastating to large numbers of people (United Nations Environmental Program, 2002). The United Nations and other international organizations have therefore tried to make protection of the environment an integral part of all economic development policy. However, environmental protection specialists say that to translate policy into action, conservation programs must be supported by the people and the major sources of the problem must also be addressed: overpopulation and poverty (United Nations Environmental Program, 2002).

Solid, Toxic, and Nuclear Wastes

Even with a rapidly growing world population and ongoing economic development in industrialized nations, the planet might be able to sustain life for a long time if it weren't for all the solid and toxic chemical waste that is dumped into the environment.

Solid Waste

In the United States and some other high-income nations, people consume a vast array of products and—in these *disposable societies*—throw away huge quantities of paper, plastic, metal, and other materials. U.S. residences, businesses, and institutions produce more than 236 million tons of municipal solid waste each year (greenprintdenver.org 2008). The typical North American creates over 1,500 pounds of municipal solid waste per year, compared to slightly more than 700 pounds produced by the average Western European. *Solid waste* is any and all unwanted and discarded materials that are not liquids or gases, including sewage solids. For example, each year people in the United States throw away the following:

- 16 billion disposable diapers
- 2 billion razors and razor blades
- 220 million tires
- More glass and aluminum than existed in the entire world before World War II (Petersen, 1994:107)

One partial solution is *recycling*—reusing resources that would otherwise be discarded. Although there has been an increase in recycling, some cities have found they are running out of landfill space and consequently have been moving their garbage to other regions as a temporary solution.

Toxic Waste

At the same time that technology has brought about improvements in the quality and length of life, it has created the potential for new disasters. One source of a potential disaster is *toxic waste,* the hazardous chemical by-products of industrial processes. Perhaps the most widely known U.S. case of toxic waste is Love Canal. In the late 1970s, residents of Niagara Falls, New York, learned that their children were attending a school that

In travel brochures, Hawaii is known for its beautiful, unlittered beaches; however, as the trash piled on this Oahu beach shows, some formerly pristine areas are now endangered by environmental pollution.

had been built on top of a toxic landfill (Gibbs, 1982). After large numbers of children became ill and the smell and appearance of the chemicals permeated the entire area, many people mobilized against Hooker Chemical Company, which had dumped tons of chemicals there (Gibbs, 1982). Eventually, the federal government bought many of the houses, moved the residents out, and removed as much of the toxic waste as possible. Today, families again live in the area, but they have a highly visible neighbor: a forty-acre grassy landfill, thirty feet high at the center, with an eight-foot-high chainlink fence surrounding it. The landfill contains 21,000 tons of toxic chemical waste and the remains of 239 contaminated houses (Hoffman, 1994).

Today, the U.S. government regulates the disposal of toxic wastes, but some hazardous wastes are not covered by regulations, and some corporations avoid the regulations by locating their factories in other countries (see Chapters 2 and 13). In addition, there is often nowhere to safely dispose of the chemicals. Many people take a "not in my backyard" attitude toward toxic chemical waste dumps (Dunlap, 1992; Freudenberg and Steinsapir, 1992).

What is it like to discover that your neighborhood is being polluted by toxic waste? A resident of the East Swallow Road neighborhood in Fort Collins, Colorado, describes the uncertainty and worry caused by pools of petroleum leaking out of a service station's underground tanks (Erikson, 1994:115):

> [Y]ou just sort of live your life on hold. I'm always saying, "God, will it ever end so we can get on with our lives?" You can't really make any plans, you just sort of live your life in limbo. Sometimes it's almost unbearable. It's like you really don't live, you just sort of exist, and you wait and you wait and you wait for it to end. But it doesn't, so you just struggle through each day and you worry. You know, it's really, really a pretty sad way to have to live.

Nuclear Waste

Nuclear, or radioactive, wastes are the most dangerous of all toxic wastes. Radioactive waste comes primarily from manufacturers of nuclear weapons and nuclear power plants, although small amounts of waste are by-products of certain medical procedures. Weapons-manufacturing plants in Washington, South Carolina, and Colorado store huge amounts of radioactive waste and chemicals in underground tanks. Inspectors have found that some of the older tanks leak and others are empty. When tanks leak, they contaminate groundwater and thousands of cubic feet of soil. Nuclear waste remains deadly for prolonged periods of time. For example, uranium waste from nuclear power plants (an estimated 50,000 tons by the early 2000s) will remain dangerously radioactive for the next 10,000 years, and plutonium waste will be radioactive for the next 240,000 years (Petersen, 1994).

Technological Disasters

Technological disasters, such as the 1986 meltdown and radiation leak at the Chernobyl nuclear power plant in the Ukraine, have increased global awareness of the problems associated with radioactive waste. However, despite the disaster, Russia was using 31 nuclear reactors in 2005 (World Nuclear Association, 2005), giving evidence to sociologist Kai Erikson's remarks. According to Erikson (1991:15), the world faces a new species of trouble today:

> [Environmental problems] contaminate rather than merely damage... They pollute, befoul, taint, rather than just create wreckage... They penetrate human tissue indirectly rather than just wound the surfaces by assaults of a more straightforward kind.... And the evidence is growing that they scare human beings in new and special ways, that they elicit an uncanny fear in us.

The chaos that Erikson (1994:141) describes is the result of *technological disasters*—"meaning everything that can go wrong when systems fail, humans err, designs prove faulty, engines misfire, and so on." Chernobyl and Love Canal were technological disasters, as was radiation leakage at the Three Mile Island nuclear power plant in Pennsylvania in 1979 and the leakage of lethal gases at the pesticide plant in Bhopal, India, in 1984. In the worst-case scenario, technological disasters kill tens of thousands of people; in the best-case scenario, they place tremendous stress on the world's ecosystems and greatly diminish the quality of life for everyone.

SOCIOLOGICAL PERSPECTIVES AND SOLUTIONS FOR POPULATION AND ENVIRONMENTAL PROBLEMS

As sociologists have examined how human behavior affects population and environmental problems, the subdiscipline of environmental sociology has emerged (see Box 15.3 on page 328). According to Cable and Cable (1995:5), "*environmental sociology* examines people's

Critical Thinking and You

Box 15.3

Do We Have a Problem or Not? Learning from Environmental Sociology

- "I take care of the environment. I recycle my paper and soft drink cans, and I don't throw stuff out the window when I'm driving."
- "My sorority participated in Clean Up Day last year. We cleared out brush and trash at an old person's house and made it look a lot better."
- "With gas prices what they are now, I'll probably walk the rest of my life. That'll probably help the environment." (Author's files)

Comments such as these by college students are typical expressions of how many of us think about our relationship to the environment. We think of ourselves as "good" or "bad" based on how our actions might affect the environment. And, indeed, sociologists who specialize in environmental sociology believe that reciprocal interactions between the physical environment, social organization, and social behavior are an extremely important topic to study. So, on the one hand, what we do as individuals is important. However, on the other hand, what corporations, governmental agencies, and political leaders do at the macrolevel is also important.

In 2005 a news item stated that, for the first time, a number of U.S. senators now acknowledge that "the Earth's climate is changing and that human activity is the cause" (Nesmith, 2005). Are our political leaders among the last to notice problems such as global warming, environmental pollution, and other deteriorating conditions that contribute to a diminished quality of life on planet Earth? Of course, these leaders might say that it is not so much a matter of acknowledging that the environment is a major international problem as it is determining how we might reduce or solve the problem. Some analysts believe that economic growth and the introduction of new technologies and alternative forms of energy can bring about vast improvements in the environment. Other analysts believe that without significant changes in national and global laws and policies, the environment that is problematic now will be largely unsustainable in future generations.

Questions for Critical Thinking

1. One school of thought suggests that there is a positive relationship between economic growth and the environment. In your own community, can you give examples of situations in which economic growth contributed to the quality of the environment? How about situations in which economic growth contributed to environmental problems?

2. We often hear people being criticized for driving "gas-guzzling" vehicles or eating at fast-food restaurants that dispense millions of sacks, wrappers, cups, and other disposable products, some of which eventually litter the nation's roadways and dump sites. Do you think that our individual choices—such as the vehicle we own or where we eat our food—really affect the quality of our environment? Or are environmental problems beyond our control because they are caused by natural causes or decisions of large corporations and governmental agencies over which we have no control?

3. The United States uses 25 percent of the world's energy, and some scientists believe we are experiencing global warming because of this vast energy consumption. Is global warming a national issue? An international issue? Can you think of ways in which we might make an aggressive effort to deal with environmental problems now and in the future?

beliefs about their environment, their behavior toward it, and the ways in which the structure of society influences them and contributes to the persistent abuse of the environment." Like all sociologists, environmental sociologists—as well as demographers—approach their study from one or another perspective.

The Functionalist Perspective

Some functionalists focus on the relationship between social structure, technological change, and environmental problems. On the one hand, they say, technological innovation serves important functions in society. For example, automation and mass production have made a wide array of goods—from automobiles and computers to McDonald's burgers—available to many people. On the other hand, technological innovation has latent dysfunctions; automation and mass production, for example, create air pollution, overuse and depletion of natural resources, and excessive solid waste. From this point of view, some environmental problems are the price a society pays for technological progress. If this is true, the best way to alleviate the problem is to develop new technologies. This is what happened, some functionalists note, when the catalytic converter and other antipollution devices were developed for automobiles.

Other functionalists take a neo-Malthusian perspective and believe that to reduce food shortages and environmental problems, population must be controlled. In other words, the more people there are alive, the greater are the overuse of finite resources and degradation of soil, water, and land.

No matter which view functionalist environmental sociologists take, they believe that solutions to overpopulation and environmental degradation lie in social institutions such as education and the government. Educators can encourage population control by teaching people about the limits to agriculture and the difficulty of feeding rapidly increasing populations. Government leaders and international organizations such as the United Nations can cooperate to find far-reaching and innovative solutions and develop understandings about more equitable use of the world's resources (Ehrlich and Ehrlich, 1991).

The Conflict Perspective

Analysts using a conflict framework believe that population and environmental problems have less to do with overpopulation and shortages of resources than they have to do with power differentials in societies and in the larger global economy. For example, early conflict theorists, such as Karl Marx and Friedrich Engels (1976/1848), did not think that the food supply was threatened by overpopulation because agricultural technology (even in their era) could meet the food needs of the growing world population if it were not for poverty. According to Marx and Engels (1976/1848), poverty exists because workers are exploited by capitalists. They argued, for example, that poverty existed in England because the capitalists skimmed off some of the workers' wages as profits. Thus the labor of the working classes was used by capitalists to earn profits, which, in turn, were used to purchase machinery that could replace the workers rather than supply food. From this classical Marxist point of view, population growth is encouraged by capitalists who use unemployed workers (the industrial reserve army) to keep other workers from demanding higher wages or better working conditions.

According to contemporary conflict theorists, corporations and the government are the two main power institutions in society. As a result, when economic decisions made by members of the capitalist class and elite political leaders lead to environmental problems, the costs are externalized, or passed along to the people (Cable and Cable, 1995:13):

> [The externalization of environmental costs of production] . . . means that the costs of production's negative impact on the environment (for example, the expense of cleaning polluted water to make it suitable for drinking) are not included in the price of the product. The company neither pays for the privilege of polluting the water nor cleans it; it saves the cost of proper waste disposal and makes environmentally conscious competition impossible. Not even the consumer of the product pays the environmental costs of production directly. Rather, the public at large essentially subsidizes the company, by either paying for the cleanup of the environment or enduring degraded environmental quality.

Although most conflict approaches to studying the environment focus on the relationship between members of the capitalist class and political elites, there is also an approach known as *ecofeminism*—the belief that patriarchy is a root cause of environmental problems. According to ecofeminists, patriarchy results in not only the domination of women by men but also the belief that nature is to be possessed and dominated rather than treated as a partner (Ortner, 1974; Merchant, 1983, 1992; Mies and Shiva, 1993).

Another conflict approach uses an *environmental justice framework*—examining how race and class intersect in the struggle for scarce environmental resources. Of particular interest to these theorists is ***environmental racism*—the belief that a disproportionate number of hazardous facilities are placed in areas populated primarily by poor people and people of color** (Bullard and Wright, 1992). Hazardous facilities include waste disposal and treatment plants and chemical plants (Schneider, 1993). A 1987 study by the Commission for Racial Justice concluded, "Race was the most potent variable in predicting the location of uncontrolled (abandoned) and commercial toxic waste sites in the United States" (Bullard and Wright, 1992:41). For example, the Carver Terrace housing subdivision in Texarkana, Texas, which is composed of 100 African-American households, was built over an area that had been previously contaminated by a creosote wood treatment facility (Capek, 1993). The federal government eventually bought out some of the homeowners and relocated the subdivision, but not until a number of years after it was determined that toxins in the neighborhood had caused the deaths of twenty-six people and the illnesses of many others (Capek, 1993).

The Symbolic Interactionist Perspective

Since symbolic interactionists take a microlevel approach, viewing society as the sum of all people's interactions, they look at environmental problems in terms of individuals. Specifically, they think environmental problems are exacerbated by people's subjective assessment of reality. They point out that children learn core values that are considered important in the United States through socialization, but some of these values can be detrimental to the environment. Consider the following widely held beliefs (Cable and Cable, 1995:11–12):

- *A free market system provides the greatest good for the greatest number of people:* Economic decision making works best in private hands.
- *The natural world is inexhaustible:* There will always be more natural resources.
- *Faith in technology:* Any challenge can be met through technology.
- *The growth ethic:* Growth equals progress; bigger is better.
- *Materialism:* Success can be measured in terms of consumption.
- *Individualism:* Individual rights and personal achievement are most important.
- *An anthropocentric worldview:* Human beings are at the center of the world, and humans are superior to other species. Standing *apart from* nature rather than recognizing that we are *part of* nature, we attempt to conquer and subdue the environment.

It might be, however, that as people become aware of the effects of environmental degradation, concern for the environment will emerge as a core value in the United States. To eliminate the global problems posed by overpopulation and environmental degradation, all societies must make the following changes (based on Petersen, 1994:109):

- Reduce the use of energy.
- Shift from fossil fuels to solar-based energy systems or other energy-efficient systems such as water power, wind power, or geothermal energy.
- Develop new transportation networks and city designs that reduce automobile use.
- Work for redistribution of land and wealth so that the poor in all nations can make a positive contribution.
- Push for equality between women and men in all nations, emphasizing literacy training, educational opportunities, and health care (including reproduction and contraception information) for women.
- Effect a rapid transition to smaller families.
- Cooperate internationally to reduce the consumption of resources by the wealthy nations and bring higher living standards to poorer nations.

Are these changes likely to occur? Some social analysts think that it will take a threatening event—a drastic change in the earth's weather patterns or a sudden increase in natural disasters—to capture the attention of enough of the earth's people and to convince political leaders that a serious change in direction is required if the planet is to continue to support human life (Petersen, 1994). We can only hope that people will not wait until it is too late.

SUMMARY

■ *What is the global population and why is population growth a problem?*

The world's population is more than 6.72 billion; it doubled in the last fifty years and, if this trend continues, will double again in the next fifty years. The concern is whether the earth's resources can support this rapid population growth.

■ *What are the primary factors that affect population growth?*

Three factors affect population growth: fertility, the actual number of children born to an individual or a population; mortality, the number of deaths that occur in a specific population; and migration, the movement of people from one geographic area to another for the purpose of changing residency.

■ *How does population growth affect a society?*

Population growth affects population composition, the biological and social characteristics of a population, including such attributes as age, sex, race, marital status, education, occupation, income, and size of household. In the United States, for example, the age distribution of the population affects the need for schools, employment opportunities, health care, and age-appropriate housing.

■ *What are the major theoretical perspectives on overpopulation?*

According to the Malthusian perspective, population expands geometrically while the food supply increases arithmetically; disaster can be averted through positive checks (e.g., famine, disease, war) or preventive checks (e.g., sexual abstinence, delayed marriage). The neo-Malthusians believe that the earth is a ticking bomb because population problems exacerbate environmental problems. The third perspective is more hopeful. According to demographic transition theory, societies move from high birth and death rates to low birth and death rates as a result of technological development. However, critics say that demographic transition theory applies chiefly to Western societies.

■ *What solutions do we have to world hunger?*

Two of the most far-reaching initiatives have been the green revolution (the growing of high-yield "miracle" crops) and the biotechnological revolution, which involves "improving" plants or animals or using microorganisms in innovative ways. However, some social analysts believe that the solution is not to produce more food but to control fertility.

■ *How is immigration changing the population composition of the United States?*

Today, the proportion of U.S. immigrants in the population is the highest it has been since 1940. If immigration continues at the present rate, it will account for two-thirds of the expected population growth in the next fifty years. (The United States is otherwise almost at zero population growth—a stable population.) Immigration leads to higher taxes, but it also brings substantial economic benefits.

■ *What is environmental degradation and what are its causes?*

Environmental degradation is caused by disruptions to the environment that have negative consequences for ecosystems. Human beings, particularly as they pursue economic development and growth, cause environmental degradation.

■ *What is the major source of air pollution and what are its effects?*

The major source is fossil fuel pollution, especially from vehicles but also from industry. One of the most serious consequences of air pollution is the greenhouse effect, an environmental condition caused by excessive quantities of carbon dioxide, water vapor, methane, and nitrous oxide in the atmosphere leading to global warming.

■ *What water, soil, and forest problems do we face?*

Water scarcity is increasing around the world, and water pollution further diminishes the available water supply. One of the major water polluters in the United States is the paper-manufacturing industry. About 15 million acres of soil are lost each year to desertification (the process by which usable land is turned into desert because of overgrazing and harmful agricultural practices) and deforestation (excessive removal of trees). Desertification is greatest in middle- and low-income nations.

■ *Why are solid, toxic, and nuclear wastes a problem?*

High-income nations are running out of space for the amount of solid waste produced by their "disposable societies." Toxic waste (hazardous chemical by-products of industry) causes death and disease if it is not disposed of properly. Nuclear, or radioactive, waste is a problem because of the length of time it remains deadly.

■ *What is the functionalist perspective on population and the environment?*

On the subject of environment, functionalists say that the latent dysfunctions of technology cause problems but that new technologies can solve these problems. Most functionalists take a neo-Malthusian perspective on population but believe that social institutions, especially education and the government, can cooperate to solve population and environmental problems.

■ *What is the conflict perspective on population and the environment?*

In the classical Marxist view, there would be enough food for all people if poverty were alleviated, and poverty exists because capitalists skim workers' wages for profits. Contemporary conflict theorists believe that the two main power institutions in society—corporations and the government—make economic decisions that result in environmental problems. An approach known as ecofeminism says that patriarchy is a root cause of environmental problems: Nature is viewed as something to be possessed and dominated. The environmental justice approach examines how race and class intersect in the struggle for scarce environmental resources.

■ *What is the symbolic interactionist perspective on population and environment?*

Symbolic interactionists see population and environment problems in microlevel—individual—terms. Through socialization, children learn core values that are often detrimental to the environment. However, there is some indication that concern for the environment is becoming a core value in the United States.

KEY TERMS

acid rain, p. 323
demographic transition theory, p. 314
demography, p. 311
desertification, p. 325
environmental degradation, p. 321
environmental racism, p. 329
fertility, p. 311
greenhouse effect, p. 324
migration, p. 312
mortality, p. 311
population composition, p. 312
zero population growth, p. 318

QUESTIONS FOR CRITICAL THINKING

1. Which perspective on population growth do you favor—neo-Malthusian or demographic transition theory—and why?
2. How do political leaders describe the "immigration problem" in the United States? Are these biased or unbiased views? Explain.
3. If you had to focus on a single aspect of environmental degradation—air pollution; water, soil, or forest problems; solid, toxic, or nuclear waste disposal—which would it be and why? What would you do to make people aware of the seriousness of the problem? What new solutions could you propose?

Chapter 16

Urban Problems

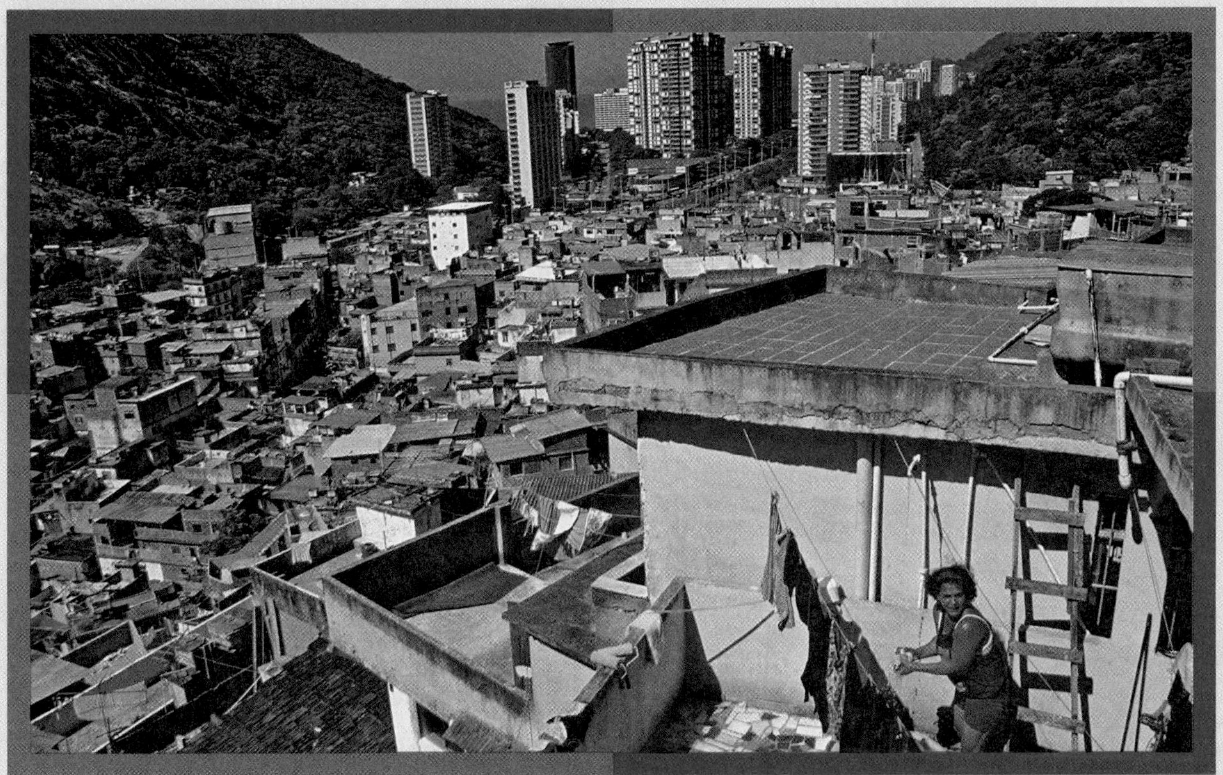

THINKING SOCIOLOGICALLY

- Why do people living in the same city often have divergent perspectives on and experiences in that city?
- Can contemporary urban problems such as fiscal crises, housing shortages, and high rates of homelessness be traced to growth and development patterns of the past?
- How does globalization influence urban and rural areas around the world?

As I was down on Green St... I took a break to stroll around the neighborhood. It's got the Lucky Dog, Coral Seafood, a few other places I know of. But I wasn't interested in the Worcester [Massachusetts] I know. I glanced a block away, and an old building caught my eye. I walked to a parallel street, down to Beach St. and its surrounding area. What I saw killed me; it felt like I was seeing a different city than the one I thought I was living in. Empty warehouses and dilapidated buildings, sure, but there were gaping holes in the street literally four feet deep, chairs and tables in the road, multiple baby carriers sitting on the sidewalk now that the kids have gotten too big. This area covers maybe two blocks, tops, and is wedged between two respectable, if run-down, areas of the city. What are these shadow places?

... These shadow places are certainly not on the maps of the city planners, the developers, or City Hall. I take that back—you can point to Beach St. on their maps, but nobody will listen. And no entity truly exists if nobody will recognize its existence.

The city itself does not exist in an objective map. No city does. The city is a conglomeration of experiences and stories, a weave of narratives and ghosts of narratives. The city is a different subjective experience for everyone who lives in it. And for every resident of Worcester, there is a secret map.

—College student Darius Kazemi (2005), writing in his college newspaper,* WPI Tech News, *describes the experience of getting out of his "comfort zone" in the city and briefly looking at other people's lives and homes, which clearly were not like his own.

What is life like in the city? As Darius suggests, people living in the same city have very divergent perspectives and experiences because of their positions in the social structure and particularly as their position is affected by race, class, gender, and age. Although the rich and the poor may live near one another in many cities, they are worlds apart in lifestyles and life chances. At the individual, microlevel, each of us has a secret map of the city in which we live. According to Darius, these secret maps are subjective: "We leave out some parts of the original map, and we add our own embellishments" (Kazemi, 2005). As social science research shows, differences in lifestyle and life chances can be attributed partly to the fact that most U.S. cities are enclaves of geographic, socioeconomic, and racial-ethnic isolation (Higley, 1995). This was certainly true of what Darius Kazemi found on his exploration of Worcester, the city in which his college is located.

In this chapter, we examine how people *experience* urban life as well as looking at some of the most pressing urban problems in the United States and other nations. Many social problems discussed in this book—including the wide gap between the rich and the poor, racial and ethnic strife, inadequate educational opportunities, and homelessness—are found in rural areas, but, of course, they are much more pronounced in densely populated urban areas. For example, crime rates typically are higher in urban areas, and schools tend to be dilapidated. As a framework for examining urban problems today, let's briefly look at the changes in U.S. cities that have led to these problems.

CHANGES IN U.S. CITIES

Urban problems in the United States are closely associated with the profound socioeconomic, political, and spatial changes that have taken place since the Industrial Revolution. Two hundred years ago, most people (about 94 out of 100) lived in sparsely populated rural areas, where they farmed. In the twenty-first century, about 80 percent of the U.S. population lives in urban areas, and many of these people live in cities that did not exist two hundred years ago (U.S. Census Bureau, 2008).

Early Urban Growth and Social Problems

Industrialization and urbanization bring about profound changes in societies and frequently spawn new social problems, such as housing shortages, overcrowding, unsanitary living and working conditions, environmental pollution, and crime (see Chapter 1). By definition, a city involves population density. According to sociologists, a *city* is a relatively dense and permanent settlement of people who secure their livelihood primarily through nonagricultural activities (Weeks, 2005). Although cities existed long before the Industrial Revolution, the birth of the factory system brought about rapid *urbanization,* which we defined in Chapter 1 as the process by which an increasing proportion of a population lives in cities rather than in rural areas. For example, the population of New York City swelled by 500 percent between 1870 and 1910 as rural dwellers and immigrants from Ireland, Italy, Germany, Poland, and other nations arrived in massive numbers, seeking jobs in factories and offices.

Early cities were a composite of commercial, residential, and manufacturing activities located in close proximity. But even then, rapidly growing cities such as New York had a few blocks (e.g., Upper Fifth Avenue) of houses where the wealthy lived (Palen, 1995). These residences were located near the center of the city, and their addresses were considered a sign of social and economic success (Baltzell, 1958; Birmingham, 1967). With the introduction of horse-drawn streetcar lines in the 1850s and electric streetcars in the 1880s, people were able to move more easily from place to place within the core city and to commute between the core city and outlying suburban areas. As a result, many middle-class families moved out of the central areas (Palen, 1995).

City leaders established municipal governments for building and repairing streets, fire protection, crime control, sewage disposal, lighting, and other general needs. In the late nineteenth and early in the twentieth century, improved transportation and new technologies for supplying water and disposing of waste enabled cities to grow even faster. However, municipal governments had trouble keeping pace with the negative side effects of "progress," including urban slums, traffic congestion, and high crime rates. Despite these problems, people continued to move to northeastern and midwestern cities in unprecedented numbers, looking for jobs, educational opportunities, and such new amenities as big department stores, parks, libraries, and theaters.

Contemporary Urban Growth

The growth of suburbs and outlying areas forever changed the nature of city life in this country. Suburban areas existed immediately adjacent to many city centers as early as the nineteenth century, but in the 1920s, these communities began to grow in earnest because of the automobile. They were referred to as "bedroom communities" because most of the residents were there on nights and weekends but went into the city for jobs, entertainment, and major shopping. During the 1930s, about 17 million people lived in suburban areas (Palen, 1995). With the exception of a few cities—for example, New York and Chicago—that built subways or other forms of mass transit, most suburban dwellers drove to work each day, establishing a pattern that would result, decades later, in traffic congestion and air pollution, problems that have drastically worsened in the past two decades (Palen, 1995).

Between the end of World War II (1945) and 1970, suburbanization brought about a dramatic shift in the distribution of the U.S. population. During the war, construction of apartments and single-family dwellings had halted as industry produced war-related goods. When the war ended, many veterans returned home, married, and had children (the "baby boom" generation). Consequently, in the late 1940s, as many as 6 million families were unable to find housing; many had to live with relatives or friends until they could find a place of their own (Palen, 1995).

To reduce the housing shortage, the federal government subsidized what became a mass exodus from the city to outlying suburbs. Congress passed the Housing Act of 1949, which gave incentives to builders to develop affordable housing. In addition, federal agencies such as the Veterans Administration (VA) and the Federal Housing Adminisitration (FHA) established lenient lending policies so that war veterans could qualify to buy homes for their families (Palen, 1995). Other factors also contributed to the postwar suburban boom, including the availability of inexpensive land, low-cost mass construction methods for building tract houses, new federally financed freeway systems, inexpensive gasoline, racial tension in city centers, and consumers' pent-up demands for single-family homes on individually owned lots (Jackson, 1985). The most widely known and perhaps the most successful suburban developer of this era was Abraham Levitt and Sons, the company that developed Levittown (on Long Island, New York). Levittown was the first large-scale, mass-produced housing development in this country (see Map 16.1). Eventually, more than 17,000 single-family residences—occupied by more than 82,000 people—were located in Levittown. Sometimes referred to as "cracker boxes" because of their simple, square construction, Levitt houses were typically two-bedroom, one-bath Cape Cod–style homes built on concrete slabs. Driveways were unpaved, and each home had its own small lawn with a couple of small bushes (Nieves, 1995).

Although early suburbanization provided many families with affordable housing, good schools and parks, and other amenities not found in the city, the shift away from city centers set up an economic and racial division of interests between cities and suburbs that remains in place even today. Although many people in the suburbs still rely on the city centers for employment, entertainment, or other services, they pay taxes to their local governments and school districts. As a result, suburban police and fire departments, schools, libraries, and recreational facilities are usually well funded and well staffed, with up-to-date facilities. Suburbs also have newer infrastructures (such as roads, sewers, and water treatment plants) and money to maintain them. In contrast, many cities have aging, dilapidated schools and lack funds for essential government services (see Chapter 12). According to national estimates, African-American and Latino/a students who attend school in predominantly subordinate-group city districts have substantially less access to computers at school than do white schoolchildren in suburban schools (Reid, 2001).

Since 1970, cities in the South, Southwest, and West have been considered postindustrial cities because their economic production largely consists of information-processing or service jobs (Orum, 1995). Whereas cities in the Northeast and Midwest grew up around heavy manufacturing, the newer Sunbelt cities have grown through light industry (e.g., computer software manufacturing), information-processing services (e.g., airline and hotel reservation services), educational complexes,

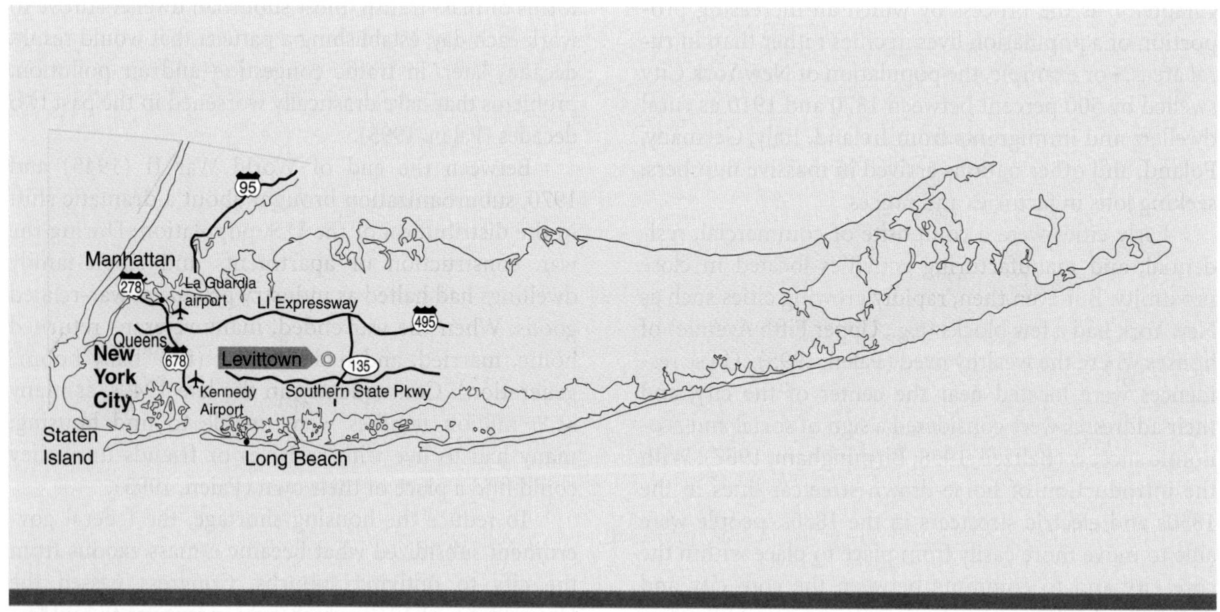

Map 16.1 *Levittown, New York*

medical centers, convention and entertainment centers, and retail trade centers and shopping malls (Sawers and Tabb, 1984). In these postindustrial cities, most families do not live near the central business district.

Today, edge cities are springing up beyond the cities and existing suburbs. An ***edge city*** **is a middle- to upper-middle-class area that has complete living, working, shopping, and leisure activities so that it is not dependent on the central city or other suburbs** (Garreau, 1991). The Massachusetts Turnpike Corridor, west of Boston, and the Perimeter Area, north of Atlanta, are examples of edge cities. Edge cities begin as residential areas; then retail establishments and office parks move into the adjacent area, creating an unincorporated edge city. Automobiles are the primary source of transportation in many edge cities, and pedestrian traffic is discouraged—and even dangerous—because streets are laid out to facilitate high-volume automobile traffic, not walkers or bicyclists. Some edge cities do not have a governing body, so they drain taxes from cities and older suburbs. Many businesses and industries move their physical plants—and tax dollars—to these areas because land is cheaper, workers are better educated, and utility rates and property taxes are lower than those in the city. As a result, many jobs move away from poor, subordinate-group workers in cities, creating structural unemployment.

Over time, large-scale metropolitan growth produces a ***megalopolis*****—a continuous concentration of two or more cities and their suburbs that have grown until they form an interconnected urban area.** The East Coast, for example, is a megalopolis, with Boston, Providence, Hartford, and their suburbs merging into New York City and its suburbs, which in turn, merge southward into Newark, Philadelphia, Baltimore, and Washington, D.C., and their suburbs. It is almost impossible to tell where one metropolitan area ends and another begins. When metropolitan areas merge into a megalopolis, there are big population changes that can bring about or exacerbate social problems and inequalities based on race, class, and gender.

URBAN PROBLEMS IN THE UNITED STATES

Even the most optimistic of observers tends to agree that cities in the United States have problems brought on by years of neglect and deterioration. As we saw in previous chapters, poverty, crime, racism, homelessness, inadequate public school systems, alcoholism and other drug abuse, and other social problems are most visible and acute in urban settings. Intertwined with and exacerbating these problems in many older cities are periodic fiscal crises.

Fiscal Crises in Cities

Not all U.S. cities are in a state of fiscal crisis and decline, but over the past four decades, there have been some that have teetered on the brink of bankruptcy. New York City was on the edge of financial collapse in 1975 until the federal government provided an elaborate bailout plan; Cleveland went into financial default in 1978. When federal aid to cities was slashed during the recession of the early 1980s, some state governments provided additional monies to cities, but most did not have the means to do so (Clark and Walter, 1994). As a result, the governments of Detroit, Boston, and New York had to drastically reduce services; they closed some public hospitals and other facilities, laid off employees, significantly cut public transit, and all but stopped maintaining the cities' infrastructures. Finding a solution to the fiscal crises of the 1980s was a real dilemma, and the situation hasn't gotten much better. As middle- and upper-income people have moved to the suburbs, retail businesses and corporations have followed them or moved their operations to other countries. The shrinking central cities have been left with greatly reduced sources of revenue, and municipal governments can't very well increase taxes when their taxes are already much higher than those in the more affluent suburbs or in Sunbelt cities such as Las Vegas, Phoenix, and Arlington and Austin, Texas (Moore and Stansel, 1992). Although increasing numbers of upper-middle and upper-class individuals and families are choosing to reside in cities proper, many residents who remain in central cities . . . are poor, unemployed, or older people living on fixed incomes. These individuals cannot pay additional taxes but still need city services such as hospitals, police and fire departments, and public transportation.

Joblessness and declining wages among central city residents further diminish the tax base in many cities and create tremendous social dislocation. To understand the extent of job loss and its impact on many cities, consider this description by sociologist William J. Wilson (1996:34–35) of the predominantly African-American community of North Lawndale in Chicago:

> After more than a quarter century of continuous deterioration, North Lawndale resembles a war zone. . . . Two large factories anchored the economy of

Signe Wilkinson, Cartoonist & Writers Syndicate/cartoonweb.com

> this West Side neighborhood in its good days—the Hawthorne plant of Western Electric, which employed over 43,000 workers and an International Harvester plant with 14,000 workers. The world headquarters for Sears, Roebuck and Company was located there, providing another 10,000 jobs. The neighborhood also had a Copenhagen snuff plant, a Sunbeam factory, and a Zenith factory, a Dell Farm food market, an Alden's catalog store, and a U.S. Post Office bulk station. But conditions rapidly changed. Harvester closed its doors in the late 1960s. Sears moved most of its offices to the Loop in downtown Chicago in 1973; a catalogue distribution center with a workforce of 3,000 initially remained in the neighborhood but was relocated outside the state of Illinois in 1987. The Hawthorne plant gradually phased out its operations and finally shut down in 1984. The departure of the big plants triggered the demise or exodus of the smaller stores, the banks, and other businesses that relied on the wages paid by the large employers. . . . In 1986, North Lawndale, with a population of over 66,000, had only one bank and one supermarket; but it was also home to forty-eight state lottery agencies, fifty currency exchanges, and ninety-nine licensed liquor stores and bars.

In the twenty-first century, efforts have been made by community-based organizations to revitalize North Lawndale and improve the quality of life there. Economic development, affordable and mixed-income housing, and education have all been part of the revitalization plan. The latest study available on this revitalization project shows that some progress has been made; however, much more redevelopment is needed because the community continues to have high rates of poverty, unemployment, and crime and low rates of education and commercial activity. North Lawndale remains disproportionately African American (94.2 percent) but has seen an increase in the Latino/a population, which now accounts for 4.5 percent of the community (Lane, Ryan, Wilson, and Yeftich, 2007). The future of North Lawndale, as with many other areas like it throughout the country, depends on the commercial development, an adequate supply of affordable and mixed-income housing, and improved academic performance and educational opportunities in local schools.

Given the acute shortage of funds in many cities, these problems will not be solved any time soon. Many cities have also experienced natural disasters such as floods, brushfires, earthquakes, hurricanes, or tornados—all of which add to the cities' financial burdens by creating new infrastructure problems at the same time that relief must be provided for the hardest-hit residents.

The Crisis in Health Care

The growing problems in health care are most evident in the nation's largest cities. Although hospitals and other medical facilities are subject to cutbacks and closings because of economic problems, poor people who live in central cities are more likely to become ill or injured than are people in more affluent suburbs. Poverty is associated with many medical problems, including certain diseases (such as tuberculosis) and problems associated with inadequate nutrition and lack of preventive care (many children are not immunized against the basic childhood diseases). Moreover, drug-related problems and HIV/AIDS place tremendous financial burdens on already underfunded community clinics, hospitals, and other medical facilities. According to the National Centers for Disease Control and Prevention in Atlanta, both the number of AIDS patients and the costs of caring for AIDS patients are highest in cities.

Because lack of funding has caused many community clinics and publicly financed hospitals to close, finding affordable health care is a major problem for city residents. Essential services have been cut back in many metropolitan hospitals. Furthermore, as managed care plans and large hospital chains have taken over the ownership of privately funded hospitals, some private hospitals now claim that they cannot afford to provide uncompensated care, and some refuse to admit uninsured patients except in life-threatening circumstances. As a result, although public hospitals cannot legally deny care to an individual, a patient might have to wait hours (sometimes even days) to see a physician or other medical personnel, who must deal with one life-and-death medical emergency after another. Today, many poor people use emergency rooms for all medical services because they do not have—and cannot afford to pay—a private physician. Consequently, the cost of providing medical services is driven higher at a time when public hospitals have greatly diminished resources. The growing homeless population in major urban areas has simply added to the cost of providing health care.

Housing Problems

Many regions in the United States lack affordable housing for low-income individuals and families (see Chapter 2). Over the last ten years, there has been a significant increase in homelessness, especially among families with children. Each year, we are made aware of the plight of homeless people through extensive media coverage during the Thanksgiving to Christmas holiday season. During the rest of the year, many people view the homeless with less compassion (see Box 16.1 on page 340).

The Housing Shortage

When people speak of "the housing shortage," they typically are referring to the availability of affordable or relatively low-cost housing. Throughout the United States, millions of apartments and houses in a wide variety of price ranges are available to rent, lease, or purchase. However, the presence of these housing units does not mean that there is adequate housing available in all price ranges and locations throughout the nation.

Over the past thirty years, the number of low-cost (affordable) housing units has continued to decrease in the United States. Some of these units became more expensive apartments or condominiums that were no longer within the price range of individuals who might have previously lived in properties located at that site. Millions of other low-cost units have been abandoned. Although it might seem surprising that landlords will abandon rental property that they own, single-room-occupancy (SRO) hotels and inexpensive apartments for lower-income residents sometimes become so great an economic liability that landlords simply abandon the properties. Landlords are most likely to give up their property when they find themselves caught between increasing property taxes, demands from the city to maintain or upgrade the property to comply with safety standards or building codes, and tenants who demand services but do not pay their rent or severely damage the units.

Abandoned buildings increase fear and isolation in the residents of adjoining properties. The empty buildings often become hiding places for drug dealers or fugitives, and some are dangerous places for children to play. In some cities, however, *urban squatters*—people who

Efforts to reduce the problem of homelessness are addressed by volunteers with organizations such as this Habitat for Humanity project in New Orleans. How might a combination of public and private initiatives be used to provide homes for a larger percentage of the U.S. population?

Social Problems in the Media

Box 16.1

Media Framing of Stories about Homelessness and the Holidays

> In a *Doonesbury* comic strip, cartoonist Gary Trudeau shows a homeless man standing in line waiting for his free meal on Thanksgiving Day. A journalist walks up and talks to the homeless man: "You're getting a free meal today... but afterwards... what do you hope for?" The homeless man replies, "Seconds." The journalist counters: "No, no... I mean in the long term." The homeless man replies, "Dessert... definitely dessert." *(Kendall, 2005:124)*

As this cartoon shows, the homeless man and the journalist are operating under different assumptions about life and what the future should hold for people. In four quick cartoon frames, Trudeau captures the essence of much media reporting about holiday assistance to the poor by showing how out of place most reporters are when they try to impose their own thinking on the homeless people they are interviewing.

In recent research I conducted on how the media frame stories about the poor and homeless, I identified two central frames that often are used in the news—thematic framing and episodic framing (Kendall, 2005). *Thematic framing* is used in news stories that emphasize statistics and trends in homelessness over the experiences of homeless persons, meaning that journalists primarily write about *facts* regarding homelessness, such as changes in rates of homelessness, hunger, and poverty. Thematic framing also focuses on how the government defines poverty and homelessness and what changes have occurred over a specific period of time in regard to these statistics. By contrast, *episodic framing* in news stories examines homelessness and poverty in terms of personal experience, particularly how these conditions affect an individual or family. This type of framing provides a human face for homelessness or poverty, but it often ignores the larger structural factors (such as high rates of unemployment) that contribute to the problem.

One of the most benevolent media messages contained in episodic framing is that the poor are down on their luck and just need a helping hand. This type of framing is especially popular in news stories published near holidays such as Thanksgiving or Christmas, asking readers for assistance in temporarily meeting some of the needs of the poor. Reporting of this type gradually increases in the fall of each year, reaches its height during the Thanksgiving and Christmas holiday season and the cold weather months, and then drops sharply from late winter to early spring. During the peak period of these human interest stories, members of the press barrage service providers at soup kitchens and homeless shelters for interviews, and volunteers are shown serving turkey dinners to the poor at Thanksgiving and

occupy land or property without any legal title to it—have moved into abandoned apartment buildings and fixed them up. As people take up unofficial residence in the buildings, they create a sense of community by watching out for each other's possessions. However, most of these projects have been short-lived. Developers who recognize potential in the area demand that the buildings be razed to make way for new hotels and office towers.

In recent years, some cities have instituted programs to provide low-cost owner-occupied housing, but some social analysts believe that these programs promote the interests of the housing industry and protect property values more than they actually help people to acquire housing. One of the best-known federal government housing initiatives, the urban homesteading program, has been fraught with problems. The program was designed to allow low-income families to purchase—for a nominal fee—abandoned properties. In return, the purchasers had to agree to live in the property and make improvements to it for a period of time, after which the property could be sold. Unfortunately, it appears that the government did not provide sufficient housing units in a given area to meet the demand and offset the urban deterioration. In addition, the Federal Housing Administration (FHA) flooded central city neighborhoods with federally insured loans that were attractive to lenders and real estate agents, who often arranged for families to purchase homes that they were then unable to maintain when repairs became necessary. As a result, massive foreclosures occurred, causing people to lose their homes, bringing about further deterioration of city neighborhoods (Squires, 1994).

Although the Department of Housing and Urban Development (HUD) continues to explore ways to provide affordable housing for low-income and

Box 16.2 (continued)

preparing baskets of food for indigent families at Christmas. An example of this type of media coverage is found in an annual series, "The Neediest Cases," published in the *New York Times.* One article, "Offering a Hand, and Hope, in a Year of Record Homelessness in New York," describes the problems of Gloria Hernandez, a homeless woman residing in New York City:

> Gloria Hernandez tries to be strong for her five children, but strength, like privacy or full stomachs, does not come easily when you and your family live in a shelter for the homeless. "The children say, 'Mommy, when are we going to get out of here?'" Ms. Hernandez, forty, said softly, her eyes downcast. "You see it in their faces: they don't speak, but they show it. They say it's your fault." (Bovino, 2003:A25)

The photo accompanying the article shows Hernandez, looking depressed, standing with her nine-year-old son, whose arm is protectively wrapped around her neck.

Although one important function of the media is to make the public aware of social problems, why do the media increase coverage at *this* time of year—during the holidays? Part of the explanation may come from sociologist Lewis A. Coser, who says "we have only so much emotional energy and yet we live in a world filled with inhumanity and suffering" (1969:104). Thus, sympathy for the afflicted in a society fluctuates over time. Otherwise, we would be emotionally overwhelmed. Another reason comes from Emile Durkheim, who points to the holidays as the time that most people express sympathy for the homeless: Holidays are times of ritual, opportunities to affirm shared values. In the United States, where individualism is highly valued but people believe that they are responsive to social problems, the holidays reassert community solidarity by redistributing goods in the community (Barnett, 1954). What have you observed in the media's coverage of homelessness? Can you identify other framing devices used by journalists and television entertainment writers to convey certain messages to media audiences about homelessness and poverty?

Questions for Consideration

1. If you watch television situation comedies, can you recall an episode where a lead character served homeless people in a soup kitchen during the Thanksgiving or Christmas holiday? If so, how were the show's stars portrayed? How were the individuals in the soup kitchen portrayed?
2. Are news reports and the storylines of television entertainment shows a reflection of readers' and viewers' interests and preferences in content material, or are these reports and storylines a reflection of the corporate interests that own the media? What, if anything, do transnational media giants gain by providing coverage of the poor and homeless in their publications and broadcasts?

poverty-level people, its efforts have not been successful. Federal housing policy continues to reinforce the patterns and practices of private housing industries, as sociologist Gregory D. Squires (1994:51) explains:

> Working through their trade associations like the National Association of Homebuilders, the National Association of Realtors, the Associated General Contractors, the American Bankers Association, the U.S. League of Savings Institutions, and many others, housing-related industries have for over fifty years secured federal housing policies that focus on the provision of low-interest loans, mortgage interest subsidies, rent supplements, and other market-based inducements. Lobbyists have successfully kept public housing to a minimum in the United States (approximately 3% of all housing), labeling it as "socialistic" and, therefore, un-American. Again, it is the winners in the competitive market that have been the primary beneficiaries of housing policy.

The federal government's involvement in housing has been criticized on several fronts. Some critics believe that federal housing aid, which is supposed to provide decent housing for the poor, has done a better job of providing housing for more affluent people. Begun in the 1950s, federally funded urban renewal projects were supposed to replace housing units in slums with better-quality, affordable housing for the poor. However, some analysts say that once the slums were cleared, more expensive housing or commercial properties were built (Jacobs, 1961). Moreover, they say, sometimes the worst, most dilapidated housing units were not chosen for redevelopment because they were not in strategic locations for economic development. Because the power of *eminent domain* gives government officials the authority to condemn certain properties, individual owners' wishes regarding their property were not always taken into consideration (Flanagan, 2002). The most successful recent initiatives

The media provide extensive coverage of hunger and homelessness during the holiday season that extends from Thanksgiving to Christmas. Such stories typically include photos of people being served a holiday dinner at a homeless shelter or church. Do you think these reports are an accurate reflection of the true nature of this pressing social problem?

for replacing substandard housing and building lower-cost housing for poor and lower-income families have come from community groups and volunteer organizations. One of the best known of these is Habitat for Humanity, which has received extensive press coverage because of former President Jimmy Carter's participation.

A second major criticism of federal housing initiatives has been directed at public housing. Most federal and state housing projects have been huge, high-rise constructions that have intensified many problems and created new ones. Most urban sociologists agree that public housing works best when it is situated in less densely populated areas with a small number of families in any one housing project. In Charleston, South Carolina, for example, one public housing project is located in a neighborhood of historic residences that tourists visit on horse-drawn carriage tours. Tour guides even point to the housing unit as a sign that their community has overcome housing segregation. But when some communities place federally funded housing projects in neighborhoods of middle-income apartments and housing, adjoining property owners object, fearing that the value of their property and their personal safety will be diminished.

Since the 1970s, some middle- and upper-middle-class families have reentered city areas and gentrified properties. ***Gentrification* is the process by which people renovate or restore properties in cities.** Centrally located, naturally attractive areas are the most likely candidates for gentrification (Palen and London, 1984). Some people view gentrification as the way to revitalize the city. Others think that it further depletes the stock of affordable housing for the poor and pushes low-income people out of an area where they had previously lived (Palen and London, 1984). The worst outcome of the housing shortage has been a significant increase in the number of homeless people in the United States.

Homelessness

Accurate data about the actual number of homeless people in the United States is unavailable. The total is probably somewhere between 500,000 and the 3.5 million estimated by advocates for the homeless. It is extremely difficult to count the number of homeless people because most avoid interviews with census takers and social scientists. Each year, however, the U.S. Conference of Mayors conducts a survey on urban homelessness, and some consistent patterns have emerged. Among the homeless, people of color are overrepresented; African Americans make up the largest part of the homeless population (42 percent), when compared to whites (39 percent), Latinas/os (13 percent), Native Americans (4 percent), and Asian Americans (2 percent) (U.S. Conference of Mayors, 2007). Single men comprise 51 percent of the homeless population, families with children 30 percent, single women 17 percent, and unaccompanied youth 2 percent (U.S. Conference of Mayors 2007). Families and children are the fastest-growing segment of the homeless population in both urban and rural areas of this country. Today, infants, preschoolers, school-age children, and their parents account for almost half of the homeless.

Many people think that "the homeless" are all alike, but homeless people come from all walks of life and include Vietnam war veterans; people with mental illnesses, physical disabilities, or AIDS; the elderly; runaway children and teenagers; alcoholics and other substance abusers; recent immigrants; and families with young children (U.S. Conference of Mayors, 2007). Some recent efforts by governmental agencies to reduce homelessness have focused on individuals with specific problems, such as those suffering from chronic alcoholism or HIV/AIDS, in addition to being without a domicile (see Box 16.2).

Some perspectives on homelessness look at larger structural issues in society, such as lack of educational opportunities and jobs, that contribute to this problem. However, other perspectives are rooted in

Social Problems and Social Policy

Box 16.2

Persons Living with HIV/AIDS and Homelessness: What Should the Government Do?

> To the Editor:
>
> The encouraging medical advances in the fight against AIDS will not bare its full impact if infected individuals fall victim to yet another killer: homelessness. . . . With an estimated 500,000 people (in 2001) with HIV or AIDS in the United States lacking suitable housing, it is simply impossible for most of them to find access to health care and adhere to strict treatment regimes. While we have made progress toward addressing the treatment of AIDS, we still have a long way to go toward eradicating conditions like homelessness that are significant barriers to long-term survival of people living with AIDS.
>
> —*Regina Quattrochi (2001), Executive Director, Bailey House, New York*

As the Executive Director of Bailey House, Regina Quattrochi sees first-hand how difficult it is for low-income people living with HIV/AIDS to find long-term housing and gain access to the services they need. In New York City, Bailey House seeks to help people meet this need and, as such, is one of about fourteen agencies that receive some funding from the U.S. Department of Housing and Urban Development (HUD) through the Housing Opportunities for Persons with AIDS (HOPWA) Program. Housing assistance and related services are funded by this program in the belief that they are vital to the overall care system needed by individuals living with HIV or AIDS. As a HUD (2005) publication states, "A stable home environment is critical for low-income persons managing complex drug therapies and potential side effects from their treatment." Bailey House and other HOPWA Program recipients develop and implement new integrated modes of housing, client services, vocational training, rehabilitation, and job placement for persons living with HIV or AIDS and their families. Although it may sound like a lot of money when we read that the HOPWA Program awards total grants of about $19 million per year to agencies such as Bailey House, this amount is tiny when we realize that these funds are spread across thirteen states, and the amount received by each agency provides only a small portion of its total operating budget. For example, out of the $18.8 million in grants awarded in 2005, New York's Bailey House received only $991,478.

Should the federal government do more to provide funding for organizations that seek to meet the housing needs of low-income people living with HIV/AIDS? How about for other people who may experience chronic homelessness? Those who are opposed to "government handouts for the poor" typically argue that providing funding for homeless shelters and for agencies that assist homeless people does not accomplish the goal of getting them off the streets and out of a cycle of dependency. By contrast, those who believe the government should be doing more to help the homeless typically argue that more money is needed for all low-income people with a variety of issues and concerns. HUD (2005) refers to itself as "the nation's housing agency" and states that it is "committed to increasing homeownership, particularly among minorities; creating affordable housing opportunities for low-income Americans; and supporting the homeless, elderly, people with disabilities, and people living with HIV/AIDS." Some analysts believe that if we as a nation are truly committed to ending homelessness, political leaders and ordinary citizens alike should be concerned at how little money is being spent overall for such a major task.

Questions for Critical Thinking

1. What are the strengths of federal grants that provide money for organizations that serve a specific category of individuals, such as people living with HIV/AIDS or those experiencing chronic homelessness, rather than providing larger sums for general "homeless" programs? What are the limitations of a targeted approach?
2. Another HUD program (Housing for People Who Are Homeless and Addicted to Alcohol Program) provides money to assist homeless persons who also struggle with chronic alcoholism. What are the strengths of having a funding program specifically directed at agencies that "serve those in the grips of alcoholism who perpetually call the streets or emergency shelters their home," as HUD states? What are the limitations of this approach?
3. Do government funding programs targeting homeless persons living with HIV/AIDS or those who are addicted to alcohol have the potential to negatively stereotype *all* homeless people as being seriously ill or addicted? What do you think?

the assumption that homelessness is primarily a problem of individuals and how they live their lives. According to social scientists, studies that focus exclusively on personal problems of the homeless, such as mental illness or substance abuse, may result in *specialism*—the assumption that individual characteristics of poor people cause their homeless condition and that, therefore, the only way to alleviate homelessness is to cure the individual's personal problems (Wagner, 1993). This approach downplays the significance of structural factors such as the unavailability of low-income housing and of mental health care, which are the most important determinants of homelessness. According to sociologists Marta Elliott and Lauren J. Krivo (1991:128), any solution to the problem of homelessness must take into account these two structural factors:

> [A]ttempts to lower levels of homelessness in U.S. metropolitan areas must address the structural conditions which underlie this phenomenon. More specifically, mental health-care services for the indigent mentally ill must be made more available to those who are or would become homeless without them. Furthermore, the structure of the housing market must be altered in order to have the greatest effects on reducing homelessness. This means that more low-cost rental housing needs to be made available to reach the most marginal and disadvantaged members of society. Such a restructuring of the housing market is unquestionably one of the primary means by which people will avoid or overcome homelessness. Without this basic resource of cheap housing in an area, some individuals fall out of the housing market completely, a problem exacerbated by an economic environment with proportionately higher numbers of unskilled jobs. Stable well-paid employment must replace this segment of the economy to reduce current levels of homelessness.

Racial and Ethnic Segregation

Problems in housing are closely intertwined with racial and ethnic segregation in the United States. Despite passage of the Federal Fair Housing Act in 1968, segregation of African Americans and whites in major metropolitan areas declined only slightly since 1970. According to sociologists Douglas S. Massey and Nancy A. Denton (1992), no other racial or ethnic group in the history of this country has ever experienced the sustained high levels of residential segregation that African Americans have experienced in central cities. Moreover, residential segregation not only affects living conditions but is also associated with other problems (Massey and Denton, 1992:2):

> Residential segregation is not a neutral fact; it systematically undermines the social and economic well-being of blacks in the United States. Because of racial segregation, a significant share of black America is condemned to experience a social environment where poverty and joblessness are the norm, where a majority of children are born out of wedlock, where most families are on welfare, where educational failure prevails, and where social and physical deterioration abound. Through prolonged exposure to such an environment, black chances for social and economic success are drastically reduced.

Although African Americans have experienced the longest and most harmful effects of housing segregation in the United States, other groups have also suffered from housing discrimination (Santiago and Wilder, 1991; Menchaca, 1995; Santiago and Galster, 1995). A number of studies have documented a history of restrictive covenants that have prohibited Mexican Americans from living in white (Anglo) areas. These covenants were frequently supported by racial harassment and violence (see Menchaca, 1995). In some cases, local custom has dictated residential segregation patterns that continue into the present. In one study of Mexican-American segregation, one woman recalls that Twelfth Street was the dividing line between the white (Anglo) American and Mexican-American neighborhoods in Santa Paula, California (Menchaca, 1995:27):

> *La calle doce* was the main division. The ranchers owned the homes in the northeast, and that was for the people whose parents worked in agriculture—which would be the lemon or the orange.... If you worked for them in the packing house or picking lemons, that's where you would live.... They used to tell us, You live in that side and we live in this side.... The rednecks used to tell us that.

Vestiges of similar patterns of residential segregation based on race or ethnicity remain in many cities. In Austin, Texas, the historic geographic and political divide between Mexican Americans and white (Anglo) Americans is an interstate highway. In other communities, the divide is a river or some other geographic or social boundary that is well known to local residents, whether or not they acknowledge its existence. Although there is less overt discrimination, and courts have ruled that racial and ethnic restrictive covenants on property are unenforceable, housing segregation continues through custom.

Some analysts argue that residence is a personal choice and that people voluntarily segregate themselves on the basis of whom they want to live near. But many people are involuntarily segregated because of certain attributes—such as race, religion, age, or disability—that others devalue. Some landlords, homeowners, and white realtors perpetuate residential segregation through a discriminatory practice known as *steering*—guiding people of color to different neighborhoods than those shown to their white counterparts. Banks sometimes engage in a discriminatory (and illegal) practice known as *redlining*—refusing loans to people of color for properties in certain areas. The behavior of neighbors can also perpetuate residential segregation (see Feagin and Sikes, 1994; Squires, 1994).

Unequal property taxation is another kind of residential segregation problem. In a study of suburban property taxes, social scientist Andrew A. Beveridge found that African-American homeowners are taxed more than white homeowners are on comparable homes in 58 percent of the suburbs and 30 percent of the cities (cited in Schemo, 1994). This might happen because African Americans are more likely to move to suburbs with declining tax bases because they have limited finances or are steered there by real estate agents or because white flight occurs as African-American homeowners move in. Because houses are often reassessed when they are sold, newcomers face a heavier tax burden than longer-term residents, whose taxes might not go up for some period of time or until they sell their own houses (Schemo, 1994).

The continual influx of immigrants into urban areas is changing the population composition in many of the nation's largest cities, including Los Angeles, Houston, Miami, Chicago, and New York. For example, Monterey Park, California, which is about a ten-minute drive east of Los Angeles during non-rush-hour traffic, has been slowly transformed from a white (Anglo) community in the 1960s to a predominantly Asian community. Indeed, within the Asian community, younger Chinese newcomers are replacing older U.S.-born Japanese Americans as the largest group (Horton, 1995).

The 1990 Census (which provides the latest available data with the exception of studies of some selected metropolitan regions) showed that for the first time, minorities had experienced a higher percentage of growth in the nation's suburbs than in its cities. One subsequent study of fifteen major metropolitan areas across the nation, including cities such as Atlanta, Boston, Chicago, Detroit, Houston, Los Angeles, Miami, New York, San Diego, and Washington, D.C., found that 49 percent of African Americans and 63 percent of Hispanic (Latino/a) residents lived in the suburbs. However, this did not mean that the suburbs were fully integrated: 71 percent of the neighborhoods in this study remained racially segregated. The study found that 63 percent of whites lived in predominantly white neighborhoods, while 71 percent of African Americans lived in predominantly black or black Hispanic neighborhoods, and 61 percent of Hispanics (Latinos/as) lived in predominantly Hispanic or African-American neighborhoods (Institute on Race and Poverty, 2006).

The persistence of racial segregation in suburban areas is closely intertwined with growing economic inequality in the United States. Some of the "first" suburbs—those developed earliest and located closest to the older city—have increasingly become the home for high concentrations of low-income persons, recent immigrants, and older individuals who live on small, fixed incomes. Cities that are becoming gentrified, along with some fast-growing outer suburbs, now have significantly more affluent populations, newer facilities, and fewer urban problems than these first suburbs (Lambert, 2006). Some newer suburbs are located in Sun Belt states such as Texas and are predominantly occupied by middle- and upper-middle income white Americans. By contrast, low-income immigrants, older

Although racial segregation persists in some suburban areas of our nation, other suburbs have become more diverse. These neighbors are having a friendly conversation that offers hope for positive social encounters across racial and ethnic lines in the future.

persons on fixed incomes, and African Americans, Asian Americans, and Hispanic Americans now comprise more than one-third of the population in first suburbs (Lambert, 2006).

Despite an increased minority presence, some suburbs remain predominantly white, and many upper-middle-class and upper-class suburbs remain virtually all white. In the suburbs, people of color (especially African Americans) often become resegregated. Chicago, for example, remains one of the most segregated metropolitan areas in the country in spite of its fair-housing ordinance. Most of the African Americans who have fled the high crime of Chicago's South Side live in nearby suburbs such as Country Club Hills and Chicago Heights; suburban Asian Americans are most likely to live in Skokie and Naperville; and suburban Latinos/as live in Maywood, Hillside, and Bellwood (DeWitt, 1994).

What will be the future of racial and ethnic relations in the cities and suburbs of this country? Sociologist John Horton is optimistic and uses Monterey Park as an example of a community that has moved gradually and peacefully toward a culture of diversity (Horton, 1995:225):

> Although the pressure to be American without "foreign" influence is increasing in California, in places like Monterey Park, where the world has already imploded, an Anglo or Eurocentric American identity is giving way to greater openness. The transformation happens unconsciously and on an incremental basis through compromise and accommodation in the pragmatic process of getting things done. It is also undertaken consciously at public events and festivals where diversity and patriotism come together, using a formula that varies with the ethnicity and politics of those who plan the events.... The results may be small and seemingly trivial, but in an era of virulent nationalism and ethnic genocide, these local experiments in multiculturalism are advances to be celebrated.

Still, we must acknowledge that some dominant-group members, especially those in the upper classes, strive to perpetuate their position at the top of the societal pyramid not only by living in certain areas of the city, but also by isolating themselves from the "Other"—the poor and many subordinate group members (see Baltzell, 1958; Birmingham, 1967; Domhoff, 1983). Thus racial segregation in the United States today remains interlocked with class-based residential segregation (Santiago and Galster, 1995), as the vignettes at the beginning of the chapter show.

PROBLEMS IN GLOBAL CITIES

Although people have lived in cities for thousands of years, the time is rapidly approaching when more people worldwide will live in or near a city than live in a rural area. In 1900, only one person out of ten lived in a city; today, one out of every two lives in a city. Moreover, two-thirds of the world's population will live in cities by 2030 (United Nations, 2005). Of all the middle- and low-income regions, Latin America is becoming the most urbanized: Four megacities—Mexico City, Buenos Aires, Lima, and Santiago—already contain more than half of the region's population and continue to grow rapidly. By 2015, no U.S. city will be among the ten most populous in the world (see Table 16.1).

Rapid global population growth is producing a wide variety of urban problems, including overcrowding, environmental pollution, and the disappearance of farmland. In fact, many cities in middle- and low-income nations are quickly reaching the point at which food, housing, and basic public services are available to only a limited segment of the population. With rapidly growing urban populations, cities such as Cairo, Lagos, Dhaka, Beijing, and São Paulo are likely to soon have acute water shortages; Mexico City is already experiencing a chronic water shortage.

Natural increases in population (higher birth rates than death rates) account for two-thirds of new urban growth, and rural-to-urban migration accounts for the rest. Some people move from rural areas to urban areas because they have been displaced from their land. Others move because they are looking for a better life. No matter what the reason, migration has caused rapid growth in cities in sub-Saharan Africa, India, Algeria, and Egypt. At the same time that the population is growing rapidly, the amount of farmland that is available for growing crops to feed people is decreasing. In Egypt, for example, land that was previously used for growing crops is now used for petroleum refineries, food-processing plants, and other factories (Kaplan, 1996). Some analysts believe that the United Nations should encourage governments to concentrate on rural development; otherwise, acute food shortages brought about by unchecked rural-to-urban migration may lead to riots (Kaplan, 1996).

As global urbanization has increased over the past three decades, differences in urban areas based on economic development at the national level have become apparent. According to sociologist Immanuel Wallerstein

TABLE 16.1 Populations of the World's Ten Largest Cities (in millions, estimated)

1996		2015	
Tokyo, Japan	26.8	Tokyo, Japan	28.7
São Paulo, Brazil	16.4	Bombay, India	27.4
New York City, U.S.A.	16.3	Lagos, Nigeria	24.4
Mexico City, Mexico	15.6	Shanghai, China	23.4
Bombay, India	15.1	Jakarta, Indonesia	21.2
Shanghai, China	15.1	São Paulo, Brazil	20.8
Los Angeles, U.S.A.	12.4	Karachi, Pakistan	20.6
Beijing, China	12.4	Beijing, China	19.4
Calcutta, India	11.7	Dhaka, Bangladesh	19.0
Seoul, South Korea	11.6	Mexico City, Mexico	18.8

Source: New York Times, 1996.

(1984), nations occupy one of three positions in the global economy: core, semiperipheral, and peripheral. ***Core nations*** **are dominant capitalist centers characterized by high levels of industrialization and urbanization.** The United States, Japan, and Germany, among others, are core nations. Some cities in core nations are referred to as *global cities*—interconnected urban areas that are centers of political, economic, and cultural activity. New York, Tokyo, and London are generally considered the largest global cities. They are also considered postindustrial cities because their economic base has shifted largely from heavy manufacturing to information technologies and services such as accounting, marketing, finance, mergers and acquisitions, telecommunications, and other highly specialized fields (Friedmann, 1995). Global cities are the sites of new and innovative product development and marketing, and they often are the "command posts" for the world economy (Sassen, 1995). But economic prosperity is not shared equally by all people in the core nation global cities. Growing numbers of poor people work in low-wage service sector jobs or in assembly production, in which they are paid by the item (piecework) for what they produce, but they have no employment benefits or job security. Sometimes the living conditions of these workers more closely resemble the living conditions of workers in semiperipheral nations than those of middle-class workers in their own country.

Most African countries and many countries in South America and the Caribbean are ***peripheral nations*—nations that depend on core nations for capital, have little or no industrialization (other than what may be brought in by core nations), and have uneven patterns of urbanization.** According to Wallerstein (1984), the wealthy in peripheral nations support the exploitation of poor workers by core nation capitalists in return for maintaining their own wealth and position. Poverty is thus perpetuated, and the problems worsen because of the unprecedented population growth in these countries.

Between the core and the peripheral nations are the ***semiperipheral nations*****, which are more developed than peripheral nations but less developed than core nations.** Only two global cities are located in semiperipheral nations: São Paulo, Brazil, the center of the Brazilian economy, and Singapore, the economic center for a multicountry region in Southeast Asia (Friedmann, 1995). Like peripheral nations, semiperipheral nations—such as India, Iran, and Mexico—are confronted with unprecedented population growth. In addition, a steady flow of rural migrants to large cities is creating enormous urban problems. Semiperipheral nations exploit peripheral nations, just as the core nations exploit both the semiperipheral and the peripheral nations.

According to Wallerstein, it is very difficult—if not impossible—for peripheral and semiperipheral nations to ever occupy anything but their marginal positions in the classlike structure of the world economy because of their exploitation by the core nations (Wallerstein, 1984). Capital investment by core nations results in uneven economic growth, and in the process, the disparity between the rich and the poor in the major cities increases. Such economic disparity and urban growth is obvious at the U.S.–Mexican

Some cities in core nations, such as Tokyo, Japan, are referred to as "global" cities. They are also considered "postindustrial" cities because their economic base has shifted from heavy manufacturing to information technologies and services.

border, where transnational corporations have built *maquiladora plants*—factories where goods are assembled by low-wage workers to keep production costs down—on the Mexican side. The demand for workers in these plants caused thousands of people to move from the rural areas of Mexico to urban areas along the border in hope of earning higher wages. The influx has pushed already overcrowded cities far beyond their capacity. Because their wages are low and affordable housing is nonexistent, many people live in city slums or at the edge of cities in *shanty towns,* where houses are made from discarded materials. Squatters are the most rapidly growing segment of the population in many Mexican cities.

Social analysts are just beginning to develop comprehensive perspectives on the position of cities in the contemporary world economy, and not all analysts agree with Wallerstein's hierarchy (1984). However, most scholars acknowledge that nations throughout the world are influenced by a relatively small number of cities (e.g., New York) and transnational corporations that have brought about a shift from an international to a more global economy (see Knox and Taylor, 1995; Wilson, 1997). In middle- and low-income nations, all social problems are "incubated and magnified in cities" (Crossette, 1996b:A3).

SOCIOLOGICAL PERSPECTIVES AND SOLUTIONS TO URBAN PROBLEMS

For more than 100 years, sociologists have analyzed urban problems to determine the causes and consequences of rapid industrialization and urbanization on people's daily lives and the structure of society. The conclusions they reach about the underlying problems and possible solutions depend on the framework they apply.

The Functionalist Perspective

In examining urban problems, most functionalists focus on three processes that have contributed to social disorganization and the disruption of social institutions. First, mass migration from rural areas to urban areas during the Industrial Revolution contributed to social disorganization by weakening personal ties in the family, religion, education, and other institutions. Second, large-scale immigration in the late nineteenth and early twentieth centuries was more than most cities could absorb, and many individuals were never fully assimilated into the cultural mainstream. With larger numbers of strangers living close together in central cities, symptoms of social disorganization, such as high rates of crime, mental illness, and suicide, grew more pronounced. According to Emile Durkheim (1933/1893), urban life changes people's relationships. Rural areas are characterized by ***mechanical solidarity*****—social bonds based on shared religious beliefs and a simple division of labor**—but these bonds are changed with urbanization. Urban areas are characterized by ***organic solidarity*****—social bonds based on interdependence and an elaborate division of labor (specialization).** Although Durkheim was optimistic that urbanization could be positive, he also thought that some things were lost in the process. Third, mass suburbanization created additional social disorganization, and most cities have been unable to reach an equilibrium since the mass exodus to the suburbs following World War II. According to urban ecologist Amos Hawley (1950, 1981), new technologies, such as commuter railways and automobiles, have led to the decentralization of city life and the movement of industry from the central city to the suburbs, with disastrous results for some people. Although urbanization, mass immigration, and suburbanization have had functional consequences—including U.S. citizenship, job opportunities, and home ownership—for many people, they have also created problems, particularly for people who are left behind in rapidly declining central cities and people who experienced discrimination.

How do functionalists suggest that urban problems may be reduced? To alleviate the fiscal crisis facing many cities and level the inequality in services provided in cities and suburbs, sociologist Anthony M. Orum (1995) suggests establishing metropolitan or regional governments. Problems such as water supply, pollution, and traffic congestion, which are not confined to one geographic area, could be dealt with more effectively through metropolitan or regional planning. However, as Orum acknowledges, it is unlikely that officials of cities and suburban municipalities will willingly give up some of their power, and people living in the more affluent suburbs are unlikely to be willing to take on the problems of the cities.

Another option for alleviating urban problems is expanding the urban tax base by creating urban enterprise zones. Cities could offer tax incentives for industries to open plants in cities and provide job training for workers, so a match could be made between jobs and workers. Critics of enterprise zones argue that business tax incentives alone won't improve conditions in cities (see Cozic, 1993).

The Conflict Perspective

Conflict analysts do not believe that cities grow or decline by chance. Members of the capitalist class and political elites make far-reaching decisions about land use and urban development that benefit some people at the expense of others (Castells, 1977; Feagin and Parker, 1990). According to conflict theorists, the upper classes have successfully maintained class-based and sometimes racially based segregation through political control and legal strategies such as municipal incorporation, defensive annexation, restrictive covenants, and zoning regulations (Feagin and Parker, 1990; Higley, 1995). But where do these practices leave everyone else? Karl Marx suggested that cities are the arenas in which the intertwined processes of class conflict and capital accumulation take place; class consciousness and worker revolt are more likely to develop when workers are concentrated in urban areas.

Contemporary conflict theorists Joe R. Feagin and Robert Parker (1990) speak of a *political economy model*, believing that both economic *and* political factors affect patterns of urban growth and decline. Urban growth, they say, is influenced by capital investment decisions, power and resource inequality, class and class conflict, and government subsidy programs. Members of the capitalist class choose corporate locations, decide on sites for shopping centers and factories, and spread the population that can afford to purchase homes into sprawling suburbs located exactly where the capitalists think they should be located (Feagin and Parker, 1990). In this view, a few hundred financial institutions and developers finance and construct most major and many smaller urban development projects, including skyscrapers, shopping malls, and suburban housing projects. These decision makers can make housing more affordable or totally unaffordable for many people. Ultimately, their motivation rests not in benefiting the community, but rather in making a profit, and the cities they produce reflect this mindset (Feagin and Parker, 1990).

The concept of *uneven development*—the tendency of some neighborhoods, cities, or regions to grow and prosper while others stagnate and decline—is a by-product of the political economy model of urban development (Perry and Watkins, 1977). Conflict theorists argue that uneven development reflects inequalities of wealth and power in society. Uneven development not only affects areas in decline, but also produces external costs that are paid by the entire community. Among these costs are increased pollution, traffic congestion, and rising rates of crime and violence. According to sociologist Mark Gottdiener (1985:214), these costs are "intrinsic to the very core of capitalism, and those who profit the most from development are not called upon to remedy its side effects." One advantage of the political economy framework is that it can be used to study cities in middle- and low-income nations as well as high-income nations (see Jaffee, 1990; Knox and Taylor, 1995; Wilson, 1997). Short of major changes in the political economy, most analysts who take a conflict perspective believe that urban problems can be reduced only through political activism and organized resistance to oppressive conditions. Some believe that central cities are powder kegs of urban unrest that periodically threaten to explode because of massive job loss and economic hardship, racial tensions, allegations of police brutality, controversial court cases, and similar issues.

The Symbolic Interactionist Perspective

Symbolic interactionists examine urban problems from the standpoint of people's *experience* of urban life and how they subjectively define the reality of city living.

How does city life affect the people who live in a city? According to early German sociologist Georg Simmel (1950), urban life is so highly stimulating that people have no choice but to become somewhat insensitive to events and individuals around them. Urban residents generally avoid emotional involvement with one another and try to ignore the events—including violence and crime—that take place nearby. They are wary of other people, looking at others as strangers; some people act reserved to cloak deeper feelings of distrust or dislike toward others. At the same time, Simmel thought that urban living could be liberating because it gives people opportunities for individualism and autonomy.

On the basis of Simmel's observations of social relations in the city, early University of Chicago sociologist Louis Wirth (1938) suggested that urbanism is a "way of life" that increases the incidence of both social and personality disorders in individuals. *Urbanism* refers to the distinctive social and psychological patterns of life that are typically found in the city. According to Wirth, the size, density, and heterogeneity of urban populations result in an elaborate division of labor and in spatial segregation of people by race/ethnicity, social class, religion, and/or lifestyle. The division of labor and spatial segregation produce feelings of alienation, powerlessness, and loneliness.

In contrast to Wirth's gloomy analysis of urban life, sociologist Herbert Gans (1982/1962) believed that not everyone experiences the city in the same way. On the basis of research in the West End of Boston in the late 1950s, Gans concluded that many residents develop strong loyalties and a sense of community in city areas that outsiders often view negatively. According to Gans, personal behavior is shaped by the type of neighborhood a person lives in within the larger urban area. For example, *cosmopolites*—students, artists, writers, musicians, entertainers, and professionals—view the city as a place where they can be close to cultural facilities and people with whom they share common interests. *Unmarried people and childless couples* live in the city because they want to be close to work and entertainment. *Ethnic villagers* live in ethnically segregated neighborhoods because they feel most comfortable within their own group. The *deprived* and the *trapped* live in the city because they believe they have no other alternatives. Gans concluded that the city is a pleasure and a challenge for some urban dwellers and an urban nightmare for others.

According to symbolic interactionists, the deprived and the trapped contribute to a social construction of reality that stereotypes city dwellers as poor, down-and-out, and sometimes dangerous, whereas many city dwellers are not this way at all. Because movies, television shows, and, particularly, extensive media coverage of crime or racial unrest in the nation's largest metropolitan areas present a very negative image of cities, an antiurban bias remains strong among many nonurban dwellers.

To reduce problems of loneliness and alienation in city life, some symbolic interactionists propose that people who live in large metropolitan areas develop subcultural ties to help them feel a sense of community and identity. A ***subculture* is a group of people who share a distinctive set of cultural beliefs and behaviors that set them apart from the larger society.** Joining an interest group—from bowling with friends from the office to volunteering in a literacy program—is one way of feeling connected. Ethnic neighborhoods are an example of subcultures; some are tightly knit, whereas others have little influence on residents' daily lives. Interactionists note that members of subcultures, especially those based on race, ethnicity, or religion, sometimes come into conflict with each other. These conflicts can result in verbal exchanges, hate crimes, or other physical violence, or they can cause the individuals to withdraw almost entirely from the larger

■ *Cities typically have large numbers of people living, working, and playing in close proximity to each other. In New York City, urban street life is further intensified by the presence of large numbers of pedestrians and heavy traffic.*

community and become more intensely involved with the subculture.

In the twenty-first century, the problems of cities are both global and local. In nations around the globe, the wealthiest people establish enclaves in which they enjoy safety and prosperity while the poorest people live in areas where neither safety nor prosperity is available. Urban change that will benefit the greatest number of people will require a revised way of looking at our social world. Fixing a pothole in the street or opening a shelter for the homeless, although a worthy activity, will not solve the problems of our cities. Larger structural changes in how we conduct business and how political decisions are made—and who benefits from that business and those decisions—must also occur.

SUMMARY

■ *How did urbanization come about?*

Urbanization—the process by which an increasing proportion of a population lives in cities rather than rural areas—began with industrialization. Before the Industrial Revolution, most people lived in sparsely populated rural areas, where they farmed. Industrialization led to the growth of cities, and urbanization brought about profound changes in societies and spawned new social problems such as housing shortages, overcrowding, unsanitary conditions, environmental pollution, and crime.

■ *How did mass suburbanization occur and what were the results?*

Mass suburbanization began with government efforts to correct the housing shortage that followed World War II. The Housing Act of 1949 gave incentives to builders to develop affordable housing, while government agencies made it possible for returning veterans to qualify for home mortgages. Other factors included the availability of inexpensive land, low-cost mass construction methods, new federally financed highway systems, inexpensive gasoline, racial tension in cities, and consumers' pent-up demands for single-family homes on individually owned lots. Mass suburbanization brought about a dramatic shift in the distribution of the U.S. population and set up an ongoing economic and racial division of interests between cities and suburbs.

■ *Why are many cities in fiscal crisis?*

Large numbers of middle- and upper-income people have moved out of the central cities to the suburbs, and more recently, many retail businesses and corporations have also moved to the suburbs or moved their operations abroad. The shrinking central cities have been left with greatly reduced sources of revenue. Many of the remaining central city residents are poor, unemployed, or older people living on fixed incomes who cannot afford to pay higher taxes. At the same time, city governments must still provide city services for them. Moreover, suburbanites who regularly use city services do not pay taxes to the city to keep up these services.

■ *Why is health care a crisis in U.S. cities?*

Health care is a problem in big cities because hospitals and other medical facilities are subject to cutbacks and closings when cities face economic problems. Also, people in impoverished sections of cities are more likely to become ill or injured because poverty is associated with many medical problems. Drug-related problems and HIV/AIDS put an added burden on facilities. All of these problems are exacerbated when managed care plans and large hospital chains take over urban hospitals and streamline services to turn a profit.

■ *Why is there a housing shortage in the United States and what is being done about it?*

When city agencies demand that a landlord comply with safety standards and building codes, many landlords abandon their buildings rather than make the investment. A bigger reason, however, is that the United States has yet to find a way to provide safe, livable, low-income housing. The urban homesteading program, for example, has been criticized for promoting the interests of the building industry instead of actually helping people to get good housing. Federal housing projects have characteristically been monolithic high-rises that intensify many problems and create new ones. One of the most successful initiatives for creating affordable housing is the volunteer organization Habitat for Humanity.

■ *How great a problem is homelessness? Are there any solutions?*

Accurate data on the actual number of the homeless are extremely difficult to get because homeless people avoid interviews with census takers and social researchers. The U.S. Conference of Mayors surveys show that people of color are overrepresented in the homeless population, and the fastest-growing segment of the homeless population is families and children. Most experts agree that any long-term, successful solution to homelessness must take structural factors into account, especially low-income housing and mental health care.

■ *Why does residential segregation exist even if it is illegal?*

In some cases, housing segregation continues through custom. Sometimes landlords, homeowners, and white realtors perpetuate residential segregation through steering—guiding people of color to different neighborhoods than those shown to their white counterparts. Unequal property taxation is another kind of residential segregation problem.

■ *What are the major problems in global cities?*

Almost one out of every two people in the world today lives in a city. Increasing population accounts for two-thirds of the new urban growth, and rural-to-urban migration accounts for the rest. Rapid urban growth brings a wide variety of problems, including overcrowding, environmental pollution, and the disappearance of farmland. The exploitation of semiperipheral nations by core nations and of peripheral nations by both semiperipheral and core nations serves to increase the urban problems in these nations. Core nations are dominant capitalist centers that are characterized by high levels of industrialization and urbanization. Peripheral nations depend on core nations for capital, have little or no industrialization (other than what is brought in by core nations), and have uneven patterns of urbanization. Semiperipheral nations are more developed than peripheral nations but less developed than core nations.

■ *What are the functionalist and conflict perspectives on urban problems?*

Functionalists believe that today's urban problems are the result of mass migration from rural areas during the Industrial Revolution, large-scale immigration in the late nineteenth and early twentieth centuries, and mass suburbanization. One solution is to create metropolitan governments. Conflict theorists believe that cities grow or decline according to decisions made by capitalists and the political elite. In other words, conflict theorists use a political economy model. Urban problems can be reduced through political activism and organized resistance to oppressive conditions.

■ *What is the symbolic interactionist perspective on urban problems?*

Symbolic interactionists look at how people subjectively experience urban life. According to German sociologist Georg Simmel, urban life is so stimulating that people have no choice but to become somewhat insensitive to people and events around them. On the other hand, urban living gives people opportunities for individualism and autonomy. Sociologist Louis Wirth expanded on Simmel's ideas, saying that urbanism produces feelings of alienation and powerlessness. Herbert Gans concluded from his research that city life is a pleasure for some and a nightmare for others. The way to avoid alienation is to develop subcultural ties.

KEY TERMS

core nations, p. 347
edge city, p. 337
gentrification, p. 342
mechanical solidarity, p. 348
megalopolis, p. 337
organic solidarity, p. 348
peripheral nations, p. 347
semiperipheral nations, p. 347
subculture, p. 350

QUESTIONS FOR CRITICAL THINKING

1. Where do you live: in the core central city, an edge city, a suburb, a rural area, a megalopolis? What examples from your everyday life can you give that relate to the problems described in this chapter? Which sociological perspective do you think best explains the urban problems you observe?
2. The government has so far failed to provide adequate low-income and poverty-level housing. What new initiatives can you suggest?
3. Why do you think families with children are the fastest-growing segment of the homeless population in both urban and rural areas of this country? What can be done about the problem?

Chapter 17

Global Social Problems: War and Terrorism

THINKING SOCIOLOGICALLY

- Why do some people see war as a *problem* while others see war as a *solution* to certain social problems?
- What are the major types of international and domestic terrorism?
- Has the "war on terror" affected individual rights and liberties in the United States?

Terrorism in London, 2005:
I was in a tube [subway car] at King's Cross [station] when one of the explosions happened. I was stuck in a smoke-filled blackened tube that reeked of burning for over thirty minutes. So many people were hysterical. I truly thought I was going to die.... I felt genuine fear but kept calm. Eventually people smashed through the windows, and we were lifted out [and] all walked up the tunnel to the station. There was chaos outside, and I started to walk down Euston Road—my face and clothes were black—towards work, and all of a sudden there was another huge bang, and people started running up the road in the opposite direction to where I was walking and screaming and crying. I now realize this must have been one of the buses exploding.

—Jo Herbert, an eyewitness to the July 2005 London terrorist bombings, describes that tragic day (*Guardian Unlimited*, 2005).

The War in Iraq:
It was raining when I stepped off the plane and into a chilly Georgia morning. The line of soldiers, heads down, struggled underneath the weight of their gear across the tarmac and into a long, low building full of Red Cross coffee and doughnuts.... It has been just over a year since I had last been at that airport; that first time there had been banners and flags, family members waving fervently at the departing plane. This time the weather, I guess, had kept them home and the gray sky was the only real witness to our return.... When the war is over, you pick up your gear, walk down the hill and back into the world, where people smile, congratulate you, and secretly hope you won't be a burden on society now that you've done the dirty work they shun.

—John Crawford (2005:WK12), a Florida National Guardsman and author of* The Last True Story I'll Ever Tell, *describes how he felt when he returned to the United States after serving in the war in Iraq.

The anguish these writers express shows why terrorism and war are of great concern to individuals and to society and why, at the national and international level, terrorism and war are among the most pressing social problems of our times. Through sporadic and random acts of violence, terrorism creates widespread fear and injures or kills victims from all walks of life. Similarly, war takes its toll on human life and damages billions of dollars in property, some of which—such as hospitals, schools, and residences—primarily serve a civilian population that can be devastated by the ravages of war and its aftermath. Moreover, the countries that finance wars, such as the current operations in Afghanistan and Iraq, shoulder massive economic burdens as they pay for expensive weapons and communications systems, transportation of equipment and personnel, the direct and indirect costs of military personnel, and all of the many other costs of war. Billions of dollars are spent in the war effort that could have been used for domestic and international spending that might have benefited people and improved their quality of life.

Sometimes, war—or the threat of military action—is viewed as the way to remedy social problems such as terrorism, religious or ethnic conflicts, or nations encroaching on the territory of other nations. However, many believe that war is the *problem,* not the *solution* to many social ills of our time. In this chapter, we examine the sociological implications of war, terrorism, and future prospects for peace.

WAR AS A SOCIAL PROBLEM

What is war? ***War* is organized, armed conflict between nations or distinct political factions.** Although many people think of war as being between two nations (general warfare) or between rival factions located within a specific geographic area of a country (regional warfare), sociologists define war more broadly to include not only *declared* wars between nations or parties but also *undeclared* wars, civil and guerrilla wars, covert operations, and some forms of terrorism. Social scientists also say that societies that remain prepared at all times for war possess a ***war system*—components of social institutions (e.g., the economy, government, and education) and cultural beliefs and practices that promote the development of warriors, weapons, and war as a normal part of the society and its foreign policy** (Cancian and Gibson, 1990).

How, then, do social scientists define *peace?* Although some sociologists simply refer to peace as the absence of violent conflict, others, including the sociologists Francesca M. Cancian and James William Gibson (1990), argue that peace is a less clearly defined concept than war. According to Cancian and Gibson, most people agree that peace is highly desirable but often have different ideas of what constitutes peace. Some equate peace with harmonious relations in a world where there is no bloodshed between groups; but sometimes nations equate peace with prevailing in battle (Gibson and Cancian, 1990). Despite the problems associated with distinguishing between war and peace, we can conclude that both consist of actions and beliefs held by people like ourselves and that these actions and beliefs have serious consequences for individuals, groups, and nations.

The Nature of War

First and foremost, war is an institution that involves *violence*—behavior that is intended to bring pain, physical injury, and/or psychological stress to people or to harm or destroy property. As we have seen, violence is a component of many social problems, particularly violent crime and domestic violence. Both of these forms of *interpersonal violence* typically involve a relatively small number of people who are responding to a particular situation or pursuing their own personal goals. In contrast, war is a form of ***collective violence* that involves organized violence by people seeking to promote their cause or resist social policies or practices that they consider oppressive.**

Except for media coverage and for those who go into combat or are friends or relatives of those who go, war is only a concept to most people in the United States. Early in our country's history, during the Civil War or the war with Mexico, for example, just the opposite was true: War took place at home or close to home. But in the twentieth century, the nature of U.S. military action was transformed. First, wars were fought on foreign soil; second, vastly more U.S. military personnel were involved. In World War I, for example, about 5 million people served in the U.S. armed forces, and more than 16 million men and women served in World War II (Ehrenreich, 1997).

The two world wars were different from each other in a very significant way. In World War I, killing civilians was considered unduly violent, but in World War II, civilians were killed intentionally. The targeting of civilians during World War II added a new dimension to war (Hynes, 1997). This is how social critic Barbara Ehrenreich (1997:206–207) describes the shift to civilians as the targets of war-related violence:

> By World War II, the destruction (and exploitation) of civilians was deliberate policy on all sides. The British used air power to "de-house" the German population; the U.S. bombed the civilian populations of Hiroshima, Nagasaki, and Dresden; the Germans and Japanese destroyed cities and exploited defeated populations as slave labor.... Air power made the mass bombings of civilians possible.

In 2001, terrorists with ties to al Qaeda used a different form of "air power"—hijacked commercial airplanes—to bring war and terror back to U.S. soil, intentionally killing thousands of civilians in the process. However, when the United States launched the so-called War on Terror, first in Afghanistan and then in Iraq, major combat again took place in nations other than the United States.

One of the most significant characteristics of war is its persistence. According to Ehrenreich (1997), World War II not only provided the United States with the opportunity to declare itself the "leader of the free world," but also gave political and economic leaders the impetus to perpetuate this nation's position as a world military superpower. Accordingly, Congress established defense spending as a national priority, and the U.S. military-industrial complex that had emerged during World War II became a massive industrial infrastructure that today produces an array of war-related goods such as uniforms, tanks, airplanes, and warships. The military-industrial complex flourished during the 1950s, when the international arms race brought about what became known as the *Cold War*—a conflict between nations based on military preparedness and the threat of war but not actual warfare. Between 1950 and the mid-1990s, the U.S. government responded to the perceived Soviet threat by spending approximately $10.2 trillion for its arms buildup. In 1991 alone, the defense industry received more than $121 billion in government contracts, giving some corporations a virtual monopoly over an entire market in which there was only one buyer (the U.S. government) and very few (if any) competitors.

The Consequences of War

The direct effects of war are loss of human life and serious physical and psychological effects on survivors. It is impossible to determine how many human lives have been lost in wars throughout human history. Were we to attempt to do so, we would need a more precise definition of what constitutes war, and we would have to assume that there would always be survivors available to count the dead (Hynes, 1997).

Despite these difficulties, social analyst Ruth Sivard (1991, 1993) tackled the problem in a limited way. She determined that 589 wars were fought by 142 countries between 1500 and 1990 and that approximately 142 million lives were lost. But according to Sivard, more lives were lost in wars during the twentieth century than in all of the other centuries combined. World War I took the lives of approximately 8 million combatants and 1 million civilians. The toll was even higher in World War II: More than 50 million people (17 million combatants and 35 million civilians) lost their lives. During World War II, U.S. casualties alone totaled almost 300,000, and more than 600,000 Americans were wounded (see Table 17.1).

The consequences of all these wars, however, pale when compared to the consequences of an all-out nuclear war. The devastation would be beyond description. Although the development of nuclear weapons might have contributed to peace among the major world powers since the late 1940s, we can see the potentially destructive effects of nuclear war in the U.S. attacks on Hiroshima and Nagasaki, Japan. In an effort to end World War II, a U.S. aircraft dropped a 1.5-kiloton atomic bomb on Hiroshima, killing 130,000 people either instantly or over the next few months as a result of

TABLE 17.1 U.S. Armed Forces Personnel Casualties in Wars

War	Battle Deaths (in thousands)	Wounds, Not Mortal (in thousands)
Spanish-American War	[a]	2
World War I	53	204
World War II	292	671
Korean conflict	34	103
Vietnam War	47	153
War in Iraq[b]	4	30

[a]Fewer than 500 total deaths.
[b]Through September 1, 2008 (rounded)
Source: U.S. Census Bureau, 2008; icasualties.org, 2008.

the deadly radiation that rained on the city (Erikson, 1994). Today, some nuclear warheads held by governments throughout the world are more than 4,000 times as powerful as the bombs that were dropped on Japan. In fact, scientists estimate that a nuclear war would kill more than 160 million people outright and that more than 1 billion people would die in the first few hours as a result of radiation poisoning, environmental contamination and destruction, and massive social unrest (Friedman and Friedman, 1996).

This all-too-common scene of war reflects only a small part of the continuing devastation from our nation's lengthy and troubling wars. What do you think are the most important consequences of war?

Even though an international treaty bans underground nuclear tests, it is believed that a number of nations are developing and stockpiling nuclear weapons. In the case of the 2003 U.S.-led invasion of Iraq, for example, the Bush Administration claimed that the regime of Iraqi President Saddam Hussein was in possession of ***weapons of mass destruction (WMD)*****—nuclear, biological, chemical, or radiological weapons that can kill thousands of people and destroy vast amounts of property at one time**—and had to be overthrown as a preemptive measure to protect the United States and other nations. When no weapons of mass destruction were found in Iraq, extensive public debate and much criticism of the Bush Administration followed for having inaccurately represented the scope and immediacy of the threat posed (Moeller, 2004). Media coverage of the WMD debate is one example of how the media frame stories about war (see Box 17.1 on page 358).

Today, military strategy calls for deploying bombs and long-range missiles to eliminate the enemy's weapons production plants and supply centers. Because these plants are located in major cities, civilians are more likely to be killed than they were in the past. And whereas Europe was the primary battleground for most wars from 1500 through World War II, middle- and low-income nations with their growing populations are now the primary sites.

The trend toward more civilian casualties that began in World War II has continued in subsequent wars, including the Vietnam War and the 1991 Gulf War (Ehrenreich, 1997). Some analysts believe that civilians accounted for 75 percent of all war-related deaths in the 1980s and nearly 90 percent in the 1990s (Renner, 1993). Other social analysts disagree. In their book *The Future of War* (1996), George Friedman and Meredith Friedman argue that the use of precision-guided munitions ("smart weapons") in Desert Storm (another name for the 1991 Gulf War) made it possible for the United States to strike particular parts of particular buildings without striking noncombatants, hence keeping the civilian death count low. However, a demographer employed by the U.S. Census Bureau has calculated that 40,000 Iraqi soldiers were killed during that war, but more than 80,000 Iraqi civilians, mostly women and children, were killed in air strikes—13,000 in "precision" bombing and 70,000 as a result of disease associated with the systematic destruction of water purification and sewage treatment systems in their country (Colhoun, 1992). Moreover, many hospitals were damaged or destroyed. In some cases, when nearby power plants were hit, hospitals could no longer operate basic equipment or provide emergency medical care to people who had been injured by bombs (Burleigh, 1991).

Patriotism—supporting "our troops" and "our cause"—is another consequence of war. In this way, war is functional because it provides an external enemy for people to hate. A dysfunctional aspect of war, however, is that the enemy is dehumanized—that is, seen as an object to obliterate rather than as another human being. According to sociologist Tamotsu Shibutani (1970), prolonged conflicts such as wars tend to be turned into a struggle between good and evil; one's own side is, of course, righteous and just, while the other side has no redeeming social or moral value.

In 2006, more than 2.6 million dollars were paid to U.S. veterans who were receiving compensation from the government for injuries they sustained in war-related activities (U.S. Census Bureau, 2008). However, not all injuries that are sustained in wars are physical. We have no accurate count of the soldiers and civilians—of all nations involved—who experience psychological trauma that affects them the remainder of their lives. Consider, for example, the psychological effects of war on Vietnam War veteran Rod Kane, who was asked by a nurse whether he was having trouble with his concentration (Hynes, 1997:219–220):

> "Trouble with concentration?" I stare at her defensively. I forgot her name already. "Not necessarily. I concentrate on the war, or drinking... but I'm not here because of my concentration problems, or my memory. I will say that if I've had trouble with anything since Nam, it's been sleeping.... One reason I drink so much, so I could pass out and not have to worry about nightmares. Of course, after a while, all the booze in the world couldn't keep them down.... I mean, there are booby-trap nightmares that speak for themselves. Instant replay nightmares where, asleep or awake, I play the same scene over and over again. There are nightmares that combine Viet Nam action with stateside stuff.... Do I have to get into all this right away?"

Kane was diagnosed with a disorder known as post-traumatic stress disorder (PTSD). Symptoms include difficulty sleeping and concentrating;

Social Problems in the Media

Box 17.1

"Weapons of Mass Destruction": Political Spin and Media Framing of a War

June 25, 2008: What I do know is that war should only be waged when necessary, and the Iraq war was not necessary.

—Scott McClellan (2008), former White House press secretary, wrote in his memoir, What Happened: Inside the Bush White House and Washington's Culture of Deception, *that he had been mislead by Administration officials about the necessity for war with Iraq and that he, in turn, unintentionally misinformed the media and the general public about the alleged importance of the war to spread democracy in the Middle East.*

March 17, 2003: Intelligence gathered by this and other governments leaves no doubt that the Iraq regime continues to possess and conceal some of the most lethal weapons ever devised.... [We] cannot live under the threat of blackmail. The terrorist threat to America and the world will be diminished the moment that Saddam Hussein is disarmed....

—President George W. Bush (2003b) in an address to the nation

March 19, 2003: The people of the United States and our friends and allies will not live at the mercy of an outlaw regime that threatens the peace with weapons of mass murder.

—President George W. Bush (2003a) in an address to the nation

These statements by a former government official and by then President George W. Bush show the contentious nature of what has happened in the United States in regard to the war in Iraq. During the weeks before the U.S. invasion of Iraq on March 20, 2003, former President George W. Bush conveyed the message to journalists and the general public that he believed an invasion of Iraq, with the subsequent removal of president Saddam Hussein from office and the establishment of a new government, were necessary to protect vital security interests of the United States and other nations. Through extensive media coverage of the president's comments on weapons of mass destruction and the imminent threat posed by Saddam Hussein, the "War on Terror" was launched, making Iraq the "big" international news story and overshadowing coverage of the U.S. military's unsuccessful search in Afghanistan for Osama bin Laden, the alleged mastermind behind a number of terrorist attacks.

Many news reporters and television anchors quickly embraced the language of war, including terms such as "weapons of mass destruction" (WMD) and "War on Terror." Stations that carry "all news, all the time," such as the FOX cable news network, had a dramatic increase in the number of viewers because of their patriotic spin on the "situation" in Iraq and what the U.S. should do about it (BBC News, 2003). And, although he now apparently regrets his decision, Scott McClellon helped to publicize this perspective to the world as the President's press secretary.

Does it matter how the media cover topics such as war and terrorism? According to one media scholar, "The public relies on the media to separate facts and tangible realities from assumptions and spin" (Moeller, 2004). How well did the media perform in this case? Not very well, according to journalism

anxiety; and recurring flashbacks or nightmares, many of which are triggered by loud, sudden noises such as thunder, automobiles backfiring, or other things that sound like gunshots or explosions. When some stimulus triggers a flashback, the individual reexperiences the horror of some deeply traumatic event. Some medical specialists link high rates of drug abuse and suicide among Vietnam War veterans with PTSD. According to one congressional study, more than 475,000 of the 3.5 million Vietnam veterans have severe symptoms of PTSD, and another 350,000 have moderate symptoms (Witteman, 1991).

Although we cannot put a price tag on loss of life, physical disability, or psychological trauma associated with war, we know that the direct economic costs of war are astronomical. Consider, for example, that the 2007 federal budget allocated $439 billion for defense spending *plus* $120 billion for military operations in Iraq and Afghanistan (U.S. Government Printing Office, 2008). To put defense and war-related expenditures in perspective, twenty-five years ago,

Box 17.1 (continued)

scholar Susan D. Moeller (2004), whose study provides insights on how *political spin* may be incorporated into *media framing* of news stories about war and terror. *Spin* is the act of selectively describing or deliberately shading an event in a way that favors one partisan response over another or that attempts to control a negative political reaction before it fully emerges and becomes detrimental to the spinners' interests (based on Safire, 1993). As you will recall, journalists use a variety of frames to shape the news stories they present to their audiences: *Frames* are cognitive shortcuts that help readers and viewers make sense of social life. Facts have no intrinsic meaning and instead take on meaning when they are embedded in a frame or story line that organizes them and gives them coherence.

Anticipating opposition to launching a war against Saddam Hussein, particularly when U.S. military personnel were already deployed in Afghanistan and the country had numerous other pressing problems, political leaders used "spin" in their speeches and conversations with the media to aggressively market the war before their critics could attempt to refute claims that Hussein possessed WMDs or disagree about linkages between Iraq and international terrorist activity. Many journalists and news commentators absorbed the political language of the WMD debate when they framed their news reports, adding credibility to the administration's claims (Moeller, 2004). The following are findings in Moeller's (2004:11) study of media coverage of the weapons of mass destruction issue:

- Virtually all news coverage of WMDs did not question the political formulation of "weapons of mass destruction" as a single category of threat.
- Based on political spin, the media associated mass destruction agents with the phenomenon of terrorism despite the fact that no terrorist organization had demonstrated the capability of performing an act of mass destruction under a strict definition of that term.
- Media framing of stories on WMDs and war results less from political bias on the part of journalists, editors, and producers than from the use of standard journalistic procedures such as the "inverted pyramid" style of news writing that gives the "lead" in stories to the "most important" information and/or the "most important" players. In the case of reporting on WMDs and problems in Iraq, the president of the United States and other top officials in his administration would be considered the most important players (Moeller, 2004:iii).

From a sociological perspective, Moeller's findings should encourage us to take a new look at how political spin and media framing might influence our beliefs on war, as well as other social problems.

Questions for Critical Thinking

1. Should we be concerned if we think that political leaders and journalists are not providing us with the information we need to make informed judgments about what we think our country should do in regard to domestic and international problems?
2. What part does national security play in the kind of information we receive from the government and the media? Is national security a more pressing priority today than the right of individuals to know what is going on in their nation? What do you think?

one analyst calculated that a single aircraft carrier would build 12,000 high schools and the cost of developing one new bomber would pay the annual salaries of 250,000 teachers to staff the schools (de Silva, 1980).

Today, more middle- and low-income nations are involved in defense buildups than in the past. Map 17.1 on page 360 shows the nations that purchase military equipment and supplies from the United States. In 2007, the nations of the world spent about $1.34 trillion on their military (GlobalSecurity.org, 2008).

MILITARY TECHNOLOGY AND WAR

War is conducted on the basis of the technology that is available in given societies at a specific point in time. However, wars are not necessarily won or lost on the basis of military technology alone. In the Vietnam War, for example, many factors contributed to the inability of the United States to declare a victory. Among these factors were conflicting ideologies and war strategies set

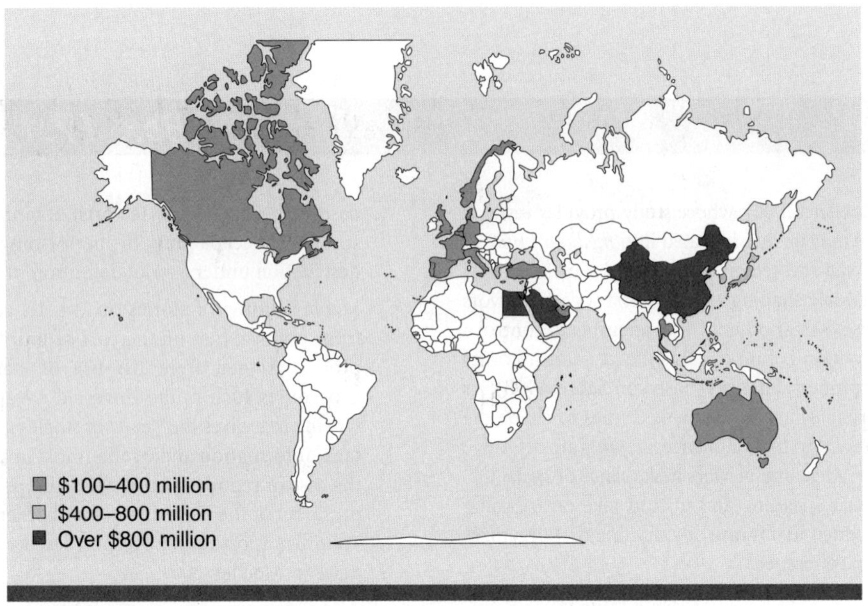

■ Map 17.1 *U.S. military sales to foreign governments, 2005 (in millions of dollars)*

Source: U.S. Census Bureau, 2008.

forth by government officials and the fact that U.S. troops could not readily distinguish the Viet Cong ("the enemy") from the South Vietnamese ("the ally") (Hynes, 1997).

The most significant military technology is referred to as the ***weapons system*, which comprises a weapons platform (e.g., a ship, aircraft, or tank), a weapon (e.g., a gun, missile, or torpedo), and the means of command and communication** (Kaldor, 1981). The importance of the weapons system is pointed out by Friedman and Friedman (1996:25): "The rise and fall of strategically significant weapons systems is the history of the rise and fall of nations and epochs. The ***strategically significant weapon* is the one that brings force to bear in such a way that it decisively erodes the war-making capability of the enemy"** [bold in original]. According to Friedman and Friedman (1996:25–26), the use of strategically significant weapons determines the "winners" and "losers" in war:

> [L]et us assume that the greatest threat presented by the enemy is the ability to move weapons platforms around quickly, and that by destroying his petrochemical production facilities we could impede his mobility. Strategically significant weapons would be those that would destroy petrochemical plants. So, in World War II, bombers with the range to reach these targets were such weapons. In Vietnam, the enemy's war-making ability could not be decisively crippled by the same sort of long-range bombers. There, the strategic weapon was North Vietnamese infantry, able to move stealthily and impose a rate of attrition on American troops that was politically unacceptable to the United States. The failure to recognize strategically decisive weapons is catastrophic. The Soviet Union's illusion that intercontinental ballistic missiles and swarms of tanks were strategically decisive led it to disaster.

In other words, though factors other than military technology may determine a nation's ability to win or lose a war, military technology is a dominant factor. For example, in the fourteenth century, Europeans used a simple new technology—black powder, an explosive made from charcoal, sulfur, and saltpeter—to overwhelm larger armies. Black powder could destroy the enemy's walls and other fortifications. When it was discovered that black powder could be exploded at the base of a metal tube and propel a projectile to a target, the gun became the basis of European and Western military power. Gunpowder made it possible for a small number of troops to overwhelm a much larger army that had only nonexplosive weapons (Friedman and Friedman, 1996).

Although black powder weapons remained the primary type of weaponry for many years, the platform that was used for carrying the weapons changed over time. With the development of such weapons platforms as coal-powered ships, petroleum-driven ships, and railroad locomotives, it became possible to move explosive-based technology virtually anywhere to destroy enemy forces. From the early 1900s to the end of World War II, the battleship, the tank, and the bomber were the primary weapons platforms. Today, the battleship has been replaced by the aircraft carrier, but the tank and the bomber continue to be important sources of weapons transportation.

As the U.S. military sought to enhance traditional weapons platforms to deal with enemy threats, new precision-guided munitions were developed, rendering many of the older ideologies and technologies obsolete, including the concept of the battlefield. No longer do foot soldiers have to engage in skirmishes for war to take place; missiles can be fired from sites located ten thousand miles from the target (Friedman and Friedman, 1996). Unfortunately, the same technology that makes possible the expanded battlefield brings with it a new system of intelligence that makes global warfare possible. According to Friedman and Friedman (1996:37–38), sensors, guidance systems, satellite communications, and other technologies that make it possible to hit a target ten thousand miles away also make it possible for weapons fired from one continent to guide themselves to targets on other continents very quickly and relatively inexpensively:

> The hyperintelligent, hypersonic, long-range projectile is almost here. Born of the air age, it will destroy the old way of making war, while securing the new geopolitical system for generations. Where guns were inaccurate, these projectiles are extraordinarily precise. Where guns must travel to within miles of a target before firing, precision munitions can devastate an enemy from any distance. Where gun/petrochemical technology requires total commitment of resources and mass production, precision munitions require technical skill. The new weaponry places inherent limits on war, both in terms of scope and in terms of damage to unintended targets. The age of total war is at an end and a more limited type of war is at hand. . . . [A]s the new weapons culture [has] slowly emerged, the United States has been at war with itself over the nature of its military power and the principles that ought to guide that power. At its core, this has been a struggle to define the proper place of technology—and of technologies—in American military doctrine. More precisely, it has been an agonizing search for a doctrine that could define and control the overwhelming claims that technology makes on all aspects of American life—a search for principles of waging war that transcend mere weaponry.

Although the high-technology weaponry that is used in warfare has received widespread media coverage, less attention has been paid to the potential significance of poison gas manufacturing and the use of chemical and biological toxic agents by international and domestic terrorists (Vetter and Perlstein, 1991).

GLOBAL TERRORISM

***Terrorism* is the use of calculated, unlawful physical force or threats of violence against a government, organization, or individual to gain some political, religious, economic, or social objective.** Terrorist tactics include bombing, kidnapping, hostage taking, hijacking, assassination, and extortion. Although terrorists sometimes attack government officials and members of the military, they more often target civilians as a way of pressuring the government.

As collective violence, terrorism shares certain commonalities with war. Both terrorism and war are major threats to world stability and domestic safety. Terrorism and war also extract a massive toll on individuals and societies by producing rampant fear, widespread loss of human life, and extensive destruction of property.

One form of terrorism—political terrorism—is actually considered a form of unconventional warfare. *Political terrorism* uses intimidation, coercion, threats of harm, and other violent attempts to bring about a significant change in or overthrow an existing government. There are three types of political terrorism: revolutionary terrorism, repressive terrorism, and state-sponsored terrorism.

***Revolutionary terrorism* refers to acts of violence against civilians that are carried out by enemies of a government who want to bring about political change.** Some dissident groups believe that if they perpetrate enough random acts of terrorism, they will achieve a political goal. Modern terrorism is not always based in a single country, as we have learned from efforts to apprehend Osama bin Laden and the al Qaeda network, who are accused of being the planners of the September 11, 2001, attacks on the United States and attacks at other times and sites associated with U.S. interests and citizens.

Money usually is a crucial ingredient in terrorism, and following the so-called money trail has been a key way in which law enforcement agencies have sought to apprehend those accused of violent terrorist attacks and of financing terrorism. Underground economic activities that allegedly support terrorism in the United States have been traced to seemingly innocent religious organizations in such places as Richardson, Texas, and Buffalo, New York.

Unlike revolutionary terrorism, ***repressive terrorism* is conducted by a government against its own citizens for the purpose of protecting an existing political order.** Repressive terrorism has taken place in many countries around the world, including Haiti, the People's Republic of China, and Cambodia, where the Pol Pot regime killed more than one million people in the four years between 1975 and 1979.

In the third type of political terrorism, ***state-sponsored terrorism,* a government provides financial resources, weapons, and training for terrorists who conduct their activities in other nations.** In Libya, for example, Colonel Muammar Qaddafi has provided money and training for terrorist groups such as the Arab National Youth Organization, which was responsible for skyjacking a Lufthansa airplane over Turkey and forcing the Bonn government to free the surviving members of Black September. Black September is the terrorist group responsible for killing Israeli Olympic athletes in the 1970s (Parry, 1976). Other countries that have been charged with using terrorism as a form of surrogate warfare include Iran, Syria, Yugoslavia, Bulgaria, Israel, and the United States (Vetter and Perlstein, 1991). The United States conducted surrogate warfare when it supported the Contras, who waged war against the Sandinista government of Nicaragua, until the Sandinistas were defeated in a 1990 election (Vetter and Perlstein, 1991).

Terrorism extracts a high toll on people and social life around the world. Emergency workers in Togliatti, Russia, shown here, treat a victim of a bus explosion that was believed to be the work of terrorists.

Although many terrorist attacks in recent years have been attributed to people from other nations, that has not always been the case; our country also has a history of domestic terrorism.

TERRORISM IN THE UNITED STATES

Scholars have identified four types of terrorism that offer the greatest potential threat to U.S. citizens:

1. *Foreign-sponsored terrorism on U.S. soil.* Because of their unprecedented magnitude and destruction, the terrorist attacks in 2001 garnered more media coverage—both in this country and abroad—than virtually any other event in U.S. history. Since the date of those attacks by al Qaeda, a multinational terrorist organization led by Osama bin Laden, terrorism and/or potential terrorist attacks have routinely captured newspaper headlines and top billing on other media sources such as television and the Internet. Government intelligence reports recently have suggested that, rather than operating through a large-scale organization under the leadership of bin Laden, al Qaeda works through hundreds of radical Islamic operatives who train in terrorist camps and work in "sleeper cells" that lie dormant in the United States and elsewhere until they receive word from higher-up that it is time to attack.
2. *Domestic-sponsored terrorism.* Although less attention has been paid to "home-grown" terrorists since 2001, the FBI and other federal agencies remain concerned about domestic groups that could engage in acts of terrorism for political and religious reasons such as violent protests against abortion clinics. The worst act of domestic terrorism in the United States took place in 1995 when a bomb destroyed the Alfred P. Murrah Federal Building in Oklahoma City, taking 168 lives and injuring 850 other people. The longest series of terrorists acts in the United States was carried out by the "Unabomber," later identified as Theodore Kaczynski, who allegedly mailed sixteen bombs that caused three deaths and twenty-two injuries. Primary targets for the self-described anarchist's bombs were business executives and university researchers. It is believed that likely targets of internal terrorist groups today (such as radical

environmental organizations) might include academic research facilities, government facilities, and different components of the infrastructure such as water plants, power stations, and pipelines.

3. *Terrorism in other nations that might affect U.S. citizens who are residing or traveling in other countries.* The U.S. Department of State and media outlets worldwide continually issue travel advisories for U.S. citizens abroad for fear that some terrorist group might attack tourist sites or other public accommodations that are frequently visited by U.S. citizens. The government also is concerned that U.S. embassies in other countries might be attacked by terrorists, and from time to time the media report on temporary embassy closings or extra precautions that are being taken to protect certain embassies.
4. *Information terrorism—the destruction of computer systems and/or records.* According to media sources and the Terrorism Research Center, information terrorism ranges from outright intrusions and denial-of-service attacks to remote code injection for future exploitation. Terrorist-sponsored computer hackers could bring down entire educational, economic, and governmental information networks if information terrorists are able to bypass built-in safeguards.

What is the best way to let people know of a potential terrorist attack? Different agencies of the United States government have grappled with this problem, and the Department of Homeland Security devised a color-coded system displaying five levels of alert: severe, high, elevated, guarded, and low. For the most part, the nation has stayed in the elevated to high categories in recent years to show the potential for an act of terrorism at any time or place. Although all of us want to be informed by governmental authorities and the media when our lives or homes may be in danger, the more frequently we are reminded of possible terrorism and bombarded by daily coverage of this sort, the more difficult it is to put fear out of our minds.

Is there a middle ground in times such as these? This question will remain a concern as communications technologies make it possible for news—whether fact or fiction—to reach us instantantly and without filters from persons who may (or may not) have accurate information about possible threats. Recall, however, that terrorists—as well as the general public—have access to media sources, and widespread coverage of terrorist activities might encourage terrorists to act or might provide them with helpful information for circumventing existing safeguards against such attacks.

Do human beings have biological predispositions toward aggressive behavior? How do analysts using a biological perspective differ in their answers to this question as compared to those using a sociological perspective?

EXPLANATIONS OF WAR AND TERRORISM

What causes collective violence such as war and terrorism? Can war and acts of terrorism be reduced? Despite centuries of war and terrorism, we still know little about the origins of violence or how to reduce such acts (Turpin and Kurtz, 1997). In Chapter 9, we discussed biological, psychological, and sociological explanations for violence. We will now examine these approaches as they relate to war and terrorism.

Biological Perspectives

Analysts who use a biological framework for explaining war and terrorism emphasize that people inherit a tendency (or predisposition) toward aggressive behavior, which can culminate in warfare or terrorist acts. Contemporary policy makers who trace violent behavior to chemical or physical abnormalities such as a brain lesion, brain dysfunction, endocrine disorder, hormonal imbalance, or other genetic factors are taking such an approach (Turpin and Kurtz, 1997).

Perhaps the most widely known advocate for biological explanations of war and terrorism is anthropologist Konrad Lorenz (1966:261), who stated, "To the humble

Military training often involves a lengthy socialization process that teaches recruits how to dispense and cope with aggressive behavior.

seeker of biological truth there cannot be the slightest doubt that human militant enthusiasm evolved out of a communal defense response of our prehuman ancestors." According to Lorenz, just as our hominid ancestors confronted and repelled predatory animals, we have an almost instinctive desire to protect ourselves from our perceived enemies. Therefore, people engage in terrorism or fight wars when stimuli trigger their predisposition toward aggression. Lorenz believes that although the predisposition toward violence was functional at one time because it ensured survival of the most "fit," this instinct is a problem in contemporary societies. Philosopher William James suggested that the kind of courage and altruism people bring to war could be better directed toward some more worthy enterprise (cited in Ehrenreich, 1997).

Some scholars have sought to identify genetic influences on violence and warfare. Among the earliest was sociobiologist Edward O. Wilson (1975), who believed that aggressive tendencies are part of human nature but that people can learn not to engage in violent behavior. More recently, anthropologists Richard Wrangham and Dale Peterson, who study aggression in animals and humans, published their findings in *Demonic Males: Apes and the Origins of Human Violence* (1996). According to Wrangham and Peterson, both human and nonhuman animals, such as chimpanzees, have the inherent capacity to commit premeditated assaults. Premeditated violence is used by humans (especially males) and lower animals to intimidate enemies, beat them up, and destroy their ability to bring future challenges. Wrangham and Peterson believe that female chimps and humans are less apt to murder or take part in war. Women were deliberately excluded from participating in war-related activities in fifty-eight of the sixty-seven human societies that Wrangham and Peterson studied (Wheeler, 1997). But this brings up another question: Do women not participate in war by choice, or are they categorically excluded by social norms and customs? More research is needed to answer this and other questions about a biological origin for warfare and terrorism. Thus far, no scientific evidence conclusively demonstrates than humans are innately violent or that biological factors are more important than social factors in producing violent behavior (Turpin and Kurtz, 1997).

Psychological Perspectives

Psychologists have provided significant insights into violence, but they do not focus on collective violence in the form of war and terrorism. In fact, most psychological explanations emphasize individualistic sources of violence, resulting from such causes as abnormal psychological development. For example, Sigmund Freud contended that violent behavior occurs when the three aspects of the human personality come into conflict with one another. If the individual's *id* (unconscious drives and instincts) conflicts with the *superego* (internalized social values), and the *ego* (the mediator between the id and superego) is unable to resolve the conflict, violent behavior might ensue, particularly if the individual has an overdeveloped id, which contains the aggressive drive, or an underdeveloped superego (Turpin and Kurtz, 1997).

Contemporary social psychologists generally believe that both individual and cultural factors must be considered in explaining why people go to war or engage in terrorism. Some social psychologists focus primarily on the processes by which cultural influences make some individuals, but not others, behave violently. From these studies, they conclude that it is easier to harm enemies when they have been depersonalized (Milgram, 1974). People also are more likely to behave violently when they are placed in positions in which they have a great deal of power and authority over others (Haney, Banks, and Zimbardo, 1984).

An interesting insight into the psychological processes that are involved in violence comes from the work of Robert Jay Lifton (1997), who studied violence inflicted by Nazi doctors at Auschwitz. According to Lifton, these doctors—who had previously been committed to saving lives—were able to commit horrible atrocities because of the psychological principle of *doubling*—"the division of the self into two functioning wholes, so that a part-self acts as an entire self" (Lifton, 1997:30). Through the process of doubling, the doctors could embrace evil without restraint, remorse, or guilt and, at the same time, be loving parents and normal members of society. According to Lifton (1997), not only can doubling save the life of a soldier in combat who is confronted with the enemy, but it also can contribute to extreme wartime brutalities and the embracing of evil.

If social psychologists are correct in believing that individual personality factors contribute to war and terrorism, then how can such behavior be reduced? The answer is to emphasize social and cultural factors that head off violence and deadly conflict. In other words, societies should deemphasize violence and encourage peaceful behavior in daily life. However, social critic Barbara Ehrenreich (1997:76) believes that our impulse to make war resides in a deep ancestral memory of our role as prey and that we live in a society that still glorifies such impulses:

> Why...would human beings want to reenact...the terror of predation? Probably for the same reason that "civilized" people today pay to see movies in which their fellow humans are stalked and devoured by flesh-eating ghouls, vampires, and extraterrestrial monsters. Nothing gets our attention like the prospect of being ripped apart, sucked dry, and transformed into another creature's meal.

Although she concedes that people enjoy such fictional encounters because they are "fun," Ehrenreich also thinks that today's films and television programming pose interesting questions about why many people enjoy watching acts of violence and terrorism.

Ehrenreich's analysis brings up a larger question: Why are many people relatively positive about war, and why do they seemingly condone the violence associated with war? According to sociologists Jennifer Turpin and Lester R. Kurtz (1997:1), many people are deeply ambivalent about war because they believe that the only way to fight violence is with more violence:

> Since most people believe they can be secure only by repelling violence with violence, they simultaneously deplore and condone it. The use of violence is considered taboo almost universally in modern society except under certain conditions. It is widely abhorred yet widely used to promote social control in settings ranging from the household to the global socioeconomic order. Because of that ambivalence, elaborate social mechanisms have been institutionalized to distinguish between legitimate and illegitimate violence. Not only are individuals threatened by violence, but so are whole societies, and now—in the nuclear age—the species itself. Ironically, the very structures supposedly created to provide security against violence instead threaten everyone.

Sociological Explanations

Sociological explanations for war and terrorism use a functionalist, conflict, or interactionist perspective. We'll look at all three, starting with the functionalist.

The Functionalist Perspective

Some functionalist explanations focus on the relationship between social disorganization and warfare or terrorism. According to these explanations, disorganization in social institutions, for example, the government, contributes to overall political instability. Militia members believe that the U.S. government no longer serves the purpose for which it was intended, namely, to protect the individual's rights and freedom. In their eyes, the U.S. government has become dysfunctional, and they engage in acts of terrorism to undermine the government so that it will change radically or be abolished.

Other functionalists focus on the functions that war serves. Looked at from this perspective, war can settle disputes between nations. However, in the age of nuclear weaponry, many nations seek other means to deal with their disagreements. Among these means are *economic sanctions,* cutting off all trade. In some instances, the United States has imposed economic sanctions, rather than engaging in war or military action, against countries engaging in terrorism, environmental violations, abuse of workers' rights, regional strife, drug trafficking, human and political rights abuses, and nuclear proliferation (Myers, 1997). However, some political analysts argue that the United States is cutting off its nose to spite its face when it imposes economic sanctions against other governments: Economic sanctions are dysfunctional for another social institution—the economy. Also, even though the United States has used sanctions against other nations from its earliest days, corporations are concerned that the sanctions deny them access to the world's markets and the profits in those markets (Myers, 1997).

Some functionalists believe that we will always have wars because of other important functions that they serve in societies. First, war demonstrates that one nation or group has power over another. Historically, conquering forces acquire the "spoils of war," including more territory and material possessions. Second, war functions as a means of punishment in much the same manner that the U.S. government uses sanctions to force other nations to comply with our viewpoint on certain issues. Third, war is a way to disseminate ideologies, usually political or religious. For example, under the slogan "making the world safe for democracy," the United States has fought its largest wars in defense of a democratic form of government (Crossette, 1997). According to sociologist Seymour Martin Lipset, "We are a revolutionary country with a revolutionary tradition. We want everyone to be democrats" (cited in Crossette, 1997:E3). But not all democracies are friends of the United States. Larry Diamond, a scholar who has examined new democracies in other nations, explains (cited in Crossette, 1997:E3):

> Political freedom has deteriorated in several of the longest-surviving democracies of the developing world, including India, Sri Lanka, Colombia, and Venezuela.... It isn't enough to have elections.... Democracy is not something that is simply present or absent. It's not like a light switch that you flip on or off. It emerges in different fragments in different sequences in different countries and in different historical periods.

Finally, many functionalists point out the economic function of war. War benefits society because it stimulates the economy through increased war-related production and provides jobs for civilians who otherwise might not be able to find employment. In 2002, for example, the United States sold more than 10.4 billion dollars in military equipment and supplies to other countries (refer back to Map 17.1 on page 360). Conflict analysts also see an economic side to war, but they are not so optimistic.

The Conflict and Symbolic Interactionist Perspectives

Conflict theorists view war from the standpoint of how militarism and aggressive preparedness for war contribute to the economic well-being of some, but not all, people in a society. According to sociologist Cynthia Enloe (1987:527), people who consider capitalism the moving force behind the military's influence "believe that government officials enhance the status, resources, and authority of the military in order to protect the interests of private enterprises at home and overseas." In other words, the origins of war can be traced to corporate boardrooms, not to the U.S. government's war room. Those who view war from this standpoint note that workers come to rely on military spending for jobs. Labor unions, for example, support defense spending because it provides well-paid, stable employment for union members.

A second conflict explanation focuses on the role of the nation and its inclination toward coercion in response to perceived threats. From this perspective, nations inevitably use force to ensure compliance within their societies and to protect themselves from outside attacks.

A third conflict explanation is based on patriarchy and the relationship between militarism and masculinity. Across cultures and over time, the military has been a male institution, and the "meanings attached to masculinity appear to be so firmly linked to compliance with military roles that it is often impossible to disentangle the two" (Enloe, 1987:531).

Symbolic interactionists would call this last perspective the *social construction of masculinity.* That is, certain assumptions, teachings, and expectations that serve as the standard for appropriate male behavior—in this case, values of dominance, power, aggression, and violence—are created and recreated presumably through gender socialization, particularly in military training. Historically, the development of manhood and male superiority has been linked to militarism and combat—the ultimate test of a man's masculinity (Enloe, 1987; Cock, 1994).

SOLUTIONS TO WAR AND TERRORISM

What will happen as we move further into the twenty-first century? How will nations deal with the proliferation of arms and nuclear weapons? Will the United States continue to be a nation at war? What should be done with the masses of nuclear waste being produced? No easy answers are forthcoming, as Ehrenreich explains (1997:239):

> War... is a more formidable adversary than it has ever been.... war has dug itself into economic systems, where it offers a livelihood to millions.... It has lodged in our souls as a kind of religion, a quick tonic for political malaise and a bracing antidote to the moral torpor of consumerist, market-driven cultures. In addition, our incestuous fixation on combat with our own kind has left us ill-prepared to face many of the larger perils of the situation in which we find ourselves: the possibility of drastic climatic changes, the depletion of natural resources, the relentless predations of the microbial world. The wealth that flows ceaselessly to the project of war is wealth lost, for the most part, to the battle against these threats.

But Ehrenreich, like most other social analysts, is not totally pessimistic about the future. She believes that human resistance to war can provide a means to spare this nation and the world from future calamities. According to Ehrenreich, the antiwar movements of the late twentieth century show that "the passions we bring to war can be brought just as well to the struggle *against* war." But, she notes, people must be willing to educate, inspire, and rally others to the cause. Like other forms of warfare, the people who are fighting for peace must be willing to continue the struggle even when the odds seem hopeless. Ehrenreich's point is supported by sociologists James William Gibson and Francesca M. Cancian (1990:9), who believe that making peace can be more difficult than making war:

> [M]aking peace requires democratic relationships: soldiers who refuse to fight in a war they do not support; citizens who claim the right to participate in making decisions instead of accepting rule by elites who make decisions in secret; newspaper reporters, magazine editors, movie makers, and others in the mass media who question the necessity of casting another nation as an "enemy" and instead look for ways to communicate with other human beings who are potentially our friends.

What about the future of terrorism in the United States and other nations? One thing appears certain: Countries such as the United States, the United Kingdom, and Spain that have experienced terrorist attacks on their own soil will be forever changed in how they deal with security and surveillance of citizens and of those seeking to enter these countries. In the United States, for example, the security procedures we go through before boarding an airplane or attending public gatherings, including sporting events, political conventions, and concerts, have increased significantly in the post-9/11 era. Likewise, passage of the USA PATRIOT Act greatly expanded the powers of law enforcement officials in this country and intelligence agencies working abroad to track and intercept communications and to crack down on activities that in any way may be linked to terrorist operations. Some people may view this law as infringing on their rights and privacy (see Box 17.2).

Why do we end our discussion of social problems with war and terrorism? They are the ultimate category of social problems. When class, race, ethnicity, or any of

Social Problems and Social Policy

Box 17.2

Does the USA PATRIOT Act Protect Us or Threaten Our Liberties? Ask Your Librarian

> **United States Department of Justice, Washington, D.C.:**
> We are waging a war that defends the lives of all Americans. And we wage that war each day in a way that values and protects the civil liberties and the constitutional freedoms that make our Nation so special.
>
> —*Alberto R. Gonzales, then U.S. Attorney General, defending the USA PATRIOT Act when Congress renewed vital provisions of the Act in 2005 (U.S. Department of Justice 2005)*
>
> **Vanderbilt University, Nashville, Tennessee:**
> Although the Jean and Alexander Heard Library system [at Vanderbilt University] has an existing Privacy Policy, these enhanced surveillance statutes [in the USA PATRIOT Act] override state laws pertaining to library confidentiality and pose a challenge to privacy and confidentiality in the library. We are developing detailed procedures for responding to requests for information, as well as undertaking a review of our recordkeeping practices.
>
> —*From "Libraries and the USA PATRIOT Act," Stevenson Science and Engineering Library, Vanderbilt University (2005)*

Messages such as the one posted on the Vanderbilt University library website are increasingly common in libraries throughout the nation because of the 2001 USA PATRIOT Act (an acronym for "United and Strengthening America by Providing Appropriate Tools Required to Intercept and Obstruct Terrorism"), which became law shortly after the September 11 terrorist attacks.

In brief, the USA PATRIOT Act "amended over 15 federal statutes, including the laws governing criminal procedure, computer fraud and abuse, foreign intelligence, wiretapping, immigration, and the laws governing the privacy of student records" in order to expand the authority of the FBI and other law enforcement agencies to gain access to suspected terrorists' business records, medical records, educational records, and library records, including stored electronic data and communications. This Act also expanded the laws governing use of telephone wiretaps and "trap and trace" devices to Internet and electronic communications (American Library Association, 2005).

(*continued*)

Box 17.2 (continued)

Libraries throughout the nation were particularly concerned about enhanced surveillance procedures that posed a challenge to privacy and confidentiality in the library. Under Section 215, "Access to Records Under Foreign Intelligence Security Act," the FBI is permitted to obtain a search warrant for "any tangible thing," including books, records, papers, floppy disks, data tapes, and computers with hard drives. The FBI can also demand to see library circulation records, Internet use records, and registration information stored in any medium. FBI agents do not have to demonstrate "probable cause" (the existence of specific facts to support the belief that a crime has been committed or that the items sought are evidence of a crime) to gain access to this information. The agents only need to claim a belief that the records they are seeking are related to an ongoing investigation pertaining to terrorism or intelligence activities. Librarians and libraries are prohibited from informing a patron that his or her records were given to the FBI or that he or she is the subject of an FBI investigation.

In 2005, Congress began the process of reauthorizing portions of the PATRIOT Act, and organizations such as the American Library Association (ALA) passed resolutions in opposition to "any use of governmental power to suppress the free and open exchange of knowledge and information or to intimidate individuals exercising free inquiry." When the PATRIOT Act was reauthorized in 2006, it contained a section addressing the issue of privacy protection for library patrons, making library records beyond the need of national security as long as the library did not operate as an electronic communication service to provide users with the ability to send or receive wire or electronic communications.

Is the USA PATRIOT Act a threat to intellectual freedom and civil liberties? Some analysts believe that it will be possible to eventually "tweak" this law so that it provides law enforcement officials with the powers they need to get the job done while, at the same time, it provides us with safeguards we need against abuse. Others believe that the Act was an overreaction to the terrorist attacks and that, in the name of the "war on terror," the government has been given the ability to "take away our freedom" (ACLU, 2005). Clearly, not everyone agrees on this (or any other) law; however, it behooves us to become familiar with the USA PATRIOT Act and to learn how it might affect our own college library, local bookstore, and home. To learn more about this debate, you may wish to visit these websites: U.S. Department of Justice (http://www.usdoj.gov), the American Library Association (http://www.ala.org), and the American Civil Liberties Union (http://www.aclu.org).

the other dominant/subordinate categories discussed in this book escalate to a level of "doing something about it" regardless of the consequences, terrorism or war can be the result. Redressing inequality is an admirable goal, but perhaps the goal should be the one stated by Tim O'Brien, who wrote about his tour of duty in Vietnam (quoted in Hynes, 1997:283–284):

> I would wish this book could take the form of a plea for everlasting peace, a plea from one who knows, from one who's been there and come back, an old soldier looking back at a dying war.... That would be good. It would be fine to integrate it all to persuade my younger brother and perhaps some others to say "No" to wars and other battles.

The international society—the community of all the nations of the world—must work to alleviate inequalities and create a better—peaceful—world for future generations. What role will you and I play during the years to come? Will we be part of the problem or part of the solution? The answer is up to us.

SUMMARY

■ *How do social scientists define war?*

Social scientists define war broadly. The term *war* includes armed conflict between two countries, undeclared wars, civil and guerrilla wars, covert operations, and some forms of terrorism. War is a form of collective violence that involves organized violence by people seeking to promote their cause or resist social policies or practices that they consider oppressive.

■ *What are the consequences of war?*

The most direct effect of war is loss of human life. In World War I and before, it was mostly military personnel who lost their lives, but in World War II and thereafter, war was waged against civilians. If a nuclear war were to take place, the devastation would be beyond description. Other consequences for both military personnel and civilians are physical and psychological damage, including post-traumatic stress syndrome. Finally, the economic costs of war and war preparedness are astronomical.

■ *How important is military technology to winning a war?*

Military technology is a dominant factor, as military history shows. In the fourteenth century, smaller European and Western armies defeated bigger armies by using the newly discovered black powder. Today, precision-guided munitions render old technologies obsolete and global warfare possible. But wars can be won on the basis of factors other than military technology, too, as the U.S. experience in Vietnam shows.

■ *What is terrorism?*

Terrorism is the use of calculated unlawful physical force or threats of violence against a government, organization, or individual to gain some political, religious, economic, or social objective. Tactics include bombing, kidnapping, hostage taking, hijacking, assassination, and extortion.

■ *What are the three types of political terrorism?*

Revolutionary terrorism involves acts of violence against civilians that are carried out by enemies of the government who want to bring about political change. Repressive terrorism is conducted by a government against its own citizens for the purpose of protecting an existing political order. In state-sponsored terrorism, a government provides financial resources, weapons, and training for terrorists who conduct their activities in other nations.

■ *What forms of terrorism represent the greatest potential threat to U.S. citizens?*

Some analysts identify the following as forms of terrorism that offer the greatest potential threat to U.S. citizens: (1) foreign-sponsored terrorism on U.S. soil such as the 9/11/2001 terrorist attacks; (2) domestic-sponsored terrorism with political or religious motivations such as violent protests against abortion clinics; (3) terrorism in other nations such as attacks at tourist sites or other public accommodations that are frequently visited by U.S. citizens; and (4) information terrorism—the destruction of computer systems and/or records.

■ *What are the biological perspectives on war and terrorism?*

Some biological proponents say that humans, especially males, are innately violent, but there is no conclusive scientific evidence to support this view or the view that biological factors are more important than social factors.

■ *What are the psychological perspectives on war and terrorism?*

Most strictly psychological perspectives focus on individualistic sources of violence, but social psychologists take both individual and cultural factors into account. Their research findings show that it is easier to harm enemies when they are depersonalized and that people are more likely to act violently when they are in positions of power. Some individuals can commit horrible atrocities without feeling guilt through the process of doubling. Social psychologists say that, to reduce war and terrorism, society must emphasize peace, not glorify violent impulses.

■ *What is the functionalist perspective on war and terrorism?*

Some functionalists focus on the relationship between social disorganization and warfare or terrorism. Examining the growth of militias, they note that disorganization in social institutions contributes to overall political instability. Other functionalists say that war serves certain functions: It settles disputes; demonstrates that one nation or group has power over another; punishes; is one way to disseminate religious and political ideologies; and, finally, stimulates the economy.

■ *What are the conflict and interactionist perspectives on war and terrorism?*

Some conflict theorists say that militarism and preparedness for war contribute to the economic well-being of some—not all—people. Another conflict perspective says that nations inevitably use force to ensure compliance within their society and to protect themselves from outside attacks. A third conflict perspective is based in patriarchy: Across cultures and over time, the military has been a male institution; it is almost impossible to untangle masculinity from militarism. Interactionists call this last perspective the *social construction of masculinity*—the connection between manhood and militarism is historically created and recreated through gender socialization.

KEY TERMS

collective violence, p. 355
repressive terrorism, p. 362
revolutionary terrorism, p. 361
state-sponsored terrorism, p. 362
strategically significant weapon, p. 360
terrorism, p. 361
war, p. 355
war system, p. 355
weapons of mass destruction, p. 357
weapons system, p. 360

QUESTIONS FOR CRITICAL THINKING

1. In World War II and every war since, more civilians than military personnel have died. Given the technology that is available, how can we safeguard civilians?
2. How do you perceive the problem of domestic terrorism in the United States? Do you think militias pose a growing threat? What solutions can you suggest?
3. Consider the question posed in the last paragraph of this chapter: What can you yourself do to make the world a better—peaceful—place in the future?

Chapter 18

Can Social Problems Be Solved?

THINKING SOCIOLOGICALLY

- What shocking lessons did we learn from the 2001 terrorist attacks, the 2005 Hurricane Katrina disaster, and similar catastrophic events about the importance of prevention and/or preparedness in dealing with national emergencies and massive social problems?
- When do macrolevel efforts work better than mid-range or microlevel attempts to deal with social problems?
- What do social movements and special-interest groups have in common in their ideologies and efforts to influence politicians and other influential people? How do they differ in their goals and methods?

Before 9/11 the Federal Emergency Management Agency listed the three most likely catastrophic disasters facing America: a terrorist attack on New York, a major earthquake in San Francisco, and a hurricane strike in New Orleans. "The New Orleans hurricane scenario," The Houston Chronicle *wrote in December 2001, "may be the deadliest of all." It described a potential catastrophe very much like the one [that occurred in August, 2005]. So why were New Orleans and the nation so unprepared?*

—Paul Krugman (2005), a noted author and columnist for the **New York Times, *criticizing the slow response by the federal government to Hurricane Katrina's devastation***

It really makes us look very much like Bangladesh or Baghdad. I'm 84 years old. I've been around a long time, but I've never seen anything like this.

—David Herbert Donald, a retired Harvard historian and a native of Mississippi, describing his reaction to the devastation caused by the hurricane (quoted in Purdum, 2005)

I was surprised and not surprised. It's not just a lack of preparedness. I think the easy answer is to say that [the victims of Hurricane Katrina] are poor people and black people and so the government doesn't give a damn. That's O.K., and there might be some truth to that. But I think we've got to see this as a serious problem of the long-term neglect of an environmental system on which our nation depends.

—Andrew Young, a former civil rights worker, mayor of Atlanta, and U.S. Ambassador to the United Nations, who was born in New Orleans, expressing his feelings about the hardship and heartbreak caused by the hurricane (quoted in Purdum, 2005)

Described as the worst natural disaster in U.S. history, Hurricane Katrina in 2005 not only left a wide path of death and destruction in its wake but also raised many serious questions about emergency preparedness and how we deal with social problems in this country. Some analysts suggest that local, state, and federal governments were not adequately prepared for unprecedented emergencies such as this devastating hurricane on the Gulf Coast (Shane and Lipton, 2005). Lack of adequate funding, resulting in part from federal income tax cuts and shifting national priorities after the 2001 terrorist attacks, coupled with the continuing conflict in Afghanistan and Iraq, have left many emergency programs in a "bare-bones" condition. Funding problems and lack of long-range planning may also contribute to failures in components of the infrastructure at a time when it is most needed. ***Infrastructure* refers to a framework of support systems, such as transportation and utilities, that makes it possible to have specific land uses** (commercial, residential, and recreational, for example) **and a built environment** (buildings, houses, highways, and such) **that facilitate people's daily activities and the nation's economy.** Problems with the infrastructure create major crises, such as when transportation systems malfunction, utilities fail or are inadequate, and *infrastructural capital* (including bridges, dams, and levees) is unable to fulfill its purpose. Infrastructure failure contributed to existing problems in New Orleans when, in the aftermath of Hurricane Katrina, water pumps and several levees on Lake Pontchartrain were breached, spilling millions of gallons of polluted water onto the city's already-flooded streets, forcing residents from their homes, and leaving thousands of people homeless. Many Gulf Coast communities, including Gulfport, Biloxi, and Hattiesburg, Mississippi, were also hard-hit by this hurricane, but media coverage typically focused on New Orleans because of the magnitude of the crisis there (see Box 18.1).

The tragedy in New Orleans also reflects social problems experienced by many people but seldom seriously discussed in this country, including the high rate of poverty (28 percent) among African Americans living in that city, which is more than double the national poverty rate for all U.S. citizens (Whitesides, 2005).

Social Problems in the Media

Box 18.1

Covering the Hurricane Katrina Disaster: Journalists as Advocates in New Orleans

> It's a disgrace, and don't think the world isn't watching. Where is the federal government? Where is food and water for these people?"
>
> —*On-air comment by Jack Cafferty, a CNN reporter, as the screen showed New Orleans hurricane victims huddled together in overcrowded, smelly shelters (quoted in Madigan, 2005)*

> I don't know why they're being ignored. It just may be disorganization and chaos.
>
> —*Shepard Smith, a Fox News correspondent, expressing his concern when the New Orleans mayor arranged for buses to remove 400 stranded tourists from downtown hotels while leaving thousands of his predominantly African-American constituents to fend for themselves for days (quoted in Madigan, 2005)*

> Did the government learn anything from 9/11 about how to handle a major catastrophe?
>
> —*On ABC's* World News Tonight, *correspondent Elizabeth Vargas questions the federal government's relief efforts for hurricane victims (quoted in Madigan, 2005)*

Should reporters such as these become emotionally involved in the stories they cover? Journalists are human beings who may lose their professional "detachment" when they see the magnitude of a major disaster such as Hurricane Katrina and when they observe the desperate plight of helpless victims.

Images of destruction, death, and desperation have become all too common a sight on our television screens and computer monitors and in magazines and daily newspapers. Through published photos, video clips, and journalists' accounts, we have witnessed terrorism in London, war in Iraq, and the deadly 2004 tsunami wave that killed nearly 300,000 people in nations such as Indonesia, Sri Lanka, India, and Thailand. Then, in 2005, we were faced with the graphic shock of news coverage from New Orleans, coverage that looked as if it were coming from a war-torn country or a Third World nation rather than a major U.S. city (Farmer, 2005).

Initially, reporters found people crying out to be rescued from rising flood waters. Then, after the initial images of shock and loss, reporters found thousands more struggling to survive without food, water, medication, and protection from other people who might harm them. As the hours and days passed, it became apparent to journalists and other observers alike that the federal government's immediate response to the disaster was going to be completely inadequate for the task at hand. At that time, some reporters shifted from feeling empathy for the victims to feeling anger and skepticism regarding this nation's emergency preparedness (Madigan, 2005). Images of death and despair that media audiences saw from afar were close and personal for reporters, some of whom temporarily left behind their dispassionate, journalistic demeanor and began to tell the story with a tone of advocacy, making demands on political leaders and relief workers to explain why help for the victims was arriving so slowly (Holloway, 2005).

Should reporters become emotionally involved in the stories they cover? The answer to this question, like many others relating to social problems, is ambiguous at best. Terry Michael, founder of the Washington Center for Politics and Journalism, believes that journalists' strong displays of emotions or discussions of their personal feelings about issues tend to compromise television reporters' effectiveness:

> In the early days of television, when reporters came from [a newspaper background], they would never feel it was appropriate to display emotions because they would have felt it would have compromised their objectivity. [These days, many television reporters] forget their responsibility as dispassionate interpreters of reality and they end up being part of the story (quoted in Madigan, 2005).

On the other hand, journalists who occasionally take on an advocacy role may help their readers or viewers feel more

(*continued*)

Box 18.1 (continued)

connected to a story or bring audiences a better understanding of the true magnitude of a disaster or other major social problem, including its causes, effects, and possible remedies. Some middle- and upper-middle class journalists showed empathy toward New Orleans hurricane victims who, for the most part, were low-income African Americans. As Marcy McGinnis, a vice president for CBS News, stated, "Just because you're a reporter doesn't mean you're made of stone and have no feelings whatsoever" (Madigan, 2005). When a reporter or news anchor expresses genuine emotion about the unmet needs of others, he or she may call attention to organizations and institutions that have failed those individuals for years, decades, or even centuries.

Are we more likely to help people in need if we see journalists or other public figures showing their own emotions and revealing their concern for those far less fortunate than they? What do you think?

Questions to Consider

1. Throughout this text, we have looked at how the media frame stories about various social problems. We have also examined media representations of race, class, gender, age, and other ascribed characteristics. How might media framing of stories about major disasters or other important social problems influence readers' and viewers' perceptions about the causes, effects, and possible solutions to those problems?

2. Under what circumstances do you think that it is *most* acceptable for reporters, television news anchors, and other journalists to show their emotions in a news report? Under what circumstances do you believe it is *least* acceptable for them to do so? Explain your answer.

Many people across a variety of political spectrums, lifestyles and economic conditions, and racial/ethnic categories were extremely critical of the length of time that it took for political leaders, the military, and other governmental agencies to mobilize and help rescue victims, care for the ill and dying, and bring some order to the city (Dowd, 2005; Purdum, 2005).

Although Hurricane Katrina was a *natural disaster* (which includes floods, hurricanes, tornadoes, and earthquakes), from a sociological perspective it also was a *social disaster.* If Hurricane Katrina's first wave was the storm itself, the second wave of this hurricane was a *manmade disaster* because large numbers of injuries, deaths, and property damage may have resulted not from the devastating effects of the hurricane itself but rather from earlier decisions about priorities, allocation of funds, and the importance of certain kinds of preparedness. In this regard, *New York Times* columnist John Tierney (2005:A29) stated, "Members of Congress will always have higher priorities than paying for levees in someone else's state." Infrastructure failures and inadequate preparedness for emergencies increased the amount of hardship, the death toll, and the extent of property damage resulting from Hurricane Katrina. These factors also contributed to civil disturbances such as looting, shootings, arson, riots, and other lawlessness. In essence, Hurricane Katrina revealed that our nation may have "penny pinched" in the wrong places, ignoring deep divisions of race, class, gender, and age that we usually do not examine or seek to remedy except when faced with massive disaster such as terrorist attacks or natural disasters of great magnitude. Then, we question the role of the U.S. government in aiding its citizens and maintaining necessary infrastructure before we move on to other issues that regain top billing in politics, the media, and everyday "water cooler" discussions. Persistent underlying social problems, such as the growing gap between the rich and the poor and the continuing significance of racial inequality in the United States, also momentarily rise to the surface for analysis in times of national crisis. In this chapter, we look at what might be done to reduce or eliminate social problems. Thinking sociologically about the causes and effects of, and possible solutions for, problems such as natural disasters like Hurricane Katrina helps focus our attention on what needs to be done to reduce some pressing social problems while examining social problems on a global basis raises an even more complex array of issues that we must consider.

THE PROBLEM WITH TACKLING SOCIAL PROBLEMS

Solving social problems is a far more complex undertaking than simply identifying them and pinpointing their social locations. It is much easier for us to call attention to a problem than it is to carry out a solution. Designing and implementing programs to solve social problems may take years while the needs of individuals and groups are immediate. According to some analysts, programs to bring about positive social change face "innumerable obstacles, delays, and frustrations," and require that we have "immense dedication and perseverance" (Weinberg, Rubington, and Hammersmith, 1981:6).

Ideal vs. Practical Solutions Perhaps the first obstacle that we face in trying to reduce or solve social problems is in dealing with the difference between *ideal* solutions and *practical* solutions. As the sociologists Martin S. Weinberg, Earl Rubington, and Sue Kiefer Hammersmith (1981:6) state, "There is usually considerable conflict between what the *ideal* solution would be and what a *workable* solution might be." Sometimes the ideal solution to a problem entails prohibitive costs. In regard to natural disasters, for example, there is no ideal solution (given the fact that we cannot stop most natural disasters) but we can do far better than we have in regard to advance warnings about a potential disaster, evacuation of individuals regardless of who they are or their ability to pay, immediate help for those who must remain behind, and better fortification against naturally occurring hazards to protect communities and infrastructure.

Preventive measures such as these are costly and time consuming, which means that they typically are allocated only a small percent of the money and resources actually needed or they are entirely swept off the table in political discussions by being labeled as "prohibitive" in cost or "impractical" in view of other seemingly more urgent budget demands. Consequently, rather than employing preventive measures to deal with social problems, we frequently rely on *after-the-fact measures* (such as trying to remedy a problem or reduce its effects after it has occurred) to deal with issues and crises. In the case of Hurricane Katrina, for example, engineers, members of the media, and many others had long asserted that money for storm protection needed to be spent to protect New Orleans from massive flooding. The Louisiana Congressional delegation had also asked for money for storm protection in the past but had received only a small portion of the amount they requested. After Hurricane Katrina hit, Alfred C. Naomi, a senior program manager for the Army Corps of Engineers, pointed out how "penny wise and pound foolish" many decisions about spending money for flood protection had been:

> It would take $2.5 billion to build a Category 5 (the highest) protection system, and we're talking about tens of billions in losses, all that lost productivity, and so many lost lives and injuries and personal trauma you'll never get over. People will be scarred for life by this event. (Revkin and Drew, 2005:A14)

Spending tens of billions after a disaster rather than $2.5 billion in advance to protect the infrastructure is an example of the after-the-fact approach to social problems. This approach is also used in education, crime, and health care. When leaders do not allocate necessary funds for schools and juvenile prevention programs, for example, they later find that more money must be spent on programs to deal with school dropouts, juvenile offenders, and others who are left behind (or left out) in the existing system. Similar situations occur in health care when patients do not receive preventive care that might reduce their risk for certain illnesses or disease (such as cardiovascular accidents, diabetes, and cancer) but instead receive expensive "high tech" medical treatment after the onset of their medical condition—if they are among the fortunate ones who have money, insurance, or a social welfare program (such as Medicare or Medicaid) that partly covers the cost of their treatment.

Defining the Problem vs. Fixing It Sometimes there is no agreement about what the problem *is* and what efforts should be made to reduce or eliminate it. After all, the people and organizations involved in the problem-*defining* stage of a social problem generally are not the same people and organizations involved in the problem-*solving* stage of a social problem. Social problems are often identified and defined by political or social activists, journalists, social scientists, and religious leaders. In contrast, the problem-solving stage usually involves elected officials and/or people working in agencies and governmental bureaucracies. Moreover, sometimes a proposed solution to a problem may only give rise to a whole new set of problems (Weinberg, Rubington, and Hammersmith, 1981). Fixing the problem is no easy matter because it often involves social change, which makes many people uncomfortable because they believe that things could indeed get worse rather than better when individuals and groups start to tinker with the status quo (things as they currently are).

SOCIAL CHANGE AND REDUCING SOCIAL PROBLEMS

It should be clear from what was said in the preceding section that the concept of social change is important to our discussion of reducing social problems. ***Social change* is the alternation, modification, or transformation of**

public policy, culture, or social institutions over time. Notice that this definition states that social change occurs "over time." Thus social change has temporal dimensions. Some efforts to deal with social problems are *short-term* strategies, whereas others are *middle-term* remedies, and still others constitute *long-term* efforts to alleviate the root causes of a social problem. In other words, efforts to alleviate individual unemployment or reduce unemployment rates in a community have a different temporal dimension than efforts to change the political economy in such a manner that high levels of employment and greater wage equity are brought about throughout a nation or nations. Clearly, efforts to alleviate individual unemployment are a short-term solution to the problem of unemployment, while efforts to reduce unemployment in a community or to change the political economy are middle-term and long-term solutions. Sometimes discussions of social change sound idealistic or utopian because they are middle-term or long-term strategies that attempt to target the root causes of a social problem. For many social problems, however, a combination of strategies is required to reduce social problems.

MICROLEVEL ATTEMPTS TO SOLVE SOCIAL PROBLEMS

In Chapter 1, we described sociologist C. Wright Mills's (1959b) belief that we should apply the sociological imagination to gain a better understanding of social problems. According to Mills, the sociological imagination is the ability to see the relationship between individual experiences and the larger society. For Mills, social problems cannot not be solved at the individual level because they are more than personal troubles or private problems. However, sometimes social institutions cannot deal with a problem effectively, and political and business leaders are unwilling or unable to allocate the resources that are necessary to reduce a problem. In these situations, we have no choice but to try to deal with a problem in our own way.

Seeking Individual Solutions to Personal Problems

Microlevel solutions to social problems focus on how individuals operate within small groups to try to remedy a problem that affects them, their family, or friends. Usually, when individuals have personal problems, they turn to their ***primary groups*****—small, less specialized groups in which members engage in face-to-face, emotion-based interactions over an extended period of time.** Primary groups include one's family, close friends, and other peers with whom one routinely shares the more personal experiences in life.

How can participation in primary groups help us to reduce personal problems? According to sociologists, members of our primary groups usually support us even when others do not. For example, some analysts believe that we have many more people who are without a domicile (technically homeless) than current statistics suggest but that, whenever possible, these people live with relatives or friends, many of whom may already live in overcrowded and sometimes substandard housing. Most people who seek individualized solutions to personal troubles believe the situation will be temporary. However, if the problem is widespread or embedded in the larger society, it might stretch out for months or years without resolution. At best, individualized efforts to reduce a problem are short-term measures that some critics refer as the "Band-Aid approach" to a problem because these efforts do not eliminate the causes of the problem.

Some microlevel approaches to reducing social problems focus on how individuals can do something about the problems they face. For example, a person who is unemployed or among the "working poor" because of low wages, seasonal employment, or other factors might be urged to get more education or training and work experience in order to find a "better" job and have the opportunity for upward mobility. Individuals who appear to have eliminated problems in their own lives through such efforts are applauded for their determination, and they are often used (sometimes unwillingly or unknowingly) as examples that others are supposed to follow.

An example of this approach is columnist John Tierney's assessment of Hurricane Katrina and his encouragement to readers to "fight floods like fires, without the feds." According to Tierney, urbanites in cities such as New York have learned to protect themselves from fire losses by purchasing insurance, and the people of New Orleans and along the Gulf Coast should do likewise:

> Here's the bargain I'd offer New Orleans: the feds will spend the billions for your new levees, but then you're on your own. You and others along the coast have to buy flood insurance the same way we all buy fire insurance—from private companies with more at stake than Washington bureaucrats.... If Americans had to pay premiums for living in risky areas, they'd think twice about building oceanfront villas. Voters and insurance companies would

> put pressure on local politicians to take care of the levees, prepare for the worst—and stop waiting for that bumbling white knight from Washington. (Tierney, 2005:A29)

Although Tierney raises an interesting point, his approach does not take into account the fact that many who experienced devastating losses in this disaster were individuals and families with the fewest material possessions and little or no hope of ever affording an oceanfront villa much less the insurance to protect it from fire and hurricanes.

Limitations of the Microlevel Solutions Approach

Although individuals must certainly be responsible for their own behavior and must make decisions that help solve their own problems, there are serious limitations to the assumption that social problems can be solved one person at a time. When we focus on individualistic solutions to reducing social problems, we are not taking into account the fact that secondary groups and societal institutions play a significant part in creating, maintaining, and exacerbating many social problems. ***Secondary groups*** **are larger, more specialized groups in which members engage in impersonal, goal-oriented relationships for a limited period of time.** Without the involvement of these large-scale organizations, which include government agencies and transnational corporations, it is virtually impossible to reduce large-scale social problems. Consider, for example, the problem of air pollution. According to scholars Mike Budd, Steve Craig, and Clay Steinman (1999:169–170):

> Sport utility vehicles, for example, pollute the air and add to global warming far more than the cars they displaced on the nation's roads. Indeed, if a legal loophole did not consider them "light trucks" instead of cars, the environmental damage they cause would keep them off the road altogether. Light trucks, which also include pickup trucks and minivans, are the fastest-growing source of global warming gasses in the country, contributing nearly twice as much per vehicle as cars, according to a study by the Environmental Protection Agency.

I can stay inside all the time so that I do not inhale polluted air, but this individual solution does not solve the problem of air pollution and does not address the role of others (vehicle manufacturers, gasoline producers, and consumers) in the creation of air pollution. With rapid acceleration in the price of gasoline and other fuel costs due to factors such as the war in Iraq and damage to oil producing facilities as a result of Hurricane Katrina, people may seek out more fuel-efficient vehicles as an economic survival strategy. At the bottom line, however, personal choices alone cannot do much to reduce most national and global problems. Even if one person decides to give up a sport utility vehicle or to stay inside all day when cities have smog alert warning days, the environment continues to be contaminated, and the air quality for future generations comes more and more into question. On the other hand, suppose a group of people banded together in a grassroots effort to deal with a social problem: What effect might their efforts have on reducing it?

MIDRANGE ATTEMPTS TO SOLVE SOCIAL PROBLEMS

Midrange solutions to social problems focus on how secondary groups and formal organizations can deal with problems or assist individuals in overcoming problems such as drug addiction or domestic violence. Some groups help people to cope with their own problems, and some groups attempt to bring about community change.

Groups That Help People Cope with Their Problems

Most midrange solutions to social problems are based on two assumptions: (1) that some social problems can best be reduced by reaching one person at a time and (2) that prevention and intervention are most effective at the personal and community levels. Groups that attempt to reduce a social problem by helping individuals cope with it or by eliminating it from their own lives are commonplace in our society (see Table 18.1 on page 378). Among the best known are Alcoholics Anonymous (AA) and Narcotics Anonymous (NA); however, a wide range of "self-help" organizations exist in most communities. Typically, self-help groups bring together individuals who have experienced the same problem and have the same goal: Quitting the behavior that has caused the problem, which can be anything from abuse of alcohol, tobacco, and other drugs to overeating, gambling, or chronic worrying. Volunteers who have had similar problems (and believe that they are on the road to overcoming them) act as role models for newer members. For example, AA and NA are operated by alcoholics and/or other substance abusers who

TABLE 18.1 Selected Self-Help Groups

Alcoholics Anonymous www.alcoholics-anonymous.org	Diabetes Support Group www.diabetes.org
Al-Anon and Alateen www.al-anon-alateen.org	Gamblers Anonymous www.gamblersanonymous.org
Alzheimer's Support Group www.alz.org	Narcotics Anonymous www.na.org
Breast Cancer Support Group www.komen.org	National Coalition for the Homeless www.nationalhomeless.org
Bulimia, Anorexia Self-Help www.nationaleatingdisorders.org	Overeaters Anonymous www.overeatersanonymous.org
Children of Lesbians and Gays Everywhere www.colage.org	Parents Without Partners www.parentswithoutpartners.org
Cocaine Anonymous www.ca.org	Step-Families Association of America www.stepfam.org
Co-Dependents Anonymous www.codependents.org	United Fathers of America www.unitedfathers.org

try to provide new members with the support they need to overcome alcohol addiction or drug dependency. According to some analysts, AA is a subculture with distinct rules and values that alcoholics learn through their face-to-face encounters with other AA members (Maxwell, 1981). Social interaction is viewed as central for individual success in the programs. Confessing one's behavioral problems to others in an organizational setting is believed to have therapeutic value to those who are seeking help. Like other midrange approaches, organizations such as AA and NA may bring changes in the individual's life; however, they do not systematically address the structural factors (such as unemployment, work-related stress, and aggressive advertising campaigns) that might contribute to substance abuse problems. For example, AA typically does not lobby for more stringent laws pertaining to drunk driving or the sale and consumption of alcoholic beverages. As a result, larger, societal intervention is necessary to reduce the problems that contribute to individual behavior.

Grassroots Groups That Work for Community-Based Change

Some grassroots organizations focus on bringing about a change that may reduce or eliminate a social problem in a specific community or region. ***Grassroots groups*** **are organizations started by ordinary people who work in concert to change a perceived wrong in their neighborhood, city, state, or nation.** Using this approach, people learn how to empower themselves against local and state government officials, corporate executives, and media figures who determine what constitutes the news in their area:

> By their nature, grassroots groups emerge to challenge individuals, corporations, government agencies, academia, or a combination of these when people discover they share a grievance. In their search for redress, they have encountered unresponsive, negative public agencies, self-serving private businesses, or recalcitrant individuals and groups. The answer for them is to select specific issues and find like-minded others. (Adams, 1991:9)

A central concern of those who attempt to reduce a social problem through grassroots groups is the extent to which other people are apathetic about the problem. Some analysts suggest that even when people are aware of problems, they do not think that they can do anything to change them or do not know how to work with other people to alleviate them:

> The biggest problem facing Americans is not those issues that bombard us daily, from homelessness and failing schools to environmental devastation and the federal deficit. Underlying each is a deeper crisis. Some see that deeper problem in the form of obstacles that block problem solving: the tightening concentration of wealth, the influence of money in politics, discrimination, and bureaucratic rigidity, to name a few. These *are* powerful barriers. But for us the crisis is deeper still. The crisis is

> that *we as a people don't know how to come together to solve these problems.* We lack the capacities to address the issues or remove the obstacles that stand in the way of public deliberation. Too many Americans feel powerless. (Lappé and Du Bois, 1994:9)

According to social analysts, more community dialogue is needed on social issues, and more people need to become involved in grassroots social movements. **A *social movement* is an organized group that acts collectively to promote or resist change through collective action** (Goldberg, 1991). Because social movements when they begin are not institutionalized and are outside the political mainstream, they empower outsiders by offering them an opportunity to have their voices heard. For example, when residents near Love Canal, located in Niagara Falls, New York, came to believe that toxic chemicals were damaging the health of their children, they banded together to bring about change in government regulations concerning the disposal of toxic wastes. Indeed, Love Canal was the birthplace of the environmental movement against dumping toxic waste. Social movements such as Mothers Against Drunk Driving (MADD), Earth First!, People for the Ethical Treatment of Animals (PETA), and the National Federation of Parents for Drug Free Youth began as community-based grassroots efforts. Over time, many midrange organizations evolve into national organizations; however, their organization and focus often change in the process (Adams, 1991). Table 18.2 provides examples of activist organizations that seek to reduce specific social problems in communities.

Grassroots organizations and other local structures are crucial to national social movements because national social movements must recruit members and gain the economic resources necessary for nationwide or global social activism. Numerous sociological studies have shown that the local level constitutes a necessary microfoundation for larger-scale social movement activism (Buechler, 2000). According to social movement scholar Steve M. Buechler (2000:149),

Midrange attempts to solve social problems typically focus on how secondary groups and formal organizations deal with problems or seek to assist individuals in overcoming problems. An example is this grassroots social movement, whose members are protesting the placement of a low-level radioactive dumping site in their neighborhood.

TABLE 18.2 Selected Organizations That Seek to Reduce a Social Problem

Category	Organization	Web Site Address
Environment	Earth First!	www.earthfirst.com
	Sierra Club	www.sierraclub.org
	Student Environmental Action Coalition	www.seac.org
Driving While Drinking	Mothers Against Drunk Driving	www.madd.org
Wages and Working Conditions	Industrial Workers of the World	www.iww.org
Neighborhoods and Poverty	National Low Income Housing Coalition	www.nlihc.org
	National Neighborhood Coalition	www.neighborhoodcoalition.org
Violence and War	Food Not Bombs	www.foodnotbombs.net
	The Nonviolence Web	www.nonviolence.org

> [S]ome forms of activism not only require such microfoundations but also thematize local structures themselves as the sources of grievances, the site of resistance, or the goal of change. By consciously identifying local structures as the appropriate areas of contention, such movements comprise a distinct subset of the larger family of movements that all rely on microfoundations but do not all thematize local structures in this way.

To understand how grassroots organizations aid national social movements, consider the problem of environmental degradation. Leaders of national environmental organizations often participate in local or regional rallies, protests, and letter-writing or e-mail campaigns, particularly when politicians are making decisions that environmentalists believe will have a negative effect on the environment. By working with local and regional activists and seeking to influence local and regional power structures—city councils, statewide planning commissions, and legislatures—national organizations assert the need for their existence and attempt to garner additional supporters and revenue for their efforts nationwide or around the globe. By intertwining local, regional, and national organizational structures, these groups create a powerful voice for social change regarding some issue.

Limitations of the Midlevel Solutions Approach

Although local efforts to reduce problems affecting individuals and collectivities in a specific city or region bring about many improvements, they typically lack the sustained capacity to produce the larger, systemic changes at the national or international levels that are necessary to actually reduce or eliminate the problem. For example, New York City's Coalition for the Homeless recently challenged the city's attempt to impose work requirements at its homeless shelters. Although this effort certainly helped some of the city's homeless people, it did not address the structural factors in the political economy, such as job loss and lack of affordable housing, that contribute to homelessness.

Many people who are involved in midrange organizations see themselves primarily as local activists. Some display a bumper sticker saying, "Think globally, act locally" (Shaw, 1999). Many activists believe that in the absence of any sustained national agenda, national problems such as child poverty, low wages, and lack of affordable housing can be reduced by community-based organizations; but some analysts now believe that local activists must demand large-scale political and economic support to bring about necessary changes.

According to Randy Shaw (1999:2–3), the director of the Tenderloin Housing Clinic in San Francisco, California, and the founder of Housing America, a national mobilization campaign to increase federal housing funds,

> America's corporate and political elite has succeeded in controlling the national agenda because citizen activists and organizations are not fully participating in the struggles shaping national political life. As the constituencies central to reclaiming America's progressive ideas bypass national fights to pursue local issues, their adversaries have faced surprisingly little opposition in dismantling federal programs achieved by six decades of national grassroots struggle. Citizen activities and organizations have steadfastly maintained their local focus even as national policy making drastically cut the resources flowing to communities. From 1979 to 1997, for example, federal aid to local communities for job training, housing, mass transit, environmental protection, and economic development fell by almost one trillion real dollars.

As this statement suggests, those working in grassroots organizations might be fighting a losing battle because the loss of federal aid can only diminish their future efforts. Accordingly, some grassroots activists have changed their motto to "think locally and act globally" (Brecher and Costello, 1998), and now work at the macrolevel, attempting to educate national leaders and corporate executives about the part that governments and transnational corporations must play if social problems are to be reduced or solved.

MACROLEVEL ATTEMPTS TO SOLVE SOCIAL PROBLEMS

Macrolevel solutions to social problems focus on how large-scale social institutions such as the government and the media can be persuaded to become involved in remedying social problems. Sometimes individuals who view themselves as individually powerless bind together in organizations to make demands on those who make decisions at the national or global level. As one social analyst explains,

> Most individuals are largely powerless in the face of economic forces beyond their control. But because millions of other people are affected in the same way, they have a

> chance to influence their conditions through collective action. To do so, people must grasp that the common interest is also their own personal interest. This happens whenever individuals join a movement, a union, a party, or any organization pursuing a common goal. It happens when people push for a social objective—say universal health care or human rights—which benefits them by benefiting all those similarly situated. It underlies the development of an environmental movement which seeks to preserve the environment on which all depend. (Brecher and Costello, 1998:107)

For example, when U.S. workers organize to support the rights of workers in low-income nations and are able to bring about changes that keep them from having to compete with these workers, they not only help workers abroad, but also help themselves (Brecher and Costello, 1998).

Working Through Special-Interest Groups for Political Change

At the national level, those seeking macrolevel solutions to social problems may become members of a ***special-interest group*—a political coalition composed of individuals or groups sharing a specific interest they wish to protect or advance with the help of the political system** (Greenberg and Page, 1993). Examples of special-interest groups are the AFL-CIO and public interest or citizens groups such as the American Conservative Union and Zero Population Growth.

Through special-interest groups, which are sometimes called *pressure groups* or *lobbies,* people can seek to remedy social problems by exerting pressure on political leaders. These groups can be categorized on the basis of these factors:

1. *Issues.* Some groups focus on *single issues,* such as abortion, gun control, or school prayer; others focus on *multiple issues,* such as equal access to education, employment, and health care (Ash, 1972; Gamson, 1990).
2. *View of the present system of wealth and power.* Some groups make *radical demands* that would involve the end of patriarchy, capitalism, governmental bureaucracy, or other existing power structures; others do not attack the legitimacy of the present system of wealth and power but insist on specific social reforms (Ash, 1972; Gamson, 1990).
3. *Beliefs about elites.* Some groups want to *influence* elites or incorporate movement leaders into the elite; others want to *replace* existing elites with people whom they believe share their own interests and concerns (Ash, 1972; Gamson, 1990).

In recent decades, more special-interest groups have been single-issue groups that focus on electing and supporting politicians who support their views. There might be more than one single-interest group working to reduce or eliminate a specific social problem. Usually, however, these groups do not agree on the nature and extent of the problem or on proposed solutions to the problem. For this reason, competing single-interest groups aggressively place their demands in front of elected officials and bureaucratic policy makers (see Chapter 13).

Working Through National and International Social Movements to Reduce Problems

Collective behavior and national social movements are significant ways in which people seek to resolve social problems. ***Collective behavior* is voluntary, often spontaneous, activity that is engaged in by a large number of people and typically violates dominant group norms and values.** Public demonstrations and riots are examples of collective behavior. Since the civil rights movement in the 1960s, one popular form of public demonstration has been ***civil disobedience*—nonviolent action that seeks to change a policy or law by refusing to comply with it.** People often use civil disobedience in the form of sit-ins, marches, boycotts, and strikes to bring about change. When people refuse to abide by a policy or law and challenge authorities to do something about it, they are demanding social change with some sense of urgency.

Groups that engage in activities that they hope will achieve specific political goals are sometimes referred to as *protest crowds.* For example, during the 2008 Republican National Convention, about 10,000 protesters marched in St. Paul, Minnesota, to show their opposition to the war in Iraq and to call for the return of American troops to the United States. A second group of about 2,000 people marched on behalf of the homeless and the poor and to call attention to injustices they believed were perpetuated and exacerbated by government policies implemented during the Bush Administration. Among those in the protest crowds were members of Veterans for Peace, Iraq Veterans Against the War, Military Families Speak Out, the Teamsters, Code Pink, the American Indian Movement, and the Poor People's Economic Human Rights Campaign.

Demonstrators are a common sight at events such as the Republican National Convention where many people in 2008 called attention to their opposition to the war in Iraq. The individual shown here claims that he was injured by riot police while protesting at this convention. What effect, if any, do protestors have on bringing about social change?

What types of national and international social movements can be used to reduce social problems? National social movements can be divided into five major categories: reform, revolutionary, religious, alternative, and resistance movements. *Reform movements* seek to improve society by changing some specific aspect of the social structure. Environmental groups and disability rights groups are examples of groups that seek to change (reform) some specific aspect of the social structure. Reform movements typically seek to bring about change by working within the existing organizational structures of society, whereas *revolutionary movements* seek to bring about a total change in society. Examples of revolutionary movements include utopian groups and radical terrorist groups that use fear tactics to intimidate and gain—at least briefly—concessions from those with whom they disagree ideologically. Some radical terrorists kill many people in their pursuit of a society that more closely conforms to their own worldview.

Religious movements (also referred to as expressive movements) seek to renovate or renew people through inner change. Because these groups emphasize inner change, religious movements are often linked to local and regional organizations that seek to bring about changes in the individual's life. National religious movements often seek to persuade political officials to enact laws that will reduce or eliminate what they perceive to be a social problem. For example, some national religious movements view abortion as a problem and therefore lobby for a ban on abortions. In contrast, *alternative movements* seek limited change in some aspects of people's behavior. Currently, alternative movements include a variety of so-called New Age movements that emphasize such things as the development of a new national spiritual consciousness.

Finally, *resistance movements* seek to prevent change or undo change that has already occurred. In public debates over social policies, most social movements advocating change face resistance from reactive movements, which hold opposing viewpoints and want social policy to reflect their own beliefs and values. Examples of resistance movements include groups that oppose domestic partnership initiatives for gay or lesbian couples; antiabortion groups such as "Operation Rescue," which seek to close abortion clinics and make abortion illegal; and anti-immigrant groups that seek to close U.S. borders to outsiders or place harsher demands on immigrant workers.

Can national activism and social movements bring about the changes that are necessary to reduce social problems? Some analysts believe that certain social problems can be reduced through sustained efforts by organizations committed to change. According to social activist Randy Shaw (1999), efforts by Public Interest Research Groups and the Sierra Club, the nation's two largest grassroots environmental groups, have stimulated a new national environmental activism that is having an effect. Wanting to strengthen the Clean Air Act of 1967, these two organizations engaged in affirmative national environmental activism, mobilizing people who had previously been disconnected from national environmental debates (Shaw, 1999). As a result, a strong working relationship developed between grassroots activists at the local level and the leaders of the national movement. In the past, national groups had believed that their national leaders knew what was best for the environmental movement and had relied solely on their leadership's relationship with lawmakers to bring about change (Shaw, 1999). However, this belief changed as activists sought to strengthen the Clean Air Act:

> The Clean Air Act standards became a battle over framing the issue. If the public saw the new standards as a health issue environmentalists would prevail. Industry would win if, as in the health care debate [of the 1990s], it could define its campaign as trying to stop Big Government from hampering the private sector's ability to improve people's lives. The campaign would revisit the philosophical battleground where corporate America had increasingly

> prevailed in the past decade. Whether environmentalists' new emphasis on national grassroots mobilizing would change this would soon be seen. (Shaw, 1999:157)

Eventually, supporters declared that the clean air campaign had been a success and vowed that they would continue to demand changes that they believed would benefit the environment and improve the quality of life (Shaw, 1999).

What about global activism? Once again, we turn to the environmental movement for an example. According to Jared Diamond, a physiology professor and director of World Wildlife Fund, some transnational corporations are becoming aware that they have a responsibility for the environment. Diamond (2000) believes that a new attitude has taken hold of corporations such as Chevron and Home Depot, both of which now claim to realize that it is better to have a clean operation than to have costly industrial disasters. Of course, consumers have also demanded that corporations become more accountable for their actions: "Behind this trend lies consumers' growing awareness of the risks that environmental problems pose for the health, economies, and political stability of their own world and their children's world" (Diamond, 2000:A31). For example, growing consumer awareness has led some companies that buy and retail forest products to no longer sell wood products from environmentally sensitive areas of the world and instead give preference to certified wood—that is, lumber that has been derived from forests where guidelines for environmentally sound logging practices have been met (Diamond, 2000).

According to some analysts, what is needed is "globalization-from-below" (Brecher and Costello, 1998). In other words, people cannot rely on corporations to solve environmental problems. Indeed, it is necessary to develop a human agenda that will offset the corporate agenda that has produced many of the problems in the first place. Social activists Jeremy Brecher and Tim Costello (1998) suggest these criteria for any proposed human agenda:

- It should improve the lives of the great majority of the world's people over the long run.
- It should correspond to widely held common interests and should integrate the interests of people around the world.
- It should provide handles for action at a variety of levels.
- It should include elements that can be at least partially implemented independently but that are compatible or mutually reinforcing.
- It should make it easier, not harder, to solve noneconomic problems such as protection of the environment and reduction of war.
- It should grow organically out of social movements and coalitions that have developed in response to the needs of diverse peoples.

On the basis of these guidelines, the only way in which a major global social problem, such as environmental degradation or world poverty, can be reduced is through a drastic redirection of our energies, as Brecher and Costello (1998:184) explain:

> The energies now directed to the race to the bottom need to be redirected to the rebuilding of the global economy on a humanly and environmentally sound basis. Such an approach requires limits to growth—in some spheres, sharp reduction—in the material demands that human society places on the environment. It requires reduced energy and resource use; less toxic production and products; shorter individual worktime; and less production for war. But it requires vast growth in education, health care, human caring, recycling, rebuilding an ecologically sound production and consumption system, and time available for self-development, community life, and democratic participation.

Do you believe that such human cooperation is possible? Will it be possible for a new generation of political leaders to separate *politics* from *policy* and focus on discovering the best courses of action for the country and the world? Where do ideas regarding possible social policies come from? Some of the ideas and policies of tomorrow are being developed today in public policy organizations and think tanks (see Table 18.3 on page 384). If, as some analysts believe, these think tanks are increasingly setting the U.S. government's agenda, how much do we know about these groups, their spokespersons, and the causes they advocate?

Perhaps gaining more information about the current state of U.S. and global affairs is the first step toward our individual efforts to be part of the solution rather than part of the problem in the future.

Limitations of the Macrolevel Solution Approach

As C. Wright Mills stated, social problems by definition cannot be resolved without organizational initiatives that bring about social change. Therefore macrolevel approaches are necessary for reducing or eliminating many social problems. However, some analysts believe that macrolevel approaches overemphasize structural barriers

TABLE 18.3 Examples of Public Policy Organizations and Think Tanks

Action Institute for the Study of Religion and Liberty	Family Research Council
Adam Smith Institute	Fight Internet Taxes!
The AFL-CIO	Frontiers of Freedom Institute
Alliance for America	Galen Institute
American Civil Liberties Union	Goldwater Institute
American Conservative Union	Heartland Institute
American Enterprise Institute	Heritage Foundation
The American Institute for Full Employment	Hoover Institute
Americans for a Balanced Budget	Hudson Institute
Americans for Democratic Action	Independence Institute
Americans for Hope, Growth and Opportunity	Institute for Civic Values
Americans for Tax Reform	Institute for Economic Analysis, Inc.
Amnesty International	Institute for First Amendment Studies
Atlas Economic Research Foundation	Institute for Global Communications
Brookings Institution	Institute for Justice
Campaign for America's Future	Institute for Policy Innovation
The Carter Center	Leadership Institute
Cascade Policy Institute	League of Conservative Voters
Cato Institute	League of Women Voters
Center of the American Experiment	Ludwig von Mises Institute
Center for Defense Information	Madison Institute
Center for Equal Opportunity	Manhattan Institute
Center for Individual Rights	National Organization for Women
Center for Law and Social Policy	National Rifle Association
Center for Policy Alternatives	OMB Watch
Center to Prevent Handgun Violence	People for the American Way
Center for Public Integrity	Pioneer Institute for Public Policy Research
Center for Responsive Politics	Planned Parenthood
Century Foundation	Progress and Freedom Foundation
Children's Defense Fund	Project for Defense Alternatives
Christian Coalition	Public Citizen
Citizens Against Government Waste	RAND Corporation
Citizens for an Alternative Tax System	Reason Foundation
Citizens for Tax Justice	Tax Reform NOW!
Clare Boothe Luce Policy Institute	Union of Concerned Scientists
Claremont Institute	U.S. Term Limits
Discovery Institute	Worldwatch Institute
Economic Policy Institute	Young America's Foundation
Empower America	

in society and give people the impression that these barriers are insurmountable walls that preclude social change. Macrolevel approaches might also deemphasize the importance of individual responsibility. Reducing the availability of illegal drugs, for example, does not resolve the problem of the individual drug abuser who still needs a means to eliminate the problem in her or his personal life. Similarly, macrolevel approaches usually do not allow for the possibility of positive communication and the kind of *human cooperation* that transcends national boundaries (Brecher and Costello, 1998). Experience, however, has shown us that positive communication and global cooperation are possible.

According to sociologist Immanuel Wallerstein, a former president of the International Sociological Association:

> We live in an imperfect world, one that will always be imperfect and therefore always harbor injustice. But we are far from helpless before this reality. We can make the world less unjust; we can make it more beautiful; we can increase our cognition of it. We need but to construct it, and in order to construct it we need but to reason with each other and struggle to obtain from each other the special knowledge that each of us has been able to seize. We can labor in the vineyards and bring forth fruit, if only we try. (Wallerstein, 1999:250)

In any case, a sociological approach to examining social problems provides us with new ideas about how to tackle some of the most pressing issues of our times (see Box 18.2).

We have seen that different theoretical approaches to analyzing social problems bring us to a variety of conclusions about how we might reduce or eliminate certain problems. Let's take a last look at the major sociological theories we have studied so that we can relate them one more time to social problems, an activity which you will hopefully continue in the future as new challenges arise and older problems continue to need resolution.

FINAL REVIEW OF SOCIAL THEORIES AND SOCIAL PROBLEMS

The underlying theoretical assumptions that we hold regarding social problems often have a profound influence on what we feel may be the best solution for a specific problem. Do we believe society is based on

Critical Thinking and You

Box 18.2

Applying Sociology to the Ordinary and the Extraordinary in Everyday Life

> [In the aftermath of Hurricane Katrina in New Orleans], you're now looking at a situation in which, when people return, they may have to find work.... Both close ties [with others] and extended relationships will be very important, and it's likely the people who have both will do best.
>
> —*Jeanne Hulbert, a sociologist at Louisiana State University in Baton Rouge, talks about studies on hurricane disasters she and her colleagues conducted that show a clear link between people's mental health and the kinds of social relationships they have. (Carey, 2005:A20)*

> People don't know until something like this comes along how much the shape of their house, the texture of their house, the mood of their neighborhood, are important parts of who they are. People take all of this so much for granted that when they return and the house is gone or not habitable it disorients them, makes them more lonely and more afraid, and they don't know why. This is true of public spaces and streets, too. You have no idea how much they mean to you until they are gone or permanently altered.
>
> —*Kai Erikson, a sociologist at Yale University and author of several books about disasters, including* Everything In Its Path: Destruction of Community in the Buffalo Creek Flood, *looks at the sociological psychology of how people deal with disasters. (Carey, 2005:A20)*

In times of crisis, including natural disasters, terrorist attacks, war, and other cataclysmic events, sociologists are often called

(continued)

Box 18.2 *(continued)*

upon to discuss these events as they affect individuals, groups, and nations. Because sociologists in academic and research settings are continually engaged in research in their areas of specialization, they are authorities on topics such as the social psychology of survival. As a result of years of theorizing and research, scholars such as Jeanne Hulbert and Kai Erikson (quoted above) gain and share with others significant insights on social phenomenon such as how people react to disasters.

However, we do not necessarily need to be experts in order to put basic sociological ideas into practice. Sociological insights on social problems can be used in a variety of fields, including criminal justice, community and human services, health care and substance abuse programs, and disaster relief efforts. But, perhaps more importantly to each of us, sociology can be used in our everyday life to help us understand what is going on around us and to evaluate the quality of life in our own community. As a final critical thinking activity in this course, let's take a new look at the city where you live.

Questions for Critical Thinking

1. Media discussions about the disaster in New Orleans often called attention to a "rich section" or "poor section" of the city. Can you identify areas of your city that could be classified as upper, middle, or lower class? If so, what sociological factors did you use to distinguish among the various areas and the people who live in each?

2. Can you identify distinct racial or ethnic patterns with regard to where people live in your city? If a reporter asked you the following question, how would you answer: "Do you think that race or class is the most important factor in determining where people in your community live?" In answering this question, is it possible that race and class are so intertwined as factors relating to privilege or deprivation that giving the reporter an "either/or" answer is virtually impossible?

stability or conflict? Is conflict typically good for society or bad for society? According to the functionalist perspective, society is a stable, orderly system that is composed of a number of interrelated parts, each of which performs a function that contributes to the overall stability of the society. From the functionalist perspective, social problems arise when social institutions do not fulfill the functions they are supposed to perform or when dysfunctions (undesirable consequences of an activity or social process that inhibit a society's ability to adapt or adjust) occur. For example, in the aftermath of Hurricane Katrina, all levels of government were severely criticized for the excessive amount of time it took to get military personnel and emergency evacuation crews to disaster sites and to provide food, water, sanitation, and transportation for those who were displaced by the storm. If the vast problems experienced by individuals living in the Gulf Coast states are symptomatic of larger gaps in national emergency preparedness, the U.S. government will continue to be accused of indifference, incompetence, or even worse. According to the functionalist approach, dysfunctions create social disorganization, which in turn causes a breakdown in the traditional values and norms that serve as social control mechanisms. As shown in Table 18.4, the social disorganization approach traces the causes of social problems to social change that leaves existing rules inadequate for current conditions. In societies undergoing social change—for example, high rates of immigration, rapid changes in technology, and increasingly complex patterns of social life—social disorganization produces stress at the individual level and inefficiency and confusion at the institutional and societal levels. Thus, the functionalist approach to reducing social problems has as central factors the prevention of rapid social changes, the maintenance of the status quo, and the restoration of order.

In contrast, the conflict perspective assumes that conflict is natural and inevitable in society. Value conflict approaches focus on conflict between the values held by members of divergent groups. These approaches also highlight the ways in which cultural, economic, and social diversity may contribute to misunderstandings and problems. According to Marxist (or critical-conflict) theorists, groups are engaged in a continuous power struggle for control of scarce resources. As a result of the unjust use of political, economic, or social power, certain groups of people are privileged while others are disadvantaged. Thus for

TABLE 18.4 Perceived Problems and Possible Solutions

Perspective	Causes	Possible Solutions
Functionalist:		
Social disorganization	Social change; inadequacy of existing social rules	Development and implementation of social rules that are explicit, workable, and consistent
Conflict:		
Value conflict	Conflict between different groups' values; economic, social, and cultural diversity	Group action involving confrontation of opponents and working for lasting changes in policy or legislation
Critical conflict (Marxist)	Relations of domination and subordination are reinforced by the global capitalist economy and political leaders who put other priorities ahead of the good of the people	Changing the nature of society, particularly inequalities that grow more pronounced as the wealthy grow richer and the poor worldwide become increasingly impoverished
Symbolic Interactionist:		
Deviant behavior	Inappropriate socialization within primary groups	Resocialize or rehabilitate people so that they will conform
Labeling	How people label behavior, how they respond to it, and the consequences of their responses	Changing the definition through decriminalization; limit labeling

Source: Based on Weinberg, Rubington, and Hammersmith, 1981; Feagin, Baker, and Feagin, 2006.

critical-conflict theorists, social problems arise out of major contradictions that are inherent in the ways in which societies are organized. When this approach is used, the root causes of social problems—patriarchy, capitalism, and massive spending on the U.S. military-industrial complex at the expense of human services, for example—must be radically altered or eliminated altogether. Focusing on the political economy, one critical-conflict approach states that the capitalist economy, which is now global, maintains and reinforces domination and subordination in social relations. This approach also examines how political leaders might put their own interests ahead of any common good that might exist. Clearly, any solutions to social problems by this approach would require radical changes in society and thus are not always viewed positively in societies in which economic prosperity based on individual attributes rather than collective activities is considered a mark of personal and social achievement. Other conflict theorists view the interlocking nature of race, class, and gender as systems of domination and subordination as central concerns to social problems. Therefore their solutions for reducing or eliminating social problems that are embedded in racial and ethnic relations, class relationships, and gender inequalities also require dramatic changes in society.

At the macrolevel, globalization theories make us aware that many social problems transcend the borders of any one nation and are often international in their causes and consequences. As some social scientists have suggested, any solution to global social problems will require new thinking about how business, politics, and civil society ought to work together and how nation-states worldwide must establish policies and enact legislation that will benefit not only their own constituents but also the global community (Richard, 2002).

If we shift to the microlevel, the symbolic interactionist perspective focuses on how people act toward one another and make sense of their daily lives. From this perspective, society is the sum of the interactions of individuals and groups. Thus symbolic interactionists often study social problems by analyzing the process whereby a behavior is defined as a social problem and how individuals and groups come to engage in activities that a significant number of people view as major social concerns. Symbolic interactionist theories of deviance note that inadequate socialization or interacting with the "wrong" people may contribute to deviant behavior and crime. Similarly, interactionists who use the labeling framework for their analysis of social problems study how people label behavior, how they respond to people engaged in such behavior, and the consequences of their behavior (Weinberg, Rubington, and Hammersmith, 1981). Essentially, a symbolic interactionist approach helps us to understand why certain actions are significant to people and how people communicate what these actions mean to them. For example, fear of potential terrorism can affect how people think and behave, whether or not they are actually in harm's way and have real cause to modify their daily routines and encounters with others.

Why were some people referred to as "looters" in the aftermath of Hurricane Katrina while others were described as "appropriating what they needed to survive"? According to symbolic interactionists, social problems may be viewed differently based on who is participating in the activity and what is believed to be the cause of their conduct.

A symbolic interactionist approach can also help us understand how low-income people caught up in a natural disaster such as Hurricane Katrina might engage in illegal behavior that they otherwise might never have considered, such as pilfering and looting, because of the magnitude of the tragedy facing them and the brief opportunity that presents itself to get "free" food, supplies, and perhaps "luxury" items such as expensive television sets or jewelry they otherwise would never have been able to afford. Moreover, only limited plans had been made by officials to successfully evacuate these individuals should the need ever arise, as one journalist stated:

> The victims...were largely black and poor, those who toiled in the background of the tourist havens, living in tumbledown neighborhoods that were long known to be vulnerable to disaster if the levees failed. Without so much as a car or bus fare to escape ahead of time, they found themselves left behind by a failure to plan for their rescue should the dreaded day ever arrive. (Gonzalez, 2005:A1, A19)

And, indeed, when that day did arrive, the majority of the victims who were hardest hit were those who lived at the margins of society and who were left behind not only when people were initially evacuated from the city before the storm hit but also when initial rescue efforts were so slow getting started. From a symbolic interactionist perspective, an ordeal such as resulted from Hurricane Katrina is likely to affect how people think and feel about themselves and others, how they view "reality," and the labels they use to identify themselves and their needs in relation to others. For example, some of the poor and black victims who prior to the disaster were struggling mightily now find themselves with new labels, including "homeless," "destitute," and "refugee."

Each of these sociological perspectives suggests ways in which social problems may be identified and remedies may be sought. In doing so, these theories provide divergent views on social change that might reduce or eliminate social problems. We are left with one final question as we conclude this book and our time together: Won't you join with sociologists and others who seek to face up to one of the greatest challenges of the twenty-first century, which is how to bring peace, justice, and greater social equality to as many of the world's people as possible?

SUMMARY

■ *Why is it difficult to reduce or eliminate social problems?*

According to social scientists, reducing or solving social problems is more complex than simply identifying such problems and pinpointing their social locations because many obstacles, delays, and frustrations confront those who attempt to bring about social changes that might alleviate the problems. Solving a problem can entail prohibitive costs and may only give rise to a whole new set of problems.

■ *What is social change and why is it important in reducing social problems?*

Social change refers to the alternation, modification, or transformation of public policy, culture, or social institutions over time. Social change is important in reducing social problems because a combination of strategies, some previously untried, are usually required to reduce major social problems.

■ *What are microlevel solutions to social problems? What are the limitations of this approach?*

Microlevel solutions to social problems focus on how individuals operate within small groups to try to remedy a problem that affects them, their family, or friends. Most people turn to their primary groups to help them deal with a problem. However, solving social problems one person at a time does not take into account the fact that secondary groups and societal institutions play a significant part in creating, maintaining, and exacerbating many social problems.

■ *What are midrange attempts to deal with social problems? What are the limitations of this approach?*

Midrange attempts to deal with social problems focus on how secondary groups and formal organizations deal with problems or seek to assist individuals in overcoming problems such as addiction to drugs or alcohol. Grassroots groups often work to change a perceived wrong in their neighborhood, city, state, or nation. Although local efforts to reduce problems that affect individuals and collectivities in a specific city or region have brought about many improvements in the social life of individuals and small groups, they usually lack the sustained capacity to produce the larger systemic changes needed at the national or international levels to reduce or eliminate the problems.

■ *What are macrolevel attempts to deal with social problems? What are the limitations of this approach?*

Macrolevel solutions to social problems focus on how large-scale social institutions such as the government and the media can become involved in remedying social problems. Some people work through social movements, others through special-interest groups, and still others through various forms of collective behavior. Although macro-level approaches are necessary for reducing or eliminating many social problems, some analysts believe that these approaches overemphasize structural barriers in society and give people the impression that these barriers constitute insurmountable walls that preclude social change. Macrolevel approaches can also deemphasize the importance of individual responsibility.

■ *What are three key factors that can be used to differentiate special-interest groups?*

The three factors by which special-interest groups may be categorized are (1) issues (single issue versus multiple demands), (2) view of the present system of wealth and power (positive versus negative), and (3) beliefs about elites (whether to try to influence elites or seek to replace them).

■ *What is collective behavior? How does civil disobedience occur?*

Collective behavior is voluntary, often spontaneous activity that is engaged in by a large number of people and typically violates dominant group norms and values. As a form of collective behavior, civil disobedience refers to nonviolent action that seeks to change a policy or law by refusing to comply with it.

■ *What are the key characteristics of the five major categories of national social movements?*

National social movements are divided into five major categories: reform, revolutionary, religious, alternative, and resistance movements. Reform movements seek to improve society by changing some specific aspect of the social structure. Revolutionary movements seek to bring about a total change in society. Religious movements seek to renovate or renew people through "inner change." Alternative movements seek limited change in some aspects of people's behavior and currently include a variety of so-called New Age movements. Resistance movements seek to prevent change or undo change that has already occurred.

■ *What is a human agenda? What might be the major criteria for such an agenda?*

According to some analysts, we need to develop a human agenda that focuses on the needs of people and offsets the corporate agenda that is currently taking precedence over other issues and concerns. Social activists Jeremy Brecher and Tim Costello suggest that any proposed human agenda should (1) improve the lives of the great majority of the world's people, (2) correspond to widely held common interests, as well as integrate the interests of people worldwide, (3) provide handles for action at a variety of levels, (4) include elements that can be implemented independently, at least in part, but that are compatible or mutually reinforcing, (5) make it easier to solve noneconomic problems such as environmental pollution, and (6) grow out of social movements and coalitions that have developed in response to the needs of diverse peoples.

■ *What is the primary focus of functionalist, conflict, and interactionist approaches to solving social problems?*

From the functionalist perspective, social problems arise when social institutions do not fulfill the functions they are supposed to or when dysfunctions occur; therefore, social institutions need to be made more effective, and social change needs to be managed carefully. According to critical-conflict theorists, social problems arise out of the major contradictions inherent in the way societies are organized (particularly factors such as patriarchy and capitalism). Consequently, attempting to solve social problems requires major changes in the political economy. Symbolic interactionists focus on how certain behavior comes to be defined as a social problem and why some individuals and groups engage in that behavior. To reduce problems entails more adequate socialization of people as well as a better understanding of how labeling affects people's behavior.

KEY TERMS

civil disobedience, p. 382
collective behavior, p. 381
grassroots groups, p. 378
infrastructure, p. 372
primary groups, p. 376
Secondary groups, p. 377
social change, p. 375
social movement, p. 379
special-interest group, p. 381

QUESTIONS FOR CRITICAL THINKING

1. Do you believe that corporations can be trusted to do the right thing when it comes to reducing or eliminating existing social problems? Is good corporate citizenship a possibility in the global economy today? Why or why not?
2. Suppose that you were given the economic resources and political clout to reduce a major social problem. Which problem would you choose? What steps would you take to alleviate this problem? How would you measure your success or failure in reducing or eliminating the problem?
3. What is most useful about applying a sociological perspective to the study of social problems? What is least useful about a sociological approach? How can you contribute to a better understanding of the causes, effects, and possible solutions to social problems?

Glossary

absolute poverty a condition that exists when people do not have the means to secure the most basic necessities of life.

acid rain rainfall containing large concentrations of sulfuric and nitric acids (primarily from the burning of fuel and car and truck exhausts).

acquaintance rape forcible sexual activity that meets the legal definition of rape and involves people who first meet in a social setting.

acute diseases illnesses that strike suddenly and cause dramatic incapacitation and sometimes death.

ageism prejudice and discrimination against people on the basis of age.

amalgamation (the melting pot model) a process in which the cultural attributes of diverse racial-ethnic groups are blended together to form a new society incorporating the unique contributions of each group.

Anglo-conformity model a pattern of assimilation whereby members of subordinate racial-ethnic groups are expected to conform to the culture of the dominant (white) Anglo-Saxon population.

anti-Semitism prejudice and discriminatory behavior directed at Jews.

assimilation the process by which members of subordinate racial and ethnic groups become absorbed into the dominant culture.

blaming the victim a practice used by people who view a social problem as emanating from within the individual who exhibits the problem.

blended family a family that consists of a husband and wife, children from previous marriages, and children (if any) from the new marriage.

capitalism an economic system characterized by private ownership of the means of production, from which personal profits can be derived through market competition and without government intervention.

chronic diseases illnesses that are long-term or lifelong and that develop gradually or are present from birth.

civil disobedience nonviolent action that seeks to change a policy or law by refusing to comply with it.

class system a system of social inequality based on the ownership and control of resources and on the type of work people do.

codependency a reciprocal relationship between the alcoholic and one or more nonalcoholics who unwittingly aid and abet the alcoholic's excessive drinking and resulting behavior.

cohabitation two adults living together in a sexual relationship without being legally married.

collective behavior voluntary, often spontaneous, activity that is engaged in by a large number of people and typically violates dominant-group norms and values.

collective violence organized violence by people seeking to promote their cause or resist social policies or practices that they consider oppressive.

comparable worth the belief that wages ought to reflect the worth of a job, not the gender or race of the worker.

conflict perspective a framework for viewing society that is based on the assumption that groups in society are engaged in a continuous power struggle for control of scarce resources.

contingent work part-time work, temporary work, and subcontracted work that offers advantages to employers but can be detrimental to workers' welfare.

core nations dominant capitalist centers characterized by high levels of industrialization and urbanization.

corporate crime illegal acts committed by corporate employees on behalf of the corporation and with its support.

crime a behavior that violates criminal law and is punishable by a fine, a jail term, or other negative sanctions.

criminal justice system the network of organizations, including the police, courts, jails, and prisons, involved in law enforcement and the administration of justice.

cultural capital social assets, such as values, beliefs, attitudes, and competencies in language and culture, that are learned at home and required for success and social advancement.

culture the knowledge, language, values, customs, and material objects that are passed from person to person and from one generation to the next in a human group or society.

deinstitutionalization the practice of discharging patients from mental hospitals into the community.

democracy a political system in which the people hold the ruling power either directly or through elected representatives.

demographic transition theory the process by which some societies move from high birth and death rates to relatively low birth and death rates as a result of technological development.

demography the study of the size, composition, and distribution of populations.

dependency ratio the number of workers necessary to support people under age fifteen and over age sixty-three.

desertification the process by which usable land is turned into desert because of overgrazing, harmful agricultural practices, or deforestation.

deviance a behavior, belief, or condition that violates social norms.

differential association theory the belief that individuals have a greater tendency to deviate from societal norms when they frequently associate with people who tend toward deviance rather than conformity.

disability a restricted or total lack of ability to perform certain activities as a result of physical limitations or the interplay of these limitations, social responses, and the social environment.

discrimination actions or practices of dominant- group members (or their representatives) that have a harmful impact on members of subordinate groups.

domestic partnership a household partnership in which an unmarried couple lives together in a committed, sexually intimate relationship and is granted the same rights and benefits accorded to a married couple.

dominant group a group that is advantaged and has superior resources and rights in a society.

drug any substance—other than food or water—that, when taken into the body, alters its functioning in some way.

drug addiction (or drug dependency) a psychological and/or physiological need for a drug to maintain a sense of well-being and avoid withdrawal symptoms.

drug subculture a group of people whose attitudes, beliefs, and behaviors pertaining to drug use differ significantly from those of most people in the larger society.

dual-earner marriages marriages in which both spouses are in the labor force.

economy the social institution that ensures that a society will be maintained through its production, distribution, and consumption of goods and services.

edge city an area of middle- to upper-middle-class residences with complete working, shopping, and leisure activities so that it is not dependent on the central city or other suburbs.

education the social institution responsible for transmitting knowledge, skills, and cultural values in a formally organized structure.

elite model a view of society in which power in political systems is concentrated in the hands of a small group, whereas the masses are relatively powerless.

environmental degradation disruptions to the environment that have negative consequences for ecosystems.

environmental racism the belief that a disproportionate number of hazardous facilities are placed in areas populated primarily by poor people and people of color.

environmental tobacco smoke the smoke in the air as a result of other people's tobacco smoking.

erotica materials that depict consensual sexual activities that are sought by and pleasurable to all parties involved.

ethnic group a category of people who are distinguished, by others or by themselves, as inferior or superior, primarily on the basis of cultural or nationality characteristics.

ethnic pluralism the coexistence of diverse racial-ethnic groups with separate identities and cultures within a society.

ethnocentrism the assumption that one's own group and way of life are superior to all others.

extended family a family unit composed of relatives in addition to parents and children, all of whom live in the same household.

families relationships in which people live together with commitment, form an economic unit and care for any young, and consider the group critical to their identity.

family of orientation the family into which a person is born and in which early socialization takes place.

family of procreation the family that a person forms by having or adopting children.

felony a serious crime, such as murder, rape, or aggravated assault, that is punishable by more than a year's imprisonment or even death.

feminization of poverty the trend whereby women are disproportionately represented among individuals living in poverty.

fertility the number of children born to an individual or a population.

fetal alcohol syndrome (FAS) a condition characterized by mental retardation and craniofacial malformations that may affect the child of an alcoholic mother.

field research the study of social life in its natural setting: observing and interviewing people where they live, work, and play.

forcible rape the act of forcing sexual intercourse on an adult of legal age against her will.

framing the manner in which news content and its accompanying visual images are linked together to create certain audience perceptions and give specific impressions to viewers and readers.

functionalist perspective a framework for viewing society as a stable, orderly system composed of a number of interrelated parts, each of which performs a function that contributes to the overall stability of society.

functionally illiterate being unable to read and/or write at the skill level necessary for carrying out everyday tasks.

gender culturally and socially constructed differences between females and males that are based on meanings, beliefs, and practices that a group or society associates with "femininity" or "masculinity."

gender bias a situation in which favoritism is shown toward one gender.

gendered division of labor the process whereby productive tasks are separated on the basis of gender.

gendered racism the interactive effect of racism and sexism in exploiting women of color.

gender gap the difference between a candidate's number of votes from women and men.

genocide the deliberate, systematic killing of an entire people or nation.

gentrification the process by which people renovate or restore properties in city centers.

glass ceiling the invisible institutional barrier constructed by male management that prevents women from reaching top positions in major corporations and other large-scale organizations.

government a formal organization that has legal and political authority to regulate relationships among people in a society and between the society and others outside its borders.

grassroots groups organizations started by ordinary people who work in concert to change a perceived wrong in their neighborhood, city, state, or nation.

greenhouse effect an environmental condition caused by excessive quantities of carbon dioxide, water vapor, methane, and nitrous oxide in the atmosphere.

hate crime a physical attack against a person because of assumptions regarding his or her racial group, ethnicity, religion, disability, sexual orientation, national origin, or ancestry.

health maintenance organization (HMO) an organization that provides, for a fixed monthly fee, total health care with an emphasis on prevention to avoid costly treatment later.

hegemony theory the view that the media are instruments of social control and are used by members of the ruling classes to create "false consciousness" in the working classes.

hidden curriculum how certain cultural values and attitudes, such as conformity and obedience to authority, are transmitted through implied demands in the everyday rules and routines of schools.

high-income nations countries with highly industrialized economies; technologically advanced industrial, administrative, and service occupations; and relatively high levels of national and per capita (per person) income.

homophobia excessive fear or intolerance of homo-sexuality.

hospices organizations that provide a homelike facility or home-based care (or both) for people who are terminally ill.

illegitimate opportunity structures circumstances that allow people to acquire through illegitimate activities what they cannot achieve legitimately.

income the economic gain derived from wages, salaries, income transfers (governmental aid such as Temporary Aid to Needy Families, known as TANF), or ownership of property.

individual discrimination one-on-one acts by members of the dominant group that harm members of the subordinate group or their property.

industrialization the process by which societies are transformed from a dependence on agriculture and handmade products to an emphasis on manufacturing and related industries.

infant mortality rate the number of deaths of infants under one year of age per 1,000 live births in a given year.

infrastructure a framework of support systems, such as transportation and utilities, that makes it possible to have specific land uses and a built environment that facilitate people's daily activities and the nation's economy.

institutional discrimination the day-to-day practices of organizations and institutions that have a harmful impact on members of subordinate groups.

interactionist perspective a framework that views society as the sum of the interactions of individuals and groups.

internal colonialism a process that occurs when members of a racial-ethnic group are conquered or colonized and forcibly placed under the economic and political control of the dominant group.

juvenile delinquency a violation of law or the commission of a status offense by a young person under a specific age.

kinship a social network of people based on common ancestry, marriage, or adoption.

labeling theory the proposition that delinquents and criminals are those people who have been successfully labeled as such by others.

latent functions hidden, unstated, and sometimes unintended consequences of activities in an organization or institution.

life chances the extent to which individuals have access to important societal resources such as food, clothing, shelter, education, and health care.

life expectancy an estimate of the average lifetime of people born in a specific year.

lifestyle–routine activity approach the belief that the patterns and timing of people's daily movements and activities as they go about obtaining the necessities of life—such as food, shelter, companionship, and entertainment—are the keys to understanding violent personal crimes and other types of crime in our society.

low-income nations primarily agrarian countries with little industrialization and low levels of national and personal income.

macrolevel analysis focuses on social processes occurring at the societal level, especially in large-scale organizations and major social institutions such as politics, government, and the economy.

managed care any system of cost containment that closely monitors and controls health care providers' decisions about medical procedures, diagnostic tests, and other services that should be provided to patients.

manifest functions open, stated, and intended goals or consequences of activities within an organization or institution.

mass murder the killing of four or more people at one time and in one place by the same person.

master status the most significant status a person possesses because it largely determines how individuals view themselves and how they are treated by others.

mechanical solidarity social bonds based on shared religious beliefs and a simple division of labor.

media concentration the tendency of the media industries to cluster together in groups with the goal of enhancing profitability.

media industries major businesses that own or own interests in radio and television production and broadcasting; motion pictures, movie theaters, and music companies; newspaper, periodical (magazine), and book publishing; and Internet services and content providers that influence people and cultures worldwide.

medical-industrial complex a term that encompasses both local physicians and hospitals as well as global health-related industries such as the pharmaceutical and medical supply companies that deliver health care today.

megalopolis a continuous concentration of two or more cities and their suburbs that have grown until they form an interconnected urban area.

melting pot model *see* amalgamation.

microlevel analysis focuses on small-group relations and social interaction among individuals.

middle-income nations countries undergoing transformation from agrarian to industrial economies.

migration the movement of people from one geographic area to another for the purpose of changing residency.

military-industrial complex the interdependence of the military establishment and private military contractors.

misdemeanor a relatively minor crime that is punishable by a fine or less than a year in jail.

mixed economy an economic system that combines elements of both capitalism (a market economy) and socialism (a command economy).

monogamy a marriage between one woman and one man.

monopoly a situation that exists when a single firm controls an industry and accounts for all sales in a specific market.

mortality the number of deaths that occur in a specific population.

murder the unlawful, intentional killing of one person by another.

norms established rules of behavior or standards of conduct.

nuclear family a family unit composed of one or two parents and their dependent children who live apart from other relatives.

obscenity the legal term for pornographic materials that are offensive by generally accepted standards of decency.

occupational (white-collar) crime illegal activities committed by people in the course of their employment or normal business activity.

oligopoly a situation in which a small number of companies or suppliers control an entire industry or service.

organic solidarity social bonds based on interdependence and an elaborate division of labor (specialization).

organized crime a business operation that supplies illegal goods and services for profit.

patriarchy a hierarchical system of social organization in which cultural, political, and economic structures are controlled by men.

peripheral nations nations that depend on core nations for capital, have little or no industrialization (other than what may be brought in by core nations), and have uneven patterns of urbanization.

permanent government the top-tier civil service bureaucrats who have a strong power base and play a major role in developing and implementing government policies and procedures.

perspective an overall approach or viewpoint toward some subject.

pink-collar occupations relatively low-paying, nonmanual, semi-skilled positions that are held primarily by women.

plea bargaining a process in a criminal trial whereby the prosecution negotiates a reduced sentence in exchange for a guilty plea.

pluralistic model the view that power is widely dispersed throughout many competing interest groups in our political system.

political action committees (PACs) special-interest groups that fund campaigns to help elect (or defeat) candidates based on their positions on specific issues.

political economy the interdependent workings and interests of political and economic systems.

politics the social institution through which power is acquired and exercised by some people and groups.

population composition the biological and social characteristics of a population, including such attributes as age, sex, race, marital status, education, occupation, income, and size of household.

pornography the graphic depiction of sexual behavior through pictures and/or words—including by electronic or other data retrieval systems—in a manner that is intended to be sexually arousing.

poverty rate the proportion of the population whose income falls below the government's official poverty line—the level of income below which a family of a given size is considered to be poor.

power the ability of people to achieve their goals despite opposition from others.

power elite rulers of the United States, which at the top is composed of business leaders, the executive branch of the federal government, and the military (especially the "top brass" at the Pentagon).

prejudice a negative attitude based on faulty generalizations about members of selected racial and ethnic groups.

prestige the respect, esteem, or regard accorded to an individual or group by others.

primary deviance the initial act of rule breaking.

primary groups small, less specialized groups in which members engage in face-to-face, emotion-based interactions over an extended period of time.

primary prevention programs that seek to prevent drug problems before they begin.

primary sector production the extraction of raw materials and natural resources from the environment.

property crime the taking of money or property from another without force, the threat of force, or the destruction of property.

prostitution the sale of sexual services (of oneself or another) for money or goods and without emotional attachment.

punishment any action designed to deprive a person of things of value (including liberty) because of an offense the person is thought to have committed.

racial group a category of people who have been singled out, by others or themselves, sometimes as inferior or superior, on the basis of subjectively selected physical characteristics such as skin color, hair texture, and eye shape.

racism a set of attitudes, beliefs, and practices used to justify the superior treatment of one racial or ethnic group and the inferior treatment of another racial or ethnic group.

relative poverty a condition that exists when people may be able to afford basic necessities, such as food, clothing, and shelter, but cannot maintain an average standard of living in comparison to that of other members of their society or group.

repressive terrorism terrorism conducted by a government against its own citizens for the purpose of protecting an existing political order.

revolutionary terrorism acts of violence against civilians that are carried out by internal enemies of the government who want to bring about political change.

scapegoat a person or group that is blamed for some problem causing frustration and is therefore subjected to hostility or aggression by others.

secondary analysis of existing data a research design in which investigators analyze data that originally were collected by others for some other purpose.

secondary deviance the process that occurs when a person who has been labeled a deviant accepts that new identity and continues the deviant behavior.

secondary groups larger, more specialized groups in which members engage in impersonal, goal-oriented relationships for a limited period of time.

secondary sector production the processing of raw materials (from the primary sector) into finished products.

second shift the domestic work that many employed women perform at home after completing their work day on the job.

segregation the spatial and social separation of categories of people by race/ethnicity, class, gender, religion, or other social characteristics.

self-fulfilling prophecy the process by which an unsubstantiated belief or prediction results in behavior that makes the original false belief come true.

semiperipheral nations nations that are more developed than peripheral nations but less developed than core nations.

serial murder the killing of three or more people over more than a month by the same person.

sex the biological differences between females and males.

sexism the subordination of one sex, usually female, based on the assumed superiority of the other sex.

sexual harassment unwanted sexual advances, requests for sexual favors, or other verbal or physical conduct of a sexual nature.

sexuality attitudes, beliefs, and practices related to sexual attraction and intimate relationships with others.

sexual orientation a preference for emotional-sexual relationships with individuals of the same sex (homosexuality), the opposite sex (heterosexuality), or both (bisexuality).

situational approach the belief that violence results from a specific interaction process, termed a "situational transaction."

social bond theory the proposition that criminal behavior is most likely to occur when a person's ties to society are weakened or broken.

social change the alteration, modification, or transformation of public policy, culture, or social institutions over time.

social control the systematic practices developed by social groups to encourage conformity and discourage deviance.

social disorganization the conditions in society that undermine the ability of traditional social institutions to govern human behavior.

social gerontology the study of the social (nonphysical) aspects of aging.

socialism an economic system characterized by public ownership of the means of production, the pursuit of collective goals, and centralized decision making.

social learning theory a theory that is based on the assumption that people are likely to act out the behavior they see in role models and media sources.

social movement an organized group that acts collectively to promote or resist change through collective action.

social problem a social condition (such as poverty) or a pattern of behavior (such as substance abuse) that people believe warrants public concern and collective action to bring about change.

social stratification the hierarchical arrangement of large social groups on the basis of their control over basic resources.

society a large social grouping that shares the same geographical territory and is subject to the same political authority and dominant cultural expectations.

sociological imagination the ability to see the relationship between individual experiences and the larger society.

sociology the academic and scholarly discipline that engages in systematic study of human society and social interactions.

special-interest group a political coalition composed of individuals or groups sharing a specific interest they wish to protect or advance with the help of the political system.

state-sponsored terrorism political terrorism resulting from a government providing financial resources, weapons, and training for terrorists who conduct their activities in other nations.

statutory rape the act of having sexual intercourse with a person who is under the legal age of consent as established by state law.

stereotypes overgeneralizations about the appearance, behavior, or other characteristics of all members of a group.

strain theory the proposition that people feel strain when they are exposed to cultural goals that they cannot reach because they do not have access to culturally approved means of achieving those goals.

strategically significant weapon one that brings force to bear in such a way that it decisively erodes the war-making capability of the enemy.

subculture a group of people who share a distinctive set of cultural beliefs and behaviors that set them apart from the larger society.

subculture of violence hypothesis the hypothesis that violence is part of the normative expectations governing everyday behavior among young males in the lower classes.

subordinate (or minority) group a group whose members, because of physical or cultural characteristics, are disadvantaged and subjected to unequal treatment by the dominant group and regard themselves as objects of collective discrimination.

survey research a poll in which researchers ask respondents a series of questions about a specific topic and record their responses.

terrorism the use of calculated, unlawful physical force or threats of violence against a government, organization, or individual to gain some political, religious, economic, or social objective.

tertiary sector production providing services rather than goods as the primary source of livelihood.

theory a set of logically related statements that attempt to describe, explain, or predict social events.

theory of limited effects a theory that states that the media have a minimal effect on the attitudes and perceptions of individuals.

theory of racial formation a theory that states that the government substantially defines racial and ethnic relations.

tolerance a condition that occurs when larger doses of a drug are required over time to produce the same physical or psychological effect that was originally achieved by a smaller dose.

total institution a place where people are isolated from the rest of society for a period of time and come under the complete control of the officials who run the institution.

tracking assigning students to specific courses and educational programs on the basis of their test scores, previous grades, or both.

transnational corporation a large-scale business organization that is headquartered in one country but operates in many countries, which has the legal power (separate from individual owners or shareholders) to enter into contracts, buy and sell property, and engage in other business activity.

urbanization the process by which an increasing proportion of a population lives in cities rather than in rural areas.

values collective ideas about what is right or wrong, good or bad, and desirable or undesirable in a specific society.

victimless crime a crime that many people believe has no real victim because it involves willing participants in an economic exchange.

violence the use of physical force to cause pain, injury, or death to another, or damage to another's property.

violent crime actions involving force or the threat of force against others.

wage gap the disparity between women's and men's earnings.

War an organized, armed conflict between nations or distinct political fractions.

war system components of social institutions (e.g., the economy, government, and education) and cultural beliefs and practices that promote the development of warriors, weapons, and war as a normal part of the society and its foreign policy.

wealth the value of all economic assets, including income, personal property, and income-producing property.

weapons of mass destruction (WMD) nuclear, biological, chemical, or radiological weapons that can kill thousands of people and destroy vast amounts of property at one time.

weapons system military technology comprising a weapons platform (e.g., a ship, aircraft, or tank), a weapon (e.g., a gun, missile, o r torpedo), and the means of command and communication.

welfare state a program under which the government takes responsibility for specific categories of citizens by offering them certain services and benefits, such as employment, housing, health, education, or guaranteed income.

withdrawal a variety of physical and/or psychological symptoms that habitual drug users experience when they discontinue drug use.

zero population growth a situation in which a population is totally stable, one that neither grows nor decreases from year to year because births, deaths, and migration are in perfect balance.

References

aaionline. 2002. "Welcome to the Africa-America Institute." Retrieved Dec. 11, 2002. Online: http://www.aaionline.org.

AAUW Educational Foundation. 2001. *Hostile Hallways: Bullying, Teasing, and Sexual Harassment in School.* Washington, DC: American Association of University Women Educational Foundation.

Abbott, Sharon. 2000. "Motivation for Pursuing an Acting Career in Pornography." In Ronald Weitzer (Ed.), *Sex for Sale: Prostitution, Pornography, and the Sex Industry.* New York: Routledge, pp. 17–34.

ABC TV. 2007. "Cavemen." Retrieved April 29, 2008. Online: http://abc.go.com/primetime/cavemen/index?pn=about.

Abraham, Laurie Kaye. 1993. *Mama Might Be Better Off Dead: The Failure of Health Care in Urban America.* Chicago: University of Chicago Press.

Acuna, Rodolfo. 1984. *A Community Under Siege: A Chronicle of Chicanos East of the Los Angeles River, 1945–1975.* Los Angeles: Chicano Studies Research Center, University of California at Los Angeles.

Adams, Karen L., and Norma C. Ware. 1995. "Sexism and the English Language: The Linguistic Implications of Being a Woman." In Jo Freeman (Ed.), *Women: A Feminist Perspective* (5th ed.). Mountain View, CA: Mayfield Publishing, pp. 331–346.

Adams, Tom. 1991. *Grass Roots: How Ordinary People Are Changing America.* New York: Citadel Press.

Aday, David P., Jr. 1990. *Social Control at the Margins: Toward a General Understanding of Deviance.* Belmont, CA: Wadsworth.

Adorno, Theodor W., Else Frenkel-Brunswick, Daniel J. Levinson, and R. Nevitt Sanford. 1950. *The Authoritarian Personality.* New York: Harper & Row.

Alexander, Karl L., Doris Entwisle, and Maxine Thompson. 1987. "School Performance, Status Relations, and the Structure of Sentiment: Bringing the Teacher Back In." *American Sociological Review,* 52:665–682.

Allen, Robert L. 1974. *Reluctant Reformers.* Washington, DC: Howard University Press.

Almaguer, Tomás. 1995. "Chicano Men: A Cartography of Homosexual Identity and Behavior." In Michael S. Kimmel and Michael A. Messner (Eds.), *Men's Lives* (3rd ed.). Boston: Allyn and Bacon, pp. 418–431.

American Association of University Women. 1992. *The AAUW Report: How Schools Short-Change Girls.* Washington, DC: The AAUW Educational Foundation and National Educational Association.

American Civil Liberties Union. 2005. "FBI Uses Patriot Act to Demand Information with No Judicial Approval from Organization with Library Records." ACLU.org (August 25, 2005). Retrieved August 26, 2005. Online: http://www.aclu.org/SafeandFree/SafeandFree.cfm?ID=18957&c=262.

American Heritage Dictionary. 2000. *American Heritage Dictionary of the English Language.* Boston: Houghton Mifflin.

American Library Association. 2005. "USA PATRIOT Act and Intellectual Freedom." Retrieved August 29, 2005. Online: http://www.ala.org/ala/oif/fissues/usapatriotact.htm.

American Psychiatric Association. 1994. *Diagnostic and Statistical Manual of Mental Disorders IV.* Washington, DC: American Psychiatric Association.

Amott, Teresa, and Julie Matthaei. 1991. *Race, Gender, and Work: A Multicultural Economic History of Women in the United States.* Boston: South End Press.

Anders, George. 1996. *Health against Wealth: HMOs and the Breakdown of Medical Trust.* Boston: Houghton Mifflin.

Andersen, Margaret L., and Patricia Hill Collins (Eds.). 2001. *Race, Class, and Gender: An Anthology* (4th ed.). Belmont, CA: Wadsworth.

Anderson, Elijah. 1990. *Streetwise: Race, Class, and Change in an Urban Community.* Chicago: University of Chicago Press.

Anderson, Makebra. "HIV/AIDS and the Elderly." Retrieved July 28, 2005. Online: http://www.finalcall.com/artman/publish/article_2010.shtml.

Angel, Ronald J., and Jacqueline L. Angel. 1993. *Painful Inheritance: Health and the New Generation of Fatherless Families.* Madison, WI: University of Wisconsin Press.

Angier, Natalie. 1990. "New Anti-depressant Is Acclaimed but Not Perfect." *New York Times* (March 29):B9.

Angier, Natalie. 1993. "Report Suggests Homosexuality Is Linked to Genes." *New York Times* (July 16):A1, C18.

Angier, Natalie. 1995. "If You're Really Ancient, You May Be Better Off: The Rise of the 'Oldest Old.' " *New York Times* (June 11):E1.

Anyon, Jean. 1980. "Social Class and the Hidden Curriculum of Work." *Journal of Education,* 162:67–92.

Apple, Michael W. 1982. *Education and Power: Reproduction and Contradiction in Education.* London: Routledge & Kegan Paul.

Applebome, Peter. 1995a. "For the Ultimate Safe School, Official Eyes Turn to Dallas." *New York Times* (September 20): A1, B8.

Applebome, Peter. 1995b. "Record Cost Cited to Fix or Rebuild Nation's Schools." *New York Times* (December 26):A1, A11.

Applebome, Peter. 1996. "Dilapidated Schools Are Busting at Frayed Seams." *New York Times* (August 25):8.

Applebome, Peter. 1997. "Mixed Results for Public School Proponents." *New York Times* (April 16):A17.

Archibold, Randal C. 2008. "Arizona Weighs Bill to Allow Guns on Campuses." *New York Times* (March 5):A1.

Arenson, Karen W. 1997. "Standard for Equivalency Degree Is Raised." *New York Times* (April 9):A18.

Arnold, Regina A. 1990. "Processes of Victimization and Criminalization of Black Women." *Social Justice,* 17(3):153–166.

Ash, Roberta. 1972. *Social Movements in America.* Chicago: Markham.

Asher, David. 2000. "Who Owns What?" Retrieved Dec. 21, 2002. Online: http://www.naa.org/presstime/0101/whoownswhat.html.

Associated Press. 2008. "China Bars Olympics Coverage From Tiananmen Square." *New York Times* (March 24). Retrieved: September 1, 2008. Online: http://www.nytimes.com/2008/03/24/business/media/24square.html.

Atchley, Robert C. 2004. *Social Forces and Aging: An Introduction to Social Gerontology* (10th ed.). Belmont, CA: Wadsworth.

Atchley, Robert C. 2000. *Social Forces and Aging: An Introduction to Social Gerontology* (9th ed.) Belmont, CA: Wadsworth.

Atlas, James. 1995. "Here's the Future. Look Familiar?" *New York Times* (December 31):EI, E5.

Atwood, Nina. 1008. "The Bachelor: Does Matt Have a Broken Chooser?" singlescoach.com (April 2). Retrieved: June 4, 2008. Online: http://www.singlescoach.com/blog/?p=293.

Austin American-Statesman. 1995. "Abuse of Elderly Is Increasing, Report Says" (May 2):A6.

Austin American-Statesman. 1997a. "Indonesia's Riady Family Wants into U.S. Banking" (April 27):A30.

Austin American-Statesman. 1997b. "Nation Needs Readers" (April 21):A6.

Austin American-Statesman. 2005. "Consumer Fraud: Most ID Theft Victims Find the Problem on Their Own." (July 29):C1.

Axinn, William G., and Arland Thornton. 1992. "The Relationship between Cohabitation and Divorce: Selectivity or Casual Influence?" *Demography,* 29(3):357–374.

Bachu, Amara, and Martin O'Connell. 2001. *Fertility of American Women: June 2000.* Current Population Reports, Series P20-543RV. Washington, DC: U.S. Census Bureau.

Baculinao, Eric. 2004. "China Grapples With Legacy of Its 'Missing Girls.'" MSNBC.com (September 14). Retrieved July 14, 2005. Online: http://www.msnbc.com/id/5953508.

Bailey, J. Michael, and D. S. Benishay. 1993. "Familial Aggregation of Female Sexual Orientation." *American Journal of Psychiatry,* 150 (February):272–277.

Bailey, J. Michael, and Richard C. Pillard. 1991. "A Genetic Study of Male Sexual Orientation." *Archives of General Psychiatry,* 48 (December):1089–1098.

Baker, Al. 2008. "Where Illegal Guns Can Do No More Harm." *New York Times* (June 3): A22.

Baldwin, James. 1963. *The Fire Next Time.* New York: Dial Press.

Bales, Kevin. 2002. "Because She Looks Like a Child." In Barbara Ehrenreich and Arlie Russell Hochschild (Eds.), *Global Woman: Nannies, Maids, and Sex Workers in the New Economy.* New York: Metropolitan/Owl, pp. 207–229.

Ballantine, Jeanne H. 2009. *The Sociology of Education: A Systematic Analysis* (6th ed.). Upper Saddle River, NJ: Pearson/Prentice Hall.

Ballantine, Jeanne H., and Floyd M. Hammack. 2009. *The Sociology of Education: A Systematic Analysis, 6/e.* Upper Saddle River, NJ: Prentice Hall.

Baltzell, E. Digby. 1958. *Philadelphia Gentlemen: The Making of a National Upper Class.* New York: Free Press.

Bandura, Albert. 1973. *Aggression: A Social Learning Analysis.* Englewood Cliffs, NJ: Prentice Hall.

Bandura, Albert, and R. H. Walters. 1977. *Social Learning Theory.* Englewood Cliffs, NJ: Prentice Hall.

Bane, Mary Jo. 1986. "Household Composition and Poverty: Which Comes First?" In Sheldon H. Danziger and Daniel H. Weinberg (Eds.), *Fighting Poverty: What Works and What Doesn't.* Cambridge, MA: Harvard University Press.

Banta, Bob. 1996. "Hyde Hopes to Be Example to Drivers." *Austin American-Statesman* (September 27):A1, A11.

Banta, Carolyn. 2005. "Trading for a High." *Time* (August 1):35.

Barber, Benjamin R. 1996. *Jihad vs. McWorld: How Globalism and Tribalism Are Reshaping the World.* New York: Ballantine Books.

Barboza, David. 2005. "China, New Land of Shoppers, Builds Malls on Gigantic Scale." *New York Times* (May 25):A1,C7.

Barlett, Donald L., and James B. Steele. 1996. *America: Who Stole the Dream?* Kansas City, MO: Andrews and McMeel.

Barlow, Hugh D., and David Kauzlarich. 2002. *Introduction to Criminology* (8th ed.). New York: HarperCollins.

Barnett, James H. 1954. *The American Christmas: A Study in National Culture.* New York: Macmillan.

Baron, Harold M. 1969. "The Web of Urban Racism." In Louis L. Knowles and Kenneth Prewitt (Eds.), *Institutional Racism in America.* Englewood Cliffs, NJ: Prentice Hall, pp. 134–176.

Barr, Bob. 2004. "Testimony Submitted by Bob Barr, Former Member of Congress, to the House Judiciary Committee, Subcommittee on the Federal Marriage Amendment." Retrieved April 6, 2004. Online: http://www.aclu.org/LesbianGayRights/LesbianGayRights.cfm?ID=15382&c=101.

Barrows, Sydney Biddle, with William Novak. 1986. *Mayflower Madam: The Secret Life of Sydney Biddle Barrows.* New York: Ivy Books.

Barry, Kathleen. 1995. *The Prostitution of Sexuality.* New York: New York University Press.

Barry, Tom. 1997. "'Burb-arians Pay Share of Austin's Sales Tax." *Austin American-Statesman* (May 27):A13.

Bartlett, Donald L., and James B. Steele. 2004a. "Who Left the Door Open?" Time.com (September 20). Retrieved July 28, 2005. Online: http://www.time.com/time/archive/preview/0,10987,995145,00.html.

Bartlett, Donald L. and James B. Steele. 2004b. *Critical Condition: How Health Care in America Became Big Business and Bad Medicine.* New York: Doubleday.

Basow, Susan A. 1992. *Gender Stereotypes and Roles* (3rd ed.). Pacific Grove, CA: Brooks/Cole.

Bassi, Laurie J., and Amy B. Chasanov. 1996. "Women and the Unemployment Insurance System." In Cynthia Costello and Barbara Kivimae Krimgold (Eds.) for the Women's Research and Education Institute, *The American Woman 1996–97: Women and Work.* New York: W.W. Norton, pp. 104–126.

Bauerlein, Monika. 1995. "The Borderless Bordello." *Utne Reader* (November–December):30–32.

Bawer, Bruce. 1994. *A Place at the Table: The Gay Individual in American Society.* New York: Touchstone.

Bayan, Rick. 2001. "Confessions of an Internet Addict." *The Cynics Sanctuary: "Some Cynical Guy":* (June 3). Retrieved: August 31, 2008. Online: http://www.i-cynic.com/weekly_40asp.

BBC. 2008a. "Families' Shopping List." *BBC News* (March 11). Retrieved April 18, 2008. Online: http://news.bbc.co.uk/go/pr/fr/-/2/hi/talking_point/7287793.stm.

BBC. 2008b. "World Bank Tackles Food Emergency." *BBC News* (March 14). Retrieved April 18, 2008. Online: http://newsvote.bbc.co.uk/mpapps/pagetools/print/news.bbc.co.uk/2/hi/business/7344892.stm.

BBC News. 2003. "Who Won the US Media War?" BBC News. Retrieved August 26, 2005. Online: http://news.bbc.co.uk/go/pr/fr/-/2/hi/americas/2959833.stm.

BBC News. 2004. "China Acts to Protect Baby Girls." BBCNews (July 15). Retrieved

July 14, 2005. Online: http://news.bbc.co.uk/go/pr/fr/-/2/hi/asiapacific/389669.stm.

Becker, Gary S. 1964. *Human Capital.* New York: Columbia University Press.

Becker, Howard S. 1963. *Outsiders: Studies in the Sociology of Deviance.* New York: Free Press.

Beckett, Katherine, Kris Nyrop, Lori Pfingst, and Melissa Bowen. 2005. "Drug Use, Drug Possession Arrests, and the Question of Race: Lessons from Seattle." *Social Problems* (August):419–441.

Beeghley, Leonard. 1989. *The Structure of Social Stratification in the United States.* Boston: Allyn and Bacon.

Belknap, Joanne. 1996. *The Invisible Woman: Gender, Crime, and Justice.* Belmont, CA: Wadsworth.

Belluck, Pam. 1997. "A Woman's Killer Is Likely to Be Her Partner, a Study Finds." *New York Times* (March 31):A12.

Belsky, Janet. 1999. *The Psychology of Aging: Theory, Research, and Interventions* (3rd ed.). Belmont, CA: Wadsworth.

Bennett, Niel G., Ann Klimas Blanc, and David E. Bloom. 1988. "Commitment and the Modern Union: Assessing the Link between Premarital Cohabitation and Subsequent Marital Stability." *American Sociological Review,* 53:127–138.

Benokraitis, Nijole V. 2008. *Marriages and Families: Changes, Choices, and Constraints* (6th ed.). Upper Saddle River, NJ: Prentice Hall/Pearson.

Benokraitis, Nijole V., and Joe R. Feagin. 1995. *Modern Sexism: Blatant, Subtle, and Covert Discrimination.* Englewood Cliffs, NJ: Prentice Hall.

Berger, Peter. 1963. *Invitation to Sociology: A Humanistic Perspective.* New York: Anchor.

Berger, Peter, and Hansfried Kellner. 1964. "Marriage and the Construction of Reality." *Diogenes,* 46:1–32.

Berger, Peter, and Thomas Luckmann. 1967. *The Social Construction of Reality: A Treatise in the Sociology of Knowledge.* Garden City, NY: Anchor Books.

Berger, Ronald J., Patricia Searles, and Charles E. Cottle. 1991. *Feminism and Pornography.* Westport, CT: Praeger.

Bergmann, Barbara R. 1986. *The Economic Emergence of Women.* New York: Basic Books.

Berke, Richard L. 1996. "Is Age-Bashing Any Way to Beat Bob Dole?" *New York Times* (May 5):E1, E6.

Bernard, Jessie. 1982. *The Future of Marriage.* New Haven, CT: Yale University Press.

Bertram, Eva, Morris Blachman, Kenneth Sharpe, and Peter Andreas. 1996. *Drug War Politics: The Price of Denial.* Berkeley, CA: University of California Press.

Best, Joel. 1999. *Random Violence: How We Talk about New Crimes and New Victims.* Berkeley, CA: University of California Press.

Best, Joel. 2001. *Damned Lies and Statistics: Untangling Numbers from the Media, Politicians, and Activists.* Berkeley, CA: University of California Press.

Bethel, Martha A. 1995. "Terror in Montana." *New York Times* (July 20):A13.

Biagi, Shirley. 1998. *Media Impact: An Introduction to Mass Media* (3rd ed.). Belmont, CA: Wadsworth.

Biagi, Shirley. 2009. *Media/Impact: An Introduction to Mass Media* (8th ed.). Belmont: Wadsworth/Cengage.

Bieber, Irving, and the Society of Medical Psychoanalysts. 1962. *Homosexuality: A Psychoanalytic Study.* New York: Basic Books.

Birmingham, Stephen. 1967. *The Right Places.* Boston: Little, Brown.

Blauner, Robert. 1972. *Racial Oppression in America.* New York: Harper & Row.

Blount, Jeb. 1996. "Saltwater Spirituals and Deeper Blues." *Houston Chronicle* (February 25):24A.

Boller, Gregory. 1997. "Sugar Daddies." *Mother Jones* (May–June):45.

Bonacich, Edna. 1972. "A Theory of Ethnic Antagonism: The Split Labor Market." *American Sociological Review,* 37: 547–549.

Bonacich, Edna. 1976. "Advanced Capitalism and Black White Relations in the United States: A Split Labor Market Interpretation." *American Sociological Review,* 41:34–51.

Bonger, Willem. 1969. *Criminality and Economic Conditions* (abridged ed.). Bloomington, IN: Indiana University Press (orig. published in 1916).

Bonnin, Julie. 1997. "Knockout Drugs." *Austin American-Statesman* (February 2):E1, E12.

Bosman, Julie. 2008. "So a Senior Citizen Walks Into a Bar ..." *New York Times* (March 9): A4.

Botvin, Gilbert, and Stephanie Tortu. 1988. "Preventing Adolescent Substance Abuse through Life Skills Training." In Richard M. Price, Emory L. Cowen, Raymond P. Lorion, and Julia Ramos-McKay (Eds.), *Fourteen Ounces of Prevention: A Casebook for Practitioners.* Washington, DC: American Psychological Association, pp. 98–110.

Bourdieu, Pierre, and Jean-Claude Passeron. 1990. *Reproduction in Education, Society, and Culture.* Newbury Park, CA: Sage.

Bourdon, Karen H., Donald S. Rae, Ben Z. Locke, William E. Narrow, and Darrel A. Regier. 1992. "Estimating the Prevalence of Mental Disorders in U.S. Adults from the Epidemiological Catchment Area Survey." *Public Health Reports,* 107:663–668.

Bourgeois, Philippe. 1995. *In Search of Respect: Selling Crack in el Barrio.* New York: Cambridge University Press.

Bovino, Arthur. 2003. "Offering a Hand, and Hope, in a Year of Record Homelessness in New York." *New York Times* (November 2):A25.

Bowers, William J. 1984. *Legal Homicide: Death as Punishment in America, 1864–1982.* Boston: Northeastern University Press.

Bowles, Samuel, and Herbert Gintis. 1976. *Schooling in Capitalist America: Education and the Contradictions of Economic Life.* New York: Basic Books.

Bragg, Rick. 1997. "Many Find Satisfaction, but Few Find Any Joy." *New York Times* (June 14):8.

Bramlett, M. D., and W. D. Mosher. 2002. "Cohabitation, Marriage, Divorce, and Remarriage in the United States." *Vital and Health Statistics,* 23(22). Hattsville, MD: National Center for Health Statistics.

Brecher, Jeremy, and Tim Costello. 1998. *Global Village or Global Pillage: Economic Reconstruction From the Bottom Up* (2nd ed.). Cambridge, MA: South End Press.

Brennan, Denise. 2002. "Selling Sex for Visas: Sex Tourism as a Stepping-stone to International Migration." In Barbara Ehrenreich and Arlie Russell Hochschild (Eds.), *Global Woman: Nannies, Maids, and Sex Workers in the New Economy.* New York: Metropolitan/Owl, pp. 154–168.

Brody, Jane E. 1996. "Good Habits Outweigh Genes as Key to a Healthy Old Age." *New York Times* (February 28):B9.

Brooks, A. Phillips, and Jeff South. 1996. "In Town after Town, Minorities Fill Programs." *Austin American-Statesman* (December 1):A1, A14.

Brown, J. Larry. 2002. "Child Hunger and Food Insecurity: The Scientific Evidence and Possible Solutions." Retrieved Aug. 11, 2002. Online: http://www.jeffbridges.com/Larry.html.

Brown, Phil. 1985. *The Transfer of Care: Psychiatric Deinstitutionalization and Its Aftermath.* Boston: Routledge & Kegan Paul.

Browne, Jan, and Kirk R. Williams. 1987. "Gender Specific Effects on Patterns of Homicide Perpetration." Presented to the American Psychological Association (cited in Barlow, 1996).

Browne, Jan, and Victor Minichiello. 1995. "The Social Meanings behind Male Sex Work: Implications for Sexual Interactions." *British Journal of Sociology*, 46(4):598–623.

Bruni, Frank. 1996. "Gay Couples Cheer Adoption Ruling, Saying It Lets Law Reflect Reality." *New York Times* (November 5):16.

Buechler, Steven M. 2000. *Social Movements in Advanced Capitalism: The Political Economy and Cultural Construction of Social Activism.* New York: Oxford University Press.

Bullard, Robert D., and Beverly H. Wright. 1992. "The Quest for Environmental Equity: Mobilizing the African-American Community for Social Change." In Riley E. Dunlap and Angela G. Mertig (Eds.), *American Environmentalism: The U.S. Environmental Movement, 1970–1990.* New York: Taylor & Francis, pp. 39–50.

Bullough, Vern, and Bonnie Bullough. 1987. *Women and Prostitution: A Social History.* Buffalo, NY: Prometheus.

Burleigh, Nina. 1991. "Watching Children Starve to Death." *Time* (June 10):56–58.

Burnham, M. Audrey, Richard L. Hough, Marvin Karno, Javier I. Escobar, and Cynthia A. Telles. 1987. "Acculturation and Lifetime Prevalence of Psychiatric Disorders among Mexican Americans in Los Angeles." *Journal of Health and Social Behavior,* 28:89–102.

Busfield, Joan. 1996. *Men, Women and Madness: Understanding Gender and Mental Disorder.* Houndmills, Basingstoke, Hampshire, England: MacMillan Press.

Bush, George W. 2001. Quoted in National Campaign for Jobs and Income Support, "Leaving Welfare, Left Behind: Employment Status, Income, and Well-Being of Former TANF Recipients." Retrieved Sept. 15, 2002. Online: http://www.nationalcampaign.org.

Bush, George W. 2003a. "President Bush Addresses the Nation." Retrieved September 3, 2005. Online: http://www.whitehouse.gov/news/releases/2003/03/20030319-17.html.

Bush, George W. 2003b. "President Says Saddam Hussein Must Leave Iraq Within 48 Hours. Remarks by the President in Address to the Nation, March 17, 2003." Retrieved September 3, 2005. Online: http://www.whitehouse.gov/news/releases/2003/03/20030317-7.html.

Bush, George W. 2003c. "President's Radio Address, February 8, 2003." Retrieved September 3, 2005. Online: http://www.whitehouse.gov/news/releases/2003/02/20030208.html.

Butler, Robert N. 1969. "Ageism: Another Form of Bigotry." *The Gerontologist,* 9:243–246.

Butterfield, Fox. 1996. "Crimes of Violence among Juveniles Decline Slightly." *New York Times* (August 9):A1, A9.

Bynum, Jack E., and William E. Thompson. 1996. *Juvenile Delinquency: A Sociological Approach.* Boston: Allyn and Bacon.

Cable, Sherry, and Charles Cable. 1995. *Environmental Problems, Grassroots Solutions: The Politics of Grassroots Environmental Conflict.* New York: St. Martin's Press.

Canadian Institute for Health Insurance. 2004. "The Cost of Health Care." Retrieved August 1, 2005. Online: http://secure.cihi.ca/cihiweb/dispPage.jsp?cw_page=media_09jun2004_b1_e.

Cancian, Francesca M. 1990. "The Feminization of Love." In C. Carlson (Ed.), *Perspectives on the Family: History, Class, and Feminism.* Belmont, CA: Wadsworth, pp. 171–185.

Cancian, Francesca M., and James William Gibson. 1990. *Making War, Making Peace: The Social Foundations of Violent Conflict.* Belmont, CA: Wadsworth.

Capek, Stella M. 1993. "The 'Environmental Justice' Frame: A Conceptual Discussion and an Application." *Social Problems,* 40:5–24.

Carey, Benedict. 2005. "Storm Will Have a Long-term Emotional Effect on Some, Experts Say." *New York Times* (September 4):A20.

Carmichael, Stokely, and Charles V. Hamilton. 1967. *Black Power: The Politics of Liberation in America.* New York: Vintage.

Carnahan, Ira. 2003. "Pork Report: From IBM to Rock 'N' Roll." Retrieved August 8, 2005. Online: http://www.forbes.com/2003/04/23/cz_ic_0423beltway.html.

Carrier, James G. 1986. *Social Class and the Construction of Inequality in American Education.* New York: Greenwood Press.

Cass, Vivien C. 1984. "Homosexual Identity Formation: Testing a Theoretical Model." *Journal of Sex Research,* 20: 143–167.

Castells, Manuel. 1977. *The Urban Question.* London: Edward Arnold.

Catalano, Ralph A., and William McConnell. 1996. "A Time-Series Test of the Quarantine Theory of Involuntary Commitment." *Journal of Health and Social Behavior,* 37: 381–387.

Catalyst. 2003. "What Keeps Women from Reaching the Top?" Retrieved July 26, 2005. Online: http://www.womensmedia.com/new/Catalyst-Women-Executives.shtml.

Cato Institute. 2006. "More Welfare, More Poverty." Based on an article by Michael D. Tanner in the *Charlotte Observer,* September 12, 2006. Washington, D.C.: Cato Institute. Retrieved April 20, 2008. Online: http://www.cato.org/pub_display.php?pub_id=6698.

Cavender, Gray. 1995. "Alternative Approaches: Labeling and Critical Perspectives." In Joseph F. Sheley (Ed.), *Criminology: A Contemporary Handbook* (2nd ed.). Belmont, CA: Wadsworth, pp. 349–367.

CBS News. 2003. "Infant Girls For Sale in China." CBSNews.com (March 24). Retrieved July 14, 2005. Online: http://www.cbsnews.com/stories/2003/03/24/world/main545861.shtml.

CBS News. 2004. "The Issues: Child Care." *CBS Evening News* (July 12). Retrieved April 4, 2005. Online: http://www.cbsnews.com/stories/2004/07/12/eveningnews/main628891.shtml.

Center for Responsive Politics, 2008. "Blue Chip Investors: Top 10 Donors." Retrieved August 29, 2008. Online: http://www.opensecrets.org/orgs/index.pnp.

Centers for Disease Control and Prevention. 2007. "Life Expectancy at Birth … by Race and Sex." Hyattsville, MD: U.S. Department of Health and Human Services, Centers for Disease Control and Prevention, National Center for Health Statistics.

Centers for Disease Control and Prevention. 2008. "HIV/AIDS in the United States: CDC HIV/AIDS Facts, March 2008." Atlanta, GA: U.S. Department of Health and Human Services, CDC.

Chambliss, William J. 1988. *Exploring Criminology.* New York: Macmillan.

Chan, Sucheng (Ed.). 1991. *Entry Denied: Exclusion and the Chinese Community in America, 1882–1943.* Philadelphia: Temple University Press.

Chang, Robert S. 1999. *Disoriented: Asian Americans, Law, and the Nation State (Critical America).* New York: New York University Press.

ChannelOne.com 2005. "About Channel One." Retrieved August 4, 2005. Online: http://www.channelone.com/common/about.

Chavez, Leo R. and Rebecca Martinez. 1996. "Mexican Immigration in the 1980s and Beyond: Implications for Chicanas/os." In David R. Maciel and Isidro D. Ortiz (Eds.), *Chicanas/Chicanos at the Crossroads: Social Economic, and Political Change.* Tucson, AZ: University of Arizona Press, pp. 25–41.

Chavez, Linda. 1991. *Out of the Barrio: Toward a New Politics of Hispanic Assimilation.* New York: Basic Books.

Chen, Hsiang-shui. 1992. *Chinatown No More: Taiwan Immigrants in Contemporary New York.* Ithaca: Cornell University Press.

Cherlin, Andrew J. 1992. *Marriage, Divorce, and Remarriage* (rev. and enlarged ed.). Cambridge, MA: Harvard University Press.

Chermak, Steven M. 1995. *Victims in the News: Crime and the American News Media.* Boulder, CO: Westview.

Chilcoat, Howard D., and Naomi Breslau. 1996. "Alcohol Disorders in Young Adulthood: Effects of Transitions into Adult Roles." *Journal of Health and Social Behavior,* 37(4):339–349.

Children's Defense Fund. 2001. *The State of America's Children Yearbook 2001.* Boston: Beacon.

Children's Defense Fund. 2003. "Early Childhood Development: Frequently Asked Questions." Retrieved April 23, 2005. Online: www.childrensdefense.org/earlychildhood/childcare/faq.aspx.

Children's Defense Fund. 2004. *The State of America's Children Yearbook 2004.* Boston: Beacon.

Children's Express. 1993. "Voices from the Future: Our Children Tell Us about Violence in America." Edited by Susan Goodwillie. New York: Crown.

Chin, Rockwell. 1999. "Long Struggle for Justice." *ABA Journal* (November): 66–67.

Cholbi, Wendy. 1998. "Paying for Performance." Retrieved Dec. 13, 2002. Online: http://www.boardmember.com/issues/archive.pl?article_id=10569.

Chronicle of Higher Education. 2002. "Attitudes and Characteristics of Freshman." Almanac Issue (August 30):26.

Chronicle of Higher Education. 2008. "Should Prostitution Be Legalized?" (March 28): B4.

Chudacoff, Howard P. 1989. *How Old Are You? Age Consciousness in American Culture.* Princetion: Princeton University Press.

City of Austin. 1996. Internal communication from Information Systems Department (October 23).

Clark, Cal, and Oliver Walter. 1994. "Cuts, Cultures, and City Limits in Reagan's New Federalism." In Terry Nichols Clark (Ed.), *Urban Innovation: Creative Strategies for Turbulent Times.* Thousand Oaks, CA: Sage, pp. 169–196.

Cleary, Paul D. 1987. "Gender Differences in Stress-Related Disorders." In Rosalind C. Barnett, Lois Biener, and Grace K. Baruch (Eds.), *Gender and Stress.* New York: Free Press, pp. 39–72.

Clinard, Marshall B., and R. F. Meier. 1989. *Sociology of Deviant Behavior* (7th ed.). Fort Worth, TX: Holt, Rinehart and Winston.

Cloud, John. 2002. "Is Pot Good For You?" *Time* (Nov. 4):62–66.

Cloward, Richard A., and Lloyd E. Ohlin. 1960. *Delinquency and Opportunity: A Theory of Delinquent Gangs.* New York: Free Press.

CNN.com. 2002. "Senate Approves Campaign Finance Bill." CNN.com. Retrieved Dec. 7, 2002. Online: http://www.cnn.com/2002/ALLPOLTICS/03/20/campaign.finance/index.html.

Coale, Ansley. 1973. "The Demographic Transition." Proceedings of the International Population Conference, Liege. Vol. 1, pp. 53–72. (Cited in Weeks, 1992.)

Cock, Jacklyn. 1994. "Women and the Military: Implications for Demilitarization in the 1990s in South Africa. *Gender and Society,* 8(2):152–169.

Codina, G. Edward, and Frank F. Montalvo. 1994. "Chicano Phenotype and Depression." *Hispanic Journal of Behavioral Sciences,* 16 (August):296–307.

Cohen, Lawrence E., and Marcus Felson. 1979. "Social Change and Crime Rate Trends: A Routine Activity Approach." *American Sociological Review,* 44:588–608.

Cohen, Richard M. 2004. *Blindsided.* New York: HarperCollins.

Cohn, Jonathan. 1997. "Reform School." *Mother Jones* (May–June):62.

Cole, Thomas B., and Annette Flanagin. 1999. "Editorial: What Can We Do About Violence?" *JAMA* (August 4): 481–482.

Coleman, Eli. 1981/2. "Developmental Stages of the Coming Out Process." *Journal of Homosexuality,* 7:31–43.

Coleman, James S. 1966. *Equality of Educational Opportunity.* Washington, DC: U.S. Government Printing Office.

Coles, Gerald. 1987. *The Learning Mystique: A Critical Look at "Learning Disabilities."* New York: Pantheon.

Colhoun, J. 1992. "Census Fails to Quash Report on Iraqi Deaths." *The Guardian* (April 22):5.

Collins, James. 1997. "Day of Reckoning." *Time* (June 16):27–29.

Collins, Patricia Hill. 1990. *Black Feminist Thought: Knowledge, Consciousness, and the Politics of Empowerment.* London: HarperCollins Academic.

Collins, Patricia Hill. 1991. *Black Feminist Thought: Knowledge, Consciousness, and the Politics of Empowerment.* New York: Routledge.

Collins, Patricia Hill. 1995. "Symposium: On West and Fenstermaker's 'Doing Difference.'" *Gender and Society,* 9(4) (August):491–494.

Collins, Randall. 1979. *The Credential Society: An Historical Sociology of Education.* New York: Academic Press.

Coltrane, Scott. 1989. "Household Labor and the Routine Production of Gender." *Social Problems,* 36:473–490.

Comstock, Gary David. 1991. *Violence against Lesbians and Gay Men.* New York: Columbia University Press.

Conant, Marcus. 1997. "This Is Smart Medicine." *Newsweek* (February 3):26.

Congressional Budget Office. 2005. "Historical Budget Data." Retrieved August 8, 2005. Online: http://www.cbo.gov/showdoc.cfm?index=1821&sequence=0.

Congressional Budget Office. 2008. "Monthly Budget Review." Washington, DC: Congressional Budget Office. Retrieved: August 10, 2008. Online: http://www.cbo.gov.

Conlon, Michael. 2005. "Gun Victims Speak Out on Scars of Violence." Reuters News Service (April 11). Retrieved June 25, 2005. Online: http://www.commondreams.org/headlines05/0411-10.htm.

Connell, Christopher. 1995. "Birth Rate for Unmarried Women Surges." *Austin American-Statesman* (June 7):A18.

Cooper, Michael. 2004. "Statement of Michael Cooper, 15, Springfield, VA on the Federal Marriage Amendment." Retrieved April 6, 2004. Online: http://www.aclu.org/LesbianGayRights/LesbianGayRights.cfm?ID=15322&c=101.

COPS. 2008. "Solving Crime Problems." Office of Community Oriented Policing Services, U.S. Department of Justice Retrieved: June 7, 2008. Online: http://www.cops.usdoj.gov/Item-154.

Corr, Charles A., Clyde M. Nabe, and Donna M. Corr. 1994. *Death and Dying, Life and Living.* Pacific Grove, CA: Brooks/Cole.

Cortese, Anthony J. 1999. *Provocateur: Images of Women and Minorities in Advertising.* Lanham, MD: Rowman & Littlefield.

Cose, Ellis. 1993. *The Rage of a Privileged Class.* New York: HarperCollins.

Coser, Lewis A. 1969. "The Visibility of Evil." *Journal of Social Issues,* 25:101–109. In Bunis, William K., Angela Yancik, and David Snow. 1996. "The Cultural Patterning of Sympathy toward the Homeless and Other Victims of Misfortune." *Social Problems* (November):387–402.

Costello, Cynthia, Anne J. Stone, and Betty Dooley. 1996. "A Perspective on America's Working Women." In Cynthia Costello and Barbara Kivimae Krimgold (Eds.) for the Women's Research and Education Institute, *The American Woman 1996–97: Women and Work.* New York: W.W. Norton, pp. 23–32.

Cottle, Charles E., Patricia Searles, Ronald J. Berger, and Beth Ann Pierce. 1989. "Conflicting Ideologies and the Politics of Pornography." *Gender and Society,* 3:303–333.

Cowan, Gloria, and Margaret O'Brien. 1990. "Gender and Survival vs. Death in Slasher Films: A Content Analysis." *Sex Roles,* 23:187–196.

Cowan, Gloria, C. Lee, D. Levy, and D. Snyder. 1988. "Domination and Inequality in X-Rated Videocassettes." *Psychology of Women Quarterly,* 12:299–311.

Cowgill, Donald O. 1986. *Aging around the World.* Belmont, CA: Wadsworth.

Cowley, Geoffrey. 1997. "Can Marijuana Be Medicine?" *Newsweek* (February 3):22–27.

Cox, Oliver C. 1948. *Caste, Class, and Race.* Garden City, NY: Doubleday.

Coy, Peter, and Heather Timmons. 2002. "Consumer Credit: Is a Crunch Coming?" *BusinessWeek Online* (Aug. 2). Retrieved Dec. 13, 2002. Online: http://www.businessweek.com/print/bwdaily/dnflash/aug2002/nf2002082_0656.htm?gl.

Cozic, Charles P. (Ed.). 1993. *America's Cities: Opposing Viewpoints.* San Diego: Greenhaven Press.

Crawford, John. 2005. "Coming Home." *New York Times* (August 14):WK12.

Crichton, Michael. 1994. *Disclosure.* New York: Random House.

Crosnoe, Robert, Chandra Muller, and Kenneth Frank. 2004. "Peer Context and the Consequences of Adolescent Drinking." *Social Problems* (May): 288–304.

Crossette, Barbara. 1996. "Agency Sees Risk in Drug to Temper Child Behavior: Worldwide Survey Cites Overuse of Ritalin." *New York Times* (February 29):A7.

Crossette, Barbara. 1997. "Democracies Love Peace, Don't They?" *New York Times* (June 1):E3.

Cumming, Elaine C., and William E. Henry. 1961. *Growing Old: The Process of Disengagement.* New York: Basic Books.

Curatolo, Peter W., and David Robertson. 1983. "The Health Consequences of Caffeine." *Annals of Internal Medicine,* 98:641–653. (Cited in Levinthal, 1996.)

Curran, James, Michael Gurevitch, and Janet Woollacott. 1982. "The Study of the Media: Theoretical Approaches." In Michael Gurevitch, Tony Bennett, James Curran, and Janet Woollacott (Eds.). *Culture, Society and the Media.* London: Methuen, pp. 5–35.

Cushman, John H., Jr. 1997. "E.P.A. Seeks Cut, Not End, to Pollution by Paper Mills." *New York Times* (May 21):A10.

Dahl, Robert A. 1961. *Who Governs?* New Haven, CT: Yale University Press.

Dalaker, Joseph. 2001. *Poverty in the United States.* Current Population Reports, Series P60-214. Washington, DC: U.S. Census Bureau.

Daly, Kathleen, and Meda Chesney-Lind. 1988. "Feminism and Criminology." *Justice Quarterly,* 5:497–533.

Davidson, Julia O'Connell. 1996. "Sex Tourism in Cuba." *Race and Class,* 38(1):39–49.

Davis, F. James. 1991. *Who Is Black? One Nation's Definition.* University Park, PA: Pennsylvania State University Press.

Davis, Kingsley. 1937. "The Sociology of Prostitution." *American Sociological Review,* 2:744–755.

De Castro, Steven. 1994. "Identity in Action: A Filipino American's Perspective." In Karin Aguilar-San Juan (Ed.), *The State of Asian America: Activism and Resistance in the 1990s.* Boston: South End Press, pp. 295–320.

Department of Health and Human Services, Centers for Disease Control and Prevention, National Center for Health Statistics.

DeNavas-Walt, Carmen, Bernadette D. Proctor, and Jessica Smith. 2007. "Current Population Reports, P60-233, Income, Poverty, and Health Insurance Coverage in the United States: 2006." Washington, DC.: U.S. Government Printing Office.

DeNavas-Walt, Carmen, Bernadette D. Proctor, and Jessica Smith. 2007. "Income, Poverty, and Health Insurance Coverage in the United States: 2006." U.S. Census Bureau, Current Population Reports, P60-233. Retrieved January 12, 2008. Online: http://www.census.gov/prod/2007pubs/p60-233.pdf.

DePasquale, Katherine M. 1999. "The Effects of Prostitution." Retrieved December 3, 1999. Online: http://www.feminista.com/v1n5/depasquale.html.

de Silva, Rex. 1980. "Developing the Third World." *World Press Review* (May):48.

Devereaux, Anna. 1987. "Diary of a Prostitute." *Cosmopolitan* (October 1987):164, 166.

DeWitt, Karen. 1994. "Wave of Suburban Growth Is Being Fed by Minorities." *New York Times* (August 15):A1, A12.

Dews, Peter B. 1984. "Behavioral Effects of Caffeine." In Peter B. Dews (Ed.), *Caffeine: Perspectives from Recent Research.* Berlin: Springer-Verlag, pp. 86–103. (Cited in Levinthal, 1996.)

Diamond, Jared. 2000. "The Greening of Corporate America." *New York Times* (January 8):A31.

Diamond, Timothy. 1992. *Making Gray Gold: Narratives of Nursing Home Care.* Chicago: University of Chicago Press.

Dietz, P. 1986. "Mass, Serial and Sensational Homicide." *Bulletin of the New England Medical Society,* 62:477–491.

DiFranza, Joseph R., and Robert A. Lew. 1995. "Effect of Maternal Cigarette Smoking on Pregnancy Complications and Sudden Infant Death Syndrome." *The Journal of Family Practice,* 40:385–394.

Dignity USA.com 2008. "Transgendered Persons—a Primer to Better Understanding." Retrieved: May 26, 2008. Online: http://www.dignityusa.org/transgender/t-primer.html.

Dobrzynski, Judith H. 1996. "When Directors Play Musical Chairs." *New York Times* (Nov. 17): F1, F8, F9.

Dollard, John, Neal E. Miller, Leonard W. Doob, O. H. Mowrer, and Robert R. Sears. 1939. *Frustration and Aggression.* New Haven, CT: Yale University Press.

Domhoff, G. William. 1978. *The Powers That Be: Processes of Ruling Class Domination in America.* New York: Random House.

Domhoff, G. William. 1983. *Who Rules America Now?* New York: Touchstone.

Domhoff, G. William. 1990. *The Power Elite and the State: How Policy Is Made in America.* New York: Aldine De Gruyter.

Donziger, Steven R. (Ed.). 1996. *The Real War on Crime: The Report of the National Criminal Justice Commission.* New York: HarperPerennial.

Doss, Yvette. 1996. "Network TV: Latinos Need Not Apply." *Frontera Magazine* (Issue 2: n.d.). Retrieved November 11, 1999. Online: http://www.frontramag.com.

Dowd, Maureen. 2005. "United States of Shame." *New York Times* (September 3):A29.

Doyle, James A. 1995. *The Male Experience* (3rd ed.). Madison, WI: Brown and Benchmark.

D'Souza, Dinesh. 1999. "The Billionaire Next Door." *Forbes* (October 11):50–62.

Duhigg, Charles. 2008. "Bilking the Elderly, With a Corporate Assist." *New York Times* (May 20): A1, A18.

Dull, Diana, and Candace West. 1991. "Accounting for Cosmetic Surgery: The Accomplishments of Gender." *Social Problems,* 38(1):54–70.

Duncan, David F. 1991. "Violence and Degradation as Themes in 'Adult' Videos." *Psychology Reports,* 69(1):239–240.

Dunlap, David W. 1995. "Court Upholds Anti-Homosexual Initiative." *New York Times* (May 14):10.

Dunlap, David W. 1996. "Role of Openly Gay Episcopalians Causes a Rift in the Church." *New York Times* (March 21):A8.

Dunlap, Riley E. 1992. "Trends in Public Opinion toward Environmental Issues: 1965–1990." In Riley E. Dunlap and Angela G. Mertig (Eds.), *American Environmentalism: The U.S. Environmental Movement, 1970–1990.* New York: Taylor & Francis, pp. 89–113.

Dunn, Ashley. 1995. "Cram Schools: Immigrants' Tools for Success." *New York Times* (January 28):1, 9.

Du Phuoc Long, Patrick (with Laura Ricard). 1996. *The Dream Shattered: Vietnamese Gangs in America.* Boston: Northeastern University Press.

Duran, Lisa. 1997. "Ignorance about Immigrants." *Austin American-Statesman* (May 19):A7.

Durkheim, Emile. 1893. *The Division of Labor in Society.* New York: The Free Press.

Durkheim, Emile. 1933. *Division of Labor in Society.* Trans. George Simpson. New York: Free Press (orig. published in 1893).

Durkheim, Emile. 1964. *The Rules of Sociological Method.* Trans. Sarah A. Solovay and John H. Mueller. New York: Free Press (orig. published in 1895).

Duster, Troy. 1995. "Symposium: The Bell Curve." *Contemporary Sociology: A Journal of Reviews,* 24(2):158–161.

Dworkin, Andrea. 1988. *Letters to a War Zone.* New York: Dutton/New America Library.

Dye, Thomas R., and Harmon Zeigler. 2009. *The Irony of Democracy: An Uncommon Introduction to American Politics* (14th ed.). Belmont: Cengage/Wadsworth.

Dynes, Wayne R. (Ed.). 1990. *Encyclopedia of Homosexuality.* New York: Garland.

Eaton, William W. 1980. "A Formal Theory of Selection for Schizophrenia." *American Journal of Sociology,* 86:149–158.

Eckholm, Erik. 2002. "Desire for Sons Drives Use of Prenatal Scans in China." *New York Times* (June 21):A3.

Eckholm, Erik. 2006. "A Welfare Law Milestone Finds Many Left Behind." *New York Times* (August 22): A1.

The Economist. 2002. "Over 60 and Overlooked." (Aug. 10):51.

EEOC. 2002. "Facts About Sexual Harassment." Retrieved Oct. 16, 2002. Online: http://www.eeoc.gov/facts/fs-sex.html.

Ehrenreich, Barbara. 1997. *Blood Rites: Origins and History of the Passions of War.* New York: Metropolitan Books.

Ehrenreich, Barbara. 1999. "Nickel-and-Dimed: On (Not) Getting by in America." *Harper's Magazine* (January):37–52.

Ehrenreich, Barbara. 2001. *Nickel and Dimed: On (Not) Getting By in America.* New York: Metropolitan.

Ehrenreich, Barbara, and Arlie Russell Hochschild. 2002. "Introduction." In Barbara Ehrenreich and Arlie Russell Hochschild (Eds.), *Global Woman: Nannies, Maids, and Sex Workers in the New Economy.* New York: Metropolitan/Owl, pp. 1–13.

Ehrlich, Paul R., and Anne H. Ehrlich. 1991. *The Population Explosion.* New York: Touchstone/Simon & Schuster.

Eichenberg, Stephan. 2008. "Plot Summary for 'Coal Black and de Sebben Dwarfs' (1943)." The Internet Movie Database. Retrieved April 30, 2008. Online: http://www.imdb.com/title/tt0035743/plotsummary.

ELCA World Hunger. 2005. "World Hunger Facts." Retrieved August 20, 2005. Online: http://www.elca.org/hunger/printfriendly/facts.html.

Elliott, Marta, and Lauren J. Krivo. 1991. "Structural Determinants of Homelessness in the United States." *Social Problems,* 38(1):113–131.

Energy Information Administration. 2004. "Mexico: Environmental Issues." Retrieved August 20, 2005. Online: http://www.eia.doe.gov/emeu/cabs/mexenv.html.

Engelhardt, H. Tristan, Jr. 1996. *Foundations of Bioethics.* New York: Oxford University Press.

Engels, Friedrich. 1972. *The Origins of the Family, Private Property, and the State.* (Ed. Eleanor Burke Leacock). New York: International.

Enloe, Cynthia H. 1987. "Feminists Thinking about War, Militarism, and Peace." In Beth Hess and Myra Marx Ferree (Eds.), *Analyzing Gender: A Handbook of Social Science Research.* Newbury Park, CA: Sage, pp. 526–547.

Epstein, Cynthia Fuchs. 1988. *Deceptive Distinctions: Sex, Gender, and the Social Order.* New Haven, CT: Yale University Press.

Epstein, Cynthia Fuchs. 1993. *Women in Law* (3rd ed.). Urbana, IL: University of Illinois Press.

Erikson, Kai T. 1962. "Notes on the Sociology of Deviance." *Social Problems,* 9:307–314.

Erikson, Kai T. 1991. "A New Species of Trouble." In Stephen Robert Crouch and J. Stephen Kroll-Smith (Eds.), *Communities at Risk: Collective Responses to Technological Hazards.* New York: Peter Land, pp. 11–29.

Erikson, Kai T. 1994. *A New Species of Trouble: Explorations in Disaster, Trauma, and Community.* New York: Norton.

Espiritu, Yen Le. 1995. *Filipino American Lives.* Philadelphia: Temple University Press.

Essed, Philomena. 1991. *Understanding Everyday Racism.* Newbury Park, CA: Sage.

Factbook on Global Sexual Exploitation. 1999. "United States of America: Facts on Trafficking and Prostitution." Retrieved December 3, 1999. Online: http://www.uri.edu/artsci/wms/hughes/catw/usa.htm.

Fairstein, Linda A. 1995. *Sexual Violence: Our War against Rape.* New York: Berkley.

FAO. 1995. *FAO Yearbook 1995.* Rome, Italy: Food and Agricultural Organization of the United Nations.

Farley, Melissa, and Victor Malarek. 2008. "The Myth of the Victimless Crime." *New York Times* (March 12): A27.

Farrey, Tom. 1999. "Images from Sports Carry Racial Weight." *ESPN Sports.* Retrieved August 15, 1999. Online: http://espn.go.com/gen/features/race/farrey.html.

F.B.I. 2006. *Crime in the United States 2006.* Retrieved January 4, 2008. Online: www.fbi.gov/ucr.cius2006.

Feagin, Joe R. 1975. *Subordinating the Poor: Welfare and American Beliefs.* Englewood Cliffs, NJ: Prentice-Hall.

Feagin, Joe R., David Baker, and Clairece Booher Feagin. 2006. *Social Problems: A Critical Power-Conflict Perspective* (6th ed.). Upper Saddle River, NJ: Prentice Hall.

Feagin, Joe R., and Clairece Booher Feagin. 2008. *Racial and Ethnic Relations* (8th ed.). Upper Saddle River, NJ: Prentice-Hall.

Feagin, Joe R., and Robert Parker. 1990. *Building American Cities: The Urban Real Estate Game* (2nd ed.). Englewood Cliffs, NJ: Prentice Hall.

Feagin, Joe R., and Melvin P. Sikes. 1994. *Living with Racism: The Black Middle-Class Experience.* Boston: Beacon Press.

Feagin, Joe R., and Hernán Vera. 1995. *White Racism: The Basics.* New York: Routledge.

Fedders, Charlotte, and Laura Elliott. 1987. *Shattered Dreams.* New York: Dell.

Federal Bureau of Investigation (FBI). 2007. *Crime in the United States: 2006.* Washington, DC: U.S. Government Printing Office.

Federal Bureau of Investigation (FBI). 2008. *Crime in the United States, 2007.* Washington, DC: U.S. Government Printing Office.

Fenstermacher, Gary D. 1994. "The Absence of Democratic and Educational Ideals from Contemporary Educational Reform Initiatives." The Elam Lecture, presented to the Educational Press Association of America. Chicago, June 10.

Fernandez, Joseph M. 1991. "Bringing Hate Crime into Focus." *Harvard Civil Rights-Civil Liberties Law Review,* 26(1):261–293.

Fields, Jason, and Lynne M. Casper. 2001. *America's Families and Living Arrangements: March 2000.* Current Population Reports, Series P20-537. Washington, DC: U.S. Census Bureau.

Fine, Gary Alan. 1987. *With the Boys: Little League Baseball and Preadolescent Culture.* Chicago: University of Chicago Press.

Fine, Michelle. 1991. *Framing Dropouts: Notes on the Politics of an Urban Public High School.* Albany, NY: State University Press of New York.

Finkelhor, David. 1984. *Child Abuse: New Theory and Research.* New York: Free Press.

Finkelhor, David, and Kersti Yllo. 1985. *License to Rape: Sexual Abuse of Wives.* New York: Free Press.

Firestone, Shulamith. 1970. *The Dialectic of Sex.* New York: Morrow.

Fisher, Lawrence M. 1996. "Health on Line: Doctor Is In, and His Disk Is Full." *New York Times* (June 14):C1, C8.

Fletcher, Heather. 2006. "Drink Up, It's Not Like You Have Lines to Learn." *New York Times* (October 29): C1.

Flexner, Abraham. 1910. *Medical Education in the United States and Canada.* New York: Carnegie Foundation.

Flynn, Joseph, Andrew Kemp, and Samara Madrid. 2008. "When the Shooting Started." *The Chronicle of Higher Education* (February 29): C1, C4.

Foner, Philip S., and Daniel Rosenberg (Eds.). 1993. *Racism, Dissent, and Asian Americans from 1850 to Present.* Westport, CT: Greenwood Press.

Forbes. 2008. "The Forbes 400: A Billion Dollars Is No Longer Enough." Retrieved: July 5, 2008. Online: http://www.forbes.com/2007/09/19/richest-americans-forbes-lists-richlist07-cx_mm_0920rich_land.html.

Forbes. 2008. "World's Billionaires." Retrieved April 18, 2008. Online: http://www.forbes.com/2008/03/05/richest-billionaires-people-billionaires08-cx_lk_0305intro.html.

Ford, Peter. 2001. "Injustice Seen As Fertile Soil for Terrorists." *The Christian Science Monitor* (28 Nov.). Retrieved Dec. 12, 2002. Online: http://www.csmonitor.com/2001/1128/p7s1woeu.html.

Foreman, Judy. 1993. "Older Adults May Face Obstacles on Job." *San Antonio Express-News* (December 15):B7.

Foreman, Judy. 1996. "Caring for Parents Long-Distance Is a Baby Boomer's Nightmare." *Austin American-Statesman* (November 3):E1, E14.

Fortune. 2005. "Women CEOs of Fortune 500 Companies." Retrieved August 27, 2005. Online: http://www.fortune.com/fortune/subs/fortune500/womenceos/0,23621,,00.html.

FOXNews.com. 2005. "Justifiable Shooting?" *The O'Reilly Factor* (July 15). Retrieved July 20, 2005. Online: http://www.foxnews.com/story/0,2933,162806,00.html.

Frankenberg, Ruth. 1993. *White Women, Race Matters: The Social Construction of Whiteness.* Minneapolis: University of Minnesota Press.

Franklin, John Hope. 1980. *From Slavery to Freedom* (3rd ed.). New York: Knopf.

French, Dolores, with Linda Lee. 1988. *Working: My Life as a Prostitute.* New York: E.P. Dutton.

French, Howard W. 2005. "A Village Grows Rich Off Its Main Export: Its Daughters." *New York Times* (January 3). Retrieved: June 2, 2008. Online: http://www.nytimes.com/2005/01/03/international/asia/03/china.html.

Freudenberg, Nicholas, and Carl Steinsapir. 1992. "Not in Our Backyards: The Grassroots Environmental Movement." In Riley E. Dunlap and Angela G. Mertig (Eds.), *American Environmentalism: The U.S. Environmental Movement, 1970–1990.* New York: Taylor & Francis, pp. 27–37.

Freund, Matthew, Nancy Lee, and Terri Leonard. 1991. "Sexual Behavior of Clients with Street Prostitutes in Camden, New Jersey." *Journal of Sex Research,* 28(4) (November):579–591.

Friedan, Betty. 1993. *The Fountain of Age.* New York: Simon & Schuster.

Friedman, George, and Meredith Friedman. 1996. *The Future of War* New York: St. Martins Griffin.

Friedman, Thomas L. 2000. "Boston E-Party." *New York Times* (January 1):A31.

Friedman, Thomas L. 2008a. *Hot, Flat, and Crowded.* New York: Farrar, Straus and Giroux.

Friedman, Thomas L. 2008b. "Postcard from South China." *New York Times* (August 31): WK10.

Friedmann, John. 1995. "The World City Hypothesis." In Paul L. Knox and Peter J. Taylor (Eds.), *World Cities in a World-System.* Cambridge, England: Cambridge University Press, pp. 317–331.

Friedrichs, David O. 1996. *Trusted Criminals: White Collar Crime in Contemporary Society.* Belmont, CA: Wadsworth.

Friend, Tim. 1996. "Teens and Drugs: Today's Youth Just Don't See the Dangers." *USA Today* (August 21):1A, 2A.

Fry, Richard. 2002. "Latinos in Higher Education: Many Enroll, Too Few Graduate." Report for the Pew Hispanic Center. Retrieved Dec. 10, 2002. Online: http://www.pewhispanic.org/site/docs/pdf/latinosinhighereducationsept5-02.pdf.

FTC. 2005. "Federal Trade Commission Cigarette Report for 2004." Retrieved March 23, 2006. Online: http://www.ftc.gov/reports/cigarette05/050809cigrpt.pdf.

Fuller, Thomas. 2005. "The Workplace: For French, Cheap Labor is a Threat." *International Herald Tribune* (May 25). Retrieved July 11, 2005. Online: http://www.iht.com/articles/2005/05/25/business/workcol25.php.

Fullilove, Mindy Thompson, E. Anne Lown, and Robert E. Fullilove. 1992. "Crack 'Hos and Skeezers: Traumatic Experiences of Women Crack Users." *Journal of Sex Research,* 29(2):275–288.

Funderburg, Lise. 1994. *Black, White, Other: Biracial Americans Talk about Race and Identity.* New York: William Morrow.

The Future of Children. 2001. *Caring for Infants and Toddlers.* Retrieved March 27, 2005. Online: http://www.futureofchildren.org/pubsinfo2825/pubsinfo_show.htm?doc_id=79324.

Gabriel, Trip. 1995a. "A New Generation Seems Ready to Give Bisexuality a Place in the Spectrum." *New York Times* (June 12):C10.

Gabriel, Trip. 1995b. "Some On-Line Discoveries Give Gay Youths a Path to Themselves." *New York Times* (July 2):1, 9.

Gailey, Christine Ward. 1987. "Evolutionary Perspectives on Gender Hierarchy." In Beth B. Hess and Myra Marx Ferree (Eds.), *Analyzing Gender: A Handbook of Social Science Research.* Newbury Park, CA: Sage, pp. 32–67.

Galbraith, John Kenneth. 1985. *The New Industrial State* (4th ed.). Boston: Houghton Mifflin.

Gamson, Joshua. 1994. *Claims to Fame: Celebrity in Contemporary America.* Berkeley, CA: University of California Press.

Gallup Poll. 2008. "Economy Widely Viewed as Most Important Problem." Gallup.com (March 13). Retrieved March 22, 2008. Online: http://www.gallup.com/poll/104959/Economy-Widely-Viewed-Most-Important-Problem.aspx?.

Gamson, William. 1990. *The Strategy of Social Protest* (2nd ed.). Belmont, CA: Wadsworth.

Ganley, Elaine. 2005. "Polish Plumber Flushes Fears in France." *USAToday* (June 29). Retrieved July 11, 2005. Online: http://www.usatoday.com/travel/destinations/2005-06-29-polish_x.htm?POE=TRVISVA.

Gans, Herbert. 1962. *Urban Villagers.* New York: The Free Press.

Gans, Herbert. 1982. *The Urban Villagers: Group and Class in the Life of Italian Americans* (updated and expanded ed.; orig. published in 1962). New York: Free Press.

Gardner, Carol Brooks. 1995. *Passing By: Gender and Public Harassment.* Berkeley, CA: University of California Press.

Gardner, Tracey A. 1994. "Racism in Pornography and the Women's Movement." In Alison M. Jaggar (Ed.), *Living with Contradictions: Controversies in Feminist Social Ethics.* Boulder, CO: Westview, pp. 171–176.

Garfinkel, Irwin, and Sara S. McLanahan. 1986. *Single Mothers and Their Children: A New American Dilemma.* Washington, DC: Urban Institute Press.

Garner, Abigail. 2005. *Families Like Mine.* New York: HarperCollins.

Garreau, Joel. 1991. *Edge City: Life on the New Frontier.* New York: Doubleday.

Gatz, Margaret (Ed.). 1995. *Emerging Issues in Mental Health and Aging.* Washington, DC: American Psychological Association.

Garvin, Glenn. 2007. "(GEICO) 'Cavemen' Series Gets a New Criticism: It's Racist." *Miami Herald* (July 26). Retrieved April 27, 2008. Online: http://www.freerepublic.com/focus/f-news/1872285/posts.

Gates, Gary J. 2006. *Same-sex Couples and the Gay, Lesbian, Bisexual Population: New Estimates from the American Community Survey.* UCLA School of Law: The Williams Institute on Sexual Orientation, Law and Public Policy. Retrieved: May 27, 2008. Online: http://www.law.ucla.edu/williamsinstitute/publications/SameSex Couplesand GLBpopACS.pdf.

Gawin, F. H., and E. H. Ellinwood, Jr. 1988. Cocaine and Other Stimulants: Actions, Abuse, and Treatment. *New England Journal of Medicine,* 318:1173–1182.

GEICO.com. 2008. "The Cavemen." Retrieved April 27, 2008. Online: http://www.geico.com.

Gelfand, Donald E. 1994. *Aging and Ethnicity: Knowledge and Services.* New York: Springer.

Gelman, David. 1991. "Clean and Sober—And Agnostic." *Newsweek* (July 8). Retrieved July 26, 2005. Online: http://www.a1associates.com/AA/newspapers.htm.

Gentry, Cynthia. 1995. "Crime Control through Drug Control." In Joseph F. Sheley (Ed.), *Criminology: A Contemporary Handbook* (2nd ed.). Belmont, CA: Wadsworth, pp. 477–493.

Gerbner, George, 1995. "Television Violence: The Power and the Peril." In Gail Dines and Jean M. Humez (Eds.), *Gender, Face, and Class in Media: A Text-Reader.* Thousand Oaks, CA: Sage, pp. 547–557.

Gerstel, Naomi, and Harriet Engel Gross. 1995. "Gender and Families in the United States: The Reality of Economic Dependence." In Jo Freeman (Ed.), *Women: A Feminist Perspective* (5th ed.). Mountain View, CA: Mayfield, pp. 92–127.

Gessen, Masha. 1993. "Lesbians and Breast Cancer." *The Advocate* (February 9):22–23.

Gibbs, Lois Marie, as told to Murray Levine. 1982. *Love Canal: My Story.* Albany, NY: State University of New York Press.

Gibson, James William, and Francesca M. Cancian. 1990. "Is War Inevitable?" In Francesca M. Cancian and James William Gibson (Eds.), *Making War, Making Peace: The Social Foundations of Violent Conflict.* Belmont, CA: Wadsworth, pp. 1–10.

Gilbert, Matthew. 2008. "Merely Beloved: *Brothers & Sisters* Uses a Civil Union to Draw Viewers. How Times Have Changed." *Boston Globe* (May 11). Retrieved: May 29, 2008. Online: http://www.boston.com/ae/tv/articles/2008/05/10/merely beloved?mode=PF.

Gilbert, Richard J. 1986. *Caffeine: The Most Popular Stimulant.* New York: Chelsea House.

Giobbe, Evelina. 1993. "Surviving Commercial Sexual Exploitation." In Diana E. H. Russell (Ed.), *Making Violence Sexy: Feminist Views on Pornography.* New York: Teachers College Press, pp. 37–41.

Giobbe, Evelina. 1994. "Confronting the Liberal Lies about Prostitution." In Alison M. Jaggar (Ed.), *Living with Contradictions: Controversies in Feminist Social Ethics.* Boulder, CO: Westview, pp. 120–136.

GLAAD. 2007a. "GLAAD's 12th Annual Diversity Study Examines 2007-2008 Primetime Television Season." Retrieved: May 27, 2008. Online: http://www.glaad.org/eye/ontv/07-08/overview2007.php.

GLAAD. 2007b. "Network Responsibility Index: Primetime Programming 2006-2007. Retrieved: May 27, 2008. Online: http://www.glaad.org/2007/PDFS/GLAAD_NRI2007.pdf.

Gladwell, Malcolm. 1997. "Damaged: Why Do Some People Turn into Violent Criminals?" *The New Yorker* (February 24–March 3):132–147.

Glaser, Barney, and Anselm Strauss. 1968. *Time for Dying.* Chicago: Aldine.

Gleick, Elizabeth. 1996. "The Children's Crusade." *Time* (June 3):30–35.

GlobalSecurity.org. 2005. "World Wide Military Expenditures." Retrieved August 25, 2005. Online: http://www.globalsecurity.org/military/world/spending.htm.

GlobalSecurity.org.2008. "Global Military Spending Equal to $200 Per Person Annually." Retrieved: October 3, 2008. Online: http:www.globalsecurity.org/military/library/news/2008/06/mil-080609-rianovosti03. htm.

Goffman, Erving. 1961. *Asylums: Essays on the Social Situation of Mental Patients and Other Inmates.* Chicago: Aldine.

Goffman, Erving. 1963. *Stigma: Notes of the Management of Spoiled Identity.* Englewood Cliffs, NJ: Prentice-Hall.

Golay, Michael, and Carl Rollyson. 1996. *Where America Stands: 1996.* New York: John Wiley.

Gold, Rachel Benson, and Cory L. Richards. 1994. "Securing American Women's Reproductive Health." In Cynthia Costello and Anne J. Stone (Eds.), *The American Woman, 1994–1995.* New York: W.W. Norton, pp. 197–222.

Goldberg, Robert A. 1991. *Grassroots Resistance: Social Movements in Twentieth Century America.* Belmont, CA: Wadsworth.

Goldstein, Amy. 2002. "Health Coverage Falls: Uninsured Numbers Up after 2 Years of Decline." *Washington Post* (Sept. 30):A1.

Golombisky, Kim. 2004. "Women of a Certain Age, Magazine Advertising, and a Politics of the Unmarked." Paper presented at the Association for Education in Journalism and Mass Communication, Toronto, Canada (August). Retrieved July 23, 2005. Online: http://list/mus/edu/cgibin/wa?A2=ind0410e&L=aejmc&F=&S=&P=2802.

Gonyea, Judith G. 1998. "Midlife and Menopause: Uncharted Territories for Baby Boomer Women." *Generations* 22(Spring):87.

Gonzalez, David. 2005. "From Margins of Society to Center of the Tragedy." *New York Times* (September 2):A1, A19.

Goode, Erich. 1989. *Drugs in American Society* (3rd ed.). New York: McGraw-Hill.

Goode, Erich. 1996. "Deviance, Norms, and Social Reaction." In Erich Goode (Ed.), *Social Deviance.* Boston: Allyn and Bacon, pp. 36–40.

Goode, William J. 1982. "Why Men Resist." In Barrie Thorne with Marilyn Yalom (Eds.), *Rethinking the Family: Some*

Feminist Questions. New York: Longman, pp. 131–150.

Goodman, Emily Jane. 1999. "Seducers, Harassers, and Wimps in Black Robes." *New York Times* (December 19):AR47, 51.

Goodman, Peter S. 1996. "The High Cost of Sneakers." *Austin American-Statesman* (July 7):F1, F6.

Goodman, Peter S. 2008a. "From Welfare Shift in '96, a Reminder for Clinton." *New York Times* (April 11): A1.

Goodman, Peter S. 2008b. "Workers Get Fewer Hours, Deepening the Down Furn." *New York Times* (April 18) A1, A21.

Gordon, David M. 1996. *Fat and Mean: The Corporate Squeeze of Working Americans and the Myth of Managerial "Downsizing."* New York: Martin Kessler Books/The Free Press.

Gordon, Milton M. 1964. *Assimilation in American Life: The Role of Race, Religion, and National Origins.* New York: Oxford University Press.

Gottdiener, Mark. 1985. *The Social Production of Urban Space.* Austin, TX: University of Texas Press.

Gover, Tzivia. 1996a. "Fighting for Our Children." *The Advocate* (November 26):22–30.

Gover, Tzivia. 1996b. "Occupational Hazards." *The Advocate* (November 26):36–38.

Gover, Tzivia. 1996c. "The Other Mothers." *The Advocate* (November 26):31.

Graham, Lawrence Otis. 1995. "It's No Longer the Back of the Bus, but ..." *New York Times* (May 21):F13.

Graham, Lawrence Otis. 2000. *Our Kind of People: Inside America's Black Upper Class.* New York: HarperPerennial.

Graham, Paul. 2004. *Hackers & Painters: Big Ideas from the Computer Age.* Sebastopol, CA: O'Reilly.

Grasmuck, Sherri, and Patricia R. Pessar. 1991. *Between Two Islands: Dominican International Migration.* Berkeley, CA: University of California Press.

Gray, Herman. 1995. *Watching Race: Television and the Struggle for "Blackness."* Minneapolis: University of Minnesota Press.

Gray, Paul. 1996. "Gagging the Doctors." *Time* (January 8):50.

Greenberg, Edward S., and Benjamin I. Page. 1993. *The Struggle for Democracy.* New York: HarperCollins.

Greenprintdenver.org. 2008. "Did You Know? Fact Sheet." Published by the City and County of Denver, Colorado. Retrieved: September 11, 2008. Online: http://www.greenprintdenver.org/about/facts.php.

Greene, Vernon L., and J. I. Ondrich. 1990. "Risk Factors for Nursing Home Admissions and Exits." *Journal of Gerontology,* 45:S250–S258.

Grieco, Elizabeth M., and Rachel C. Cassidy. 2001. U.S. Census Bureau Brief. "Overview of Race and Hispanic Origin." Retrieved Sept. 25, 2002. Online: http://www.census.gov/prod/2001pubs/c2kbr01-1.pdf.

Grobe, Jeanine (Ed.). 1995. *Beyond Bedlam: Contemporary Women Psychiatric Survivors Speak Out.* Chicago: Third Side Press.

Gross, Jane. 1997. "More AIDS Is Seen in People over 50." *New York Times* (March 16):23.

Guardian Unlimited. 2005. "I Thought I Was Going to Die: Accounts From People Who Witnessed the Explosions in Central London Today." *Guardian Unlimited* (July 7). Retrieved August 25, 2005. Online: http://www.guardian.co.uk/terrorism/story/0,12780,1523183,00.html.

Hacker, Andrew. 1995. *Two Nations: Black and White, Separate, Hostile, Unequal* (rev. ed.). New York: Ballantine Books.

Hamilton, James T. 1998. *Channeling Violence: The Economic Market for Violent Television Programming.* Princeton, NJ: Princeton University Press.

Hamper, Ben. 1991. *Rivethead: Tales from the Assembly Line.* New York: Warner Books.

Haney, Craig, Curtis Banks, and Philip Zimbardo. 1984. "A Study of Prisoners and Guards in a Simulated Prison." In E. Aronson (Ed.), *Readings about the Social Animal.* New York: W.H. Freeman.

Haney, Walter. 1993. "Testing and Minorities." In Lois Weis and Michelle Fine (Eds.), *Beyond Silenced Voices: Class, Race, and Gender in United States Schools.* Albany, NY: State University of New York Press, pp. 45–73.

Hansell, Saul. 2000. "America Online Agrees to Buy Time Warner for $165 Billion; Media Deal Is Richest Merger." *New York Times* (January 11):A1, C11.

Hardy, Eric S. 1996. "Annual Report on American Industry." *Forbes* (January 1):76–79.

Harlow, C. W. 1991. *Female Victims of Violent Crime.* Washington, DC: U.S. Department of Justice, Bureau of Justice Statistics.

Harrington Meyer, Madonna. 1990. "Family Status and Poverty among Older Women: The Gendered Distribution of Retirement Income in the United States." *Social Problems,* 37:551–563.

Harrison, Roderick J. 2001. "Residential Segregation Persists as African Americans Move to Suburbs." Retrieved August 26, 2005. Online: http://www.findarticles.com/p/articles/mi_qa3812/is_200109/ai_n8972848.

Hartlaub, Peter. 2004. "New Grand Theft Auto Will Rob You of Your Life." *SFGate.com.* Retrieved July 13. Online: http://www.sfgate.com/cgibin/article.cgi?f=/c/a/2004/11/19/DDG659TC0K1.DTL&hw=grand+theft+auto+san+andreas&sn=001&sc=1000.

Hartley, Nina. 1994. "Confessions of a Feminist Porno Star." In Alison M. Jaggar (Ed.), *Living with Contradictions: Controversies in Feminist Social Ethics.* Boulder, CO: Westview, pp. 176–178.

Hartmann, Heidi. 1976. "Capitalism, Patriarchy, and Job Segregation by Sex." *Signs: Journal of Women in Culture and Society,* 1(Spring):137–169.

Hartmann, Heidi. 1981. "The Family as the Locus of Gender, Class, and Political Struggle: The Example of Housework." *Signs,* 6:366–394.

Hauchler, Ingomar, and Paul M. Kennedy (Eds.). 1994. *Global Trends: The World Almanac of Development and Peace.* New York: Continuum.

Hauser, Robert M. 1995. "Symposium: The Bell Curve." *Contemporary Sociology: A Journal of Reviews,* 24(2):149–153.

Havighurst, Robert J., Bernice L. Neugarten, and Sheldon S. Tobin. 1968. "Disengagement and Patterns of Aging." In Bernice L. Neugarten (Ed.), *Middle Age and Aging.* Chicago: University of Chicago Press, pp. 161–172.

Hawley, Amos. 1950. *Human Ecology.* New York: Ronald Press.

Hawley, Amos. 1981. *Urban Society* (2nd ed.). New York: Wiley.

Hays, Constance L. 1995. "If the Hair Is Gray, Con Artists See Green: The Elderly Are Prime Targets." *New York Times* (May 21):F1, F5.

Healy, Patrick O'Gilfoil. 2007. "Run! Hide! The Illegal Border Crossing Experience." *New York Times* (February 4). Retrieved: September 10, 2008. Online: http://travel.nytimes.com/2007/02/04/travel/04HeadsUp.html.

Heilbrunn, Leslie. 2000. "Mind Control?" *Brill's Content* (January):105–109.

Helms, Marisa. 2005. "Shooting Fuels Debate Over Safety of Prozac for Teens." Minnesota Public Radio: News & Features (March 25). Retrieved July 25, 2005. Online: http://news.minnesota.publicradio.org/features/2005/03/25_helmsm_prozacfolo/.

Hendriks, Aart, Rob Tielman, and Evert van der Veen. 1993. *The Third Pink Book: A Global View of Lesbian and Gay Liberation and Oppression.* Buffalo, NY: Prometheus.

The Henry J. Kaiser Family Foundation. 2004. "The HIV/AIDS Epidemic in the United States." Retrieved July 30, 2005. Online: http://www.kff.org/hivaids/upload/Fact-Sheet-The-HIV-AIDS-Epidemic-in-the-United-States-March-2004.pdf.

Henry, William A., III. 1990. "Beyond the Melting Pot." *Time* (April 9):28–35.

Herd, D. 1988. "Drinking by Black and White Women: Results from a National Survey." *Social Problems,* 35(5):493–520.

Herek, Gregory M. 1995. "Psychological Heterosexism and Anti-Gay Violence: The Social Psychology of Bigotry and Bashing." In Michael S. Kimmel and Michael A. Messner (Eds.), *Men's Lives* (3rd ed.). Boston: Allyn and Bacon, pp. 341–353.

Hernandez, Raymond. 1997. "New York Offers Pollution Permits to Lure Companies." *New York Times* (May 19):A1, B8.

Herrnstein, Richard J., and Charles Murray. 1994. *The Bell Curve: Intelligence and Class Structure in American Life.* New York: Free Press.

Herz, Diane E., and Barbara H. Wootton. 1996. "Women in the Workforce: An Overview." In Cynthia Costello and Barbara Kivimae Krimgold (Eds.) for the Women's Research and Education Institute, *The American Woman 1996–97: Women and Work.* New York: W.W. Norton, pp. 44–78.

Hetzel, Lisa, and Annetta Smith. 2001. *The 65 Years and Over Population: 2000.* Census 2000 Brief, C2KBR/01-10. Washington, DC: U.S. Census Bureau.

Higginbotham, Elizabeth. 1994. "Black Professional Women: Job Ceilings and Employment Sectors." In Maxine Baca Zinn and Bonnie Thornton Dill (Eds.), *Women of Color in U.S. Society.* Philadelphia: Temple University Press, pp. 113–131.

Higley, Stephen Richard. 1995. *Privilege, Power and Place: The Geography of the American Upper Class.* Lanham, MD: Rowman & Littlefield.

Hills, Stuart L. 1971. *Crime, Power, and Morality.* Scranton, PA: Chandler.

Hirsch, Amanda. 2008. "Confessions of an Internet Addict." Retrieved: August 31, 2008. Online: http://www.creativedc.org/blog/2008/07/confessions-of-internet-addict.html.

Hirschi, Travis. 1969. *Causes of Delinquency.* Berkeley, CA: University of California Press.

Hirschi, Travis, and Michael J. Hindelang. 1977. "Intelligence and Delinquency: A Revisionist Review." *American Sociological Review,* 42:571–586.

Hispanic Association on Corporate Responsibility. 2004. "Corporate Governance Report 2004." Retrieved July 23, 2005. Online: http://www.hacr.org/mediacenter/pubID.21/pub_detail.asp.

Hoberman, John. 1997. *Darwin's Athletes: How Sport Has Damaged Black America and Preserved the Myth of Race.* Boston: Houghton Mifflin.

Hochschild, Arlie Russell, with Ann Machung. 1989. *The Second Shift: Working Parents and the Revolution at Home.* New York: Viking/Penguin.

Hodson, Randy, and Teresa A. Sullivan. 2008. *The Social Organization of Work* Belmont: Wadsworth.

Hoffman, Andrew J. 1994. "Love Canal Lives." *E Magazine* (November–December): 19–22.

Hoffman, Jan. 1997. "Crime and Punishment: Shame Gains Popularity." *New York Times* (January 16):A1, A11.

Holloway, Diane. 2005. "Images of Death, Desperation Put Us in the Midst." *Austin American-Statesman* (September 3):A8.

Holmes, Robert M. 1988. *Serial Murder.* Beverly Hills, CA: Sage.

Holmes, Robert M., and Stephen T. Holmes. 1993. *Murder in America.* Newbury Park, CA: Sage.

Holmes, Ronald M. 1983. *The Sex Offender and the Criminal Justice System.* Springfield, IL: Charles C. Thomas.

Holmes, Steven A. 1996a. "1996 Cost of Teen Pregnancy Is Put at $7 Billion." *New York Times* (June 13):A11.

Holmes, Steven A. 1996b. "Education Gap Between Races Closes." *New York Times* (September 6):A8.

Holt, John C. 1964. *How Children Fail.* New York: Dell.

Hooker, Evelyn. 1957. "The Adjustment of the Male Overt Homosexual." *Journal of Projective Techniques,* 21:18–31.

Hooker, Evelyn. 1958. "Male Homosexuality and the Rorschach." *Journal of Projective Techniques,* 22:33–54.

Hooyman, Nancy and H. Asuman Kiyak. 2008. *Social Gerontology: A Multidisciplinary Perspective,* 8th ed. Boston: Allyn and Bacon.

Hopkins, Evans D. 1997. "Lockdown: Life Inside Is Getting Harder." *The New Yorker* (February 24/March 3):66–71.

Horowitz, Allan V. 1982. *Social Control of Mental Illness.* New York: Academic.

Horton, John. 1995. *The Politics of Diversity: Immigration, Resistance, and Change in Monterey Park, California.* Philadelphia: Temple University Press.

Hostetler, A. J. 1995. "Joe Camel Blamed for Rise in Teen Smoking." *Austin American-Statesman* (July 21):A2.

Houghton, Brian K., and Neal A. Pollard. 2002. "The Media and Terrorism: Second-Hand Terrorism." The Terrorism Research Center. Retrieved Dec. 23, 2002. Online: http://www.terrorism.com/terrorism.Media.shtml.

Hounsell, Cindy. 1996. "Women and Pensions: A Policy Agenda." In Cynthia Costello and Barbara Kivimae Krimgold (Eds.) for the Women's Research and Education Institute, *The American Woman 1996–97: Women and Work.* New York: W.W. Norton, pp. 166–173.

HUD. 2005. "News Release: HUD Awards $18.8 Million to Help People & Families Living With HIV/AIDS." (August 19). Washington, D.C.: U.S. Department of Housing and Urban Development.

Huddle, Donald. 1993. *The Net National Cost of Immigration.* Washington, DC: Carrying Capacity Network.

Huesmann, R. Rowell, Jessica Moise-Titus, Cherly-Lynn Podolski, and Leonard D. Eron. 2003. "Longitudinal Relations Between Children's Exposure to TV Violence and Their Aggression and Violence Behavior in Young Adulthood: 1977–1992." *Developmental Psychology* (March):201–221.

Hughey, Matthew W. 2008. "Walking Upright but not Alright: The Trivialization of Discrimination and Identity Politics in ABC's *Cavemen.*" *Social Problems Forum* (Winter): 38-39.

Human Rights Campaign. 2003. "HRC Decries Two Recent Hate Crimes Against GLBT People of Color." Human Rights Campaign (May). Retrieved July 1, 2005. Online: http://www.hrc.org.

Human Suffering Index. 1992. Washington, DC: Population Crisis Committee (now Population Action International).

Huston, Aletha C. 1985. "The Development of Sex Typing: Themes from Recent Research." *Developmental Review,* 5:2–17.

Hutchison, Ray, and Charles Kyle. 1993. "Hispanic Street Gangs in Chicago's Public Schools." In Scott Cummings and Daniel J. Monti (Eds.), *Gangs: The Origins and Impact of Contemporary Youth Gangs in the United States.* Albany, NY: State University of New York Press, pp. 113–136.

Hynes, Samuel. 1997. *The Soldiers' Tale: Bearing Witness to Modern War.* New York: Allen Lane/Penguin.

iCasualties.org. 2005. "Iraq Coalition Casualty Count." Retrieved September 3, 2005. Online: http://icasualties.org/oif.

iCasualties.org. 2008. "Iraq Casualty Count." Retrieved: October 3, 2008. Online: http://www.casualties.org.

Inciardi, James A., Ruth Horowitz, and Anne E. Pottieger. 1993a. *Street Kids, Street Drugs, Street Crime: An Examination of Drug Use and Serious Delinquency in Miami.* Belmont, CA: Wadsworth.

Inciardi, James, Dorothy Lockwood, and Anne E. Pottieger. 1993b. *Women and Crack-Cocaine.* New York: Macmillan.

Institute on Race and Poverty, 2006. "Minority Suburbanization, Stable Integration, and Economic Opportunity in Fifteen Metropolitan Regions." Institute on Race and Poverty, University of Minnesota Law School. Retrieved: September 5, 2008. Online: http://www.irpumn.org/uls/resources/projects/Minority_Suburbanization_full_report_032406.pdf.

Iyengar, Shanto. 1990. "Framing Responsibility for Political Issues: The Case of Poverty." *Political Behavior* 12 (March): 19–40.

Iyengar, Shanto. 1991. *Is Anyone Responsible? How Television Frames Political Issues.* Chicago: University of Chicago Press.

Jack, Dana Crowley. 1993. *Silencing the Self: Women and Depression.* New York: HarperPerennial.

Jackson, Kenneth T. 1985. *Crabgrass Frontier: The Suburbanization of the United States.* New York: Oxford University Press.

Jacobs, Jane. 1961. *The Death and Life of Great American Cities.* New York: Random House.

Jaffee, David. 1990. *Levels of Socio-economic Development Theory.* Westport, CT: Praeger.

JAMA: The Journal of the American Medical Association. 1996. "Health Care Needs of Gay Men and Lesbians in the United States" (May 1):1354–1360.

James, William H., and Stephen L. Johnson. 1996. *Doin' Drugs: Patterns of African American Addiction.* Austin, TX: University of Texas Press.

Jankowski, Martín Sánchez. 1991. *Islands in the Street: Gangs and American Urban Society.* Berkeley, CA: University of California Press.

Janofsky, Michael. 1996. "Home-Grown Courts Spring Up as Judicial Arm of the Far Right." *New York Times* (April 17):A1, A13.

Janofsky, Michael. 1997. "Old Friends, Once Felons, Regroup to Fight Crime." *New York Times* (March 10):A1, A10.

Jarrett, Robin L. 1997. "Living Poor: Family Life among Single Parent, African-American Women." In Diana Kendall (Ed.), *Race, Class, and Gender in a Diverse Society: A Text-Reader.* Boston: Allyn and Bacon, pp. 344–365.

Jayson, Sharon. 1997. "Case of Channel One." *Austin American-Statesman* (January 22):B1, B6.

Jencks, Christopher, Marshall Smith, Henry Acland, Mary J. Bane, David Cohen, Herbert Gintis, Barbara Heyns, and Stephan Michelson. 1972. *Inequality: A Reassessment of the Effect of Family and Schooling in America.* New York: Basic Books.

Jensen, Michael. 2007. "*Ugly Betty* Is Freaking Fabulous (and Gay)." Afterelton.com. Retrieved: May 26, 2008. Online: http://www.afterelton.com?TV/2007/3/uglybetty.

Johnson, Bruce D., Paul J. Goldstein, Edward Preble, James Schmeidler, Douglas S. Lipton, Barry Spunt, and Thomas Miller. 1985. *Taking Care of Business: The Economics of Crime by Heroin Abusers.* Lexington, MA: Lexington Books.

Johnson, Reed. 2008. "Mexican Town Offers Illegal Immigration Simulation Adventure." *Los Angeles Times* (May 24). Retrieved: September 10, 2008. Online: http://www.latimes.com/news/nationworld/nation/la-et-border24-2008may24,0,4295754,print.story.

Joint Center for Political and Economic Studies. 2000. "Joint Center Releases 1999 National Count of Black Elected Officials." Retrieved Sept. 25, 2002. Online: http://www.jointcenter.org/pressrel/2000_beo.htm.

Jolin, Annette. 1994. "On the Backs of Working Prostitutes: Feminist Theory and Prostitution Policy." *Crime and Delinquency,* 40(1):69–83.

Jones, Gerard. 2002. *Killing Monsters: Why Children Need Fantasy, Super Heroes, and Make-Believe Violence.* New York: Basic.

Jones, M. Gail, and Jack Wheatley. 1990. "Gender Differences in Teacher-Student Interactions in Science Classrooms." *Journal of Research in Science Teaching,* 27(9):861–874.

Jung, John. 1994. *Under the Influence: Alcohol and Human Behavior.* Pacific Grove, CA: Brooks/Cole.

Kahn, Joseph. 2007. "Murdoch's Dealings in China. It's Business, and It's Personal." *New York Times* (June 26). Retrieved: September 1, 2008. Online: http://www.nytimes.com/2007/06/26/world/asia/26murdoch.html.

Kaiser Family Foundation. 2004. "*Inside*-OUT: A Report on the Experiences of Lesbians, Gays and Bisexuals in America and the Public's Views on Issues and Policies Related to Sexual Orientation." Retrieved: May 27, 2008. Online: http://www.kff.org/kaiserpolls/upload/New-Surveys-on-Experiences-of Lesbians-Gays-and Bisexuals-and-the-Public-s-Views-Related to Sexual-Orientation-Report.pdf.

Kalb, Claudia. 1999. "No Green Light Yet: A Long-Awaited Report Supports Medical Marijuana Use. So Now What?" *Newsweek* (March 29):35.

Kaldor, Mary. 1981. *The Baroque Arsenal.* New York: Hill and Wang.

Kalish, Richard A. 1985. *Death, Grief, and Caring Relationships* (2nd ed.). Monterey, CA: Brooks/Cole.

Kalish, Richard A., and D. K. Reynolds. 1981. *Death and Ethnicity: A Psychocultural Study.* Farmingdale, NY: Baywood.

Kaminer, Wendy. 1990. *A Fearful Freedom: Women's Flight from Equality.* Reading, MA: Addison-Wesley.

Kane, Hal. 1995. "Leaving Home." *Transaction: Social Science and Modern Society* (May–June):16–25.

Kantrowitz, Barbara. 1993. "Live Wires." *Newsweek* (September 6):42–48.

Kaplan, David A. 1993. "Dumber Than We Thought." *Newsweek* (September 20): 44–45.

Kaplan, Robert D. 1996. "Cities of Despair." *New York Times* (June 6):A19.

Karmen, Andrew A. 2000. "Victims of Crimes: Issues and Patterns." In Joseph F. Sheley (Ed.), *Criminology: A Contemporary Handbook* (3rd ed.). Belmont, CA: Wadsworth, pp. 165–185.

Kasindorf, Jeanie. 1988. "Hustling: Working Girl." *New York Times* (April 18):56.

Katz, Janet, and William J. Chambliss. 1995. In Joseph F. Sheley (Ed.), *Criminology: A Contemporary Handbook* (2nd ed.). Belmont, CA: Wadsworth, pp. 275–303.

Kaysen, Susanna. 1993. *Girl, Interrupted.* New York: Vintage.

Kazemi, Darius. 2005. "I Love It Here: The Secret Maps of Worcester." *WPI Tech News* (April 12). Retrieved August 20, 2005. Online: http://www.wpi.edu/News/TechNews/article.php?id=973.

Keck, William. 2008. "Top This: A Gay Ceremony of ABC's *Brothers & Sisters.*" Retrieved: May 29, 2008. Online: http://abcnews.go.com/print?id=4824155.

Kelso, William A. 1994. *Poverty and the Underclass: Changing Perceptions of the Poor in America.* New York: New York University Press.

Kemp, Alice Abel. 1994. *Women's Work: Degraded and Devalued.* Englewood Cliffs, NJ: Prentice Hall.

Kempadoo, Kamala, and Jo Doezema (Eds.). 1998. *Global Sex Workers: Rights,*

Resistance, and Redefinition. New York: Routledge.

Kempe, C. Henry, F. Silverman, B. Steele, W. Droegemueller, and H. Silver. 1962. "The Battered-Child Syndrome." *Journal of the American Medical Association,* 181:17–24.

Kempe, Ruth S., and C. Henry Kempe. 1978. *Child Abuse.* Cambridge, MA: Harvard University Press.

Kendall, Diana. 2002. *The Power of Good Deeds: Privileged Women and the Social Reproduction of the Upper Class.* Lanham, MD: Rowman & Littlefield.

Kendall, Diana. 2005. *Framing Class: Media Representations of Wealth and Poverty in America.* Lanham, MD: Rowman & Littlefield.

Kennedy, Paul. 1993. *Preparing for the Twenty-First Century.* New York: Random House.

Kessler, Ronald C. 1994. "Lifetime and 12-Month Prevalence of DSM-III-R Psychiatric Disorders in the United States: Results of the National Comorbidity Survey." *JAMA, The Journal of the American Medical Association,* 271 (March 2):654D.

Kessler. 2005. "Failure and Delay in Initial Treatment Contact After First Onset of Mental Disorders in the National Comorbidity Survey Replication." *Archives of General Psychiatry,* 62: 6 (June): 603–613.

Kessler-Harris, Alice. 1990. *A Woman's Wage: Historical Meanings and Social Consequences.* Lexington, KY: University Press of Kentucky.

Kiel, Douglas P., David T. Felson, Marian T. Hanna, Jennifer J. Anderson, and Peter W. F. Wilson. 1990. "Caffeine and the Risk of Hip Fracture: The Framington Study." *American Journal of Epidemiology,* 132:675–684.

Kilborn, Peter T. 1993. "Voices of the People: Struggle, Hope and Fear." *New York Times* (November 14):4A1, 4A14.

Kilborn, Peter T. 1996. "With Welfare Overhaul Now Law, States Grapple with the Consequences." *New York Times* (August 23):A1, A10.

Kilbourne, Jean. 1994. "Still Killing Us Softly: Advertising and the Obsession with Thinness." In Patricia Fallon, Melanie A. Katzman, and Susan C. Wooley (Eds.), *Feminist Perspectives on Eating Disorders.* New York, Guilford, pp. 395–454.

Kilbourne, Jean. 1999. *Deadly Persuasion: Why Women and Girls Must Fight the Addictive Power of Advertising.* New York: Free Press.

Kim, Elaine H., and Eui-Young Yu. 1996. *East to America: Korean American Life Stories.* New York: New Press.

Kimmel, Michael S. 1987. "The Contemporary 'Crisis' in Masculinity in Historical Perspective." In Harry Brod (Ed.), *The Making of Masculinities.* Boston: Allen and Unwin, pp. 121–153.

Kimmel, Michael S. (Ed.). 1990. *Men Confront Pornography.* New York: Crown Books.

King, Leslie, and Madonna Harrington Meyer. 1997. "The Politics of Reproductive Benefits: U.S. Insurance Coverage of Contraceptive and Infertility Treatments." *Gender and Society,* 11(1):8–30.

Kinsey, Alfred C., Wardell B. Pomeroy, Clyde E. Martin, and Paul H. Gebhard. 1948. *Sexual Behavior in the Human Male.* Philadelphia: Saunders.

Kipnis, Laura. 1996. *Bound and Gagged: Pornography and the Politics of Fantasy in America.* New York: Grove Press.

Kitano, Harry H. L., and Roger Daniels. 1995. *Asian Americans: Emerging Minorities* (2nd ed.). Englewood Cliffs, NJ: Prentice Hall.

Kitch, Carolyn. 2003. "Selling the 'Boomer Babes' *more, my generation,* and the 'New' Middle Age." *Journal of Magazine and New Media Research* (Spring). Retrieved July 23, 2005. Online: http://aejmcmagazine.bsu.edu/journal/archive/Spring_2003/Kitch.htm.

Kivel, Paul. 1996. *Uprooting Racism: How White People Can Work for Racial Justice.* Philadelphia: New Society Publishers.

Klockars, Carl B. 1979. "The Contemporary Crises of Marxist Criminology." *Criminology,* 16:477–515.

Klonoff, Elizabeth A. 1997. *Preventing Misdiagnosis of Women: A Guide to Physical Disorders That Have Psychiatric Symptoms.* Thousand Oaks, CA: Sage.

Kluger, Richard. 1996. *Ashes to Ashes: America's Hundred-Year Cigarette War, the Public Health and the Unabashed Triumph of Philip Morris.* New York: Alfred A. Knopf.

Knox, Paul L., and Peter J. Taylor (Eds.). 1995. *World Cities in a World-System.* Cambridge, England: Cambridge University Press.

Knudsen, Dean D. 1992. *Child Maltreatment: Emerging Perspectives.* Dix Hills, NY: General Hall.

Kolata, Gina. 1996a. "Experts Are at Odds on How Best to Tackle Rise in Teen-Agers' Drug Use." *New York Times* (September 18):A17.

Kolata, Gina. 1996b. "New Era of Robust Elderly Belies the Fears of Scientists." *New York Times* (February 27):A1, B10.

Kolata, Gina. 1996c. "On Fringes of Health Care, Untested Therapies Thrive." *New York Times* (June 17):A1, C11.

Kosmin, Barry A., and Seymour P. Lachman. 1993. *One Nation under God: Religion in Contemporary American Society.* New York: Crown Trade Paperbacks.

Kozol, Jonathan. 1986. *Illiterate America.* New York: Plume/Penguin.

Kramer, Peter D. 1993. *Listening to Prozac.* New York: Viking.

Kreider, Rose M., and Jason M. Fields. 2002. "Number, Timing, and Duration of Marriages and Divorces: Fall 1996." U.S. Census Bureau, Current Population Reports, P70-80. Retrieved Dec. 3, 2002. Online: www.census.gov/prod/2002pubs/p70-80.pdf.

Kristof, Nicholas D. 1996a. "Aging World, New Wrinkles." *New York Times* (September 22):E1, E5.

Kristof, Nicholas D. 1996b. "Asian Childhoods Sacrificed to Prosperity's Lust." *New York Times* (April 14):1, 6.

Krohn, Marvin. 2000. "Sources of Criminality: Control and Deterrence Theories." In Joseph F. Sheley (Ed.), *Criminology: A Contemporary Handbook* (3rd ed.). Belmont, CA: Wadsworth, pp. 373–399.

Krufka, Marci M. 2001. "Women Lawyers: From Changing Policies to Changing Perceptions." Retrieved July 26, 2005. Online: http://www.altmanweil.com/about/articles/pdf/womenlawyers.pdf.

Krugman, Paul. 2005a. "A Can't Do Government." *New York Times* (September 2):A23.

Krugman, Paul. 2005b. "Passing the Buck." *New York Times* (April 22):A23.

Kübler-Ross, Elisabeth. 1969. *On Death and Dying.* New York: Macmillan.

Kurz, Demie. 1989. "Social Science Perspectives on Wife Abuse: Current Debates and Future Directions." *Gender and Society,* 3(4):489–505.

Kurz, Demie. 1995. *For Richer, for Poorer: Mothers Confront Divorce.* New York: Routledge.

Lacey, Marc. 2008. "Across Globe, Empty Bellies Bring Rising Anger." *New York Times* (April 18): A1, A11.

Lakoff, George. 2002. *Moral Politics: How Liberals and Conservatives Think.* Chicago: University of Chicago Press.

Lamanna, Mary Ann, and Agnes Riedmann. 2009. *Marriages and Families: Making Choices in a Diverse Society* (10th ed.). Belmont, CA: Wadsworth/Cengage.

Lambert, Bruce. 2006. "'First' Suburbs Growing Older and Poorer, Report Warns." *New York Times* (February 16): A1.

Landler, Mark. 2005. "A Crucible in Turkey: Steel Maker Lies at the Heart of a

Struggle Over Privatization." *New York Times* (August 5):C1,C4.

Lane, Michael; Amanda Ryan; Shelly Wilson; and Taylor Yeftich. 2004. "A Path to Renewal: The Revitalization of North Lawndale." DePaul University PPS (Winter 2007). Retrieved: September 5, 2008. Online: http://condor/depaul.edu/~fdemissi/lawndale1.pdf.

Langelan, Martha J. 1993. *Back Off! How to Confront and Stop Sexual Harassment and Harassers.* New York: Fireside/Simon & Schuster.

Lantigua, Juleyka. 2000. "Latinos Missing from Network Television." Retrieved Sept. 25, 2002. Online: http://secure.progressive.org/pmplvj10.htm.

Lantos, T. 1992. "The Silence of the Kids: Children at Risk in the Workplace." *Labor Law Journal,* 43:67–70.

Lappé, Frances Moore. 2008. "World Hunger: Its Roots and Remedies." In John Germov (ed.), *A Sociology of Food and Nutrition: The Social Appetite* (3rd ed.). New York: Oxford University Press. Retrieved April 18, 2008. Online: http://www.smallplanet.org/worldhungerchapter.pdf.

Lappé, Frances Moore, and Paul Martin Du Bois. 1994. *The Quickening of America: Rebuilding Our Nation, Remaking Our Lives.* San Francisco: Jossey-Bass.

Lasswell, Harold D. 1969. "The Structure and Function of Communication in Society." In Wilbur Schramm (Ed.), *Mass Communications.* Urbana, IL: University of Illinois Press, pp. 103–130.

Lauber, Almon W. 1913. *Indian Slavery in Colonial Times within the Present Limits of the United States.* New York: Columbia University Press.

Lauderback, David, and Dan Waldorf. 1993. "Whatever Happened to ICE: The Latest Drug Scare." *Journal of Drug Issues,* 23:597–613.

Lauer, Robert H. 1995. *Social Problems and the Quality of Life* (6th ed.). Madison, WI: Brown.

Lauer, Robert H., and Jeannette C. Lauer. 1991. "The Long-Term Relational Consequences of Problematic Family Backgrounds." *Family Relations,* 40:286–290.

Laumann, Edward O., John H. Gagnon, Robert T. Michael, and Stuart Michaels. 1994. *The Social Organization of Sexuality: Sexual Practices in the United States.* Chicago: University of Chicago Press.

Laurence, Leslie, and Beth Weinhouse. 1994. *Outrageous Practices: The Alarming Truth About How Medicine Mistreats Women.* New York: Fawcett Columbine.

Lawrence, Mike. 1996. "Prisoners of Another Reality." *The Mission,* 23 (Spring). San Antonio, TX: The University of Texas Health Science Center at San Antonio.

Lazare, Daniel. 1999. "Your Constitution Is Killing You (Right to Bear Arms)." *Harper's Magazine* (October):57.

Leaf, Clifton. 2002. "Enough Is Enough: They Lie, They Cheat, They Steal, and They've Been Getting Away with It for Too Long." *Fortune* (March 18). Retrieved Nov. 23, 2002. Online: http://www.fortune.com/indext.jhtml?channel=print_article.jhtml&doc_id=206659.

Leaper, Campbell. 1994. *Childhood Gender Segregation: Causes and Consequences.* San Francisco: Jossey-Bass.

Leary, Warren E. 1996. "Even When Covered by Insurance, Black and Poor People Receive Less Health Care." *New York Times* (September 12):A10.

Lee, D. J., and Kyriakos S. Markides. 1990. "Activity and Mortality among Aged Persons over an Eight Year Period." *Journal of Gerontology,* 45:S39–S42.

Lee, Felicia R. 1996. "Infertile Couples Forge Ties within Society of Their Own." *New York Times* (January 9):A1, A7.

Lefrançois, Guy R. 1999. *The Lifespan* (6th ed.). Belmont, CA: Wadsworth.

Lehmann, Jennifer M. 1994. *Durkheim and Women.* Lincoln, NE: University of Nebraska Press.

Lehne, Gregory K. 1995. "Homophobia among Men: Supporting and Defining the Male Role." In Michael S. Kimmel and Michael A. Messner (Eds.), *Men's Lives* (3rd ed.). Boston: Allyn and Bacon, pp. 325–336.

Leinen, Stephen. 1993. *Gay Cops.* New Brunswick, NJ: Rutgers University Press.

Lemert, Edwin. 1951. *Social Pathology.* New York: McGraw-Hill.

Lemonick, Michael D. 2005. "The Scent of a Man: What the Brain and the Nose Tell Scientists about Sexual Orientation—in the Human Nose." *Time* (May 23). Retrieved July 30, 2005. Online: http://www.time.com/time/archive/prview/0,10987,1061508,00.html.

Leong, Wai-Teng. 1991. "The Pornography 'Problem': Disciplining Women and Young Girls." *Media, Culture, and Society,* 13:91–117.

Lerman, Hannah. 1996. *Pigeonholing Women's Misery: A History and Critical Analysis of the Psychodiagnosis of Women in the Twentieth Century.* New York: Basic Books.

LeVay, Simon, and Dean H. Hamer. 1994. "Evidence for a Biological Influence in Male Homosexuality." *Scientific American* (May):45–49.

Levin, Jack, and Jack McDevitt. 1993. *Hate Crimes: The Rising Tide of Bigotry and Bloodshed.* New York: Plenum.

Levin, William C. 1988. "Age Stereotyping: College Student Evaluations." *Research on Aging,* 10(1):134–148.

Levine, Peter. 1992. *Ellis Island to Ebbets Field: Sport and the American Jewish Experience.* New York: Oxford University Press.

Levinthal, Charles F. 2007. *Drugs, Behavior, and Modern Society* (5th ed.). Boston: Allyn & Bacon.

Levy, Steven, and Brad Stone. 2005. "Grand Theft Identity." *Newsweek* (July 4):38–47.

Lewin, Tamar. 1995. "The Decay of Families Is Global, Study Says." *New York Times* (May 30):A5.

Lewis, Neil A. 1995. "Administration Won't Join Attack on Gay Rights Ban." *New York Times* (June 9):A11.

Lewis, Oscar. 1966. *La Vida: A Puerto Rican Family in the Culture of Poverty—San Juan and New York.* New York: Random House.

Liebow, Elliot. 1993. *Tell Them Who I Am: The Lives of Homeless Women.* New York: Free Press.

Lifton, Robert Jay. 1997. "Doubling: The Faustian Bargain." In Jennifer Turpin and Lester R. Kurtz (Eds.), *The Web of Violence: From Interpersonal to Global.* Urbana and Chicago: University of Illinois, pp. 31–44.

Lindblom, Charles. 1977. *Politics and Markets.* New York: Basic Books.

Lindsey, Linda L. 1994. *Gender Roles: A Sociological Perspective* (2nd ed.). Englewood Cliffs, NJ: Prentice Hall.

Link, Bruce G., and Bruce P. Dohrenwend. 1989. "The Epidemiology of Mental Disorders." In Howard E. Freeman and Sol Levine (Eds.), *Handbook of Medical Sociology* (4th ed.). Englewood Cliffs, NJ: Prentice Hall, pp. 102–127.

Lips, Hilary M. 1993. *Sex and Gender: An Introduction* (2nd ed.). Mountain View, CA: Mayfield.

Liptak, Adam. 2008. "More Than 1 in 100 Adults Are Now in Prison in U.S." *New York Times* (February 29): A14.

Liptak, Adam. 2008. "Same-Sex Marriage and Racial Justice Find Common Ground." *New York Times* (May 17): A10.

Loftus, Tom. 2004a. "Game Mocks Real Tragedy, Gang Experts Say." *MSNBC* (November 6). Retrieved November 7, 2004. Online: http://www.msnbc.msn.com/id/6409148/.

Loftus, Tom. 2004b. "'Grand Theft Auto' Back With a Vengeance." *MSNBC.com* (November 5). Retrieved November 7, 2004. Online: http://www.msnbc.msn.com/id/6399463/.

Logan, John R. 2001. "The New Latinos: Who They Are, Where They Are." Retrieved Sept. 25, 2002. Online: http://mumford1.dyndns.org/cen2000/HispanicPop/HspReport/HspReportpage1.html.

Lollock, Lisa. 2002. *The Foreign Born Population in the United States: March 2000.* Current Population Reports, Series P20-534. U.S. Census Bureau, Washington, DC.

Lopez, Edison. 2005. "Survivors Tell of Horror on Sunken Boat." SFGATE.com (August 18). Retrieved August 19, 2005. Online: http://www.sfgate.com/cgibin/article.cgi?f=/n/a/2005/08/18/international/i133453D87.DTL.

Lorber, Judith. 1994. *Paradoxes of Gender.* New Haven, CT: Yale University Press.

Lorenz, Konrad. 1966. *On Aggression.* New York: Bantam.

Lottes, Ilsa. 1993. "Reactions to Pornography on a College Campus: For or Against?" *Sex Roles: A Journal of Research,* 29(1–2):69–90.

Lubrano, Alfred. 2004. *Limbo: Blue-Collar Roots, White-Collar Dreams.* Hoboken, NJ: John Wiley.

Luckenbill, David F. 1977. "Criminal Homicide as a Situated Transaction." *Social Problems,* 25:176–186.

Luker, Kristin. 1996. *Dubious Conceptions: The Politics of Teenage Pregnancy.* Cambridge, MA: Harvard University Press.

Lundy, Katherine Coleman. 1995. *Sidewalk Talk: A Naturalistic Study of Street Kids.* New York: Garland Publishing.

Maccoby, Eleanor E., and Carol Nagy Jacklin. 1987. "Gender Segregation in Childhood." *Advances in Child Development and Behavior,* 20:239–287.

MacCorquodale, Patricia, and Gary Jensen. 1993. "Women in the Law: Partners or Tokens?" *Gender and Society,* 7(4):582–593.

MacDonald, Kevin, and Ross D. Parke. 1986. "Parental-Child Physical Play: The Effects of Sex and Age of Children and Parents." *Sex Roles,* 15:367–378.

Macdonald, Scott. 1995. "The Role of Drugs in Workplace Injuries: Is Drug Testing Appropriate?" *Journal of Drug Issues,* 25(4):703–723.

Macintyre, Donald. 2002. "Base Instincts." *Time* (August 5). Retrieved July 30, 2005. Online: http://www.time.com/time/asia/magazine/article/0,13673,501020812333899,00.html.

MacKinnon, Catharine. 1987. *Feminism Unmodified: Discourses on Life and Law.* Cambridge, MA: Harvard University Press.

Macy, Marianne. 1996. *Working Sex: An Odyssey into Our Cultural Underworld.* New York: Carroll & Graf.

MADD. 1999. "Rating the States 2000 Report Card." Mothers Against Drunk Driving and the GuideOne Foundation. Retrieved December 4, 1999. Online: http://www.madd.org.

Madden, Patricia A., and Joel W. Grube. 1994. "The Frequency and Nature of Alcohol and Tobacco Advertising in Televised Sports, 1990 through 1992." *The American Journal of Public Health,* 84(2):297–300.

Madigan, Nick. 2005. "Anger, Empathy, Skepticism Crackling Through Journalistic Objectivity." *Baltimore Sun* (September 4). Retrieved September 4, 2005. Online: http://www.baltimoresun.com/features/lifestyle/balte.to.journalist04sep04,1,3081718.story.

Magrane, Diane, and Jonathan Lang. 2006. "An Overview of Women in U.S. Academic Medicine, 2005-06." *Analysis in Brief: Associaton of American Medical Colleges* 6 (October). Washington, D.C. : Association of American Medical Colleges.

Malinowski, Bronislaw. 1964. "The Principle of Legitimacy: Parenthood, the Basis of Social Structure." In Rose Laub Coser (Ed.), *The Family: Its Structure and Functions.* New York: St. Martin's Press.

Malthus, Thomas R. 1965. *An Essay on Population.* New York: Augustus Kelley, Bookseller (orig. published in 1798).

Mam, Teeda Butt. 1997. *Children of Cambodia's Killing Fields.* New Haven, CT: Yale University Press.

Mann, Coramae Richey. 1993. *Unequal Justice: A Question of Color.* Bloomington, IN: Indiana University Press.

Mann, Patricia S. 1994. *Micro-Politics: Agency in a Post-Feminist Era.* Minneapolis: University of Minnesota Press.

Marable, Manning. 1995. *Beyond Black and White: Transforming African-American Politics.* New York: Verso.

Marcus, Eric. 1992. *Making History: The Struggle for Gay and Lesbian Equal Rights.* New York: HarperCollins.

Marger, Martin N. 1994. *Race and Ethnic Relations: American and Global Perspectives.* Belmont, CA: Wadsworth.

Marine, William M., and Tracy Jack. 1994. "Analysis of Toxology Reports from the 1992 Census of Fatal Occupational Injuries." *Compensation and Working Conditions,* 46(10):1–7.

Marquart, James W., Sheldon Ekland-Olson, and Jonathan R. Sorensen. 1994. *The Rope, the Chair, and the Needle.* Austin, TX: University of Texas Press.

Marriott, Michel. 2004. "The Color of Mayhem." *New York Times* (August 12): E1,E7.

Marshall, Victor W. 1980. *Last Chapters: A Sociology of Aging and Dying.* Monterey, CA: Brooks/Cole.

Marshall, Victor W., and Judith Levy. 1990. "Aging and Dying." In Robert H. Binstock and Linda George (Eds.), *Handbook of Aging and the Social Sciences* (3rd ed). New York: Academic Press.

Martin, Carol L. 1989. "Children's Use of Gender-Related Information in Making Social Judgments." *Developmental Psychology,* 25:80–88.

Martin, Laura. 1992. *A Life without Fear.* Nashville, TN: Rutledge Hill Press.

Marx, Karl, and Friedrich Engels. 1971. "The Communist Manifesto." [orig. published in 1847]. In Dirk Struik (Ed.), *The Birth of the Communist Manifesto.* New York: International.

Marx, Karl, and Friedrich Engels. 1976. *The Communist Manifesto.* New York: Pantheon (orig. published in 1848).

Massey, Douglas S., and Nancy A. Denton. 1992. *American Apartheid: Segregation and the Making of the Underclass.* Cambridge, MA: Harvard University Press.

Massey, James L., and Marvin D. Krohn. 1986. "A Longitudinal Examination of an Integrated Social Process Model of Deviant Behavior." *Social Forces,* 65:106–134.

Mastrofski, Stephen D. 2000. "The Police in America." In Joseph F. Sheley (Ed.), *Criminology: A Contemporary Handbook* (3rd ed.). Belmont, CA: Wadsworth, pp. 405–441.

Matthew's Place (matthewsplace.com). 1999. "Dennis Shepard's Statement to the Court" (November 4). Retrieved November 15, 1999. Online: http://www.matthewsplace.com/dennis2.htm.

Maxwell, Milton A. 1981. "Alcoholics Anonymous." In Martin S. Weinberg, Earl Rubington, and Sue Kiefer Hammersmith (Eds.), *The Solution of Social Problems: Five Perspectives* (2nd ed.). New York: Oxford University Press, pp. 152–156.

Mayall, Alice, and Diana E. H. Russell. 1993. "Racism in Pornography." In Diana E. H. Russell (Ed.), *Making Violence Sexy: Feminist Views on Pornography.*

New York: Teachers College Press, pp. 167–177.

Mayell, Hillary. 2004. "As Consumerism Spreads, Earth Suffers, Study Says." *National Geographic News* (January 12). Retrieved: August 6, 2005. Online: http://news.nationalgeographic.com/news/2004/01/0111_040112_consumerism.html.

Maynard, Joyce. 1994. "To Tell the Truth." In Jay David (Ed.), *The Family Secret: An Anthology.* New York: William Morrow, pp. 79–85.

McCaffrey, Barry R. 1997. "We're on a Perilous Path." *Newsweek* (February 3):27.

McCall, Nathan. 1994. *Makes Me Wanna Holler: A Young Black Man in America.* New York: Vintage.

McCain, John. 2008. "Remarks by John McCain on the Economy." Retrieved: August 19, 2008. Online: http://www.johnmccain.com/action/center/print.aspx

McChesney, Robert W. 1999. *Rich Media, Poor Democracy: Communication Politics in Dubious Times.* Urbana, IL: University of Illinois Press.

McChesney, Robert W. 2004. *The Problems of the Media: U.S. Communications Politics in the 21st Century.* New York: Monthly Review Press.

McClellan, Scott. 2008. *What Happened: Inside the Bush White House and Washington's Culture of Deception.* New York: PublicAffairs Books.

McDaniel, Mike. 2002. "Issues of Originality, Diversity Loom Large for Networks." *Houston Chronicle* (July 15). Retrieved Sept. 28, 2002. Online: http://www.chron.com/cs/CDA/printstory.hts/ae/tv/1492774.

McDonnell, Janet A. 1991. *The Dispossession of the American Indian, 1887–1934.* Bloomington, IN: Indiana University Press.

McElvogue, Louise. 1997. "Making a Killing Out of Nature." *Television Business International* (November):52.

McIntosh, Peggy. 1995. "White Privilege and Male Privilege: A Personal Account of Coming to See Correspondences through Work in Women's Studies." In Margaret A. Andersen and Patricia Hill Collins (Eds.), *Race, Class, and Gender: An Anthology.* Belmont, CA: Wadsworth, pp. 76–87.

McKinlay, John B. 1994. "A Case for Refocusing Upstream: The Political Economy of Illness." In Peter Conrad and Rochelle Kern (Eds.), *The Sociology of Health and Illness.* New York: St. Martin's, pp. 509–530.

McLanahan, Sara, and Gary D. Sandefur. 1994. *Growing Up with a Single Parent: What Hurts, What Helps.* Cambridge, MA: Harvard University Press.

McLarin, Kimberly J. 1994. "A New Jersey Town Is Troubled by Racial Imbalance between Classrooms: Would End to Tracking Harm Quality?" *New York Times* (August 11):A12.

McLean, Mora. 1999. "The 'Africa Story' in American News." *Foreign Policy* (Fall):6.

McNamara, Robert P. 1994. *The Times Square Hustler: Male Prostitution in New York City.* Westport, CT: Praeger.

McNeil, Legs, Jennifer Osborne, and Peter Pavia. 2005. *The Other Hollywood: The Uncensored Oral History of the Porn Film Industry.* New York: ReganBooks.

McWilliams, Carey. 1968. *North from Mexico: The Spanish-Speaking People of the United States.* Westport, CT: Greenwood (orig. published in 1948).

McWilliams, Peter. 1996. *Ain't Nobody's Business If You Do: The Absurdity of Consensual Crimes in Our Free Country.* Los Angeles: Prelude Press.

Mead, Margaret. 1966. "Marriage in Two Steps." *Redbook,* 127:48–49, 85–86.

Mead, Rebecca. 1994. "Playing It Straight: In and out of the Closet." *New York* (June 20):40–46.

Mechanic, David, and David A. Rochefort. 1990. "Deinstitutionalization: An Appraisal of Reform." *Annual Review of Sociology,* 16:301–350.

Medpagetoday.com. 2005. "Coffee Sends Wake Up Call to the Brain." Retrieved July 25, 2005. Online: http://www.medpagetoday.com/PrimaryCare/SleepDisorders/TB/927.

Meers, Erik Ashok. 1996. "Murder, He Wrote." *The Advocate* (March 5):49–52.

Melendez, Edgardo. 1993. "Colonialism, Citizenship, and Contemporary Statehood." In Edwin Melendez and Edgardo Melendez (Eds.), *Colonial Dilemma: Critical Perspectives on Contemporary Puerto Rico.* Boston: South End Press, pp. 41–52.

Menchaca, Martha. 1995. *The Mexican Outsiders: A Community History of Marginalization and Discrimination in California.* Austin, TX: University of Texas Press.

Méndez-Méndez, Serafin, and Diane Alverio. 2001. "Network Brownout 2001: The Portrayal of Latinos in Network Television News, 2000. Retrieved Sept. 25, 2002. Online: http://www.nahj.org/pdf/brownout.pdf.

Mendoza, Manuel. 1995. "Minority Actors Scarce on TV." *Austin American-Statesman* (June 12):B12.

Merchant, Carolyn. 1983. *The Death of Nature: Women, Ecology, and the Scientific Revolution.* San Francisco: Harper and Row.

Merchant, Carolyn, 1992. *Radical Ecology: The Search for a Livable World.* New York: Routledge.

Mercy, James A., and Linda E. Saltzman. 1989. "Fatal Violence among Spouses in the United States, 1976–1985." *The American Journal of Public Health,* 79:595–599.

Merton, Robert. 1938. "Social Structure and Anomie." *American Sociological Review,* 3(6):672–682.

Merton, Robert King. 1968. *Social Theory and Social Structure* (enlarged ed.). New York: Free Press.

Messer, Ellen, and Kathryn E. May. 1994. *Back Rooms: Voices from the Illegal Abortion Era.* Buffalo, NY: Prometheus.

Michael, Robert T., John H. Gagnon, Edward O. Laumann, and Gina Kolata. 1994. *Sex in America: A Definitive Survey.* New York: Warner Books.

Michigan Department of Education. 1990. *The Influence of Gender Role Socialization on Student Perceptions.* Lansing, MI: Michigan Department of Education, Office of Sex Equity in Education.

Mickelson, Roslyn Arlin, and Stephen Samuel Smith. 1995. "Education and the Struggle Against Race, Class, and Gender Inequality." In Margaret L. Andersen and Patricia Hill Collins (Eds.), *Race, Class, and Gender* (2nd ed.). Belmont, CA: Wadsworth, pp. 289–304.

Mies, Maria, and Vandana Shiva. 1993. *Ecofeminism.* Atlantic Highlands, NJ: Zed Books.

Milgram, Stanley. 1974. *Obedience to Authority.* New York: Harper & Row.

Milkman, Harvey, and Stanley Sunderwirth. 1987. *Craving for Ecstasy: The Consciousness and Chemistry of Escape.* Lexington, MA: Heath.

Miller, Casey, and Kate Swift. 1991. *Words and Women: New Language in New Times* (updated). New York: HarperCollins.

Miller, Eleanor M. 1986. *Street Woman.* Philadelphia: Temple University Press.

Miller, Michael W. 1994. "Quality Stuff: Firm Is Peddling Cocaine, and Deals Are Legit." *Wall Street Journal* (October 17):A1, A14.

Miller, Patricia G. 1993. *The Worst of Times.* New York: HarperCollins.

Mills, C. Wright. 1959a. *The Power Elite.* Fair Lawn, NJ: Oxford University Press.

Mills, C. Wright. 1959b. *The Sociological Imagination.* London: Oxford University Press.

Mills, C. Wright. 1976. *The Causes of World War Three.* Westport, CT: Greenwood Press.

Mills, Robert J. 2002. "Health Insurance Coverage: 2001." Retrieved Nov. 30, 2002. Online: http://www.census.gov/hhes/hlthins/hlthin01/hlth01asc.html.

Minow, Newton N., and Craig L. LaMay. 1999. "Changing the Way We Think." In Robert M. Baird, William E. Loges, and Stuart E. Rosenbaum (Eds.), *The Media and Morality.* Amherst, NY: Promethus Books, pp. 309–330.

Mirowsky, John. 1996. "Age and the Gender Gap in Depression." *Journal of Health and Social Behavior,* 37 (December):362–380.

Mirowsky, John, and Catherine E. Ross. 1980. "Minority Status, Ethnic Culture, and Distress: A Comparison of Blacks, Whites, Mexicans, and Mexican Americans." *American Journal of Sociology,* 86:479–495.

Moeller, Susan D. 2004. "Media Coverage of Weapons of Mass Destruction." Center for International Security Studies at Maryland, University of Maryland, College Park. Retrieved August 28, 2005. Online: http://www.cissm.umd.edu/documents/WMDstudy_full.pdf.

Moffitt, Robert, Andrew Cherlin, Linda Burton, Mark King, and Jennifer Roff. 2002. "The Characteristics of Families Remaining on Welfare." Retrieved Sept. 15, 2002. Online: http://www.jhu.edu/~welfare/19505(19459)Welfare_Brief.pdf.

Mohawk, John. 1992. "Looking for Columbus: Thoughts on the Past, Present, and Future of Humanity." In M. Annette Jaimes (Ed.), *The State of Native America: Genocide, Colonization, and Resistance.* Boston: South End Press, pp. 439–444.

Monahan, John. 1992. "Mental Disorder and Violent Behavior: Perceptions and Evidence." *American Psychologist,* 47: 511–521.

Moore, Joan W. (with Harry Pachon). 1976. *Mexican Americans* (2nd ed.). Englewood Cliffs, NJ: Prentice Hall.

Moore, Stephen, and Dean Stansel. 1992. "The Myth of America's Under-Funded Cities." *Cato Policy Analysis* (December). (Reprinted in Charles P. Cozic (Ed.), *America's Cities: Opposing Viewpoints.* San Diego: Greenhaven Press, 1993, pp. 25–32.)

Morgenson, Gretchen. 2008. "Given a Shovel, Digging Deeper Into Debt." *New York Times* (July 20): A1, A18.

Morales, Ed. 1996. "The Last Blackface." *Si Magazine* (Summer 1996):44–47, 85.

Mosher, Steven W. 1994. *A Mother's Ordeal: One Woman's Fight against China's One-Child Policy.* New York: HarperPerennial.

Mowbray, Carol T., Sandra E. Herman, and Kelly L. Hazel. 1992. "Gender and Serious Mental Illness." *Psychology of Women Quarterly,* 16(March):107–127.

MSNBC.com 2007. "Witness: Gunman 'Didn't Say A Single Word.'" *MSNBC.com* (April 16). Retrieved March 24, 2008. Online: http://www.msnbc.msn.com/id/18139889.

Mumford Center for Comparative Urban and Regional Research. 2002. "Choosing Segregation: Racial Imbalance in American Public Schools, 1990–2000." Retrieved Sept. 25, 2002. Online: http://mumford1.dyndns.org/cen2000/SchoolPop/SPReport/page1.html.

Mumford Center for Comparative Urban and Regional Research. 2001. "Ethnic Diversity Grows, Neighborhood Integration Lags Behind." Retrieved Sept. 25, 2002. Online: http://mumford1.dyndns.org/cen2000/WholePop/WPreport/page1.html.

Murphy-Milano, Susan. 1996. *Defending Our Lives: Getting Away from Domestic Violence and Staying Safe.* New York: Anchor.

Mydans, Seth. 1997. "Brutal End for an Architect of Cambodian Brutality." *New York Times* (June 14):5.

Myers, Steven Lee. 1997. "Converting the Dollar into a Bludgeon." *New York Times* (April 20):E5.

Myerson, Allen R. 1996. "A Double Standard in Health Coverage." *New York Times* (March 17):F1, F13.

Nagourney, Adam. 1996. "Affirmed by the Supreme Court." *New York Times* (May 26):E4.

National Center for Educational Statistics. 2006. "Number and Percentage of Gifted and Talented Students in Public Elementary and Secondary Schools, by Sex, Race/Ethnicity, and State: 2002." Washington, D. C.: U. S. Department of Education. Retrieved: August 17, 2008. Online: http://nces.ed.gov/programs/digest/d06/tables/dt06_051.asp.

National Center for Health Statistics. 2003a. "Births: Final Data for 2002." Retrieved August 20, 2005. Online: http://www.cdc.gov/nchs/data/nvsr/nvsr52/nvsr52_10.pdf.

National Center for Health Statistics. 2003b. "Deaths: Final Data for 2002." Retrieved August 20, 2005. Online: http://www.cdc.gov/nchs/data/nvsr/nvsr53/nvsr53_05.pdf.

National Center for Health Statistics. 2004. *Health, United States, 2004.* Hyattsville, MD: National Center for Health Statistics.

National Center for Health Statistics, 2007. *Health, United States, 2007.* Hyattsville, MD: National Center for Health Statistics.

National Center for Health Statistics, 2007a. "Births: Final Data for 2005." Retrieved: September 12; 2008. Online: http://www.cdc.gov/nchs.data/nvsr56/nvst56_06.pdf

National Center for Health Statistics, 2007b. "Deaths: Final Data for 2005." Retrieved: september 12, 2008. Online: http://www.cdc.gov/nchs/data/nvsr/nvsr56/nvsr56_10.phd

National Center for Statistics and Analysis. 2004. "Traffic Safety Facts, 2003: Alcohol-Related Crashes and Fatalities." Washington, DC: U.S. Department of Transportation.

National Center on Elder Abuse. 2005. "Elder Abuse Prevalence and Incidence." Retrieved July 28, 2005. Online: http://www.elderabuse-center.org/pdf/publication/FinalStatistics050331.pdf.

National Collegiate Athletic Association. 2001a. "NCAA Year-by-Year Sports Participation 1982–2001." Retrieved Oct. 20, 2002. Online: www.ncaa.org/library/research/participation_rates/1982-2001/009-056.pdf.

National Collegiate Athletic Association. 2001b. "Sports and Recreation Programs of Universities and Colleges, 1957–1982. Retrieved Oct. 20, 2002. Online: www.ncaa.org/library/research/participation_rates/1982-2000/153-164.pdf.

National Council on Crime and Delinquency. 1969. *The Infiltration into Legitimate Business by Organized Crime.* Washington, DC: National Council on Crime and Delinquency.

National Federation of State High School Associations. 2001. "2001 Athletics Participation Totals." Retrieved Oct. 20, 2002. Online: http://www.nfhs.org/Participation/SportsPart01_files/sheet001.htm.

National Highway Transportation Safety Administration. 2002. "Motor Vehicle Traffic Crash Fatality and Injury Estimates for 2001." Retrieved Nov. 2, 2002. Online: http://www-nrd.nhtsa.dot.gov/pdf/nrd-30/NCSA/Rpts/2002/Assess01.pdf.

National Highway Transportation Safety Administration. 2004. "Traffic Safety Facts: Alcohol-Related Crashes and Fatalities." Retrieved July 25, 2005. Online: http://www-nrd.nhtsa.dot.gov/pdf/nrd-30/NCSA/TSF2003/809761.pdf.

National Institute on Drug Abuse. 1999. "NIDA Info-Facts: Cigarettes and Other Nicotine Products." Retrieved Nov. 2, 2002. Online: http://www.nida.nih.gov/Infofax/tobacco.html.

National Institute of Mental Health. 2008. "Statistics." Washington, D.C.: National Institutes of Health.

New York Times. 2007. "The High Cost of Health Care." Editorial, *New York Times* (November 25): WK9.

National Television Violence Study. 1998. "Executive Summary," *National Television Violence Study*, vol. 3. Retrieved October 31, 1999. Online: http://www.ccsp.ucsb.edu/execsum.pdf.

National Victim Center. 1992. *Rape in America: A Report to the Nation*. Arlington, VA/Charleston, SC: National Victim Center.

National Victims Resource Center. 1991. *Juvenile Prostitution: Fact Sheet*. Rockville, MD: Victims Resource Center.

Nava, Michael, and Robert Dawidoff. 1994. *Created Equal: Why Gay Rights Matter to America*. New York: St. Martin's Press.

Navarro, Mireya. 1996. "Marijuana Farms Are Flourishing Indoors, Producing a More Potent Drug." *New York Times* (November 24):13.

Navarro, Mireya. 2002. "Trying to Get beyond the Role of the Maid." *New York Times* (May 16):B1, B4.

NBC.com/Will&Grace. 1999. "Will & Grace." Retrieved November 25, 1999. Online: http://www.nbc.com/will&grace.

Nechas, Eileen, and Denise Foley. 1994. *Unequal Treatment: What You Don't Know about How Women Are Mistreated by the Medical Community*. New York: Simon & Schuster.

Neckerman, Kathryn M., and Joleen Kirschenman. 1991. "Hiring Strategies, Racial Bias, and Inner-City Workers." In Diana Kendall (Ed.), *Race, Class, and Gender in a Diverse Society*. Boston: Allyn and Bacon, pp. 388–404.

Neergaard, Lauran. 1996. "FDA Prepares to Regulate Medical Info on the Internet." *Austin American-Statesman* (October 20):A7.

Nelesen, Andy. 2008. "College Shootings Trigger Heated National Gun Debate." *greenbaypressgazette.com* (March 30). Retrieved March 31, 2008. Online: http://www.greenbaypressgazette.com/apps/pbcs.dll/article? AID=/20080330/GPG0101/803300737/1978.

Nesmith, Jeff. 2005. "Senators Acknowledge Global Warming, But Question Solutions." Austin360.com (Cox News Service). Retrieved August 20, 2005. Online: http://www.austin360.com/search/content/shared/news/nation/stories/07/22CLIMATE.html.

Newman, Katherine S., Cybelle Fox, David J. Harding, Jal Mehta, and Wendy Roth. 2004. *Rampage: The Social Roots of School Shootings*. New York: Basic Books.

Newman, Katherine S., Cybelle Fox, David Harding, Jal Mehta, and Wendy Roth. 2005. *Rampage: The Social Roots of School Violence,*. New York: Basic Books.

Newsweek. 1999a. "An Editorial: Guns in America: What Must Be Done" (August 23):23–25.

Newsweek. 1999b. "The Gun War Comes Home" (August 23):26–32.

New York Times. 1993. "Despite 6-Year U.S. Campaign, Pornography Industry Thrives" (July 4):10.

New York Times. 1994. "Educating Elderly on AIDS" (August 9):A8.

New York Times. 1995. "Malnutrition Hits Many Elderly" (July 3):A7.

New York Times. 1996a. "Aging World, New Wrinkles" (September 22):E1.

New York Times. 1996b. "Where the Drugs Come From" (March 2):5.

New York Times. 1997a. "A New Study of Day Care Shows Benefit of Attention" (April 5):A10.

New York Times. 1997b. "Public's Assessment of Presidents and Problems" (January 20):A10.

New York Times. 1997c. "Sugar's Sweet Deal" (April 27):E14.

New York Times. 1997d. "The Militia Threat" (June 14):18.

New York Times. 1999a. "Editorial: The Collapse in Seattle" (December 6):A28.

New York Times. 1999b. "What's the Problem?" (August 1):WK4.

New York Times. 2005. "Editorial: Excessive Powers." (August 27):A24.

New York Times. 2007. "High Cost of Health Care." Editorial, *New York Times* (November 25): WK9.

Nieves, Evelyn. 1995. "Wanted in Levittown: One Little Box, with Ticky Tacky Intact." *New York Times* (November 3):A12.

Norman, Michael. 1993. "One Cop, Eight Square Blocks." *New York Times Magazine* (December 12):62–90, 96.

Nyhart. Nick. 2001. "Raising Hard-Money Limits: An Incumbent Protection Plan." Retrieved Dec. 14, 2002. Online: http://www.rollcall.com/pages/columns/observers/01/guest0329.html.

Oakes, Jeannie. 1985. *Keeping Track: How Schools Structure Inequality*. New Haven, CT: Yale University Press.

O'Briant, Erin. 2008. "Do Kids Raised by Lesbians Turn Out Different?" Gay.com. Retrieved: May 24, 2008. Online: http://www.gay.com/families/article.html?coll=rela_article&sernum=382.

Obama, Barack. 2008. "Remarks of Senator Barack Obama: Town Hall on the Economy, August 2, 2008." Retrieved: August 19, 2008. Online: http://www.barackobama.com/speeches/index.php.

O'Connell, Helen. 1994. *Women and the Family*. Prepared for the UN-NGO Group on Women and Development. Atlantic Highlands, NJ: Zed Books.

Oliver, Melvin L., and Thomas M. Shapiro. 1995. *Black Wealth/White Wealth: A New Perspective on Racial Inequality*. New York: Routledge.

Olzak, Susan, Suzanne Shanahan, and Elizabeth H. McEneaney. 1996. "Poverty, Segregation, and Race Riots: 1960 to 1993." *American Sociological Review*, 61(August):590–613.

Omi, Michael, and Howard Winant. 1994. *Racial Formation in the United States: From the 1960s to the 1990s* (2nd ed.). New York: Routledge.

Orenstein, Peggy (in association with the American Association of University Women). 1994. *School Girls: Young Women, Self-Esteem, and the Confidence Gap*. New York: Anchor/Doubleday.

Orenstein, Peggy. 1996. "For Too Many Schoolgirls, Sexual Harassment Is Real." *Austin American-Statesman* (October 4):A15.

Ortner, Sherry B. 1974. "Is Female to Male as Nature Is to Culture?" In Michelle Rosaldo and Louise Lamphere (Eds.), *Women, Culture, and Society*. Stanford, CA: Stanford University Press.

Orum, Anthony M. 1995. *City-Building in America*. Boulder, CO: Westview.

Otis, Leah. 1985. *Prostitution in Medieval Society*. Chicago: University of Chicago Press.

Oxendine, Joseph B. 1995. *American Indian Sports Heritage*. Lincoln, NE: University of Nebraska Press (orig. published in 1988).

Palen, J. John. 1995. *The Suburbs*. New York: McGraw-Hill.

Palen, J. John, and Bruce London. 1984. *Gentrification, Displacement, and Neighborhood Revitalization*. Albany, NY: State University of New York Press.

Parenti, Michael. 1988. *Democracy for the Few* (5th ed.). New York: St. Martin's Press.

Parenti, Michael. 1998. *America Besieged.* San Francisco: City Lights Books.

Parker, Keith D., Greg Weaver, and Thomas Calhoun. 1995. "Predictors of Alcohol and Drug Use: A Multiethnic Comparison." *Journal of Social Psychology,* 135(5):581–591.

Parker, Robert Nash. 1995. "Violent Crime." In Joseph F. Sheley (Ed.), *Criminology: A Contemporary Handbook* (2nd ed.). Belmont, CA: Wadsworth, pp. 169–185.

Parker-Pope, Tara. 2008. "Drinking to Extremes to Celebrate 21." *New York Times* (April 8): A1.

Parry, A. 1976. *Terrorism: From Robespierre to Arafat.* New York: Vanguard Press.

Parsons, Talcott. 1951. *The Social System.* New York: Free Press.

Parsons, Talcott. 1955. "The American Family: Its Relations to Personality and to the Social Structure." In Talcott Parsons and Robert F. Bales (Eds.), *Family, Socialization, and Interaction Process.* Glencoe, IL: Free Press, pp. 3–33.

Pateman, Carole. 1994. "What's Wrong with Prostitution?" In Alison M. Jaggar (Ed.), *Living with Contradictions: Controversies in Feminist Social Ethics.* Boulder, CO: Westview, pp. 127–132.

Patterson, Charlotte J. 1992. "Children of Lesbian and Gay Parents." *Child Development,* 63:1025–1042.

Patterson, James, and Peter Kim. 1991. *The Day America Told the Truth.* Englewood Cliffs, NJ: Prentice Hall.

Patterson, Martha Priddy. 1996. "Women's Employment Patterns, Pension Coverage, and Retirement Planning." In Cynthia Costello and Barbara Kivimae Krimgold (Eds.) for the Women's Research and Education Institute, *The American Woman 1996–97: Women and Work.* New York: W.W. Norton, pp. 148–165.

PBS. 2008. "Bill Moyers Journal: Food Is the Big Story This Week" (April 11). Retrieved April 15, 2008. Online: http://www.pbs.org/moyeers/journal/04 112008/transcript4.html

Pear, Robert, and Erik Eckholm. 2006. "A Decade After Welfare Overhaul, a Shift in Policy and Perception." *New York Times* (August 21): A1.

Pear, Robert, 1994. "Health Advisers See Peril in Plan to Cut Medicare." *New York Times* (August 31):A1, A10.

Pearce, Diana M. 1978. *The Feminization of Poverty: Women, Work, and Welfare.* Chicago: University of Illinois Press.

Pedersen-Pietersen, Laura. 1997. "You're Sober at Last. Now Prove It to the Boss." *New York Times* (January 12):F10.

Perry, David C., and Alfred J. Watkins (Eds.). 1977. *The Rise of the Sunbelt Cities.* Beverly Hills, CA: Sage.

Petersen, John L. 1994. *The Road to 2015: Profiles of the Future.* Corte Madera, CA: Waite Group Press.

Peterson, V. Spike, and Anne Sisson Runyan. 1993. *Global Gender Issues.* Boulder, CO: Westview Press.

Pettigrew, Thomas. 1981. "The Mental Health Impact." In Benjamin Bowser and Raymond G. Hunt (Eds.), *Impacts of Racism on White Americans.* Beverly Hills, CA: Sage, p. 117.

Pew Research Center for the People and the Press. 1995. "A Content Analysis: International News Coverage Fits Public's Ameri-Centric Mood." Retrieved August 8, 2005. Online: http://peoplepress.org/reports/pds/19951031.html.

Phillips, Kevin. 1995. *Arrogant Capital: Washington, Wall Street, and the Frustration of American Politics.* Boston: Little, Brown.

Phillips, Peter. 1999. *Censored 1999: The News That Didn't Make the News.* New York: Seven Stories Press.

Phillips, Peter. 2005. "Big Media Interlocks with Corporate America." Project Censored: The News that Didn't Make the News (July). Retrieved August 8, 2005. Online: http://www.projectcensored.org/newsflash/big_media_interlocks.html.

Pierce, Jennifer L. 1995. *Gender Trials: Emotional Lives in Contemporary Law Firms.* Berkeley, CA: University of California Press.

Pizzo, Steve, M. Fricker, and P. Muolo. 1991. *Insider Job: The Looting of America's Savings and Loans.* New York: HarperPerennial.

Polakow, Valerie. 1993. *Lives on the Edge: Single Mothers and Their Children in the Other America.* Chicago: University of Chicago Press.

The Polling Report. 2005. "Problems and Priorities." Retrieved June 23, 2005. Online: http://www.pollingreport.com/prioriti.htm.

Ponse, Barbara. 1978. *Identities in the Lesbian World: The Social Construction of Self.* Westport, CT: Greenwood Press.

Poovey, Bill. 2003. "Tyson Says Top Bosses Didn't Know." *CBSnews.com* (February 7). Retrieved July 30, 2005. Online: http://www.cbsnews.com/stories/2003/02/05/national/main539521.shtml.

Poovey, Bill. 2004. "Ala. Doctor Starts 'Mothers Against Meth.'" PhillyBurbs.com. Retrieved July 25, 2005. Online: http://www.phillyburbs.com/pb-dyn/news/1-09032004359691.html.

Popenoe, David. 1996. *Life without Father: Compelling New Evidence That Fatherhood and Marriage Are Indispensable for the Good of Children and Society.* New York: Martin Kessler/Free Press.

Portes, Alejandro, and Dag MacLeod. 1996. "Educational Progress of Children of Immigrants: The Roles of Class, Ethnicity, and School Context." *Sociology of Education,* 69(4):255–276.

Potterat, John J., Donald E. Woodhouse, John B. Muth, and Stephen Q. Muth. 1990. "Estimating the Prevalence and Career Longevity of Prostitute Women." *Journal of Sex Research,* 27(May):233–243.

Preston, Jennifer. 1996. "Hospitals Look on Charity Care as Unaffordable Option of Past." *New York Times* (April 14):1, 15.

Proctor, Bernadette D., and Joseph Dalaker, 2002. U.S. Census Bureau, Current Population Reports, P60-219, *Poverty in the United States, 2001.* Washington, DC: U.S. Government Printing Office.

Proctor, Bernadette D., and Joseph Dalaker. 2003. *Poverty in the United States: 2002.* U.S. Census Bureau, Current Population Reports, P60-222. Washington, DC: U.S. Census Bureau.

Purdum, Todd S. 1997. "Legacy of Riots in Los Angeles: Fears and Hope." *New York Times* (April 27):1, 16.

Purdum, Todd S. 2005. "Across U.S. Outrage at Response." *New York Times* (September 3): A1, A11.

Quan, Tracy. 2008. "Really Dangerous Liaisons." *New York Times* (March 12, 2008): A27.

Quattrochi, Regina. 2001. "Homeless With AIDS: Letter to the Editor." *New York Times* (June 9):A14.

Raffalli, Mary. 1994. "Why So Few Women Physicists?" *New York Times Supplement* (January):Sect. 4A, 26–28.

Rank, Mark Robert. 1994. *Living on the Edge: The Realities of Welfare in America.* New York: Columbia University Press.

Raphael, Ray. 1988. *The Men From the Boys: Rites of Passage in Male America.* Lincoln, NE: University of Nebraska Press.

Raymond, Janice G. 1999. "Health Effects of Prostitution." Retrieved Nov. 2, 2002. Online: http://www.uri.edu/artsci/wms/hughes/mhvhealt.htm.

Razvi, Zainub. 2007. "Confessions of Webaholics: Internet Addiction Exposed." Retrieved: August 31, 2008. Online: http://desicritics.org/2007/09/19/065010.php.

Reagan, Brad. 2002. "Home Bankruptcies Jump 8 Percent." Retrieved Dec. 13,

2002. Online: http://www.msnbc.com/news/831322.asp.

Reckless, Walter C. 1967. *The Crime Problem.* New York: Meredith.

Reid, Karla Scoon. 2001. "Racial Disparities." Retrieved Dec. 21, 2002. Online: http://www.edweek.org/sreports/tc01/tc01article.cfm?slug=35race.h20.

Reid, Sue Titus. 1987. *Criminal Justice.* St. Paul, MN: West.

Reiss, I. L. 1986. *Journey into Sexuality: An Exploratory Voyage.* Englewood Cliffs, NJ: Prentice Hall.

Relman, Arnold S. 1992. "Self-Referral—What's at Stake?" *New England Journal of Medicine,* 327 (November 19):1522–1524.

Renner, Michael. 1993. *Critical Juncture: The Future of Peacekeeping.* Washington, DC: Worldwatch Institute.

Renzetti, Claire M., and Daniel J. Curran. 1995. *Women, Men, and Society* (3rd ed.). Boston: Allyn and Bacon.

Reskin, Barbara F., and Heidi Hartmann. 1986. *Women's Work, Men's Work: Sex Segregation on the Job.* Washington, DC: National Academy Press.

Reskin, Barbara F., and Irene Padavic. 1994. *Women and Men at Work.* Thousand Oaks, CA: Pine Forge.

Revkin, Andrew C., and Christopher Drew. 2005. "The Levee: Intricate Flood Protection Long a Focus of Dispute." *New York Times* (September 1):A14.

Rich, Frank. 2003. "When You Got It, Flaunt It." *New York Times* (November 23): AR1, AR34.

Richard, J. F. 2002. *High Noon: Twenty Global Problems, Twenty Years to Solve Them.* New York: Basic.

Richardson, Laurel. 1993. "Inequalities of Power, Property, and Prestige." In Virginia Cyrus (Ed.), *Experiencing Race, Class, and Gender in the United States.* Mountain View, CA: Mayfield, pp. 229–236.

Rios, Delia M. 2004. "Amendments raise question: What is the Constitution for?" *Austin American-Statesman* (March 28): A17.

Risling, Greg. 2005. "Autopsy Shows LAPD Gunfire Killed Toddler." *MercedSun-Star.com* (July 13). Retrieved July 30, 2005. Online: http://www.mercedsun-star.com/24hour/nation/story/2553521p-10958581c.html.

Ritter, Malcolm. 2003. "Children-TV Violence Link Has Effect." Associated Press (March 9). Retrieved June 30, 2005. Online: http://www.freerepublic.com/focus/news/860791/posts.

Ritzer, George. 1995. *Expressing America: A Critique of the Global Credit Card Society.* Thousand Oaks, CA: Pine Forge.

Roberts, Nickie. 1992. *Whores in History: Prostitution in Western Society.* London: HarperCollins.

Roberts, Sam. 1993. *Who We Are: A Portrait of America Based on the Latest U.S. Census.* New York: Times Books.

Rockstargames.com 2004. "Grand Theft Auto: San Andreas." Retrieved July 13, 2005. Online: http://www.rockstargames.com/sanandreas/.

Rogers, Deborah D. 1995. "Daze of Our Lives: The Soap Opera as Feminine Text." In Gail Dines and Jean M. Humez (Eds.), *Gender, Race and Class in Media: A Text-Reader.* Thousand Oaks, CA: Sage, pp. 325–331.

Rogg, E. 1974. *The Assimilation of Cuban Exiles: The Role of Community and Class.* New York: Aberdeen.

Romo, Harriett D., and Toni Falbo. 1996. *Latino High School Graduation.* Austin, TX: University of Texas Press.

Ropers, Richard H. 1991. *Persistent Poverty: The American Dream Turned Nightmare.* New York: Plenum.

Rosenberg, Janet, Harry Perlstadt, and William Phillips. 1993. "Now That We Are Here: Discrimination, Disparagement and Harassment at Work and the Experience of Women Lawyers." *Gender and Society,* 7(3):415–433.

Rosenthal, Elisabeth. 1993. "The Inner City: Lack of Doctors for the Poor Is Obstacle to Health Plans." *New York Times* (November 14):HD6.

Rosenthal, Elisabeth. 1997. "The H.M.O. Catch: When Healthier Isn't Cheaper." *New York Times* (March 16):E1, E4.

Ross, Stephen L., and Margery Austin Turner. 2005. "Housing Discrimination in Metropolitan America: Explaining Changes between 1989 and 2000. *Social Problems,* 52, no. 2: 152–180.

Rosser, Sue V. 1994. *Women's Health—Missing from U.S. Medicine.* Bloomington, IN: Indiana University Press.

Rossi, Peter H. 1989. *Down and Out in America: The Origins of Homelessness.* Chicago: University of Chicago Press.

Rothchild, John. 1995. "Wealth: Static Wages, Except for the Rich." *Time* (January 30):60–61.

Rowley, Ian, and Kiroko Tashiro. 2005. "Japan: Crazy for Cramming." *BusinessWeek.com* (April 18). Retrieved August 1, 2005. Online: http://www.businessweek.com/magazine/content/05_16/b3929071.htm.

Rubin, Lillian B. 1976. *Worlds of Pain: Life in the Working-Class Family.* New York: Basic Books.

Rubin, Lillian B. 1994. *Families on the Fault Line.* New York: HarperCollins.

Rubington, Earl, and Martin S. Weinberg (Eds.). 1996. *Deviance: The Interactionist Perspective* (6th ed.). Boston: Allyn and Bacon.

Ruggles, Patricia. 1990. *Drawing the Line: Alternative Policy Measures and Their Implications for Public Policy.* Washington, DC: Urban Institute Press.

Ruggles, Patricia. 1992. "Measuring Poverty." *Focus,* 14(1):1–5.

Russell, Diana E. H. 1993. "Introduction." In Diana E. H. Russell (Ed.), *Making Violence Sexy: Feminist Views on Pornography.* New York: Teachers College Press, pp. 1–20.

Rutenberg, Jim, and Corey Kilgannon. 2005. "2 More White Men Are in Custody in Attack on Black MAN." *New York Times* (July 1):A15.

Ryan, William. 1976. *Blaming the Victim* (rev. ed.). New York: Vintage.

Sachs, Aaron. 1994. "The Last Commodity: Child Prostitution in the Developing World." *World Watch,* 7(4) (July–August):24–31.

Sadker, Myra, and David Sadker. 1994. *Failing at Fairness: How America's Schools Cheat Girls.* New York: Scribner.

Safilios-Rothschild, Constantina. 1969. "Family Sociology or Wives' Family Sociology? A Cross-Cultural Examination of Decision-Making." *Journal of Marriage and the Family,* 31(2):290–301.

Safire, William. 1993. *Safire's New Political Dictionary.* New York: Random House.

Sale, Kirkpatrick. 1990. *The Conquest of Paradise.* New York: Knopf.

Sampson, Robert J. 1986. "Effects of Socioeconomic Context on Official Reactions to Juvenile Delinquency." *American Sociological Review,* 51(December):876–885.

Sanday, Peggy Reeves. 1996. *A Woman Scorned: Acquaintance Rape on Trial.* New York: Doubleday.

Sanger, David E. 1999. "Global Economy Dances to Political Tune." *New York Times* (December 20):C21.

Sang-Hun, Choe. 2008. "A Taste of Failure Fuels an Appetite for Success at South Korea's Cram Schools." *New York Times* (August 13). Retrieved: August 17, 2008. Online: http://www.nytimes.com/2008/08/13/world/asia/13cram.html.

Sanger, David E. 2000. "In Leading Nations, a Population Bust?" *New York Times* (January 1):YNE8.

Santiago, Anna M., and George Galster. 1995. "Puerto Rican Segregation in the United States: Cause or Consequence of Economic Status?" *Social Problems,* 42:361–389.

Santiago, Anna M., and Margaret G. Wilder. 1991. "Residential Segregation and Links to Minority Poverty: The Case of Latinos in the United States." *Social Problems,* 38:701–723.

Sapon-Shevin, Mara. 1993. "Gifted Education and the Protection of Privilege: Breaking the Silence, Opening the Discourse." In Lois Weis and Michelle Fine (Eds.), *Beyond Silenced Voices: Class, Race, and Gender in United States Schools.* Albany, NY: State University of New York Press, pp. 25–44.

Sassen, Saskia. 1995. "On Concentration and Centrality in the Global City." In Paul L. Knox and Peter J. Taylor (Eds.), *World Cities in a World-System.* Cambridge, England: Cambridge University Press, pp. 63–75.

Sawers, Larry, and William K. Tabb (Eds.). 1984. *Sunbelt/ Snowbelt: Urban Development and Regional Restructuring.* New York: Oxford University Press.

Schemo, Diana Jean. 1994. "Suburban Taxes Are Higher for Blacks, Analysis Shows." *New York Times* (August 17):A1, A16.

Schickler, Rob. 1999. "Society's Reaction to Killings Getting Predictable." *Baylor Lariat* (November 4):2.

Schiesel, Seth. 2008. "Forget It, Niko, It's Liberty City, a Dystopian Dream." *New York Times* (April 28): B1, B6.

Schiller, Herbert I. 1996. *Information Inequality: The Deepening Social Crisis in America.* New York: Routledge.

Schindehette, Susan, and Jeff Truesdell. 2005. "Crystal Meth Killed Her Brother." *People* (July 11):101–102.

Schneider, Keith. 1993. "The Regulatory Thickets of Environmental Racism." *New York Times* (December 19):E5.

Schreuder, Cindy. 1996. "What Kindergartners Can Teach Us about Living in a Multicultural World." *Austin American-Statesman* (July 7):F1, F5.

Schrof, Joanne M. 1993. "The Gender Machine." *U.S. News and World Report* (August 2):42–44.

Schur, Edwin M. 1965. *Crimes without Victims: Deviant Behavior and Public Policy.* Englewood Cliffs, NJ: Prentice Hall.

Schwartz, Emma. 2008. "In Congress, the Uphill Battle for Gun Control." *U.S. News and World Report* (March 6, 2008). Retrieved March 31, 2008. Online: http://www.usnews.com/articles/news/politics/2008/03/06/in-congress-the-uphill-battle-for-gun-control.htm.

Scott, Alan. 1990. *Ideology and the New Social Movements.* Boston: Unwin & Hyman.

Scott, Denise Benoit. 1996. "Shattering the Instrumental-Expressive Myth: The Power of Women's Networks in Corporate-Government Affairs." *Gender and Society,* 10(3):232–247.

Searight, H. Russell, and Priscilla R. Searight. 1988. "The Homeless Mentally Ill: Overview, Policy Implications, and Adult Foster Care as a Neglected Resource." *Adult Foster Care Journal,* 2:235–259.

Seelye, Katharine Q. 1997a. "Future U.S.: Grayer and More Hispanic." *New York Times* (March 27):A18.

Seelye, Katharine Q. 1997b. "Trickle of Television Liquor Ads Releases Torrent of Regulatory Uncertainty." *New York Times* (January 12):8.

Segal, Lynn. 1990. "Pornography and Violence: What the 'Experts' Really Say." *Feminist Review,* 36:29–41.

Seligman, Martin E. P. 1975. *Helplessness: On Depression, Development and Death.* San Francisco: Freeman.

Serrill, Michael S. 1992. "Struggling to Be Themselves." *Time* (November 9):52–54.

Serrin, Judith. 1997. "Immigration Helps Economy, Analysis Shows." *Austin American-Statesman* (May 18):A7.

Shah, Sonia. 1994. "Presenting the Blue Goddess: Toward a National Pan-Asian Feminist Agenda." In Karin Aguilar-San Juan (Ed.), *The State of Asian America: Activism and Resistance in the 1990s.* Boston: South End Press, pp. 147–158.

Shane, Scott, and Eric Lipton. 2005. "Storm Overwhelmed Government's Preparation." *New York Times* (September 2): A1, A14.

Shannon, Kelley. 1996. "Allocations, Segregation Hurt Latinos' Schooling." *Austin American-Statesman* (September 13): A11.

Shaw, Randy. 1999. *Reclaiming America: Nike, Clean Air, and the New National Activism.* Berkeley, CA: University of California Press.

Shea, Christopher. 1996. "A Scholar Links Sexual Orientation to Gender Roles in Childhood." *Chronicle of Higher Education* (November 22):A11, A12.

Shedler, J., and J. Block. 1990. "Adolescent Drug Users and Psychological Health." *American Psychologist,* 45:612–630.

Sheff, David. 1995. "If It's Tuesday, It Must Be Dad's House." *New York Times Magazine* (March 26):64–65.

Sheldon, William H. 1949. *Varieties of Delinquent Youth: An Introduction to Constitutional Psychiatry.* New York: Harper.

Sheley, Joseph F. (Ed.). 2000. *Criminology: A Contemporary Handbook* (3rd ed.). Belmont, CA: Wadsworth.

Shelton, Beth Ann. 1992. *Women, Men and Time: Gender Differences in Paid Work, Housework and Leisure.* Westport, CT: Greenwood.

Shenon, Philip. 1996a. "Jet Makers Preparing Bids for a Rich Pentagon Prize." *New York Times* (March 12):A1, C4.

Shenon, Philip. 1996b. "When 'Don't Ask, Don't Tell' Means Do Ask and Do Tell All." *New York Times* (March 3):E7.

Sher, Kenneth J. 1991. *Children of Alcoholics: A Critical Appraisal of Theory and Research.* Chicago: University of Chicago Press.

Shibutani, Tamotsu. 1970. "On the Personification of Adversaries." In Tamotsu Shibutani (Ed.), *Human Nature and Collective Behavior.* Englewood Cliffs, NJ: Prentice Hall, pp. 223–233.

Shilts, Randy. 1993. *Conduct Unbecoming: Lesbians and Gays in the U.S. Military, Vietnam to the Persian Gulf.* New York: St. Martin's Press.

Shweder, Richard A. 1997. "It's Called Poor Health for a Reason." *New York Times* (March 9):E5.

Sidel, Ruth. 1996. *Keeping Women and Children Last: America's War on the Poor.* New York: Penguin.

Simmel, Georg. 1950. *The Sociology of Georg Simmel.* Trans. Kurt Wolff. Glencoe, IL: Free Press (orig. written in 1902–1917).

Simon, Brenda M. 1999. "*United States* v. *Hilton.*" *Berkeley Technology Law Journal* 14:385–403.

Simon, David R. 1996. *Elite Deviance* (5th ed.) Boston: Allyn and Bacon.

Singer, Bennett L., and David Deschamps. 1994. *Gay and Lesbian Stats.* New York: New Press.

Sivard, Ruth L. 1991. *World Military and Social Expenditures—1991.* Washington, DC: World Priorities.

Sivard, Ruth L. 1993. *World Military and Social Expenditures—1993.* Washington, DC: World Priorities.

Skolnick, Jerome H. 1975. *Justice without Trial* (2nd ed.). New York: Wiley.

Sleeter, Christine E. 1996. "White Silence, White Solidarity." In Noel Ignatiev and John Garvey (Eds.), *Race Traitor.* New York: Routledge, pp. 257–265.

Smith, Alexander B., and Harriet Pollack. 1994. "Deviance as Crime, Sin, and Poor Taste." In Patricia A. Adler and Peter Adler (Eds.), *Constructions of Deviance:*

Social Power, Context, and Interaction. Belmont, CA: Wadsworth.

Smith, M. Dwayne. 2000. "Capital Punishment in America." In Joseph F. Sheley (Ed.), *Criminology: A Contemporary Handbook* (3rd ed.). Belmont, CA: Wadsworth, pp. 621–643.

Snell, Cudore L. 1995. *Young Men in the Street: Help-Seeking Behavior of Young Male Prostitutes.* Westport, CT: Praeger.

Snitow, Ann Barr. 1994. "Mass Market Romance: Pornography for Women Is Different." In Alison M. Jaggar (Ed.), *Living with Contradictions: Controversies in Feminist Social Ethics.* Boulder, CO: Westview, pp. 181–188.

Snow, David A., and Leon Anderson. 1993. *Down on Their Luck: A Study of Homeless Street People.* Berkeley, CA: University of California Press.

Snyder, Benson R. 1971. *The Hidden Curriculum.* New York: Knopf.

Soble, Alan. 1986. "Pornography in Capitalism: Powerlessness." In Alan Soble, *Pornography: Marxism, Feminism and the Future of Sexuality.* New Haven, CT: Yale University Press, pp. 78–84.

Spagat, Elliot. 2005. "Novel Media Campaign Aims to Deter Illegal Border Crossings." SFGATE.com (August 18). Retrieved August 19, 2005. Online: http://www.sfgate.com/cgi-bin/article.cgi?f=/n/a/2005/08/18/state/n110452D22.DTL.

Spinelli, Corey. 1998. "A Tale of Two Trials." *Scholastic Magazine* (September 10):16–19.

Squires, Gregory D. 1994. *Capital and Communities in Black and White: The Intersections of Race, Class, and Uneven Development.* Albany, SUNY Press.

Stanko, Elizabeth. 1990. *Everyday Violence: How Women and Men Experience Sexual and Physical Danger.* London: HarperCollins.

Stanley, Alessandra. 1995. "Russian Mothers, from All Walks, Walk Alone." *New York Times* (October 21):A1.

Stanley, Julia P. 1972. "Paradigmatic Woman: The Prostitute." Paper presented at South Atlantic Modern Language Association, Jacksonville, FL, cited in Jessie Bernard, *The Female World.* New York: Free Press, 1981.

Stares, Paul B. 1996. *Global Habit: The Drug Problem in a Borderless World.* Washington, DC: Brookings Institution.

Starr, Paul. 1982. *The Social Transformation of American Medicine.* New York: Basic Books.

Stead, Deborah. 1997. "Corporations, Classrooms, and Commercialism." *New York Times Education Supplement* (January 5):30–33.

Steering Committee of the Physicians' Health Study Group. 1989. "Final Report on the Aspirin Component of the Ongoing Physician's Health Study." *New England Journal of Medicine,* 321:129–135.

Steffensmeier, Darrell, and Emilie Allan. 2000. "Looking for Patterns: Gender, Age, and Crime." In Joseph F. Sheley (Ed.), *Criminology: A Contemporary Handbook* (3rd ed.). Belmont, CA: Wadsworth, pp. 85–127.

Stein, Rob. 2008. "As Abortion Rate Drops, Use of RU-486 Is On Rise." *Washington Post* (January 22): A1.

Steingart, R. M., M. Packer, P. Hamm, and others. 1991. "Sex Differences in the Management of Coronary Artery Disease." *New England Journal of Medicine,* 325:226–230.

Stern, Christopher. 1998. "Researchers Shocked to Find—TV Violence." *Variety* (April 20–26):24.

Stevens, Jane Ellen. 2001. In "Reporting on Violence: New Ideas for Television, Print and Web." Edited by Lori Dorfman. Berkeley, CA: Berkeley Media Studies Group. Retrieved June 30, 2005. Online: http://www.bmsg.org/content/handbook2ndEd.pdf.

Stevens, William K. 1997. "How Much Is Nature Worth? For You, $33 Trillion." *New York Times* (May 20):B7, B9.

Stevenson, Seth. 2007. "Neanderthal TV." *Slate* (March 19). Retrieved April 27, 2008. Online: http://www.slate.com/toolbar.aspx?action=print&id=2162149.

Stewart, Charles T., Jr. 1995. *Healthy, Wealthy, or Wise? Issues in American Health Care Policy.* Armonk, NY: M.E. Sharpe.

Stobbe, Mike. 2008. "Report: School Slayings Down From 1990s." *FoxNews.com* (July 18). Retrieved: August 17, 2008. Online: http://www.foxnews.com/wires/2008Jan18/0,4675,School/Murders.00.html.

Stolberg, Sheryl Gay. 1997. "Breaks for Mental Illness: Just What the Government Ordered." *New York Times* (May 4):E1, E5.

Stoller, Robert J. 1991. *Porn: Myths for the Twentieth Century.* New Haven, CT: Yale University Press.

Story, Paula. 1997. "L.A. Police Assess Robbers' Greater Firepower." *Austin American-Statesman* (March 2):A5.

Straus, Murray A., Richard J. Gelles, and Suzanne K. Steinmetz. 1980. *Behind Closed Doors: Violence in the American Family.* New York: Anchor.

Substance Abuse and Mental Health Services Administration. 2001. "2001 National Household Survey on Drug Abuse: Illicit Drug Use." Retrieved Nov. 16, 2002. Online: http://www.samhsa.gov/oas/NHSDA/2k1NHSDA/vol1/Chapter2.htm.

Sugarmann, Josh. 1999. "Laws That Can't Stop a Bullet." *New York Times* (November 4):A27.

Suggs, Welch. 2005. "Gender Quotas? Not in College Sports." *The Chronicle of Higher Education* (July 1):A24–26.

Sullivan, Bob. 2005. "The Secret List of ID Theft Victims." *MSNBC.com* (January 29). Retrieved July 30, 2005. Online: http://www.msnbc.msn.com/id/6814673.

Sullivan, Maureen. 1996. "Rozzie and Harriet? Gender and Family Patterns of Lesbian Coparents." *Gender and Society,* 10(6):747–767.

Sutherland, Edwin H. 1939. *Principles of Criminology.* Philadelphia: Lippincott.

Sutherland, Edwin H. 1949. *White Collar Crime.* New York: Dryden.

Swedish Institute. 2003. "The Health Care System in Sweden." Retrieved August 1, 2005. Online: http://www.sweden.se/templates/cs/BasicFactsheet_6856.aspx.

Takaki, Ronald. 1993. *A Different Mirror: A History of Multicultural America.* Boston: Little, Brown.

Talbot, Margaret. 2002. "Men Behaving Badly." *New York Times Magazine* (Oct. 13):52–57, 82, 84, 95.

Tatum, Beverly Daniel. 2003. *Why Are All the Black Kids Sitting Together in the Cafeteria? And Other Conversations About Race.* New York: Basic Books.

Taylor, Howard F. 1995. "Symposium: The Bell Curve." *Contemporary Sociology: A Journal of Reviews,* 24(2):153–157.

Taylor, J., and B. Jackson. 1990. "Factors Affecting Alcohol Consumption in Black Women." *International Journal of the Addictions,* 25(12):1415–1427.

Terkel, Studs. 1996. *Working: People Talk About What They Do All Day and How They Feel About What They Do.* New York: New Press.

Texas Lawyer. 1997. "A.G.'s Opinions: *Hopwood*/Scholarship Programs/Equal Protection" (February 17):24–25.

Thoma, Mark. 2006. "Econoblog: The Costs and Benefits of Immigration: A *Wall Street Journal Online* Econoblog."

Retrieved: September 13, 2008. Online: http://economistsview.typepad.com/economistsview/2006/06/econoblog_the_c.html.

Thomas, Gale E. 1995. "Conclusion: Healthy Communities as a Basis for Healthy Race and Ethnic Relations." In Gail E. Thomas (Ed.), *Race and Ethnicity in America: Meeting the Challenge in the 21st Century.* Bristol, PA: Taylor & Francis, pp. 335–342.

Thomson, Elizabeth, and Ugo Colella. 1992. "Cohabitation and Marital Stability: Quality or Commitment?" *Journal of Marriage and the Family,* 54:259–267.

Thorne, Barrie. 1995. "Girls and Boys Together ... But Mostly Apart: Gender Arrangements in Elementary School." In Michael S. Kimmel and Michael A. Messner (Eds.), *Men's Lives* (3rd ed.). Boston: Allyn and Bacon, pp. 61–73.

Thornton, Arland. 1989. "Changing Attitudes toward Family Issues in the United States." *Journal of Marriage and the Family,* 51 (November):873–893.

Thornton, Michael C., Linda M. Chatters, Robert Joseph Taylor, and Walter R. Allen. 1990. "Sociodemographic and Environmental Correlates of Racial Socialization by Black Parents." *Child Development,* 61:401–409.

Thornton, Russell. 1984. "Cherokee Population Losses during the Trail of Tears: A New Perspective and a New Estimate." *Ethnohistory,* 31:289–300.

Thornton, Russell. 1987. *American Indian Holocaust and Survival.* Norman: University of Oklahoma Press.

Tienda, Marta, and Haya Stier. 1996. "Generating Labor Market Inequality: Employment Opportunities and the Accumulation of Disadvantage." *Social Problems,* 43(2):147–165.

Tierney, John. 1994. "Porn, the Low-Slung Engine of Progress." *New York Times* (January 9):H1, H18.

Tierney, John. 2005. "Fight Floods Like Fires, Without the Feds." *New York Times* (September 3):A29.

Toner, Robin. 1993. "People without Health Insurance." *New York Times* (November 14):HD16.

Toner, Robin. 1995. "No Free Rides: Generational Push Has Not Come to Shove." *New York Times* (December 31): E1, E4.

Torrey, E. Fuller. 1988. *Nowhere to Go: The Tragic Odyssey of the Homeless Mentally Ill.* New York: Harper and Row.

Tower, Cynthia Crosson. 1996. *Child Abuse and Neglect* (3rd ed.). Boston: Allyn and Bacon.

Travis, John. 1995. "X Chromosome Again Linked to Homosexuality." *Science News,* 148 (November 4):295.

Triggle, Nick. 2005. "Has the Prescription Worked?" *BBCNews* (July 31). Retrieved August 1, 2005. Online: http://news.bbc.co.uk/1/hi/health/4716901.stm.

Tsiko, Sifelani. 2005. "Western Media's Coverage of Africa Biased." Mediachannel.org (August 7). Retrieved August 7, 2005. Online: http://mediachannel.org/blog/node/503.

Tumulty, Karen. 1996. "Why Subsidies Survive." *Time* (March 25):46–47.

Turk, Austin T. 1966. "Conflict and Criminality." *American Sociological Review,* 31:338–352.

Turk, Austin T. 1971. *Criminality and Legal Order.* Chicago: Rand McNally.

Turpin, Jennifer, and Lester R. Kurtz. 1997. "Introduction: Violence: The Micro/Macro Link." In Jennifer Turpin and Lester R. Kurtz (Eds.), *The Web of Violence: From Interpersonal to Global.* Urbana and Chicago: University of Illinois, pp. 1–27.

Tyson, Eric K. 1993. "Credit Crackdown: Control Your Spending Before It Controls You." *San Francisco Examiner* (November 28):E1. (Cited in Ritzer, 1995.)

Uchitelle, Louis. 1995. "Retirement's Worried Face: For Many, the Crisis Is Now." *New York Times* (July 30):F1, F4.

United Nations. 1995. *The World's Women 1995: Trends and Statistics.* New York: United Nations.

United Nations. 2000. *The World's Women 2000: Trends and Statistics.* New York: United Nations Publications.

United Nations. 2005. "World's Population Reaches 6.5 Billion This Year, Could Reach 7 Billion by 2012, UN Says." Retrieved August 26, 2005. Online: http://www.un.org/apps/printnewsAr.asp?nid=13379.

United Nations Development Programme. 1999. *Human Development Report: 1999.* New York: Oxford University Press.

United Nations Development Programme. 2004. "Human Development Reports: HDR 2004." Retrieved August 20, 2005. Online: http://hdr.undp.org/statistics/data/indic/indic_1_1_1.html.

United Nations Development Programme. 2005. *Human Development Report 2005.* New York: United Nations Development Programme.

United Nations Development Programme. 2007. *Human Development Report: 2007.* New York: United Nations Development Programme.

United Nations Environmental Program. 2002. *Global Environmental Outlook 3.* Retrieved Dec. 14, 2002. Online: http://www.unep.org/geo/geo3/english/overview/020.htm.

United Nations Food and Agriculture Organization. 2006. "The State of Food Insecurity in the World 2006." United Nations: Rome. Retrieved April 19, 2008. Online: http://www.fao.org/docrep/007/y5650e/y5650e00.htm.

U.S. Administration on Aging. 1998. "The National Elder Abuse Incidence Study; Final Report September 1998. Retrieved Oct. 19, 2002. Online: http://www.aoa.gov/abuse/report/default.htm.

U.S. Bureau of Justice Statistics. 2005. "Capital Punishment Statistics." Retrieved August 3, 2005. Online: http://www.ojp.usdoj.gov/bjs/cp.htm.

U.S. Bureau of Justice Statistics. 2008. "Capital Punishment Statistics." Retrieved: August 20, 2008. Online: http://www.0/p.usdoj.gov/bjs./cp.htm

U.S. Bureau of Labor Statistics. 2004. "Highlights of Women's Earnings in 2003. Report 978." Retrieved March 17, 2005. Online: www.bls.gov/cps/cpswom2003.pdf.

U.S. Bureau of Labor Statistics. 2005a. "Employment Status by Sex, Presence and Age of Children, Race, and Hispanic or Latino Ethnicity, 2004." Retrieved August 6, 2005. Online: http://www.bls.gov/cps/wlf-table5-2005.pdf.

U.S. Bureau of Labor Statistics. 2005b. "Usual Weekly Earnings of Wage and Salary Workers: Second Quarter 2005." Retrieved July 26, 2005. Online: http://www.bls.gov/news.release/wkyeng.nr0.htm.

U.S. Bureau of Labor Statistics. 2007. "Highlights of Women's Earnings in 2006." Retrieved May 13, 2008. Online: http://www.bls.gov/cps/cpswom2006.pdf.

U.S. Bureau of Labor Statistics. 2008. "Employment Status of the Civilian Noninstitutional Population by Educational Attainment, Sex, Race, and Hispanic or Latino Ethnicity." Retrieved April 28, 2008. Online: http://www.bls.gov/web/cpseea17.pdf.

U.S. Census Bureau. 2004a. "Hispanic and Asian Americans Increasing Faster Than Overall Population." Retrieved July 23, 2004. Online: http://www.census.gov/PressRelease/www/releases/archives/race/001839.html.

U.S. Census Bureau. 2004b. "Presence of Children Under 18 Years Old—Households, by Total Money Income in 2003, Type of

Household, Race and Hispanic Origin of Reference Person." Current Population Survey, 2004 Annual Social and Economic Supplement. Retrieved July 23, 2005. Online: http://pubdb3.census.gov/macro/032004/hhinc/new04_000.htm.

U.S. Census Bureau. 2008a. "Health Insurance Coverage: 2006." Washington, D.C.: U.S. Census Bureau. Retrieved: July 8, 2008. Online: http://www.census.gov/hhes/www.hlthins/hlthin06/hlth06asc.html.

U.S. Census Bureau. 2008b. *Statistical Abstract of the United States: 2008* (127th ed.). Washington, DC: U.S. Government Printing Office. Online: http://www.census.gov/statb/www/.

U.S. Conference of Mayors. 2004. "Hunger and Homelessness Survey: 2004." Retrieved August 26, 2005. Online: http://www.usmayors.org/uscm/hungersurvey/2004/onlinereport/HungerAndHomelessnessReport2004.pdf.

U. S. Conference of Mayors. 2007. "Hunger and Homelessness Survey: 2007." Retrieved: September 5, 2008. Online: http://www.usmayors.org/HHSurvey2007/hhsurvey07.pdf.

U.S. Department of Education. 2004. "A Guide to Education and No Child Left Behind." Retrieved August 6, 2005. Online: http://www.ed.gov/nclb/overview/intro/guide/guide.pdf.

U. S. Department of Education. 2008. "25th Annual Report to Congress on the Implementation of the Individuals with Disabilities Education Act (2003)." Washington, D.C.: U. S. Department of Education. Retrieved: August 17, 2008. Online: http://www.ed.gov/about/reports/annual/osep/25th-vol-1-sec-1.pdf.

U.S. Department of Education. 2005. "Youth Indicators, 2005: Trends in the Well-Being of American Youth." Retrieved August 6, 2005. Online: http://nces.ed.gov/pubsearch/pubsinfo.asp?pubid=2005050.

U.S. Department of Housing and Urban Development. 2002. "Welcome to the Community Renewal Initiative." Retrieved Dec. 21, 2002. Online: http://www.hud.gov/offices/cpd/economicdevelopment/programs/rc/index.cfm.

U.S. Department of Justice. 2005. "USA PATRIOT Act." Retrieved August 26, 2005. Online: http://www.lifeandliberty.gov.

U.S. Department of Labor. 2002. "Nontraditional Occupations for Women in 2001." Retrieved Oct. 12, 2002. Online: http://www.dol.gov/wb/wb_pubs/nontrad2001.htm.

U.S. Department of State. 1996. *International Narcotics Control Strategy Report.* Washington, DC: U.S. Department of State.

U.S. Department of State. 2002. "World Military Expenditures and Arms Transfers, 1999–2000." Retrieved Dec. 22, 2002. Online: http://www.state.gov/t/vc/rls/rpt/wmeat/99_00/.

U.S. Government Printing Office. 2005. "Budget of the United States Government: Browse Fiscal Year 2006." Retrieved August 9, 2005. Online: http://www.gpoaccess.gov/usbudget/fy06/browse.html.

U. S. Government Printing Office. 2008. Budget of the United States Government. Retrieved: October 3, 2008. Online: http://www.gpoaccess/govlusbudget/fy08/browse.html.

U.S. House of Representatives, Committee on Ways and Means. 1994. *1994 Green Book.* Washington, DC: U.S. Government Printing Office.

Valdez, Avelardo. 1993. "Persistent Poverty, Crime, and Drugs: U.S.-Mexican Border Region." In Joan Moore and Raquel Pinderhughes (Eds.), *In the Barrios: Latinos and the Underclass Debate.* New York: Russell Sage Foundation, pp. 173–194.

Valic.com 2003. "Experienced Workers are Good Business." AIG VALIC Education and Planning Center (November 24). Retrieved July 23, 2005. Online: http://www.valic.com/fpc2003/stcu.nsf/contents/workers.

Vanderbilt University. 2005. "Libraries and the USA PATRIOT Act." Retrieved: August 29, 2005. Online: http://www.library.vanderbilt.edu/science/info/patriot.htm.

Vanneman, Reeve, and Lynn Weber Cannon. 1987. *The American Perception of Class.* Philadelphia: Temple University Press.

Velasco, Manuel Simón. 2002. "Editorial." *Migrant Workers: International Labour Conference, Labor Education 2002/4, No. 129.* Geneva, Switzerland: ILO. Retrieved August 19, 2005. Online: http://www.ilo.org/public/english/dialogue/actrav/publ/129/129.pdf.

Venis, Sarah. 2002. "Violence against Women: A Global Burden." *The Lancet* (April 6):1172.

Vergakis, Brock. 2007. "Utah Allows Guns On College Campuses." *FOXNews.com* (April 27). Retrieved April 5, 2008. Online: http://www.foxnews.com/2007Apr27/0,4675,CampusGuns,00.html

Vetter, Harold J., and Gary R. Perlstein. 1991. *Perspectives on Terrorism.* Pacific Grove, CA: Brooks/Cole.

Vito, Gennaro F., and Ronald M. Holmes. 1994. *Criminology: Theory, Research and Policy.* Belmont, CA: Wadsworth.

Wagner, David. 1993. *Checkerboard Square: Culture and Resistance in a Homeless Community.* Boulder, CO: Westview.

Wald, Matthew L. 1996a. "A Fading Drumbeat against Drunken Driving." *New York Times* (December 15):E5.

Wald, Matthew L. 1996b. "Group Says Alcohol-Related Traffic Deaths Are Rising." *New York Times* (November 27):A11.

Walmartclass.com. 2005. "Women Speak Out." Declaration of Melissa Howard in Support of Plaintiffs' Motion for Class Certification in the United States District Court, Northern District of California, Case No. C-01-2252MJJ, Betty Dukes et al. v. Wal-Mart Stores, Inc. Retrieved July 14, 2005. Online: http://www.walmartclass.com/walmartclass_forthepress.html.

Wallerstein, Immanuel. 1984. *The Politics of the World Economy.* Cambridge, England: Cambridge University Press.

Wallerstein, Immanuel. 1999. *The End of the World as We Know It: Social Science for the Twenty-First Century.* Minneapolis: University of Minnesota Press.

Wang, Philip S., Patricia Berglund, Mark Olfson, Harold A. Pincus, Kenneth Wells, and Ronald C. Kessler. 2005. "Failure and Delay in Initial Treatment contact After First on set of Mental Disorders in the national Comorbidity Survey Replication." *Archives of General Psychiatry,* 62: 6(June): 603–613.

Warr, Mark. 2000. "Public Perceptions of and Reactions to Crime." In Joseph F. Sheley (Ed.), *Criminology: A Contemporary Handbook* (3rd ed.). Belmont, CA: Wadsworth, pp. 13–31.

Warshaw, Robin. 1994. *I Never Called It Rape.* New York: HarperPerennial.

Wartella, Ellen. 1995. "The Commercialization of Youth: Channel One in Context." *Phi Delta Kappan,* 76 (February):448–451.

Waters, Malcolm. 1995. *Globalization.* New York: Routledge.

Watney, Murdoch. 2004. "Identity Theft—The Dangerous Imposter." *De Rebus: South African Attorney's Journal* (July):20. Retrieved July 30, 2005. Online: http://www.derebus.org.za/archives/2004Jul/articles/identitytheft.htm.

Watson, Roy E. L., and Peter W. DeMeo. 1987. "Premarital Cohabitation Versus Traditional Courtship and Subsequent Marital Adjustment: A Replication and a Follow-Up." *Family Relations,* 36:193–197.

Ways and Means Republicans. 2007. "'Official' Poverty Data Ignore Most Government Anti-Poverty Benefits." (August). Washington, D.C.: U. S. House of

Representatives, 110th Congress, Authored by: Ways and Means Republicans. Retrieved April 19, 2008. Online: http://republicans.waysandmeans.house.gov/showarticle.asp?ID=98.

Watts, Charlotte, and Cathy Zimmerman. 2002. "Violence against Women: Global Scope and Magnitude." *The Lancet* (April 6):1232–1237.

Webster, Bruce H., Jr., and Alemayehu Bishaw. 2007. "Income, Earnings, and Poverty Data from the 2006 American Community Survey." U.S. Census Bureau. Retrieved April 26, 2008. Online: http://www.census.gov/prod/2007pubs/acs-08.pdf.

Weeks, John R. 2005. *Population: An Introduction to Concepts and Issues* (9th ed.). Belmont, CA: Wadsworth.

Weinberg, Martin S., Earl Rubington, and Sue Kiefer Hammersmith. 1981. *The Solution of Social Problems: Five Perspectives* (2nd ed.). New York: Oxford University Press.

Weinberg, Martin S., Colin J. Williams, and Douglas W. Pryor. 1994. *Dual Attraction: Understanding Bisexuality.* New York: Oxford University Press.

Weiner, Tim. 1995. "Serial Bomber Threatens Blast aboard a Los Angeles Airliner." *New York Times* (June 29):A1, A6.

Weisman, Steve. 2005. "Identity Theft in the Global Village: 50+ Perspective." AARP.org (June). Retrieved July 30, 2005. Online: http://www.aarp.org/research/international/perspectives/jun_05_identity_theft.html.

Weisner, Thomas S., Helen Garnier, and James Loucky. 1994. "Domestic Tasks, Gender Egalitarian Values, and Children's Gender Typing in Conventional and Nonconventional Families." *Sex Roles,* 30:23–54.

Weiss, Gail. 1995. "Sex-Selective Abortion: A Relational Approach." Originally published in *Hypatia,* Winter 1995 (12:3) (Bloomington: Indiana University Press, 1995). Retrieved: October 13, 2002. Online: http://www.hsph.harvard.edu/rt21/medicalization/WEISS_Sex-selective.html.

Weiten, Wayne, and Margaret A. Lloyd. 1994. *Psychology Applied to Modern Life: Adjustment in the 90s.* Pacific Grove, CA: Brooks/Cole.

Weitz, Rose. 2007. *The Sociology of Health, Illness, and Health Care: A Critical Approach* (4th ed.). Belmont, CA: Wadsworth.

Weitzer, Ronald. 2000. "The Politics of Prostitution in America." In Ronald Weitzer (Ed.), *Sex for Sale: Prostitution, Pornography, and the Sex Industry.* New York: Routledge, pp. 159–180.

Weitzman, Lenore J. 1985. *The Divorce Revolution.* New York: Free Press.

Wellman, David T. 1993. *Portraits of White Racism* (2nd ed.). New York: Cambridge University Press.

Westoff, Charles F. 1995. "International Population Policy." *Society* (May–June):11–15.

Wheeler, David L. 1997. "The Animal Origins of Male Violence." *Chronicle of Higher Education* (March 28):A15–A16.

Whitesides, John. 2005. "Katrina Devastation Highlights Poverty of U.S. Blacks." Reuters.com (September 2). Retrieved September 3, 2005. Online: http://today.reuters.com.

Wilkie, Jane Riblett. 1993. "Changes in U.S. Men's Attitudes toward the Family Provider Role, 1972–1989." *Gender and Society,* 7(2):261–279.

Williams, Christine L. 1995. *Still a Man's World: Men Who Do Women's Work.* Berkeley, CA: University of California Press.

Williams, David R., David T. Takeuchi, and Russell K. Adair. 1992. "Socioeconomic Status and Psychiatric Disorders among Blacks and Whites." *Social Forces,* 71:179–195.

Williams, Gregory Howard. 1996. *Life on the Color Line: The True Story of a White Boy Who Discovered He Was Black.* New York: Plume/Penguin.

Williams, Richard G. 1997. "Once a Doctor, Now a 'Provider.' " *Austin American-Statesman* (March 19): A19.

Williams, Robin M., Jr. 1970. *American Society: A Sociological Interpretation* (3rd ed.). New York: Knopf.

Williamson, Robert C., Alice Duffy Rinehart, and Thomas O. Blank. 1992. *Early Retirement: Promises and Pitfalls.* New York: Plenum Press.

Willis, Brian M. 2000. "Global Health Impact of Child Prostitution." Retrieved Nov. 2, 2002. Online: http://apha.confex.com/apha/128am/techprogram/paper_17865.htm.

Willis, Ellen. 1981. *Beginning to See the Light.* New York: Alfred Knopf.

Willis, Ellen. 1983. "Feminism, Moralism, and Pornography." In Ann Snitow, Christine Stansell, and Sharon Thompson (Eds.), *Powers of Desire: The Politics of Sexuality.* New York: Monthly Review Press, pp. 460–466.

Wilson, David (Ed.). 1997. "Globalization and the Changing U.S. City." *The Annals of the American Academy of Political and Social Science,* 551(May). Special Issue. Thousand Oaks, CA: Sage.

Wilson, Edward O. 1975. *Sociobiology: A New Synthesis.* Cambridge, MA: Harvard University Press.

Wilson, William Julius. 1996. *When Work Disappears: The World of the New Urban Poor.* New York: Knopf.

Wines, Michael. 2005. "Niger's Anguish Is Reflected in Its Dying Children." *New York Times* (August 5): A1, A6.

Wirth, Louis. 1938. "Urbanism as a Way of Life." *American Journal of Sociology,* 40:1–24.

Wirth, Louis. 1945. "The Problem of Minority Groups." In Ralph Linton (Ed.), *The Science of Man in the World Crisis.* New York: Columbia University Press, p. 38.

Witt, Susan. 1997. "Parental Influence on Children's Socialization to Gender Roles." *Adolescence* 32(126):253–259.

Witteman, P. 1991. "Lost in America." *Time* (February 11):76–77.

Wolfgang, Marvin E., and Franco Ferracuti. 1967. *The Subculture of Violence: Towards an Integrated Theory in Criminology.* Beverly Hills, CA: Sage.

Women for Sobriety. 2005. "Introduction to Women for Sobriety." Retrieved July 28, 2005. Online: http://www.womenforsobriety.org.

Women's International Network. 1995. "Sex Trade Flourishing in Japan." *WIN News* 21(1) (Winter):42.

Woods, James D., with Jay H. Lucas. 1993. *The Corporate Closet: The Professional Lives of Gay Men in America.* New York: Free Press.

World Health Organization. 1946. *Constitution of the World Health Organization.* New York: World Health Organization Interim Commission.

World Health Organization. 2002. *The World Health Report 2002: Reducing Risks, Promoting Health Life.* Geneva, Switzerland: World Health Organization.

World Nuclear Association. 2005. "Nuclear Power in Russia." Retrieved August 20, 2005. Online: http://www.world-nuclear.org/info/inf45.htm.

World Resources Institute. 1992. *World Resources 1992–93.* New York: Oxford.

Wrangham, Richard, and Dale Peterson. 1996. *Demonic Males: Apes and the Origins of Human Violence.* New York: Houghton Mifflin.

Wren, Christopher. 1996a. "Clinton Declares That Columbia Has Failed to Curb Drug Trade." *New York Times* (March 2):1, 5.

Wren, Christopher. 1996b. "Teen-Agers Find Drugs Easy to Obtain and Warnings Easy to Ignore." *New York Times* (October 10): A12.

Wright, Erik Olin. 1979. *Class Structure and Income Determination.* New York: Academic Press.

Wright, Erik Olin. 1985. *Class.* London: Verso.

Wright, Erik Olin. 1997. *Class Counts: Comparative Studies in Class Analysis.* Cambridge, England: Cambridge University Press.

Wright, Erik Olin, Karen Shire, Shu-Ling Hwang, Maureen Dolan, and Janeen Baxter. 1992. "The Non-Effects of Class on the Gender Division of Labor in the Home: A Comparative Study of Sweden and the U.S." *Gender and Society,* 6(2):252–282.

Wright, Quincy. 1964. *A Study of War.* Chicago: University of Chicago Press.

Wright, Richard T., and Scott Decker. 1994. *Burglars on the Job: Streetlife and Residential Break-ins.* Boston: Northeastern University Press.

WuDunn, Sheryl. 1996. "In Japan, Even Toddlers Feel the Pressure to Excel." *New York Times* (January 23):A3.

Young, J. H. 1961. *The Toadstool Millionnaires: A Social History of Patent Medicine in America before Federal Regulation.* Princeton, NJ: Princeton University Press.

Young, Jeffrey. 2005. "Identity Theft Now Global Problem." PoliticsOL.com (April 27). Retrieved July 20, 2005. Online: http://www.politicsol.com/news/2005/04-27-identity-theft-now-global-problem.html.

Young, Michael Dunlap. 1994. *The Rise of the Meritocracy.* New Brunswick, NJ: Transaction.

Zate, Maria. 1996. "Hispanics Struggle for Corporate Stature." *Austin American-Statesman* (August 11):H1, H3.

Zelizer, Viviana. 1985. *Pricing the Priceless Child: The Changing Social Value of Children.* New Haven, CT: Yale University Press.

Zimring, Franklin E., and Gordon Hawkins. 1997. *Crime Is not the Problem: Lethal Violence in America* (Studies in Crime and Public Policy). New York: Oxford University Press.

Zuger, Abigail. 1998. "Many Prostitutes Suffer Combat Disorder, Study Finds." Retrieved Nov. 2, 2002. Online: http://www.prostitutionresearch.com/nytimes1998.html.

Name Index

Subject Index

Photo Credits

p. 1: William Whitehurst/Corbis; p. 5: James Nielsen/Getty Images/Newscom; p. 12: Richard Carson/Reuters/Bettmann/Corbis; p. 13: Mario Tama/Getty Images; p. 16: AP Wide World Photos; p. 17: Vicki Silbert/PhotoEdit; p. 24: AP Wide World Photos; p. 27: AFP/Getty Images; p. 32: Tomas del Amo/Photolibrary; p. 32: Tony Freeman/PhotoEdit; p. 37: Rob Melnychuk/Photodisc/Getty Images; p. 37: Robert Brenner/PhotoEdit; p. 38: Joel Stettenheim/Corbis; p. 45: Carla Van Wagoner/Wirelmage/Getty Images; p. 49: AP Photo/NYPD; p. 49: AP Photo/Diane Bondareff; p. 56: Miguel Gandert/Bettmann/Corbis; p. 57: AP Wide World Photos; p. 59: Geoff Hansen/Getty Images; p. 63: Strauss/Curtis/Bettmann/Corbis; p. 68: Mark Peterson/Corbis; p. 72: Ariel Skelley/Corbis; p. 74: Hazel Hankin; p. 77: Copyright 2006 ABC News/ABC Photography Archives/Craig Sjodin; p. 82: Cindy Charles/PhotoEdit; p. 84: Ben Baker/Redux; p. 90: David Young-Wolff/PhotoEdit; p. 100: Lewin Studio Elyse/Image Bank/Getty Images; p. 101: Jeffery Allan Salter/Corbis; p. 104: Greg Nikas/Meditrust Corporation; p. 105: Bob Daemmrich/Stock Boston; p. 109: Tom & Dee Ann McCarthy/Corbis; p. 113: Mario Perez/ABC/Everett Collection; p. 116: Newscom; p. 117: Human Rights Campaign; p. 120: Mark Richards/PhotoEdit; p. 123: Marilyn Humphries Photography; p. 124: Dan Callister/Getty Images; p. 128: Sean Murphy/Stone/Getty Images; p. 133: Stephen Shaver/AFP/Getty Images/Newscom; p. 140: Ed Kashi/Corbis; p. 144: AP Wide World Photos; p. 148: Topham/The Image Works; p. 156: Tom & Dee Ann McCarthy/Corbis; p. 160: John Chiasson; p. 167: Mario Tama/Getty Images; p. 174: John Boykin/The Stock Connection; p. 182: PhotoEdit; p. 185: AP Photo/Rogelio V. Solis; p. 192: Ed Maynard/Alamy; p. 196: A. Ramey/Woodfin Camp & Associates; p. 202: Sebastian Pfuetze/Zefa/Corbis; p. 207: AP Photo/Stuart Ramson; p. 210: Eli Reed/Everett Collection; p. 212: Dung Vo Trung/Sygma/Corbis; p. 218: John Moore/Getty Images/Newscom; p. 220: eff Greenberg/PhotoEdit; p. 224: Christopher Thomas/Photographer's Choice/Getty Images; p. 229: HBO/Photofest: P. 231: Ariel Skelley/Taxi/Getty Images; p. 233: Getty Images; p. 237: Creasource/Corbis; p. 240: Mark Burnett/Photo Researchers; p. 245: Bob Daemmrich/Stock Boston; p. 248: Will & Deni Mclntyre/Corbis; p. 255: Jim West/The Image Works; p. 256; Michael Newman/PhotoEdit; p. 260: Alan Oddie/PhotoEdit; p. 260: Jon Levy; p. 269: AP Photo/Mary Altaffer; p. 269: AP Photo/Chris Carlson; p. 273: Paulo Fridman; p. 275: Tony Law/Redux; p. 276: David Young-Wolff/PhotoEdit; p. 277: AP Photo/U.S. Air Force, Airman 1st Class Courtney Witt; p. 289: Phillippe Lopez/AFP/Getty Images; p. 295: Columbia/Suzanne Hanover/The Kobal Collection; p. 298: Edouard Berne/Stone/Getty Image; p. 301: Everett Collection; p. 303: Newscom; p. 304: Teh Eng Koon/AFP/Getty Images; p. 309: AP Photo/Denis Poroy; p. 315: Bruce Brander/Photo Researchers; p. 318: Bob Daemmirch/ The Image Works; p. 323: Stephanie Maze/Woodfin Camp & Associates; p. 326: Paul Mccormick/Image Bank Getty Images; p. 333 ABBAS/ Magnum Photos; p. 339: Jim West/PhotoEdit; p. 342: Joseph Sohm/Visions of America/Corbis; p. 345; John Henley/Corbis; p. 348: PictureQuest; p. 350: Stockbyte/Getty Images p. 353: AP Photo/U. S. Army/Marshall Independent; p. 356 REUTERS/Andrea Comas; p. 362: REUTERS/Stringer; p. 363: J&B Photographers/Animals Animals/Earth Scenes; p. 364: Scott Olson/Getty Images; p. 371: AP Photo/Marcio Jose Sanchez; p. 379: Bob Daemmrich/Stock Boston; p. 382: AP Photo/Jim Mone; p. 388: AP Wide World Photos.